The QuarkXPress Book
Fourth Edition for Macintosh

The Quark XPress Book

Fourth Edition for Macintosh

by
David
Blatner

and

Eric Taub

edited by
Stephen F.
Roth

AN OPEN HOUSE BOOK

PEACHPIT PRESS

The QuarkXPress Book, Fourth Edition for Macintosh
David Blatner and Eric Taub
Edited by Stephen F. Roth

Peachpit Press, Inc.
2414 Sixth Street
Berkeley, CA 94710
510/548-4393
510/548-5991 (fax)

Cover design: Ted Mader + Associates
Interior design: Olav Martin Kvern
Production: Glenn Fleishman and Mike Arst

Permissions

The following photographs were used with permission of Special Collections Division, University of Washington Libraries. Figures 8-5, 8-8, 8-14, pages 458, 461, and 469, photo by Todd, negative no. 10511; figures 8-11 and 8-18, pages 465 and 476, photo by A. Curtis, negative no. 4103; and figure 8-17, page 473, photo by A. Curtis, negative no. 30744.

Distribution

Peachpit Press books are distributed to the US book trade by Publishers Group West, 4065 Hollis, PO Box 8843, Emeryville, CA 94609, phone 800/788-3123 or 510/658-3453, fax 510/658-1834. Peachpit books are also available from wholesalers throughout the US including Baker & Taylor Books, Golden-Lee Book Distributors, and Ingram Book Company. Resellers outside the book trade can contact Peachpit directly at 800/980-8999.

Notice of Rights

Notice of Liability

ISBN 1-56609-129-2
9 8 7 6 5 4 3 2 1
Printed and bound in the United States of America

Printed on recycled paper

Quark
XPress
Secrets

▼▼

When we introduced QuarkXPress back in 1987, we had no idea of the broad impact it would have on the world of publishing. Now, if you look at any random collection of magazines and newspapers, the chances are that many of them were produced using Quark-XPress. From high-end, four-color publishing to short newsletters and brochures, the methods used to produce professional-looking documents have changed completely in the last seven years. And QuarkXPress has been a major force catalyzing that change. The power of XPress has overshadowed the power of the old, expensive, dedicated high-end publishing systems.

But, with this power came complexity. That is, until the release of QuarkXPress 3.0. When we were developing 3.0, it was immediately apparent that we had to make a radical shift in the way the user interacts with the computer. To add more features, we had to make using XPress simpler. The 3.0 user interface made Quark-XPress both more powerful and easier to use. In successive releases of version 3, we added substantial new features to make navigating and creating documents, importing and linking images, and printing to PostScript devices simpler and more robust. Version 3.3 is just the latest iteration of an ongoing process of refining, developing, and improving.

Even with all of the new publishing and color-oriented features, however, we still take a very broad view of our audience.

The XPress documentation takes you only so far. The uses of the product are as varied as the backgrounds of the users. To get all the information that everyone wants takes much more. That's where *The QuarkXPress Book* comes in.

Back in 1990, when David asked me to write a foreword for *The QuarkXPress Book,* I thought, "Yeah, sure. I'll write something generic that says how nice the book is and that it will be a good addition to your library." Then, I actually got to read it. It is more than a good book on XPress. It is a great book. With every release of QuarkXPress, *The QuarkXPress Book* has paced the release date, providing up-to-the-last-minute information on all of the new functionality and utilities in QuarkXPress.

This book covers more than just QuarkXPress, however. It is a book on Macintosh. The information that's covered has broader uses to anyone who owns a Mac. It explains lots of secrets about how the Mac really works. And with tips ranging from simple step-by-step procedures for creating fancy drop caps to hidden details of the Finder and resources, the information provided is invaluable.

Users like David and Eric are one of the reasons that Quark-XPress has been successful. Making a great product takes more than just a bunch of clever people in research and development. It takes actual users telling us what we did right and what we did wrong. David and Eric both use QuarkXPress. Each edition of this book was produced with QuarkXPress. Its quality is not a testament to what QuarkXPress can do; it is a testament to what QuarkXPress can do in the hands of skilled and knowledgeable operators. No matter what your level of expertise, this book will help you know more and work better. It will be one of the most useful books you own for QuarkXPress and the Macintosh.

Tim Gill
Founder and Senior Vice President
of Research and Development
Quark, Inc.

The Amazon Explorers

▼ ▼

"You're doing what?"

"We've got one QuarkXPress document here to print the borders for each page, and then in this other document we have all the text in galleys. We tried to put them together, but because we don't know the program well enough, it's faster just to use our production people for pasteup."

"If you're just going to paste it up, why are you using Quark-XPress at all?"

"A consultant suggested we buy a Macintosh and QuarkXPress. But we haven't had a chance to really learn it. Besides, Quark-XPress lets us make really good borders."

It was a story both of us had heard before. Designers, ad agencies, small and large businesses bought Macintoshes and Quark-XPress with the idea that everything was going to be easier, faster, and cooler. All that can be true, but let's face it: QuarkXPress is not a magical solution. Desktop publishing on the Macintosh requires knowledge, experience, and expertise.

It seems there is a need for a consultant who not only knows the computer and graphic design, but also one who can sit there, patiently, and—at 11 PM—walk with you through building a better registration mark, making a drop cap, or explaining how master pages work. All for a $29.95 flat fee. That consultant is this book.

▼ ▼

The Early Days

But how did this book come to be? What possessed us to write over 250,000 words on a piece of computer software? Let's start at the beginning of our QuarkXPress story.

The early days of desktop publishing were much simpler than they are now. When a new program came out, we asked some basic, hard-hitting questions.

▶ Can you put text on a page?

▶ Can you put graphics on a page?

▶ Does the page print?

Once we had a satisfactory answer to those three questions, we could get down to brass tacks, ripping it to pieces to make it do all the things it wasn't designed to do. It was a wild time, much like trudging through the Amazon forests with only a machete and a match.

To be blunt, I'm not ordinarily the quiet type. So it is telling that, when I saw the first copy of QuarkXPress 1.0, all I could say was, "Wow." Here was, at last, a program to use instead of Page-Maker. No more eyeballing the measurements, no more relying on built-in algorithms. Those were the days of PageMaker 1.2, and QuarkXPress was a glimmer of hope in the dark ages.

But it was the beginning of the Macintosh Way, and we were so gung-ho on not acting like IBM-PC users that we would do almost anything not to look in the manuals. Even if we had wanted to peek every once in a while, peer pressure was stiff. No, we had to play by the rules and learn QuarkXPress the hard way.

Perhaps all those years of system crashes and blank pages coming out of the printer paid off. While frequenting cocktail parties, we can blithely hint at the magnificent techniques we've come upon for using QuarkXPress in a networked environment. Our friends and family are amazed as we stand tall, knowing which menu to pull down to create style sheets. But is it really enough?

Making Pages

Even more important than fancy party talk has been the ability to use all our QuarkXPress tips and tricks to make good-looking pages quickly and efficiently. And back in 1990, we knew it was finally time to put finger to keyboard and get this information out to you, the real world users of QuarkXPress. To find even more tips, tricks, and techniques for QuarkXPress users, we searched the on-line systems, looked through back issues of computer magazines, and even resorted to books on other Macintosh software.

We've continued that search for the last four years, squirreling away every trick and tip we could find, storing them up for the next edition, or the one after that. Everything we've collected, right up the time we made PostScript dumps of this edition, we managed to squeeze into this book, one place or another.

But books full of tips and tricks tell just half the story. And we think the simple menu-by-menu approach that most computer books use deserves the phrase "tastes filling, less great!" We knew there should be more.

So we sat down and listed all the ways in which we use Quark-XPress in our work: books, magazines, newsletters, flyers, and brochures. The most striking thing we found was that we rarely used QuarkXPress by itself. Aldus FreeHand, Adobe Illustrator, Post-Script programming, Microsoft Word, Adobe Photoshop, and numerous system extensions and utilities all play a large part in our publishing process. We figured that if we weren't publishing in a vacuum, you probably weren't either. So we gathered up information about using those programs in conjunction with QuarkXPress.

Our idea was to roll together tips and tricks, a full overview of the program, and in-depth discussions of core concepts behind using QuarkXPress in the real world. So, we've included discussions on fonts, PostScript printing, color models, and much more, alongside examples of how we've been using QuarkXPress for the past eight years. We also describe the way QuarkXPress operates and how to take advantage of its sometimes strange methods.

Of course, this is a lot of information for a single book. But what did you shell out $29.95 for? Chopped liver? No, this book is meant not only to be read, but to be used. We wanted to include a Post-It pad so you could mark the pages you'll use the most, but it didn't work out. Don't let that stop you, though.

▼ ▼

About this Book

Although we expect you to know the basics of using a Macintosh (moving the mouse, pulling down menus, and so on), we have purposely taken a wide spectrum of potential readers into account, from Macintosh beginners to seasoned professionals. We did this because we've found that those seasoned professionals are delighted to learn new tricks, techniques, and concepts, and people who have used the Macintosh very little sometimes surprise us with their intuitive grasp of the Big Picture.

Remember, this book was written for you. It's designed to work for you—as your personal consultant—whoever you are. It's also designed to help you get a sure footing on a sometimes uneven path and to help you make pages like the pros.

Organization

We have organized this book to reflect what we think QuarkXPress is all about: producing final camera-ready output from your computer. So we start with an overview of the program, move on to building a structure for the document, then discuss the basics—such as putting text and pictures on a page. Next we move into some fine-tuning aspects of QuarkXPress, and finally to printing. That's the speed-reading rundown; now here's a play-by-play of the chapters.

Introduction. In the Introduction we lay out QuarkXPress on the table, telling you what it is and what it does. We also run down each of the new features in version 3.3.

Chapter 1: QuarkXPress Basics. The first step in understanding Quark-XPress is learning about its structure from the ground up. This involves an investigation of QuarkXPress's menus, palettes, and dialog boxes. We also look at everything from file management, to navigating through your document, to the basics of the library, grouping, and alignment controls. Even advanced users tell us they find features and techniques in this chapter that they never knew.

Chapter 2: Document Construction. Without a sturdy foundation, your document won't be reliable or flexible when you need it to be. This chapter discusses the basics of making earthquake-proof infrastructures for your pages: opening a new document, creating master pages, and setting up column guides and linking for text flow.

Chapter 3: Word Processing. If you wanted a drawing program, you would have bought one. Words are what QuarkXPress is all about, and this chapter is where words start. We talk here about simple text input, the Find/Change feature, and checking spelling.

Chapter 4: Type and Typography. Once you've got those words in the computer, what do you do with them? Chapter 4 discusses the details of formatting text into type—fonts, sizes, styles, indents, drop caps—all the things that turn text into type.

Chapter 5: Copy Flow. You bought the computer, so why not let it do the work for you? This chapter explains how to use style sheets to automate aspects of copy processing, and how to use importing and exporting effectively.

Chapter 6: Pictures. Who reads text anymore? We like to look at the pictures. And pictures are what Chapter 6 is all about. We discuss every Macintosh graphics file format and how to work with each in your documents. We also cover rotating, skewing, and other manipulations of images.

Chapter 7: Where Text Meets Graphics. This is the frontier-land: the border between the two well-discussed worlds of type and pictures. Life gets different on the edge, and in this chapter we discuss how to handle it with grace—using inline boxes, paragraph rules, and the new text runaround features.

Chapter 8: Modifying Images. Here's where a good eye can help you improve a bitmapped image, and a creative eye can help you make those graphics do flips. In this chapter we look at brightness, contrast, gamma correction, and halftoning for bitmapped images such as scans.

Chapter 9: Color. QuarkXPress is well-known for its powerful color capabilities. Chapter 9 covers color models, building a custom color palette, applying colors, and the first steps in understanding color separation.

Chapter 10: Printing. This chapter is where everything we've talked about is leading: getting your document out of the machine and onto film or paper. In this chapter we cover every step of printing—from the Chooser to color separations. We also discuss the finer points of working with service bureaus and how to troubleshoot your print job.

Appendix A: EfiColor. EfiColor, a color-management system that improves the correspondence between colors on screen, on color printer output, and on printed results from offset printing, was the single biggest new feature in QuarkXPress over the past year. It's covered in detail in this appendix.

Appendix B: Macintosh/PC File Transfers. More and more people are using QuarkXPress in a cross-platform environment. In Appendix B, we explore the ins and outs of moving files between the two programs and operating systems.

Appendix C: AppleEvent Scripting. Although AppleEvent scripting has appeared in the press a lot, people don't really know what to make of it. In Appendix C, we cover the wild world of scripting Quark-XPress using AppleScript. Don't worry, we're not really programmers ourselves; if *we* can understand this stuff, so can you.

Appendix D: Resources. The last appendix is an extensive directory of Quark XTensions, software, user groups, and magazines and publications that we've found useful while working with QuarkXPress. We also cover little tidbits like how to get an educational Lab-Pak, and show a few examples of QuarkLibraries.

Finding What You Need

There are many ways to read this book. First, there's the cover-to-cover approach. This is the best way to get every morsel we have included. On the other hand, that method doesn't seem to work for some people. As we said, this book is meant to be used, right off the shelf, no batteries needed.

We've done everything in our power to make it easy to find topics throughout this book. However, there's so much information that sometimes you might not know where to look. The table of contents breaks each chapter down into first- and second-level headings. So you can jump to a particular topic fast.

If you are primarily looking for the new 3.3 features, you should take a look at the description of new features in the Introduction. That will also tell you where in the book we describe the feature fully. Also, throughout the book we've added margin icons that point out the new features.

If it's a tip that you're looking for, you can look through the tips list at the beginning of the book. We've also started the tips in the text with the word "Tip" to make them stand out. Finally, if you can't find what you're looking for, or are trying to find an explanation for a single concept, try the index.

Faith

Just to be honest with you, there's almost no way to explain one feature in QuarkXPress without explaining all the rest at the same time. But that would make for a pretty confusing book. Instead, we're asking you to take minor leaps of faith along the path of reading these chapters. If we mention a term or function you don't understand, trust us that we'll explain it all in due time. If you are able to do that you will find that what we are discussing all makes sense. For example, we're not going to talk about the details of creating a new document until the second chapter, *Document Construction*, even though we need to talk about working with documents in Chapter 1, *QuarkXPress Basics*.

▼ ▼

Acknowledgments

No book is an island. So many people have directly and indirectly contributed to this book's production that we would have to publish a second volume to thank them all. We do want to thank a few people directly, however.

First of all, a great thanks to the people at Quark who not only put out a great product, but also worked with us to get this book out to you with as much information in it as we've got. In particular, Tim Gill, Ralph Risch, Fred Ebrahimi, Mark Niemann-Ross, Elizabeth Jones, Becky "our fave" Lefebvre, Sid "the build's almost done" Little, Jay "the Guy" McBeth, Kathleen "hold on, I'll check" Thurston, Peter Warren, and Dave Shaver.

Other folks: Tami Stodghill and Buck Buckingham at the XChange, Bob "Windows" Weibel, Robert Hoffer, Scott Lawton, Tony DeYoung, Dacques Viker, and the mavens at EFI: Adam Stock, Stephanie "stop processing" Arvizu, and Danielle Beaumont.

And many thanks go to all the people who wrote, called, and e-mailed us their comments and suggestions. We've tried to incorporate their ideas into this fourth edition.

Keith Stimely

Some of our readers may notice that Keith Stimely's name has been removed from the cover of the book. We are sorry to say that Keith passed away in November 1992. In the process of preparing this fourth edition, the text has been revised to the degree that the publisher removed his name from the cover. However, his work is not forgotten, and for every copy of this book sold, Peachpit Press is making a contribution in his name to the Our House hospice in Portland, Oregon.

The People Who Made This Book

Guy Kawasaki wrote about Steve Roth in *The Macintosh Way*: "If you find an editor who understands what you are trying to do, brings the best out of you, and doesn't botch up your work, 'marry' him as fast as you can." I can't think of a better description of Steve, so that'll have to do. Steve's already married to Susie Hammond, who—along with Cindy Bell—was excellent in making sure our t's were dotted and i's crossed, and—most of all—making sure that we didn't sound like fools. Steve's new managing editor, Glenn Fleishman, contributed greatly to making this book as good as the reviewers have said it is.

I also want to thank our publisher, Ted Nace. We gave it the wings, but he made it fly. Also, much appreciation and astonishment goes toward my officemates: our excellent book designer Olav Martin Kvern, our wordsmith Don "reference-man" Sellers, Steve "It All Looks the Same!" Broback, John "it's not lunchtime yet" Cornicello, Marci "patience is a virtue" Eversole, Kim "ping-pong" Rush, Michele Dionne, and all the other folks who helped poke and prod the book until it was done. Cary Norsworthy, Keasley, Gregor, and everyone else at Peachpit Press have been an incredible help in both getting us on and off press in record time as well as getting the books out to you. The people at Torrefazzione and Spot Bagels, for mind- and body-sustaining espresso. Mike Arst for making pages, saving our butts, and helping us get our figures in shape. Doug "Aldus" Peltonen for help with technical edits. Neil Kvern at Seattle Imagesetting for delivering our color pages from the imagesetter.

And, finally, there are those people even further behind the scenes who helped along the road. Vincent Dorn at LaserWrite in Palo Alto, who said, "Hey, let's go to Burger King." Steve Herold at

LaserGraphics in Seattle, who said, "Meet Steve Roth." All my parents, Alisa and Paul, Debbie Carlson, and other friends who were such a support over the past few decades. It wouldn't have happened without you.

Thanks.

David Blatner

Overview

▼ ▼

Contents

▼ ▼

▼ ▼

Chapter 6   Pictures

▼ ▼

▼ ▼

▼ ▼

Tips

▼ ▼

▼ ▼

▼ ▼

Chapter 3   **Word Processing** 179

▼ ▼

Chapter 4   **Type and Typography** 205

▼ ▼

▼ ▼

▼ ▼

▼ ▼

INTRODUCTION

Trying to figure out what type of program Quark-XPress is reminds us of a scene from an old *Saturday Night Live* episode, when a couple bickered over their new purchase. "It's a floor wax," said one. "No, it's a dessert topping," replied the other. The answer soon became clear: "It's a floor wax *and* a dessert topping." QuarkXPress is a program with the same predicament. Some people insist it's a typesetting application. Others bet their bottom dollar that it's a word processor. Still others make QuarkXPress a way of life.

The truth is that QuarkXPress is all these things, and more. However, no matter how you use it, it is never more than a tool. And a tool is never more than the person behind it.

We like to think of machetes. You can use a machete as an exotic knife to cut a block of cheese. Or, you can use it as your only means of survival while hacking through the Amazon jungles. It's all up to you.

Here in the Introduction, we talk about the big picture: Quark-XPress and how it fits into the world of desktop publishing. We also talk about the new QuarkXPress, version 3.3, and how it's different from earlier versions of the program. Most importantly, we set the stage for the real thrust of this book: how to use Quark-XPress to its fullest.

1

▼▼

What QuarkXPress Is

QuarkXPress combines word processing, typesetting, page layout, drawing, image control, and document construction in a single program. From text editing to typography, page ornamentation to picture manipulation, it offers precision controls that you'll be hard pressed to find in other programs.

Who QuarkXPress is For

Just because it has all these powers, though, doesn't mean that only trained publishing professionals or graphic designers can or should use it. Anyone who can run a Macintosh ("the computer for the rest of us") can use it. In fact, many of the people who swear by QuarkXPress aren't even in the "publishing" business. They use it for internal corporate communications, product brochures, stationery, display advertisements, name tags, labels, forms, posters, announcements, and a hundred other things.

Of course, it does "real" publishing, too, and has become a top choice in that realm. It's used by book publishers such as Simon and Schuster and Peachpit Press; magazines such as *Newsweek, People, Spy, Entertainment Weekly, Rolling Stone,* and *Premiere*; newspapers such as *The New York Times, USA Today, The Washington Times,* and *The Denver Post*; design firms, art studios, advertising agencies, and documentation departments throughout the world.

▼▼

What QuarkXPress Does

When it comes right down to it, QuarkXPress is built to make pages. You can place text and graphics as well as other page elements on an electronic page and then print that out in a number of different formats. But how can you do that? What tools are at your disposal? Before we spend the rest of the book talking about how to use

QuarkXPress and its tools, we had better introduce you to them. And perhaps the best way to introduce QuarkXPress in real world terms is to provide a digest of some of its most basic options.

Page sizes. You can specify the page sizes for each of your documents, along with their margins. Page dimensions can range from one by one inch to 48 by 48 inches, and margins can be any size that'll fit on the page. QuarkXPress's main window presents you with a screen representation of your full page, and guidelines indicate margin areas. You can view pages at actual size or any scale from 10 percent to 400 percent. If your document consists of multiple pages, you can scroll through them all or see them in miniature. If pages are larger than the maximum paper size handled by the target printer, QuarkXPress will *tile* the document, printing it in overlapping sections for you to assemble manually.

Page layout. QuarkXPress provides tools so you can design your pages by creating and positioning columns, text boxes, picture boxes, and decorative elements. There's a facility to set up "text chains" that automatically flow text from one text box to another, whether the boxes are on the same or different pages. QuarkXPress can automate the insertion of new pages and new columns, the creation of elements that are common to all pages, and the page numbering/renumbering process itself.

Word processing. QuarkXPress's word processing tools let you type directly into pages and edit what you type, and your text can appear as either a full-page background (as on paper in a typewriter) or wrapping into overlaying text boxes that can be moved and resized. Text always automatically rewraps to fit new box boundaries.

Formatting type. You have full control over character-level formatting (font, size, style, etc.) and paragraph-level formatting (indents, drop caps, leading, space before and after, etc.). You can also build style sheets for different types of paragraphs that include both character and paragraph formatting.

Importing text. Various import filters let you bring in formatted text from other programs (again, either onto full pages or smaller text boxes), while simultaneously reformatting using style sheets.

Graphic elements. Drawing tools let you create lines, boxes, ovals, and polygons in different styles, sizes, and shapes, with different borders, fills, and colors. You can even make those ugly rounded-corner rectangles if you want to.

Importing graphics. You can import computer graphics into picture boxes. These graphics can include scanned images, object-oriented and bitmapped graphics, in color, grayscale, or black and white. Once you've imported them into picture boxes, they can be cropped, fitted, rotated, skewed, and—with bitmaps—manipulated for brightness, contrast, and special effects.

▼ ▼

The Birth of an Upgrade

If you've never watched an artist create an image with oil paints, you may not understand what all the fuss and expense is about. When you see the end result, it's easy to think that they just picked up a brush and painted the whole thing. What you'd be missing is the hours of slowly building, changing, covering, modifying, pondering, and dreaming. Half of what makes a piece of art special is the *process* it went through in its creation.

Art isn't the only thing that is born out of process. Computer software is very similar. And so it's with great admiration that we can look forward to each new revision of QuarkXPress, where code has been modified, other parts ripped out and replaced with something better, and then—in fits of inspiration—whole new features are added, making the final piece (at least for this version) one step better, more usable, and simply *cooler* (see Figure I-1).

We don't know if QuarkXPress 3.3 was born out of a secret desire to make users frustrated ("*another* upgrade!?") or perhaps

Figure I-1
Evolution of
the species

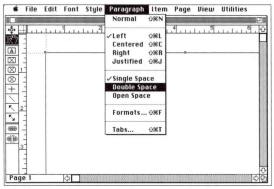

Version 1.10

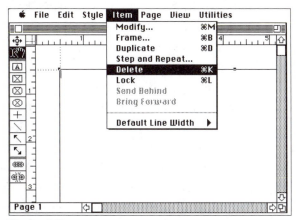

Version 2.12

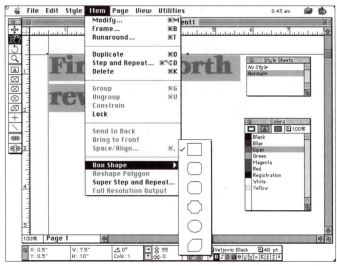

Version 3.3

simply a desire on Quark's part to make the hottest new technology available as quickly as possible, but we do know that they'll succeed in both. Our only suggestion to you is to try to focus on the latter. There's no doubt that it's a hassle to upgrade, but when you have, life will be better. In this chapter we want to quickly show you how much better it can be.

The History

One of the frustrating things about writing books about computer software is how often the software gets updated. And every time the software is updated, we're right behind it with an update to the book (actually, because we usually work with early beta software, our books sometimes come out even before the new update really ships).

We've gone through three updates so far on this book. In the first edition, we told you about the many exciting new features that appeared in QuarkXPress 3.0, including the pasteboard, the polygon tool, and the overall interface that was a quantum leap beyond earlier versions. In the second edition, we covered version 3.1 and its automatic ligatures, color blends, and the disappearance of the XPress Data file. The last edition of the book included an introduction to EfiColor as well as new style sheet commands, new preferences, and a score of other new features.

Now we're taking the next step. QuarkXPress 3.3, while only a minor upgrade, has several features in it that are really cool (see Table I-1). Here's a quick rundown of what they are, and where you can find more information on them. (Note that some of these features were incorporated in Quark's free XTensions—Bob, Son of Bob, FeaturesPlus, and Bobzilla—before they were integrated into the application itself. See Appendix D, *Resources*, for a rundown of which free XTension added which features in which version of QuarkXPress.)

Table I-1

New features
in recent versions

Feature . . .	First appeared in version . . .	3.2	3.3	See page
Accents for All Caps		●		291
Anchored box paragraph indent improved			●	437
AppleEvents		●		661
Auto Backup		●		33
Auto Save		●		32
Box skew		●		73
Collect for Output		●		594
Color drag		●		506
Cool Blends		●		507
Copying linked text boxes		●		105
DCS 2.0		●		381
Deselecting items			●	61
Display preferences		●		126
Document previews		●		32
Drag-and-Drop text		●		183
EfiColor		●		611
Font reporting		●		208
Forced Justify		●		276
Grayscale/Color TIFF		●		126
Get Text settings sticky			●	10
High-resolution TIFF screen previews			●	450
Importing EPS color names			●	498
Increased number of open documents		●		35
Indent Here improved			●	303
Interactive text resizing		●		220
JPEG import filter			●	382
Keep with Next ¶ improved			●	282
Kern to space			●	9
Local formatting on style sheets		●		341
Low-resolution output		●		563
Mirror imaging (flipping)		●		74
Multiple Masters font support		●		687
Multiple-monitor tiling		●		36
New math procedures (multiply, divide)		●		686
Next Style		●		355

Feature . . .	First appeared in version . . .	3.2	3.3	See page
Opening libraries in Open dialog box		●		115
Pantone color sets		●		489
PCX Filter			●	383
PDF folder			●	22
Photo CD filter			●	382
Picture Usage suppression checkmark		●		411
Polygonal text boxes			●	428
PPD support			●	549
Printing ASCII or binary		●		550
Redraw speedup		●		52
Registration information		●		20
Renaming incoming style sheets		●		349
Revert to Last Autosave			●	51
Shading grayscale TIFFs			●	454
Smart Quotes		●		128
Speed Scroll		●		125
Stacking windows		●		36
Tiling windows		●		36
Toyo and DIC color models			●	492
Trapping Preferences		●		518
Two-character tab leaders			●	267
Undoing multiple-item deletions			●	53
Vertical Scaling		●		226
Windows QuarkXPress		●		645
Windows submenu		●		35
XTension folder			●	22

The Big Fixes

When users speak, Quark listens (though sometimes they listen so quietly that it appears as though they don't hear). Sooner or later they get around to responding with changes in the program (their wish list for upgrades to QuarkXPress is very long). In fact, most of the features in version 3.3 are either bug fixes or modifications to existing features that make them better. Let's start with a look at what features have been enhanced.

Tab leaders. PageMaker and QuarkXPress are forever in a game of feature catch-up. Perhaps the first thing Quark's engineers saw on the PageMaker 5.0 spec sheet was two-character tab leaders. Now Quark does it, too. (See "Tabs," page 263.)

Document Layout palette. The Document Layout palette has been enhanced in several relatively minor ways, though some people might feel the changes are more of a de-evolution. (See "Document Layout Palette," page 100; and "Master Pages and the Document Layout Palette," page 159.)

Indent Here character. People were forever screaming at Quark because paragraphs with an Indent Here character wouldn't continue indenting when a paragraph broke across two text boxes. Instead of plugging their ears, Quark decided to change the feature. It now works correctly. (See "Special Characters," page 301.)

Keep with Next ¶/Keep Lines Together. Strangely enough, sometimes it takes Quark a *long* time to fix something the majority of users complain about. One such complaint has been the inability to string together more than two paragraphs with Keep with Next ¶. Now you can. Plus, Keep Lines Together now works much better in conjunction with Keep with Next ¶. (See "Widow and Orphan Control," page 281.)

Spaceband kerning. You may not have even noticed that Quark-XPress ignored all spaceband kerning (automatic kerning pairs in which one character is a space). Well, it no longer does. Also, you can now make spaceband kerning pairs in the Kerning Editor. (See "Kerning," page 229, and "Fine-Tuning Type," page 288.)

Deleting multiple items. It's funny how little aggravations can build up throughout a day until finally you just get fed up with it all and kick your computer off the desk. One tiny non-feature that has always added to this escalation has been the inability to undo a deletion when you're deleting more than one item from your page. Your computer will sport fewer bruises now that Quark fixed this problem. (See "Undo and Cancel," page 52.) There are a few tricks to this, which we cover, notably that if one of the items you delete is a linked text box, when you undo the deletion, the box doesn't relink.

Displaying high-resolution images. In the past, when you imported TIFF images, QuarkXPress would provide you with a 72-dpi screen image only if you held down the Shift key at import time. Now, the program imports at 72 dpi as a matter of course (see page 450).

Paragraph Indents for Anchored Boxes. In Chapter 7, *Where Text Meets Graphics*, there's a tip called "Anchored Boxes as Initial Caps," page 303, in which we point out a bug in pre-3.3 versions of QuarkXPress. The problem was that text ran around anchored boxes at the same distance as their left indent. If an anchored box sat at the beginning of a paragraph that had a half-inch left indent, then the text indented half an inch from the anchored box. We never met anyone who likes this. Fortunately, Quark has changed this so that the text only indents from the side of the text box rather than any anchored box you have pasted in.

Shading TIFFs. If you've needed to ghost back or desaturate a grayscale TIFF image, you've probably gotten intimate with the Other Contrast dialog box while wondering why QuarkXPress didn't just let you apply a Shade to it. In version 3.3, you can forget all that and go directly to the Style menu's Shade feature. Note that you still have to use Other Contrast to desaturate color TIFFs. (See "The Style Menu" page 454.)

Sticky Get Text settings. Another minor improvement that makes life just that much more pleasurable is that the Convert Quotes and Include Style Sheets checkboxes in the Get Text dialog box are now sticky. That is, the programs remembers the settings you chose last time you imported text (helpful especially when you're importing a number of stories into your document; see Chapter 3, *Word Processing*).

▼ ▼

Tip: Use the Right XTensions. QuarkXPress 3.3 shipped with new versions of several of its XTension filters, including XPress Tags and Kern/Track Editor. In order to get the full functionality of the program, make sure you're using those new versions. You can check version numbers by selecting the XTension's icon in the Finder and choosing Get Info from the File menu (or pressing Command-I).

▼ ▼

New and Exciting

So far the changes we've been discussing are all pretty minor enhancements to already existing features. But 3.3 isn't all just bug fixes and minor improvements; there are a few full-fledged new features included, too.

Polygonal Text Boxes. This is the hottest and coolest new feature in version 3.3. You can turn any text box into a polygon by selecting Box Shape from the Item menu. Then you can edit the polygon by turning on Reshape Polygon and using normal polygon-editing features. This should not only turn a few heads, but it also makes funky text wraps much easier to create (see page 303).

Importing Colors. If you work much with FreeHand or Illustrator EPS files (or Photoshop duotones), you'll really appreciate this one: QuarkXPress now imports named spot colors from those files and adds them to the color list. That means you can apply the colors from within QuarkXPress, as well as ensure that the spot-color jobs will separate correctly (see page 498).

JPEG. If you work with large images, you may be using some form of JPEG compression. And if you are compressing files with JPEG, you probably want to figure out how to get them into QuarkXPress. Now there's a JPEG filter that lets you import JPEG files directly into QuarkXPress. Every time you print, QuarkXPress automatically decompresses the image and sends it to the printer. (See "Macintosh Graphic File Formats," page 372.) Note that you don't need this filter to import JPEG *EPS* files, but you *do* need to be using a PostScript Level 2 printer for JPEG EPS files to print.

Photo CD. The second new import filter for QuarkXPress lets you import Photo CD files directly into picture boxes. This feature sounds about eight times better than it really is. We explore why in Chapter 6, *Pictures*.

PCX. Last and certainly least, QuarkXPress 3.3 also comes with a PCX filter XTension. This lets you import PCX graphics into picture boxes. But think for a moment: why would you ever want to do that? Oh well. As always, it's nice to have the option.

▼ ▼

Requirements

To take advantage of all these great new features in QuarkXPress, you need, at a minimum, a Quadra 840av with 128Mb of RAM, a one-gigabyte hard disk drive, twin removable hard drives, a 600Mb magneto-optical drive and 2Gb DAT tape storage system for secondary backup, a 32-bit color drum scanner, a high-res imagesetter with a PostScript Level 2 RIP, a Printware LQ 1200-by-600-dpi laser (for rough comps), a SuperMac Proof Positive 11-by-17-inch color dye-sub printer, a 21-inch color monitor with 24-bit video and graphics accelerator cards, and, of course, an NTSC video capture board and genlock control panel.

Just kidding! All you really need is a Mac Plus system and five megabytes of RAM. But, as few things are more frustrating than being all psyched up to start something only to discover that you can't, for lack of an essential component, here is a résumé of the components you need to know about.

Hardware and System Software

If you haven't yet made the plunge to System 7.0 or 7.1 (even though it was introduced in May 1991), you really should go ahead and do it now. You don't *need* System 7 to run QuarkXPress, but we find it helpful. To run the program effectively you'll need a hard drive and eight megabytes of RAM. You'll also need a 1.4Mb floppy drive just to install the program (if you really need 800K install disks Quark will send them to you on request; however, it takes four to six weeks to get them). Note that some features of QuarkXPress, such as AppleEvent scripting and Publish and Subscribe, are only available under System 7 or higher.

But let's be honest: we really can't recommend using Quark-XPress to its fullest on any Macintosh without a 68030 or higher processor (which means you can use almost every Macintosh sold in the last four years) and a 12-inch monitor. And, although you can use a black-and-white monitor, unless you're really never going to be doing even a two-color job, we think you should have one that displays color. Ultimately, that means we'd use a 68030 Mac II (not the plain II), many of the newer Performas, or any of the Centris or Quadra models. (We use several computers at our respective offices, including a few IIs, Centrises, and Quadras, a Duo 210, and miscellaneous other machines.)

Keyboards

QuarkXPress is a keyboard- and mouse-intensive program. You'll be spending a lot of your time selecting items or text, dragging, or choosing menus. If you have an extended keyboard—one that has the 15 function keys, page up and down keys, and a keypad—you can save yourself hours (or days!) by using built-in shortcuts. You can also assign style sheets to keys (this is where the keypad comes in handy). And if you get a utility like CE Software's Quic-Keys, you can use the keyboard even more effectively. Apple's new Adjustable Keyboard isn't as helpful because it puts the function and page keys in a separate unit that's hard to position well.

Hard Disks

The Iron Law of Hard Disk Storage is that your needs expand to equal and then exceed the storage capacity available. Get the biggest hard disk you can. If you think you'll never need more than

100Mb of storage, then get double that. You may be sorry later if you don't. Most of the new Macintoshes don't come with anything smaller than a 230Mb hard drive; we think that's a pretty good minimum.

Random Access Memory

RAM is good. Put as much into your computer as you possibly can afford. To run System 7 you need a minimum of eight megabytes (Apple says you can do it with four, but we think that's foolish). If you're doing serious publishing, chances are you'll want to run QuarkXPress along with several other applications, and probably want at least 16Mb. David feels pretty comfortable with the 24Mb in his Quadra 650; but when he's doing a lot of Photoshop work, he wishes he had more. You'll want the extra RAM to move around smoothly when you have those programs open along with much-needed extensions and control panel devices, such as ATM and SuperBoomerang. The more color work you're doing, the more RAM you should have.

▼ ▼

QuarkXPress and You

Version 3.3 of QuarkXPress is clearly a pretty impressive package. But don't let it intimidate you. Remember, QuarkXPress is not only a machete, it's a Swiss Army machete. If you want to use it for writing letters home, you can do it. If you want to create glossy four-color magazines, you can do that too. The tool is powerful enough to get the job done, but sometimes—if you're trying to get through that Amazon jungle—you need to wield your machete accurately and efficiently.

Let's look at how it's done.

CHAPTER 1

QUARKXPRESS BASICS

Whoever thought that something called a "gooey" would ever be so important to the way we use a computer? While most of the world clutched their crib sheets to remember "how-to" keyboard codes for saving a document, moving to the end of a line, or drawing a box, a few visionary researchers came upon a simple idea: a *graphical user interface*, or GUI ("gooey"). "Why not," these researchers asked, "make using a computer more intuitive?" These researchers developed the underpinnings of the Macintosh GUI, which in turn laid the groundwork for desktop publishing to take off.

The basics of the Macintosh GUI are simple: create an environment in which somebody can get the most out of a computer without having to remember too much, or even think too much in order to get the job done. The GUI comes between the person using the computer and the computer itself. For example, when you want to move a file from one disk to another, you click on it and drag it across the screen. The GUI handles all the internal computer stuff for you.

When you work with QuarkXPress, you work with the Macintosh GUI. You don't have to remember long codes or read a computer language, or even understand what's going on behind the scenes. We must say that it's been our experience that the more you know about how computers work, the better you can use them. However, this book is not meant for programmers. This book, like QuarkXPress, is—to steal a line from Apple—"for the rest of us."

We hear mumbling in the halls, "Who cares about gooey users and interfaces? We just want to use the program." Well, hold on; you can't tell the players without a program, and you can't effectively use QuarkXPress without understanding how it relates to you. So, we'll play emcee and introduce the players: the members of the QuarkXPress interface.

▼ ▼

First Steps in Quarking

We're going to start with a quick discussion of installing Quark-XPress; if you're not installing but rather updating your program, hold on and we'll cover that, too (see also "Tip: Installing with an Updater," below).

When you take QuarkXPress out of the package, you're faced with a whole mess o' disks. If you're like us, you bypass the manual entirely and just start shoving disks into the computer to see what there is to see. You'll find that all the peripheral files for the program are located intact on the disks, while the program itself is compressed and segmented onto three different disks. The installer (or updater) is the only thing that can piece together and decompress the application onto your hard drive. However, if you want to copy the other filters, XTensions, or files over by hand later, you can do that, too. (We just let the installer do it for us; it's easier and it knows where all the proper files are.)

▼ ▼

Tip: Installing with an Updater. Quark has three utilities it sends out to install version 3.3: an installer, an upgrader, and an updater. The installer is made for people who purchase new versions. The upgrader upgrades versions 3.0, 3.1, and 3.2 to 3.3. And the up-dater only updates version 3.2 to 3.3. Both the updater and the upgrader require that you have a copy of the older version present on your hard disk in order to install 3.3.

But what if you need to re-install the latest version at some point due to a hard disk failure or some other obscure reason? Do you need to re-install version 3.2 and then upgrade it? No. Just hold down the Option key while you click the OK button in the first flash screen of the upgrader (see Figure 1-1). This installs a copy without an older version having to be around.

Figure 1-1
The upgrader (labeled
Updater in the splash
screen) and the
3.2-to-3.3 updater

Hold down Option while clicking OK in the upgrater (3.0, 3.1, or 3.2 to 3.3) to re-install a full copy of QuarkXPress without the original application.

The 3.2-to-3.3 updater must have a copy of 3.2 to update.

This doesn't work with the version 3.2-to-3.3 updater. Because the move from 3.2 to 3.3 was so slight, Quark didn't want to put a lot of money into sending out a whole bunch of expensive disks. So, instead, this updater can't re-install—it can only update.

▼ ▼

Installing 3.3

Installing QuarkXPress is a snap. In earlier versions you had to either install everything on all the disks, or go through a series of dialog boxes, checking which files you wanted to install. However, beginning with version 3.3, Quark uses a single dialog box that asks you which files, text filters, XTensions, and other files you want to install (see Figure 1-2).

If you leave the settings as they are, everything is copied to your hard drive except for the tutorials and sample files (those you have to either copy yourself or explicitly tell the installer to copy for you by turning on the checkmark).

Figure 1-2

Installing
QuarkXPress 3.3

> **QuarkXPress 3.3 Installation**
>
> Please check the items you want installed. Click on an item's checkmark to check or uncheck it. Click on an item to obtain item information.
>
> | Install | Name | Size |
> |---|---|---|
> | √ | QuarkXPress Application | 3366 KB |
> | √ | AppleEvents Preview | 1400 KB |
> | √ | Advanced AppleEvents Scripting | 600 KB |
> | √ | EfiColor Color Management | 1400 KB |
> | √ | XTension Updaters | 60 KB |
> | √ | Word Processing Filters | 400 KB |
> | √ | Frame Editor | 100 KB |
> | √ | QuarkXPress Release Notes | 128 KB |
> | √ | Output Request Template | 10 KB |
>
> Size of Checked Items: 7464 KB
>
> Item Information:
>
> [**Install**]
>
> [Cancel]
>
> [**Destination Folder**] Disk Space Available: 7380 KB
>
> Lb. of Fleish :QuarkXPress 3.3 Folder

You can tell QuarkXPress not to install certain files or XTensions by clicking on the checkmarks. A running tally at the bottom tells you how much space the total number of files will take up on your hard disk.

In David's opinion, the best result of this new tell-what-you-want interface is that you don't have to install the infamous Frame Editor anymore (more later on that and why David doesn't like it).

Note that the installer still installs all the XTensions and filters, but the items that aren't checked in the second dialog box are placed in a separate folder. At least this helps keep your Quark-XPress folder tidy, and speeds up launching XPress, though it doesn't save any disk space.

By the way, you'll probably notice that XTension Updaters is listed in the Installation dialog box. However, as of this writing, almost no XTension developers are including updaters on the disks. In fact, the only ones we've seen are updaters for Tableworks and TruNew. (There's a small chance that will change by the time you read this.) So, unless you're using one of those XTensions, you can just turn off that install checkmark. In the prerelease versions of QuarkXPress that we've been working with, the QuarkPrint updater (which you need in order to make QuarkPrint work with version 3.3) is actually on the AppleScript disk and doesn't get copied over automatically. We find this awfully strange, so maybe it will have been changed by the time you read this.

Updating to 3.3 from 3.2

Because 3.3 involves only minor changes in the application itself, Quark released an updater program on a single disk. When you double-click on the 3.3 updater icon, you get a dialog box prompting you to find your copy of QuarkXPress 3.2. Select your copy of QuarkXPress 3.2, and the updater changes the appropriate program code to bring it up to version 3.3.

Because the updater actually changes your existing copy of the application, we recommend a few things before updating.

▶ Make a backup copy of the QuarkXPress application itself, just in case your machine crashes or you get an error during the update.

▶ Turn off *all* virus protection software before updating. Better yet, turn off all extensions (see "Tip: Starting Clean," below).

▶ Make a backup of the updated 3.3 application before running it for the first time, just in case you need a "clean" copy in the future.

The updater disk also comes with an updater for Quark's basic XTensions. The XTension updater lets you select which ones to update and then prompts you to find the old version. You may have to reinstall the old XTension off the 3.2 disks in some cases.

Note that printer descriptions (PDF files) are handled a little differently under version 3.3. See Chapter 10, *Printing*, and "Tip: XTensions Folder and PDF Folder" later in this chapter, for specific details.

▼ ▼

Tip: Starting Clean. Note that Quark recommends that you turn off all your system extensions and control-panel devices before you install QuarkXPress. You can do this by holding down the Shift key while restarting your Macintosh. (Hold it down until you see the message "Extensions Off.") This is especially important if you use any sort of automatic virus-detection utility.

▼ ▼

Registration

When you first install QuarkXPress, you are required to fill out a survey. The information you provide is saved onto a registration disk that you send back to Quark. There were myths going around saying Quark was secretly saving all sorts of other information on this disk, including what software you use and so on. This is not true. The registration disk *does* take one piece of information with it that it doesn't ask you for: your system configuration (what Macintosh model you use, what system, and so on). Theoretically, this information could help the people in technical support, should you ever talk to them about a problem.

▼ ▼

Tip: If You Sell Out. Why you'd ever want to sell your copy of QuarkXPress is beyond us. However, in case you do, you'd better know Quark's rules about such things. First of all, you have to notify Quark that you want to sell their product. (The closest thing to this that we've encountered in real life is someone telling their parents that they wanted to buy birth control pills.) Quark's customer service will send you a Transfer Request form, and a license agreement for the person to whom you're selling. After both of you sign the forms and you return them with $25 "transfer fee," Quark updates their database and the deed is done. The only reason we even bring this up is that we've heard of people getting into weird situations because they didn't follow the rules. So now you know.

▼ ▼

Other Files

When the installer, upgrader, or updater is done doing its thing, you'll find a slew of files on your hard disk. These include several files for getting text from word processors, a dictionary, and several other files that help QuarkXPress do its business. Figure 1-3 shows a folder containing QuarkXPress and its application files.

Figure 1-3
A standard
QuarkXPress folder

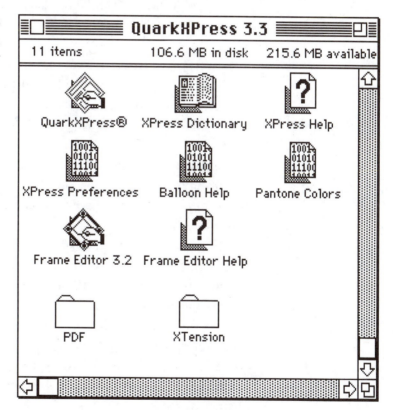

Most of the files are in the QuarkXPress program folder. Note that some may have made their way into your System Folder, too—particularly the EfiColor Processor and database.

▼ ▼

Tip: Clean Up Your Folder. Unless you have and use more software than we do (which is hard to imagine), you don't need all the files that get installed with QuarkXPress. We never seem to have enough room on our hard disks, so we have gotten in the habit of throwing away any files that we don't need. If you're never going to use the Frame Editor, just throw it away, along with its Help file. (We can't think of many reasons why you'd want to; it only lets you create bitmapped frames.) If you only use Microsoft Word as your text editor, go ahead and throw away the MacWrite, Word-Perfect, WriteNow, and MS-Works text filters. If you ever need to get them back, you'll find them on one of the disks in the installation package.

However, if you really don't want to throw out those files, make an "Other XTensions" folder and put the ones you don't use in there. The more supplementary files you have floating around in QuarkXPress's folder, the longer QuarkXPress takes to launch.

▼ ▼

Tip: XTension and PDF Folders. In every version of QuarkXPress up to 3.2, most Printer Description Files (PDFs) were included in the application itself, and XTensions were kept loose in the Quark-XPress folder. Now with 3.3, the times they are a changin'. Quark has reorganized the contents of the QuarkXPress folder by adding a PDF folder that includes all the PDFs and an XTension folder to hold all of the filters and XTensions you use (see Figure 1-4). If you want to turn off an XTension or remove a PDF, you can move it to another folder (called, for example, "Other XTensions") and QuarkXPress won't load them. If you don't use a DuPont 4Cast printer (few people do these days), you just move that PDF someplace else and it won't show up in the Page Setup dialog box (see Chapter 10, *Printing*).

We like this new setup because it makes it easier for us to customize and organize our system. However, note that if you change the name of the folders even a little, QuarkXPress might not be able to find them at all.

Figure 1-4

Some of the items
in the XTension
and PDF folders

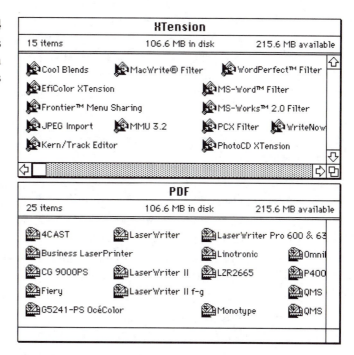

▼ ▼

Tip: Where To Put All Those Files. Just a quick digression on the topic of hard-disk management. Apparently, one of the most difficult techniques for Macintosh users to understand and control is the effective management of files on their hard disks. Now, we know that *you* wouldn't do something like this, but there are those who just toss their files and applications all over their hard disks, sometimes into folders and sometimes not. They are making their lives hard for themselves.

The Macintosh's folder system is designed to make life easy for you. We like to keep one folder called "Quark Folder" that contains the actual QuarkXPress application and all the filters and supplemental files we need. We have a folder inside of that one for keeping extra add-on modules and filters that we sometimes need but don't want around most of the time. Then, in a different folder from the Quark Folder, we keep our QuarkXPress documents (usually a specific folder for each project we're working on).

If you aren't familiar with folders and how they work, we heartily suggest you look into the matter (see "File Management," below). You may not self-actualize from using folders well, but your life is sure to be the better for it.

▼ ▼

Know Thy Program

Before we go any further into the wild world of QuarkXPress, we think it's necessary to take a quick look at two parts of the program: the Environments dialog box and the old XPress Data file (now deceased). The first can tell you where you are; the second is a QuarkXPress history lesson.

About That About Box

There are times when it's helpful to know the state of your Mac. One of those times is when you're on the telephone with Quark technical support. Another is when you're troubleshooting a weird problem yourself. QuarkXPress can tell you about itself and its environment via the Environment dialog box (see Figure 1-5). You can get to this dialog box in two ways.

▶ Hold down the Option key and select About QuarkXPress from the Apple menu.

▶ If you have an extended keyboard, you can press Command-Home. (The Home key is up near the Delete and Page Up keys.)

The Environment dialog box tells you familiar information about your Mac's system and your version of QuarkXPress. It also displays a list of XTensions that you have currently running, and if you click on one, you'll see the XTension's serial number (if it has one; most don't). Plus, there's a button for displaying your user-registration information, and another for creating a registra-

Figure 1-5

QuarkXPress
Environment
dialog box

tion disk with your information which you can send back to Quark. Quark uses these disks to plug your information directly into its customer-support database.

Why create a registration disk if it's already created as part of the installation process? Sometimes Quark receives registration disks that have been damaged in transit. Until now, there was no way they could ask you to easily recreate such a damaged disk; once you installed and mailed in your disk, it was *gone!* Now you have the option of creating a new one. Kind of obscure, rarely needed, but when you gotta do it . . . .

The Demise of XPress Data

Once upon a time, QuarkXPress users always had to keep track of a little file called XPress Data. This file kept all sorts of important information with it, and if it got lost or deleted or corrupted, hours of your work could be toast. The most annoying thing about XPress Data, though, was that every time you sent your document to a service bureau to be printed, you had to include the XPress Data file with it. Most people either didn't know that or they simply forgot, and their output was often screwed up because of it.

The XPress Data file was the place where QuarkXPress stored all custom (user-defined) kerning tables, tracking tables, frames, and hyphenation information (see Chapter 4, *Type and Typography*). Now, when you create a kerning table (or a tracking table, a custom frame, or hyphenation exceptions) while in a document, the information is stored in two places: in XPress Preferences (essentially the same as XPress Data, but with a different name), and *within the file itself.*

If you bring that file to another machine with a different XPress Preferences file, that machine alerts you that something is different (the tables in the Preferences file are different from those in the document). It then asks you whether you want to use the information that was stored with the document or the application's default preferences data (see Figure 1-6). If you respond that you don't want to use the document's original information, Quark-XPress reflows your pages using the built-in XPress Preferences information from the version of QuarkXPress you're using. If you respond that you do want to use the document's original information, it is used and continues to be saved right along with that file.

Figure 1-6
QuarkXPress saves
some information
with the document

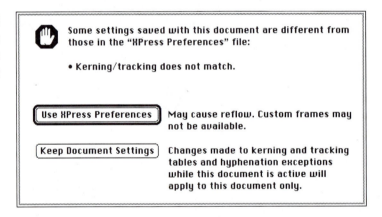

This means that when you send your QuarkXPress documents to a service bureau, you no longer need to include that elusive XPress Data file. The service bureau just tells the program to use the document's information, and no text reflow occurs.

Plus, beginning with version 3.2, an important bit of information is added to each document that 3.0 and 3.1 inadvertently left out. If you've defined any special trapping information, that is now also contained in documents. So there'll be no more nasty trapping surprises when you look at your press run (or fewer, anyway).

Suppose you create custom information for a document, but don't want that information to be used in the next document you create. When you save and close that first document, you can reset kerning or tracking tables, or clear out the Hyphenation Exceptions dictionary for the next document. If you don't clear and reset these controls, the XPress Preferences file remembers them, and they are used for each document that you create.

▼ ▼

Tip: Resetting and Switching Preferences. The truth of the matter is that the XPress Preferences file is basically the same as the XPress Data file; they just changed its name. If you delete the XPress Preferences file (or move it out of the System Folder and the QuarkXPress folder), then QuarkXPress creates a clean, new one for you. This is a great method for starting over from scratch with the default tracking and kerning tables, and with no items in Hyphenation Exceptions.

If you have two or more XPress Preferences files with varying information, you can move them in and out of your QuarkXPress folder (in the Finder, or preferably with a utility like PrairieSoft's DiskTop that you can use without switching to the Finder). However, you do have to quit and relaunch QuarkXPress for the new items to take effect.

▼ ▼

Tip: Using Your Old Data Files. By the way, don't worry about your old XPress Data files. They're obsolete, but you can still use them. Just put them in your QuarkXPress folder, make sure there are no XPress Preferences files floating around, and start QuarkXPress. The XPress Data file is magically transformed into an XPress Preferences file!

▼ ▼

File Management

Getting a good grasp on file management is essential to working most efficiently and happily with QuarkXPress. When we talk about file management with QuarkXPress, we are talking primarily about opening, closing, and saving your documents. These are pretty basic concepts, so if you've used other Macintosh programs you should feel right at home with these actions. If you haven't used a Macintosh before, you're soon to learn a great way of organizing computer files.

Opening Documents

We won't talk in depth about creating new files until Chapter 2, *Document Construction.* However, we do want to talk about opening them here. (In case you don't have any to play with, there are several QuarkXPress documents available on the Tutorial and Sample disks.)

There are three ways to open an existing QuarkXPress document. You can double-click on the document's icon in the Finder, which launches QuarkXPress and opens the file. Or, if you're running System 7, you can drag the document's icon onto the Quark-XPress icon (or an alias of QuarkXPress). If you are in QuarkXPress, you can select Open from the File menu (or press Command-O). QuarkXPress then asks you if you want to view either documents, or templates, or both (All Types). We discuss templates and their function in "Saving Your Document," below.

▼ ▼

Tip: Hope for Lost Icons. Sometimes QuarkXPress documents and libraries get confused and lose their desktop icons. One side-effect of this is that you often can't double-click on the icons to automatically open them. You can do two things to get around this.

▶ **Rebuild the desktop.** If you hold down the Option and Command keys while the Macintosh is starting up (after the Extensions have loaded and before the hard drives appear on the desktop), you'll be asked if you really want to rebuild the desktop. If you click OK, there's a good chance that the icons will appear again.

▶ **Drag and drop.** For a less complete solution, you can drag the icon onto the QuarkXPress program icon using System

7's "drag-and-drop" ability. This opens the document or library. If the program's not running, the system launches it. Then you can Save As with the same or different name, which rebuilds the icon and its link to the application.

▼ ▼

Tip: Launching QuarkXPress. When you launch QuarkXPress (double-click on the QuarkXPress icon) the program performs all sorts of operations while it's loading. For example, it figures out which fonts are in the system and which XTensions are available for its use. While it's doing all this, you don't see too much happening on the screen.

When it loads certain XTensions, it scrolls a little image of the XTensions in the Quark splash screen; some XTensions don't have animated icons, so they don't appear. If the icon is scrolling across too quickly, you can hold down the mouse key and it slows down. Conversely, if you want to speed up a slow one, the mouse key speeds it across.

Finally, you know that the computer is ready to go when you see QuarkXPress's menu bar across the top of the screen and the Tool and Measurements palettes appear.

▼ ▼

Closing Documents

You have four choices for closing a document.

▶ Click the close box in the upper-left corner of the document window.

▶ Press Command-W.

▶ Choose Close from the File menu.

▶ Select Quit from the same menu. (Of course, this choice not only closes the file, but it also quits QuarkXPress.)

If changes have been made to the document since the last time you saved it, you'll see an alert box asking you if you want to save those changes.

▼ ▼

Tip: Closing Up Shop. If you want to quickly close all open documents, you can either press Command-Option-W or Option-click the Close box.

▼ ▼

Saving Your Document

Until you save your document to a disk, it exists only in the computer's temporary memory (called RAM), ready to disappear forever in the event of a power disruption or system crash. You should save any new document as soon as it opens, and make frequent saves during your work session. All it takes is Command-S. We suggest developing it into a nervous tic. We cannot tell you how many times we and our clients have lost hours of work because we didn't save frequently enough. David even made a little sign to post above his computer that said, "Save Every 10 Minutes." You can also use Quark's Auto Save feature (see "Auto Save," below).

Let's look at the commands in QuarkXPress that let you save your documents, along with two other powerful features: one for autosaving and one for making backups.

Save. If you want to save your document with the same name that it already has, you can select Save from the File menu (or press Command-S). If you haven't yet saved your document, and it is unnamed, selecting Save automatically acts like Save As.

Save As. Selecting Save As from the File menu (or pressing Command-Option-S) lets you save the document you're working on under a different name. For example, David often saves different versions of a document with each version number attached. The first one might be called "Brochure 1.1", the next "Brochure 1.2", and so on. Whenever he decides to create a new version, he chooses Save As from the File menu, which brings up the Save As dialog box (see Figure 1-7). He types in a file name (or edits the one that's there), then clicks the Save button to save it to disk. If

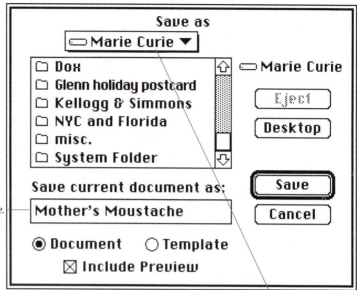

Figure 1-7
The Save As dialog box

Type the name of the file here.

Your document is saved in whatever folder is listed here.

you decide to do this, remember to delete earlier versions as soon as you decide you don't need them anymore, or else your hard disk will burst at the seams.

Like we said above, file management is an issue that too many people don't seem to "get." The Save As dialog box is a key ingredient in file management. The important issue here is that your document is saved to whatever folder is open in the Save As dialog box. If you want your document saved in a folder called Current Jobs, you must navigate your way to that folder. You have a few tools at your disposal for this. Table 1-1 shows several mouse and keyboard shortcuts.

Table 1-1
Navigating through the high seas

Press . . .	To . . .
Up Arrow	Move one item up on the displayed files list
Down Arrow	Move one item down
Command-Up Arrow	Move one folder "up"
Double-click	Open this folder
Enter or Return	Open this folder (when a folder is highlighted) Save here (if no folder is highlighted)

▼ ▼

Tip: Preview When Opening. One of the neat things about saving a document as a template (see "Templates," below) is the handy preview of the document's first page that you see whenever you select the template in QuarkXPress's file-opening dialog box. We've always loved this feature, and wondered why Quark didn't simply implement it for *all* documents, not just templates. Well, as of version 3.2, they have.

Any document that you create in QuarkXPress version 3.2 or later can have a first-page preview attached to it by checking Include Preview in the Save As dialog box. Note that QuarkXPress can't preview documents saved in earlier versions of the program. You have to open them and use Save As first. Adding a preview to a document only adds about 5K or 10K to the total size of the document.

▼ ▼

Auto Save. At first glance, Auto Save looks like a yawner. As it turns out, it's anything but. There are plenty of commercial and shareware utilities that will automatically save a document you're working on, as you're working on it. QuicKeys and Now Utilities' NowSave both come to mind.

But all these utilities work by generating the equivalent of QuarkXPress's Save command at predefined intervals. Now suppose you mistakenly delete all of a story; then, before you can Undo your deletion, QuicKeys or NowSave kicks in, saving your document (and your mistake) for all eternity—or until you fix your mistake, or lose your job because of it! For this reason, we've stayed away from autosaving utilities.

Until now. The folks at Quark really got the design of this feature right. You turn on Auto Save by checking it in the Application Preferences dialog box (see "Changing Defaults," later in this chapter), and you can specify any interval you want between saves (the default is every five minutes). But—and here's the great part—autosaves don't automatically overwrite your original file. That only happens when you use the Save command. So if you use the Revert to Saved command, you revert to the last saved version of your original file—just as you would expect—*not* to the last autosaved one (see "Revert to Saved," below).

Auto Save exists to help you recover from a dreaded system crash or network communications failure. (When you lose the connection to your file server with a file open, sometimes Quark-XPress refuses to let you do a Save As). After you have a crash, you can restart QuarkXPress and open the autosaved file.

Whenever QuarkXPress does an autosave, it creates a file in the same folder as your document that keeps track of every change you've made since the last time you saved the document. Whenever you save your document, QuarkXPress deletes that incremental file, and starts over again.

The problem with Auto Save is that it creates a file the same size as the one you're working on. If your file is 12Mb large, then you'd better have at least 12Mb available on your hard drive when you turn on Auto Save. It's a nice system, but far from perfect.

Auto Backup. Until recently, revision control with QuarkXPress has been strictly up to you. If you wanted to keep previous versions of a document, you had to be sure to copy them to another location, or use Save As frequently, slightly changing the name of your file each time. (We always name our files with version numbers: 1.1, 2.4, etc.) However, starting with version 3.2, those days are gone.

You can use Auto Backup (also found in the Application Preferences dialog box, under the Edit menu; or press Command-Option-Shift-Y) to tell QuarkXPress to keep up to 100 previous versions of your document on disk (the default is five). By clicking the Destination button, you can specify exactly where you want revisions to be stored. The default, "<document folder>", is simply the folder in which your original document resides. If you ever need to open a previous version of a file, just look in the destination folder. The file with the highest number appended to its name is the most recent revision. Note that it's often a good idea to change the backup destination folder to a different hard drive, just in case the one you're working on goes south.

▼ ▼

Tip: Fill 'Er Up with Backups. After working with Auto Backup for a couple of weeks, you may find your hard drive mysteriously filling up. Remember, those backup files (as many per file as you've specified in Application Preferences) don't go away by themselves. You need to delete them when you're done with them. One suggestion: Set your Auto Backup to save to a special backup folder on a seldom-used drive.

▼ ▼

Templates

To some people, the concept of templates seems shrouded in more mystery than the Druids of old. Here's an area that seems complicated because people make it complicated. But it's not.

You have the choice of saving your document as a template when you're in the Save As dialog box. When a file is saved as a template, nothing changes except that you cannot accidentally save over it. For example, let's say you create a document and save it as a normal document called "Newsletter Template." Then, a couple of days later you go back into the document and create the newsletter: you make changes, flow text in, and place pictures. You then select Save from the File menu. The file, "Newsletter Template," is modified with the changes you made, and there is no way to "go back" to the original untouched file (unless you've made a backup somewhere).

Okay, now let's say you create that same "Newsletter Template," then save it as a template by clicking Template in the Save As dialog box. Then, when you make changes to that document and select Save from the File menu, QuarkXPress doesn't automatically erase the old file and replace it with the new one. Instead, it gives you the Save As dialog box and lets you choose a different name. When you open a template, it opens as an "Untitled" document.

▼ ▼

Tip: Resaving Templates. If QuarkXPress gives you the Save As dialog box when you try to save a document specified as a template, how can you change the template itself? Simple. You can replace the old template with a new one by giving it exactly the same name in the Save As dialog box. (Don't forget to click the Template button if you still want it to be a template.)

▼ ▼

Tip: Alternate Templates. System 7 introduced the concept of Stationery, which hasn't caught on yet. Instead of saving a file as a document or as a template, you save it as a document or a stationery pad. QuarkXPress doesn't implement this, but you can use the Finder's Get Info command on a document, and then click the Stationery Pad box. Then, when you open that file, it automatically opens it as an "Untitled" window. Stationery isn't only for QuarkXPress documents; any Macintosh document can be made into a template using this Get Info feature. In some programs, this has replaced the Template option in Save As.

▼ ▼

Multiple Documents

QuarkXPress lets you open up to 25 document windows at a time. However, the actual number and size of documents you can have open depends on both the amount of memory available and the number of files open. (QuarkXPress internally opens more files than just the documents you work with; see "Tip: Too Many Files Open," below.)

Window management. Having so many document windows open at once could mean massive clutter and confusion (especially for Eric, who thinks that the Mac's "desktop metaphor" was created to let him make his virtual desktop as messy as his physical one); fortunately, Quark has provided two solutions.

First, under the View menu, the Windows submenu lists all open document windows (including the Clipboard and Help and Find/Change windows). Just selecting a window makes it active, which is particularly convenient if the window you want happens to be hidden beneath a slew of other windows.

Second, there are two items in the Windows submenu: Stack Documents and Tile Documents (see Figure 1-8). The Stack Documents command arranges your windows somewhat like a slightly fanned hand of cards. There's always at least a tiny smidgen of each window showing, even the hindmost one, so you can select any window by clicking on it.

Figure 1-8
The Windows
submenu

Tiling resizes every document window so that each takes up an equal portion of your Mac's screen. So if you have three document windows, tiling sizes and arranges them so that each takes up one-third of your screen. We often use this when dragging objects or pages from one document to another.

▼ ▼

Tip: Windows Menu Shortcut. The Windows submenu sure is useful, but getting to its hierarchical commands is a pain in the mouse, especially since Quark has placed it right in the middle of the View menu. Fortunately, there's an easy and eminently logical shortcut. Hold down the Shift key and drag on the title bar of your active document window; up pops an exact replica of the Windows menu, from which you can select any window, or stack or tile them all (see Figure 1-9). What better place for a Windows menu than in a window itself?

▼ ▼

Tip: Tiling to Multiple Monitors. Our associate Glenn runs Quark-XPress from his Macintosh Duo, and when he's in the office he uses both the Duo screen and an additional monitor. It turns out that if you have more than one monitor attached to your Mac, you can have QuarkXPress tile documents so that the tiling spreads across all your available monitors. So if you have two monitors and four open documents, two documents will appear

Figure 1-9

Popup menu from
the title bar of a
document window

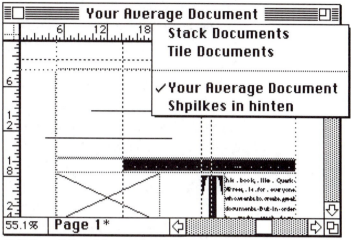

Hold down Shift and drag on the title bar.

in each monitor. You can turn on this feature by checking the Tile
to Multiple Monitors box in the Application Preferences dialog
box. If you leave this box unchecked, QuarkXPress tiles all the
open documents within your main monitor only (the one that's
displaying the menu bar).

▼ ▼

Tip: Full-Screen Documents. You've probably noticed that whenever
you open a document or make a new one, the document window
sizes itself nicely to the size of your screen, except that it leaves
some room at the left and bottom edges for the default locations
of the Tool and Measurements palettes. Even if you click on the
window's Zoom box, the document expands but leaves the
palette area untouched.

However, you can choose how you want QuarkXPress to
behave when you zoom a window. In the Application Preferences
dialog box, under the Display section, there's a checkbox labeled
Full-Screen Documents. Check the box (the default is unchecked),
and whenever you open or create a new document, or zoom a
document window, it'll fill your entire screen. Leave it unchecked,
and zooming respects the default location of the Tool and Measurements palette.

▼ ▼

Tip: Too Many Files Open. Here's a tip that's only relevant if you use an operating system earlier than 7.0. The early Macintosh systems only let you have a limited number of files open at one time. This number was determined for the original Finder, and—for some obscure reason—was never raised when MultiFinder was created. Obviously, the more applications you have running at a time, the more files you have open. This is especially true because many applications open "invisible" files that you don't ordinarily know about. For example, QuarkXPress opens one file for each XTension you have available in your QuarkXPress folder, plus a file for the XPress Dictionary, XPress Hyphenation, and so on.

When we ran two or more applications at a time under System 6.0.x, we found ourselves staring at warning dialog boxes that said we couldn't open another file, and listening to mysterious beeps when we tried to open anything from the Apple menu. Then we learned that we could use a utility such as Fedit (or an option in the old Suitcase II) to increase Apple's limit. Any utility that lets you alter the boot blocks of your system should work fine. This is a very easy process. We set ours to 40 (which, for some technical reasons, actually meant that we could have up to 200 files open), and we never had another problem of this sort.

We still think the best workaround for this problem, though, is simply to upgrade to System 7 or later, in which case this isn't an issue.

▼ ▼

Locking Documents

There's one other method of insuring against undesirable changes to documents: locking the file. This, like the Stationery feature we talked about earlier, is a function of the Macintosh system rather than QuarkXPress. You can lock an entire document by selecting the document in the Finder, choosing Get Info from the File menu, and clicking the Locked checkbox in the lower-left corner of the Get Info dialog box. Another way to lock a file is by using PrairieSoft's DiskTop utility. You can select a file, press Command-I (for Get Info), then click the Locked checkbox. This is handy for locking documents on the fly.

If you open a locked QuarkXPress document by double-clicking on it, you are told that this is a locked file and that you won't be able to save your changes. If you open the locked file from within QuarkXPress and later try to save it, you get a nasty "Can't Save to Disk" error. The only way to save a locked file is to perform a Save As under a different name.

We don't really recommend this method for creating templates. It's kind of a hassle, and makes us a little nervous. Locking documents is good, however, for making sure someone else doesn't come in and inadvertently screw up the work you've done.

▼ ▼

QuarkXPress's Interface

While working in QuarkXPress, you have access to its powerful tools and features through several areas: menus, palettes, dialog boxes, and keystrokes. Let's look carefully at each of these methods and how you can use them.

Menus

There are several conventions used in QuarkXPress's menus. One is the hierarchical menu, which we call a submenu. These allow multiple items to be, literally, offshoots of the primary menu item. Another convention is the checkmark. A checkmark next to a menu item shows that the feature is enabled or activated. Selecting that item turns the feature off—or disables it—and the checkmark goes away. If a menu item has an ellipsis (. . .) after it, you know that selecting it will bring up a dialog box. Finally, menus show the main keystroke shortcut for a menu item. Figure 1-10 shows these three menu conventions. Other conventions are discussed as needed throughout the book.

Figure 1-10

Menu conventions

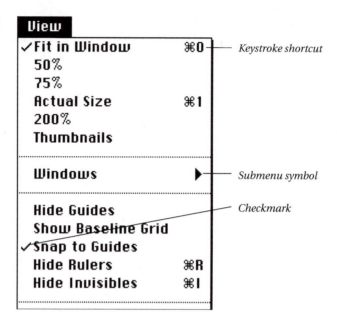

Keystroke shortcut

Submenu symbol

Checkmark

We don't need to talk a great deal about menus and what's on them here, because we discuss their contents throughout the book. However, you should note that certain types of features fall under particular menus. Let's go through a quick rundown.

File. Items on the File menu relate to disk files (entire documents). Commands to open, save, and print disk files are located here.

Edit. The Edit menu contains features for changing items within QuarkXPress. The last section of the Edit menu contains features to edit internal defaults on a document- or application-wide level, such as the color palette, the text style sheets, and specifications for each tool on the Tool palette (see "Tool palette," below).

Style. The Style menu changes depending on what item you have selected on your document page. Selecting a picture box results in one Style menu, selecting a text box results in a different one, and rules (lines) result in a third menu. The items on the Style menu enable you to change specific style attributes of the selected item.

Item. Whereas the Style menu contains commands for changing the contents of a picture or text box, the Item menu's commands change the box or rule itself. For example, changing the style of a picture box's contents might involve changing the shade of a picture. Changing an attribute of the box itself may involve changing the frame thickness of the picture box.

Page. The Page menu is devoted to entire pages in your document. Controls for master pages (see Chapter 2, *Document Construction*) are located here, as well as several features for adding, deleting, and navigating among pages.

View. Almost every feature based on what you see and how you see it is located in the View menu. This menu also includes several other items, such as Show Guides, that involve QuarkXPress's interface. We'll be discussing these later in this chapter.

Utilities. This menu is, in many ways, a catch-all that contains assorted goodies for helping make pages. The spelling checker, libraries, and so forth are kept here. Also, most XTensions add items to the Utilities menu, so the more XTensions you have, the longer this menu is.

▼ ▼

Tip: Adding Your Own Keystrokes. This is *not* a paid political announcement. We love QuicKeys. To be fair, there are other macromakers around (*e.g.,* Tempo II), but we know QuicKeys the best and we're continually amazed at what it helps us do (see Figure 1-11). For those who don't know what making macros is all about, let us elucidate. Macros are miniprograms that you can build that tell the computer to do something.

For example, if you use the Move to Front function from the Item menu often (we do), you may want to create a macro that selects Move to Front for you in a keystroke rather than having to pull down a menu yourself. We have one of these: Command-Control-F. This saves more time than you can imagine (or, if it doesn't, it at least feels like it does—which is just as good).

Figure 1-11

QuicKeys 3.0's main window

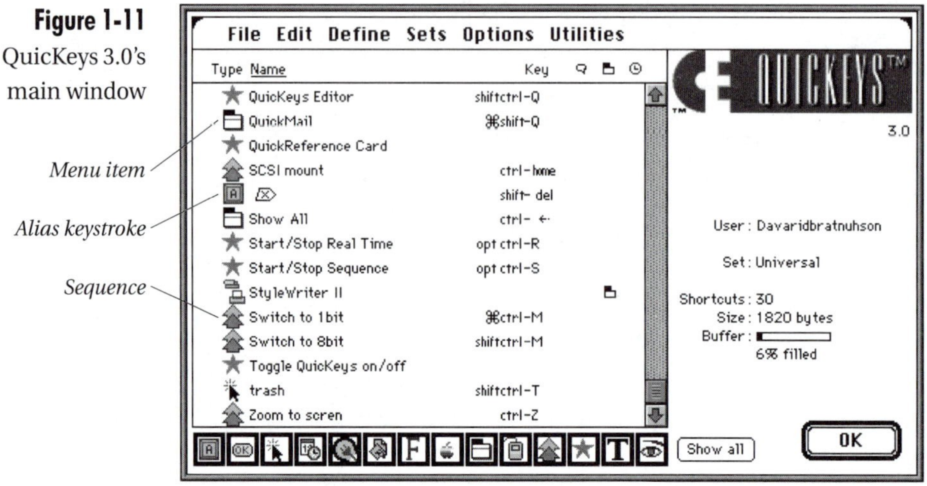

Menu item

Alias keystroke

Sequence

Macros don't have to be as simple as just selecting a menu item, though. For example, one macro we have selects a paragraph, applies a style, puts an extra rule above the paragraph, and places a special character after the paragraph's last word. One keystroke sets the macro off and running.

▼ ▼

Palettes

One of the key elements in QuarkXPress's user interface is the palette structure. A palette in QuarkXPress is similar to a painter's palette insofar as a palette contains a selection of usable and changeable items that you can put wherever suits you best. A left-handed painter may hold a paint palette in her right hand, while a short ambidextrous painter might place the palette on the floor. QuarkXPress has several palettes, each with a different function, which can be placed anywhere you like on the screen. They're additional windows on the screen that, although they can overlap one another, never go "behind" a document window. Because of this, we call them *floating* palettes.

You can manipulate palettes in the same manner as you would move a Macintosh window. For example, to move a palette, drag the window from the top shaded area. To close a palette, click the Close box in the upper-left corner. Also, two palettes we'll talk about (the Document Layout palette and the Libraries palette) have Zoom boxes in their upper-right corners. Click the Zoom box once and the palette expands; again, and it reduces in size.

QuarkXPress comes with seven palettes: Tool, Measurements, Document Layout, Colors, Style Sheets, Trap Information, and Library (see Figure 1-12). When you first launch QuarkXPress, you can see two of these seven: the Tool palette and the Measurements palette.

QuarkXPress remembers which palettes are open or closed and where each palette is placed, so palettes show up where you left them next time you launch the program.

Let's take a look at each of these palettes.

Tool palette. The Tool palette is the most elementary and functional of the palettes. There's not a lot you can do without it. Here you have the tools for making boxes in which you place your pictures and text, tools for rotating, tools for drawing lines, and tools for linking the text boxes together to allow the flow of text. Selecting a tool is easy: just click on it (see "Tip: Keyboard Palettes," below). We won't go into each tool here, as we discuss them in "Using the Tools," later in this chapter.

Measurements palette. Like the Style menu, the Measurements palette is dynamic: it changes depending on what sort of item is selected. Text boxes have one type of Measurements palette, Picture boxes have a second type, and rules and lines have a third type (see Figure 1-13). Which tool from the Tool palette you have selected also has an effect on how the Measurements palette looks. The Measurements palette's purpose in life is to show you an item's vital statistics and save you a trip to the Style or Item menu for making changes to those page elements.

For example, if you select a text box, the Measurements palette shows the dimensions of the text box, the coordinate of its upper-left corner, the number of columns in the box, the rotation angle of the box, and the style, font, and size of the text you've selected in the box.

Figure 1-12

QuarkXPress's
seven palettes

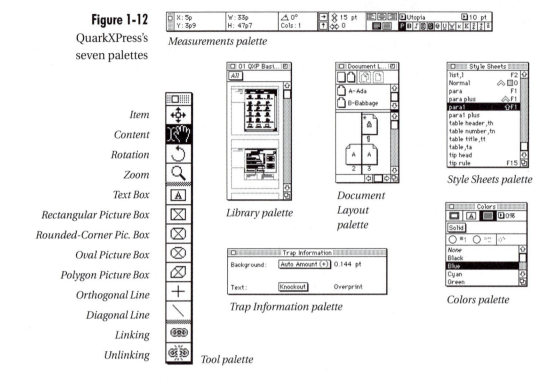

Measurements palette

Item
Content
Rotation
Zoom
Text Box
Rectangular Picture Box
Rounded-Corner Pic. Box
Oval Picture Box
Polygon Picture Box
Orthogonal Line
Diagonal Line
Linking
Unlinking

Tool palette

Library palette

Document Layout palette

Style Sheets palette

Trap Information palette

Colors palette

Not only does the Measurements palette display this information, but you can click on an item in the palette and change it. For example, if you want to rotate a picture box 10 degrees, you replace the "0" with "10" and then press either Return or Enter. (Pressing Return or Enter tells QuarkXPress that you've finished; it's like clicking an OK button.)

Note that the left half of a Measurements palette displays information about a page element (an "item"), and the right half displays information about the contents or the style of the item (see "Items and Contents" page 54).

▼ ▼

Tip: Keyboard Palettes. You can access and select items on either the Tool palette or the Measurements palette using keyboard commands. To show or hide the Tool palette, press the F8 key (if you have an extended keyboard). To select the next tool down on the Tool palette, press Command-Tab or Option-F8. To select the next higher tool, press Command-Shift-Tab or Shift-Option-F8. If

Figure 1-13

The Measurements palette's displays for the three kinds of item selections

For text boxes

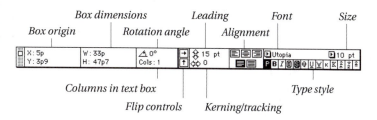

For picture boxes

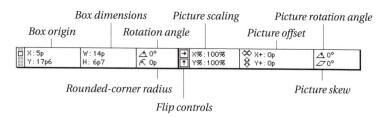

For lines (rules)

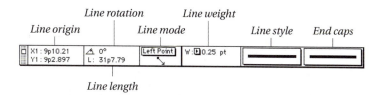

you have closed (hidden) the Tool palette, you can open it by pressing any of these key commands.

You also can use the Tab key to move through the Measurements palette. You can jump to the first item on this palette by pressing Command-Option-M (this also opens the palette, if it was closed).

David finds it much faster to toggle between items on the Tool palette using keystrokes, especially when moving between the Content tool and the Item tool. And he hardly ever uses the mouse to click in the Measurements palette, preferring to press Command-Option-M, then tabbing through the items until he gets where he wants. You can also press F9 to show and hide the Measurements palette.

▼ ▼

Tip: Jump to Fonts. If you've ever wondered how the Research and Development department at Quark decides what features to put into QuarkXPress, this might amuse you. Tim Gill, founder and senior vice-president for R&D at Quark, attended the first annual Quark Users' International Conference in New York City back in 1991. In the middle of a question-and-answer session, someone stood up and asked if there was a way to change quickly from one font to another. He thought about it for a few moments and replied, "How about a keystroke that places you in the font field of the Measurements palette?" After a round of applause, he said, "Okay, it'll be in the next version." That keystroke, we're proud to report, is Command-Shift-Option-M (the same as jumping to the Measurements palette, but adding the Shift key).

doesn't work — ?

▼ ▼

Document Layout palette. You can find the Document Layout palette by selecting Show Document Layout from the View menu (or pressing the F10 key). This palette displays a graphic representation of your document, page by page. When you first start using it, it's slightly weird, but the more you work with it, the more you realize how amazingly cool it is.

We discuss the Document Layout palette in "Manipulating Your Document," later in this chapter, but—in a nutshell—you can use this palette for creating, deleting, and shuffling pages, assigning master pages, and creating multipage spreads. Generally, many of the functions of the Page menu can be performed by dragging icons in the Document Layout palette.

Style Sheets palette. The principle is simple: whenever you're working with text, you can apply, edit, and view style sheets on the fly by using the Style Sheets palette. This palette lists all the styles in your document, along with their keyboard shortcuts if they have any. (If you have lots of styles, you can make the palette larger or just scroll through them.) We discuss the Style Sheets palette (including what style sheets are, if you don't know already) in Chapter 5, *Copy Flow*.

Colors palette. Just like styles, you can apply and edit colors with a click, using the Colors palette. This floating palette contains a list of every available color, along with a tint-percentage control and three icons. Depending on what tool and object you have selected, some icons are grayed out. When you select a text box, the icons represent frame color, text color, and background color for that box. When you select a line, two icons gray out, and only the line-color icon remains. We'll cover this in more detail in Chapter 9, *Color.*

Trap Information palette. Unlike most palettes in QuarkXPress, where you have the option either to use them or to use menu items, the Trap Information palette is the only way that you can use object-by-object trapping (we cover trapping in detail in Chapter 9, *Color*). The palette shows you the current trap information for a selected page object, gives you "reasons" for why it's trapping the object that way, and lets you change that object's trap value. Unless you've changed the trap value, the Trap Information palette displays all objects at their default trap.

Libraries. Here's another QuarkXPress feature which we discuss in much greater detail later in this chapter (we're not trying to tease; we're just taking things one step at a time). The Library looks like a simple palette, but it has some very powerful uses. You can have more than one Library palette open at a time (each floating palette represents one Library file), and you are able to store up to 2,000 items in each library. Libraries are slightly different from other palettes in that they're not accessed by the View menu; you use the New Library command to create them, and the standard Open dialog box to access them (both under the File menu).

Dialog Boxes

You can perform almost every function in QuarkXPress with only the palettes and the menus. However, it is rarely efficient to work this way. Dialog boxes are areas in which you can usually change many specifications for an item at one time. For example, Figure

1-14 shows the Text Box Specifications dialog box. In this dialog box, you can modify any or every item quickly, then click OK to make those changes take effect.

Figure 1-14

A typical dialog box

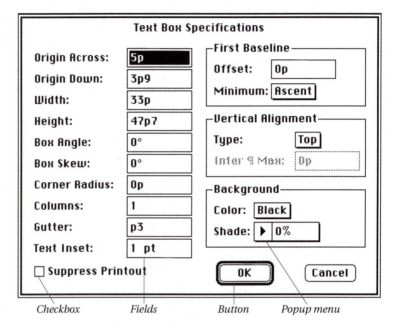

Checkbox   *Fields*   *Button*   *Popup menu*

Dialog box terminology. Here's a quick lesson in terminology, if you're unfamiliar with dialog boxes. The area in which you enter a value is called a *field*. Oftentimes there are *checkboxes* that can be checked on or off, or grayed out if undefined. Many dialog boxes also contain *popup menus*, which act much like the menus at the top of the screen: just position the cursor on them, press the mouse button, and drag the mouse up or down until you have selected the item you want. Then let go of the mouse button.

Typically, dialog boxes have two buttons: OK and Cancel. Clicking OK closes the dialog box and puts your changes into effect. Cancel closes the dialog box and ignores the changes you've made. Some dialog boxes have a Save option, which acts as OK. Other dialog boxes have an Apply button. Clicking this button temporarily applies the settings you've made to the document so that you can see them. If you like what you see, you can then click OK. If you don't like it, you can usually press Command-Z to revert the dialog box to the last setting. In any case, you can click Cancel to rid yourself of the dialog box and the changes you've made, even after applying them (see "Undo and Cancel," page 52).

▼ ▼

Tip: Pushing Your Buttons. Almost every button in QuarkXPress's dialog boxes can be replaced with a keystroke. The keystroke is usually the first letter in the button's name. For example, if a dialog box has Yes and No buttons, you can select them by pressing Command-Y and Command-N. When you're checking spelling in a story, you can select the Skip button by pressing Command-S. Note that any button that is highlighted (has a darker border than a normal button) can be selected by pressing Enter or Return (This is usually OK, but might be something else, such as Find Next in the Find/Change dialog box.) Cancel is always selected by pressing Command-period.

▼ ▼

Tip: Continuous Apply. As we said earlier, the Apply button temporarily applies the change you made in a dialog box. You can then decide whether you want to actually make that change, revert, or cancel the operation entirely. Even though pressing Command-A speeds up the process some, we often find it helpful to be in a Continuous Apply mode by pressing Command-Option-A (or holding down the Option key while clicking Apply). Pressing this highlights the Apply button (turns it black), as if you were holding the button down continuously. Now, every change you make in the dialog box is immediately applied to your page item. You can still press Command-Z to undo the last change, or Command-Period to cancel the dialog box. To turn off Continuous Apply, just press Command-Option-A again.

By the Numbers

Unless you raise horses and measure everything in "hands," chances are that you and QuarkXPress share a common measurement system. QuarkXPress understands measurements in points, picas, inches, ciceros, centimeters, and millimeters. You can use these measurement units at any time, no matter what the default setting is (see "Changing Defaults" later in this chapter). Table 1-2 shows how to specify a value for each system.

Table 1-2

Measurement systems

You can spec . . .	By typing . . .	Examples
points	pt or p	6pt or p6
picas	p	10p or 2p6 (2 picas, 6 points)
inches (decimal)	"	6" or 6.5" or 6.888832"
ciceros	c	2c or 6c3 (6 ciceros, 3 points)
centimeters	cm	3cm
millimeters	mm	210mm
Q (Japanese unit)	Q	4Q

If you're like us, our mathematical abilities have degenerated to the point of having to use calculators to "be fruitful and multiply." Realizing this, Quark incorporated the ability to calculate into every entry field. You can specify measurements with a plus or minus sign to build simple equations using one or more measurement units. For example, if a measurement was set to "10p", and you wanted to add 4 cm, you could type "10p+4cm". Similarly, if you wanted to take away one pica, two points (ever since calculators, our math skills have degenerated horribly), we could type "10p-1p2". Note that the first example mixes measurement systems; you don't have to be consistent here because the program does all the math for you.

Similarly, you can use * (the asterisk) for multiplication and / (the slash) for division in any field. If you have a text box that measures 4.323 inches, and you want to make it two-thirds as wide, just add "*2/3", to the right of the inch mark. Or, if you want to make a picture box 120 percent of its current size, just type "*1.2" after the width measurement. Remember that you can mix up and match all the measurements, too; so even "3p+24mm/3*9" is valid (though we can't think why you'd need it).

The Value Converter palette (see Figure 1-15) lets you type numbers in any measurement system and shows you the conversion dynamically in all measurement systems that XPress supports. You must have the FeaturesPlus or Thing-a-ma-bob XTension in the same folder as QuarkXPress to access this feature.

Figure 1-15
Value Converter
palette

The Value Converter palette is added by the FeaturesPlus XTension (or the Thing-a-ma-bob XTension in version 3.3)

After You Click OK

Mistakes are common in the world of desktop publishing. In fact, one of the great benefits of working on a computer, in our opinion, is that we can make as many mistakes as we want and always recover from them. In QuarkXPress, there are several methods to recover from a mistake or a decision you later regret.

Revert To Saved

As we said above, no changes are permanent until you save them. If you want to discard all changes made to a document since the last save, you can do it by closing the document (choose Close from the File menu) and telling QuarkXPress that you don't want to save the changes. Or, if you wish to continue working on it without interruption, choose Revert to Saved from the File menu. For example, if—in the name of improvement—you have managed to mess up your document beyond redemption, you can revert to the version that you last saved.

Tip: Revert to Last Minisave. The Auto Save feature we talked about above goes by another name, too: PageMaker calls these things minisaves. Sometimes you want to use a minisave as something other than crash insurance. In version 3.3, you can actually revert to the last autosave instead of going back all the way to the last full save (for instance, if you like the changes you made 10 minutes ago, but not the ones you made five minutes ago). Just hold down the Option key when you select Revert from the File menu.

▼ ▼

Undo and Cancel

Since we're on the topic of reverting back and ignoring changes to the document, we really need to take a quick detour and look at the Undo and Cancel commands. Undo is found under the Edit menu, and is a staple of all Macintosh programs. If you make a mistake, you can almost always Undo it (press Command-Z or the F4 key). And if you're in the middle of making a mistake, you can press Command-period to cancel the action.

While it's just that simple in most Macintosh programs, Quark-XPress has some interesting extra features which might be helpful to know about.

Interruptible screen redraw. QuarkXPress 3.2 introduced a new feature that can make life much better: interruptible screen redraw. If you have 43 pictures and text boxes on your page and it's taking forever to draw them, you can press Command-period to cancel the redraw. QuarkXPress stops drawing as soon as it finishes drawing the next object (that's slightly different from some other programs, such as Adobe Photoshop, which stop immediately).

Text. Any text you type can be undone until you move the cursor point. For example, if you type three words, then move back a word and add a letter, QuarkXPress resets its Undo "memory" so an Undo would only remove the added letters. This can be frustrating if you don't really know what's going on because it seems like it forgets stuff. It's not forgetful; we are.

Type styles. Typographic styles are also remembered and can be undone. Note that QuarkXPress undoes all the styles you've applied since you last started applying styles. We know that sounds strange, so here's an example: if you select a word and make it bold and italic and small caps (we'll show you how to do all that later in the book), and then press Command-Z, Quark-XPress reverts to how the text was before you applied any type styles. However, if you move the text insertion point by clicking somewhere else or moving with keystrokes, then the program resets its Undo memory again and you can't Undo any of it.

Multiple items. One of the banes of our existence has been the inability to undo the deletion of multiple items—until now. QuarkXPress version 3.3 now gives you the chance to undo any action that removes more than one item at a time. That means that you can delete two or 200 picture boxes, text boxes, lines, or anchored boxes without fear of screwing up royally. But there's a catch: if you do anything even so slight as to click someplace else on the page, the program resets its memory and can't recover your action. Deleting a group unlinks all linked text boxs; it doesn't relink them when you Undo. Undo is a fragile thing; in the words of Arthur Miller, "attention must be paid."

Dialog boxes and palettes. You can get yourself out of a bad situation in every dialog box or palette in QuarkXPress by remembering the ubiquitous and powerful features: Command-period (Cancel) and Command-Z (Undo). For instance, if you change the x or y coordinates for a text box, and then decide what you're doing is a mistake, you can undo it even before the change takes place. Pressing Command-Z reverts to the previous state and keeps the field highlighted. Pressing Command-period reverts and takes you out of the palette or dialog box altogether.

Using the Tools

Up to now, we've primarily talked about the general interface: this does this, that does that. Now our emphasis shifts toward the practical. Let's look at each tool on the Tool palette in turn.

Items and Contents

If you only learn one thing from this chapter it should be the difference between items and contents. This is a concept that some people find difficult to understand, but it is really pretty simple. Moreover, the concept of items and contents is central to working efficiently in QuarkXPress.

Let's take it from the beginning. In order to put text on a page, you must place it in a text box. To put a graphic image on a page, you must place it in a picture box. Text boxes act as a sort of corral that holds all the words. There's almost no way a word can get outside the bounds of a text box. Picture boxes act as a sort of window through which you can see a picture. In both cases, the content of the box is different from the box itself.

Boxes are *items*. What goes inside them is *content*. You can modify either one, but you need to use the correct tool at the correct time.

Item tool. The Item tool is the first tool on the Tool palette (or "Pointer tool"; though sometimes it's called by its technical name: "the pointy-thingy"). It's used for selecting and moving items (picture and text boxes, rules, and so on). You can use the Item tool by either choosing it from the Tool palette or holding down the Command key while any other tool is selected (though you can't select or work with multiple items unless you actually have the Item tool selected). We discuss all the things you can do with items later in "Manipulating Items," page 66.

Content tool. The second tool on the Tool palette is the Content tool (sometimes called the "Hand tool"). This tool is used for adding, deleting, or modifying the contents of a text or picture box. Note that its palette icon consists of a text-insertion mark and a hand. When you have selected this tool from the Tool palette, QuarkXPress turns the cursor into one of these icons, depending on what sort of box you have highlighted (as we'll see in Chapter 6, *Pictures*, the hand is for moving images around within a picture box).

▼ ▼

Tip: Where Did the Rest of My Page Go? QuarkXPress novices, and even experienced users, often get a rude shock when working on complicated page layouts because of a curious side effect of the Content tool. Whenever you select a text or picture box, that box hides all page elements it overlaps. This feature can be useful because it lets you edit the contents of a box free of any distractions caused by other page elements. However, the sudden disappearance of many or most of the elements on a page can make even the most experienced users momentarily confused.

Of course, these "vanished" elements return to view if you deselect the box you're editing. Click someplace else or switch to the Item tool. (Remember, you can quickly switch from the Content tool to the Item tool by pressing Command-Shift-Tab or Option-Shift-F8, and back again with Command-Tab or Option-F8.)

▼ ▼

Text Boxes

In this chapter we're mostly talking about items, which we sometimes call page elements or objects. The first tool on the Tool palette that lets us make a page element is the Text Box tool. Creating text boxes is simple: choose the Text Box tool from the Tool palette, and then click and drag a text box. You can see exactly how large your text box is by watching the width and height values on the Measurements palette. Note that you can keep the text box square by holding down the Shift key while dragging.

Text boxes—as items—have five basic attributes: position, size, background color, columns, and text inset. They also have border or frame attributes, rotation and skew angle, and (in version 3.3) corner radius. We discuss each of these later in this chapter.

▼ ▼

Tip: Keeping Your Tools Around. After you use a tool like the text or picture box tool, the Tool palette automatically reverts back to either the Content or the Item tool (depending on which of the two you last used). This becomes a hassle if you want to use the same tool again. Instead, you can hold down the Option key as you select a tool. The tool remains selected until you choose another one.

▼ ▼

Position and size. All boxes are positioned by their upper-left corner. This point is called their *origin*. The first two fields in the Text

where is Text Specs ? ——Specifications dialog box (select the box and press Command-M) and the text box Measurements palette are Origin Across and Origin Down. The size of the box is then specified by its width and height (the distances to the right and down from the origin). Note that if you've rotated the box, it still thinks of the origin as its original corner. So if you rotate 90 degrees clockwise, the upper right corner (formerly the upper-left corner) is still the origin point.

▼ ▼

Tip: Quick Accurate Boxes. Some people tend toward a visual approach to creating and sizing boxes in QuarkXPress, while others work with a more mathematical or coordinate-based method. Fortunately, both work equally as well. You can click and drag page elements out to the size you want them, if you prefer to make a decision based on seeing what it looks like.

Or, if you're working on a grid, you can draw a box to any size, and then go into the Measurements palette or Item Specifications dialog box to specify the origin coordinates, the width, and the height.

▼ ▼

Tip: Moving an Item's Origin. PageMaker lets you set the origin of a page element from a number of locations, rather than just the upper-left corner. Until QuarkXPress does the same, we can only offer a somewhat weak workaround for specifying alternate origins: use the built-in math functions. If you want the right side of a 12-pica-wide picture box to be set at the 2.75-inch mark, type "2.75"-12p" into the x-origin field of the Measurements palette. That is, simply subtract the width of the box from the right point. Or, if you want the center of a 16-pica-wide text box to be at the 18 cm mark, you can type "18cm-16p/2".

▼ ▼

Background color. Every picture or text box has a background color (see Chapter 9, *Color*), or can have a background set to None. Any background color other than None can be set to a specific tint.

Note that zero percent of a color is not transparent; it's opaque white. This background color reaches all the way to the inside edge of the frame around the box. There is a subtle distinction between going to the edge of the box and the edge of the frame: if you specified a frame on a box, the background color only fills to the frame, rather than the edge of the box (see "Frames," page 112). If you have not specified a frame around a box, however, then the background color fills the box up to the border.

Columns. While the last two items were applicable to both text and picture boxes, the columns attribute is text-box specific. Text boxes can be divided into a maximum of 30 columns. Each column's size is determined by the size of the *gutter* (blank space) between columns. You can set the gutter width only in the Text Box Specifications dialog box, although you can set the number of columns in either this dialog box or the Measurements palette.

Note that you cannot have columns with negative widths: the number of columns you can have is determined by the gutter width. For example, if your gutter width is one pica and your text box is 20-picas wide, you cannot have more than 20 columns; however, that many columns would leave no room for text.

Text Inset. The last attribute particular to text boxes is Text Inset. The Text Inset value determines how far your text is placed inside the four sides of the text box. For example, a Text Inset value of zero places the text right up against the side of the text box. A text inset value of "3cm" places the text no closer than three centimeters from the side of the box.

The default setting for text inset is one point. We can't tell you why; we find it rather obnoxious. In "Changing Defaults," page 122, we discuss how to change these default settings. We usually just change it to zero for Text Inset. You can only specify the Text Inset value in the Text Box Specifications dialog box.

Note that there are XTensions, like The Kitchen Sink and Text Inset XT, that let you specify the Text Inset value for each of the four sides rather than simply one value for all sides. That can be very helpful in certain situations.

▼ ▼

Tip: That Ol' Specifications Dialog Box. We use the Specifications dialog box for picture boxes, text boxes, and rules so much that we're glad to have some variance in how we get to it. You can open a Specifications dialog box for a page element in three ways.

► Double-click on the page element with the Item tool. (Remember, you can hold down the Command key to temporarily work with the Item tool.)

► Select the item with either the Content or the Item tool and press Command-M.

► Select the item with either the Content or the Item tool and choose Modify from the Item menu.

Once you're in the dialog box, you can tab through the fields to get to the value you want to change. After a while, you memorize how many tabs it takes to get to a field, and you can press Command-M, Tab, Tab, Tab, Tab, Tab, type the value, press Return, and be out of there before QuarkXPress has time to catch up with you. That's when you know you're becoming an XPress Demon.

▼ ▼

Picture Boxes

As we said above, picture boxes are made to hold pictures. That's part of the truth, but let's hold off on that subject for a bit. Chapter 6, *Pictures*, tells us all about importing pictures. QuarkXPress gives us four different tools for creating picture boxes. Each makes a box of a different shape: rectangles, rounded-corner rectangles, ovals, and polygons. Let's take a brief look at each of these and why you should use them.

Rectangular Picture Box tool. This is the basic, no-frills picture box maker. As with the Text Box tool above, just click and drag a box to the size you want it. We use this box for 95 percent of the picture boxes we make.

Rounded-Corner Picture Box tool. The Rounded-corner Picture Box tool makes rectangular picture boxes that have rounded corners. Is this of interest to you? Not to be biased, but some of the all-time worst designs that have come off a Macintosh use rounded-corner picture boxes. We really dislike them. But, then again, it's your design, and you can do what you like with it.

Plus, to be frank for a moment: this tool is redundant. Why? Any rectangular picture box can have rounded corners simply by an adjustment to the Corner Radius value in the Picture Box Spec-ifications dialog box or the Measurements palette. Unless you use a lot of rounded-corner picture boxes (and if you do, we don't want to know about it), you probably could get by with just using the Rectangular Picture Box tool and adjusting the Corner Radius.

Oval Picture Box tool. When you need circles and ovals, the Oval Pic-ture Box tool is the way to get them. Ovals are constrained to circles when you hold the Shift key down while dragging. Note that oval picture boxes are still defined by the rectangle that bounds them. That is, you modify an oval's shape by its height and width.

Polygon Picture Box tool. The Polygon Picture Box tool lets you make a picture box in almost any shape you'd like. The key is that the shape must be made of straight lines only .

The basic method for creating this type of frame is to click on the Polygon Picture Box tool, click where you want your first point to be (it doesn't matter which corner of the frame you begin with), then keep clicking at successive corners to create the shape you want. You'll notice that when the mouse hovers over the first point on the line, the cursor turns into a hollow circle. This indicates that it will close the path and finish the polygon when you click.

Polygonal picture boxes must have at least three points on them, but there's no limit that we can tell (and we've done some pretty complex picture boxes; see "Tip: Making Your Grayscale Picture Transparent" in Chapter 8, *Modifying Images*).

Once you have created a polygon, QuarkXPress places an invisible rectangular border around it. The corner handles of this border, like the bounding border of ovals, define the polygon's height and width. Whenever you select the polygonal picture box, you see these corner handles. You can use them to stretch the polygonal picture box, but not to reshape it. We cover reshaping and resizing polygons and other picture boxes in "Manipulating Items," later in this chapter.

Now, starting in version 3.3, you can create polygonal text boxes, too. We'll talk more about that in "Transforming Box Shapes," below.

▼ ▼

Tip: The Polygon Blues. Here's a quick one that can help you out of a jam. If you're drawing a complex polygon and can't find the first point of the polygon, don't fret, and—whatever you do—don't restart your Mac! You've got two reasonable choices. First, you can press Command-period to cancel the polygon operation. However, that kills the polygon entirely. The second choice is better: just double-click somewhere. Double-clicking automatically closes the polygon for you. Then you can go back and edit it to the shape you want.

▼ ▼

Selecting Items

The most basic action you can take with a page item in Quark-XPress is to select it. Once again: to select and modify an item itself, you need to use the Item tool. To select and modify the contents of a picture or text box, you need to use the Content tool.

You can select more than one item at a time only with the Item tool selected. You can do this by one of two methods.

Shift-click. You can select multiple items by Shift-clicking on them with the Item tool. If you have more than one item selected and you want to deselect one, you can Shift-click on it again (shift-clicking acts as a toggle for selecting and deselecting).

▼ ▼

Tip: Grab Down Deep. There are plenty of times we've found that we need to reach through one or more objects on our page and grab a picture or text box that's been covered up. Moving everything on top is a real hassle. Instead, you can select through page items to get hold of objects that are behind them. Hold down the Command-Option-Shift keys while clicking with the either the Item or Content tool to select the object one layer down. The second click selects the object on the next layer down, and so on. With the Item tool and an object selected, we've occasionally been unable to grab down deep without first deselecting the object.

▼ ▼

Marquee. If you drag with the Item tool, you can select more than one item in one fell swoop. This is called dragging a *marquee* because QuarkXPress shows you a dotted line around the area that you're dragging over. Every picture box, text box, and line that falls within this marqueed area gets selected, even if the marquee only touches it slightly.

We love the ability to drag a marquee out with the Item tool in order to select multiple objects. It's fast, it's effective, and it picks up everything in its path. However, sometimes it even picks up things you don't want it to pick up. For example, let's say you have an automatic text box on your page and then place some picture boxes on it. If you drag a marquee across the page to select the picture boxes, chances are you'll select the text box, too. You may not notice this at first, but if you group the selection or start dragging it off into a library or someplace else, you'll be taking the text box along for the ride. This spells havoc (press Command-Z quick to undo the last action).

So, just a quick lesson from people who've been there: watch out for what you select and group. And if you do select more than you want, remember that you can deselect items by holding down the Shift key and clicking on them.

▼ ▼

Tip: Deselecting *En Masse*. Starting in version 3.3, you can deselect every selected page item in one stroke by pressing Tab when the

Item tool is selected. We find this really helpful when we're zoomed in on the page and can't tell what's selected and what isn't. Note that this is the same keystroke as in FreeHand. Also, remember that the Tab key means something different with the Content tool: it makes a tab.

▼ ▼

Picture Box Attributes

Picture boxes are similar to text boxes in several ways. First, they are positioned according to their origin (upper-left corner of the box). Second, they are generally sized by their width and height. Third, they have background color (see "Text Boxes," page 55, for a discussion of these three items). However, some picture boxes have two attributes that text boxes don't: Corner Radius and Suppress Picture Printout. We'll hold off on covering the latter until Chapter 6, *Pictures*.

Corner Radius. The Corner Radius attribute is applicable to rectangular and rounded-corner rectangle boxes (including text boxes in 3.3). We've already told you how we feel about rounded corners on boxes, but—just in case you still want to make them—you can use this value to set how rounded those corners should be. Corner Radius defines the size of the radius of a circle tangent to the sides of the box (see Figure 1-16). You can change the corner radius of a rectangular picture box either in the Picture Box Specifications dialog box or in the Measurements palette (you can change the corner radius of a text box in version 3.3, but only in the Text Box Specifications dialog box).

Transforming Box Shapes

Once you have created a text or picture box, you can change it into another shape using the Box Shape submenu under the Item menu (see Figure 1-17). For example, if you made a rectangular picture box on your page you could turn it into an oval by first selecting the picture box, and then selecting the oval picture box icon in the Box Shape submenu.

Figure 1-16
Corner Radius defines
how rounded
the corners are

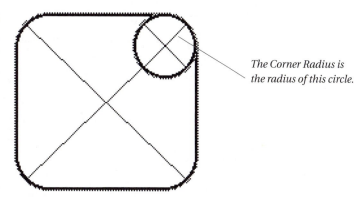

*The Corner Radius is
the radius of this circle.*

This submenu has two other preset picture boxes that you might find useful. One is a beveled corner box, another is a photo-frame box. The "depth" of the bevel or the concave curve depends on the Corner Radius setting.

The last item on the Box Shape submenu is an icon representing a polygonal picture box. When you select a picture box and then choose this last icon, the picture box does not change in any obvious way. However, this is an extremely useful technique for making slight modifications to a picture box as we'll see later when we discuss the Reshape Polygon feature.

Note that polygonal text boxes are new in QuarkXPress version 3.3.

Figure 1-17
Box Shape
submenu

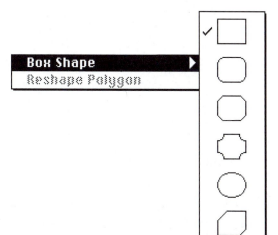

Lines and Arrows

The Tool palette contains two tools to draw lines and arrows on your page. To be precise, you really only draw lines, but those lines can be styled in several fashions, plus they can have arrowheads and tailfeathers. You can create these lines with any thickness between .001 and 864 points (that's a pretty thick line—more than 11 inches thick), and at any angle. The two tools are the Orthogonal Line tool and the Line tool.

Orthogonal Line tool. For those of you who aren't in arm's reach of a dictionary, *orthogonal* means that the lines you draw with this tool can only be horizontal or vertical. Drawing a line is easy: choose this tool from the Tool palette, then click and drag to where you want to go. This tool is somewhat redundant, insofar as you can constrain the movement of the Line tool orthogonally by holding down the Shift key. However, since many of the rules we make are horizontal or vertical, it's nice to have this option.

Line tool. The Line tool can make a line at any angle. If you hold down the Shift key while dragging out the line, you can constrain the line to 45 or 90 degrees. Don't worry if the line looks jaggy; that will smooth out when the file is printed.

Line Attributes

Once you have created a line, you can apply certain attributes to it, including line weight, style, endcaps, and color. Each of these can be specified in the Style menu or in the Line Specifications dialog box. Several also can be specified in the Measurements palette.

Line weight. We always use the word "weight" rather than "width," which is what QuarkXPress calls the thickness of a line. (When we talk about the width of horizontal lines, people often think we're talking about length.) The line weight is centered on the line. That is, if you specify a six-point line, three points fall on one side of the line, and three points fall on the other side.

This value appears in both the Line Specifications dialog box and the Measurements palette. However, we never such mundane methods; instead, we press Command-Shift-\ (backslash) to bring up the Line Width dialog box. Table 1-3 shows several other ways to change a line's weight with keystrokes. (You can use the same keystrokes to specify type size.)

Table 1-3
Changing line weight

To ...	Press ...
Increase weight by preset amount	Command-Shift-period
Increase weight by one point	Command-Shift-Option-period
Decrease weight by preset amount	Command-Shift-comma
Decrease weight by one point	Command-Shift-Option-comma

Color and shade. You can set the line's color to any color in the document (see Chapter 9, *Color*), then tint it to any value from zero to 100 percent, in .1-percent increments (zero percent is white). This specification is available in the Line Specifications dialog box or in the Colors palette.

Style and endcaps. Lines don't have to be boring; spice them up with a new style, or add endcaps to turn them into arrows. You can choose one of 11 different line styles and one of six endcap combinations by selecting them from two popup menus in either the Line Specifications dialog box or the Measurements palette (see Figure 1-18).

Figure 1-18
Line styles
and endcaps

Six of the line styles are defined as multiple lines. The weight of each line of the group is determined by a ratio. For example, each line in the double line style is given a third of the total weight (one third for a black line, another third for the clear part—the space—and so on). So if you specify the double line with a 12-point thickness, each black line is four points thick, and the white (clear) space between them is four points across.

Even though you have six to choose from, the endcap styles are limited: basically with arrowheads and tailfeathers, or without them. Because QuarkXPress defines all its lines as going from left to right or top to bottom, you can control which side the arrow head should be on by choosing the proper endcap from the popup menu. For example, if your line was drawn from left to right, and you want the head of the arrow to be on the left end of the line, you should select an endcap that has the arrow pointing to the left. Note that if you later change the line so that the left is farther to the right, QuarkXPress shifts the arrowhead so that it stays in the same position (as you'd expect).

▼ ▼

Manipulating Items

Once you've created a page element (item) such as a picture box or a line, what can you do with it? A lot. In this section we talk about how to move, rotate, skew, resize, reshape, lock, duplicate, suppress the printout of, and delete items. Remember that we're talking only about the items themselves here, so you need to select the items with the Item tool to make most of these changes.

Moving Items

You can move an entire page element in several ways. First, you can select the Item tool, then click on the object and drag it. This sometimes gets tricky if you have many different overlapping objects on a page. For example, you can click anywhere within an empty picture box to select it. However, if there's a picture in the picture box, you must click on part of the picture itself.

The second method for moving an item is by changing its origin coordinates in the Measurements palette or the Item Specifications dialog box. We find this method especially useful if we need to move the item a specific amount. For example, let's say we have a text box with its origin at one inch across and one inch down. If we want to move a text box horizontally 18 picas, we change the Origin Across coordinate in the Measurements palette to "1"+18p", then press Enter. The box automatically moves over.

A third method for moving items is by selecting them and pressing the arrow keys on the keyboard. Each time you press an arrow key, the item moves one point in that direction. Pressing Option-arrow moves the item .1 point.

[handwritten margin note: ? Doesn't it work (works for lines)]

▼ ▼

Tip: Techniques for Item Placement. If you have a style of placing and sizing your page elements—such as lines and picture boxes—that works for you, stick to it. To paraphrase an anonymous poet, "A manner of picture-box placement is a real possession in a changing world." Nonetheless, here are some basic guides that we've found helpful.

▶ Use picas and points for everything except basic page size. These are the standard units among designers and printers, and allow precision without having to deal with numbers like .08334 inches (which is six points, or half a pica). If you're working with type, this also makes it easier since type is generally specified in picas and points .

▶ Try to use round numbers for most of your measurements. Creating a box at the Fit in Window size usually gives you measurements that have coordinates out to the thousandth of a point, such as "6p3.462". It might seem like a picky detail, but, in the long run, it can come in handy to either create your boxes at Actual Size and then resize them if needed, or—if you must work at a reduced or enlarged view—go into the Measurements palette or the Item

Specifications dialog box (double-click on the box or press Command-M) and change the coordinates and the sizes to round numbers.

▶ Use the oval- or polygon-shaped boxes only when you must have that shape. Using a rectangle or square box for the majority of your pictures can cut your printing time to half or a third of what it takes when you use ovals.

▼ ▼

Tip: Viewing Changes as You Make Them. It's always a hassle to move, resize, or rotate a picture or text box because while you're doing it, QuarkXPress only shows you the outline of the box rather than the whole box. Or does it?

If you hold the mouse button down on a picture-box handle for half a second before dragging it, you can see the picture crop (or scale, if you have the Command key held down, too) as you move the handle. Similarly, if you move or rotate the box, you can see the text or picture rotate while dragging if you simply pause for half a second before starting to drag. No, you don't have to count out half a second; just wait until you see the object flash quickly before you start dragging.

▼ ▼

Resizing and Reshaping Items

Resizing an object is just about as simple as moving it. Reshaping it may be that simple, or it may be slightly more complex. Resizing and reshaping lines is a little different from resizing or reshaping picture or text boxes, so let's take them one at a time.

Picture and text boxes. Before we get into the world of reshaping polygons, let's discuss the basics: resizing and reshaping rectangular and oval boxes. Once again, you have a choice between using QuarkXPress's interactive click-and-drag style or working in measurements.

▶ **Resizing by dragging.** To resize by clicking and dragging, you place the screen cursor over one of the box's handles.

Boxes have eight handles (one on each side, one on each corner) that you can drag to resize. Dragging a side handle resizes the box in one direction—horizontally or vertically. Dragging a corner handle resizes the box in two directions (horizontally *and* vertically). As long as Reshape Polygon is not selected from the Item menu (if it's selected, it has a checkmark next to it), you can resize polygons using this same click-and-drag method.

► **Resizing by the numbers.** The second method of resizing and reshaping picture and text boxes is by changing their height and width values. These values are located in both the Item Specifications dialog box and the Measurements palette. Unless you're a wizard at math, it's difficult to keep an object's aspect (width-to-height) ratio this way (see "Tip: Proportional Resizing by the Numbers," below). Instead, this is a great way to make a box exactly the size you want it. For example, if you want an eight-by-10-inch picture box, you can draw one to any size you'd like, then change its width and height coordinates to eight inches and 10 inches.

▼ ▼

Tip: Maintain the Ratios. In order to maintain an item's width and height ratio while stretching it, you can hold down the Option and Shift keys while dragging. If you want to constrain the box into a square or circle, just hold down the Shift key while dragging. (If the object were rectangular or oval, it would snap into a square or a circle.)

▼ ▼

Tip: Proportional Resizing by the Numbers. Don't forget that Quark-XPress can do a lot of math work for you. This can come in handy in situations where you're trying to resize items on a page. For example, if you know that the one-by-two-inch box (two inches tall) on the page should be five inches wide, you can type five inches into the width box. But what do you put in the height box? If you want to keep the aspect ratio, you can let the program do a little math for you: just type "*newwidth/oldwidth" after the height value. In this example, you'd type "*5/2" after the height. This multiplies the value by the percentage change in width (if you divide five by two, you get a 250 percent change, or 2.5 times the value).

▼ ▼

Polygonal picture boxes. Once you make that last segment of a polygon by clicking on its beginning/ending point, it seems as though the game is over. If the Reshape Polygon item is not selected from the Item menu, then QuarkXPress places a rectangular bounding box around the polygonal picture box and there's no way to move a corner or a line segment. The key there, of course, is the Reshape Polygon feature from the Item menu. If you select a polygonal picture box and then enable Reshape Polygon, each corner point has its own handle.

To move a corner point, simply click on it and drag it someplace else. You also can move an entire line segment, including the two points on either end of it, by just clicking and dragging it. To add a new corner point, you can hold down the Command key and click where you want it. Or, if you want to delete a corner point that was already there, you can hold down the Command key and click on top of it.

Lines. Most people define lines by their two endpoints. However, QuarkXPress can define any line in four different ways. Each line description is called a *mode*, and it shows up in both the Line Specifications dialog box and the Measurements palette. The four modes are as follows.

- ▶ **Endpoints.** This mode describes the line by two sets of coordinates, x1,y1 and x2,y2. In the Line Specifications dialog box, these may be called the Left Endpoint and the Right Endpoint, or the Top Endpoint and the Bottom Endpoint, depending on how steep the line is.

- ▶ **Left Point.** In Left Point mode, QuarkXPress describes a line by three values: its left or bottom endpoint, its length, and its angle.

▶ **Right Point.** QuarkXPress uses the same three values for the Right Point mode, except that it uses the right or top coordinate.

▶ **Midpoint.** The fourth mode, Midpoint, defines lines by their length and angle based on the coordinate of the center point. That is, if a line is two inches long, QuarkXPress draws the line one inch out on either side from the midpoint, at the specified angle.

You can define a line while in one mode, modify it with another, and move it with another.

For example, let's say you draw a line someplace on your page. You then find you want to rotate it slightly. You have the choice to rotate the line from its left point, right point, or midpoint by selecting the proper mode from the Measurements palette or the Line Specifications dialog box, then changing the line's rotation value. If you want to move over just the left point of the line three points, you can switch to Endpoints mode and alter the x1, x2 coordinate.

To resize a line by a given percentage, you can multiply its length by the percentage. If you want a line to be 120 percent as long, just multiply the length value in the Measurements palette or Line Specifications dialog box by 1.2. To make it half as long, multiply by .5 or divide by two.

▼ ▼

Tip: Constraining Lines Along an Angle. We all know that you can hold down the Shift key while you resize or reshape a line to constrain the line horizontally and vertically. However, you also can constrain a line along its angle of rotation by holding down the Option and Shift keys together while dragging an endpoint. This is similar to constraining boxes to their width/height proportions.

▼ ▼

Tip: Making Line Joins Join. We're putting a bid in here for a Line tool that can draw more than one segment at a time (like a polygon that doesn't have to be closed). Until then, however, we are forced to use single-segment lines, carefully joining them at their corners. Note that if you place two lines' endpoints together, they won't necessarily join properly. That is, if two lines come together at a 90-degree angle, and their endpoints are specified as exactly the same, the corner joint looks chiseled out (see Figure 1-19).

Figure 1-19
Lines don't always
join properly

*Extend the line to fill
in the missing piece.*

You can fill this missing piece in two ways. First, you can move the endpoint of one of the lines half the line thickness. For example, if you are using 12-point lines, one of the lines should be extended six points. Remember, you can adjust the line mode and specify an endpoint coordinate as an equation (for example, "45p3.6+6pt").

The next method is probably easier: use Space/Align from the Item menu. If you align the left edges of the two lines, the notch disappears.

Rotating Items

You can rotate an item numerically using the Item Specifications dialog box or the Measurements palette, or by eye with the Rotation tool (the third item in the Tool palette). Note that positive rotation values rotate the object counterclockwise; negative values rotate it clockwise (this is arguably counterintuitive). Most objects are rotated from their center. This center may not be where you think it is, however. The center is defined as the middle of the object's bounding box. Figure 1-20 shows an example of an object whose center is not where you might expect.

Lines are the main exception when it comes to the center of rotation. Lines rotate differently depending on their Mode (see "Lines," above). For example, if a line is in Right Point mode when you specify a rotation, the line rotates around the right endpoint.

Figure 1-20
QuarkXPress rotates
from the center of an
object's bounding box

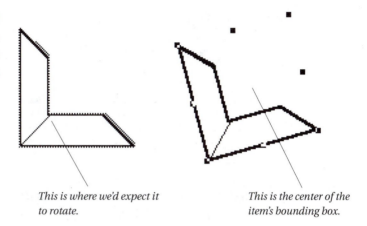

*This is where we'd expect it
to rotate.*

*This is the center of the
item's bounding box.*

If you are more visually minded, you can rotate items using
the Rotation tool.

1. Select a page item.

2. Choose the Rotation tool from the Tool palette.

3. Click where you want the center of rotation.

4. Drag the Rotation tool. As you drag, the object is rotated in
   the direction you drag. The farther from the center of rotation you drag, the more precise the rotation can be.

We don't like to use this tool, but that's just our bias. It may suit
you well. However, it's significantly harder to control the rotation
by using the tool rather than entering a specific value.

Skewing Items

QuarkXPress lets you skew text and picture boxes and their contents. (Skewing a box is much like skewing a picture, which we talk
about in Chapter 6, *Pictures*.) You can skew a text box, and all the
text within the box is skewed to the same angle—and you're still
able to edit the text. By combining QuarkXPress's ability to skew
and rotate text boxes, you can create some interesting effects, like
a 3-D cube with angled text on each side (see Figure 1-21).

Figure 1-21

Box skew

> *Oh my goodness gracious, I'm falling to the right, I'm falling! Help me! I'm caught in a skewed text box and I can't get out. Please call for help before I am skewed too far... Oh my goodness gracious, I'm falling to the right, I'm falling! Help me! I'm caught in a skewed text box and I can't get out. Please call for help before I am skewed too far... Oh my goodness gracious, I'm falling to the right, I'm falling! Help me!*

Text Box Skew. To skew a text box and its contents, just select the box and choose the Modify command on the Item menu. In the Text Box Specifications dialog box (press Command-M, or double-click with the Item tool), go to the Box Skew field, and enter the number of degrees you want the box to be skewed (it only lets you enter values between -75 and 75 degrees). Enter a positive number to skew the box and its contents to the right; a negative number skews them to the left.

Picture Box Skew. You've been able to skew the contents of picture boxes in QuarkXPress since version 3.0; but since version 3.2, you can skew the box *and* its contents, all in one fell swoop. Just go to the Picture Specifications dialog box and enter a Box Skew value exactly as described above for text boxes. The only difference is that you can still skew the *contents* of a picture box independently of the box itself, using the Picture Skew field in the dialog box or Measurements palette.

Of course, if you're really bored, you can even play dueling skewing by setting values in Box Skew and Picture Skew that cancel each other out.

Flipping Out

It used to be that if you wanted to flip a picture or text along the vertical or horizontal axis—so that you could mirror it on facing pages, for instance—you had to dive into a graphics program, flip the image, save it as a picture, then bring it into your QuarkXPress document.

Well, no longer. Just select the object, then go to the Style menu and choose Flip Vertical or Flip Horizontal. Note that you have to use the Content tool to do this, as this is actually mirroring the contents of the box rather than the box itself. Not only does this command let you flip pictures and text, but flipped text remains fully editable (to do this, you have to practice reading the newspaper in the mirror).

You can also use the icons for flipping contents in the Measurements palette (see Figure 1-22). The top icon controls horizontal flipping; the lower one controls vertical flipping.

Figure 1-22

Flip Horizontal/
Vertical

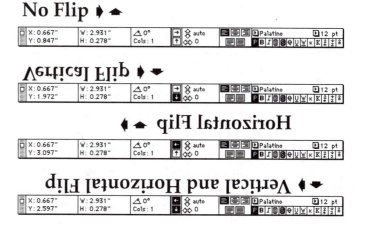

Locking Items

There are times when you want an item to stay how and where it is. For example, if you've painstakingly placed multiple text boxes on your page, you probably don't want to move or resize them accidentally. You can lock any page item down to its spot, making it invulnerable to being moved or resized with the Item tool. Just select the item with either the Item or the Content tool and choose Lock from the Item menu (or press Command-L).

If an item is locked, the Item tool cursor turns into a padlock when passed over it. You cannot move it by clicking and dragging either the item or its control handles. We find this feature especially helpful when we're working on a complex page and don't want an accidental click here or a drag there to ruin our work.

However, note that the item might move when you least expect it. For example, if you use the Space/Align feature, QuarkXPress ignores the Locked status and moves the object (this really bugs us). Also, you can always change the contents of the items; locking only affects the item, not the contents within.

To unlock an item, select it and press Command-L again (or choose Unlock from the menu).

▼ ▼

Tip: Moving Locked Items. As usual, no matter how much we say you can't do something, there is a way to get around it. The one way you can move a locked item is by changing its Origin Across and Origin Down settings in the Item Specifications dialog box or in the Measurements palette (see "Resizing and Reshaping Items," above).

▼ ▼

Suppress Printout and Suppress Picture Printout

If you turn on Suppress Printout (in the Line, Picture Box, or Text Box Specifications dialog box) for any object on your page, QuarkXPress won't print that object. Ever. Period. This is helpful for when you want nonprinting notes to be placed in your document, or for setting runaround objects that affect your text but don't print out on your final page. (Just because the object doesn't print doesn't mean runaround goes away.)

The Picture Box Specifications dialog box also gives you a second checkbox: Suppress Picture Printout. If you check this one, it keeps the picture from printing, but the box itself still prints. The difference? If the picture has a frame around it, the frame prints and the picture doesn't.

Duplicating Items

The last set of features we discuss in this section on manipulating items revolves around duplicating items on your page. There are three ways to duplicate a page element such as a picture or text box: copy and paste it, duplicate it, or use Step and Repeat.

Copy and paste. Selecting an item, copying it, and pasting it (Command-C and Command-V) is the Macintosh Way, though it's not

??? Does latest ITEM
on page created stay
on most front part
of table top or screen,
even after duplicating
previous item does it
stay at original
layer on screen as
the copied ITEM ???

Default Settings ???
again

always the most efficient or precise way. Many people get confused when they copy and paste picture and text boxes, because they don't use the correct tools. Remember, the Item tool is for working with *items* (boxes and lines), and the Content tool is for working with the *contents* of boxes. If you have the Content tool selected and you try to copy a text box, you only copy text. Copying with the Item tool actually copies the text box.

In PageMaker there's a thing called "power pasting," which pastes an object at the same place on the page as you copied or cut it from. QuarkXPress doesn't have this capability at this time, though some commercial XTensions such as Kitchen Sink can do it (see Appendix D, *Resources*). See also "Tip: Clone Item," below. Without one of these XTensions, when you paste a page item, the program places it in the middle of your screen.

Duplicate. If you select an item with the Item tool or the Content tool, then choosing Duplicate from the Item menu (or pressing Command-D) duplicates that item, displacing it from the original with the horizontal and vertical offsets last used in Step and Repeat (see below). You can then move the new item around to where you want it. The default setting for Duplicate is ¼ of an inch down and to the right from the original object.

UN-DO

✱ Command Z does NOT
work when duplicating
more than one ITEM,
But you can select
and press delete
or Command K

Step and Repeat. The Step and Repeat feature can best be described as a powerhouse, and we wish every program had it. The Step and Repeat command (under the Item menu, or press Command-Option-D) lets you select one or more objects and duplicate them with specific horizontal and vertical offsets as many times as you like. For example, if you want 35 lines, each nine points away from each other across the page, you select the line, choose Step and Repeat from the Item menu, and enter "35" in the Repeat Count field, "9pt" in the Horizontal Offset field, and "0" in the Vertical Offset field. After you use Step and Repeat, you can press Command-Z to Undo all of the duplications.

Both Duplicate and Step and Repeat have certain limitations. First, you cannot duplicate an item so that any part of it falls off the pasteboard. If you are working with constrained items (see "Constraining Items," below), you cannot duplicate them so that any of the copies would fall outside of the constraining box. Any items you do duplicate from within a constrained group become part of that constrained group. Note that duplicating an item from a set of grouped objects does not result in the copy being part of the group.

If you have the free XTension called Bobzilla, you'll also see a feature under the Item menu called Super Step and Repeat. This is exactly what it sounds like: a super-duper, over-and-above-the-norm Step and Repeat function. We'll cover it a little further in Appendix D, *Resources*.

▼ ▼

Tip: Clone Item. If you're an Aldus FreeHand user, you're probably familiar with the Command-= keystroke to duplicate an item without any offset. This is called *cloning*. QuicKeys lets us make QuarkXPress do the same thing. We built a macro that selects Step and Repeat from the Item menu, types "1", presses Tab, "0", Tab, "0", then clicks OK. This makes a duplicate of an item that sits precisely on top of the original.

▼ ▼

Tip: Moving Objects to Other Documents. QuarkXPress's ability to drag objects around the page (or from one page to another) doesn't stop at the boundaries of the document window. You can use the Item tool to drag an object or group of objects to another document (see "Moving Items Between Documents," page 101). You need to have both documents open and visible on the screen—we often use the Tile command in the Windows submenu under the View menu to move the document windows into place quickly.

Confused — What does it do TILE?

▼ ▼

Deleting Items

As we suggested above, there is a difference between deleting the contents of a picture or text box and deleting the box itself. When the contents of a box (such as a picture or text) are deleted, the box still remains. When the box itself is deleted, everything goes. There are three basic ways to delete a page item.

▶ We think the easiest way to delete a page item is to select it (with either the Item or the Content tool) and press Command-K. This is the same as selecting Delete from the Item menu. (If you're still using version 3.2, try holding down various combinations of Shift, Command, and Option when you do this; you might find that there is alien life on the planet after all.)

▶ The second easiest way to delete an item is to select it with the Item tool and press the Delete key on your keyboard. Remember that if you use the Content tool, you delete the text or picture rather than the box.

▶ A third way to delete an item is to select it with the Item tool and select Cut or Clear from the Edit menu. Of course, cutting it actually saves the item on the Clipboard so that you can place it somewhere else later.

? Group of what

The only one of these methods that works for deleting an item from a group is Command-K. That's because to remove this kind of page item, you must first select it with the Content tool (or else you end up deleting the entire group).

Note that until version 3.3, you couldn't perform an Undo after deleting multiple objects. Fortunately, that's been changed now (see "Undo and Cancel," page 52).

▼ ▼

Tip: Alien Deletions. Macintosh software has a long history of "Easter eggs": wacky little useless features that programmers include late at night after too many hours of staring at the screen. QuarkXPress has its fair share of Easter eggs. One is the little Martian that walks out on your screen and kills an object on your page (see Figure 1-23). You can call this little fella' up from the depths by pressing Command-Option-Shift-K (in version 3.2, you only have to press Command-Option-K); or you can hold down the modifiers while selecting Delete from the Item menu.

Figure 1-23
The Martian

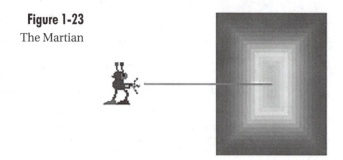

Relationships Between Items

Page-layout programs like QuarkXPress are designed so that you can put a number of text and picture objects on a page. That's the whole point. And anytime you have more than one object on a page, you're going to be concerned about the relationships between those objects. For instance, if you have a block of text and a picture next to it, you probably have an idea about how you want those two items to relate: Do they align on their left edges? Are they centered next to each other? Should the picture always follow the text?

Curiously, some page-layout software developers don't understand this fundamental element of page layout, and they haven't included tools for handling these relationships in their programs. Fortunately for us, however, Quark *does* understand.

In this section we talk about controlling relationships between items: layering, grouping, constraining, and, finally, their position on the page relative to other page elements.

Layering Items

QuarkXPress, like most desktop publishing programs, handles multiple objects on a page by *layering* them. Each page item (picture box, text box, or line) is always on a higher or lower layer than the other page items. This is generally an intuitive approach to working with page elements; it's just what you would do if each of the objects were on a little piece of paper in front of you. The one difference is that while on paper you can have multiple objects on the same layer, each and every item on a QuarkXPress page is on its own layer. When you're placing objects on your page, you work from the bottom layer up. The first object you place is the bottommost object, the second object is on top of it, and so on.

If none of your page elements touch or overlap one another, then layering has almost no relevance to you. However, when they do touch or overlap in some way, you want to be able to control which objects overlap which. The primary methods for controlling layering are the Bring to Front and Send to Back commands in the Item menu.

Bring to Front and Send to Back function as sweeping controls, moving a selected object all the way to the back or all the way to the front layer. When you hold down the Option key while selecting the Item menu, the Send to Back and Bring to Front items become Send Backward and Bring Forward. These functions move objects one layer at a time. They're not as powerful as the layering controls in FreeHand or Illustrator 5, but they're equally important.

Note that you can also use the function keys to move things up and down through layers (see Table 1-4).

Table 1-4	**Press . . .**	**To . . .**
Layering keystrokes	F5	Bring to Front
	Shift-F5	Send to Back
	Option-F5	Bring Forward
	Shift-Option-F5	Send Backward

Grouping Objects

Objects on a page are rarely lone creatures. Often, they like to bunch together to form single units, like organic cells grouping to form a vital organ in your body. Similarly, you can create groups of page items. A group of objects can include any number of text boxes, picture boxes, and/or lines. When you select one member of the group with the Item tool, the whole group gets selected. Or, you can select and modify individual members of the group with the Content tool.

Here's what you do.

1. Using the Item tool, select the items you want grouped. You can hold down the Shift key to select multiple items. Or, you can drag a marquee over or around the objects (any object that the marquee touches is selected).

2. Select Group from the Item menu or press Command-G.

It's that easy. When the group is selected with the Item tool, a dotted line shows the bounding box of the grouped objects (see Figure 1-24).

To ungroup a bunch of objects, select the grouped object with the Item tool and select Ungroup from the Item menu (or press Command-U).

• *also obviosly to see what is in the group*

Figure 1-24
Grouped objects

Bounding box shows the grouped objects

Tip: Multilevel Grouping. Not only can you group multiple objects, but you can group multiple groups, or groups and objects. This means that you can build levels of grouped objects. For example, on a catalog page you may have six picture boxes, each with a caption in a text box. You can group each caption box with its picture box, then select these six grouped objects and group them together. Later, if you ungroup the six objects, each picture box is still grouped with its caption box.

Modifying Grouped Objects

As we mentioned above, once you have grouped a set of objects, you can still modify each of them using the Content tool. Just select the element and change it. Each item can be rotated, re-sized, or edited just as usual. To move a single object in a grouped selection, hold down the Command key to get a temporary Item tool. Then move the object where you want it and release the Command key.

QuarkXPress lets you do some pretty nifty things with grouped items. If you select Modify from the Item menu (or press Command-M, or double-click on the group with the Item tool), Quark-XPress gives you a specifications dialog box for the group. If every object in a group is the same type of object (all rules, all text boxes, etc.), QuarkXPress gives you a modified specifications dialog box for that type of object. The Origin Across and Origin Down values are the measurements for the upper-left corner of the group, rather than any one object within the group.

If you change a value in one of these composite specifications dialog boxes, you change that value for every one of the objects in the group. For example, if you specify a background color for the grouped objects, the background color is applied to all the boxes in the group. If you set the Picture Angle to 20 degrees for a group of picture boxes, the items in each of the picture boxes are rotated within their box (see Chapter 6, *Pictures*).

You can also change some specifications for a group of mixed-type objects. For example, you can turn on Suppress Printout for a group, and each of the objects in the group has its Suppress Print-out checkbox turned on. (We covered that feature in "Suppress Printout and Suppress Picture Printout," page 76, and discuss it a little more in Chapter 6, *Pictures*). If you later ungroup the objects, the settings you make while they were grouped remain.

If you have any lines (rules) in the group, changing the background color of the group affects the color of the line itself.

▼ ▼

Tip: Modifying Frames for Groups. If your grouped objects don't contain any other grouped objects, you can modify every frame in the

*To see what Items
are in the Group,
Highlight Frames Items shapes.*

group by selecting Frames from the Item menu (or pressing Command-B). You can't select this when there are grouped groups.

▼ ▼

Constraining

If you asked a QuarkXPress user a few years ago what one feature they would have sold their grandmother to get rid of, they would invariably have said "parent-and-child boxes." These parent-and-child boxes made it nearly impossible to be flexible with page design because boxes became "trapped" inside other boxes. These constraints were actually rather useful and accessible when you got accustomed to them. But there were many times when what we really needed was a choice of whether to enable it or not.

Let's be clear here for those not familiar with this feature. We're not talking about the type of constraining that Macintosh people usually talk about (and that we've mentioned earlier in this chapter) that refers to holding down the Shift key to constrain the movement of an object to a 45- or 90-degree angle. This is a different sort of constraint.

When David thinks about parent-and-child box constraints, it reminds him of a baby's playpen (this is probably some leftover childhood trauma, but he doesn't want to go into it). A playpen is basically a box that is a structure in its own right. However, you can place objects (or babies) into it, and they can't get out unless you physically take them out.

Similarly, a parent box is a text or picture box that has certain structural constraints so that any items that are created or placed inside its boundaries ("child" items) can't easily get outside those boundaries. For example, imagine a text box that was specified as a parent box. It acts as a normal text box. However, when you draw a line inside it using one of the Line tools, that line cannot be moved or resized to extend outside the text box. The only way you can get it out is by cutting it and pasting it elsewhere.

We know it sounds awful, but, as we said, there are some great applications. For example, building a table by adding vertical and horizontal rules to a text box is aided if those rules don't slip away when you move the box (child items move with their parents). Also, if you have a specific area in which all items must remain, creating a parental constraint makes sure that you don't accidentally mess up your specifications when your eyes are bleary at three in the morning.

You can create parent-and-child box constraints in two ways: automatic constraints and manual constraints. Let's look at each of these in turn.

Automatic constraints. Automatic constraints were the standard for early versions of QuarkXPress. With automatic constraints on, all picture and text boxes act as parent constraint boxes. You can turn automatic constraints on and off by checking the Auto Constraint box in the General Preferences dialog box. You can turn on Auto Constraint while you create boxes that you want to act as parent boxes and child items, and then turn it off to create "normal" boxes and items. This means that when you turn off Auto Constraint, the parent boxes only act as parent boxes to the child items that you created while Auto Constraint was on.

Note that the parent box and the child items are grouped when you select them with the Item tool. To unconstrain these items, see "Manual constraints," below.

Manual constraints. If you prefer, you can apply your own parent-and-child box constraints to a set of objects by manually constraining them. It's easy to do.

1. Make sure the page elements you want to be child items are totally within the boundaries of the box you want to be the parent box.

2. Make sure the soon-to-be-parent box is behind each of the objects that are soon to be constrained. Parent boxes must be on a lower layer than their children. You can think of the playpen analogy: the playpen must be under—and surrounding—the child.

3. Select and group the child and parent objects and boxes (see "Grouping Objects," page 81).

4. Select Constrain from the Item menu.

Those objects that are on top of the parent box and are in that group are constrained to the boundaries of the parent box.

You can unconstrain this group of objects by clicking on the parent-and-child group with the Item tool and selecting either Unconstrain or Ungroup from the Item menu. Unconstrain removes the constraints, but leaves the items grouped. Ungroup removes both the grouping and constraining specifications. (You cannot have parent-and-child constraints without grouping.)

[handwritten in margin: USE CONTENT TOOL to resize ITEMS that are constrained. ? why would you want to just unconstrain them? Might as well ungroup them to do both.]

Aligning and Distributing Objects

Before we knew how cool the Space/Align feature was, we simply didn't know how badly we needed it. Now we use it all the time; once you know about it, you probably will, too. Space/Align is, in some ways, the control center for setting up object relationships on your page. Let's look at why.

The whole idea of Space/Align is to move page items around to create certain relationships between them. The tools you have to work with are Between, Space, and Distribute Evenly. Here are the steps you should take.

1. Select all the items that you want to relate to one another. For instance, if you want two items to align along their left edges, select both of them.

2. Determine the nature of the relationship. Are you trying to align the objects vertically or horizontally? Or both? Turn on the appropriate checkboxes in the dialog box.

3. Decide whether you want to align or distribute the objects. We'll talk about the difference in just a moment. If you're aligning the objects, select Space and enter the amount of space you want between the items; if you're distributing them, select Distribute Evenly.

4. Tell QuarkXPress what part of the objects you want to align or distribute. For example: the left edges of two boxes, or the tops of a few lines, or the centers of five mixed items.

Starting with the second step, let's take a look at each of these.

Vertical/Horizontal. If you select some objects then choose Space/Align from the Item menu (or press Command-comma) you'll see the Space/Align Items dialog box (see Figure 1-25). This dialog box is broken down into Horizontal and Vertical sections, and you can use one or the other—or both—by clicking their respective checkboxes.

Figure 1-25

Space/Align dialog box

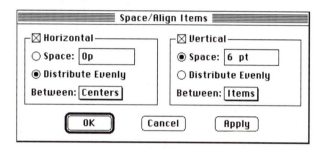

Space. Enabling the Space value (by clicking the radio button in front of it) lets you align objects. The value in the Space field determines how far apart the objects should align. For example, let's say you are horizontally aligning the left edges of two boxes. If you specify "0p" as the Space value, the left edge of the first box is at the same place as the left edge of the second box. If you specify "5p" as the Space value, the left edge of the first box is placed five picas from the left edge of the second box (see Figure 1-26).

But which box moves? The topmost or leftmost items always stay stationary; they are the reference points for alignment. Other page elements move to align with them.

As we said, we use alignment all the time. If we have four text boxes that we want to line up on their right edges, we no longer have to select each one and make sure their horizontal positioning is equal. Now, we just select them all and align their right edges with Space set to zero.

Figure 1-26
Horizontal spacing
with Space/Align

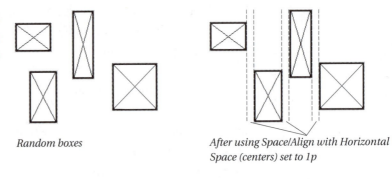

Random boxes

After using Space/Align with Horizontal
Space (centers) set to 1p

▼ ▼

Tip: Spacing with Percentages. You don't have to type an absolute
value into the Space field. You can type a percentage, too. For instance, if you want the tops of two lines to be twice as far apart as
they already are, you can type "200%" and click OK. When you're
working in percentages, the Apply button has an additional function: it lets you apply that percentage more than once. If you type
"150%" and click Apply, the objects are spaced one-and-a-half
times their existing distance. Then, if you click Apply again,
they're moved *another* one-and-a-half times, and so on.

▼ ▼

Distribute Evenly. Let's say you have three picture boxes and you
want the space between them to be equal. It could take nigh-on
forever to figure out exactly where to move the middle box so that
you've got equal space on each side. Instead, you can let the Distribute Evenly feature do it for you. We find distribution very
helpful when we have a number of items that are all the same
size, but are scattered around the page (see Figure 1-27).

Distribute Evenly always takes the leftmost and rightmost or
the topmost and bottommost page elements that you have selected, and uses them as the distribution boundaries. In other
words, those objects don't move, but all the other objects that you
selected do move.

Between. The last step in the process outlined above is figuring out
what part of the objects you want to align or distribute. Your

Figure 1-27
Distribute Evenly with
Space/Align

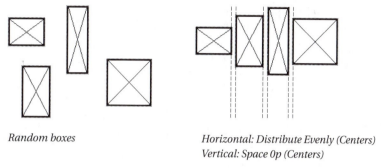

Random boxes

Horizontal: Distribute Evenly (Centers)
Vertical: Space 0p (Centers)

Distribute Evenly leaves the farthest left and right items in the same place, while dividing the rest of the space between all of the intermediate items.

choices are the edges (Top, Bottom, Right and Left), the Center, and the item itself (called Item). You choose any one of these by selecting it from the Between popup menu. Of course, the Horizontal section only lets you choose Left Edges, Right Edges, or Centers, while the Vertical section lets you choose Top Edges, Bottom Edges, or Centers.

The concept of aligning or distributing objects based on Item is sometimes confusing to people. Item refers to the bounding box of the page element. So, for example, horizontally aligning two text boxes with Space set to zero and Between set to Item results in the right side of one being aligned with the left side of the second. Another way to say this is that there is zero space between the items.

And note that we said this is based on the *bounding box* of the object, which is the smallest rectangle that can enclose the entire object. This may result in alignment that you might not expect, especially when you're working with rotated or oddly shaped polygonal picture boxes (see Figure 1-28). Typically, when you're distributing objects, you'll use Item as the Between setting.

If you have multiple objects on a page, and you want to center all of them on top of each other, you can apply both a vertical and a horizontal alignment to them, with Centers selected in the Between popup menu, and Space set to zero.

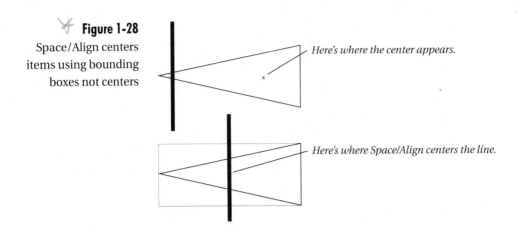

Figure 1-28
Space/Align centers items using bounding boxes not centers

Here's where the center appears.

Here's where Space/Align centers the line.

Getting Around Your Document

QuarkXPress shows you the pages in your document as though they were all spread out in order on a giant white pasteboard. However, unless you happen to work on an enormous screen, you never get to see much of the pasteboard at one time. Let's look at how you can move around to see different parts of a page, and different pages within your document.

Scrolling

The first step in moving around within your document is scrolling. *Scrolling* refers to using the horizontal and vertical scroll bars on the right and bottom sides of the document window to move your page (see Figure 1-29). If you click the arrow at the top of the vertical scroll bar, you move a bit "up" your page (closer to the top). If you click the left arrow in the horizontal scroll bar, you move to the left on your page, and so on.

We find many people never get past this elementary level of scrolling. This is conceivably the slowest method you could use. We implore you to look at our alternatives.

You can move large distances in your document by moving the little white box (some people call it the "scroll elevator") in the scroll bars. Clicking in the gray area moves you by one screen at a time. You also can use keystroke commands to move around the screen vertically. Table 1-5 shows you how.

Figure 1-29
Document Window

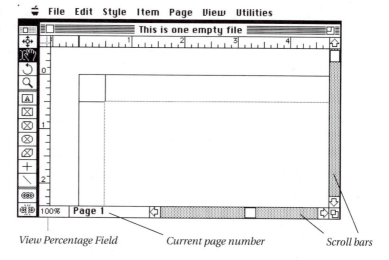

View Percentage Field   Current page number   Scroll bars

▼ ▼

Tip: Scroll Speed. If you do use the scroll bar arrows to get around, you definitely want to examine the Scroll Speed feature in the Application Preferences dialog box. This feature lets you control how far each click in a scroll-bar arrow takes you. For example, if you have the Scroll Speed set to Fast, then clicking an arrow may move you an entire screen or more. If you have it set to Slow, a click may only move the screen one or two pixels.

Don't confuse Scroll Speed with Speed Scroll. We cover the latter in "Defaults," later in this chapter.

▼ ▼

Tip: Live Scrolling. When you drag the white box along the scroll bar, it's often difficult to tell how far on the page you've gone. This is because the vertical scroll bar represents the entire length of your document, and the horizontal scroll bar represents the full width of the pasteboard. If you have multipage spreads in your document, the pasteboard can be very large (see more on spreads in Chapter 2, *Document Construction*). But if you hold down the Option key while you drag the box, the screen scrolls with you, so you can see how far you're going (this is called *live scrolling*).

You can enable live scrolling on a permanent basis by checking in the Live Scroll box in the Application Preferences dialog box. With that feature turned on, Option-dragging on the scroll bar box makes the document *not* live scroll.

To move . . .	Press . . .	Extended keyboards, press . . .
Up one screen	Control-K	Page Up
Down one screen	Control-L	Page Down
Start of document	Control-A	Home
End of document	Control-D	End
First page	Control-Shift-A	Shift-Home
last page	Control-Shift-D	Shift-End
Next page	Control-Shift-L	Shift-Page Down
Previous page	Control-Shift-K	Shift-Page Up

▼ ▼

Tip: Use the Grabber Hand. The Grabber Hand is arguably the most
important tool in QuarkXPress. The problem with the scroll bars
is that you can only scroll in one direction at a time. It's a hassle:
down a little, over to the left, down a little more, now to the right,
and so on. But if you hold down the Option key at any time, the
cursor turns into the Grabber Hand, and when you click and drag,
the page moves where you move the Grabber Hand. Try it! We
think it's one of the greatest methods for getting around the page.

In earlier versions of Quark, you could turn this feature off
entirely; since 3.2, it's always on. However, you can temporarily
disable it by turning on Caps Lock. This turns Option-click into a
zoom toggle.

▼ ▼

Zooming

If you have a brand-new 90-inch HDTV monitor, you may not
need to read this section. For the rest of us, zooming is a necessity
of life. When you zoom in and out on a page, you are using an
electronic magnifying glass, first enlarging a particular area of a
page, and then reducing your screen view so that you are seeing
the entire page or pages at once.

QuarkXPress lets you magnify or reduce your screen view
from 10 to 400 percent, in steps of .1 percent. You can jump

between several preset views quickly by selecting them from the View menu or by using keystrokes. Here's the various ways.

► View menu

► Zoom tool

► Keystrokes

► Magnification field

► Zoom marquee

View menu. The View menu lists zooming values of Fit in Window, 50%, 75%, Actual Size (which is 100 percent), 200%, and Thumbnails. Fit in Window adjusts the zoom percentage to fit whatever size window you have open at the time. If you're working with facing pages, then the scale is set to fit a two-page spread in the window. Thumbnails zooms way back so that you can see a bunch of pages at the same time (but it does more than that; see "Thumbnails," page 99).

When you select a magnification from the View menu, QuarkXPress automatically zooms to the percentage you want and centers the current page in your window. If any item on the page you're looking at is selected when you switch magnifications, QuarkXPress centers that item in the window. Or, if the item is on the pasteboard, the program centers it if any part of the item is showing when you switch views.

For example, if you select a short rule on a page while viewing at Fit in Window size, and then select Actual Size, QuarkXPress zooms in and centers that rule on your screen. If the selected item is a text box and you have the Content tool selected, the program centers the cursor or whatever text is highlighted. This makes zooming in and out on a page much easier: if you're editing some text, you can use Fit in Window to see the "big picture," then select Actual Size to zoom back to where your cursor is in the text.

Zoom tool. You can also use the Zoom tool on the Tool palette for your quick zooming pleasure. Sorry, did we say "quick?" We hardly find clicking in the Tool palette, then on our document, then back in the Tool palette "quick." However, we're in luck.

If you hold down the Control key, you get a Zoom In tool; add the Option key, and you get a Zoom Out tool. Each time you click on your page with the Zoom tool, QuarkXPress zooms in or out by a particular percentage. You can control the increments that it uses in the Tool Preferences dialog box (see "Changing Defaults," page 122).

Keystroke zooming. If we can avoid using the menus, we usually do; they're almost never the most efficient method of working. So when it comes to zooming, we much prefer to use keystrokes and clicks. Table 1-6 shows the basic keystrokes and keystroke-and-click combinations for zooming in and out. Plus, you can set up QuicKeys for the other menu items, too, if you find that useful.

Table 1-6
Zooming

Press . . .	To go to or toggle . . .
Command-1	Actual Size
Command-0	Fit in Window
Command-Option-0	Fit pasteboard in window
Option-click (with Caps Lock)	Between Actual Size and Fit in Window
Command-Option-click	Between Actual Size and 200%

There are two basic keystroke-and-click combinations that you can use to zoom in and out. Command-Option-clicking on your page alternates your view between Actual Size and 200%. When you have Caps Lock on, Option-clicking on your page alternates between zooming out to Fit in Window and zooming in to Actual Size (when Caps Lock is off, the Option key only gives you the Grabber Hand).

Magnification field. Another one of our favorite methods for zooming in and out is by adjusting the View Percent field in the lower-left corner of the document window. Note that when you're in Actual Size, this field shows "100%". Whenever you zoom in or out, this field changes. Well, you can change it yourself by clicking in the field (or pressing Control-V, which highlights the field), typing a scaling percentage (or "T" for Thumbnails view), and pressing Enter or Return.

Zoom marquee. There's no doubt that our favorite zooming technique is to hold down the Control key (to get the Zoom tool), and dragging a marquee around a specific area. When you let go of the mouse button, QuarkXPress zooms into that area at the precise percentage necessary to fit it in the window. So if you're at Actual Size and drag a marquee around one word, QuarkXPress zooms in to 400 percent and centers that word on your screen. You can use this to zoom out, too, by dragging a marquee that's larger than your screen (the screen scrolls along as you drag the marquee), but we don't find this as useful.

Moving from Page to Page

In the last section we talked about moving around your page using scrolling and zooming. Because every page in your document sits on one big pasteboard, these same techniques work for moving around your document. You can scroll from one page to another using the scroll bars and the Grabber hand, and so on. But let's be frank: this is not the fastest way to get around. It might help in moving around a two-page spread, but not for moving around a 200-page book. Instead, there are ways to move by whole pages at a time, or to jump to the page you want.

Extended keyboards. If you have an extended keyboard (we recommend these for serious desktop publishers), you can move one page forward or back by pressing Command-Page Up or Command-Page Down (you can replace the Command key with the Shift key if you like). If you don't have an extended keyboard, Control-Shift-K and Control-Shift-L also move one page at a time.

You may find yourself wanting to jump to the very beginning or end of your document. Again, on the extended keyboard, press the Home key or the End key. On standard Apple keyboards, press

Control-A or Control-D. You'll jump to the top or the bottom of the document, respectively. There is confusion just waiting to happen here. Jumping to the top or the bottom of the document does not ensure that you jump to the first or last page. Especially in the case of facing-page documents (see Chapter 2, *Document Construction*), you may find yourself out in the middle of a pasteboard, not knowing where the actual page is until you zoom out.

Instead of using the jump-to-top or -bottom keystrokes, try Command-Home (Control-Shift-A) or Command-End (Control-Shift-D). These move you to the top of the first or last page of your document. Once again, you can substitute the Shift key for the Command key for these keystrokes.

Moving to a specific page. If you're trying to get to a page somewhere in the middle of your document, there are three methods to get there quickly.

▶ Double-click the page icon in the Document Layout palette or click the page number below the icon (we'll discuss this palette in more detail in Chapter 2, *Document Construction*).

▶ If you install Quark's FeaturesPlus Xtension (with version 3.1 or 3.2) or Thing-a-ma-bob XTension (with version 3.3), you can select a page from a popup menu (see Figure 1-30). Just click on the Page Number field in the lower-left corner of the document window, and drag until you get to the page you want.

Not Me

▶ You can select Go To from the Page menu (or, better yet, press Command-J). Note that if the page you want to go to is in a differently-named section, you have to type the name exactly as it's listed in the lower-right corner of the document window. For instance, if you're using Roman numerals, and you want to jump to the fourth page, you have to type "iv". (See "Sections and Page Numbering," in Chapter 2, *Document Construction*, and "Tip: Jump to Absolute Page Numbers," below.)

Figure 1-30
Popup pages

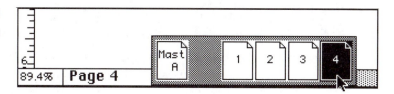

▼ ▼

Tip: Jump to Absolute Page Numbers. If you play around with sections and page numbers, you may find yourself in a quagmire when you try to print a page range. For example, let's say your document begins on page 56 and you want to print the 16th through the 20th pages. You could sit around and try to figure out what numbers to plug in to the Print dialog box's page range fields or you could just type "+16" and "+20". The plus sign before the number means that the numbers are absolute; the first page is "+1", the second page is "+2", and so on.

This is also helpful when moving to a page using Go To page. You can quickly jump to the 20th page by typing "+20".

▼ ▼

Note that for any of the keystrokes we've outlined here, there is a menu item in the Page menu. We think working with a mouse and menus is fast, but there is no doubt that once you start working with keystrokes, moving around your document becomes lightning-fast.

▼ ▼

Manipulating Your Document

Okay, now that we've covered how you can move around your document, let's talk about how you can insert, delete, and move pages within your document. There are three good ways to handle these tasks in QuarkXPress: menu items, thumbnails, and the Document Layout palette. Let's look at each one of these.

Menu Manipulations

As we said much earlier in this chapter, the Page menu holds QuarkXPress's page-manipulation tools. In this section we're primarily interested in the first three menu items: Insert, Delete, and Move. We're holding off on a discussion of inserting pages until the next chapter (see "Making Pages" in Chapter 2, *Document Construction*), so we'll talk about the last two.

Delete. When you choose Delete from the Page menu, QuarkXPress displays the Delete dialog box. This is a simple dialog box asking you which page or pages to delete. If you only want to delete one, just type it in the From field. If you want to delete consecutive pages, then type the page range in the From and To fields.

Move. If you want to move a page or a range of pages, you can select Move from the Page menu. Here you can specify which page or pages to move, and where to move them (see Figure 1-31). For example, if you want to move pages 15 through 21 to after the last page in your document, you can type "15" in the first field, "21" in the second field, and click To End of Document. You also can specify a move to before or after a specific page.

Figure 1-31
The Move Pages
dialog box

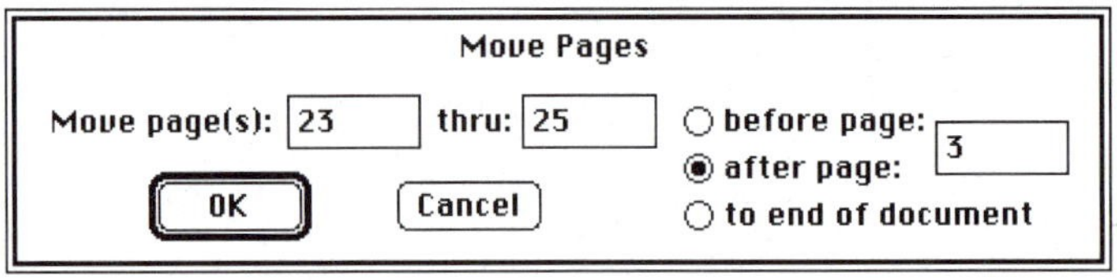

Move Pages

Move page(s): 23   thru: 25   ○ before page:
                                ● after page: 3
OK   Cancel   ○ to end of document

Tip: Doing It to the End. QuarkXPress is smarter than the average computer program. In fact, it's slowly learning plain English. For example, if you want to delete from one page to the end of the document, but you don't know what the last page number is, you can type "end" in the Thru field of the Delete dialog box. This also works in the Move dialog box. For instance, you can move all pages 15 to the end of the document by typing "15" and "end" in the appropriate fields.

Thumbnails

You can see a thumbnail view of your document in the same way as you select any other percentage scaling view: from the View menu. (Or by typing "T" into the Magnification field in the lower-left corner of the document window. Actually you can type "T", "Th", "Thu", "Thum", or "Thumb"—it just depends on how much you feel like flinging your fingers across the keyboard.) Although you can use this to look at your document as thumbnails (like looking at it in 10-percent viewing mode), Thumbnails is actually more useful as a tool for moving pages.

To move a page in Thumbnails mode, select the page and drag it to where you want it. While moving a page around in Thumbnails mode, you'll find the cursor turning into two different icons. The first looks like a minipage. If you let go of the mouse button with this icon displayed, the page is moved, but it's added as a spread. That is, the rest of the pages won't shuffle and reflow (see "Multiple Page Spreads" in Chapter 2, *Document Construction*).

The second icon, a black arrow, appears when you move the cursor directly to the left of or under another page. This arrow means that the page will be placed directly before or under a specific page. Letting go of the mouse button when you have this arrow cursor reflows the pages in the document. This is the same as moving pages using Move from the Page menu.

▼ ▼

Tip: Selecting Multiple Pages. It's easy to select more than one page at a time in Thumbnails mode or in the Document Layout palette (more on the latter in the next section). If the pages are consecutive (pages four through nine, for example), hold down the Shift key while you select each page. Or, click the first page in the range, hold down the Shift key, and click the last page in the range. Every page between the two is selected (this is just like selecting text).

You can select nonconsecutive pages (such as pages one, three, and nine), while in Thumbnails mode or in the Document Layout palette by holding down the Command key while clicking on each page.

▼ ▼

Document Layout Palette

The Document Layout palette is one of the key elements in working efficiently with multipage documents. You can move pages, delete them, insert new ones, create and apply master pages, and more, with a quick drag of an icon. Let's look at how you can use this palette to delete and move pages.

To open the Document Layout palette, select Show Document Layout from the View menu (see Figure 1-32). For our purposes right now, you only need to think about two parts of the palette: the page icons and the icons in the upper-right corner. We'll get into more advanced uses (applying master pages, for instance) in Chapter 2, *Document Construction.*

Figure 1-31

The Document Layout Palette

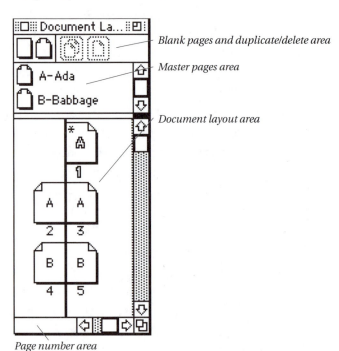

Blank pages and duplicate/delete area

Master pages area

Document layout area

Page number area

Moving pages within the Document Layout palette is just like moving them in Thumbnails mode, except that you can't see what's on the pages. Simply select the page or pages that you want to move, and drag them to their destinations. QuarkXPress uses the same icons here as in Thumbnails mode. That is, the little page icon means that you're creating a spread, and the right and down arrow icons mean that you're moving the pages into the flow (the other pages displace to accommodate the moved page).

Deleting a page with the Document Layout palette is even simpler than deleting a file while on the Macintosh desktop: in QuarkXPress versions 3.0 and 3.1 you just select it and drag it onto the trash icon; in 3.2 you had to click the Delete button. In version 3.3, however, you select the page(s) and click the Delete icon (the one with the page with an "X" through it). However, do note that while you can retrieve a file that you placed into the desktop Trash, you cannot undo your actions and retrieve a page that you throw away in QuarkXPress. Obviously, it's worth being extra careful in this area.

Moving Items Between Documents

You don't have to stop at moving items and pages just within your document. You can move them from one document to another faster than you can say, "Maybe it's time to get a larger monitor for my Mac."

To move a page item from one document to another, you must have both documents open and visible on your screen. This is sometimes difficult on small screens. You can usually resize one or both windows using the Resize area on the document window (that little icon in the lower-right corner). We also find the Tile Documents feature (in the Windows submenu under the View menu) useful for this. Then, select the item you want to move with the Item tool (or hold down the Command key to get the Item tool temporarily), and drag it across.

If you pause between the document windows, you may find the first document starts to scroll. Don't worry, it's just Quark-XPress not realizing that you want to move it all the way into the second document. Just move the item a little farther and the scrolling should stop. Once you let go of the mouse button, the item is copied over into the new document. Note that we say "copied." The item is not actually moved; rather, it is copied from one into the other. If you want to get rid of it in the first document, just delete it (Command-K).

Of course, there is always the old standby method for getting items from one document to another: Copy and Paste. Here, you want to make sure that you have the Item tool selected while in both documents, or else QuarkXPress won't know that you want to copy or paste the item itself.

Moving Pages Between Documents

Versions 1 and 2 of QuarkXPress sported a Get Document function, which was extremely useful. First of all, it let you copy whole pages from one document to another. Secondly, it let you access pages from a different document without actually opening it (this was often helpful in retrieving corrupted files). Unfortunately, the Get Document feature is now gone.

Taking its place is a feature that lets you actually drag a page from one document into another, as long as both documents are in Thumbnails view. (Hold down the Option key and select Tile Documents from the Windows submenu under the View menu or in the title bar to put *all* documents into Thumbnails mode.) This is especially handy if you like to see the pages that you're copying before you copy them. In fact, Quark's tech support still recommends this as a preferred method for saving documents that are becoming corrupted.

▼ ▼

Tip: Moving Background Windows. If you're working on a small screen and you need to resize and move your document windows in order to drag across page items or even full pages, you might find it helpful to know that you can move a window without actually selecting it. That is, normally, if you click on a window, that window is brought to the front. We say that it becomes *active.* You can move a window without bringing it to the front by holding down the Command key while you click and drag the bar at its top. Actually, this isn't a QuarkXPress feature; it's a Macintosh feature.

▼ ▼

Linking

We need to introduce a concept here that is crucial to working with text boxes: *linking*. Links, sometimes known as chains, are the connections between text boxes that allow text to flow from one into the other. You can have as many text boxes linked up as you like. There are two ways to link text boxes together: have QuarkXPress do it for you automatically, or do it yourself manually. We cover automatic text links in Chapter 2, *Document Construction*. We cover manual linking here.

Linking Text Boxes

Let's say you have two text boxes and the text in the first is overflowing (a little box with an "X" in its lower-right corner indicates a text overflow), so you want to link it to the second box. Here's what you do.

1. Choose the Linking tool from the Tool palette (it's the one that looks like three links in a chain).

2. Next, click on the first text box. A flashing dotted line should appear around it.

3. Finally, click on the second text box. When you select the second text box, an arrow should connect from the first text box to the second. We call this the *text link arrow*. This happens even if the two text boxes are on different pages.

That's it. The boxes are now linked, and text flows between them. If you want to link another box to your text chain, just follow the same procedure: click on the second text box, then on the third, and so on. You cannot link a box to another box that has text in it unless the second box is already part of the chain.

If you want to add a text box to the middle of a text chain, first click on a box that is already linked, and then click on the text box you want to add. The text now flows from the original chain through your added text box and back to the original chain (see Figure 1-33).

▾ ▾

Tip: Getting Rid of the Flashes. Many people seem to get flustered when they've selected a text box with the Linking tool and then decide they don't want to follow through and link the box to anything after all. The text box is just sitting there flashing, seeming to call for some special action. Nope, no special action required. You can either click someplace where there's no text box, or just switch tools, and the flashing stops.

▾ ▾

Unlinking Text Boxes

If you want to remove a link between two text boxes, use the Unlinking tool from the Tool palette. The process is simple. Let's say you have a link between two text boxes that you want to sever. First, click on one of the text boxes with the Unlinking tool. As soon as you click on it, you should see the gray arrow linking the two boxes. Then click on either the arrowhead or the tailfeathers of this text link arrow. The arrow disappears and the link is gone.

If other page items are on top of the text link arrow's arrowhead and tailfeathers, you may not be able to click on it. This always seems to happen at 1 AM, after everything else has gone wrong on the project, and this is the last straw. Nonetheless, the way we solve this problem is to rearrange the layers using Move to Front and Move to Back, or to temporarily shift the obstructing objects in order to get to one of the two.

Another problem some people encounter is that they can click and click on the arrowhead or tailfeather, but can't make it disappear. Quark has made it difficult to click on them so that you don't accidentally click on the wrong one. Try placing the cursor right over the very tip of the arrow or the point where the two tailfeathers meet.

▾ ▾

Tip: Unlinking a Text Box from the Middle of a Chain. If you unlink a text box from the middle of a chain by clicking on the arrowhead or tailfeathers with the Unlinking tool, the entire text chain is broken at that point. Instead, you can tell QuarkXPress to remove a text

Figure 1-33

Adding a text box to
a linked text chain

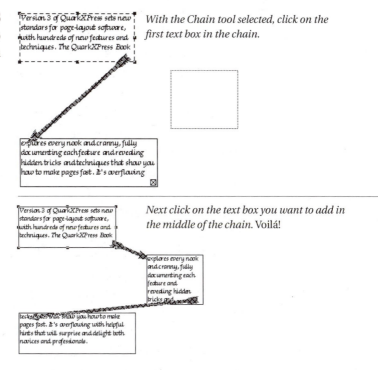

With the Chain tool selected, click on the
first text box in the chain.

Next click on the text box you want to add in
the middle of the chain. Voilá!

box from the text chain without breaking the rest of the flow by
selecting the Unlinking tool, then holding down the Shift key
while clicking on the box you want to remove.

▼ ▼

Copying Linked Text Boxes

We really love the ability to easily copy objects between documents. The only problem has been that QuarkXPress has refused
to copy linked text boxes. However, in version 3.2 this problem
was almost solved.

Copying Single Linked Text Boxes. You can copy a single linked text
box to a new document, and QuarkXPress copies, along with it,
the entire text chain from that box on. None of the text preceding
that box in the chain moves to the target—only the text from the
ensuing linked boxes (and any overflow text).

If you have Automatic Page Insertion turned on, and your new document's master page has an automatic text box, QuarkXPress creates as many new pages as necessary to contain all of the copied story. So if you move a box that's part of a long story, you may end up with quite a stack of new pages to deal with.

It'd be nice if QuarkXPress could automatically break the chains when you copy, bringing to the new document only the text within the box you're moving (if you'd like, that is). But we have to leave Quark some refinements to work on for the next version.

Copying Groups of Linked Text Boxes. Believe it or not, you can now also easily copy as a group text boxes that are linked to each other. ONLY But if you want to copy multiple text boxes that are linked to each other, as well as to boxes that you haven't selected, QuarkXPress still refuses to copy or move them, prompting you instead with the familiar, "This text box or a text box in the group has linkages that can't be duplicated." If you're in Thumbnails view, and copy multiple pages from one document to another, links between boxes on different pages are also maintained in your target document.

▼ ▼

Guides and Rulers

When you are working on your document, you usually have rulers on the top and left sides of the window. This not only gives you a perspective on where you are on the page, but it's a great visual aid in selecting coordinates. Let's say you want to change the size of a picture box by dragging a corner handle. If you're visually inclined, you may not want to bother with referring to the Measurements palette while you drag. Instead, if you watch the rulers, you'll see that gray lines show the left, right, top, and bottom edges as the box moves.

Rulers

You can turn the rulers on and off by selecting Show or Hide Rulers from the View menu, or by pressing Command-R. The only time you really need to turn the rulers off, though, is when you want to get a slightly larger view of the page. Otherwise, just leave them on.

You can specify which measurement system you want to use for your rulers in the General Preferences dialog box (from the Edit menu, or press Command-Y). The vertical and horizontal rulers don't have to use the same measurement system. For example, you can set Horizontal Measure to inches and Vertical Measure to picas. That would just confuse us, so we generally keep both the same (we always use picas).

The values you choose in the General Preferences dialog box are not only used on the rulers, but also throughout the Measurements palette and Item Specifications dialog box. For example, if you change the Vertical Measure to Ciceros, then every vertical measurement shows up in ciceros and points. You can still type in measurements using other units—see Table 1-2 on page 50—but QuarkXPress always converts them.

Item Coordinates

If you're using facing pages or multipage spreads, the ruler can measure from the upper-left corner of each page in the spread or from the upper-left corner of the whole spread. For instance, let's say you have two letter-size pages in a facing spread (like in a magazine). If you set the Item Coordinates popup menu in the General Preferences dialog box to Page (the default value when you install QuarkXPress), the horizontal ruler goes from zero to 8.5 inches on the left page, and then starts at zero again for the right page.

If you change Item Coordinates to Spread, the horizontal ruler stretches across the entire spread, beginning with zero and ending with 17 inches (two times 8.5). We almost always leave this control set to Page, but every now and again we change it to Spread, so that we can measure where objects sit across the spread.

Adjusting the rulers. You can change more than just the measurements you see in the rulers and how far the rules reach; you can also change where the rulers measure from. Typically, the zero points of the horizontal and vertical rulers begin at the upper-left corner of the page or spread. But you can move the origin—or "0,0"—point of the rulers by clicking in the little square area where the rulers meet and dragging to where you want the origin to be.

There are two great reasons to use this feature. First, this is how you control what prints out when you're manually tiling a document (see Chapter 10, *Printing*). Second, you might need to measure a number of objects from a some point on the page that's not the upper-left corner. For instance, you can set the ruler origins to the bottom-left corner instead, so that the measurements run up the page instead of down.

When you're ready to reset the ruler origins, click that same little white box at the juncture of the rulers just once. The zero points are set back to where they started.

Visual accuracy. Rulers are visually accurate. When a box or a rule looks like it is directly over a tick mark in the ruler, it really is. For example, if you want to visually place a box at the two-inch mark (as opposed to using the Measurements palette), you can follow the gray lines in the rulers as you drag the box. When the gray line is over the two-inch mark, the box is truly at two inches, even when you're at a view other than 100 percent, or if you've changed the Points/Inch value. Note that if you have Inches Decimal selected as your vertical or horizontal measurement in the General Preferences dialog box, you get 20 tick marks in each inch (each is .05 inches); if you select Inches, the rulers only have 16 tick marks (each is .0625 inches).

This might not seem like a big deal, but in earlier versions, you could never really be sure unless you checked the Measurements palette or the Item Specifications dialog box. It might have been at 1.998 or 2.01 inches.

Guides

Back in the good old days, before we started laying out pages by sitting in front of little plastic boxes, no one worked without guides. We had blueline guides on paste-up boards, straightedge guides on drafting tables for making sure we were aligning items correctly, and transparent rulers to ensure that we were measuring type and rules correctly. We certainly didn't throw any of that away when we bought our Macintoshes—they still come in handy pretty often. However, QuarkXPress gives us all those tools electronically.

You can add a vertical or a horizontal guide to your page by clicking one of the rulers and dragging guides out onto the page.

▼ ▼

Tip: Page Versus Pasteboard Guides. It turns out that there are two sorts of guides in QuarkXPress: page guides and pasteboard guides. If you drag a guide down or to the right and release it on the page itself, it runs the length of the page from top to bottom or from side to side. It doesn't cross over a spread or onto the pasteboard or anywhere beyond the page. This is called a *page guide*. If you let the guide go onto the pasteboard, however, the guide runs the length of the whole spread and all the way across the pasteboard. This is called a *pasteboard guide*. Note that you can't put pasteboard guides on master pages (we cover master pages more in the next chapter).

▼ ▼

Guides don't print, so it doesn't matter where you place them on your page. However, you may want to adjust the guides to fall in front of or behind opaque text or picture boxes. You can do this by changing the Guides setting in the General Preferences dialog box. Your two choices are Behind and In Front.

Once you've placed a guide on your page, you can move it by clicking the guide and dragging it to where you want it. Note that the guide has to be visible to do this; we almost always leave the preference set to In Front. Plus, if you have the Content tool selected, you have to click in an area where there are no other items in order to select a guide. If you have the Item tool selected, you can always grab and move it.

Conversely, if you want to select an item that's behind a guide, you can do it easily with the Content tool; with the Item tool, you often end up grabbing the guide instead. We sure wish you could Command-Option-Shift-click through guides to select objects with the Item tool. Maybe in the next version. ☺

The Measurements palette displays the coordinate of where the guide is while the guide is moving (unfortunately, once you let go of the guide, there is no way to find out the measurement of where it sits on the page without "grabbing" it again—and probably moving it in the process).

To remove a guide from your page, grab it and drag it out of the window. That means you can drag it back into either ruler, or off to the right or bottom of the window, whichever is closest to where your cursor is at the time.

▼ ▼

Tip: Getting Rid of Ruler Guides. No matter how easy it is to move guides around, it's always a hassle to add 20 guides to a page and then remove them one at a time. Well, take a shortcut: hold down the Option key while clicking once in the horizontal ruler, and all the horizontal guides disappear. Option-clicking in the vertical ruler has the same effect on vertical guides.

If the page touches the ruler when you Option-click on it, only the page guides disappear (the ones running the length of the page). If the pasteboard touches the ruler, only the pasteboard guides go away (the ones running across the whole pasteboard).

▼ ▼

Tip: Dashed Guides. If you change QuarkXPress's ruler guides to the "Black" in the Application Preferences dialog box, the guides become dashed lines. Some people like 'em that way, it turns out. For solid black guides, set the color to 99 percent "Black".

Better
(especially if use colors a lot) ✸

▼ ▼

Tip: Scale-Specific Guides. Apparently some programmer threw this feature in without telling anyone, because we found out that it's not even documented internally at Quark. If you hold down the Shift key while dragging a ruler guide rule out on the page or spread, it becomes magnification-specific. That is, if you pull it

Cool too ✸

out in Actual Size view, you'll only be able to see it at Actual Size view or higher (more zoomed in) magnification. If you zoom out (let's say to Fit in Window view), it disappears. This is great for those times when you want to see a thumbnail of the page without guides, but need the guides to work with.

▼ ▼

Snap to Guides

One of the most important values of guides is that picture and text boxes can snap to them. All guides have this feature, including margin and column guides (we'll talk more about those in Chapter 2, *Document Construction*). You can turn Snap to Guides on and off by selecting it in the View menu. For example, if you have five picture boxes that you want to align, you can pull out a guide to the position you want it, and—if Snap to Guides is enabled in the View menu—as the picture boxes are moved next to the guides, they snap to that exact line.

On the other hand, there are times when you probably want to disable Snap to Guides—so just select it again from the View menu, or use the Shift-F7 shortcut. For example, if you are working with a line very close to a column guide, it may snap to the guide when you don't want it to. Just turn off Snap to Guides. Generally, however, we leave this feature on.

The distance at which a guide pulls an item in, snapping it to the guide position, is determined by a control in the General Preferences dialog box (Command-Y). The default value is six points.

▼ ▼

Frames

There are times when you want to put a picture on your wall with a frame, and there are times when you just tape it up frameless. When you're making pages, there are times when you want a frame around a text or picture box, and there are times when you don't. QuarkXPress lets you have your choice. All picture and text boxes default to a frame of zero width, which means there's no frame at all. You can add a frame to any picture or text box by selecting it and choosing Frame from the Item menu (or pressing Command-B).

The Frame Specifications dialog box contains fields and pop-up menus that let you specify the weight, color, shade, and line style of your frame (see Figure 1-34). Color and shade are self-explanatory, but we need to talk a little about frame styles and thickness.

Frame style. In earlier versions, QuarkXPress included a bunch of wild ornamental frames that you could use. The problem was that they were all bitmapped and so they not only took a long time to print, but they sometimes looked really poor. Now you're limited to seven styles: lines, double lines, triple lines, and variations on those lines. You can apply these frames to any kind of text or picture box.

Frame weight. Quark calls the thickness of a frame its "width." We're used to calling it the *weight*. No matter what you call it, it's the thickness of the line making up the frame. And, in a manner similar to lines, if the line weight is not thick enough, the frame style may not show up properly (a triple line set to .5 point comes out looking just like a single half-point line).

Frames can grow from the box edge in, or the box edge out. That is, a 10-point frame is measured from the edge of the box either out or in. This is different from lines: their weight is measured from their center (a 10-point line falls five points on one side of the line and five points on the other).

You can control which side of the box edge the frame falls on with the Framing popup menu in the General Preferences dialog box (from the Edit menu, or press Command-Y). Choosing Inside from this menu places frames on the inside of boxes; Outside places them on the outside. The confusing thing is that even when you have Frames set to Outside, the frame looks like it's falling on the inside. That's because QuarkXPress actually makes the box

Figure 1-34
Frame Specifications
dialog box

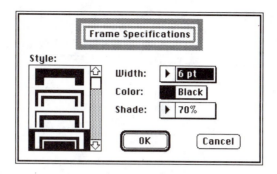

itself a little bigger to set the frame correctly *as though* it were an Inside frame. We think this method is sort of a pain in the butt, so we always leave it set to Inside.

How do you do it?

Note that you can create a frame on a box while in the Inside mode, then change the mode to Outside, and subsequent frames are built on the outside of boxes (or vice-versa). Existing boxes don't change when you change the preferences.

Frame Editor

We've mentioned the Frame Editor a couple of times throughout this chapter—usually saying that it's something to be thrown away—without really explaining what it is. Frame Editor is a separate application which ships with QuarkXPress. It lets you create borders or frames which you can apply to picture or text boxes. This program is part of history; it first shipped way back in the early days of QuarkXPress, when no one was really doing high-end work with any program on the desktop.

Unfortunately, at this point Frame Editor is sort of anachronistic and has few uses for the serious designer or production artist. The problem is that all the frames you can make are bitmapped. That means that rather than defining a border with smooth lines and curves, you have to use dots in a bitmap (see Chapter 6, *Pictures*, for more information on the differences between object-oriented and bitmapped images). The biggest problem with this is that diagonal and curved lines appear jaggy at almost any size (see Figure 1-35).

Figure 1-35
One of the many
confusing windows in
the easily avoidable
Frame Editor

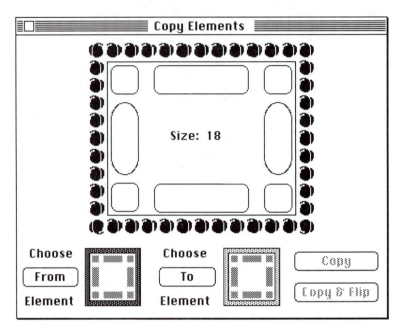

On the other hand, if you want to create frames with only horizontal and vertical lines, Frame Editor can do the trick pretty easily. However, we won't get into the details of the program here because it's just not our cup of tea.

Two items to note about frames. First, the frame information is saved in the XPress Preferences file (some frames are even included in the Preference file on the installation disks). If you apply a custom frame to a box, that frame is saved in the document as well. Second, it's recommended that if you apply a custom frame to a picture or text box, apply it at the size at which it was built. If it was built to be 18 points, you should apply it at 18 points. Otherwise, you may have difficulty printing.

Libraries

QuarkXPress lets you keep libraries full of items: picture boxes, text boxes, lines, groups of objects, and so on. These libraries are saved as external files on disk. For example, while writing this book, we placed each piece of artwork in a library, grouped with figure numbers, captions, and callouts. The artwork was later dragged out of the library by the production team onto the QuarkXPress pages. This increased the chance that nothing too weird would happen when we were making pages, and decreased the time it took to produce a chapter.

Note that a library holds page items, plus their contents. For example, you could place a text box with a particular headline in a particular style in a library. However, picture boxes in libraries don't fully contain their pictures. If a picture was imported using Get Picture, the library only remembers the link to the external file, rather than the file itself. So, although our artwork could be stored in a library, we still had to move many of our EPS and TIFF files from disk to disk (if you are lost, don't worry; we talk about all these issues in Chapter 6, *Pictures*). *phew !*

You can have more than 10 libraries open at a time (we haven't found an upper limit yet), and each library can hold up to 2,000 entries. You can even label each library entry for quick access. Let's look at how all of this is done.

Manipulating Libraries

Libraries are, in many way, just like QuarkXPress documents. Putting an item in a library is like putting it on a separate page of a document. The analogy follows in creating and opening libraries, as well. You can create a new library by selecting Library from the New submenu in the File menu (or by pressing Command-Option-N). And to open a library, you select it in the Open dialog box (the program recognizes it as a library automatically, so you don't have to do anything special). Once you choose a library, QuarkXPress brings it up on your screen as a palette. (With versions earlier than 3.2, you create and open libraries by selecting Libraries from the Utilities menu.)

As we mentioned earlier in this chapter, palettes work much like other windows (in fact, we often call them windoids). For example, like a window, you close a palette by clicking the Close box in the upper-left corner. The palette floats, so you can move the palette wherever you like on your screen. You also can expand the palette by clicking the Zoom box in the upper-right corner of the window. Note that this type of zooming doesn't have anything to do with a percentage scaling view. The first time you click on it, the palette fills your screen. The second time, it decreases back to "normal" size. You also can resize the windoid by clicking and dragging the lower-right resizing box, just like a normal window.

Adding and Moving Library Entries

You'll hardly believe how easy it is to add and remove library entries. To add a page item to an open library, just click on the item with the Item tool (or hold down the Command key to get a temporary Item tool), and drag the item across into the library. When you're in the library, your mouse cursor turns into a pair of glasses (don't ask us why; all the librarians we know wear contacts), and two triangular arrows point to your position in the library. When you let go of the mouse button, the item you're dragging is inserted in the library at the location these pointers indicate. That is, you can position your page item (or existing library items) anywhere in the library by dragging it into place.

You also can add an item to a library by using Cut or Copy and Paste. You need to use the Item tool to cut or copy an item from the page, but you can use either the Item or the Content tool to paste it in a library. Just click in the position where you want the item to go, then press Command-V (or select Paste from the Edit menu). When picking a place to paste the item, click between two items, so that you can see the positioning arrows. If you click on an item in the library before pasting, you are telling QuarkXPress to replace that item with this new one.

Note that although we're saying you can add "an item" to the library, that one item can contain a number of page items. If you want, you can select picture boxes, text boxes, and lines—whether grouped or not—and put them all into the same library item.

After you add an item to a library, then you can see a thumbnail-size representation of it (see Figure 1-36). This representation is highlighted, and you won't be able to do any work on your page until you click someplace other than the library.

You can move an item in a library from one position to another by clicking on it and dragging it to a new position. If you have more items in your library than fit in the palette, you may have some difficulty, because the library doesn't automatically scroll as you drag. We use one of two methods to get around this. First, you can cut and paste items, as we described above. Second, you can click the Zoom box to expand the size, reposition the item, and rezoom the box down to a small palette.

Removing Library Items

To take an item from an open library and place it on a page, click on it with either the Item or the Content tool and drag it onto your

Figure 1-36
Adding an item
to a library

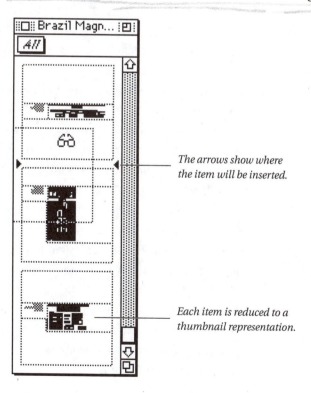

The arrows show where the item will be inserted.

Each item is reduced to a thumbnail representation.

page. This doesn't remove the item from the library; it makes a copy of it on your page. It's similar to dragging something from one document to another. If you want to delete an item from a library, click on it, then select Clear from the Edit menu (or press the Delete key). You also can use Cut from the Edit menu (Command-X), which removes the item and places it on the Clipboard. QuarkXPress always warns you before totally removing something from a library, because you can't do Undo afterwards.

Labeling Library Items

Imagine having 150 different items in a library and trying to find just the ones that are pictures of baby seals. Remember that all you can see on screen is a thumbnail representation of the items. Luckily, you have labeled each library item with a foolproof system, and you are just a popup menu item away from finding those baby seals.

Every item in a library may be labeled either for identification purposes or to group items together (or both). With your library items labeled, you can access the library items by a single label, multiple labels, and more.

To assign a label to a library item, double-click on its thumbnail representation. Up comes the Library Entry dialog box. There is only one field in this dialog box for you to type the label in. After you add one label to an item, the popup menu in this dialog box is enabled (see Figure 1-37). This popup menu lists each of the previous labels you've assigned (see "Tip: Grouping Library Items").

After you have labeled items in your library, you can select from among them with the popup menu at the top of the Library palette (see Figure 1-38). This acts as a kind of electronic card catalog. There are always two items in this popup menu: All and Unlabeled. Selecting All shows you every item in the library. Selecting Unlabeled displays only the items that have not yet been labeled. Any other labels that you have assigned to library items also appear on this popup menu. If you select one of these, you only see items that have been assigned that label.

Figure 1-37
The Library Entry
dialog box

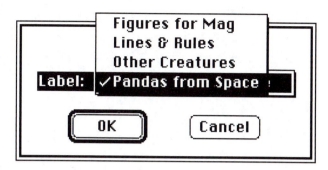

Figures for Mag
Lines & Rules
Other Creatures
Label: ✓Pandas from Space

OK   Cancel

Figure 1-38
Selecting a
subcategory in
the library

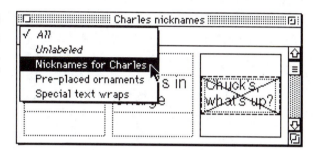

Charles nicknames

✓ All
Unlabeled
Nicknames for Charles
Pre-placed ornaments
Special text wraps

Chuck's
what's up?

Then, if you select a second label from the popup menu, that label is added to the category you're already looking at. The name on the popup menu changes to Mixed Labels which tells you that more than one label is being displayed. You can deselect one label category by rechoosing it from the popup menu (that is, these labels in the popup menu act as on-and-off toggle switches). You can deselect all the subcategories by choosing All from the popup menu.

▼ ▼

Tip: Grouping Library Items. As we mentioned above, you can group library items together (this isn't the same as grouping items on the page). You do this by giving them the same label. For example, if you have a bunch of lines that you use a lot for one magazine, you might label them all "Mag Lines." Then, when you need one, you simply pull down the Library palette's popup menu and select that label.

However, if each one of the item's labels isn't exactly the same, QuarkXPress won't know to group them together. Instead of typ-

experiment better

ing the same label over and over again for each item, you can just type it once. Then use the popup menu in the Library Entry dialog box to choose that item each time you want to assign it to an item within the library. This is faster, and you avoid typos.

▼ ▼

Saving Libraries

No matter how hard you try, you won't find a command to save the library file. This can be disconcerting, to say the least. What happens to all those items if you can't save them?

QuarkXPress normally saves a library only when you quit the program or close your current document. This is generally unacceptable, because people work for long periods without quitting or closing a document (during the production of the first edition of this book, one person lost over an hour's worth of work because of a system crash before the library was saved).

Fortunately, there's now an Auto Library Save feature in the Application Preferences dialog box that makes QuarkXPress save a library every time you place a new item in it. This may slow down your work a little if you're adding a number of items, but it could also save you lots of time if something should go wrong.

▼ ▼

Tip: Send your Libraries, Not Your Pictures. If you're preparing templates and picture libraries so that someone else can do the actual page-layout work, remember that you might not need to send them the picture files on disk. QuarkXPress captures a low-resolution preview image for each picture when you imported it into a picture box, and that's saved within the library.

If you send just the library file, the person making pages can place, see, and print the screen representations. When the document file comes back to you, QuarkXPress remembers the locations of all the original graphics files on your disks, and uses those for printing.

▼ ▼

XTensions

Here's an aspect of QuarkXPress that we think is so hot and amazing that we couldn't think of a nasty thing to say about it even if we tried. Quark has built in a system so that programmers can write add-on modules (XTensions) to work with QuarkXPress. There are over 200 developers around the world creating these XTensions. Some cost $5,000 and are designed for a very limited market, such as large newspapers. Others are free, and can (and should) be used by anyone using QuarkXPress. Appendix D, *Resources*, gives more information about how to get your hands on XTensions.

In order to use an XTension, all you have to do is place it in the same folder as QuarkXPress 3.2 (or in the XTension folder with version 3.3). When you start up QuarkXPress the XTension does its thing, whatever that may be. Usually, XTensions add an item to a menu, or even add a whole new menu. Most XTensions add items to the Utilities menu, because they are utilities. For example, Quark released a free XTension called Bobzilla which, among other things, added a feature called Line Check to the Utility menu (see "Line Check," page 301, in Chapter 4, *Type and Typography*). Again, we talk much more about XTensions and what they can do in Appendix D, *Resources*.

Zappers

There's one particular kind of XTension, called a Zapper, which we should mention at least briefly here. Zappers are XTensions that you only have to use once and then can throw away; you just put them in the QuarkXPress folder, and then start up the program. The first time you do that, QuarkXPress gets "zapped," and you don't need the Zapper anymore (although we recommend that you keep it somewhere on your disk, just in case).

Quark has only released Zappers once, after the initial release of version 3.0. Those Zappers were free, and fixed bugs that Quark discovered in the program after shipping. As of this writing, there aren't any Zappers that you need to use for versions 3.2 and 3.3. We just wanted to make sure that you knew about them, so that if one comes out at some point, you won't be surprised.

Patchers

Instead of using a Zapper to update QuarkXPress, Quark sometimes uses a Patcher. Technically, a Patcher isn't an XTension, but this is the best place to deal with it. For version 3.2 of Quark-XPress, Quark shipped a Patcher to update it to "patch level 2." The Patcher is a standalone program that changes QuarkXPress. To work it, you just double-click on it. It asks you where to find your copy of QuarkXPress, and then it does its thing. The Patcher changes just the parts of the program needed to make the corrections. This is essentially how the 3.2-to-3.3 updater works, as well.

▼ ▼

Changing Defaults

Each and every one of you reading this book is different, and you all have different ways of using QuarkXPress. Fortunately, Quark has given you a mess of options for customizing the internal default settings. A *default setting* is a value or indicates a way of doing something; QuarkXPress uses the default value or method unless you specifically choose something else.

For example, the factory default setting for picture and text boxes is that they are created with no frame around them (see "Frames," earlier in this chapter). But you can change default settings. If you're so inclined, you can modify QuarkXPress so that every text box you create is automatically framed with a two-point line. In this way, you can customize your work environment so that it best suits you.

Default settings range from how guides are displayed on the screen to how QuarkXPress builds small caps characters. There are six built-in preferences sets: Application, General, EfiColor, Typographic, Tools, and Trapping. We'll cover EfiColor Preferences in

Appendix A, *EfiColor*; Typographic Preferences in Chapter 4, *Type and Typography*; and Trapping Preferences in Chapter 9, *Color*. We'll take a look at the other three here.

▼ ▼

Tip: Document Defaults Versus Program Defaults. There's an important difference between changing your default preferences with a document open, and with no documents opens. In most cases, if you have a document open when you change a default preference, that change is specific to that document. Even if you have other documents open at the same time, the change is made to only the one that is active. If no documents are open when you set a default preference, then you are setting new defaults for the whole program and that change is made to every new document you open from then on. These changes are stored in the XPress Preferences file, and are used when creating new documents.

For example, if you set the increments on the Zoom tool (in the Tool Preferences dialog box; see below) to 100 percent while a document is open, the preference is logged for that document only. If you set it while no documents are open, that setting is made for every new document you create. However, documents that were opened using the original setting keep their defaults.

▼ ▼

Application Preferences

The main exception to the rule about whether or not a document is open when you make a change is Application Preferences (from the Edit menu, or press Command-Option-Shift-Y; see Figure 1-39). Any change made in this dialog box affects the whole program and all documents, whether they're new or old. Plus, these preferences are not saved with any document itself, so if you give a file to someone else, it may look or print slightly differently on their machine because of the mismatch of preferences. This is almost never a serious problem, though, due to the sorts of preferences found here. Here's a rundown of the options in the Application Preferences dialog box.

Figure 1-39

Application
Preferences

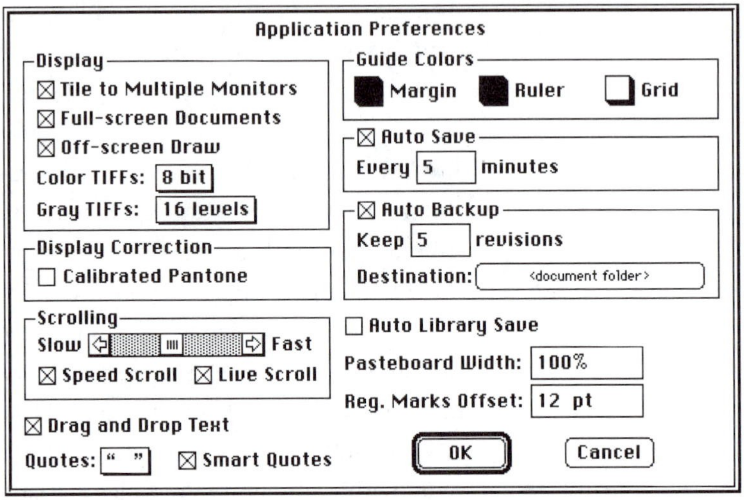

Guide Colors. The controls in the upper-right corner of the Application Preferences dialog box let you change the colors of QuarkXPress's three types of guide lines: Margin, Ruler, and Grid. The margin guides are the lines that show where the page margins are. The ruler guides are the guides you can pull out onto the page. And the grid guides are the lines that the program shows you when you have Show Baseline Grid enabled (see Chapter 4, *Type and Typography*). Note that this control is only available when your monitor is set to at least 256 levels of gray or color. (It's not available with the 16-gray-level PowerBooks or Duos without an external monitor hooked up, assigned as the startup monitor, and set to 256 colors or grays.)

Live Scroll. Steve, our editor, keeps telling us not to be redundant in our writing. And since we already gave our shpiel about Live Scroll earlier in this chapter (see "Scrolling"), we'll just say: Yes, this is a great feature, and it's great to have it built right in, but it's nowhere near as cool as the Grabber Hand.

Speed Scroll. Here's another wonderful enhancement that makes us want to bow down and give thanks in the general direction of Denver (where Quark lives). If you turn on Speed Scroll, Quark-

XPress automatically greeks the display of pictures, graphics and blends as you scroll through a document. Only when you stop scrolling does it take the time to properly display these elements.

This may not sound like a big improvement at first, but if you've died of boredom while scrolling through a long document with lots of big four-color TIFFs, you'll appreciate how much time Speed Scroll can save you (that is, unless you *like* taking a coffee break while you scroll).

Scroll Speed. Yep, now there's Speed Scroll *and* Scroll Speed. It's not confusing, is it? As we discussed earlier in the "Scrolling" section, Scroll Speed controls how fast QuarkXPress scrolls when you use the scroll bars. Note that the default Scroll Speed control setting is pretty slow. Increasing the speed (by clicking on the right arrow) can make a drastic difference in how quickly you can make your pages (although this won't speed up screen redraw any).

Tile to Multiple Monitors. Here's where you tell QuarkXPress whether or not you want it to consider *all* the monitors you have plugged into your Mac when it tiles open documents. Unless you have more than one monitor hooked up, you should just leave this turned off.

Full-Screen Documents. Checking this box lets you zoom windows to fill your entire screen; unchecking it leaves room for the Tool and Measurements palettes. We typically leave this turned off, but why should you listen to us? The options are here to make your life easier.

Off-Screen Draw. We can't find any good reason to use Off-screen Draw other than personal preference. If you don't have this on, you can see QuarkXPress redraw each page object one at a time when you scroll around the page. If you enable Off-Screen Draw, QuarkXPress redraws all the items "behind the scenes" and shows them to you all at once. It takes just as long either way, so it really comes down to how you like your computer to behave.

What's the difference?

Color TIFFs/Gray TIFFs. These controls first saw life as a simple checkbox in version 3.1 that would allow you to choose whether, on eight- or 24-bit displays, imported grayscale TIFFs would be shown using 256 or 16 levels of gray. This proved to be so popular that the interface was revised (now it's a popup menu), with similar choices extended to color TIFFs.

Specifically, you can select 16 (four-bit) or 256 (eight-bit) levels of gray for grayscale TIFFs, and 256 colors (eight-bit), thousands of colors (16-bit), or millions of colors (24-bit) display for color TIFF images.

It's a time-versus-quality issue. The lower the bit depth, the faster your screen redraw will be; the higher the bit depth, the better the screen display. You can recoup some of the performance hit from higher-quality image displays by selecting Speed Scroll, above.

Of course, if you don't have eight-, 16-, or 24-bit images, you can't display them in those modes, anyway. QuarkXPress can't improve the screen display of an image beyond the information that's contained in the file. Note that these features don't affect the images themselves or how they print—just how they're displayed on the screen.

Auto Library Save. As we said earlier, in the "Libraries" section, libraries are only saved when you close them unless you enable Auto Library Save. This makes QuarkXPress save the library every time you add an item to it. It slows down production a little, but it's worth it as a safety measure.

Display Correction. If you've installed the EfiColor XTension and system (see Appendix A, *EfiColor*), you'll see a checkbox entitled Display Correction in the Application Preferences dialog box. This lets you turn on or off the part of EfiColor that attempts to match your onscreen display of color to what's available from your selected printer.

When you turn on Display Correction, you can select your monitor (if you have a profile installed for it) from a popup menu of monitors your EfiColor system knows about. We explain this process in more detail in Appendix A, *EfiColor*.

If you haven't installed EfiColor, but you *have* installed the Pantone Professional Color Toolkit control panel, the checkbox will be called Calibrated Pantone, instead.

Mine? →

Calibrated Pantone. If you don't have EfiColor installed and you turn on the Calibrated Pantone option, QuarkXPress uses the color-matching powers of the Professional Color Toolkit control panel, if it's installed on your system. (It's available for free from Pantone, and from the usual nefarious sources.) Once you've specified your monitor and printer in the Toolkit control panel, it handles color matching of Pantone colors on screen and on printout (the Pantone spot colors being of special importance, since they're hard to simulate with CMYK inks).

It's arguable that EfiColor provides better screen representations of Pantone inks than Pantone's Toolkit does. Both base their screen colors on CIE values, but rumor has it that the Toolkit's CIE values aren't very good (there's an update in progress as we write this). For color-printer output, the Toolkit might provide better output, because it bases printing on CMYK values that are hand-tuned for each color and each printer. There's no need for color correction on separation, of course, because Pantone colors are printed with—you guessed it—Pantone inks.

Another advantage of using the Toolkit instead of EfiColor is speed; if you're just creating spot-color (read: PMS) jobs, there's no reason to suffer the processing overhead that EfiColor imposes.

Pasteboard Width. That pasteboard around each of our document's pages is great, but we usually find it a little too large (and—depending on the job—occasionally too small). Fortunately, we can control how wide the pasteboard is by specifying a percentage in the Pasteboard Width field. The default value of 100 percent tells QuarkXPress to make each side of the pasteboard the same width as one page in the document. That is, if you have an 8.5-by-11-inch page, each side of the pasteboard is 8.5 inches wide. Changing the Pasteboard Width to 50 percent makes the pasteboard half that width. Unfortunately, there's still no way to change the pasteboard space above and below each page.

Reg. Marks Offset. We don't know about you, but if we were operating a two-ton papercutting machine on a tight schedule, we wouldn't always make cuts within three or four points (.055 inch) of accuracy. That's what QuarkXPress is asking your printer to do when it prints its registration marks only six points from the edge of the page (see Chapter 10, *Printing*). However, you can adjust how far out you want the registration marks to print with the Reg. Marks Offset control in the Application Preferences dialog box. We generally set this to between 12 and 18 points. Remember, however, that if you set your Reg. Marks Offset to 18 points and then send your document to a service bureau, your setting doesn't follow the document (this is an Application Preference). They should be told to set theirs, as well.

Auto Save and Auto Backup. This is covered in detail in "Saving," earlier in this chapter.

Smart Quotes. This option both turns on the Smart Quotes feature and lets you specify which characters will be used for open and closed quotes. Smart Quotes works by looking to the left of the insertion point to determine if an open or closed quote character should go there. If the character to the left is a white space character, such as a spaceband, tab key, or return, QuarkXPress enters an open single or double quote when you press the ' or " key.

The popup menu lets you choose some alternative quote characters, including various double quotes, Spanish alternatives, and inside and outside guillemet (French quote mark) combinations, all of which can be useful if you're formatting foreign-language documents (see Figure 1-40).

Figure 1-40

Different kinds of
Smart Quotes available

"This is an example of Smart Quotes," he said.

"This is a different kind of Smart Quotes," he added.

„Here's yet another kind of Smart Quotes," he continued.

«These quotes are called guillemets,» he went on.

»So are these, but they're reversed,« he concluded.

The main place where Smart Quotes isn't so smart is when you're typing apostrophes at the beginning of a word—"In late '93," for instance. Watch out for these. (See "Tip: Getting Your Quotes Straight," in Chapter 4, *Type and Typography,* for how to type curly and straight quotes quickly.)

▼ ▼

Tip: Toggling Smart Quotes. Smart Quotes is really cool if you type a lot in QuarkXPress. However, if you ever want to enter a single or double "neutral" straight quote character, it's a hassle to turn off Smart Quotes first. Instead, hold down the Control key when typing the quote (single or double). When Smart Quotes is on, you get a straight quote; when it's off, you get a curly quote.

▼ ▼

Drag and Drop Text. We'll cover this in detail in Chapter 3, *Word Processing.*

General Preferences

Of the 14 default preferences in the General Preferences dialog box (from the Edit menu, or press Command-Y; see Figure 1-41), only two are not described elsewhere in this book: Points/Inch and Ciceros/cm. Here's a list of where you can find information on the other 12 defaults.

Horizontal Measure and Vertical Measure. See "Guides and Rulers," page 106.

Auto Page Insertion. See "Automatic Page Insertion," page 169, in Chapter 2, *Document Construction.*

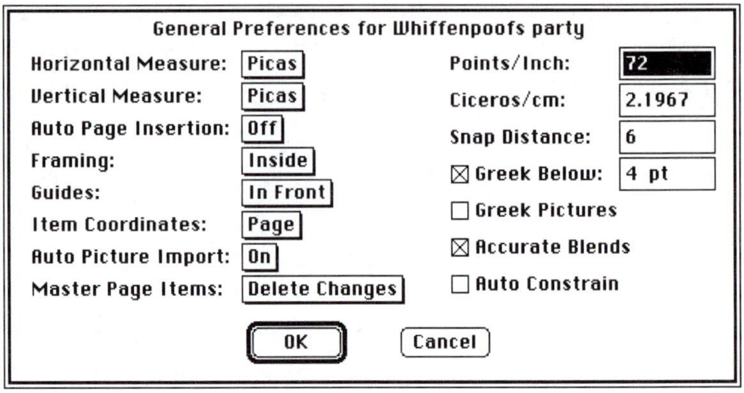

Figure 1-41

The General
Preferences
dialog box

General Preferences for Whiffenpoofs party

Horizontal Measure:	Picas	Points/Inch:	72
Vertical Measure:	Picas	Ciceros/cm:	2.1967
Auto Page Insertion:	Off	Snap Distance:	6
Framing:	Inside	☒ Greek Below:	4 pt
Guides:	In Front	☐ Greek Pictures	
Item Coordinates:	Page	☒ Accurate Blends	
Auto Picture Import:	On	☐ Auto Constrain	
Master Page Items:	Delete Changes		

OK   Cancel

Framing. See "Frames," page 112.

Guides and Item Coordinates. See "Guides and Rulers," page 106.

Auto Picture Import. See "Picture Usage," page 409, in Chapter 6, *Pictures.*

Master Page Items. See "Master Pages and Document Pages," page 155, in Chapter 2, *Document Construction.*

Greek Below. See "Text Greeking," page 334, in Chapter 4, *Type and Typography.*

Greek Pictures. See "Greeking and Suppression," page 410, in Chapter 6, *Pictures.*

Accurate Blends. See "Cool Blends," page 507, in Chapter 9, *Color.*

Auto Constrain. See "Constraining," page 84.

Points/Inch. Somebody, sometime, somewhere along the line, decided that PostScript should measure 72 points to an inch. However, as it turns out, printers and graphic designers have always measured just *over* 72 points to the inch. QuarkXPress, being the power-rich program it is, gives you the choice of how you want to measure points. If you have a burning need to work in a traditional measurement setting, you can change the value of the Points/Inch field in the General Preferences dialog box to 72.27. We tend toward progress and think that people should just throw out their old rulers and embrace a new standard. Thus, we leave it at 72 points per inch.

Ciceros/Cm. A cicero, in case you're like us (*Americanus Stupidus*), is a measurement in the Didot system, used primarily in France and other continental European countries. Just as a pica equals 12 points, the cicero equals 12 points. The difference? Differently sized points. A Didot point equals .01483 inch instead of the American-British .01383 inch. Anyway, the only really important thing about all this is that QuarkXPress defaults to 2.1967 ciceros per centimeter. This is close enough to a traditional cicero (you can do the math).

Note that if you want to work with Didot points more directly, you can change Points/Inch, above, to 67.43 (QuarkXPress 3.3 lets you enter Points/Inch values below 70.)

Tool Preferences

You may find yourself making the same change or changes repeatedly to a type of page item; for example, you always change the text inset for text boxes from one to zero points, or always change your lines to .25-point thickness after drawing them. These item attributes, as well as most other attributes for page items, are defaults you can change.

You can use the Tool Preferences dialog box to change the default settings for any of the item-creation tools on the Tool palette, plus the Zoom tool (see Figure 1-42). To change a default for an item-creation tool (the tools that create picture boxes, text boxes, or lines), select the tool's icon in the dialog box, and then click on one of the three buttons to change some aspect of that tool: Modify, Frame, or Runaround.

Figure 1-42
Tool Preferences

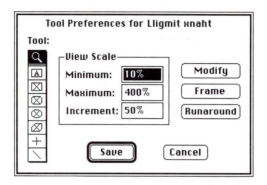

Modify. This button brings up the Item Specifications dialog box for the particular tool. As we discussed earlier in this chapter, a picture box has a different specifications dialog box than a text box, and so on. You can change any value in this dialog box that is not grayed out.

For example, you can change the default corner radius of a rounded-corner picture box, but you can't change its default width or height. We rarely want our picture boxes to have a colored background, so we have changed our picture box tool's defaults so that the Background Color is set to zero-percent black.

Frame. You can specify an automatic frame for text or picture boxes by clicking the Frame button. Let's say you specify a one-point single-line frame for the Polygon Picture Box tool. After you click OK, every polygonal picture box you make has that frame. You don't have to keep the frame if you don't want it (just remove it as you would any other frame: change its width to zero). But this is the default setting for creating new ones.

Runaround. You also can change the text runaround value for boxes made with a tool. For example, you can set the Text Box tool to make text boxes that have no runaround. Note that you can set any runaround that you normally could for a box or line except that you cannot set the default for a picture box to Manual Runaround.

▼ ▼

Tip: Get to Those Tool Preferences Quickly. As you probably can tell, we do almost anything to avoid actually making a selection from a menu. We just find that other methods are faster for us, and they should be for you, too. For example, you can jump to the Tool Preferences dialog box by double-clicking on a tool in the Tool palette. This automatically highlights the tool you chose, and you're ready to make your change. Unfortunately, this is one dialog box in which you can't use the keyboard to "push" buttons.

You can press "save"

▼ ▼

Moving On

You now know the basics of how QuarkXPress relates to you, and the general concepts of how you can use its tools to make your pages. If you weren't familiar with these tools before, a little practice will turn you into a pro in no time. If you were familiar with them, we hope you now have increased your arsenal of high-caliber techniques.

Either way, you should now be ready to move into the next chapter, in which we move away from a freeform, throw-it-all-on-a-page style of working and introduce you to systematic methods of building documents.

CHAPTER 2

DOCUMENT CONSTRUCTION

We find the design process fascinating. The designer must meld rigid, mathematical specifications with flowing, flexible sensibilities. QuarkXPress works best when you use this mix. First, build the foundation of your document with precision. Second, place items on the page with creativity.

This chapter is about starting that process: building an infrastructure for your document. We call this *document construction*. It's just like the construction of a building. First you decide on the building's specifications—how tall and wide, and so on. Next, you lay a foundation and build structural supports.

In QuarkXPress it's very similar. First we decide on the specifications of the document—how tall and wide, whether it's double- or single-sided, and so on. Next, we build the structures of the page—repeating page elements, page numbering, and text flow. If you don't take these steps first, the foundation of your work will be unreliable—and your building might just fall down.

Step with us into the building mode. First stop is opening a new document.

▼ ▼

Building a New Document

When you open QuarkXPress using the program defaults, you'll see a blank screen underneath the menu bar, with the Tool and Measurements palettes showing. The first step in creating a new document is to choose New from the File menu (or press Command-N). This brings up the New Document dialog box, shown in Figure 2-1. It is here that you take the first steps in determining a document's page dimensions, page margins, number of columns, the spacing between columns, and whether the pages are laid out facing each other or not.

Figure 2-1

The New Document dialog box

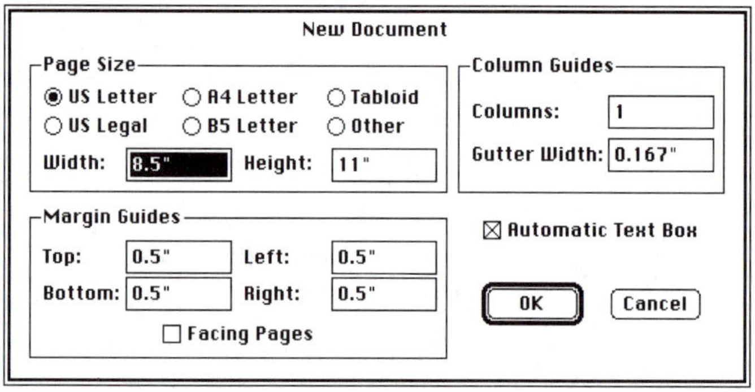

```
                          New Document
 ┌─Page Size─────────────────────┐  ┌─Column Guides──────┐
 │ ● US Letter  ○ A4 Letter  ○ Tabloid│  │                    │
 │ ○ US Legal   ○ B5 Letter  ○ Other  │  │ Columns:   [1    ] │
 │                                │  │                    │
 │ Width: [8.5"]  Height: [11"]   │  │ Gutter Width: [0.167"]│
 └────────────────────────────────┘  └────────────────────┘
 ┌─Margin Guides─────────────────┐    ☒ Automatic Text Box
 │ Top:   [0.5"]   Left:  [0.5"]  │
 │ Bottom:[0.5"]   Right: [0.5"]  │    ( OK )   ( Cancel )
 │        ☐ Facing Pages          │
 └────────────────────────────────┘
```

The New Document dialog box is the "Checkpoint Charlie" for entering the new document zone (walls may crumble, but metaphors remain). Note that there is nothing in the New Document dialog box that locks you in; you can make changes to these settings at any time within a document, even after you've worked on it a lot.

Let's take a look at each of this dialog box's items in detail.

Page Size

When you make your pass through the New Document dialog box on the way to creating a document, you have the opportunity to determine the dimensions of its pages. The *default setting*—the one QuarkXPress chooses for you if you make no change—is a standard letter-size page: 8.5-by-11 inches. You can choose among five preset choices, or you can choose a custom size page. Table 2-1 shows the measurements for each of the preset choices in three common measurement units.

Table 2-1

Preset page sizes

Name	In inches	In picas/points	In millimeters
US Letter	8.5 by 11	51p by 66p	216 by 279.4
US Legal	8.5 by 14	51p by 84p	216 by 355.6
A4 Letter	8.27 by 11.69	49p7.3 by 70p1.9	210 by 297
B4 Letter	6.93 by 9.84	41p6.9 by 59p0.7	176 by 250
Tabloid	11 by 17	66p by 102p	279.4 by 431.8

Choosing "Other" lets you create any page size from one by one inch to 48 by 48 inches. You also can select another page size by simply typing the page dimensions into the Width and Height fields. Note that if you're using one of the preset radio button choices, these fields show the measurements for those pages.

▼ ▼

Tip: Page Size is Not Paper Size. Page Size in the New dialog box refers to the size of the pages you want as your finished output—not to the size of the paper going through your printer. These may or may not be the same. In the Page Size area, type in the page dimensions of the actual piece you want to produce. For example, if you want to create a seven-by-nine inch book page, enter these values in the Width and Height fields, even if you're outputting to a laser printer capable of handling only letter-size pages.

▼ ▼

Margin Guides

The Margin Guides area allows you to specify the margin sizes on all four sides of a page: Top, Bottom, Left, and Right. When you work with facing pages (see below), Left and Right change to Inside and Outside. These margin guides can be used to define the *column area*. In the book and magazine trade, the column area is usually called the *live area*. It's the area within which the text and graphics usually sit (see Figure 2-2). Running heads, folios, and other repeating items sit outside the live area.

Figure 2-2
The Column,
or "live" area

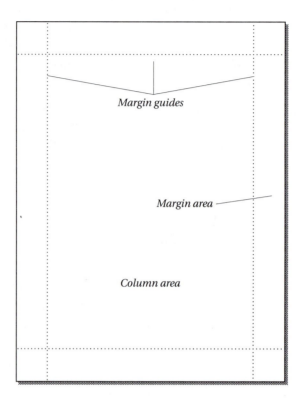

Margin guides

Margin area

Column area

The term "live area" may be slightly misleading, however, because everything that's on a page prints out, whether it's inside the margin guides or outside—or even partially on the page and partially off it. Note that the margin guides are only that: guides. You can ignore them if you want. You should also note that these guides specify the size of the automatic text box (which, again, we'll talk about later in this chapter).

There are some qualities about margin guides that make them unique. Although margin guides resemble ruler guides both in form and function, once you place margin guides you cannot change their position by dragging them; you have to change them in the Master Guides dialog box. We look at making these kinds of modifications in "Making Pages," page 165.

All pages in your document don't have to have the same margins. But they do until you create multiple master pages. Once again, we defer discussion of this process until later in the chapter. For now, let's just concentrate on building one simple document.

Note that these guides don't print out. Nor do they limit what you can do on the page. They are simply part of the general infrastructure of the document, and are meant as guides. Not only can you change these guides at any time, but (as with the printed guides on blueline grid paper) you can disregard them entirely.

Column Guides

There's another kind of automatic guide you can place on a page: column guides. If you select a value larger than one for the Columns field in the New Document dialog box, the area within the margin guides is divided into columns. For example, if you want a page that ordinarily has three columns of text on it, you can specify a value of three (see Figure 2-3).

Your next decision is the amount of gutter space. This is a different "gutter" than people sometimes use to refer to the inside page margin. In QuarkXPress, the *gutter* is the blank space between column guides.

Perhaps the best way to think about column guides is the concept of the page grid. Unfortunately, QuarkXPress can't create a true horizontal and vertical grid for your page. However, it can

[handwritten margin note: Can only make Column Guide in New Document the beginning. got it!]

Figure 2-3
Column guides

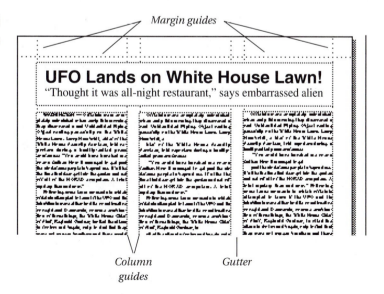

Margin guides

UFO Lands on White House Lawn!
"Thought it was all-night restaurant," says embarrassed alien

Column guides

Gutter

give you the tools to make one yourself. Column guides are the first part of that procedure: they allow you to place columns of space on a page. When Snap to Guides is selected from the View menu, items such as text boxes and lines snap to your column guides (see Chapter 1, *QuarkXPress Basics*).

▼ ▼

Tip: Snap to Guides for Box Fitting. We often find it more helpful to draw separate text boxes for each column rather than use one large text box separated into columns. Column and margin guides make this process easy (see Figure 2-4). If you have Snap to Guides turned on (under the View menu), you can quickly draw a text box that fills one column. This text box can be duplicated, then positioned in the next column, and so on, until each column is created.

Eric sometimes decides he doesn't want the column guides cluttering up his page after he's drawn these text boxes, so he simply removes them from the master page using Master Guides. David, having lived with clutter most of his life, just leaves the guides where they are.

▼ ▼

Figure 2-4
Using column guides to
make columns of
different width

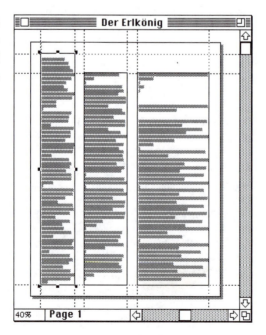

Facing Pages

Although the Facing Pages feature is located in the Margins area of the New Document dialog box (and in the Document Setup dialog box), it deserves some special attention. At this stage in the game, you have two choices for your document: single-sided or facing pages.

Single-sided pages. Single-sided pages are what most people generate from desktop-publishing equipment: single-sided pieces of paper. For example, handbills, posters, letters, memos, or one-page forms are all single-sided. In QuarkXPress a normal, single-sided document looks like a series of pages, each positioned directly underneath the next (see Figure 2-5).

Facing pages. Whereas nonfacing pages are destined to be single, facing pages are always married to another page (well, almost always). For example, pick up a book. Open it in the middle. The left page (the *verso*) faces the right page (the *recto*). In many books (like the one you're looking at), the left and right pages are almost exactly the same. However, most books have a page with a slightly larger inside margin (*binding margin*) than the outside margin (*fore-edge margin*). This is to offset the amount of the page "lost" in the binding.

QuarkXPress displays facing pages next to each other on the screen (see Figure 2-6). For example, when moving from page two to page three you must scroll "across" rather than "down." Note that even page numbers always fall on the left; odd numbers always fall on the right.

If you check Facing Pages in the New dialog box, QuarkXPress sets up two master pages: a left and a right page. These can be almost completely different from each another. Later in the chapter we'll see how.

Automatic Text Box

Here's a relatively easy choice: do you want your first page and all subsequently added pages to have text boxes automatically placed

Figure 2-5
Single-sided pages

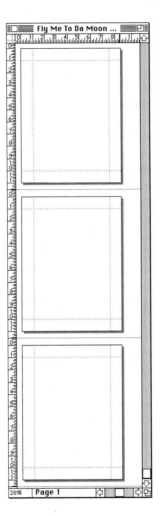

on them? If so, check this box. The text box fills the page to the margin guides. This is clearly the way to go if you're working with documents such as books or flyers that are mostly text.

If you do check Automatic Text Box, the text box that Quark-XPress makes for you is set to the same number of columns and gutter size that you specified in the Column Guides area. We discuss the Automatic Text Box checkbox in detail in "Automatic Text Boxes," page 151.

Figure 2-6

Facing pages

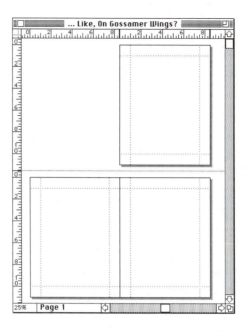

... Like, On Gossamer Wings?

25% Page 1

▼ ▼

No button to change this. Why? Oh well.

Tip: Check That New Document Dialog Box. QuarkXPress remembers what you selected in the New Document dialog box for the last document and gives you the same thing next time you start on a new document. This can be helpful or it can be a drag. You'll hear us say this throughout the book: verify each dialog box as you go. Don't just assume that you want every default setting. Pay attention to those details and you'll rarely go wrong.

▼ ▼

Master Pages: Elementary

In March of 1990, traffic was disrupted and mini-riots occurred in major American cities as thousands of employees of graphic design firms, typesetting shops, service bureaus, and other businesses took to the streets spontaneously in joyous, drunken revels upon hearing Quark's announcement that version 3.0 of QuarkXPress would significantly improve the program's implementation of master pages.

Master pages are the means of establishing repeating elements common to multiple pages within a document. For example, if you have one master page in a single-sided document, then what's on that master page shows up on every new page you create. In facing-page documents there are two master pages, one for the left page and one for the right. Master-page elements can be defined as common to all left or all right pages. Thus, in a facing-page document, all the left pages include all of the elements on the left master page.

If you're used to working with a dedicated word-processing program, you know that the way to create and edit headers and footers in it is to call up a special window and type in it, thereafter choosing to hide or show the header/footer on scrolling pages as the particular program allows. There is no way to hide headers and footers in QuarkXPress. You create them directly on your master pages as standard text or picture boxes, and they show up everywhere you go. Figure 2-7 shows a master page with headers and footers.

What Master Pages Are Good For

Although your creativity in formatting master pages may be unlimited, master pages' most common uses are for running heads, repeating graphics, and automatic page numbers. These items are perfect for master pages because creating them for every page in your document would be a chore that Hercules would shudder at and Job would give up on.

Automatic Page Numbering. We have a confession to make: before we knew better, we would put "1" on the first page, "2" on the second page, and so on. When we deleted or added pages, we just took the time to renumber every page. That seemed reasonable enough. What else could we do?

QuarkXPress lets you set up automatic page numbering for an entire document. You don't actually type any number on the master page. What you do is press the keystroke for Current Box Page Number character (Command-3). This gives you a number place-

didn't work Command-3

Figure 2-7
Headers and footers

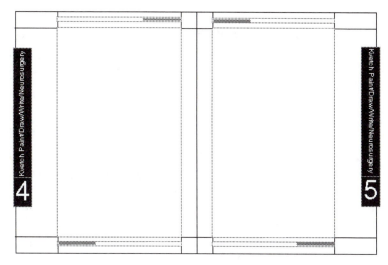

holder. This placeholder is replaced by the page number when you are looking at the document from the Document view. In master pages, the page-number placeholder looks like this: <#>.

The number appears in whatever font, size, and style you choose on the master page. For example, if you set the <#> character to nine-point Futura, all the page numbers come out in that style. This can actually cause some confusion: if you choose a font like an Expert Set or Pi collection, the numbers or the <#> characters might appear differently than you expected. But with normal typefaces, you'll see the numbers just like you'd think.

Remember, the Current Box Page Number character (Command-3) is simply a character that you type, manipulate, or delete using keyboard commands. You also can type it alongside other text, to form text blocks that read "Page <#>", or, "If you wanted to find pg. <#>, you found it."

These page numbers flow with your pages. For example, if you move page 23 to be your new page 10, every page in the document changes its position and numbering accordingly. Also, if you change the page numbering scheme to Roman numerals or whatever (see "Sections," later in this chapter), QuarkXPress automatically changes that style on every page.

▼ ▼

Tip: Big Page Numbers. The problem with checking thumbnails on screen is that you can hardly ever figure out what page number is what. One reader tells us that she sometimes adds big automatic page numbers (Command-3) that hang off the edge of the pages onto the pasteboard for the left and right master pages (see Figure 2-8). You can set these text boxes to have no runaround and turn Suppress Printout on, and QuarkXPress acts as if they aren't even there. However, even at tiny sizes, you can see them attached to each page.

Figure 2-8
Thumbnail page numbers

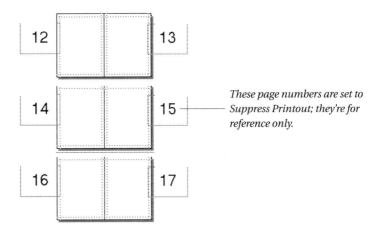

These page numbers are set to Suppress Printout; they're for reference only.

▼ ▼

Graphics and master pages. You can do anything with a graphic on a master page that you can do on a regular document page, including defining it for text runarounds. You can be subtle and put a small graphic in your header or footer, or you can put a great big graphic in the background of every page (see Figure 2-9).

The thing to remember when formatting master pages with graphics—whether as backgrounds or for runaround effects—is that what you place on the master page appears on every page of the document. If you only want a graphic on a few pages in your document, you're best off either handling such things on a page-by-page basis in the regular document view, or creating different master pages to hold different graphics.

Figure 2-9
Placing a graphic on
your master page

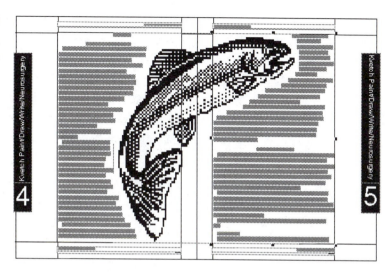

QuarkXPress offers you more flexibility in master-page creation than any other Macintosh publishing program. But if you
use other page-layout software, you should note that Quark-
XPress's master pages differ significantly from their competition's
versions in concept and function.

How PageMaker Does It

In PageMaker, master pages interact "transparently" with actual
document pages. It is common to describe them using the metaphor of transparent overlays on all pages, but really they are more
like "underlays" beneath each page. PageMaker lets you create
and edit the guts of the document on your document page, while
its master page underlay displays and prints underneath it.
Speaking metaphorically, you can "slide out" this master page
underlay at any time, change the page formatting, and then slide
it back in.

However, you cannot locally change any master-page elements within actual document pages, because although they
display and print there, they really exist only on the underlay—
untouchable unless they are slid out. Nor can you choose to base

pages on only certain of the elements on a master page; everything on the master page is either turned on or turned off. And you cannot have multiple master pages for a single document.

How QuarkXPress Does It

Master pages in QuarkXPress are totally different. You get all the retroactive formatting power found in the other programs, plus more. Elements on QuarkXPress's master pages show up on regular document pages not as view-only elements existing on an underlay, but as real elements which you can edit just like any other page element. If you change master-page formatting, you have the option of saving or eradicating any "local" modifications you've made to those master-page elements on document pages.

You can base document pages on a *formatted* or a *blank* master page (the latter is the QuarkXPress equivalent of turning a master page "off"). And you can have multiple master pages—up to 127—in any document, so you can base different document pages on different master pages. This is very useful if your document comprises multiple sections that require different looks.

We're going to stick to the basics in this elementary section on QuarkXPress's master pages, because to throw all the options and variables down on the table at once might make things seem more complicated than they really are. Working with master pages isn't complicated when taken step by step.

Your First Master Page

Two things happen simultaneously when you click OK in the New dialog box: QuarkXPress builds a master page called "A-Master A" and creates the first page of your document for you to work on. The master page and the document page are almost identical. If you checked Facing Pages in the New Document dialog box, QuarkXPress still only creates a single document page, but it makes two master pages: a left page called "L-A-Master A" and a right page called "R-A-Master A".

There are three methods for switching between viewing the master pages of a document and the document itself.

▶ **Document Layout palette.** The icons for the master pages are located at the top of the Document Layout palette. To jump to the master page you want to view, double-click its icon (see Figure 2-10).

▶ **Display submenu.** You can choose to work on either your document or your master pages by selecting them from the Display submenu located under the Page menu (see Figure 2-12).

▶ **Popup page.** If you installed Quark's free FeaturesPlus XTension (for versions 3.1 and 3.2) or Thing-a-ma-bob XTension (for version 3.3), clicking and dragging the page number in the lower-left corner of the document's window gives you a popup menu from which you can select any document page or master page (see Figure 2-12).

clik it

Figure 2-10

Viewing a
master page

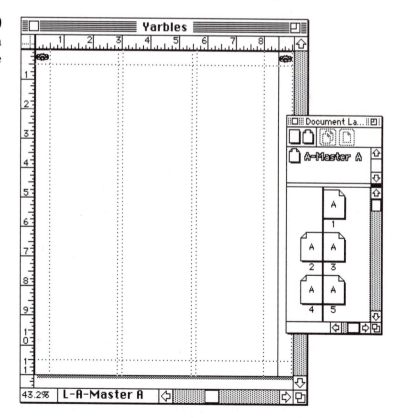

Figure 2-11
Selecting a page
to look at

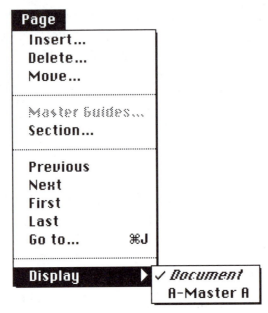

Figure 2-12
Popup pages

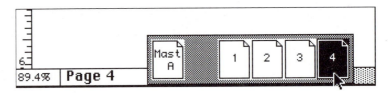

You can tell whether you're looking at a document page or a master page by three telltale signs.

▶ The page-number indicator in the lower-left corner of the document window tells you that you are looking at a document page.

▶ An automatic text-link icon is always in the upper-left corner of a master page. (We discuss what this is later in the chapter.)

▶ While viewing a master page, you can't able to perform certain functions that are usually available. For example, the Go To feature (Command-J) feature is disabled, as is Insert.

▼ ▼

Tip: Printing Master Pages. Printing master pages is simple enough, but people often can't figure out how to do it. The trick is that you have to have the master page you want printed showing when you select Print from the File menu. Note that this prints both the left and right page if the document has facing pages (you can't print only the left or the right alone). Unfortunately, this means that if you have 12 different master pages and you want them all printed, you have to print them one spread at a time.

▼ ▼

Automatic Text Boxes

Although master pages look very similar to normal document pages, there are some basic differences of which you need to be aware. These are the master guides, the automatic text-link icon, and the automatic text-link box. Each of these is integral to the construction of a well-built document.

Note that *automatic text-link icon* is our term for what Quark's documentation refers to as both the "Intact Chain Icon" and the "Broken Chain Icon." Similarly, our term *automatic text-link box* is referred to as "automatic text box" in the Quark manuals. We think our terminology is more descriptive, so that's what we use. If you like theirs, then do a mental substitution.

Master Guides

We said above that you could change the margins and column guides after you set them in the New Document dialog box. The Master Guides dialog box is the place to do it. You can get the Master Guides dialog box by selecting Master Guides from the Page menu when you're working on a master page (see Figure 2-13).

When you use the Master Guides dialog box to change the margin guides or the column guides, only the currently open

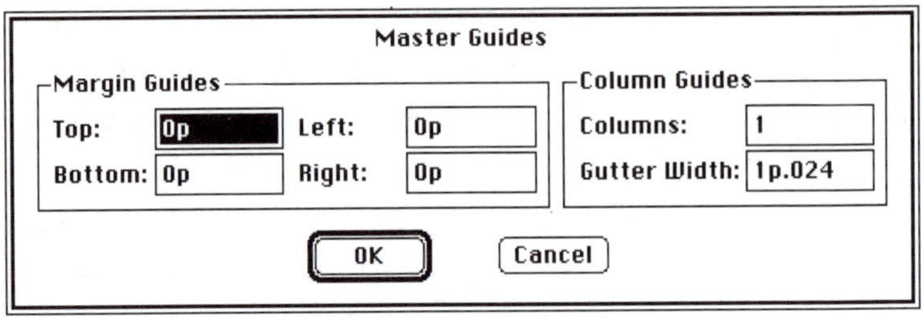

Figure 2-13

Master Guides
dialog box

```
┌─────────────────────────────────────────────────────────────┐
│                         Master Guides                         │
│  ┌─Margin Guides───────────────┐  ┌─Column Guides──────────┐  │
│  │  Top:    [0p    ]  Left:  [0p  ]│  │ Columns:     [1      ]│  │
│  │  Bottom: [0p   ]  Right: [0p  ]│  │ Gutter Width:[1p.024]│  │
│  └─────────────────────────────┘  └────────────────────────┘  │
│                  ( OK )      ( Cancel )                         │
└─────────────────────────────────────────────────────────────┘
```

master page changes. Later in this chapter, you'll learn about having multiple master pages; in that case, you can have different
margins and columns for each master page in your document.

Note that when you change the margin or column guides
using Master Guides, you affect the automatic text box on that
page. If the boundaries of the automatic text box reach to the
margin guides (they always do unless you've changed them), the
boundaries are changed to match the new margins. Similarly, if
you change the columns field in the Master Guides dialog box,
the automatic text box also gets altered (as long as you haven't
changed its boundaries or column settings).

Automatic Text-Link Icon

The automatic text-link icon is the little picture of a chain in the
upper-left corner of every master page. It is the gateway to
QuarkXPress's automatic text-linking feature. This feature allows
QuarkXPress to automatically link together text boxes that occur
on each page. This process also can be accomplished manually
but it is much slower. The automatic text-link icon works in conjunction with the automatic text-link box, which we discuss soon.

The automatic text-link icon is always either broken (disabled) or linked (enabled). You can use the Linking and Unlinking
tools while viewing your master pages to switch the automatic
linking on and off (see below).

Automatic Text-Link Box

Another item of importance to master pages is the automatic text-
link box. This is a text box that is linked through QuarkXPress's

automatic linking mechanism. Automatic linking is the way that QuarkXPress links pages together. We know this sounds confusing. Let's look at an example.

Picture a one-page document with only one master page, "A-Master A". If your text fills and overflows the text box on the first page, you can add a page by selecting Insert Page from the Page menu. If your "A-Master A" has an automatic text-link box on it, then the overflow text can automatically flow onto the newly added page. If there is no automatic text-link box on the master page, then QuarkXPress does not link your first page text box to anything, and you have to link things manually (see Chapter 1, *QuarkXPress Basics*).

There are two ways to get automatic text-link boxes on your master page.

▶ **Automatic Text Box.** If you check Automatic Text Box in the New Document dialog box when you're creating a document, QuarkXPress places a text box on your first document page and also on "A-Master A". The text box on the master page is an automatic text-link box.

▶ **Linking to the chain.** You can create your own automatic text-link box by drawing a text box on your master page and then linking it to the automatic text-link icon. Select the Linking tool, click on the automatic text-link icon in the upper-left corner of the page, then click on the text box you want automatically linked (see Figure 2-14). If you want both the left- and righthand pages to be automatic text-link boxes, you need to link both of them.

An automatic text-link box is a special-case text box. It is reserved solely for text that is typed on (or flowed into) document pages, so you cannot type any text in it while on the master page. This is different from other boxes that are on the master page, which can contain text or graphics. We'll look at why you'd want these other types a little later on.

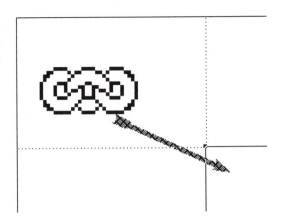

Modifying Automatic Text-Link Boxes

While you cannot type in automatic text link boxes, you can make many formatting specifications on them. For example, you can specify the number of columns, width, height, background color, and frame. While QuarkXPress originally places automatic text-link boxes so that they fill the area outlined by the margin guides (with the number of columns specified for column guides), you can move and resize them to suit your needs.

▼ ▼

Tip: Assigning a Startup Font. Although you cannot actually type in an automatic text-link box while in master-page viewing mode, you *can* assign character and paragraph formatting to the box. Just select the text box with the Content tool and specify the font, size, style, leading, and so on. You can even set the default style sheet for the box (see Chapter 5, *Copy Flow*). Then, when you return to the document page, the text you type in that box appears in the font, style, and leading that you chose. Text that is imported into that box does not necessarily appear in that font, however.

Cool

▼ ▼

Creating Multiple Automatic Text-Link Boxes

You can actually have any number of automatic text-link boxes on a master page. That is, text could flow into one, then another, then another before flowing onto the next page. What you have to do is link them all in the order in which you want text to flow into them. You define the first box as automatic, using the procedures described above. Then you click in succession with the Linking tool on the boxes you want to define as automatic text-link boxes. This defines them as part of the automatic text chain. You'll see the linking arrows shoot out with each new link that you create. To continue the link from a left master to a right master, click on the right master's automatic text-link icon before joining any boxes found on the right master.

Unlinking Automatic Text-Link Boxes

The easiest way to discard an automatic text-link box is to delete it (Command-K). But if you want to keep the box and simply negate its definition as an automatic text-link box, you can do that using the Unlinking tool. First, click on the automatic text-link icon with the Unlinking tool, thereby showing the linking arrow. Next, click on the tail of the linking arrow to break the chain and turn the box into a "normal" master-page text box. In the case of multiple successively linked boxes, the automatic linking is broken wherever you've broken the chain, though any other links remain.

Master Pages and Document Pages

There is a subtle but certain link between your master pages and document pages that goes beyond one mirroring the other. Because QuarkXPress lets you change master page items on your document pages (unlike PageMaker), you have extra power; but with that power comes—what else?—responsibility. The responsibility to pay attention to what you're doing. Here's why.

Changing Master-Page Items

After you have created a master page and applied it to a document page, you can manipulate the master-page items in either master page or document view. Which view you're in when you make a change determines what effect the change has on your document.

Changes to master items on master pages. If you are in master-page view when you make a change to a master-page item, the change is reflected on every page in your document that is based on that master page—unless that item has been changed on particular pages while in document view (see Figure 2-15).

For example, let's say you have a header with the name of the document and the page number. You have created a 30-page document with this master page, so each page has that header on it. If you change the running head because the document's title has changed, that change shows up on all 30 pages. The same thing happens if you change the typeface of the head, or anything else about the master page.

In fact, if you deleted the running head's text box from the master page, it would be deleted from every document page based on that master page, too.

Changes to master items on document pages. However, if you changed the header on page 10 while in document view before reworking the header on the master page, the header on every page except page 10 is changed. Page 10 remains unchanged because local page changes override the master-page change for that text box.

As long as no local page changes are made, if you delete the header from the master page, the header is deleted from every page of the document. But, if a change had already been made locally to the header on page 10, in this example, then that header on page 10 is *not* deleted. If you then delete the running head's text box or even the whole master page, the text boxes that appear on document pages are deleted except for the one on page 10, which was *locally* modified.

Figure 2-15

Master Page changes

*Enter a running head
and page number on the
Master Page.*

```
┌────────────────── Shpilkes in hinten ──────────────────┐
│                                                          │
│   CHAPTER·TITLE·PLACEHOLDER→      <#> ·                  │
│                                                          │
│ 281.3% R-A-Master A                                      │
└──────────────────────────────────────────────────────────┘
```

*On a document page,
the item shows up exactly
as it appears on the Master
Page with the correct page
number inserted.*

```
┌────────────────── Shpilkes in hinten ──────────────────┐
│                                                          │
│   CHAPTER·TITLE·PLACEHOLDER→        3                    │
│                                                          │
│ 281.3% Page 3                                            │
└──────────────────────────────────────────────────────────┘
```

*Edit this text for the
running head on the
document page.*

```
┌────────────────── Shpilkes in hinten ──────────────────┐
│                                                          │
│     OUR·HONKING·SKIN→             3 ·                   │
│                                                          │
│ 281.3% Page 3                                            │
└──────────────────────────────────────────────────────────┘
```

*If you then go back
and change the text on
the Master Pages . . .*

```
┌────────────────── Shpilkes in hinten ──────────────────┐
│                                                          │
│   **David Friedman's Recipes**→   <#> ·                 │
│                                                          │
│ 281.3% R-A-Master A                                      │
└──────────────────────────────────────────────────────────┘
```

*. . . the running head
remains the same on
the document page.*

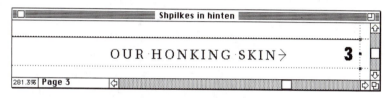

```
┌────────────────── Shpilkes in hinten ──────────────────┐
│                                                          │
│     OUR·HONKING·SKIN→             3 ·                   │
│                                                          │
│ 281.3% Page 3                                            │
└──────────────────────────────────────────────────────────┘
```

This keep-local-changes approach makes sense if you think about it, but it's often frustrating. For instance, if you forget that something is a master-page item and you change it even just a little, QuarkXPress notices and breaks the link between it and the master page. That's one reason why it's important to be clear on what's a master-page item and what's not. Note that if you change a master page item on a document page (such as that running head in the earlier example), and then you change it back to exactly the way it was, QuarkXPress forgives and forgets that you ever changed it in the first place.

Applying Master Pages to Document Pages

Once back on the actual document pages, any changes made to master items (elements derived from the master page) affect only those actual pages; master pages themselves are not affected by local page changes. To modify a master page, you have to go back into master-page view.

What happens if you assign one master page to a page that already has master items on it, or if you reapply the current master page to a document page? (We'll talk about how to do these in "Master Pages and the Document Layout Palette," later in this chapter.) Master items from the current master page are generally deleted and replaced by the master-page items. The one exception is if you have already locally modified a master item.

The determining factor for what happens to master page items that have been modified locally (while in document view) is the Master Page Items feature in the General Preferences dialog box (under the Edit menu). You have two choices.

Delete Changes. If Master Page Items is set to Delete Changes, when you reapply a master page to a document page, every master item on a page is deleted and replaced with new master items—even if changes have been made locally. If you have made changes, this is a great way to "reset" the page: reapply a master page to a document page while Delete Changes is set in the General Preferences dialog box. All the locally modified items are deleted and reset back to the original master items.

Keep Changes. The alternative to deleting locally modified master items is keeping them. When Keep Changes is selected in the General Preferences dialog box, QuarkXPress skips over any master items that you have modified (changed their position, size, shape, font, text, and so on). This is the default setting when you start a document.

Note that these settings have no effect if you simply edit a master-page item—only if you apply or reapply a master page to a document page. As discussed earlier, if you edit a master-page item which has been modified locally on a document page, that change doesn't affect the locally changed item. In this case, if you want to force the document page to reflect the master page change you made, you have to reapply the master page with General Preferences set to Delete Changes.

▼ ▼

Tip: When Are Master Pages Reapplied? One of the most frustrating occurrences to both beginner and experienced QuarkXPress users is the seemingly random way QuarkXPress automatically reapplies master pages to your document pages. However, there's really nothing random about it. Simply put, QuarkXPress automatically reapplies a master page every time a page switches sides in a facing pages layout. If you add one page before page four, then page four becomes page five, flipping from a left to a right page in the spread. In this case, QuarkXPress automatically reapplies the master page. If you added two pages before page four, then QuarkXPress wouldn't automatically reapply the master page at all. This is one reason that adding pages in even increments is so important in QuarkXPress when working with facing pages.

▼ ▼

Summing it Up

And that's really all there is to how the master page feature works. It's simple and ingenious, and any more advanced things that you do with it are based on these operational principles.

▼ ▼

Master Pages and the Document Layout Palette

If you've gotten this far, you've learned the hardest stuff about QuarkXPress's master pages. Now it's time to take the next step and learn a further level of control, by offering the following additional options.

▶ Creating new master pages

▶ Creating new master pages based on existing ones

▶ Naming and ordering master pages

▶ Applying master pages to document pages

▶ Deleting master pages

There are many ways to use multiple master pages. For example, most books are separated into several sections, including front matter, body text, and index. Each section is paginated and formatted differently from the body, with different (or no) headers or footers. You can create a master page for each of these sections. Multiple master pages are almost required for magazine production, where you may have a plethora of different sections: front matter, regular article pages, photo features, full-page ads, and small-ad sections, to name a few.

Multiple master pages are accessible through the Document Layout palette. We introduced the Document Layout palette in Chapter 1, *QuarkXPress Basics*. Now we're going to concentrate on how you can use it to work with your master pages.

Document Layout Palette

If you look at the Document Layout palette for the facing-pages document in Figure 2-16, you'll see that it is divided vertically into four areas: blank document and duplicate/delete, master page, document layout, and page numbersection.

Blank document and duplicate/delete area. At the top of the Document Layout palette is the blank document and delete/duplicate area. This is used for creating, duplicating, and deleting both document and master pages.

At the left, you see blank single-sided and facing-page icons. Next to those icons are two buttons: one to delete master or document pages, the other to duplicate master pages.

Figure 2-16

Document Layout palettes for a single-sided and a facing-pages document

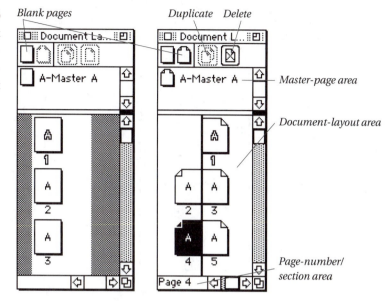

Blank pages Duplicate Delete

Master-page area

Document-layout area

Page-number/ section area

You can create a new master page by dragging a blank single or facing-page icon into the master page area (see Figure 2-17). You delete master pages and document pages by selecting them and clicking the Delete button; similarly, you duplicate master pages by selecting them and clicking Duplicate.

Deleting either a master or document page with the Delete button is not reversible with Undo (Command-Z), so make sure you really want to do it.

▼ ▼

Tip: Avoiding Alerts. We don't know about you, but we often spout spontaneous invectives when our computer alerts us to a dangerous procedure. Because we've used the program for so long, we *know* that what we're doing can't be undone or is potentially life-threatening to our document. One example is the "Are you sure you want to delete these pages" prompt when you click the Delete button in the Document Layout palette. QuarkXPress is trying to be helpful, because you can't reverse this action. But it just typically annoys us. However, if you Option-click the Delete button, the pages are deleted without a prompt. Hoorah for progress.

Figure 2-17
Creating a new
master page

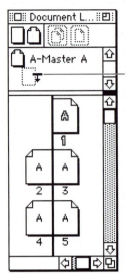

*Dragging a blank page to the master
page area changes the mouse icon to a
page insertion symbol to indicate
where the master page will be added.*

▼ ▼

Tip: Retrieving Document Layout Deletions. If you've deleted a master
page from the Document Layout palette, the only way to get it
back is by selecting Revert to Saved from the File menu. This, of
course, only works if you've saved your document recently. Bear
in mind that this method wipes out all changes you've made
since your last save, so pause a moment and reflect before you
jump into this last resort. (In version 3.3, you can also revert to
your last minisave—if you had Auto Save turned on in Application Preferences—by holding down Option and selecting the
Revert to Saved menu item.)

hmmm.....ok

▼ ▼

Master-page area. Just below the blank-document icons and Delete and Duplicate buttons is the master-page area. Here's where
you create, name, and access master pages. To create a new master page, you drag a blank page icon into this area. To duplicate
an existing master page, click the Duplicate button. Duplicating
another master page is the fastest way to make one master page
that's based on another.

A default name is assigned to a master page when it's created:
the first is "A-Master A", the second is "B-Master B", and so on. You

*Should be A-Master 1
B-Master 2
etc.*

can only rename the part following the hyphen—to name it just click on the name and type. If you delete the letter or hyphen, they get automatically reinserted at the beginning of whatever you typed. The name you assign is the name that appears in master page scroll lists and menus throughout the program.

If you create more master pages than you can see at once, you can drag on the black bar at the right, between the master page area and the document-layout area's scroll bars. Dragging up reduces space allotted to master page names, dragging down increases it. This is like the split-window feature in Microsoft Word and Excel.

If you have more than two master pages, QuarkXPress lets you move them by clicking on the scroll arrows. Note that the second master page you create is called "B-Master B", even if you place the icon in the master-page selection list before "Master A".

▼ ▼

Tip: Basing a New Master Page on Another. If you need a new master page but don't want to format it from scratch, you can base it on another that carries at least some formatting that you wish to retain. There are two ways to do this. First, you can create a new master page as described above. Then, select the icon of the particular master page whose formatting you wish to copy, and drag it over the icon of the just-created master page, releasing the mouse button when that icon is highlighted.

However, an even easier way is simply to select the master page you want to duplicate, and click the Duplicate button at the top of the Document Layout palette.

▼ ▼

Document-layout area. The largest part of the Document Layout palette is the document-layout area. This area shows icons of the document's pages, numbered and positioned in the order of their actual appearance in the document (see "Manipulating your Document" in Chapter 1, *QuarkXPress Basics*, for more on this area). Each page icon on the palette displays the master page that it is based on. When you first open a new document, only one page is visible and it is based on "A-Master A".

Page number/section area. In the lower-left corner of the Document Layout palette sits the page number/section area, which shows you what page is currently selected (highlighted) in the Document Layout palette (not necessarily what page you're looking at in the document window). This is number is in the same format as the one that you can see in the lower-left corner of the document window when you're looking at a page.

If you click the page-number box, QuarkXPress brings up the Section dialog box.

Applying Master Pages

There are two ways to apply the formatting of any master page to an existing document page. The first method is to select the page or pages you want to apply the master page to (remember that you can Shift-click to select a range, or Command-click to select individual pages out of sequential order) and Option-click on the desired master page in the master page area.

The second method is to drag a master page icon on top of a document page icon (this doesn't work in version 3.2). You can release the mouse button as soon as the page icon is highlighted. The document page assumes the formatting of that master page.

Unmodified master items (from the old master page) are deleted and replaced with the new master items. Items that you have modified may or may not be deleted (see "Changing Master Page Items," above). You can also apply one master page to another master page by the same method.

If you don't want any master page applied to a particular page (if you want to turn master pages off for a page), you can apply one of the blank document icons to it instead. Just do the same thing: either drop the icon on top of a document page in the palette or Option-click the icon with the pages selected.

▼ ▼

Tip: Copying Master Pages. Have you ever wanted to copy a master page from one document to another? Kinda' difficult, isn't it? Well, no, not really. Put both documents into Thumbnail viewing mode and drag a page from the first document into the second. The master page that was assigned to that page comes over along with the page itself. Then you can delete the page itself, and the master page stays in the second document.

Making Pages

In Chapter 1, *QuarkXPress Basics*, we discussed moving pages around and deleting them. Clearly, it was slightly premature, as we hadn't yet gotten to adding new pages to a document. We cover that procedure here.

There are two ways to add pages to your document: using the Insert Pages dialog box or using the Document Layout palette.

Insert Pages

The first way you can add pages to your document is by selecting Insert from the Pages menu. This brings up the Insert Pages dialog box (see Figure 2-18).

You can type the number of pages you want to add in the Insert field, and then select where you want those pages to be added. You have three choices: before a page, after a page, and at the end of the document. The first two require that you choose a page that the page(s) should be added before or after; the third requires no additional number, as it places the pages after the last page in the document.

Before you click OK, though, you need to think about two other things in this dialog box: the Link to Current Text Chain checkbox, and the Master Page choice. Let's look at these in reverse order.

Master Page choice. You can choose which master page you want new pages to be based on by selecting one from the Master Page popup menu. Or, if you like, you can base new pages on blank single-sided or facing pages (of course, you can choose the latter only if you're working with a facing-page document).

Figure 2-18
The Insert Pages
dialog box

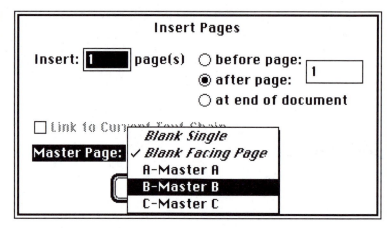

Link to Current Text Chain. If a text box is selected on your page, and the master page on which you are basing your inserted pages has an automatic text-link box, then you have the option of having the inserted pages automatically linked with the text box you have selected. This is a potentially confusing concept, so let's look at it carefully.

Let's say you have a text box on a page, and it's overflowing with text. Let's also say that your master page "C-FeatureOpener" has an automatic text-link box on it that is enabled (linked to the automatic text-link icon).

1. Select the text box on the document page.

2. Select Insert from the Page menu.

3. Add a page based on master page "C-FeatureOpener" at the end of the document.

If you check Link to Current Text Chain in the Insert Pages dialog box, then the text from your document page text box automatically links to your inserted pages. If you do not select Link to Current Text Chain, then the pages are still added, but there is no link between your text box and the text boxes on those pages. You can, however, link them up manually using the Link tool.

Document Layout Insertions

The second method for inserting pages is to insert them via the Document Layout palette. Like everything else in this palette, adding pages is performed via dragging icons. To add a page based on a master page, drag that master-page icon down into the position you want (before a page, after a page, at the end of a document, or as a page in a spread). If you don't want the page based on a master page, you can drag the single-sided or facing-page icon into place instead (as mentioned above, you can only drag a facing-page icon if you are working with a facing-page document).

If you want to add more than one page at a time, or want to add pages that are linked to the current text chain, then you must hold down the Option key while clicking and dragging the page icon into place. When you let go of the icon, QuarkXPress gives you the Insert Pages dialog box. You can select the appropriate items as described above.

Just go to Insert Pages in the first place, time is same.

▼ ▼

Tip: Unintentional Multipage Spreads. There are problems in moving pages around in spreads that are just waiting to unfurl. If you insert the pages next to an existing page, you may be unknowingly creating a multipage spread instead of adding pages the way you'd want. The trick is to be careful about what icons you see when you're dropping the page. If you see a page icon, you'll get a spread; if you see a black arrow icon, you'll add pages to the document flow.

▼ ▼

Modifying Your Pages

Fortunately for desktop publishers, you can change the foundation of your document significantly more easily than a construction worker can change the foundation of a building. Not only can you modify your master pages in all sorts of ways, as we've seen, but you can modify the underlying page size, margins, column guides, and more. Let's look at each of these controls.

Changing Page Size

Even after you've clicked OK in the New dialog box and begun adding pages to a document, you can still change the page size in the Document Setup dialog box (choose Document Setup from the File menu; see Figure 2-19). Note that this dialog box bears a striking resemblance to a portion of the New Document dialog box. The rules are just the same (see "Page Size," page 136).

Figure 2-19

The Document
Setup dialog box

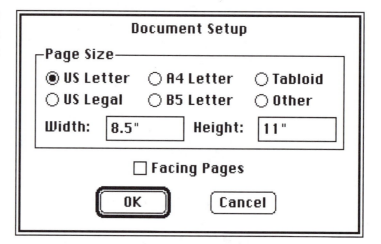

Your only real limitation in modifying page size is the size of any objects you have already placed on the page. QuarkXPress won't let you make a page so small that page elements would "fall off" the pasteboard (the size of the pasteboard surrounding each page is determined by the size of your document page). If this is a limiting factor, you may be able to work around the problem by adjusting the width of the pasteboard (see "Tip: Adjusting Your Pasteboard," in Chapter 1, *QuarkXPress Basics*). The program also prevents you from making the document so small that the margin guides bump into each other. If that's the problem, first change the margin guides (we'll tell you how to do that in just a moment).

Changing Facing Pages

You can change one other page feature with the Document Setup dialog box: facing pages. If you originally specified your document as single-sided, you can change to a facing-page document by checking Facing Pages in the Document Setup dialog box. Facing-page documents can have facing master pages (the facing-page icon is enabled in the Document Layout palette).

However, you cannot change a facing-page document to a single-sided document if you have any facing master pages. If you need to change a facing-page document to a single-sided document, first delete all the facing master pages (select them from the Document Layout palette and click the Delete button), then uncheck Facing Pages in the Document Setup dialog box.

Changing Margins

As we mentioned above, every page in your document has the same margins until you create multiple master pages, each with different margins. When you first open a master page, its margin guides are set to the values you specified in the New dialog box. You can change these margins by selecting Master Guides from the Page menu. Remember that the Master Guides menu item is only available when a master page is being displayed.

Changing Column Guides

Migrants from PageMaker should be aware that QuarkXPress's column guides cannot be repositioned by dragging them with the mouse. Instead, you change the Column Guides settings in the Master Guides dialog box. QuarkXPress lets you have a different number of columns and varied gutter sizes for each master page. If you want to have no column guides on a page, type "1" in the Columns field.

▼ ▼

Automatic Page Insertion

Importing a long text document can be a harrowing experience when you're working with automatically linked text boxes. The text flows beyond page one and—it seems—into the netherworld.

Where does the rest of the text go when the first text box is filled? QuarkXPress lets you control this through the Auto Page Insertion popup menu in the General Preferences dialog box (under the Edit menu). You have four choices: End of Story, End of Section, End of Document, and Off. The default setting (the way it's set up if you don't change anything), is End of Section.

End of Story. With this option selected, QuarkXPress inserts new pages right after the page containing the last text box in a story, and they bear the master-page formatting of the page that held that box. If, for instance, your story starts on page one and jumps to page five, any text overflow from the page five text box causes pages to be inserted following page five, not page one.

End of Section. Under this option, pages are inserted following the last page in a section (see "Sections and Page Numbering," below). Additional pages bear the master-page formatting of the last page in that section. Thus, if your page one story jumps to page five, and page five is part of a section that ends with page eight, new pages inserted because of text overflow appear right after page eight.

End of Document. This option causes pages to be inserted after the last page of the document, no matter how long it is and despite any sections you might have set up. Inserted pages bear the master page formatting of the last page of the document.

If you have only one story and one section in a document, then all three of these settings mean the same thing.

Off. When Auto Page Insertion is set to Off, QuarkXPress never adds pages automatically. Instead, you must add pages manually (see "Making Pages," earlier in this chapter).

Text Linking

Remember, the Automatic Page Insertion feature only works if the master page that's getting inserted has an automatic text-link box. That makes sense, because pages are always inserted based on text flowing through the automatic text chain. You cannot have *automatic page insertion* without an *automatic text link,* and you cannot have that without an *automatic text-link box.*

Multipage Spreads

When the rest of the world thought that facing-page spreads were pretty nifty, Quark came along and added the capability to build three-page spreads. In fact, you can quickly and easily build four-page, five-page, or any number of pages in a spread, as long as the combined width of the spread doesn't exceed 48 inches.

Once again, this is a job for the Document Layout palette. Spreads can be created in both facing-pages and single-sided documents by dragging a page icon (either a new page or one already in the document) to the right side of a right page or to the left side of a left page. Single-sided documents, for this purpose, are considered to be made entirely of right pages, but there aren't many times that you'd be doing this with a single-sided document. The pasteboard (represented by the dark gray area in the palette) automatically expands to accommodate the pages. Figure 2-20 shows an example of creating a three-page spread in a facing-page document.

Note that when you drag a page over to create a multipage spread, don't let go of the mouse button if you see the little black arrow icon. That'll reshuffle the file rather than building a spread. Instead, you should only let go when you see a dark page icon in the place that you want the spread page to be.

Sections and Page Numbering

Earlier in this chapter we discussed how to apply automatic page numbering to your document's master pages. Here we talk about

Figure 2-20

Making a three-page spread

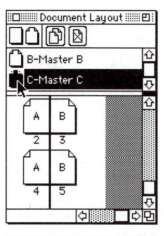

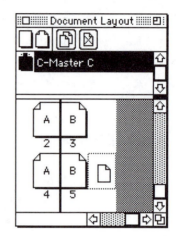

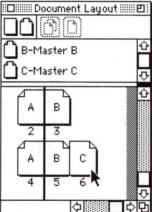

how to customize those page numbers and create multiple sections within a single document.

Ordinarily, a QuarkXPress document has one section. Page numbers start with the Arabic numeral "1" and go up consecutively, page by page (we can't figure out why they're called Arabic numerals because the numbers in Arabic are totally different; nonetheless, that's what normal, plain ol' numbers are called). However, you can change the starting page number, the style of page numbers, and add multiple sections that each have their own page-numbering styles by using the Section feature.

Changing Your Starting Page Number

Whenever you specify a section in your document, you're starting a new page numbering scheme; in fact, that's the only good reason for using sections.

For instance, let's say you're producing a book, and each chapter is saved in a separate QuarkXPress file. If the first chapter ends on page 32, you can tell QuarkXPress to start the page numbers in chapter two at page 33, and so on. To do this, go to the first page of the document (the one you want to change the numbering for), and select Section from the Page menu. Then, turn the Section feature on by clicking in the box (an "X" should appear). Type the starting page number that for your document, and click OK (see Figure 2-21).

Figure 2-21

Setting up a new section

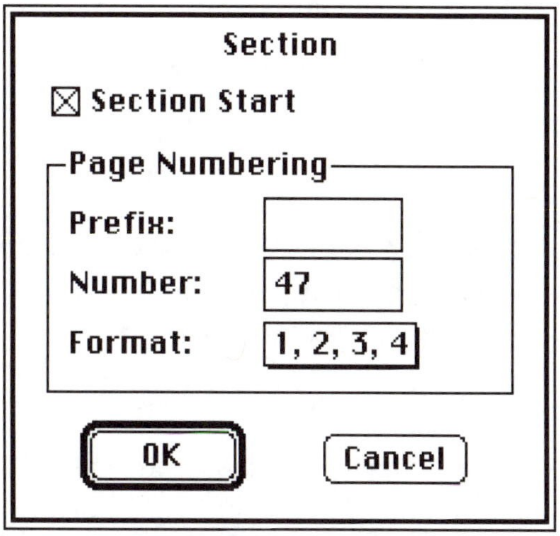

The first page of a new section always has an asterisk after its name. This doesn't print out. It's just a sign that QuarkXPress gives you on the screen, saying that this is a section beginning.

You can have as many sections in a document as you want, each starting with a different page number. If you make the fifth page in your document a new section and set it to start on page 47, then your document's page numbering goes "1, 2, 3, 4, 47, 48, 49 . . . ."

▼ ▼

Tip: Get to That Section Quickly. There's another way to get to the Section dialog box, but the method depends on which version of QuarkXPress you're using.

▶ In 3.1, you get there by clicking a page icon and then clicking the master pages name area in the Document Layout palette.

▶ In version 3.2, first you have to go to the correct page by clicking it in the Document Layout palette; then you click the page number below the icon.

 ▶ In version 3.3, they've changed it again: click the page, then click the page number field in the lower-left corner of the palette.

Any way you do it, it brings the Section dialog box up faster than having to reach for a menu.

▼ ▼

Changing the Page-Numbering Style

QuarkXPress lets you choose from five formats for numbering pages in the Section dialog box.

▶ Arabic numerals (1, 2, 3, 4, etc.)

▶ Uppercase Roman numerals (I, II, III, IV, etc.)

▶ Lowercase Roman numerals (i, ii, iii, iv, etc.)

▶ Capital letters (A, B, C, D, etc.)

▶ Lowercase letters (a, b, c, d, etc.)

To pick one of these numbering styles for a section, go to the first page in the section, select Section using one of the methods described above, and choose a numbering format from the Format popup menu.

Prefixes

Automatic page numbers can contain more than just a number in the five formats listed above. You also can include a prefix of up to four characters to the page number. For example, you may want the page numbers in a book appendix to read "A-1", "A-2", and so on. The "A-" is a prefix to the Arabic numerals. You can type this sort of prefix in the Prefix field of the Section dialog box. This prefix not only appears in the Document Layout palette and in the automatic page numbers, but it even shows at the top of the page when you print with registration marks (see Chapter 10, *Printing*).

Automatic "Continued . . ." Pagination

In magazines and newspapers, where stories can jump from page six to 96, it is often helpful to have a "Continued on Page X" message at the bottom of the column from which text is jumping, and a "Continued from Page X" message at the top of the column to which it is jumping. These are sometimes called *jump lines.* QuarkXPress can't automate creation of the lines, but it can automate the placement and revision of the page numbers in them. This is useful because you may change links, or insert or delete new pages, and such actions could change the page numbers referred to. In such cases you won't have to go through and manually update the numbers.

To Create a "Continued on . . ." Message

It's easy to create these jump lines (see Figure 2-22).

1. Make a text box the same width as the column or text box it concerns and move it on top of that text box (if this new text box is behind the original text box, you can select Bring to Front from the Item menu).

Figure 2-22

Jump lines

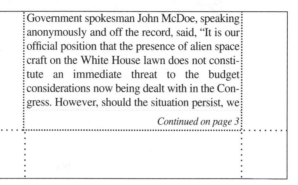

Government spokesman John McDoe, speaking anonymously and off the record, said, "It is our official position that the presence of alien space craft on the White House lawn does not consti- tute an immediate threat to the budget considerations now being dealt with in the Con- gress. However, should the situation persist, we

Continued on page 3

2. Be sure its runaround is set to Item (see Chapter 7, *Where Text Meets Graphics*). This ensures that your jump line has its own space, and isn't jumbled in on top of the other text.

3. Type the text of your jump line (for example, "Continued on"), and, when you come to placement of the page num- ber, press Command-4. This is the next text box page num- ber character. If you haven't added pages yet, the character as typed looks like this: "<None>". Of course, if the font you're using is a Pi or Expert Set font, the character will look really different than this.

If your text links change, pages get shuffled, or an act of god is invoked, QuarkXPress always knows where your text is going and updates the "Next Box Page Number."

Nonetheless, these jump lines can sometimes get confused. When QuarkXPress sees one of these jump lines, it looks at any text box that is behind the jump line. If there is more than one text box behind the jump line text box, QuarkXPress chooses the one that is "closest" to it; in other words, the text box that is on the next layer down. This is a feature which you've just got to try to understand or believe. We have no idea how the program knows that there should be a relationship between the two boxes; it's just cool that it does.

To Create a "Continued from . . ." Message

You can create a "Continued from . . ." jump line by following the same procedures for creating a "Continued on . . ." text box, but place it at the top of the column concerned. When you come to the page number, press Command-2 for the previous box page number character, which shows the page number of the previous text box in the chain. This number is also automatically updated as necessary.

Your messages don't have to read "Continued on/from . . ." You can type any words you want. For instance, "Started on page <None>" or even "If you really care about finishing this story, you'll have to flip past the bulk of this magazine and go all the way to page "<None>", where you'll find it buried among the facial cream ads." What matters is that you type the relevant placeholder character somewhere in your message text box.

▼ ▼

Foundations

Like a construction worker on the job, you are now ready to build your pages with the understanding and confidence that you've got a strong infrastructure to hold the document up. First, you can use the tools discussed in Chapter 1, *QuarkXPress Basics*, to build text and picture boxes on your master and document pages. And next you can fill those boxes with text and pictures; so that's where we're headed now.

CHAPTER 3

WORD PROCESSING

When you think of Quark-XPress, you think of typography. But before you can set type in QuarkXPress, you have to get the words onto your page somehow. In the early days of desktop publishing, you'd usually write your stories in a word-processing program, and then import the files into a page-layout program. From its inception, QuarkXPress was a capable word processor, and as it matured, it added more and more word-processing features. Style sheets, find and replace, a spelling checker, and even drag-and-drop text editing are all elements that have made this program a competent—though not exceptional—word processor.

However, all is not sugar and snails and puppy-dog tails. In complex documents and on many lower-end Macintosh models, QuarkXPress can become so slow that even a moderately skilled typist can get ahead of it. In this chapter, we'll examine the strengths and weaknesses of writing and editing in QuarkXPress, including its powerful Find/Change feature and its spelling checker (we'll hold off on style sheets until Chapter 5, *Copy Flow*). We'll also give you some tips for overcoming QuarkXPress's occasional sluggishness.

▼ ▼

Entering and Editing Text

The most basic aspect of entering text into a QuarkXPress document is making sure that what you type shows up where you want it. QuarkXPress novices often become flustered when they open a document and start typing, only to find that nothing is happening. That's because to enter text in a text box, you must use the Content tool, and you must have selected a text box.

Selecting and Navigating

As we mentioned in the Preface, we assume that you're already familiar with the basic mouse and editing techniques used by almost every Macintosh application. However, QuarkXPress goes beyond that interface, and adds many extras to the standard Macintosh methods of moving the insertion point and selecting text. One of the many things we like about QuarkXPress is that it provides more than one method for performing the same action; in the case of selecting and navigating, you can use either the mouse or the keyboard.

Using the mouse. As with any Macintosh program, you can select a range of text by dragging the pointer diagonally up or down a text column, or you can select a word by double-clicking on it. But QuarkXPress has additional multiple-click selections (see Table 3-1). If you triple-click, you select a line of text. Quadruple-clicking selects a paragraph, and quintuple-clicking selects all the text in the active box's text chain (we don't know about you, but clicking five times in succession is difficult for us; instead, we just press Command-A, which does the same thing).

If you hold down the Shift key and click anywhere in your text chain, all the text from the previous location of the insertion point to the location of your click is selected.

If you select a range of text in a text box, then deselect the box and edit other boxes, QuarkXPress remembers the selection. When you reselect that text box, the same text is still selected in it.

To Select	Click
A word and contiguous punctuation	Twice
A line	Three times
A paragraph	Four times
An entire story	Five times — *Command A*

Table 3-1

Effects of multiple clicks

▼ ▼

Tip: Extend by Word. If you continue to press down on the mouse button after your final click, you can extend your selection by dragging. If you've selected a word by double-clicking, for instance, you can drag to select more text, word by word. And if you've selected a paragraph with four clicks, you can similarly drag to increase your selection paragraph by paragraph.

▼ ▼

Using the keyboard. You can use the keyboard to duplicate most of the selections you can make with the mouse. You can also do many things with the keyboard that are not possible with the mouse alone (see Table 3-2). For instance, you can jump to the beginning of a line quickly just by pressing Command-Option-Left Arrow.

Holding down the Shift key in combination with any of the keyboard movement commands selects all text between the insertion point's original location and the location to which the key combination sends it. In the example above, you could select all the text from the cursor point to the beginning of the line just by adding Shift to the keystroke.

We find the ability to quickly jump to the beginning or end of a story by pressing Command-Option-Up Arrow or Command-Option-Down Arrow especially handy. It can save you a lot of scrolling if you forget the exact page on which a story starts or finishes; plus, we use it to quickly select all the text from the cursor to the beginning or end of the story by adding the Shift key.

▼ ▼

Tip: The Lazy Man's Way to Follow a Text Chain. QuarkXPress has a simple feature that can help if you need to follow a story through

To move to the . . .	Press . . .
Previous character	Left Arrow
Next character	Right Arrow
Previous line	Up Arrow
Next line	Down Arrow
Previous word	Command-Left Arrow
Next word	Command-Right Arrow
Start of line	Command-Option-Left Arrow
End of line	Command-Option-Right Arrow
Start of story	Command-Option-Up Arrow
End of story	Command-Option-Down Arrow

your document, but you don't exactly remember the page to or from which the text chain is jumping. All you have to do is position the insertion point at the beginning or end of the story's text box on the current page. If you're at the beginning of the text box, press the Left or Up Arrow key to move the insertion out of the current box to the previous box in the chain. If you're at the end of the box, similarly press the Right or Down Arrow key to jump the insertion point to the next box in the text chain.

As soon as you move the insertion point out of the current box, QuarkXPress follows it, scrolling automatically to the page containing the text box to which you've moved the insertion point. If possible, QuarkXPress even nicely centers the box in the document window.

▼ ▼

Deleting Text

There are a number of ways to delete text in QuarkXPress (see Table 3-3). You can, of course, use the Delete key to delete text to the left of the insertion point one character at a time, or to remove a text selection. QuarkXPress also lets you delete the character to the right of the insertion point by holding down the Shift key while

Table 3-3	To delete . . .	Press . . .
Keyboard deletions	Previous character	Delete
	Next character	Shift-Delete *or* Del key (Extended keyboard)
	Previous word	Command-Delete
	Next word	Command-Shift-Delete
	Any select text	Delete

(plus any punctuation)

pressing Delete. Similarly, Command-Delete gets rid of the entire word to the left of the insertion point, and Command-Shift-Delete removes the word to the right of the insertion point.

Drag-and-Drop Text

We thought drag-and-drop text editing was pretty cool when it was introduced to the Macintosh world in Microsoft Word 5.0. We think it's even cooler now that it's in our favorite program, introduced in version 3.2. Drag and drop is an easy way of copying or moving text from one location to another in a story.

To use drag-and-drop text editing, select some text, then drag the selection to another location in the text chain. As you move the mouse, you'll see an insertion point move along with it. When the insertion point reaches the place where you want the selected text to go, release the mouse button, and—*presto!* Your text is cut from its original location, and placed at the insertion point.

If you want to copy a selection (instead of just moving it), hold down the Shift key as you drag. Note that any text you drag-move or drag-copy also gets placed in the Clipboard (replacing whatever was there). Also, at least for now, you can't drag-copy text between unlinked text boxes, or between documents—you can do it only within continuous text chains.

If dragging and dropping sounds good to you and you want to use it, you'll have to check it on in the Application Preferences dialog box—it's turned off by default.

? How to Drag
is a drag.
? Still probs.
? Has to be text in the next text box to move to new box.

▾ ▾

Importing Text

While you may type all the text in your QuarkXPress documents, most people don't. More often than not, copy is prepared in the more word-oriented environs of a word processor, then imported into a QuarkXPress document. You import text using the Get Text command in the File menu. In order to access this command, you must have the Content tool selected, and a text box active. To bring text into the active text box, follow the steps below.

1. Position the insertion point where you want the text to be brought into the text box.

2. Choose Get Text from the File menu (Command-E).

3. When the Get Text dialog box appears, select one of the files listed. It displays all files that are in word-processing formats that QuarkXPress can import (see "What Filters Are, and How To Use Them," below).

4. Press Return, or click the Open button.

While you're in the Get Text dialog box, you have two additional options for importing the file: Convert Quotes and Include Style Sheets.

Convert Quotes. If you'd like QuarkXPress to automatically convert straight double and single quotes (",') to curly double and single quotes ("", ''), and double hyphens (--) to true em dashes (—), check Convert Quotes in the Get Text dialog box.

Include Style Sheets. If you're importing a Microsoft Word file, and you want QuarkXPress to include the file's style sheets, check Include Style Sheets. Also, if you're importing an ASCII (plain text) file that uses XPress Tags to contain formatting and style-sheet information, you must also be sure to check the Include Style

Sheets box. We cover both Style Sheets and XPress Tags fully—including what exactly happens when you import them with this feature—in Chapter 5, *Copy Flow*.

What Filters Are, and How To Use Them

QuarkXPress uses XTensions called filters to convert text to and from word-processing formats. Because they're XTensions, you can move them in and out of the QuarkXPress 3.2 folder, or the XTension folder in 3.3 (making them available or not available to the program). Also, this makes it easier for Quark to update them.

QuarkXPress has Mac-only filters for MacWrite and MacWrite II; Microsoft Word, Works, and Write; WordPerfect; and WriteNow; as well as ASCII text using XPress Tags (we wish it could read and write RTF—Rich Text Format—but unfortunately it can't). In order for QuarkXPress to understand these file formats, you must have the appropriate filter in the same folder with QuarkXPress. The same advice for XTensions applies here: if you don't need a particular filter, move it out of that folder so the program will load faster.

In Chapter 5, *Copy Flow*, we explore why you would want to be careful about what word processor you can use, and why we use Microsoft Word.

Finding and Changing

QuarkXPress's powerful Find/Change feature is one of the reasons many desktop publishers prefer to use QuarkXPress as their word processor. You can use the Find/Change feature either to look for and change occurrences of any text you specify, regardless of attributes, such as font, type style, point size, and so on, or it can look for and change these attributes with no regard to the actual words being modified. Or it can look for and change only occurrences of specified text with specified attributes.

As you read about the various options that can be set for the Find/Change dialog box, remember that you can change its defaults by opening it and modifying it with no document open. Any changes you make are stored in the XPress Preferences file and become the new defaults for your copy of QuarkXPress.

Where QuarkXPress Looks

When searching with the Find/Change feature, QuarkXPress can check either the entire text chain connected to the active text box, or it can look for and change text throughout an entire document. If you have a text box selected, QuarkXPress searches through the story from the location of the insertion point to the end of the story (note that the button in the dialog box says Find Next; that means the next one after the cursor position).

There are two ways to search an entire story from the very beginning. First, you can put the insertion point at the very beginning of the story (press Command-Option-Up Arrow). Or you can put the insertion point anywhere in the story, and hold down the Option key; the Find Next button turns into a Find First button. (For the sake of efficiency, you can also just press Option-Return or Option-Enter to immediately do a Find First.)

If you want QuarkXPress to check all the text in the document rather than just a single story, you must check the Document box in the Find/Change dialog box. However, we've heard reports that if you have a text box selected when you do this, sometimes the program doesn't always search the whole document. So we always deselect any boxes before starting this sort of search (perhaps Quark has fixed this possibly apocryphal problem by now).

Checking Document only searches the document pages; if you want to search the master pages, too, you have to do that in a separate search. If you currently are displaying a document's master pages, the Document checkbox is labeled Masters, and you can use it to search all the document's master pages at once.

Specifying Text

To change all occurrences of text regardless of text formatting attributes, you can use the Find/Change dialog box as it first appears when you select the Find/Change command from the

Edit menu (see Figure 3-1). Enter the text you want QuarkXPress to find in the Find What field, then enter the replacement text in the Change To field.

Figure 3-1
The Find/Change
dialog box

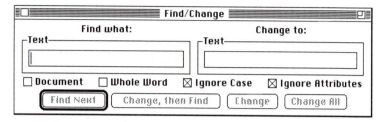

Special characters. It's easy enough to search for normal words or phrases, but what about invisible characters? It turns out that you can enter certain special characters in the Find What and Change To fields with the aid of the Command key. For example, if you want to search for all the new paragraph characters in a document (what you get when you press Return at the end of a paragraph), you select the Find What field, and press Command-Return. This appears in the field as "\p".

Table 3-4 shows characters you can enter in these fields, how to type them, and how they appear in the fields.

Table 3-4
Special characters
in the Find/Change
dialog box

To enter this character . . .	Press . . .	Or type . . .
Tab	Command-Tab	\t
New paragraph	Command-Return	\p
New line	Command-Shift-Return	\n
New column	Command-Enter	\c
New box	Command-Shift-Enter	\b
Previous box page number	Command-2	\2
Current box page number	Command-3	\3
Next box page number	Command-4	\4
Wildcard (single character)	Command-?	\?
Backslash	Command-\	\\
Punctuation space		\.
Flex space		\f

Wildcards. You can use the wildcard character ("\?") to represent any character. This is useful if you're looking for a word you may have spelled different ways, such as "gray" and "grey." Instead of running two search operations to find all occurrences of this word, you could simply type "gr\?y" in the Find What field. You can get the "\?" by pressing either Command-? or by typing a backslash followed by a question mark.

Note that the wildcard character can only be used in the Find What field. QuarkXPress doesn't let you use it in the Change To field, because the program's not sophisticated enough to do that kind of pattern-replacing.

To actually search for a backslash character itself in the Find What or Change To fields, type the backslash twice, or press Command-\.

Whole Word. Next to the Document checkbox you'll find another one labeled Whole Word. Checking this box means that QuarkXPress only finds occurrences of the Find What text if it's a whole word. That means that the text can't be bounded by other text or numerals. So a Whole Word search for "ten" finds the word "ten" when it's bounded by spaces, punctuation, or special characters such as new line or paragraph marks. It would *not* find "often," "tenuous," or "contentious." If you don't have "Whole Word" selected, QuarkXPress will find every occurrence of the text you entered, even if it's embedded in other text.

Ignore Case. If Ignore Case is on, QuarkXPress finds all occurrences of the text in the Find What field, regardless of whether the capitalization of the text found in the document exactly matches what you typed into the Find What field. For example, if you entered "Help," QuarkXPress would find "Help," "HELP," and "help."

How QuarkXPress determines the case of characters it's replacing when Ignore Case is checked depends on the capitalization of the text it finds in the document.

▶ If the found text begins with an initial capital, or is in all upper- or lowercase, QuarkXPress follows suit and similarly capitalizes the replacement text.

▶ If the found text doesn't match the above three cases, QuarkXPress capitalizes the replacement text exactly as you entered it into the Change To field.

For example, let's say you are searching for all examples of "QuarkXPress" and want to make sure the internal capital letters are proper. If you leave Ignore Case on, and the program finds "quarkxpress", it does not capitalize the proper characters. Turn off Ignore Case, and the feature replaces the word with "Quark-XPress", properly capitalized as you entered it.

Specifying Attributes

As we said earlier, you can search for more than just text in QuarkXPress. You can search for text-formatting attributes (font, size, type style), too. If you want to search for formatting, uncheck Ignore Attributes in the Find/Change dialog box. When Ignore Attributes is checked, QuarkXPress looks for all occurrences of the text no matter how it's formatted, and replaces it without making any changes to the character formatting.

When you uncheck Ignore Attributes, the Find/Change dialog box expands (see Figure 3-2). In addition to text fields under the Find What and Change To headings, there are areas under each heading for specifying font, size, and type style. Note that you can't find or change style sheets.

What to Find, What to Change

If you look closely at the Find/Change dialog box when Ignore Attributes is turned off (that is, when you're searching for text formatting as well as text), you'll notice that there's a checkbox next to the name of each area. By checking and unchecking these boxes, and by modifying what's inside each area, you can tell Quark-XPress just what attributes you're looking for, and what you want them changed to.

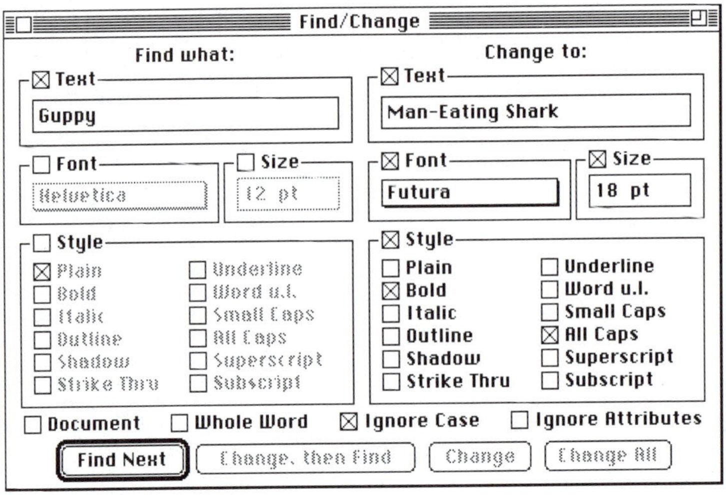

Figure 3-2

The Find/Change
Attributes dialog box

The left side of the dialog box shows all the attributes that should be searched for; the right side is what the text should be changed to. The first three areas on each side of the dialog box—Text, Font, and Size—are simple to use. If you want to specify something, make sure the area's checkbox is turned on. Then you simply enter the text or point size in the appropriate fields, and/or use the popup font menu to select the font. On the left side (the Find What side), the Font menu lists only the fonts actually used in the current document; on the right side (the Change To side), it lists all fonts currently available from your system.

If the document uses fonts that are currently not open in your system, QuarkXPress will list them in the Find What side, along with their font ID numbers. You can then use Find/Change to change the unavailable fonts to ones that are currently available (though you can expect the whole document to reflow, since the character widths vary so much between fonts).

There doesn't need to be a parallel between what you specify in the Find What side and the Change To side. In fact, such asymmetrical searches offer some of the most intriguing possibilities for finding and changing in QuarkXPress.

You could easily, for example, find all occurrences of a company name and apply a special typeface or style to it.

1. Type the company name into the Find What field.

2. Uncheck Font, Size, and Style on the left side of the dialog box. That tells the program to pay no attention to those attributes.

3. Uncheck Text and Size on the right side of the dialog box. That tells QuarkXPress to replace the words with the same text and at the same size.

4. Then set the Font and Style settings in the Change to side the way you want (see "Finding and Changing Character Styles," below).

This procedure searches for all occurrences of the text, no matter what formatting is applied, and replaces them with the same text but in a specific typeface and style, leaving the size alone (we cover all text formatting in Chapter 4, *Type and Typography*).

Finding and Changing Character Formatting

Specifying what character formatting QuarkXPress should search for or replace is a bit more complicated than what we described above; however, it's really not that bad once you get used to it. The check boxes next to most of the Style choices can be either checked, unchecked, or grayed-out. Clicking an unchecked box puts an "X" in it. Clicking a checked box makes it grayed-out. Clicking a grayed-out box unchecks it. (see Figure 3-3).

What do those various checkboxes mean? On the left side (the Find What side), a checked box means that you want Quark-XPress to only find text set to that style. An unchecked box means you *don't* want it to find text in that style. A gray box means that it doesn't matter if the text contains that style or not; you want QuarkXPress to find text either way (see Table 3-5). Another way to look at it is that blank means "no," checked means "yes," and gray means "I don't care."

The various checkboxes mean similar things on the right (Change To) side of the dialog box. Turning on a checkbox means you want QuarkXPress to apply that style when it changes text it

Figure 3-3

Check boxes in
the Find/Change
dialog box

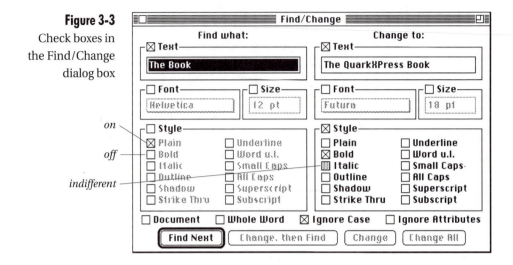

on

off

indifferent

Table 3-5

Style checkboxes in
the Find/Change
dialog box

Box is ...	Means ...
Unchecked	Find or replace text without this attribute
Checked	Find or replace text with this attribute
Grayed	Find it either way, but leave it alone when replacing

finds. An unchecked box means you *don't* want that style to be
present in the changed text (if it's there, QuarkXPress removes it).
Leaving the box gray means that QuarkXPress doesn't do anything to that style. If it's already there, it stays there; if it's not,
QuarkXPress doesn't apply it.

A word can't have both the Underline and Word Underline
styles simultaneously. So checking on one unchecks the other,
and graying one automatically makes the other gray as well. Small
Caps/All Caps and Superscript/Subscript work together similarly.

Going to It

Now that you know how to specify what you want to find, what
you want to change, and how to tell QuarkXPress where to search,
you can use the four buttons at the bottom of the dialog box to
begin finding and changing. When you first specify your Find/
Change criteria, all buttons except Find Next are grayed out (see

Figure 3-4
The Find/Change
control buttons

Figure 3-4). Hold down the Option key and click Find First, and QuarkXPress searches for the first occurrence of text matching your specifications in the current story or document. It displays this text in the document window and selects it.

You then have a choice. Clicking Find Next again takes you to the next occurrence of text meeting your specifications, without changing the currently selected text. Clicking Change, Then Find changes the selection as specified in the Change To side of the dialog box. QuarkXPress then looks for the next occurrence of matching text. The Change button changes the selected text and leaves it selected, and the Change All button has QuarkXPress search for and automatically change all occurrences in the story or document. After QuarkXPress changes all occurrences, a dialog box comes up listing the number of change made (if any).

▼ ▼

Tip: Seeing Text as It Is Found. If you are one of the unlucky sods who has a small-screen Macintosh, then you'll find that the Find/Change dialog box fills almost the entire screen when you are searching or replacing attributes. Thus, when you click Find Next, you can't see what the program found. Don't worry; there's an antidote to this poison.

You can reduce the size of the dialog box considerably by clicking the Zoom button in the box's upper right corner. The reduced view shows only the buttons you need to navigate and change what you've specified (see Figure 3-5). Clicking the Zoom button again takes you back to the larger dialog box.

Figure 3-5
Shrinking the Find/
Change dialog box

▤□	Find/Change	□▤
Find Next	Change, then Find	Change	Change All

▼ ▼

Spelling Checker

Of course, once you've got your text written or imported into QuarkXPress, you wouldn't want to print it without first running it through QuarkXPress's spelling checker. QuarkXPress (3.2 and later) comes with a 120,000-word dictionary (that's the file called XPress Dictionary), and you can create your own auxiliary dictionaries as well. The Check Spelling command is under the Utilities menu, and allows you to check a selected word, a story, or an entire document (see Figure 3-6).

Figure 3-6

The Check Spelling
hierarchical menu

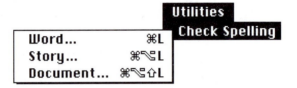

Checking a Word

If you only want to check one word, you can select it (or you can just put the cursor anywhere within the word) and choose Word from the Check Spelling submenu (or press Command-L; note that in versions before 3.2, this was Command-W—which is now the keystroke for Close Window). The Check Word dialog box appears (see Figure 3-7), listing all words in the XPress Dictionary (and the open auxiliary dictionary, if any; see below) that resemble the word you selected.

If the suspect word—the word you're checking is always called the *suspect* word, even if it's correctly spelled—appears in a dictionary, it shows up in the scrolling list and is selected automatically. This means, as far as QuarkXPress is concerned, the word is spelled correctly, and you can click Cancel to continue.

If the suspect word doesn't appear in an active dictionary, you can scroll through the list of words and select a replacement. Click on the proper word in the list, then click the Replace button. The new spelling replaces the word in your story, and the Check Word box closes.

Figure 3-7

Checking a Word

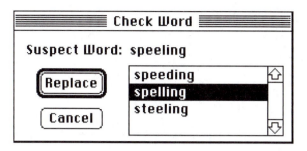

If QuarkXPress can't find any words that approximate the suspect word, it displays the message, "No similar words found." Click the Cancel button to close the Check Word dialog box.

Checking a Story

Typically, you'll be more likely to check a whole story rather than a single word. To do this, click anywhere in the story's text box (any box within the linked chain will do) with the Content tool. Then, select Story from the Check Spelling hierarchical menu (or press Command-Option-L). The Word Count dialog box appears, showing running totals as QuarkXPress scans the story, counting the total number of words, the total number of unique words (each word counted once, no matter how many times it occurs), and the number of suspect words—ones that QuarkXPress can't find in its dictionary, or in the open auxiliary dictionary, if there is one (see Figure 3-8).

When QuarkXPress is finished counting, click the OK button. If the program didn't find any suspect words, then this just returns you to your document. On the other hand, if words have been caught, then the button brings up the Check Story dialog box. This dialog box displays suspect words one at a time, in the order they

Figure 3-8

Word Count dialog box

This dialog box comes up after you select the Story or Document submenu from the Check Spelling menu. It shows how many total words in the story or document, the number of unique words, and how many unique or suspect words aren't located in the XPress Dictionary and the Auxiliary Dictionary (if one is open).

occur in the story. As each appears in the dialog box, QuarkXPress scrolls the document window to the word, and highlights it so you can see it in the context in which it's used on the page. If a suspect word is used more than once in the story, QuarkXPress tells you how many times.

Changing the spelling. When you check the spelling of a whole story rather than just a word, QuarkXPress doesn't show you possible replacement words automatically. If you know the correct spelling for a suspect word, you can enter it in the Replace With field, and click the Replace button to have the new spelling replace the one in your document. Or, if you do want QuarkXPress to look for possible spellings in the available dictionaries, you can click the Lookup button (or press Command-L). QuarkXPress displays a list of possible alternatives in the scrolling text field. You can select an alternate spelling by clicking on it, then clicking the Replace button or pressing Enter or Return. The new spelling replaces the suspect word in your document, and QuarkXPress moves on to the next suspect word in the story. If there are no more suspect words, the Check Story dialog box closes.

Note that if QuarkXPress finds more than one occurrence of a suspect word, it will replace every occurrence of the word with the new spelling you choose.

Skipping and keeping. To go to the next suspect word without changing the spelling of the current one, click the Skip button (Command-S). To add the current suspect word to an auxiliary dictionary, click the Keep button (Command-K). This button is only active when an auxiliary dictionary is open (see "Auxiliary Dictionaries," below).

▼ ▼

Tip: Speed Spelling Check. If you've ever tried to check the spelling in an enormous document, you've probably found yourself waiting for the screen to redraw. Only after the redraw can you decide to move on to the next word. Bob Martin points out that the process goes more quickly if you first reduce the document window size considerably and then zoom in to 400 percent. QuarkXPress has very little to redraw on the screen each time. Plus, the found text is almost always more visible in the small window.

▼ ▼

Checking a Document/Master Page

You can check the spelling of all the text in an entire document by selecting Document from the Check Spelling submenu (or by pressing Command-Option-Shift-L). QuarkXPress counts and checks all the words in your current document, from first page to last. It displays the Word Count dialog box, then lets you change suspect words through a Check Document dialog box that is identical in layout and function to the Check Story dialog box.

Unfortunately, this procedure only checks the spelling on the real document pages, not the master pages. To check spelling on master pages, you need to be viewing one of the master pages (it doesn't matter which, if you have more than one). When master pages are displayed, the Document item on the submenu becomes Masters. By selecting this command you can check all the text on every master page in your document, using a Check Masters dialog box that works just like the Check Story and Check Document dialog boxes.

Auxiliary Dictionaries

You can't add or change words in QuarkXPress's standard dictionary. You can, however, create and use an Auxiliary Dictionary, so you can have QuarkXPress's spelling checker take into account specialized words that aren't in the standard dictionary. Note that you can only have one Auxiliary Dictionary open at a time for each document.

Creating or opening an Auxiliary Dictionary. To open an existing Auxiliary Dictionary, or to create a new one, select the Auxiliary Dictionary item from the Utilities menu. This opens the Auxiliary Dictionary dialog box. Select a dictionary stored on any mounted volume, and click the Open button.

You can also create a new Auxiliary Dictionary by clicking the New button, which brings up a dialog box that lets you specify the name and location of the new dictionary. Enter the name of the new dictionary in the text field, and click the Create button.

Adding and removing words. When you first create an Auxiliary Dictionary, it contains no words. There are a couple of ways to add words to it. First, you can add words to the dictionary using the Keep button when you're checking spelling. This button adds the current suspect word to your Auxiliary dictionary. Another way to add words is with the Edit Auxiliary item from the Utilities menu. This feature is only available when there's an open Auxiliary Dictionary.

When you select Edit Auxiliary, a simple dialog box appears, with a scrolling list of all the words in the currently open dictionary (see Figure 3-9). To add a new word, enter it in the text field and click the Add button. Words added to the dictionary cannot contain any spaces or punctuation (not even hyphens). Plus, don't try to add words that have accents (or other foreign language markings) in the US English version of the program. They may either corrupt the dictionary, or the letters will just disappear.

To remove a word from the dictionary, scroll through the list until you find the word. Select it by clicking on it, then click the Delete button.

Figure 3-9
The Edit Auxiliary Dictionary dialog box

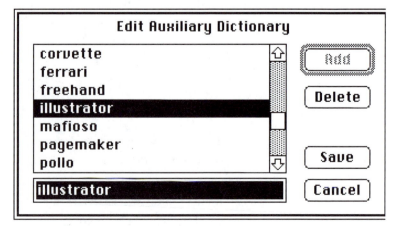

Remembering dictionaries. If you open or create an Auxiliary Dictionary with a document open, QuarkXPress automatically associates the two. Whenever you open the document, QuarkXPress also opens the dictionary, until you either close that dictionary or open a different one (this breaks the link with the first dictionary and makes a link with the new one). You can also set up an Auxiliary Dictionary that will be applied to all subsequent documents by opening a dictionary while no documents are open. However, QuarkXPress may not be able to find an auxiliary dictionary if you move either the dictionary or a document associated with it—or sometimes when you have a system crash while Quark is running—in which case, you'll receive an error message when you try to check spelling in your document. If QuarkXPress loses track of the Auxiliary Dictionary, just go back and open it again.

▼ ▼

Tip: Editing Dictionaries with a Word Processor. QuarkXPress dictionaries are text files, with one word per paragraph. They have a "type" of TEXT and a "creator" of XPR3 (you can change a file's type and creator with DiskTop, ResEdit, and several other programs). Because it's a text file, you can edit a QuarkXPress Auxiliary Dictionary with any word processor. Remember to save as Text Only.

▼ ▼

Tip: Adding Your Microsoft Word Dictionary. The user dictionaries that Microsoft Word creates are text files as well, and like QuarkXPress dictionaries, they have one word per paragraph. They're usually called "User 1." Since a Word dictionary is of type DICT, you have to use Word's Shift-F6 (the Open any file command) to open it. Or, you can select All Files from the Open dialog box's popup menu. Once it's open, you can copy the contents and paste them into your QuarkXPress Auxiliary Dictionary.

Be aware that if you edit the Word dictionary and save it, you have to sort it in Word (select Sort from the Utilities menu), save it as Text Only, and then change the file type back to DICT before Word will recognize it as a dictionary.

▼ ▼

When Not to Use QuarkXPress

As we've seen throughout this chapter, QuarkXPress does have powerful word-processing features. However, there are reasons why you may not want to use it for word processing in your documents. We think knowing when *not* to use QuarkXPress is as important as knowing when to use it, so here's a quick rundown.

Workgroup publishing. Word-processing programs tend to be much less expensive than QuarkXPress. If you're in a big office or workgroup, it may make more financial sense to do basic text entry on word processors, rather than a powerhouse page-layout program like QuarkXPress.

Features. Another reason is that powerful though QuarkXPress may be, it doesn't offer features available in the most powerful word-processors, such as outlining or automatic numbering of paragraphs. If you're working on a long, complicated document with sections that might require constant rearranging and reorganizing, you probably need the organizational power of a good outlining feature like Microsoft Word's. Since its styles work well with QuarkXPress's style sheets, Word is usually considered the best word processor to use with QuarkXPress (see Chapter 5, *Copy Flow*).

Slow Going. But perhaps the most important reason to consider *not* doing your word processing in QuarkXPress is speed. Or rather the lack of it. Sometimes writing and editing text in QuarkXPress can seem to slow to a crawl. Entering text becomes so sluggish that the program can't keep up with even a moderate typist.

Why does this happen? First, QuarkXPress often has to jump all over the document as you type, unlike a word processor, which simply scrolls top to bottom. Second, QuarkXPress has to do much more work than a typical word processor whenever it must reflow text. If you're working on a long story that goes through several pages of linked boxes, and the text has to flow through and around other page elements, this complexity also adds to the computations that QuarkXPress must perform whenever you change or add text. Plus, QuarkXPress may have to compute kerning and other type effects, which slow it down further.

▼ ▼

Tip: Use a Text Editor. Veteran QuarkXPress users have discovered that, while characters may be lost when typing rapidly into a QuarkXPress text box, type pasted in from the Clipboard never gets lost or damaged. One way to quickly get text into the Clipboard is to type it in a simple text-editing application, and then copy and paste it into QuarkXPress. There are many such small utilities on the market (under System 6 they were called DAs or Desk Accessories). You could even make do with Apple's bare-bones Note Pad. Then there are the excellent shareware programs McSink and MiniWriter, and the commercial programs Vantage and MockWrite.

The disadvantage of using text-editing applications is that whatever text you create in them can be only pure text. You must apply any formatting attributes after you've pasted the text into QuarkXPress.

▼ ▼

Modifying Preferences and Settings

You can quickly modify some of the things in QuarkXPress that affect the speed with which you can enter or edit text. Note that these two speedups really won't affect speed a lot, especially on faster computers. But they can help.

Hyphenation. If you want to speed up QuarkXPress's text reflow a little, try to turn off hyphenation as much as possible in your document. If QuarkXPress doesn't have to determine if and where it should hyphenate a word whenever it breaks a line, it will be able to incorporate new or changed text into a story more quickly. You can edit all of the H&J settings used in your document, and turn off hyphenation (see Chapter 4, *Type and Typography*). Don't forget to turn hyphenation back on when you're ready to proof or print your document.

If you're using style sheets, you can streamline this process a bit. Instead of editing your H&J settings each time you want to turn hyphenation on or off, you can create a special hyphenation setting with hyphenation off, called, perhaps, "NoHyphens." If you've based most of the styles in your document on the "Normal" style, all you have to do is edit the "Normal" style, and select the "NoHyphens" setting to turn off hyphenation in all styles based on "Normal." To turn hyphenation back on, just reselect original "Normal" H&J setting (we discuss Style Sheets in more detail in Chapter 5, *Copy Flow*).

Kerning. Another way to speed up text reflow is to turn off automatic kerning in your document. Go to the Typographic Preferences dialog box for your document (under the Edit menu), and make sure Auto Kern Above is not checked.

Note that these two suggestions affect where line breaks fall and how text will appear when printed. You should make certain to return both the H&J and kerning settings to those you intend to use for final output before you check your document for widows, orphans, or loose lines. Because of the hassle involved with these techniques and the minimal speedup, we can't say that we use them very often (if at all). We'd rather write in a word processor.

Using Dummy Text Boxes

The problem with using a text-editing application to type text is that you can't include any character-formatting attributes. And if you modify the settings of your QuarkXPress document to speed things up, you might forget to change them back, and end up printing a document with incorrect hyphenation and kerning. Moreover, if you have complicated layouts, entering text into QuarkXPress will be sluggish even if you have turned off hyphenation and kerning, as QuarkXPress must still reflow the entire story as you enter or change text.

Another solution to the text-entry problem is to create a text box in the pasteboard area of the page where you want to enter or change text. If you need to simply add text to the page, type the text into the box on the pasteboard area, copy or cut it, and then paste it into the correct location in the story's text box on the page.

If you need to edit text that's already there as well as add text, select the text to be modified from the page, and then copy and paste it into the box on the pasteboard. Make all the necessary edits there, then copy or cut the revised text, and paste it back to the same location on the page. Since QuarkXPress remembers the last selection you made in any text box, all you need to do is select the story's box on the page. It won't be necessary to reselect the text that you originally copied out. QuarkXPress does that for you automatically.

Of course, the dummy text box doesn't have to be on the pasteboard; it could just as easily be in a separate document. Moving text between two documents (the "live" file and the simple dummy file) is sometimes even easier. But there's a problem here just waiting to pop out: style sheets. We're going to cover style sheets fully in Chapter 5, *Copy Flow*, but we should say here that if you change the style sheets of your dummy text box document without making parallel changes in the "live" file, you can really mess yourself up. If you don't feel comfortable with keeping track of that sort of stuff, you should probably just use a dummy text box in the same document.

Watching Your Words

By following the tips we've shown you here, you may not be able to have QuarkXPress write your stories for you, but you'll be able to get the very most out of the program's advanced word-processing features.

In the next chapter, we'll see how you can take those blocks of plain text that you've created and turn them into type, using QuarkXPress's extensive typographic controls.

TYPE AND TYPOGRAPHY

There's an old husband's tale that says you can tell what a baby is going to grow up to become by the first real word she speaks. If she says "mama," she'll grow up to be a loving parent. If she says "teevee," chances are she will be a couch potato. If she says "QuarkXPress," she'll become a designer.

There's no doubt—even if this tale is hogwash—that Quark-XPress is often the first word on a designer's lips when the topic of desktop publishing comes up. That's because no desktop-publishing application handles typesetting as powerfully as Quark-XPress. In this chapter we will discuss the many typographic controls that QuarkXPress puts at your fingertips. We're going to start with basics: fonts and typographic principles. However, professionals should at least skim over this section (the fundamentals of fonts are rarely taught, and many people find themselves in deep . . . uh . . . water at some point because of it).

Next, we'll discuss control of both character- and paragraph-level formatting, including—among many other items—kerning and tracking, hyphenation and justification, and typographic special effects.

If you're reading this book from cover to cover, expect to spend a while here in this chapter. We've got a lot to talk about, and we expect you'll find it rewarding.

▼ ▼

Macintosh Fonts

The word "font" now has several meanings. Historically, it refers to a set of characters in a given typeface and size. Typefaces are the general look of the character set. For example, Helvetica is a typeface, while 14-point Helvetica is a font.

However, for the sake of simplicity, we're following the path that has become popularized over the past few years, defining both *typeface* and *font* as synonyms: a font or a typeface is a set of characters that share a particular look. For example, the text you're reading is in the Utopia font or typeface, while the headings for each section are in the Futura font or typeface. The more you learn about type and typography, the more you see its subtle nuances and personalities. But don't worry too much about that yet. Just start by seeing these basic differences.

Typefaces can be found cast in metal, carved from wood, or imaged on photographic negatives. In the case of the Macintosh computer, typefaces are represented digitally. That is, you can't see the typeface until you tell the computer to process the digital information and image a character either to the screen or onto paper or film. As it turns out, the Macintosh can image fonts to the screen in the same way that it prints them. What does that mean for you? It means that what you see on the screen is usually pretty close to what you get on paper.

Over the past few years, the Macintosh has undergone a quiet evolution in how it handles fonts, making font management easier but our task of describing it to you harder. That's okay; we'll do it anyway.

Adobe Type Manager

Even though we're still at the beginning of the chapter, we're going to talk as if you're using Adobe Type Manager (ATM) on your computer. If you're not using this crucial piece of software, consider it homework to purchase and install a copy of ATM by the end of this chapter.

Why should you get it? Primarily because it makes the fonts you see on the screen bear a greater resemblance to those you get from your printer. At any size. Figure 4-1 shows the difference between type on a Macintosh screen with and without ATM.

Figure 4-1
Screen type with
and without ATM

Wiz ATM

Wizzout ATM

You can get ATM in a number of ways. First, it's bundled with all of Adobe's software products—Photoshop, Illustrator, Premiere, Type On Call, and Dimensions. If you've ever purchased an Adobe font, chances are ATM came with it. Plus, it's even bundled with some third-party products. If you bought a Macintosh in the last couple of years, you probably received a card right in the box that offers it to you for only a few dollars to cover shipping.

In mid-1994, Apple will release System 7.5 Professional, which will include something called QuickDraw GX. QuickDraw GX will have ATM built right into it.

The worst case is to buy it bundled with a few dozen nice fonts for $50 from a mail-order warehouse. Take your pick.

Bitmap and Outline Fonts

Let's start simple: the Macintosh images fonts on the screen using a combination of *screen fonts* and *printer fonts*. Screen fonts are collections of bitmapped images—one bitmapped image for each character at each size. Printer fonts contain the outline of each character at no particular size; just curves and straight lines. (If you don't know the differences between bitmapped and outline graphics, take a quick peek at that section at the beginning of Chapter 6, *Pictures*.)

Screen display. When you press a key on the keyboard, the computer looks to see whether it's got a bitmap of the typeface in the size and style you're using. If it does, it displays this. If it doesn't, it goes to the printer (outline) font, and creates a bitmap by scaling the outline to the size you're using. This bitmap is then displayed.

This system almost always works. The one problem is when you don't have a printer font available or installed correctly. Most font companies distribute bitmap screen fonts for free (this is what Adobe does on their Type On Call CD-ROM) and charge for the printer font. If you're using a screen font that isn't paired with an outline font, the computer makes a rough approximation of the size by scaling the screen font up or down. For example, if you specify that you want to type some 17-point Helvetica, the computer gets the nearest screen font it has—let's say 12-point Helvetica—and then scales it up. The approximation is jaggy and hard to read, but the character widths are correct, and therefore your line endings won't change when you output from a machine that has the printer fonts (see Figure 4-2).

You can tell if you're missing the screen font by selecting Font Usage from the Utilities menu. Any font that's missing will show up as "{-2, Unknown}" or "{-122, MinionExpertRegular}". The number is the Font ID that the Macintosh uses to tell fonts apart. By the way, you'll automatically get a warning when you open a file if you're missing a needed font, and be given the option of finding it or substituting another one.

Font output. Whereas the screen font is bitmapped, the printer font is made up of outlined characters that can be scaled, rotated, and skewed in all sorts of ways without the ugly extrapolation encountered on the screen. The key issue for you to understand is that the screen font acts as a *representative* of the printer font. When you go to print your document out, whatever you see on the screen is replaced with a nice, smooth, outline font on your printed output, imaged at the full resolution of the output device.

Again, problems occur when your computer or printer can't find the outline font. In that case, it substitutes either a jaggy-look-

Figure 4-2

Bitmaps enlarged with
and without ATM

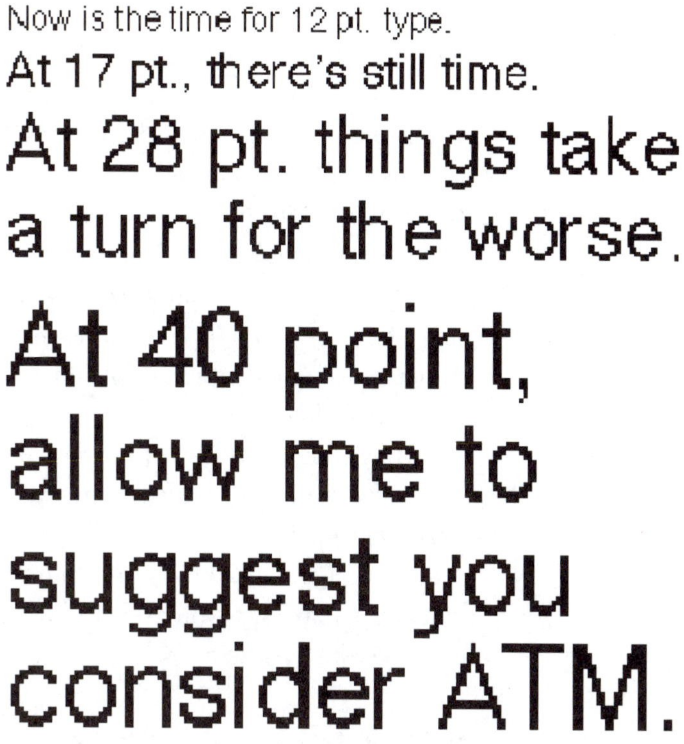

Now is the time for 12 pt. type.

At 17 pt., there's still time.

At 28 pt. things take
a turn for the worse.

At 40 point,
allow me to
suggest you
consider ATM.

Bitmaps being displayed or printed without ATM get jaggier as they get bigger.

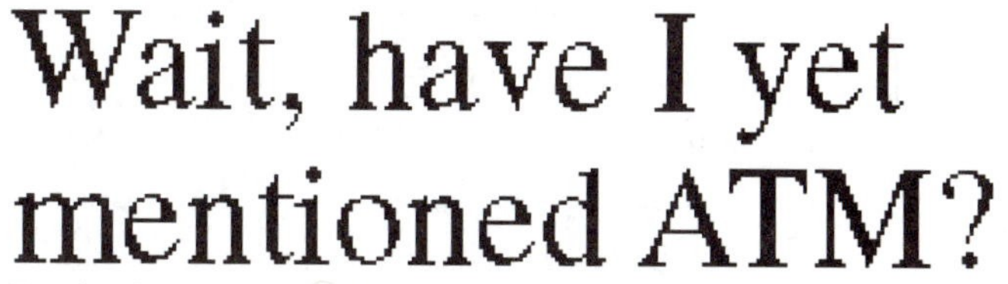

Wait, have I yet
mentioned ATM?

Type is crisp on screen and on bitmap (non-PostScript) printers with ATM.

ing bitmapped version of the font (scaled from the screen font) or
Courier (that typewriter-looking font). We'll talk more about making sure printer fonts are available in Chapter 10, *Printing*.

Fonts under System 6

The first thing you should know if you're not using System 7 or
later is that you should upgrade at least as far as system 6.0.8.
That said, we think you should go even further and upgrade to at

least System 7.0.1, and probably even later. Anyway, we're not here to tell you what you should do; rather what you *could* do.

Screen fonts. In System 6 (and earlier), all bitmapped screen fonts are saved either in suitcases (they have little suitcase icons) or in the System file itself. (As an exercise, go ahead and open your System Folder and locate the System file; most people don't know it's even there, but that's half of what makes the computer go!) To move fonts between their suitcases and the System file, you have to use a utility called Font/DA Mover. This is such a pain that we're not even going to talk about it. Suffice it to say that consultants have made fortunes just explaining this one stupid utility.

Moving fonts around this way was such a hassle that third-party developers came up with much better ways to do it (see "Font Management," below). Nonetheless, if you are using Font/DA Mover, make sure you're using version 4.2; earlier versions can damage your System file.

Printer fonts. In System 6, all printer fonts are stored loose in the System Folder; don't enclose them in another folder, or the computer won't be able to find them at output time. This means that if you use a lot of printer fonts, then your System Folder gets enormous. Font management utilities such as MasterJuggler or Suitcase help with this problem, too, because you can keep those printer fonts in some other folder along with the screen fonts.

Fonts under System 7.0

Handling fonts in System 7.0 (and 7.0.1) became significantly easier and more fun (though we still think using a font-management utility is better; see "Font Management," below).

Screen fonts. Screen fonts still live in the System file under System 7.0, but it's much easier to move them there: just drag them. The System file has become a folder of sorts; if you double-click on it, it opens like a folder. (This is sort of non-intuitive, but you get used to it quickly.) Inside this System file, you can see all the screen fonts and TrueType fonts that are available (we'll cover TrueType and why you should avoid it in just a bit). To move a screen font in, you drag it on top of the System file (or on top of the System Folder itself). To pull a screen font out, you can open the System file and drag it out.

Note that screen fonts that aren't in the System file can be in or out of suitcases. To take a font out of a suitcase in System 7, you can double-click on the suitcase file. It, too, acts like a folder and will open a window. Then you can pull out (or drag in) whatever screen fonts you want.

Printer fonts. In System 7.0, the printer (or outline) fonts live in the Extensions folder inside the System Folder. There's no doubt that this cleans up the System Folder quite a bit; however, it clutters up the Extensions folder. The nice thing about System 7 is that you can drag all the screen and printer fonts on top of the System Folder icon and the computer asks you if you want it to put the files where they're supposed to be (we like a little intelligence built into this machinery).

Fonts under System 7.1

Apple made one more change to the font-handling architecture when they took the step to System 7.1: they created a Fonts folder. This folder sits inside the System Folder and contains all fonts: great and small; screen and printer (suitcased or out in the open); bitmapped and outline. The Fonts folder makes installing and removing fonts much, much easier. Unfortunately, it's still not as easy or powerful as using a font-management utility such as MasterJuggler or Suitcase.

As in System 7.0, you can have screen fonts in or out of their suitcases within the Fonts folder. And, also similar, you can let the system do the thinking by simply dropping fonts on top of the System Folder icon. Note that if you have printer fonts inside another folder within the Fonts folder, the computer won't be able to find them. All the fonts have to be loose in the folder.

Table 4-1 shows you where the files should be for each system.

Table 4-1

Font placement

System version	Screen fonts	Printer fonts
6.0.8	System file	System Folder
7.0.x	System file	Extensions folder
7.1	Fonts folder	Fonts folder

Kinds of Fonts

We've been blithely strutting along so far with the assumption that all fonts are created equal. This, like every other sociopolitical issue, is simply not true. There are four basic kinds of fonts that you should know about on the Macintosh: Type 1, Type 3, TrueType, and bitmap-only.

Type 1. Type 1 fonts are PostScript outline fonts that come with associated screen fonts. They're typically high-quality and have reasonably good hinting (*hinting* is that magical behind-the-scenes technology that makes fonts look pretty good on low-resolution printers, such as 300-dpi desktop laser printers; without hinting, type at small sizes falls apart and looks crummy).

Type 3. Almost no one uses Type 3 fonts anymore, but you can find them here and there, especially from smaller font developers. The problems with Type 3 are manifold but come down to: they have no hinting, they don't work with ATM, and they sometimes have trouble printing (especially with the newest LaserWriter drivers). That means that they often look crummy on low-resolution printers, and they look crummy on screen. Note that hinting has no effect on high-resolution printers such as imagesetters. If you have a Type 3 font that you just can't live without, you might be able to convert it to Type 1 with a program like Metamorphosis or FontMonger.

TrueType. A couple of years ago, Microsoft and Apple came out with a new type format called TrueType (originally codenamed "Royal"). Their promise was that these fonts would be high quality, force typeface prices down, print easily and quickly, and match their PostScript counterparts identically. The first two were quickly achieved; the latter two turned out to be untrue.

Since then one thing has become clear: the graphic arts market should not use TrueType fonts. Service bureaus hate them (they often are the single offending item that makes a file not print at all); files can reflow unexpectedly if you use both True-Type and Type 1 fonts with the same names (for example, if you create a file and then give it to someone else who has fonts of the same name but different type); and, generally, they cause headaches to everyone involved.

The first thing we do after installing System 7.1 is delete all the TrueType fonts from the Fonts folder, except for those with city names—Chicago, Monaco, Geneva, and New York. These are required by the system for use in dialog boxes and the like.

If you work in an insurance office, you'll like TrueType because it has great hinting capability (you can print readable five-point type on your desktop laser printer if you're working with a well-hinted TrueType font; not all of them are). But if you're in the graphic arts world, we urge you to stay away from this format.

Bitmap-only. To be complete, we really should cover one last font format: bitmap-only. These fonts are designed to only be bit-mapped and have no outline fonts to complement them. Almost all fonts that are named after cities—such as Boston, Palo Alto, and San Francisco—are bitmap-only fonts. Monaco, New York, and Geneva are bitmap-only fonts in all systems earlier than System 7; then they've turned into TrueType fonts.

Bitmapped fonts can be scaled down to output well on some printers. For instance, 12-point Boston prints on an ImageWriter set to best quality by taking the 24-point version of the font and scaling it down (thus increasing the resolution to the Image-Writer's 144 dpi).

Nonetheless, there are almost no times when you'd want to use bitmap-only fonts unless you're trying to achieve a digital-looking effect. They will always print out jaggy, if they print out at all. (See Chapter 10, *Printing*, for more details.)

▼ ▼

Font Management

If you were only working with two or three typefaces for the rest of your life, you'd never need to think about font management. However, most people doing any kind of publishing work commonly work with hundreds of fonts. Keeping these fonts in order is critical to working efficiently with QuarkXPress.

What Font to Choose

Before we move on to how QuarkXPress handles fonts, let's look a little further into the subject of fonts in general.

You can work with thousands of different typefaces on a Macintosh with a PostScript printer. Figure 4-3 shows four potential candidates. Note that the bold, italic, and bold italic versions of a typeface are actually entirely separate faces from the "base" or "Roman" font.

Figure 4-3
Four separate fonts

Adobe Garamond Roman
the same, **Bold**
one more time *Italic*
and of course ***Bold Italic***

However, if a bold or italic (or bold italic, for that matter) version of the font is not available, the computer may generate its own version of that style or just print the base version of the font. A bold may be created by printing double, an italic may be created by skewing—also known as slanting or "obliquing"—the font. Like many things the computer does on its own, these versions are pretty awful. They're usable in certain circumstances, but quite unacceptable for anything approaching traditional typeset quality.

How do you know whether a real font is available or not? The best way is to get to know your font families by reading the manuals that come in the packages, then using the fonts and exploring whathow they look. If you want to know if an outline font is available for a particular style, you can try looking for it in the appropriate place (either in the System Folder, the Extensions folder, or the Fonts folder, depending on your system version).

Font-Management Utilities

If you have more than 20 fonts on your hard drive, you should be using a font-management utility such as Suitcase or Master-Juggler. Period. These programs let you keep all your fonts (screen and outline) together in one folder, or in multiple folders anywhere you want on your hard drives. You can arrange fonts into groups, opening just the ones you want when you need them. In this way, you keep your font menus short, you speed up font selection, and you keep your system small (the more fonts you have in your System Folder, the larger the system is going to be).

Plus, these utilities are pretty cheap (between $25 and $50) so there's almost no reason not to have them around.

Opening Fonts

He's not sure why, but David seems to have trouble remembering to open all the typefaces he needs in a document. For example, if he has a page that has four different fonts on it, he—as often as not—fails to open one of those fonts using MasterJuggler (which he prefers over Suitcase because of its simple interface; see Figure 4-4) before he starts QuarkXPress. Fortunately, starting in version 3.1, QuarkXPress can use a font as soon as you open it with Suitcase or MasterJuggler, even if you're still in the program and your document is open. We call this "instant font updating." You may notice that QuarkXPress sometimes pauses longer than usual after you open the font; it's just updating its internal font list. (In Suitcase, you need to turn on the Update Font List checkbox in the Fonts Preferences submenu.)

Figure 4-4

MasterJuggler and Suitcase's main windows

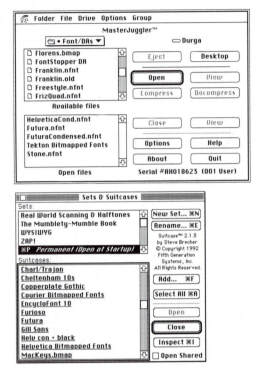

▼ ▼

Character Formatting

There are two types of typographic controls: character-based and paragraph-based. The character-based controls let you change the character formatting—typeface, size, color, bold, italic, and so on; the paragraph-based controls let you change the paragraph formatting—left and right indents, tab settings, space before and after, etc. Let's talk about character formatting first.

The character-based controls are those that affect only the text characters that you select. If you have selected only one word in a sentence and apply a character style to it, that word and only that word is changed.

Let's look at each character-formatting control, how you can change it, and why you'd want to.

Use the Content Tool. The very first thing you need to know about controlling type in QuarkXPress is that you must have selected both the Content tool and the text box that contains the text you want to change. If you want to make a character-based change, you must have those characters you want to alter selected. If you want to make a paragraph-based change, you can select the paragraph (four mouse clicks) or a portion of the paragraph. You can even just have the cursor located anywhere within the paragraph. Just remember: if you want to change the contents of a text box, use the Content tool.

Selecting a Typeface

Picking a typeface can be a very personal thing, fraught with implication and the anxiety of decision. If someone tells you they want their document set in 10-point Courier, it may be better just to stay quiet. However, once the choice is made, there are a number of ways to select the typeface. Let's look at each of them here.

The Style menu. Almost every typographic control can be accessed through an item on the Style menu. When you have the text selected that you want to change, you can select the typeface name from the Font submenu.

The Measurements palette. If you would rather avoid submenus, you can select a typeface from the Measurements palette instead. Here you have two methods of selecting.

▶ You can click on the arrow popup menu to bring up a list of fonts. It is often quicker to select from this menu than from the Style menu because it's always visible and is not a hierarchical menu (David hates these).

▶ You can type the name of the typeface you want. Do this by clicking to the left of the first character of the typeface name shown in the Measurements palette (or jump there quickly by pressing Command-Option-Shift-M), then typing a few characters of the typeface name you want. As soon as QuarkXPress recognizes the name, it inserts the rest of it for you.

For example, if you want to change from Helvetica to Avant Garde, click just to the left of the "H" and type "Ava." By the time you type these three letters, chances are it will recognize Avant Garde (as long as you have that screen font loaded). This is clearly a boon to desktop publishers who have many fonts and are tired of scrolling down a list for five minutes to select Zapf Dingbats.

▼ ▼

Tip: Jumping Forward in the Menu. If your menus are really long and you want to jump to a certain point in the menu, you can use the two methods of selecting a font in the Measurements palette together. For example, if you're looking for Zapf Dingbats but can't remember how "Zapf" is spelled, you can type "Z" in the font field of the Measurements palette (remember you can get there quickly by pressing Command-Option-Shift-M), then clicking the arrow button. You are transported directly to the end of the list as opposed to the beginning.

▼ ▼

Character Attributes. The Character Attributes dialog box is the Style menu and half the Measurements palette rolled into one, and is a simple keystroke away (Command-Shift-D). Here you can change the typeface using the same methods as described in "The Measurements palette," above.

Find/Change and Font Usage. Let's say you have half your document in Helvetica and you want to change that copy to Futura. You can use either the Find/Change or the Font Usage dialog boxes to search for all instances of characters set in the Helvetica font, and replace them with Futura. We discussed the Find/Change dialog box in some detail in Chapter 3, *Word Processing,* and we'll discuss the Font Usage feature later in this chapter.

Font Size

Selecting a font is only half the battle; once you've done that, you typically need to change the size of the typeface. You use the same options for changing the type size as we described above: Style menu, Measurements palette, Character Attributes dialog box, and the Find/Change or Font Usage dialog boxes. In addition, you can use a set of keystrokes to make your selected text larger or smaller (see Table 4-2).

Table 4-2

Font sizing keystrokes

Press . . .	To . . .
Command-Shift-period	Increase point size through a preset range
Command-Shift-comma	Decrease point size through a preset range
Command-Option-Shift-period	Increase point size in one-point increments
Command-Option-Shift-comma	Decrease point size in one-point increments

The preset range that we mention in Table 4-2 is the same range listed on the Size menu: 7, 9, 10, 12, 14, 18, 24, 36, 48, 60, and 72 points. When you increase through the preset range with a keystroke, your character size jumps from one to the next on this list. We generally use the Command-Shift-period and comma (smaller and larger) to jump through the presets until we're close to the size we want. Then we fine-tune the point size by adding the Option key to the keystroke so that it moves only one point at a time.

▼ ▼

Tip: Precision Font Sizing. If you aren't satisfied with the preset font sizes, you can enter your own—in .001-point increments—in the Font Size dialog box. You can get to this dialog box by selecting Other from the Size submenu or by pressing Command-Shift-\ (backslash). This is one of our most commonly used keystrokes.

▼ ▼

Interactive Text Resizing

For quite a while you've been able to scale a picture box and its contents by holding down the Command key while dragging on a handle (see Chapter 6, *Pictures*). But if you ever tried to do that with type, nothing would happen. However, beginning in version 3.2, you don't have to feel sheepish, because you actually can scale text within a box by Command-dragging on its handles. As you resize the box, the text size increases or decreases to fit your changes. Depending on how you reshape the box, the type size changes along with the type's horizontal or vertical scaling (see Figure 4-5).

Figure 4-5
Interactive text resizing

All the rules for resizing and scaling picture boxes apply to text boxes. In addition to Command-key scaling, hoding down Shift-Command turns rectangular boxes into squares (scaling contents appropriately), and holding down Shift-Command-Option scales the box and its contents but maintains existing horizontal and vertical proportions. And if you wait half a second after you click on a handle before you begin to drag, you can see the type change on screen as you drag (see "Tip: Viewing Changes as You Make Them," in Chapter 1, *QuarkXPress Basics*).

There are two catches to this funky feature. First, it only stretches type to the limits you could ordinarily. For example, you can't stretch type wider than 400 percent, because horizontal scaling won't go any further than that. Second, this scaling only works on unlinked text boxes, not on text boxes that are part of a longer story, as it's intended for use on headline and display type.

Think about how easily you could mess up the formatting of a long story, if by resizing a text box through which it flowed, you ended up scaling some (but not all) of the text in a paragraph.

▼ ▼

Type Styles

QuarkXPress has 13 built-in attributes that you assign at a character level. Figure 4-6 gives samples of each of these, plus examples of how to use them.

These type attributes can be assigned to selected text in four ways, which are similar to how you assign typefaces and type size.

Style menu. Perhaps the second-slowest method of selecting a type style is to choose it from the Type Style submenu under the Style menu (see Figure 4-7).

Measurements palette. Each of the type styles is displayed by an icon in the Measurements palette (see Figure 4-8). The icons either display a sample of the style or give a graphic representation of it. For example, Superscript is shown by the numeral "2" over an up arrow. To select a type style, click the icon. The icon acts as a toggle switch, so to turn the style off, you click it again. If you have several type styles selected, you can rid yourself of them by clicking the "P" (for Plain).

Keystrokes. Each type style can be selected by a keystroke, as shown in Table 4-3. Once again, the styles are toggled on and off with each keystroke. We find keystrokes especially useful while typing directly into QuarkXPress; we can enter text and change styles while never taking our hands from the keyboard.

Character attributes. The slowest method of choosing a type style is by going to the Character Attributes dialog box (Command-Shift-D). The type styles in the Character Attributes dialog box are turned on and off by checking boxes. These checkboxes can be in one of three states: on, off, or indeterminate (gray).

▶ **On.** An "X" in the check box means the style is selected for all of the selected text.

Figure 4-6
Type styles

Plain text
Italic
Bold
Underlined (everything)
Word underlining
~~Strike-Thru~~
Outline
Shadow
ALL CAPS
SMALL CAPS
Su^{per}script ---(baseline shown as dotted line)
Sub$_{script}$ ------
Superior char^{acters}

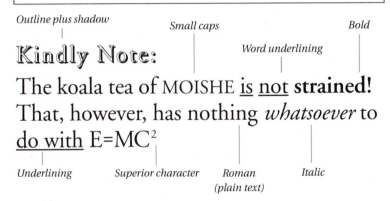

Outline plus shadow   Small caps   Bold

Word underlining

Kindly Note:
The koala tea of MOISHE is not strained!
That, however, has nothing *whatsoever* to
do with E=MC^2

Underlining   Superior character   Roman (plain text)   Italic

▶ **Off.** If the checkbox is blank, that style is not applied to any of the selected text.

▶ **Indeterminate.** A gray checkbox means that some of the characters have that style and others don't. (See "Finding and Changing Type Styles" in Chapter 3, *Word Processing*.)

Figure 4-7
The Type Style menu

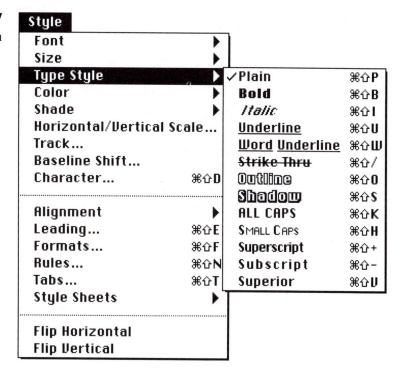

Figure 4-8
Measurement palette
type styles

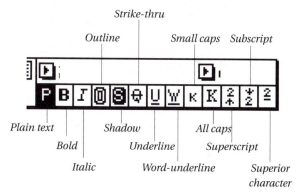

Note that these three states are also used to display the type style in the Measurements palette. However, instead of an "X," the Measurements palette inverts the symbol.

Styling by Attributes Versus Font Choice

You can style text either by applying style attributes like those described above, or by choosing a styled font itself. For example, say you're working with the Bodoni font, and you want to italicize

Keystroke	Style	Example
Command-Shift-P	Plain text	Ecce Eduardus Ursus
Command-Shift-B	Bold	**Ecce Eduardus Ursus**
Command-Shift-I	Italic	*Ecce Eduardus Ursus*
Command-Shift-O	Outline	Ecce Eduardus Ursus
Command-Shift-S	Shadow	Ecce Eduardus Ursus
Command-Shift-/	Strike through	~~Ecce Eduardus Ursus~~
Command-Shift-U	Underline	Ecce Eduardus Ursus
Command-Shift-W	Word underline	Ecce Eduardus Ursus
Command-Shift-H	Small caps	ECCE EDUARDUS URSUS
Command-Shift-K	All caps	ECCE EDUARDUS URSUS
Command-Shift-=	Superscript	Ecce Eduardus Ursus
Command-Shift-hyphen	Subscript	Ecce Eduardus Ursus
Command-Shift-V	Superior	Ecce Eduardus Ursus

Table 4-3
Type styles

some selected text. You can either choose Italic as a style, or go to the Font submenu and choose the specific Bodoni Italic screen font (assuming you have it installed). That font will show up in the submenu as "I Bodoni Italic" (or something similar to this). Either way, you'll get the same results: Bodoni Italic on your screen and on the page.

Which method is better? Choosing by formatting attribute is certainly faster, especially if you do it with keyboard commands. And it has the advantage of being font-independent. For example, if you've applied an italic formatting attribute to a range of your Bodoni text, and later decide to change your text face to Galliard, the italic formatting is retained.

On the other hand, if you choose the Bodoni Italic font for the emphasized range of text, when you make the changeover to Galliard, you get just Galliard and not Galliard Italic. Why? Because you simply switched from one font to another, and your text carried no format information. The original italicized range was an italic font with a Plain style attribute. To change fonts, you'd have to change "Bodoni" to "Galliard"; "I Bodoni Italic" to "I Galliard Italic"; "B Bodoni Bold" to "B Galliard Bold"; and so on.

Nonetheless, problems can occur if you choose a style attribute and there is no outline font of that style available. For instance, if you select Hobo and apply the Bold style to it, it will look correct on the screen but won't print correctly because there's no such thing as Hobo Bold. Again, the key is simply to know your fonts.

No matter which method you use, we urge you to be consistent in your choice. There's little chance that something will go wrong if you change type styles in some places using style attributes and in other places using the actual fonts. However, just to keep things simple, it's best to be consistent.

▼ ▼

Color and Shade

You can quickly and easily change the color or the tint (shade) of a piece of text. First, select the text and then select either the color under the Color submenu, or the tint value from the Shade submenu off the Style menu. You can also use the Colors palette to set both of these attributes. The default color palette contains nine colors (see Chapter 9, *Color,* for information about adding and editing colors in this list). The default tints are in multiples of 10 percent; however, you can assign a specific tint value by selecting Other in the Shade submenu, or by typing in a value in the upper right corner of the Colors palette (see Figure 4-9).

▼ ▼

Tip: Reversed Type. There is no specific command for reversed type—typically white-on-black type—as there is in PageMaker. But that doesn't mean you can't achieve that effect. Simply select the text and choose White from the Color submenu or from the Character Attributes dialog box (Command-Shift-D). If you want the reversed type on a black background, either place a black box behind it, or color the text box's background in the Text Box Specifications dialog box (Command-M).

Figure 4-9
Assigning a color
to type

Horizontal and Vertical Scaling

Imagine the characters in a typeface are rubber and stretchable. Now imagine stretching a typeface—one that took hundreds of hours to laboriously design at a specific width—to 160 percent of its size, warping the characters into something they were never meant to be. Now imagine the type designer's face contorting in horror as he or she sees what you've done to the type.

Okay, you get the idea: typefaces are designed to be a specific width and shouldn't be messed with unless you have some really good reasons. What are some good reasons? The best reason of all is that you want the typeface to look that way. If you're responsible for the typographic design, then you can make any choices you want. Note that we're not talking about your using 70-percent compression of Helvetica because you don't feel like buying another package from Adobe. We are talking about using Cheltenham compressed to 85 percent because it looks cool.

Another good reason to play with the horizontal scaling is if you need to make some body copy fit a particular space. Here we're talking about changing the horizontal scaling of the text plus or minus two or three percent, not 10 or 20 percent. We'd be surprised if anyone other than the designer could see the difference of a few percent, especially at small sizes. Scaling Times Bold to 50 percent of size to make it fit as a headline is a bad idea (see Figure 4-10).

If, after all these warnings, you still want to play with the horizontal or vertical scaling of your type, you can do so using the Horizontal/Vertical Scale feature under the Style menu (vertical scaling first appeared in QuarkXPress 3.2; instead of stretching the type horizontally, it makes it taller while maintaining the same width). First, select Horizontal or Vertical from the popup menu (you can't modify both at the same time). Entering values below 100 percent makes the text either narrower or shorter and squatter, depending on the Horizontal/Vertical setting; values above 100 percent stretch it wider or make it taller. Note that you don't have to type a percent sign; just the number will do.

You can also alter horizontal and vertical with keystrokes: Command-] (right square bracket) makes selected text wider in five-percent increments; Command-[(left square bracket) makes the selected text narrower in five-percent increments. (We remember the difference in an obscure way: the key on the left means narrow—or less; the key on the right means wider—or more.) The keystrokes modify horizontal or vertical scaling depending on the last modified direction.

▼ ▼

Kerning and Tracking

There are times in life when all those little letters on a page are just too far apart or too close together. The problem may be between two characters in 120-point display type, or it may be throughout an entire typeface. Whatever the case, QuarkXPress can control it through the use of kerning and tracking. They're similar, but let's look at them one at a time.

Figure 4-10
Horizontal scaling
of type

Got a problem?   *20 pt. Helvetica Condensed*

Check your compression.   *(Tracking: +2)*

Got a problem?   *20 pt. Helvetica (horizontal scaling: 60%)*

Check your compression.   *(Tracking: -2)*

Got a problem?   *20 pt. Helvetica bold (scaling: 60%)*

Check your compression.   *(Tracking: -2)*

Times bold with horizontal scaling of 50% — but with the inter-word spaces not compressed

Rats! Squashed again!

Times bold with horizontal scaling of 50% — inter-word spaces also scaled to 50%. Tracking in both examples: -1

Squashed! Rats again!

Times roman 10/11 — normal scaling

I began to experience an acute sense of panic when, despite everyone's assurances to the contrary, I began to approach the end of the line and found that I was not quite going to make it.

Times roman — scaled to 99% (same line width)

I began to experience an acute sense of panic when, despite everyone's assurances to the contrary, I began to approach the end of the line and found that I was not quite going to make it.

▼ ▼

Tip: Know Your Ems and Ens. Many typographic controls are specified using units of measure called *ems* and *ens*. (Some people call the "en" a *nut* to distinguish it aurally from an em.) These are not nearly as confusing as some people make them out to be. The default for the em in QuarkXPress is the width of two zeros side by side in the font and size you're working in. If that sounds weird, it's because it is. We can't figure out why they did it that way, but that's just the way it is. An en space is half of the em space width—the width of one zero.

Because this is so weird and unreasonable, Quark has added a checkbox in the Typographic Preferences dialog box (Command-Option-Y) labeled Standard Em Space. This sets the width of an em space to the same width every other piece of software uses: the size of the typeface you're using. So if you're using 14-point Times with the Standard Em Space checkbox on, the em space is 14 points wide. For consistency and a sense of doing the right thing, we recommend that you set this as your default (by changing the preference with no documents open).

If you're typing along and change point size, then the size of the em and en units changes as well. This can be a great aid. For example, if you change the size of a word after painstakingly kerning it, your kerning does not get lost or jumbled. The kerning was specified in ems, and therefore is scaled along with the type.

Em spaces and em dashes are not always equal in width. Usually they are (especially when Standard Em Space is turned on), but it really depends on what the typeface designer decided.

▼ ▼

Kerning

Adjusting space between two characters is referred to as *kerning* or *pair kerning*. You'll sometimes find kerning defined as purely the removal of space between characters. In QuarkXPress, kerning can be either the removal or the *addition* of space—moving two characters closer together or farther apart. Figure 4-11 shows

Figure 4-11
Kerned and
unkerned type

No automatic or manual kerning

DAVID WAVES!

Auto-kerning on; no manual kerning

DAVID WAVES!

Manual kerning applied to all character pairs

DAVID WAVES!

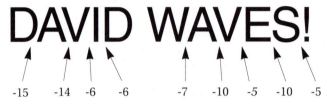

-15   -14   -6   -6   -7   -10   -5   -10   -5

some examples of type, first unkerned and then kerned. The problem is made obvious here: too much space between characters can make words look uneven or unnatural.

QuarkXPress supports two kinds of kerning: automatic and manual. Type designers usually build into the font itself kerning pair values that can be invoked automatically in QuarkXPress. Automatic kerning is global: it affects all instances of a character pair. Manual kerning is local: it affects only the pair selected.

Automatic. When we say automatic, we mean really automatic: all you have to do is turn on the function and QuarkXPress will make use of the font's built-in kerning pairs. It's up to font vendors to determine how many and which kerning pairs to include with a font, and which values to assign them. Most fonts come with anywhere between 100 and 500 such pairs. Third parties also sell kerning pairs you can import.

There's almost no good reason to turn off automatic kerning altogether, but if you want to, the switch is in the Typographic Preferences dialog box, under the Edit menu. Perhaps the only good reason to make judicious use of automatic kerning is speed: the more kerning pairs in a font, the slower it will display and print. We usually keep Auto Kern Above set to kern everything over five points (we can easily see the difference between kerned and unkerned text blocks at six points). In fonts that have a lot of kerning pairs—over 1,000—this might slow down screen redraw and printing slightly, but on the new, fast computers and printers you probably won't notice a difference.

Manual. Figure 4-11 showed a word in three renditions: with no kerning, with automatic kerning, and with manual kerning in addition to automatic kerning. The last looks best, doesn't it? (Please agree.)

Manual kerning in QuarkXPress is the adjustment of space between character pairs on a case-by-case basis. You make each adjustment in increments of fractions of an em space (see "Tip: Know Your Ems and Ens," above). Why anyone would want to kern to a precision of $\frac{1}{20,000}$ of an em space is beyond us, but QuarkXPress lets you do just that.

Manual kerning is usually reserved for larger type sizes for two reasons. First, it's harder to see poorly kerned pairs in smaller point sizes, so people say, "Why bother?" Second, you wouldn't want to go through a sizable amount of body text in the eight- to 14-point range, meticulously kerning pairs. It would take forever. Leave kerning of small type sizes to automatic kerning. If you don't like the built-in kerning pairs in a font, you can change them (see "Kerning and Tracking Tables," later in this chapter).

Manual kerning is a character-level attribute, but with a distinct difference from other character attributes. Instead of selecting the text you want to change, you place the cursor between two of the characters before applying kerning (see Figure 4-12). If you select one or more characters, you end up applying tracking rather than kerning (see "Tracking," below). Once you've clicked at an insertion point, you can control the space between the characters in four ways.

Kern. You can select the Kern feature from the Style menu, which brings up the Kern dialog box. Whole number values typed in

Figure 4-12
Cursor placement
for kerning

Manual kerning with correct cursor placement

Incorrect cursor placement for manual kerning, but right for tracking

here represent units of ½₀₀ em. For example, typing in "10" adds $^{10}/_{200}$ (½₀) of an em, and typing "-.1" removes ½,₀₀₀ of an em (typing a minus sign—a hyphen—before the value makes it negative). This is a really slow and painful way to apply kerning.

Character Attributes. You can change the kerning value between two characters by using the Character Attributes dialog box (Command-Shift-D) works just fine, but it's even slower than the Kern dialog box.

Measurements palette. The Measurements palette contains left arrow and right arrow icons that control tracking and kerning in text (they mean something different for pictures). Table 4-4 gives you a rundown on how to use them.

Table 4-4
Kerning control with
the Measurements
palette arrow icons

Click . . .	While pressing . . .	To . . .
Right Arrow		Increase space 10 units (½₀ em)
Right Arrow	Option	Increase space one unit (½₀₀ em)
Left Arrow		Decrease space 10 units (½₀ em)
Left Arrow	Option	Decrease space one unit (½₀₀ em)

Keystrokes. David hates to take his hands off the keyboard while he's working. He asks, "Why should I, when I can do just about everything I need through keystrokes?" He's got a point there. Table 4-5 shows the keystrokes you can use to control kerning.

Table 4-5	Hold down . . .	To . . .
Kerning keystrokes	Command-Shift-}	Increase space 10 units ($\frac{1}{20}$ em)
	Command-Option-Shift-}	Increase space one unit ($\frac{1}{200}$ em)
	Command-Shift-{	Decrease space 10 units ($\frac{1}{20}$ em)
	Command-Option-Shift-{	Decrease space one unit ($\frac{1}{200}$ em)

No matter which method you use to kern, you can see the kerning value in the Measurements palette (next to the left and right arrows), in the Kern dialog box, and in the Character Attributes dialog box.

▼ ▼

Tip: Kerning the Kerned. What shows up as the kern value when you want to kern a pair that is already kerned because of automatic kerning? Nothing. You'll still find a zero in the Kern Amount field. QuarkXPress regards the values applied by automatic kerning as the norm, so you don't have to worry about them.

However, if you have applied manual kerning with automatic kerning set up one way, then later you change automatic kerning settings, your kerning values may be way off.

▼ ▼

Tip: Removing Manual Kerning. Have you ever been handed a file that someone had spent many hours adding hundreds of kerning pairs to manually? What if they really didn't know what they were doing and you want to remove all that kerning before starting over? If you have Quark's free FeaturesPlus or Thing-a-ma-bob XTension installed, you'll see a feature in the Utilities menu called Remove Manual Kerning. Just select the range of text you want to affect, then select that from the menu. *Voilà!* All gone.

▼ ▼

Tracking

We know it's incredibly confusing, but it's true: There are two separate features in QuarkXPress, each called Tracking. They're similar, but we need to break them down for clarity. The first is a character-level attribute, and we're going to talk about it here. The second is a font-level attribute which changes the font as a whole, rather than just changing a set of characters, and we'll discuss it in great detail later in this chapter.

Character-level tracking. Tracking, as a character-level attribute, is the adjustment of space between all of the character pairs in a range of text. It's sometimes called "track kerning" or "kern tracking," though we think the best name for it is *range kerning* (which is what it's called in PageMaker). The idea is simple: you can add or subtract space between many pairs of characters all at one time by using tracking controls (see Figure 4-13). These controls are so similar to the kerning controls that we're not even going to waste time and paper going into much depth.

You can control tracking by selecting a range of type and using the Measurements palette, the Track feature from the Style menu (this menu item changes from "Kern" to "Track" when you have more than one character selected), the Character Attributes dialog box, or the same keystrokes as kerning. The reason all the controls are virtually the same is that QuarkXPress "decides" for you whether to kern or track, based on what is selected in the text box. In fact, though, these controls have the same functions. One is applied to a single pair of characters; the other is applied to several or many pairs.

▼ ▼

Tip: Tracking and the Single Word. The way tracking works, technically, is by adding or subtracting space to the right of each selected character. If you want to track a single word and don't want the space after the last character adjusted, you should select not the whole word, but only the characters up to the last letter. For example, if you want to apply a 10-unit track to the word "obfuscation," without changing the space after the "n," you would only select the letters "obfuscatio" and apply tracking.

▼ ▼

The crazy thing about this whole setup is that while kerning and tracking do the same thing, they are totally different features. One result of this is that kerning and tracking are cumulative. For

Figure 4-13

Tracking text

Tracking: +7

Art directors *everywhere* were ignoring me until I realized what I needed:

Much tighter tracking!
Tracking: −12

To England: That precious stone set in a silver sea

Tracking: 0. Copy doesn't fit.

To England: That precious stone set in a silver sea

Tracking: -4. Copy fits.

example, if you kern a character pair -10 units, then apply a tracking of -10 units to those characters, the space between them ends up 20 units smaller than normal. Also, if you track a word, then go in and look at the kerning between two letters, it appears as though there were no kerning applied at all. If you're a former (or present) PageMaker user, this may really throw you for a loop.

▼ ▼

Tip: When to Track. Ah, we hear the reader sighing, "But what about some real-world tips?" Okay, let's throw some rules out for you.

▶ If you're setting text in all capitals or in true small capitals from an Expert Set font, add between five and 10 units of space by tracking the word. Remember that you may not want to add tracking to the last character of the word (see "Tip: Tracking and the Single Word," above).

▶ Printing white text on a black background often requires a little extra tracking, too. That's because the negative (black) space makes the white characters seem closer together.

▶ Larger type needs to be tracked tighter (negative tracking values). Often, the larger the tighter, though there are aesthetic limits to this rule. Advertising headline copy will often be tracked until the characters just "kiss." You can automate this feature by setting up dynamic tracking tables, which we'll discuss later in this chapter.

▶ A condensed typeface, such as Futura Condensed, can usually do with a little tighter tracking. Sometimes we'll apply a setting as small as -1 to a text block to make it hold together better.

▶ When you're setting justified text and you get bad line breaks, or if you have an extra word by itself at the end of a paragraph, you can track the whole paragraph plus or minus one or two units without it being apparent. Sometimes that's just enough to fix these problems.

Remember, however, that no matter how solid a rule, you are obliged to break it if the finished design will be better.

▼ ▼

Wordspacing

Quark's free FeaturesPlus or Thing-a-ma-bob XTension adds one more option to character-level attributes: the ability to adjust kerning for spacebands within a selected range of text. As we discussed above, kerning is the adjustment of space between characters; it's often called letterspacing, but we prefer to reserve that term for justification controls (which we'll talk about later in this chapter). What Quark is calling wordspacing here is really just changing kerning between words (wherever it finds spacebands).

There are three conditions for adjusting wordspacing—spaceband kerning—over a selected range of text.

▶ You can only use keystrokes.

▶ You must have an extended keyboard.

▶ The FeaturesPlus XTension file must be in the same folder as your copy of QuarkXPress 3.2, or the Thing-a-ma-bob XTension must be in the XTension folder in version 3.3.

Table 4-6 shows the keystrokes you should use to adjust word spacing. Note that adjusting wordspacing is no magical trick: QuarkXPress is simply adding and subtracting kerning from each spaceband between words. And the biggest problem with this is that you can't go back and see how much you've added. To remove all the spaceband kerning, use the Remove Manual Kerning feature described earlier.

	Press . . .	To . . .
Table 4-6 Keystrokes for wordspacing	Command-Shift-Control-]	Increase wordspacing 10 units
	Command-Shift-Option-Control-]	Increase wordspacing one unit
	Command-Shift-Control-[	Decrease wordspacing 10 units
	Command-Shift-Option-Control-]	Decrease wordspacing one unit

Baseline Shift

The final character attribute that we discuss here is baseline shift. The baseline is the line—if you will—on which the type sits. For example, each line of text you're reading is made of characters sitting on a baseline. You can shift a character or group of characters above or below the baseline using the Baseline Shift feature under the Style menu.

The baseline shift is specified in points; negative values shift the character down, positive values shift it up. You can enter any value, up to three times the font size you're using, in tenths of a point; for example, you could shift a character off the baseline by 30 points in either direction if that character were 10-point type.

Note that baseline shift is similar to kerning and tracking in an important way: even though you specify values in points rather than fractions of an em, the value of the baseline shift changes as the font size changes. For example, if you specify a four-point baseline shift for some 15-point type, when you double the font size to 30 points, the shifted character is "reshifted" to eight points ($2 \times 4 = 8$).

The truth of the matter is that you can and will use the superscript and subscript type styles for almost every instance of raising or lowering a character. So what's the advantage of having a separate Baseline Shift control? Figure 4-14 shows several examples of how you might use baseline shift in your text.

Figure 4-14
Baseline Shift

I DON'T NEED NO BASELINE SHIFT.

I FEEL A NEED FOR A SUPERSCRIPT.

ME, I'D RATHER BE A SUPERIOR CHARACTER.

OY. I'M FEELIN' KINDA UNSTABLE, WHAT WITH ALL THIS BASELINE SHIFTING GOING ON.

▼ ▼

Paragraph Formatting

Character formatting is all very well and good, but when it comes to how text flows in a column, it don't make Bo Diddley squat. To handle text flow on a paragraph level, we move to paragraph formatting. These controls include indents, leading, tabs, and hyphenation and justification, as well as some esoteric functions such as Keep with Next ¶ and a widow and orphan control. We'll discuss each of these features and more. In addition, as usual, we'll give you lots of examples so you can see what we're talking about.

▼ ▼

Tip: Selecting Paragraphs. We often look over people's shoulders when they work, and what we see could scare a moose. One such scare is the technique of selecting a paragraph so that you can apply some paragraph formatting to it (leading, space before, or whatever). People think that they have to select the whole paragraph first. Not true! When changing paragraph formatting, you only have to have the cursor in the paragraph you want to change. That means you can have one word selected, or three sentences, or half of one paragraph and half of another, or whatever.

▼ ▼

The central headquarters of paragraph formatting is the Paragraph Formats dialog box (see Figure 4-15). Let's discuss each feature in this dialog box in turn, branching off on tangents when we need to.

Figure 4-15
The Paragraph
Formats dialog box

Paragraph Formats

Left Indent: 0p   Leading: 15 pt
First Line: 0p   Space Before: 0p
Right Indent: 0p   Space After: 0p
☐ Lock to Baseline Grid   ☐ Keep with Next ¶
☐ Drop Caps   ☐ Keep Lines Together
Alignment: Centered
H&J: Standard   Apply
OK   Cancel

▼ ▼

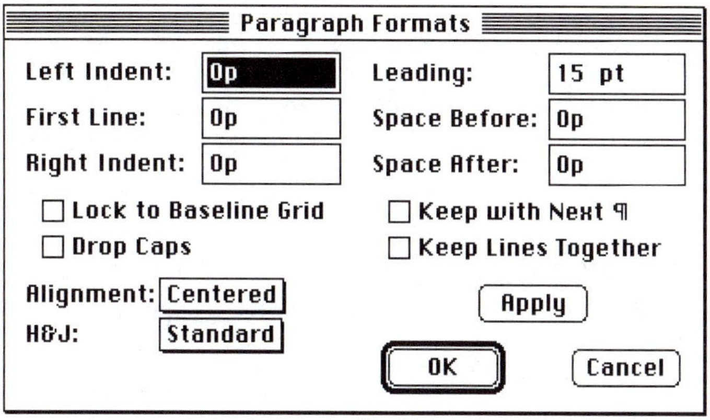

Alignment

Why not start with the most bold and blatant paragraph attribute—its alignment. Most people are familiar with the five horizontal alignment options: left aligned, right aligned, justified, force justified, and centered. We will discuss each of these first, then move on to a less-known feature: vertical alignment.

Horizontal Alignment

If you've been involved with desktop typography long enough (a day or two), you'll know that different sources have many names for the same thing. For example, what QuarkXPress calls "left aligned" others may call "left justified" or "flush left/ragged right."

We're not going to start naming names, but QuarkXPress's terms are simpler and make more sense. For one thing, "justified" means only one thing: text fitting flush on left and right. "Fully justified" is redundant, and "left-justified" is . . . well, it just isn't. Figure 4-16 shows some examples of text with various horizontal alignments.

You can specify alignment for a paragraph in any of four ways.

Figure 4-16
Horizontal alignment

We·have·heard·the·chimes·at·midnight.¶   *Left aligned*

A·hit!·A·palpable·hit!¶   *Centered*

I·am·too·much·i'·the·sun   *Right aligned*

Paragraph Formats. As we said above, the Paragraph Formats dialog box is always an option when you're changing paragraph formats. The control is a popup menu item (see Figure 4-17).

Figure 4-17
Alignment control in
the Paragraph Formats
dialog box

Paragraph Formats

Left Indent: `0p`	Leading: `15 pt`
First Line: `0p`	Space Before: `2p6`
Right Indent: `0p`	Space After: `0p`

☐ Lock to Baseline Grid   ☐ Keep with Next ¶
☐ Drop Caps   ☐ Keep Lines Together

Alignment: ✓Left
H&J: Centered
Right
Justified
Forced

(Apply)

(OK)   (Cancel)

Alignment submenu. You can select the horizontal alignment you want from the Alignment submenu under the Style menu.

Keystrokes. Note that the Alignment submenu lists a keystroke for each style. These are easy to remember as they rely on a first-let-ter mnemonic: hold down the Command and Shift keys and press

"L" for Left, "R" for Right, "C" for Centered, and "J" for Justified. The keystroke for Forced justification is a variant on Justified: Command-Option-Shift-J.

Measurements palette. Perhaps the easiest alignment method of all is to use the Measurements palette. When you have an insertion point in a paragraph, QuarkXPress displays five icons representing the five horizontal alignment selections (see Figure 4-18). To change a paragraph's alignment, click on the one you want.

While left-aligned, right-aligned, and centered paragraphs are relatively straightforward, justified and force-justified text is more complicated. However, we're putting off talking about justification and hyphenation until later in this chapter.

Figure 4-18
Horizontal alignment
in the Measurements
Palette

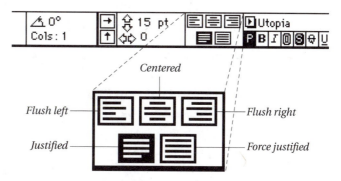

Flush left
Centered
Flush right
Justified
Force justified

▼ ▼

Tip: Limit Your Alignments. We're sure you would never do this. We know that you're a designer of reputation and flair. But we might as well mention this tip, just in case.

Don't use left-aligned, right-aligned, centered, and justified text all on the same page unless you have a reasonable design sense and a signed note from your parent. Too often people let all this high-falutin' technology go to their head and design their pages using every trick in the bag. Remember that there is strength in simplicity.

▼ ▼

Vertical Alignment

Vertical alignment is not really a paragraph attribute, but rather an attribute of each text box. Nonetheless, since we're talking about alignment, and since vertical alignment is closely related to other paragraph attributes (leading in particular), we might as well bring this into the discussion.

Just as horizontal alignment is the horizontal placement of the text within a column, vertical alignment is the vertical placement of the text within its box. You can specify attributes similar to those used in horizontal alignment: Top, Bottom, Center, and Justified. The only place you can change this setting is in the Text Box Specifications dialog box (Command-M, or double-click on the box with the Item tool selected). Here you're presented with a popup menu for each selection (see Figure 4-19).

Let's look at each of the alignment possibilities briefly.

Figure 4-19
Vertical Alignment
in the Text Box
Specifications
dialog box

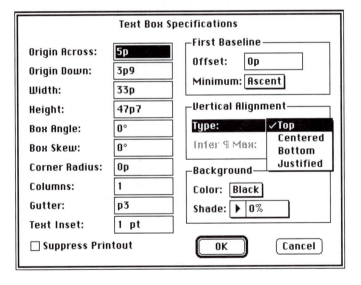

Top. This is the default setting for text boxes. It's what you're probably used to if you use QuarkXPress regularly. The text starts at the top of the text box and, as you type, fills the box. Exactly where the text starts depends on the First Baseline control (discussed later in the chapter).

Centered. When Vertical Alignment is set to Centered, the text within the text box is vertically centered. That sounds trite, but we can't explain it any better than that. See Figure 4-20 for an example of this effect. Note that blank lines can affect the positioning of the text in the text box; sometimes you have to delete them to get it to look right.

▼ ▼

Tip: Centering Text. Specifying either horizontal or vertical center alignment may not result in your text looking perfectly centered. Why? Because the mathematical horizontal centering of text may not look as "right" as an optical centering, especially if you have punctuation before or after the text. You can use invisible characters colored the same as whatever they're on top of. For example, white on top of a white background. Or, you can use altered indentation (see "Indents," below) to change the way the text looks (see Figure 4-21). Remember, what looks right is more "right" than what the computer says.

In the case of vertical centering, text in all capitals or text in fonts such as Zapf Dingbats may not appear to be centered in the box. This is because QuarkXPress does not actually find the center of the characters you've typed. Rather, it uses the full height of the font, ascent and descent combined, to calculate proper placement. We suggest using baseline shift to move the characters around until they look the way you'd like them to.

▼ ▼

Bottom. By specifying Bottom, you force the last line of text to the bottom of the box. Then, as text flows into the text box, each line pushes the type higher in the box. Note that it is the bottom of the descender, not the baseline, that sits flush with the box's bottom.

Justified. Justification here means that text will be flush with the top and bottom of the box. QuarkXPress puts the first line of the text box at the top, the last line at the bottom, and then adds or deletes space between interior lines. That means that there may be a lot of extra space between lines and paragraphs (leading settings are overridden when necessary).

Figure 4-20

The four Vertical
Alignment settings

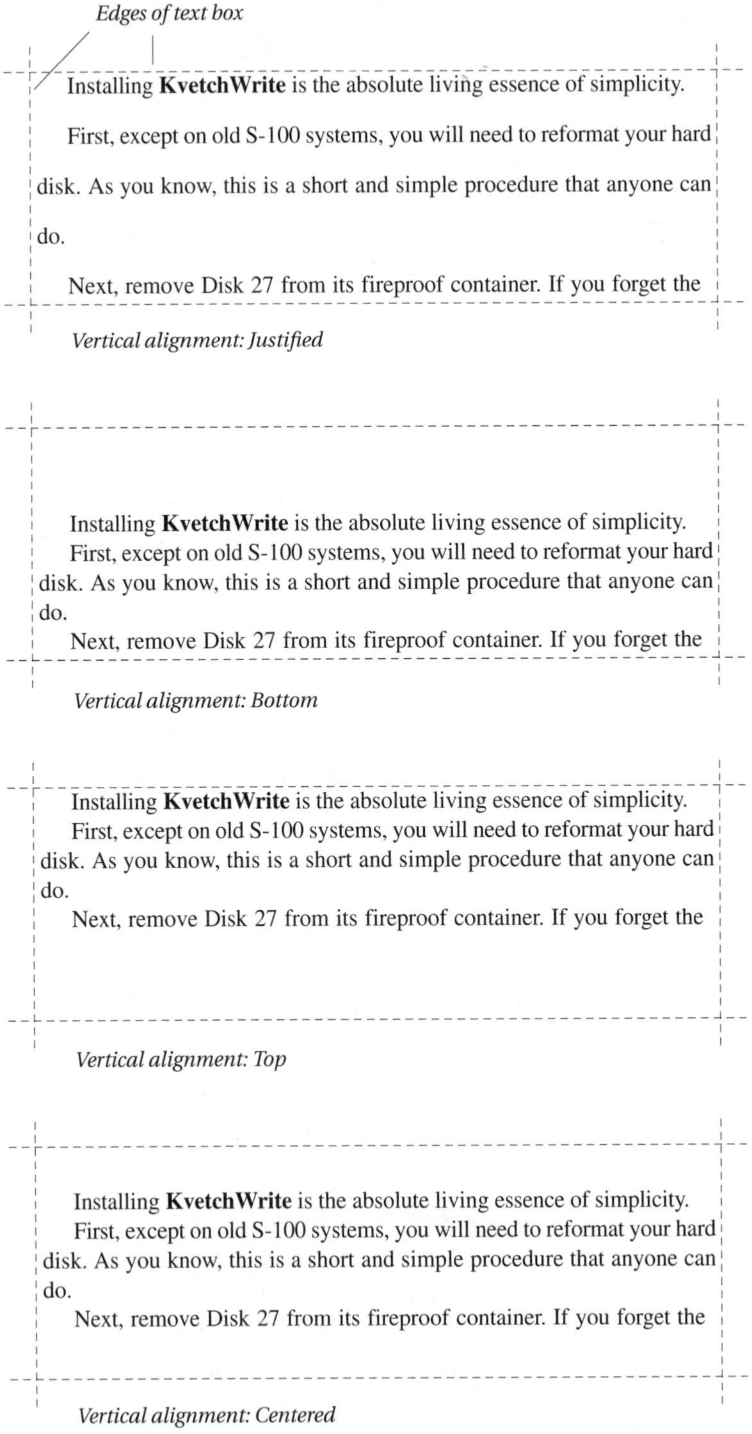

Edges of text box

Installing **KvetchWrite** is the absolute living essence of simplicity.

First, except on old S-100 systems, you will need to reformat your hard

disk. As you know, this is a short and simple procedure that anyone can

do.

Next, remove Disk 27 from its fireproof container. If you forget the

Vertical alignment: Justified

Installing **KvetchWrite** is the absolute living essence of simplicity.
First, except on old S-100 systems, you will need to reformat your hard
disk. As you know, this is a short and simple procedure that anyone can
do.
Next, remove Disk 27 from its fireproof container. If you forget the

Vertical alignment: Bottom

Installing **KvetchWrite** is the absolute living essence of simplicity.
First, except on old S-100 systems, you will need to reformat your hard
disk. As you know, this is a short and simple procedure that anyone can
do.
Next, remove Disk 27 from its fireproof container. If you forget the

Vertical alignment: Top

Installing **KvetchWrite** is the absolute living essence of simplicity.
First, except on old S-100 systems, you will need to reformat your hard
disk. As you know, this is a short and simple procedure that anyone can
do.
Next, remove Disk 27 from its fireproof container. If you forget the

Vertical alignment: Centered

Figure 4-21
When centering
is not centered

"Take your little brother swimming with a brick."

This is not visually centered because of the quotation marks.

"Take your little brother swimming with a brick."

This is adjusted by placing punctuation colored white on each line.

You can specify a maximum distance between paragraphs in a vertically justified text box by changing the Inter ¶ Max value in the Text Box Specifications dialog box. A setting of zero, which is the default, tells QuarkXPress to distribute all space evenly by adding leading. A setting higher than zero lets the program add extra space between paragraphs rather than change your leading. Figure 4-22 shows some examples of vertically justified text with different Inter ¶ Max settings.

When Quark announced they would support vertical justification, the press thought it would be the greatest thing since the transistor. Our response is: if you set up your leading grids and text boxes correctly, you shouldn't need to have some computer going through your drawers, shuffling lines around. We wouldn't want a computer to marry our daughters (if we had any), and we don't want a computer changing our leading and paragraph spacing.

No matter how picky we are about correctly setting up our documents, we do admit that there are times when vertical justification comes in handy. For example, many newspapers use this feature constantly to "bottom out" their columns.

Indents

Horizontal alignment depends entirely on where the left and right margins are. In a column of text, the margins are usually at the edges of the text box (or the column, in a multicolumn text

Figure 4-2

Varying the

Inter ¶ Max setting

Ior, auritulus cinereus ille annosus Raili, solus in silvae angulo quodam carduoso stabat, pedibus late divaricatis, capite deflexo de rerum natura meditans.

"Cur?" cogitabat, modo "quemad-

modum?"

Itaque Puo appropinquante Ior paulisper a meditatione desistere gavisus est ut maeste "Ut vales?" ei diceret.

Text is 10/11,
Inter ¶ Max setting is
zero points. The leading
is ignored completely.

Gray line represents
the text box.

Ior, auritulus cinereus ille annosus Raili, solus in silvae angulo quodam carduoso stabat, pedibus late divaricatis, capite deflexo de rerum natura meditans.

"Cur?" cogitabat, modo "quemad-modum?"

Itaque Puo appropinquante Ior paulisper a meditatione desistere gavisus est ut maeste "Ut vales?" ei diceret.

Text is 10/11,
Inter ¶ Max setting is
four points. The leading
is adjusted slightly,
while space is added
between paragraphs.

Ior, auritulus cinereus ille annosus Raili, solus in silvae angulo quodam carduoso stabat, pedibus late divaricatis, capite deflexo de rerum natura meditans.

"Cur?" cogitabat, modo "quemad-modum?"

Itaque Puo appropinquante Ior paulisper a meditatione desistere gavisus est ut maeste "Ut vales?" ei diceret.

Text is 10/11,
Inter ¶ Max setting is
one pica. The leading is
back to normal, and
space is only added
between paragraphs.

box). However, you may want the first line of every paragraph to be indented slightly. Or you might want the left or right margin to be other than the edge of the column. You control each of these by changing the values for the paragraph indents.

▼ ▼

Tip: Watch the Text Inset. The default text inset for text boxes is one point, so your text will be indented one point from each side of the box automatically. Make sure to change the value in the Text Box Specifications dialog box (Command-M) if you don't want the one-point indent.

The best way to avoid this default problem is to close all documents, and double-click the Text Box tool. This brings up the Tool Preferences dialog box, where you can click the Modify button to change the Text Inset to zero. A text inset of zero sometimes makes the text a little hard to read on screen, because it bounces up against the side of the box; so you may or may not want to do this.

Note that some XTensions, including SetInset and Kitchen Sink, let you set the Text Inset differently for each side of the box: top, bottom, left, and right.

▼ ▼

QuarkXPress lets you change three indent values: Left Indent, Right Ondent, and First Line indent. All three controls are located in the Paragraph Formats dialog box (Command-Shift-F; see Figure 4-23). We'll discuss each one and then talk about how you can use them.

Figure 4-23
Right Indent, Left
Indent, and First
Line Indent

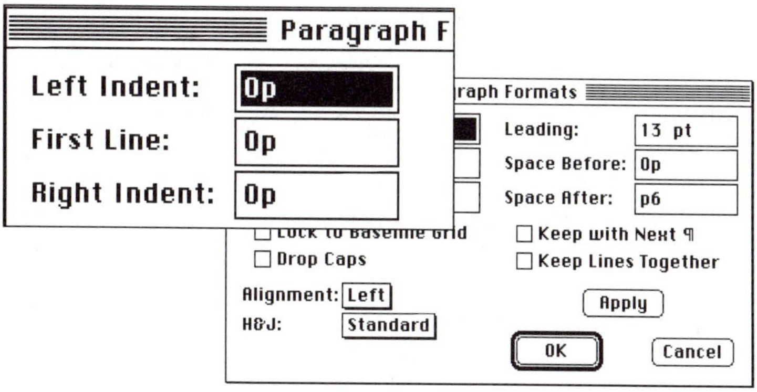

Left Indent. The Left Indent control specifies how far the paragraph sits from the left side of the text box or column guide. The Left Indent is actually measured from the Text Inset border, not the side of the box. For example, if you want your paragraph to be exactly three picas indented from the side of the text box, and your Text Inset setting is four points, then your Left Indent should be "2p8" (three picas minus four points).

Right Indent. The Right Indent control specifies how far the right edge of the paragraph will be positioned from the right edge of the text box or column guide (or text indent). For example, if you change the Right Indent to .5 inch, you can imagine an invisible line being drawn .5 inch from the right column guide. The text cannot move farther to the right than this line (see Figure 4-24).

Figure 4-24
Right Indent

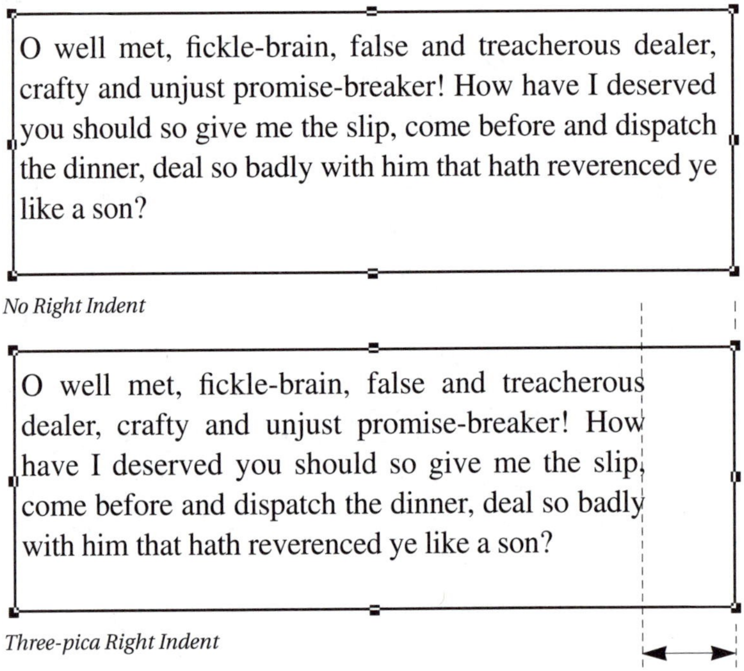

O well met, fickle-brain, false and treacherous dealer, crafty and unjust promise-breaker! How have I deserved you should so give me the slip, come before and dispatch the dinner, deal so badly with him that hath reverenced ye like a son?

No Right Indent

O well met, fickle-brain, false and treacherous dealer, crafty and unjust promise-breaker! How have I deserved you should so give me the slip, come before and dispatch the dinner, deal so badly with him that hath reverenced ye like a son?

Three-pica Right Indent

First Line. Whatever you do, wherever you go, don't type five spaces to indent the first line of each paragraph. If you must, use a tab. If you want to avoid the problem completely, use a First Line indent. The First Line indent feature does exactly what it sounds like it would do: indents only the first line of each paragraph.

How large your indent should be depends primarily on your design and the typeface you are working with. If you are working with a typeface with a large x-height (the height of the lowercase "x" in relation to the height of the capital letters), you should use a larger first line indent than if you are working with a low x-height typeface. Book designers often use a one- or two-em indent; if you're using 12-point type, the indent might be 12 points or 24 points.

▼ ▼

Tip: Hanging Indents. You can use Left Indent and First Line indent to create hanging indents (used for bullet lists and the like) by typing a negative number as the First Line indent. We often use "1p6" (one-and-a-half picas) for a left indent and "-1p6" for a first line indent. This places our first character (a bullet) at the zero mark, and the subsequent lines at the "1p6" mark (see Figure 4-25). Typing a tab after the bullet skips over to the "1p6" mark whether or not we have a tab stop there (we'll discuss tabs and tab stops later in this chapter).

Figure 4-25
Hanging indents

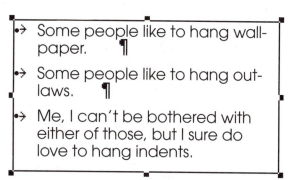

The benefit of hanging indents like this is that you don't have to painfully set your own returns after each line. If you set hard or soft returns after each line—we'll talk about the difference later in this chapter— then edit the text, or even change the typeface, it takes a long time to fix the text, removing the old returns and putting new ones in. This is horrible; if you had just used hanging indents instead, your problem would be solved automatically.

▼ ▼

Note that you don't have to specify any of the indents by typing numbers. While the Paragraph Formats dialog box is open, you are shown a ruler along the top of the active text box (see Figure 4-26). This ruler contains three triangle markers: two on the left, and one on the right. You can move these icons by clicking and dragging them along the ruler.

Figure 4-26

The text ruler associated with the Formats dialog box

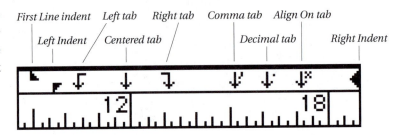

The right triangle is the Right Indent. The bottom-left triangle is the Left Indent. The top-left triangle is the First Line Indent. While moving these triangles around, the First Line indent moves with the Left Indent. This is the same as Microsoft Word and other programs (though those programs let you move the Left Ondent independently by holding down the Shift key; QuarkXPress doesn't). For example, if you set a ¼-inch First Line Indent, and then move the Left Indent triangle to ½ inch, the First Line Indent moves with it to the ¾-inch point (½ inch plus ¼ inch).

▼ ▼

Tip: Formatting Past the Boundaries. As the old Zen master said, "Frustration dissipates like the morning fog when light is shed on the problem." (Actually, we don't know any Zen masters, so we just made that up.) One frustration we've seen people get caught in is the issue of formatting past the boundaries of the text box. For example, when you open the Paragraph Formats dialog box, QuarkXPress adds a ruler along the top of the text box so that you can manually add or edit the tab stops and indents. However, if the box is too wide, you can't see the left or right side of the ruler because it runs right off the document window (see Figure 4-27).

However—and here's the shedding of the light part—it turns out that if you click in that ruler and drag to the left or right, the

Figure 4-27
The too-wide ruler

If you select a wide block of text and bring up Paragraph Tabs, the ruler just runs right off the window.

page scrolls with you. Pretty soon you get to where you want to go and you can stop dragging. Note that when you do this, you sometimes add a tab stop (we'll talk about which one later in this chapter), and you have to get rid of it by clicking on it and dragging it off the ruler.

Leading

If we could get one concept across to you in this chapter, we'd want it to be: don't follow the defaults. By not following default values, you are forced to pay attention to how the type looks, rather than letting the computer do it for you. There is perhaps no better example of why this is important than leading.

Leading (pronounced "ledding") is the space between lines of text. The name originates from the lead strips or blocks used to add space between lines (slugs) of metal type. QuarkXPress gives you considerable control over leading values for each paragraph, or it can "fly on automatic," specifying leading for you.

In this section we'll discuss the two modes and three methods for specifying leading. Pay close attention to the words "color" and "readability" in this section; they're the reasons we bother to be so meticulous.

Specifying Leading

Although QuarkXPress lets you use any measurement system you want, leading is traditionally measured in points. When talking type, most typesetters and designers say things like, "Helvetica 10 on 12," and write it out as "10/12." Designers who have grown accustomed to digital equipment (in other words, just about everybody), would say that 10/12 means setting 10-point type so that the baseline of one line is 12 points from the baseline of the next line (see Figure 4-28).

Figure 4-28
Specifying leading

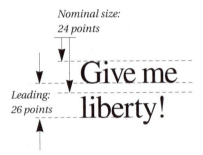

Leading is a paragraph-level attribute. That is, each paragraph can have its own leading value, but you can't have two different leading values within a paragraph. You specify your leading in one of three places: the Paragraph Formats dialog box (Command-Shift-F), the Leading dialog box (Command-Shift-E), or the Measurements palette. Whereas in the first two you can only enter the leading value (more on this below), in the Measurements palette you can change leading in two ways (see Figure 4-29).

▶ You can select the leading value and replace it with the value you want.

▶ Clicking the up or down arrow next to the leading value increases or decreases the leading value in one-point increments.

You can also use shortcuts to change a paragraph's leading. Table 4-7 shows the four keystrokes.

Leading Methods

QuarkXPress lets you specify leading values in three ways: absolutely, automatically, and relatively. Let's look at these.

Figure 4-29

Leading in the
Measurements Palette

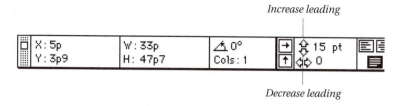

Increase leading

Decrease leading

Table 4-7	**Press . . .**	**To . . .**
Leading keystrokes	Command-Shift-'	Increase leading in one-point increments
	Command-Option-Shift-'	Increase leading in .1-point increments
	Command-Shift-;	Decrease leading in one-point increments
	Command-Option-Shift-;	Decrease leading in .1-point increments

Absolute. Setting your leading in an absolute form makes your leading as steadfast as Gibraltar. If you specify 14-point leading, you get 14-point leading—no matter what size type the paragraph contains. If the type is bigger than the leading, the type overprints preceding lines. When, as in the example given above, someone talks about "10/12" type, this is what they're talking about.

QuarkXPress lets you type any absolute leading value between zero and 1,080 points.

▼ ▼

Tip: True Zero Leading. If you set a paragraph's leading to zero, QuarkXPress decides you really mean that you want "automatic" leading (see below). But what if you really want no leading at all from baseline to baseline? If you set leading to .0001 points, the program rounds down to exactly zero. The next highest value is .001 points. The truth of the matter is that these are equivalent for all intents and purposes, but we wanted to be clear anyway.

Why would anyone want to use zero leading? Well, it wouldn't be common. Zero leading means that every line in the paragraph would be printed exactly on top of the line above it; making the whole paragraph be only one line tall. It's especially good for those postmodern designs where you don't really need to read any of the words.

▼ ▼

Automatic. Auto Leading sets leading as a percentage of the largest font size on each line. This percentage is usually 20 percent greater than the font size. For example, if the largest font size on a given line is 10 points, then your leading will be set to 12 points (10 plus 20 percent of 10). If you change the font size to 12 points, then the leading changes to 14.4 points. Note that if you change only one character on a line to a larger font size, then that line alone will have a different leading value (which just *screams* "desktop published!"), even though Auto leading is a paragraph-wide feature (see Figure 4-30).

Figure 4-30
Autoleading can result in irregular leading within a paragraph

Noodle. Oh! monstrous, dreadful, terrible! Oh! Oh! Deaf be my ears, for ever blind my eyes! **D**umb be my tongue! feet lame! all senses lost! Howl wolves, grunt bears, hiss snakes, shriek all ye ghosts!

One character can throw the leading off.

King. What does the blockhead mean?

Auto leading is the default setting of any new text box. However, to choose it specifically, you can type either "Auto" or "0" as the leading value.

You can change the automatic-leading percentage value in the Typographic Preferences dialog box. There are two things you should note about doing this, though. First, the change is document-wide; you can't change the automatic leading percentage for only one paragraph or text box.

Second, you must specify clearly what the automatic leading measurements are; that is, if you want a percent, you must type a percent sign. This is important because you can also specify the automatic leading to be a relative leading value (more on relative values in a moment).

To be honest with you, we use automatic leading when we're typing up grocery shopping lists. But when we're working on a project professionally, we define the leading explicitly using absolute or relative leading. Many professional magazines, newspapers, and newsletters use automatic leading because they don't know any better; and then they blame QuarkXPress for outputting weird-looking text.

Relative. Whereas automatic leading generally determines the leading value based on a percentage of font size, relative leading determines leading by an absolute value. You specify relative leading by including the characters + or - (plus or minus/hyphen) before your leading value. For example, applying a leading value of "+3" to 12-point type results in "12/15" leading. If you change the font size to 22 points, you get "22/25" leading (22 plus three).

By typing a negative relative value, you can tighten up the leading. However, you have a limit: the height of a capital on the lower line cannot move higher than the baseline of the upper line (to achieve that ugly effect, you have to use absolute leading).

We often use relative leading when we are specifying leading *solid*—that is, when the leading equals the point size. Instead of keying in 30-point leading for 30-point type, we type "+0". Then, if (or when) we change the font size, the leading changes with it.

Leading Modes

When specifying leading in QuarkXPress, you can work in one of two leading modes: Word Processing or Typesetting. You can select which mode to use with Typographic Preferences under the Edit menu).

Word Processing. Let's be straight here: even if you're using Quark-XPress only as a word processor, you shouldn't use Word Processing mode. There's just no point to it. Selecting Word Processing mode makes QuarkXPress use an ascent-to-ascent measurement. Ascent to ascent means that the leading value you specify will be measured from the top of a capital letter on one line to the top of a capital letter on the next line. The only reason Quark included this method was because many word-processing programs use it. You shouldn't, because the leading will change depending on the typeface you're using, and there's no way you can tell what the leading value actually is (this side of examining a font's Ascent value using ResEdit or some font utility).

Typesetting. As we noted above, the proper way to specify leading on the Macintosh is to measure from the baseline of one line to the baseline of the next. QuarkXPress calls this Typesetting Mode. It's the program default; if someone has changed it, change it back and leave it that way.

▼ ▼

Tip: When Black and White Is Colorful. When designers and typesetters talk about the *color* of a page or the color of type, they aren't talking red, green, or blue. They're referring to the degree of darkness or lightness that the text projects. The color of text is directly related to the typeface, letterspacing, wordspacing, and leading. Other design elements, such as drop caps, graphic elements, or pullquotes, can have a significant effect on the color of a page. It's usually a good practice to maintain an even and balanced color throughout your page, unless you're trying to pull the viewer's eye (as opposed to pulling the viewer's leg) to one area or another (see Figure 4-31).

One way to see the color of a page or a block of type is to hold the printed page at some distance and squint. You can also turn the page over and hold it up to light, so you can see the text blocks without being distracted by the text itself.

▼ ▼

Tip: Leading Tips. Here are a few tips and tricks for adjusting your leading. Remember, though, that ultimately it is how easily the text reads and how comfortable the color is that counts. Figure 4-32 shows some samples for each of these suggestions.

▶ Increase the leading as you increase the line length. Solid leading may read fine with a line containing five words, but will be awful for a line containing 20 words.

▶ Generally use some extra leading for sans serif or bold type. It needs the extra room.

Figure 4-31
The color of text blocks

Eduardus ursus, amicis suis agnomine "Winnie ille Pu"—aut breviter "Pu"—notus, die quodam canticum semihiantibus labellis superbe eliquans

Stone Serif 9/12

Eduardus ursus, amicis suis agnomine "Winnie ille Pu"—aut breviter "Pu"—notus, die quodam canticum semihiantibus

Stone Serif bold 9/12

Eduardus ursus, amicis suis agnomine "Winnie ille Pu"—aut breviter "Pu"—notus, die quodam canticum semihiantibus labellis superbe

Veljovic 10/13

Eduardus ursus, amicis suis agnomine "Winnie ille Pu"—aut breviter "Pu"—notus, die quodam canticum semihiantibus

Univers 55 Regular 10/13

Eduardus ursus, amicis suis agnomine "Winnie ille Pu"—aut breviter "Pu"—notus, die quodam canticum semi-hiantibus labellis superbe

Palatino with zero tracking

Eduardus ursus, amicis suis agnomine "Winnie ille Pu"—aut breviter "Pu"—notus, die quodam canticum semihiantibus labellis superbe eliquans

Palatino with -10 tracking

▶ Note the x-height of your typeface. Fonts with a small x-height can often be set tighter than those with a large x-height.

▶ Set display or headline type tightly. Big type can and should be set tightly, using either "+0" relative leading or even absolute leading smaller than the point size you're using.

▶ When you're using really tight leading, be careful not to let the ascenders of one line touch the descenders of the line above it.

A corollary tip to all of these: break the rules if it makes the design look better!

▼ ▼

Tip: Vertical Leading Ruler. One feature QuarkXPress doesn't have is a customizable vertical ruler. "Why would anyone want that?" we

Figure 4-32

Leading techniques

*The longer a line,
the more leading
you'll need.*

9/9.5

Look, s'pose some general or king is bone stupid and leads his men up a creek, then those men've got to be fearless, there's another virtue for you. S'pose he's stingy and hires too few soldiers, then they got to be a crowd of Hercule's. And s'pose he's slapdash and don't give a bugger, then they got to be clever as monkeys else their number's up.

9/11

Look, s'pose some general or king is bone stupid and leads his men up a creek, then those men've got to be fearless, there's another virtue for you. S'pose he's stingy and hires too few soldiers, then they got to be a crowd of Hercule's. And s'pose he's slapdash and don't give a bugger, then they got to be clever as monkeys else their number's up.

*Fonts with small
x-heights can be
set tighter.*

The misery of this one woman surges through my heart and marrow, and you grid imperturbed over the fate of thousands!

9/11.5

The misery of this one woman surges through my heart and marrow, and you grid imperturbed over the fate of thousands!

9/9.5

*Display type can be
set tightly.*

The best thing since sliced bread

36/31

*Watch out for your
ascenders and
descenders.*

Cagney Jads

48/39

hear you asking. Well, the best reason is to set a vertical ruler in increments of your body copy's leading. That is, if the body copy leading is set to 11 points, it's nice to have a vertical ruler in increments of 11 points. This is especially helpful for aligning objects to your leading grid.

One way to get such a custom vertical ruler is to create one on the pasteboard. Follow these steps.

1. Draw a one-pica-wide box as tall as your page (we would just draw a little box, then go into the Measurements palette and set the Origin Across and Origin Down both to zero, the width to one pica, and the height to 8.5 inches or whatever). Make sure this box has no background color and a text runaround of None.

2. Place a one-pica-wide line with a thickness of .5 point at the bottom or top of this box.

3. Step-and-repeat this line in increments of your body copy leading as many times as you need to reach from the top of the box to the bottom.

4. Select the box and every line in it (drag a marquee around them with the Item tool), and group them (Command-G).

5. Press Command-M to go to the Group Specifications dialog box, and turn on Suppress Printout.

You can now position this next to your page, or on a master page, and use it as a guide. You also may find it helpful to drag out guides and align them with the tick marks.

Space Before and After

Not only can you place interline space with leading, you can add space between paragraphs using the Space Before and Space

After attributes. You can find both of these controls in the Paragraph Formats dialog box (Command-Shift-F).

While it is entirely your prerogative to use both the Space Before and Space After attributes, you normally will only need to use one or the other. Think about it: if you add equal space before and space after a paragraph, it doubles the amount of space between each paragraph. Whichever you use is immaterial. David always uses Space Before, and Eric likes Space After. Each requires a slightly different way of thinking, but the concepts are ultimately the same.

We've seen more than one designer become flustered when applying Space Before to the first paragraph in a text box. Nothing happens. Remember that Space Before has no effect on the first paragraph in a text box. This is usually what you want, though. If the program did add space before a paragraph at the top of the text box, multiple columns might not align, and the file would look really weird. To add space before the first paragraph in a text box, use the First Baseline placement control (see "First Baseline," below).

▼ ▼

Tip: Adding Extra Space. Recently, David witnessed one of his esteemed officemates using multiple carriage returns to control the space between paragraphs and almost went apoplectic. Let's see if we can pound this idea into your head as strongly as we did with, "Don't use multiple spaces between words or punctuation."

Don't ever use an extra carriage return to add space between paragraphs. Not only will you offend the people at Quark who spent long hours implementing the Space Before and Space After features, but you will—nine out of 10 times—mess yourself up with extra blank paragraphs hanging out at tops of columns or in other places where you don't want them. If you want a full line of space between paragraphs, apply it through Space Before or Space After in the Paragraph Formats dialog box.

▼ ▼

First Baseline

The first line of a text box is always a tricky one for perfectionists. How far away from the top edge of the text box should the line sit? And how to get it there? QuarkXPress lets you set First Baseline in the Text Box Specifications dialog box (Command-M, or double-click on the text box with the Item tool selected).

The key issue to remember here is that QuarkXPress places the first line of text in the box according to three values: the size of the type, the Text Inset value, or the First Baseline Offset value. This is potentially confusing, so let's take it slowly (see Figure 4-33).

Figure 4-33

How First Baseline Offset thinks

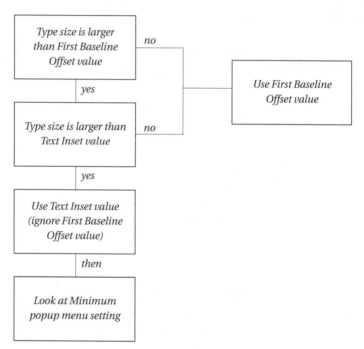

▶ QuarkXPress compares the three values (type size, Text Inset, and First Baseline Offset).

▶ If the size of the type is larger than either the First Baseline Offset value or the Text Inset value, then the Text Inset value is used.

▶ If the First Baseline Offset value is larger than both the type and the Text Inset value, then it is used as the first line's placement.

▶ If the Text Inset is the value used rather than the First Baseline Offset value, then a fourth factor is brought into the equation: the Minimum setting.

The Minimum setting specifies where the top of the text is. You can choose three values for the Minimum setting: Cap Height, Cap+Accent, and Ascent (see Figure 4-34).

For example, if your text box has a Text Inset of six points and a First Baseline Offset of three picas (36 points), QuarkXPress places the first line 36 points down from the top edge of the box. On the other hand, if the type changes to 60 points, then QuarkXPress ignores the First Baseline Offset and places the top of the text (as determined by the Minimum setting) at the Text Inset value.

Figure 4-34
The Minimum settings:
Cap Height,
Cap+Accent,
and Ascent

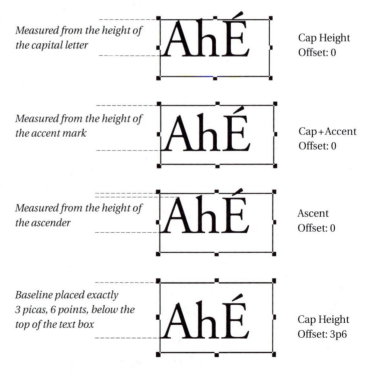

Measured from the height of the capital letter

Cap Height
Offset: 0

Measured from the height of the accent mark

Cap+Accent
Offset: 0

Measured from the height of the ascender

Ascent
Offset: 0

Baseline placed exactly 3 picas, 6 points, below the top of the text box

Cap Height
Offset: 3p6

▼ ▼

Tabs

If you've ever typed on a typewriter, you've probably encountered tabs. A tab is a jump-to signal in the form of a keyboard character. For example, if you're typing along and press the Tab key, the text cursor jumps to the next tab stop along the line. You can place these tab stops anywhere you like across the text column. Tab stops are paragraph-level formatting attributes, so each paragraph can have a different set of tab stops. If you don't specify your own tab stops, QuarkXPress sets default stops every half-inch across the text box.

▼ ▼

Tip: Don't Use Space Where You Really Want Tabs. Have you ever tried to align multiple columns using the spacebar? If you have, you have probably known frustration like no other frustration known to desktop publishers. We call it the "it-works-on-a-typewriter" syndrome. It's true; you can line up columns on a typewriter. But you shouldn't in desktop publishing. The reason has to do with fonts.

On most standard typewriters, the font you're using is a monospaced font. That means each and every character in the font is the same width. However, most typefaces on the Macintosh are *not* monospaced. Therefore, you cannot rely on an equal number of characters always being an equal distance. Figure 4-35 shows this phenomenon clearly. So, don't use multiple spaces when you're trying to align columns. In fact, don't use multiple spaces ever. Use tabs.

▼ ▼

Tip: Multiple Tabs. If you are setting up a table and you want to place tabs between each column, follow the same rule as spaces: don't type multiple tabs in a row to make your columns align. Set one tab stop for each column. Then just press Tab once to jump from column to column.

▼ ▼

QuarkXPress lets you set seven types of tab stops using two different methods. Let's look at the types of tab stops first. They

Figure 4-35

Using spaces
for alignment

Take one	from column "a"	and one	from column "b"
but here	you actually	have four	columns see?

Aligned with spaces (bad)

Take one	from column "a"	and one	from column "b"
but here	you actually	have four	columns see?

Aligned with tabs (good)

are: Left, Right, Center, Right Indent, Decimal, Comma, and Align On. Figure 4-36 shows examples of each of these types of tab stops in a common situation—a table.

▶ **Left tab stop.** This is the type of tab stop you're used to from typewriters. The text after the tab continues as left-aligned.

▶ **Right tab stop.** Tabbing to a Right tab stop causes the following text to be right aligned. That is, it will be flush right-against the tab stop.

▶ **Center tab stop.** Text typed after tabbing to a Center tab stop will center on that tab stop.

▶ **Right Indent tab.** Right Indent tabs don't show up in the popup menu because they're not really tab stops. You enter them in a text box with the Content tool selected by pressing Option-Tab. We'll talk about this more fully in just a moment.

▶ **Decimal, Comma, and Align On tab stops.** These three tab stops act similarly. They act like a right tab until a special character is entered; then the next text is flush left. The decimal and comma tabs align on the first non-numeric, non-

Figure 4-36
Using tabs

Acme Digital Frammis Corp.

"Have a *wonderful* day!"

1994 Customer Dissatisfaction as a Function of Product Color

Product Color	People Per Product	Units Sold	Unit Price ($)	Dissatisfaction Index*
Moon Maid	120/20	2001	12.95[a]	6.77
Stuck Pig	44/63	5877	19.95	13.32
Curmudgeon	56/56	31	6[b]	57.91
Haggis	1/100000	3	129.97	3244.36

Parts per million [a]Special discount [b]Sold to GK

Left tab *Align on "/"* *Centered tab* *Decimal tab* *Right tab*

punctuation character. Selecting Align On brings up a one-character entry field; you can then enter the special character that acts as the tab stop.

▼ ▼

Tip: Formatting Tabs Quickly. One reader, Barry Simon, pointed out to us that you can sometimes format tabs for a number of lines more easily by just working on a single line. If you set the proper tab settings for the first line, you can quickly apply those settings to the rest of the lines by selecting all the lines (including the first one), opening the Tabs dialog box (Command-Shift-T), and clicking OK (or pressing Return). The tab setting for the first line is applied to the rest of the lines.

▼ ▼

Tip: Hanging Tabs. There's a subtle feature in the decimal tab function which you'll love if you ever create balance sheets. The decimal tab doesn't just line up decimals. Rather, QuarkXPress thinks of any non-number that falls after a number to be a decimal point, and aligns to it. For example, if you press Tab and type "94c2.4" on a line with a decimal tab, QuarkXPress aligns to the "c" rather than the period.

We thought this was a bug, until we realized how handy it could be. For example, if you are lining up numbers in a column, the negative-balance parentheses hang outside of the column. You can even create hanging footnotes, as long as they're not numbers (see unit cost column in Figure 4-36, above).

▼ ▼

The Tabs Dialog Box

The easiest and most precise way to place your tab stops is through the Paragraph Tabs dialog box, which you can find by selecting Tabs in the Style menu, or by pressing Command-Shift-T. When this dialog box is open, QuarkXPress places a ruler bar across the box of the text box you're working in.

You can place a tab stop by first selecting the kind of tab stop you want from the Alignment choices, then either clicking in the ruler area or typing a tab-stop value into the Position box. If you type the value in, you must click either the Apply button or OK to make the tab stop appear in the ruler bar (see Figure 4-37). If you have continuous Apply on (Command-Option-A), then pressing Tab adds *and* applies the tab stop.

Figure 4-37
The Paragraph Tabs
dialog box

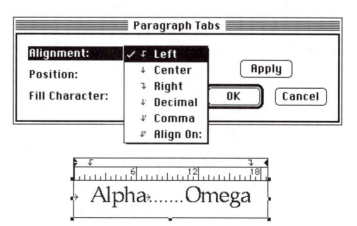

The second method for applying tabs is through the Paragraph Formats dialog box. However, in this instance, you can only create left tab stops and you must place them by clicking in the text-box ruler (in other words, it's really a very limited way to set tab stops for a paragraph).

Tab Leaders

You can also add a leader to each tab stop. A leader fills the tab space with one or two repeated characters, such as a period or a dash (two-character tab leaders are new in 3.3; see Figure 4-38). To add a leader to a tab stop which has not been created yet, set the alignment using the popup menu, type the leader characters into the Fill Character field (we prefer the word *leader* over "fill character"), and then place the tab stop.

Figure 4-38
Tab leaders and
tracking

It droppeth --------------------as the purple rain from ⓇⓇⓇⓇⓇⓇⓇⓇⓇⓇⓇⓇⓇ Hollywood Ducks and chicks ❋☞❋☞❋☞ and geese better ⬫⬫⬫⬫⬫⬫⬫⬫⬫⬫⬫⬫⬫⬫⬫⬫⬫ scurry

Other characters used as tab leaders. In the second line, the size of the tab itself was reduced to 10 points. In the fourth line, the < and > symbols were kerned together by selecting the tab character.

To add a leader to a tab stop which has already been placed, click on the tab-stop icon (the little arrow in the ruler), type the leader character(s) in the appropriate box, and then click the Apply button. If you want to place more than one tab stop with a leader using this method, you must click the Apply button for each one, or press Command-Option-A keystroke to turn on continuous Apply. When you have placed the tab stops you want, click OK to save the changes to that paragraph.

▼ ▼

Tip: Adjusting Leaders. You don't have to be content with the size and font of a tab's leaders (otherwise called "fill characters"). If you want the characters to be smaller, select the tab character itself and change the point size. If you want the characters to be in another font, change the font of that tab character. People don't often think of the tab character as a character, but that's just what it is. If you turn on Show Invisibles (select it from the View menu), you can see the character as a little gray triangle.

Changing the font and size isn't all you can do: you can even change the amount of space between the leader characters. Select the tab space and adjust its tracking/kerning value. Typically, when you change the kerning value for a single character it only changes the space between it and the next character; however, in this case it changes the space between each of the leader characters (see Figure 4-39).

Figure 4-39
Tab leaders

Period used as leader characters (18 points; same as other type on the line).

Moishe is.................................not strange.

Oh yes. . . . . he is, too.

Tab reduced to 10 points with a tracking value of 94.

▼ ▼

Changing and Deleting Tab Stops

Once you have tab stops set for a paragraph, you can go back and edit them by dragging the tab-stop icons along the ruler in either the Paragraph Tabs or the Paragraph Formats dialog box. Unfortunately, you can't simply type in a new value for a tab stop in the Position box (this just adds a new tab stop rather than moving the old one). You can edit the type of alignment or the fill character for a tab stop in the Paragraph Tabs dialog box by first clicking the tab stop icon, changing the settings you want, and clicking OK.

You can rid yourself of an unwanted tab by dragging the icon out of the ruler boundaries (see Figure 4-40). To clear all the tab stops for a paragraph, Option-click the tab ruler in either the Paragraph Tabs or Paragraph Formats dialog box.

Editing tab stops is one place that the continuous Apply feature is really helpful; again, Option-click the Apply button to turn

Figure 4-40

Dragging away
a tab stop

this on or off. When you turn it on, you can adjust tab stops and QuarkXPress updates the paragraph(s) automatically. This makes adjusting columns much faster and easier.

Right Indent Tab

Trying to set a tab stop exactly at the right margin can be very frustrating. Even worse, if your right margin or the size of your text box changes, your tab stop doesn't follow along. Typing a Right Indent tab (Option-Tab) fixes all that. This type of tab acts as though you've placed a right tab stop flush with the right margin of your paragraph. Plus, it moves as you adjust the margin or the text box. Inserting this type of tab effectively adds the tab and sets a variable tab stop at the same time. (We can hear the handful of people who "get it" sighing appreciatively in the background. Those of you who don't, just try it once and you'll understand.)

The Right Indent tab acts just like a tab character (you can even search for it the same way, using "\t"; see "Find/Change" in Chapter 3, *Word Processing*), though there's no way to set its own leader. It picks up the same leader as the previous tab stop in the paragraph. Note that you won't see a tab stop in the Paragraph Tabs dialog box's ruler: it's always set to the right margin, wherever that is. Also, you should note that Option-Tab jumps past all other tab stops in that paragraph, all the way over to the right margin.

Hyphenation and Justification

There are few items more dear to a typesetter's heart than hyphenation and justification—often called simply *H&J*. Proper hyphenation and justification of a document is often the most important single factor in the way a document looks. And if your H&J is bad . . . well, there's little that anyone can do (see Figure 4-41).

QuarkXPress has some very powerful controls over how it hyphenates and justifies text in a column. However, this is once more a situation where you won't want to go with its default settings. Let's take a look at what H&J is all about, and then get into the details of how you can make it work for you.

Figure 4-41
Hyphenation and
Justification can make
the difference

Doing a good job with the program involves knowing a little something about good hyphenation and justification settings. If y'ain't got the good settings, you don't got the good-looking type, either. This paragraph, for example, is simply atrocious.

Doing an *especially* good job with the program involves taking the time to learn about its hyphenation and justification controls. You'll be glad you did.

The Basics of H&J

Although hyphenation and justification are entirely separate functions, they almost always go together. Almost always.

The idea behind both hyphenation and justification is to make text fit into a given space and still look as good as possible. It turns out that there are three basic ways to fit text without distorting it too much.

▶ Controlling the spacing between each of the letters.

▶ Controlling the spacing between the words.

▶ Breaking the words at a line break by hyphenating.

Any one of these, if performed in excess, looks pretty awful. However, it is possible to mix them together in proper measure for a pleasing result.

▼ ▼

Tip: Check for Rivers. Often the first problem that arises when people set their text to justified alignment is that their documents start looking like a flood just hit; all these rivers of white space are flowing around little islands of words. Because our eyes are so good at seeing patterns of lines, too much space between words is disturbing to the eye (we see the space rather than the words). We told you in "Tip: When Black and White is Colorful," page 256, that turning the page over and holding it up to the light is a good way to check the color of a text block. It's also a great way to check for rivers in your text. This way your eye isn't tricked into actually looking at the words—just the spaces.

▼ ▼

Although you can't adjust the algorithms that QuarkXPress uses for H&J, you can change many variables that help in its decision-making. These values make up the Edit Hyphenation & Justification dialog box, found by first selecting H&Js from the Edit menu (or pressing Command-Option-H), selecting the H&J to edit, and then clicking the Edit button (see Figure 4-42).

Let's divide the controls in this dialog box into two groups—Auto Hyphenation and Justification—and discuss them one at a time.

Auto Hyphenation

QuarkXPress can automatically hyphenate words at the end of a line, breaking them into syllables according to an internal algorithm. When you first start up the program, make sure that Auto Hyphenation is turned on. If it's off, QuarkXPress won't hyphenate any words unless you include hyphens or discretionary hyphens (see "Formatting Characters," below). You can turn on Auto Hyphenation in the Edit Hyphenation & Justification dialog box (remember that if you turn it on when no documents are open, it stays on for all subsequent files). When you enable hyphenation, several items become active. These features are the basic controls over QuarkXPress's internal hyphenating algorithms. Let's look at them one at a time.

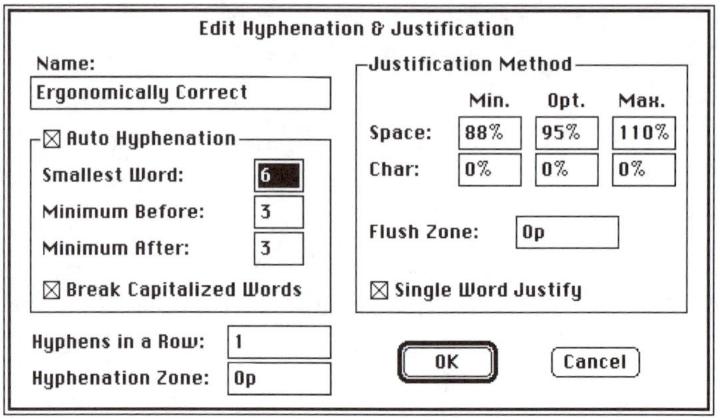

Figure 4-42

The Edit Hyphenation & Justification dialog box

```
┌─────────────────────────────────────────────────────────┐
│              Edit Hyphenation & Justification             │
│  Name:                    ┌─Justification Method──────┐  │
│  ┌──────────────────────┐ │           Min.  Opt.  Max.│  │
│  │Ergonomically Correct │ │  Space:  [88%] [95%] [110%]│  │
│  └──────────────────────┘ │                            │  │
│  ┌─⊠ Auto Hyphenation───┐ │  Char:   [0%]  [0%]  [0%] │  │
│  │ Smallest Word:   [6 ] │ │                            │  │
│  │ Minimum Before:  [3 ] │ │  Flush Zone:  [0p      ]  │  │
│  │ Minimum After:   [3 ] │ │                            │  │
│  │ ⊠ Break Capitalized Words│  ⊠ Single Word Justify   │  │
│  └───────────────────────┘ └────────────────────────────┘  │
│  Hyphens in a Row:  [1 ]                                  │
│  Hyphenation Zone:  [0p]     ( OK )      ( Cancel )       │
└───────────────────────────────────────────────────────────┘
```

Smallest Word. When QuarkXPress is attempting to hyphenate a line of text, it must decide what words are eligible for hyphenation. You can quickly discard most of the smaller words by specifying the smallest word QuarkXPress considers. For example, you might not want the word "many" to hyphenate at the end of a line. By setting the Smallest Word value to five or higher, you tell QuarkXPress to ignore this word, as well as any other word with fewer than five letters.

Minimum Before. The Minimum Before value specifies the number of letters in a word which must come before a hyphen break. Depending on your tastes and your pickiness level, you might set this to two or three. Otherwise, words like "tsetse" (as in "fly") might break after the first "t."

Minimum After. The Minimum After value specifies the number of letters in a word that must come after a hyphen break. Again, this value is based on aesthetics. Some people don't mind if the "ly" in "truly" sits all by itself on a line. (*The New York Times* breaks "doesn't" after the "s," but it's a newspaper, after all.) For most quality work, you would want a minimum setting of three. And never, ever, set it to one (the results are uglier than a vegetarian's face at a meat-packing plant).

Break Capitalized Words. This control is self-explanatory. You can tell QuarkXPress to either break capitalized words or not. The feature is there for those people who think that proper nouns should never be broken. We're picky, but not that picky.

Hyphens in a Row. One area in which we *are* that picky is the number of hyphens we allow in a row. For most work, we hate to see more than a single hyphen in a row down a justified column of text. QuarkXPress defaults to "unlimited," which is the same as typing zero. If you're creating newspapers, this might be appropriate. If you're making art books, be a bit more careful with your hyphens. We usually set this to two as a default and then go through and tweak the line breaks by hand.

Hyphenation Zone. Another way to limit the number of hyphens in a section of text is the Hyphenation Zone setting. While relatively simple in function, this feature is one of the more difficult to understand (it was for us, anyway).

The idea is that there is an invisible zone along the right margin of each block of text. If QuarkXPress is trying to break a word at the end of a line, it looks to see where the hyphenation zone is. If the word before the potentially hyphenated word falls inside the hyphenation zone, then QuarkXPress just gives up and pushes the word onto the next line (does not hyphenate it). If the prior word does not fall within the hyphenation zone, then QuarkXPress goes ahead with hyphenating the word (see Figure 4-43).

For example, if the words "robinus christophorus" came at the end of a line and QuarkXPress was about to hyphenate "christophorus," it would first look at the word "robinus" to see if any part of it fell inside the hyphenation zone. If it did, QuarkXPress would not hyphenate "christophorus" at all; if it didn't, QuarkXPress would use its standard hyphenation algorithms to break the word appropriately.

Normally, Hyphenation Zone is set to zero units. This setting specifies no hyphenation zone, so all lines can have hyphenation up to the limit of the Hyphens in a Row value.

Figure 4-43
Hyphenation zone

*Gray bar is for
reference only*

The effect of nonop-
posed interactive
hypermedia con-
tains the antitheti-
cal rhetorical
conundrum irregard-
less of the particu-
lant material

No hyphenation zone

The effect of
nonopposed
interactive hyper-
media contains the
antithetical
rhetorical conun-
drum irregardless of
the particulant

Hyphenation Zone of four picas

*"Of"and "anti-
thetical" fall in
the Hyphenation
Zone, so the fol-
lowing words
don't break.*

Justification

As we mentioned above, justifying text is the process of adding or removing space throughout a line of text to keep it flush on the left and right. You can alter several of the parameters QuarkXPress uses for determining justification by changing values found in the Edit Hyphenation & Justification dialog box. These values are controlled in the Justification Method area. It's divided into values for wordspacing, letterspacing (called "character spacing" by Quark), and Flush Zone width, plus a checkbox for Single Word Justify. Let's look at each of these.

Wordspacing. As we described above in "Character Formatting," wordspacing describes the amount of space between words. In the case of justification, it describes the spectrum of how large or small the spaces between words can be. You can specify Minimum, Optimum, and Maximum percentages of a normal space character. For example, a value of 80 percent allows a space between words that is 80 percent of a normal space. (Note that the "normal" space is the spaceband width defined by the designer of the typeface; this can vary greatly between font families.)

We almost always specify a relatively loose minimum and maximum, such as 85 percent and 140 percent, with an optimum value of 100 percent. We do this because we'd rather have Quark-XPress add wordspacing than letterspacing. However, some typefaces need tighter spacing in general; therefore, depending on the typeface, we might set Optimum to around 95 percent.

Character Spacing. You can also set Minimum, Optimum, and Maximum percentages for the spacing between characters. The percentages are based on the width of an en space (see "Formatting Characters," below). Whereas 100 percent was normal for Word Spacing, zero percent is normal for Character Spacing, and should almost always be used as the Optimum setting.

We generally don't give QuarkXPress much freedom in adjusting letterspacing because we think the type designer probably knows more about what character widths should be than we do (and certainly more than QuarkXPress does). For example, we might set Minimum to -1 percent, Maximum to five percent and Optimum to zero percent. But here, again, is an area where you need to print out a few text blocks, preferably on an imagesetter, look at the color of the type, and decide for yourself.

We also try to keep this setting tight because loose letterspacing is difficult to read. Again, we'd rather add space between words than letters any day. Some typographers who we greatly respect insist that letterspacing should always be set at "0/0/0" (that is, QuarkXPress should never change letterspacing). David's from California originally, so he's much looser than that.

Flush Zone. If you thought the Hyphenation Zone setting was obscure, you just hadn't heard about Flush Zone yet. The Flush Zone setting does one thing, but does it very well: it determines whether the last line of a paragraph gets force justified or not.

The value you type in the field is the distance from the right margin that QuarkXPress checks. If the end of the line falls into that zone, the whole line gets justified. Of course, in many instances, you can just use the Forced alignment setting, so this feature isn't something we use much.

Single Word Justify. The Single Word Justify checkbox lets you tell QuarkXPress whether you want a word that falls on a justified line by itself to be force justified (see Figure 4-44). Newspapers will probably leave this on. Art directors of fancy foreign magazines might insist that it get turned off. Personally, we don't like how the

Figure 4-44

Single Word Justify

A knock at the door!
Quickly stuffing the
long, slender, store-
bought foodstuff into a
drawer, he sprung blithe-
ly to receive his visitor,
only to be greeted by
thirty-six thousand
members of the feared
Fruit-and-Vegetablist
Majority. He knew he
was in trouble now.

A knock at the door!
Quickly stuffing the
long, slender, store-
bought foodstuff into a
drawer, he sprung blithe-
ly to receive his visitor,
only to be greeted by
thirty-six thousand
members of the feared
Fruit-and-Vegetablist
Majority. He knew he
was in trouble now.

In the example on the right, Single Word Justify is off. Note the phrase "Fruit-and-Vegetablist."

word looks either way, and we'd just as soon have the sentence rewritten, or play with other character formatting to reflow the paragraph. This feature doesn't apply to the last line of a paragraph; you still need to use the Flush Zone or force justify to get those lines to justify.

Forced Justification

Speaking of justification, when you select Forced (from the Style menu, the Measurements palette, or by pressing Command-Shift-M), QuarkXPress forces every line in a paragraph to be justified, including lines that wouldn't ordinarily extend to the margin, such as a single word on a line or a single-line paragraph.

Forced justification has basically the same effect as creating a Hyphenation and Justification setting with a very large Flush Zone. It takes a lot of steps to define and apply such an H&J setting, however, so Quark's made it easy with the Forced mode.

Note that forced justification only works with full paragraphs, and QuarkXPress defines a full paragraph as ending with a return. Therefore, if you have a text box that has only one line in it, and that line doesn't end with a return, the program won't justify it.

Setting Your Own H&J

Different paragraphs in your document may need different hyphenation and justification settings. For example, you may want each paragraph on one page to hyphenate regularly, but on another page to remain unhyphenated. Or, you might want not want headlines to hyphenate, but the rest of your document to hyphenate regularly. You can use QuarkXPress's H&Js feature to set up multiple H&J settings to be applied later at a paragraph level.

Creating an H&J Setting

When you select H&Js from the Edit menu (or by pressing Command-Option-H), the H&Js dialog box appears (see Figure 4-45). You can add, delete, edit, duplicate, or append H&J settings. The list on the left side of the dialog box shows the names of each H&J setting. A new document only contains one setting: "Standard". This is the default setting for all text paragraphs.

Figure 4-45
The H&Js for Document dialog box

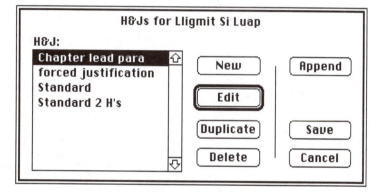

You can add a new H&J setting in two ways.

▶ Click the New button to create a new H&J setting. Change the hyphenation and justification parameters as described above, give the setting a name, and click OK. The Edit H&Js dialog box you see when you click New is a duplicate of the Standard setting.

▶ Click first on a setting (such as "Standard"), and then click the Duplicate button. You can then edit a duplicate of the setting you first clicked on. This is helpful for basing one H&J setting on another.

Deleting and Appending H&Js

To delete an H&J setting, first click on its name, then click the Delete button. If you've applied the H&J setting to any paragraph in the document, or to a style sheet, QuarkXPress prompts you for an H&J to replace it with. This is an easy way to merge several H&Js into a single one.

If you have set up H&J settings in a different document, you can append them to your current document's list by clicking the Append button, and then selecting the document to import from. If the names of any appended H&J settings are the same as settings in your open document, QuarkXPress compares them. If the settings are identical and the name is identical, it keeps everything as is. If the settings vary, you get a dialog box that asks you whether you want to rename the H&J setting you're appending, or not import it (keep existing H&J). If you choose rename, the appended H&J has an asterisk added after its name (see Figure 4-46).

Figure 4-46

Appending same-name H&Js settings

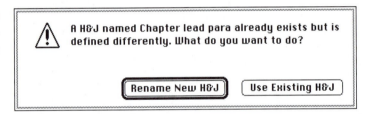

A H&J named Chapter lead para already exists but is defined differently. What do you want to do?

[Rename New H&J]   [Use Existing H&J]

There's another way to move an H&J setting from one document to another: copy and paste a text box that contains a paragraph tagged with that H&J setting. This way, you can move only selected H&J settings, rather than all at once. However, if you move a setting this way, QuarkXPress won't do the same-name check described above. If there are differences between two H&J settings with the same name, the imported settings are just ignored (same as selecting Use Existing H&J).

Applying an H&J Setting

Once you have created more than one H&J setting, you can choose which setting to use on a paragraph level by using the

Paragraph Formats dialog box. With the cursor in a paragraph, or with multiple paragraphs selected, you can select an H&J setting from the popup menu in the Paragraph Formats dialog box (see Figure 4-47). You can also set the H&J setting in a style sheet (we talk more about Style Sheets in Chapter 5, *Copy Flow*).

Figure 4-47

Appliying an H&J setting

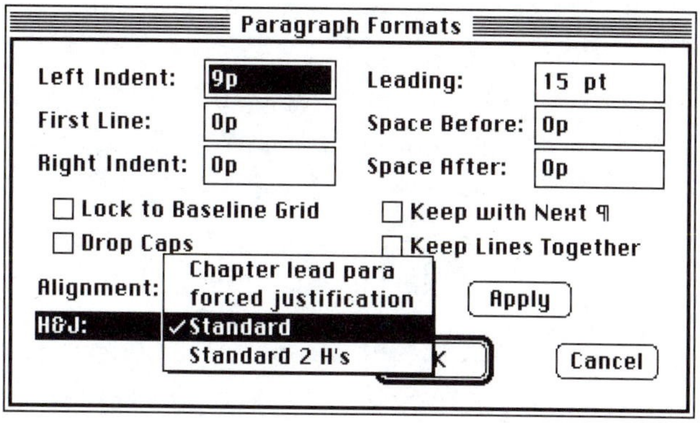

▼ ▼

Tip: Tighter and Looser H&Js. David almost always works with a minimum of three H&J settings in his document: "Standard", "Tighter", and "Looser". First, he edits the Standard H&J setting, turning on Auto Hyphenation, and tightening up (lowering the values) on the letter- and wordspacing parameters. The "Tighter" and "Looser" settings are for specialty cases. If a paragraph looks better with slightly tighter H&Js, then he applies "Tighter". If the Standard settings are too limiting for a paragraph, and having looser spacing wouldn't hurt it, then he applies "Looser".

One of the most important things to remember when fooling around with these types of settings is the color of the page. If setting a tighter H&J makes one text block look noticeably darker than the rest of the page, you may need to manually alter the paragraph rather than let the H&J settings do it for you.

▼ ▼

Tip: Find/Change H&J settings. There's just no way to find and replace H&J settings throughout a document. Or is there? Let's say someone was working on your document and applied an H&J setting called "Really Tight" to paragraphs when you weren't looking. You want to clear them out. This isn't something you need to do every day, but if you do need to do it, you can try these simple steps. (You can also use the technique described in "Tip: Overwriting Existing Styles," in Chapter 5, Copy Flow.)

1. Create a new temporary document and bring the overly tight H&J into it. The easiest way to do this is probably to apply the "Really Tight" H&J to a dummy paragraph in a dummy text box, then drag that text box over to the new dummy document (or you can use Cut and Paste). When the text box comes across to the new document, it brings the "Really Tight" H&J setting with it.

2. Delete the tight H&J from your original document. When you do this, QuarkXPress asks you which H&J setting you want to apply to paragraphs that contain the deleted H&J. In this example, when you delete "Really Tight" from the H&J list, you can replace it with "Standard," or something else. This effectively does a complete search and replace throughout the document: everywhere the "Really Tight" setting was applied, it gets changed to something else.

3. The "Really Tight" H&J setting was saved in the temporary document, so you can retrieve it by dragging that dummy text box back across (or by using Cut and Paste). Then you can close that dummy document.

A couple of caveats to this tip. First, note that this changes all the paragraphs in a document that use the offending H&J setting. There's still no way to change some and not others automatically. Also remember that this only works in versions 3.2 or later; before then, H&J settings, when deleted, were always reset to "Standard".

▼ ▼

Widow and Orphan Control

We mean no disrespect to widows and orphans, but when it comes to typesetting, we must carefully control them, stamping out their very existence when we have the chance.

If you know what we're talking about already, bear with us or skip this paragraph (or test whether you can remember which is the widow and which is the orphan). A *widow* is the last line of a paragraph that winds up all by itself at the top of a column or page. An *orphan* is the first line of a paragraph that lands all by itself at the bottom of a column or page. We sometimes also refer to a line of text comprised of only one word as an orphan. David likes the following mnemonic device: widows sounds like "windows," which are high up (top of the page), whereas orphans make him think of tiny Oliver (who was small, and thus, at the bottom of the page).

Typesetters sometimes also refer to a line of text comprised of only one word as either a widow or orphan. To avoid the confusion, in our office we prefer the word *runt*.

All typographic widows and orphans are bad, but certain kinds are really bad—for example, a widow line that consists of only one word, or even the last part of a hyphenated word. Another related typographic horror is the subhead that stands alone with its following paragraph on the next page.

Fortunately, QuarkXPress has a set of controls that can easily prevent widows and orphans from sneaking into your document. The controls are the Keep With Next ¶ and Keep Lines Together features, and you can find them in the Paragraph Formats dialog box (Command-Shift-F). Let's look at each of these.

Keep With Next ¶

The Keep With Next ¶ feature is perfect for ensuring that headings and the paragraphs that follow them are always kept together. If the paragraph is pushed onto a new column, a new page, or below an obstructing object, the heading follows right along (see Figure 4-48).

You may want to keep paragraphs together even in cases not involving subheads. For example, entries in a table or list that shouldn't be broken could each be set to Keep With Next ¶. Beginning in version 3.3, you can bind together multiple paragraphs with Keep With Next ¶ (it used to only keep two paragraphs together at a time).

Keep Lines Together

The Keep Lines Together feature is the primary control over widows and orphans for your paragraphs. When you check Keep Lines Together in the Paragraph Formats dialog box, QuarkXPress expands the dialog box to give you control parameters in this area (see Figure 4-49). Let's look at these controls one at a time.

All Lines In ¶. You can keep every line in a paragraph together by checking All Lines In ¶. For example, if a paragraph is broken onto two pages, enabling All Lines In ¶ results in that entire paragraph being pushed onto the next page to keep it together.

It's easy to confound a computer. David remembers a Star Trek episode in which a man forced a computer to commit suicide by instructing it to perform contradictory functions. Fortunately, QuarkXPress won't cause your Macintosh to blow up if you specify All Lines In ¶ for a text block larger than your column. In cases like this, QuarkXPress simply goes ahead and either breaks the paragraph, ignoring this control (in versions earlier than 3.3), or—in version 3.3 and later—pushes the whole paragraph out of the text box.

Start. You don't have to specify that all the lines in a paragraph should be kept together. Instead, you can control the number of lines that should be kept together at the beginning of the paragraph and at the end.

Figure 4-48
Keep With Next ¶

This paragraph style does not have Keep With Next ¶ set.

This paragraph style does have Keep With Next ¶ set.

The value you type in the Start field determines the minimum number of lines that QuarkXPress allows at the beginning of a paragraph. For example, specifying a two-line Start value causes paragraphs that fall at the end of a page to maintain at least two lines on the first page before it breaks. If at least two lines of that paragraph cannot be placed on the page, then the entire paragraph is pushed over to the next page.

The Start feature is set up to eliminate orphans in your documents. If you don't want any single lines sitting at the bottom of a page, you can specify a value of two for the Start control (some designers insist that even two lines alone at the bottom of a page is ugly and may want to adjust the Start value to three or greater).

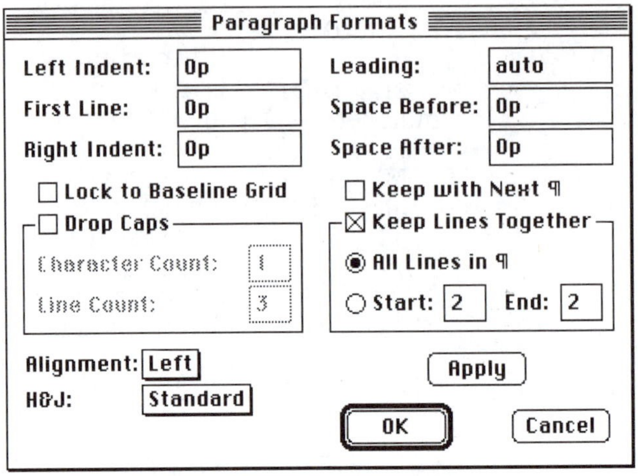

Figure 4-49

Keep Lines
Together feature

```
┌══════════════ Paragraph Formats ══════════════┐
│                                                 │
│  Left Indent:    [0p      ]   Leading:     [auto    ] │
│                                                 │
│  First Line:     [0p      ]   Space Before: [0p      ] │
│                                                 │
│  Right Indent:   [0p      ]   Space After:  [0p      ] │
│                                                 │
│     ☐ Lock to Baseline Grid    ☐ Keep with Next ¶ │
│   ┌─☐ Drop Caps───────       ┌─☒ Keep Lines Together─┐ │
│   │  Character Count:  [1]     ◉ All Lines in ¶      │ │
│   │  Line Count:       [3]     ○ Start: [2]  End: [2]│ │
│                                                 │
│  Alignment: [Left]            ( Apply )         │
│  H&J:       [Standard]    (( OK ))  ( Cancel )   │
└─────────────────────────────────────────────────┘
```

End. The value specified in the End field determines the minimum number of lines that QuarkXPress lets fall alone at the top of a column or after an obstruction. A value of two or greater rids you of unwanted widowed paragraphs (if a widow occurs, QuarkXPress "pulls" a line off the first page onto the second page or column).

▼ ▼

Tip: Other Orphan and Widow Controls. It's all very well and good to let QuarkXPress avoid widows, orphans, and runts for you, but for most documents you still need to painstakingly peruse each page, making adjustments as you go. You have many other tools to help you avoid widows and orphans. Here are some of our favorites.

▶ Adjust tracking by a very small amount over a range of text, but try to do at least a whole paragraph or a few complete lines so the color of the type doesn't vary within the paragraph. Typically, nobody can tell if you've applied -1 or -2 tracking to a paragraph or a page, but it might be enough to pull back a widow or runt.

▶ Adjust horizontal scaling by a small amount, such as 99.5 percent, or 100.5 percent.

▶ Make sure Auto Hyphenation and Auto Kern Above are on. Kerning can make a load of difference over a large area of text. Auto Hyphenation has to be changed in all of your H&Js, while Auto Kern Above affects the entire document.

▶ Change your H&J's Word Spacing to a smaller Optimal setting. If it's at 100 percent, try 98 percent.

▶ Set up different hyphenation and justification settings that you can apply to problem paragraphs. You might apply a tighter or a looser setting for a paragraph, for instance, or allow more hyphens in a row.

If none of these work for you, don't forget you can always just rewrite a sentence or two (if it's yours to rewrite). A quick rewrite of a sentence can fix up just about any problem.

Baseline Grid

In typography, the smallest change can make the biggest difference in a piece's impact. For example, look at a high-quality magazine page that has multiple columns. Chances are that each line lines up with a line in the next column. Now look at a crummy newsletter. Place a rule across a page and you'll see lines of text all over the place. What's missing is an underlying grid. You can create a grid and lock each line of text to it with QuarkXPress's Baseline Grid feature.

Each document has its own Baseline Grid setting, which is pervasive throughout every page. However, whether a block of text actually locks to that grid is determined on a paragraph level. You can set the Baseline Grid value for the document in the Typographic Preferences dialog box (from the Preferences submenu under the Edit menu, or press Command-Option-Y). You have two controls over the Baseline Grid: the Start value and the Increment value. The Start value determines where this grid begins, measured from the top of the page. Set it to start at the first baseline of your body copy.

The Increment value determines the distance from one horizontal grid line to the next. Generally, this value is the same as the leading in the majority of your body copy. For example, if your body copy has a leading of 13 points, then you should type "13pt" as your Increment value. However, sometimes it's better to use half the body copy's leading; in this example, you might use a 6.5-point grid.

Assigning a Baseline Grid

To lock a paragraph to the baseline grid that you have established, click the Baseline Grid checkbox in the Paragraph Formats dialog box (Command-Shift-F). Note that the baseline grid overrides paragraph leading. That is, if your paragraph has a leading of 10 points, when you enable Baseline Grid each line snaps to the Increment value (13 points, in the example above). If your paragraph has a leading larger than the Increment value, each line snaps to the next grid value. In other words, your leading never gets tighter, but it can get very loose. If your Increment value is 13 points and your leading is 14 points, each line snaps to the following grid line, resulting in 26-point leading (see Figure 4-50).

There is no doubt that a careful study and practice of baseline grids can make your document better looking. However, you can get the same quality from being careful with your leading and text box placement.

Showing the Grid

The baseline grid in QuarkXPress is usually invisible, so sometimes it's difficult to understand why text is sticking to weird baselines. However, you can see this underlying grid by selecting Show/Hide Baseline Grid from the View menu (or by pressing Option-F7). If you don't like the color of the baseline grid, you can set it to whatever you want in Application Preferences (Command-Option-Shift-Y).

Note that the baseline-grid guides you see when you select Show Baseline Grid act just like ruler guides. They follow the Guides control in the General Preferences dialog box (Command-

Figure 4-50
Lock to Baseline Grid

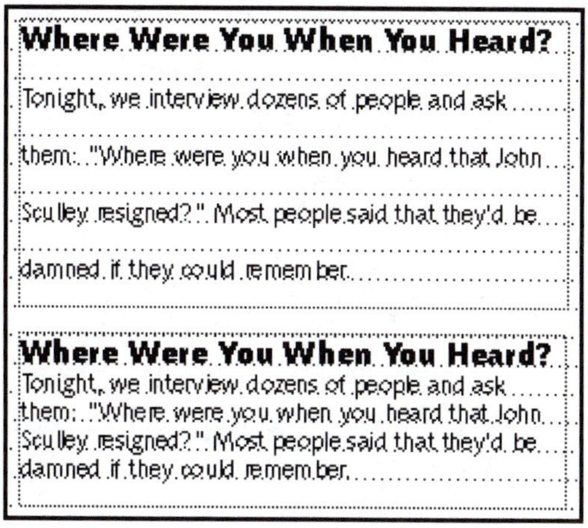

With a 13-point Baseline Grid, type with 14-point leading locked to the grid gets bumped to the next grid increment.

But 13-point leading on a 13-point grid works perfectly.

Y) as to whether they appear in front of or behind page items. Plus, when Snap to Guides is on, page items snap to the baseline grid guides (when they're showing).

Maintain Leading

If you don't use baseline grids, but still want to maintain consistent leading on your page, you might want to look closely at the Maintain Leading feature. This feature—which we usually just leave turned on in the Typographic Preferences dialog box—ensures that each line in a text box is placed according to its leading value when another object (such as a picture box or a line) obstructs the text and moves text lines around.

When Maintain Leading is turned off, two things happen. First, the line of text following an obstruction abuts the bottom of that obstruction (or its text runaround, if the runaround value is larger than zero points; we talk about text runaround in Chapter 7, *Where Text Meets Graphics*). Second, the rest of the lines of text in that text box fall on a different leading grid than do those above the obstruction. This is much easier to see than to read (or write) about, so check out Figure 4-51. This feature has no effect on paragraphs that are already set to Lock to Baseline Grid.

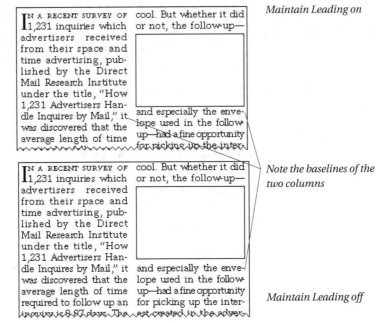

Figure 4-51
Maintain Leading

Maintain Leading on

Note the baselines of the two columns

Maintain Leading off

▼ ▼

Fine-Tuning Type

Almost everything we've talked about in this chapter has been at a character or paragraph level. Here we're going to talk about making typographic adjustments on a document level. You have control over several areas at a document level, including how superscript, subscript, superior, and small-caps characters are "built"; which words will hyphenate; and how ligatures, accents, and special spaces are dealt with. You can also create custom automatic tracking and kerning tables, and run through an automatic check for typographic problem areas.

Let's look at how you can use each of these controls in your documents.

Typographic Preferences

By selecting Typographic Preferences under the Edit menu (or pressing Command-Option-Y), you can control the way Quark-XPress handles a number of its typographic features: superscript, subscript, superior, and small caps characters, hyphenation, kerning, em spaces, baseline grid, leading, ligatures, and foreign-language accents (see Figure 4-52). Here's a run-down of all the different features in this dialog box, what they do, or where you can find information about them elsewhere in this book.

Remember that if you change items in the Typographic Preferences dialog box with no documents open, the defaults are changed for every new document you create from then on.

Figure 4-52

The Typographic Preferences dialog box

Typographic Preferences

┌─Superscript─
Offset: 33%
VScale: 100%
HScale: 100%

┌─Subscript─
Offset: 33%
VScale: 100%
HScale: 100%

┌─Baseline Grid─
Start: 0.5"
Increment: 12 pt

┌─Small Caps─
VScale: 75%
HScale: 75%

┌─Superior─
VScale: 50%
HScale: 50%

┌─Leading─
Auto Leading: +2pt
Mode: Typesetting
☒ Maintain Leading

☒ Accents for All Caps
☒ Auto Kern Above: 4 pt
Flex Space Width: 40%
Hyphenation Method: Enhanced
☒ Standard em space

☒ Ligatures
Break Above: 2
☒ Not "ffi" or "ffl"

OK   Cancel

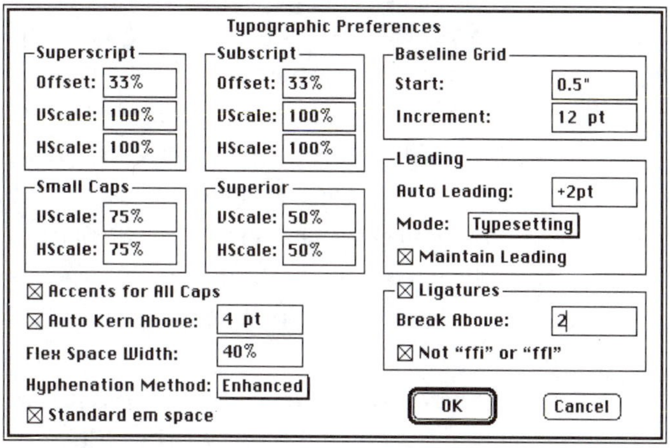

Superscript and Subscript. Few people ever bother to get into the nitty-gritty of building these type styles, but the controls are here if you ever want them. Both the Superscript and the Subscript controls are the same: Offset, VScale, and HScale. Note that if you want to make fractions, we generally recommend the Make Fraction feature of Quark's free FeaturesPlus or Thing-a-ma-bob XTension rather than fiddling with these values (see "Typographic Special Effects," later in this chapter).

▶ **Offset.** You can determine how far from the baseline your superscript or subscript characters should move by altering the Offset amount. You specify Offset as a percentage of the text size. For example, if the offset for Subscript were set to 50 percent, then a subscript character would move nine points down for 18-point type. You can specify any amount between one and 100 percent.

▶ **VScale and HScale.** These terms are short for "vertical scale" and "horizontal scale," which are responsible for how tall and wide the super- or subscript text is. The controls default to 100 percent, which we find much too large. We generally set both to a value between 70 and 80 percent, so that a superscript or subscript character doesn't stand out too much against the rest of the text. Here, too, you can set the value to anything between one and 100 percent.

Superior. You don't have to worry about the offset for superior characters because they are automatically set to be vertically flush with a capital letter in that font. So the only modifications you can make here are to the vertical and horizontal scaling of the character. This is clearly an area of aesthetic choice. We tend to like the 50-percent default that QuarkXPress gives us; though some people like to make the HScale slightly larger, such as 55 percent, so that the character has a little more weight.

Small Caps. You can also set the vertical and horizontal scaling of all small caps characters in a document. Though we think it would be nice to be able to set the characteristics of small caps on the character, paragraph, or story level, these controls are usually good enough.

There are times when adjustable (or "fake") small caps are even better than traditional (or "true") small caps, such as those found in Expert Sets. For example, we know a designer who recently specified that all small caps in a book's body copy should be 8.5 points tall. The body text was 10-point Palatino, so the company producing the templates just changed the small caps specifications to 85 percent in the horizontal direction (85 percent of 10-point type is 8.5-point type) and 90 percent in the vertical direction (making the characters slightly wider gives a slightly heavier, although stretched look). A traditional small cap would not achieve this effect; however, it would probably keep the type color in the paragraph more consistent.

Character Widths. This feature was eliminated in QuarkXPress version 3.2, which is okay with us. It's almost never used. Just for your reference, though (in case you're using an earlier version), integral character widths ignore the true widths of characters in a font, rounding them off to the nearest point. Does this seem like something we'd recommend? No. Unless you always use QuarkXPress 3.1 or earlier to print to a dot-matrix printer such as the ImageWriter II, keep the Character Widths setting to Fractional.

Accents for All Caps. This typographic refinement lets you specify whether accents appear on accented characters to which you've applied the All Caps character style. For example, when you apply the All Caps style, QuarkXPress can either keep the accents in the characters "åëìóû" or not. If it does, you get "ÅËÌÓÛ" rather than simply "AEIOU." Depending on the design of your document or what language you're working in, you may want to turn this feature on or off.

Leading Preferences. We talk about each of the Leading preferences earlier in this chapter. Leading Mode and Auto Leading are discussed in the section called "Leading." The Maintain Leading feature is discussed in the "Baseline Grid" section.

Auto Kern Above. Auto Kern Above is discussed in the "Automatic kerning" section of "Kerning and Tracking," page 227. There we told you to change this to about four or five points.

Flex Space Width. See "Formatting Characters" in the "Special Characters," page 301, for an explanation of this feature.

Hyphenation Method. We explore Hyphenation Methods a little later in the chapter, in "Tweaking Hyphenation." But we can give the rundown again now: just leave this set to Enhanced; there's almost no reason to change it to Standard.

Baseline Grid. We wrote a whole section called "Baseline Grid" earlier in this chapter; check that out.

Standard Em Space. See "Tip: Know Your Ems and Ens," in the "Kerning and Tracking" section, page 229. The low-down: turn this on and leave it on.

Ligatures. We'll discuss ligatures later in this chapter in "Special Characters," page 301. Our recommendation: turn it on.

▼ ▼

Kerning and Tracking Tables

As we noted earlier in this chapter, most fonts include built-in kerning tables of 100 to 500 pairs. However, you can modify these pairs or add your own by using Quark's Kern/Track Editor XTension (it comes with QuarkXPress, though you have an option not to install it when you update or install QuarkXPress). You must make sure that this XTension is located in the same folder as QuarkXPress 3.2, or in the XTension folder with version 3.3.

Modifying tracking and kerning tables is different from many of QuarkXPress's typographic controls in that it's font-specific. For example, if you alter the kerning table for Avant Garde, those changes are in effect whenever you use Avant Garde in any QuarkXPress document. However, the font itself isn't altered; so the changes don't show up when working in any other program.

The kerning modifications you make are stored in the XPress Preferences file and in the document itself. In version 3.0, the information was only saved in a file called XPress Data, so if you gave your document to anyone else (like a service bureau) you had to send XPress Data along with your file. Thankfully, that changed. Now, if you give the publication file to someone else, they will be prompted when they open whether or not they want to keep your preferences (such as kerning, custom framing, etc.).

If you're using QuarkPrint or XState (see Appendix D, *Resources*), you can set a preference so documents are always opened with Document Settings intact, without a prompt.

Kerning Tables

To modify a font's kerning table, choose Kerning Table Edit from the Utilities menu. This brings up the Kerning Table Edit dialog box, which presents a scrolling list of available fonts (see Figure 4-53). The list lets you choose Plain, Bold, Italic, and Bold Italic variants of each installed font.

Figure 4-53

The Kerning Table Edit dialog box

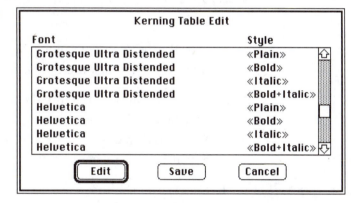

The fonts appear in styles such as "Janson Text", "B Janson Text Bold", "I Janson Text Italic", and so on. Modifying a Bold version of "B Janson Text Bold" won't help you any. Instead, choose "B Janson Text Bold" in its Plain style.

You have to edit kerning tables for one font at a time. This means that you cannot edit Palatino in its Plain style and expect all the Bold, Italic, and Bold Italic variants to be altered as well (see "Tip: Quick Kerning for Families," below).

After selecting a font from the list (you can jump through the list quickly by typing the first letter of the font name you want), click Edit to move to the Kerning Values dialog box, where you can edit an existing pair, add a new pair to the list, or delete a pair (see Figure 4-54). You can also import and export lists of these kerning pairs in a text-file format. Let's look at how each of these operations is performed.

Figure 4-54

The Kerning Values
dialog box

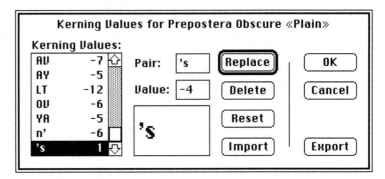

Adding a pair. You can add a new kerning pair to QuarkXPress's list in three steps.

1. Type the two characters in the Pair field. They appear in a preview window below the Value field.

2. Type a kerning amount into the Value field. This value is specified in $\frac{1}{200}$ of an em (see "Tip: Know Your Ems and Ens," earlier in this chapter). The preview updates as soon as you enter new values.

3. Click the Add button.

That's all there is to it.

Editing a pair. You can adjust kerning pairs that you have created or that come predefined in the font by clicking on a pair in the Kerning Values table, and then modifying the value in the Value field. Once you have set the value you want, click the Add button to add it back to the table.

Deleting or resetting a pair. If you don't like a kerning pair that you added, or you want to get rid of one that was built in, select the pair from the list and click the Delete button. If you have altered a kerning pair and want to reset it to its original value, click on the pair and then click the Reset button (this also works if you've deleted a pair accidentally; just retype the pair and click Reset).

Import/Export. There are those who know kerning pairs so well that they'd rather just type up a mess of them in a text-editing program and then import them all at once into QuarkXPress. You can do this by creating a text-only file within any text editor (such as Microsoft Word, Vantage, or MacWrite) in the following format.

1. Type the kerning pair (the two letters).

2. Type a space.

3. Type the kerning value in QuarkXPress's kerning units ($\frac{1}{200}$ of an em). Negative numbers mean negative kerning. Then press Return to go to the next line.

Switch back to the Kerning Values dialog box in QuarkXPress, and click the Import button to bring this text file in.

If you want to edit the kerning values that are already built into the font, you can first export those values by clicking the Export button. Then edit them and re-import them.

▼ ▼

Tip: Quick Kerning for Families. Applying kerning pairs to a number of faces can be very time-consuming and tiresome. You can speed up this process by using the Import feature to apply the same kerning tables to several typefaces. Once you've imported the kerning tables, you can go back and edit them to compensate for specifics of that typeface.

▼ ▼

Tracking Tables

Most fonts need to have tighter tracking applied to them in larger point sizes. In the past, we've just gotten used to changing the tracking for various display fonts because font vendors do not build supplemental tracking values into their fonts. Fonts come with only one tracking value: the normal letterspacing of the font as determined by the type designer. However, QuarkXPress lets you create custom tracking tables for each font you use.

A tracking table tells QuarkXPress how much tracking to apply at various sizes of a font. This, too, is part of the Kern/Track Editor XTension that comes with QuarkXPress.

Here's an example to illustrate this feature. Let's say you're creating a template for a new magazine. You've decided to use Futura Bold for your headers, which are at a number of different sizes. You know that your largest header is 60 points and should have -20 tracking, and the smallest header is 12 points and should have no tracking. Here's what you do.

1. Select Tracking Edit from the Utilities menu.

2. Choose the font that you want to edit—in this case Futura Bold—and click the Edit button. If QuarkXPress recognizes the family as "merged," then it only shows you one family name rather than breaking it down into separate fonts. For instance, it shows you one Palatino selection rather than four Palatino fonts: roman, italic, bold, and bold-italic. If the typeface is merged into one, the tracking gets applied to every font in the family. In font families that are not merged, you have to create tracking settings for each style variation. For example, one tracking table for "Bodoni", another for "B Bodoni Bold", and so on.

3. You see the Tracking Values dialog box (Figure 4-55). The vertical axis represents tracking values from -100 to 100 in increments of $\frac{1}{200}$ of an em. The horizontal axis represents type sizes from zero to 250 points; the farther to the right on the grid, the larger the type. The default setting is a horizontal bar at the zero tracking level. In other words, all point sizes start out with a zero tracking value.

4. Click on the line at the two-point size (on the far left). As you hold down the mouse button, you can see the graph values shown in the dialog box. Note that clicking on the graph places a new point on it. You can have up to four corner points on each graph. This first point we've added is the anchor at the zero tracking level.

5. Click on the line at the 60-point size and drag the graph line down to the -20 tracking level. Figure 4-55 shows these two

Figure 4-55

A tracking table graph

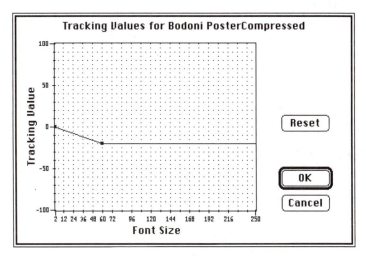

points making up the entire graph. If we saved this now, then whenever you used Futura Bold, all sizes larger than two points would have negative tracking applied to them.

6. You can add a third control handle at the 12-point type size and set it to zero tracking. Now all type larger than 12 points has tracking applied; as the text gets larger, more and more tracking is applied.

To save your changes, click OK. Then, if you're done with your tracking-table edits, click Save.

While editing a font's tracking table, you can start over by clicking the Reset button. You can always go back (even after you've saved), and click the Reset button to get the horizontal bar graph back.

Note that these tracking values are only applied to a font when Auto Kern Above is turned on. In fact, the tracking tables only apply to font sizes above the automatic-kerning limit which has been entered in the Auto Kern Above value field in the Typographic Preferences dialog box.

Like custom kerning, custom tracking is stored in your document as well as in your XPress Preferences file. So if you give one of your files with custom tracking to another person, they'll get an alert message when they open the document asking whether or not they want to retain the settings for tracking, kerning, and other customized values. If they click the Keep Settings button, the text in the file will be spaced exactly as it was on your system.

▼ ▼

Tweaking Hyphenation

Earlier in this chapter, we talked about how to create, edit, and apply H&J settings. However, there are some tools that you can fine-tune that apply throughout the whole document or application: the Hyphenation Exceptions and the Suggested Hyphenation features. Let's look briefly at each of these.

Suggested Hyphenation

The entire life's work of the Suggested Hyphenation feature is to help you figure out how QuarkXPress is going to hyphenate a word. First select Suggested Hyphenation from the Utilities menu (or press Command-H). Once you have a word selected—or have the cursor somewhere within or immediately to the right of a word—QuarkXPress shows you how it would hyphenate a word (see Figure 4-56).

QuarkXPress uses an algorithm to hyphenate words—you have a choice of algorithms: Standard and Enhanced (see "Hyphenation Method," below). Both algorithms take all sorts of things into account, including the parameters set within the Edit

Figure 4-56
Suggested
Hyphenation

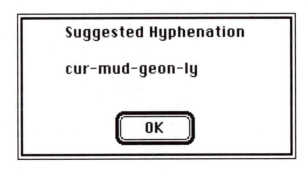

Suggested Hyphenation

cur-mud-geon-ly

OK

Hyphenation & Justification dialog box (such as the number of entries in Break Capitalized Words, Minimum Before, and so on). For example, when Minimum After is set to "3", the word "wildly" does not appear hyphenated in the Suggested Hyphenation dialog box. However, if you change Minimum After to "2" it does.

Hyphenation Method

Because QuarkXPress uses algorithms to hyphenate its words, some words don't break properly and you get strange hyphenation. The only two ways to get better hyphenation are to use Hyphenation Exceptions (see below) and get a better algorithm. Because some words, such as "academy," "appendix," and "electromechanical" were breaking incorrectly, Quark inserted into the program a new algorithm, called Enhanced. You can switch between the old way and the new way in the Typographic Preferences dialog box (Command-Option-Y).

By the way, the only reason to change Hyphenation Method from Enhanced to Standard is if you're opening old QuarkXPress (pre-3.0) documents in a newer version and the text is flowing incorrectly. Enhanced hyphenation (the default in all new versions of the program) is simply a better hyphenation algorithm.

Hyphenation Exceptions

The second method of adjusting how QuarkXPress hyphenates certain words is Hyphenation Exceptions. You can control the hyphenation fate of particular words by setting your own specific hyphenation in the Hyphenation Exceptions dialog box, which you access by selecting Hyphenation Exceptions from the Utilities menu (see Figure 4-57).

The first time you open the dialog box, the list is empty. To add a word, just type it in the available space, including hyphens where you want them. If you don't want a word to hyphenate at all, don't put any hyphens in it.

Once you've created some hyphenation exceptions, you can edit them by clicking on them, making the necessary changes,

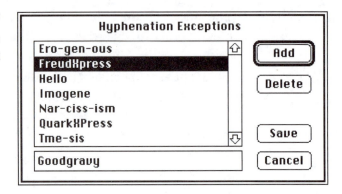

Figure 4-57
The Hyphenation
Exceptions dialog box

and then clicking the Replace button (note that the Add button changes to a Replace button in this case). You can also delete items on the list by selecting them and clicking the Delete button.

Hyphenation exceptions are stored in the XPress Preferences file, which is in the same folder as the QuarkXPress application. The changes you make are global: they affect each and every document on that machine when you create or open them. Like other information stored in the XPress Preferences file, it follows your document around onto other people's machines because it's stored inside each document as well.

▼ ▼

Tip: Watch Those Hyphens. There's nothing like giving your document a good once-over before you print it out. One of the things you want to look for is a badly hyphenated word. Remember that QuarkXPress uses an algorithm to hyphenate words rather than a look-up dictionary like some other programs. Because of this, it can hyphenate more words than other programs, but it doesn't always do it right.

For example, QuarkXPress hyphenates the word "Transeurope" as "Transeur-ope" rather than "Trans-europe." If you find these problem words, you can either change them manually (by adding discretionary hyphens), or make a global change using Hyphenation Exceptions.

▼ ▼

Line Check

David can remember the day—no, days—when his final task before taking a 530-page book to the service bureau was to scroll laboriously though his QuarkXPress files, looking for and fixing any last-minute widows, orphans, and badly hyphenated words. Of course, each fix caused a reflow of all text that followed, and so on. Would that he had Quark's free Bobzilla XTension, which adds a utility called Line Check to the Utilities menu. This handy feature automatically searches for typographically undesirable lines.

Line Check searches through a document looking for widows, orphans, automatically hyphenated words, manually hyphenated words, "loose" lines (justified lines with too much space in them), and text boxes that have overflowed. It won't fix them for you, but it sure does make cleaning up documents at the last minute a less harrowing experience.

▼ ▼

Special Characters

If you're using QuarkXPress to type letters to your mother, you probably don't need this section. If you're doing just about anything else with it, stand by.

When you look at your Macintosh keyboard, you see between 50 and 100 characters represented on the keys. What you don't see are the hundreds of special characters you can access with just a few keystrokes. In this chapter we'll look at what some of those characters are, including invisible "utility" characters, dingbats, math symbols, and special punctuation. By no means do you have to memorize most of these; instead, when you're working on documents you may want to refer back to the tables we've included.

Formatting Characters

The first set of characters we'll look at are invisible characters that are used for special formatting in your document. Several of these characters are visible when you select Show/Hide Invisibles from the View menu (or you can toggle them on and off by pressing Command-I). However, a few are not; you just have to remember where you put them. Let's take a look at what these characters are (see Table 4-7 for more information on each character and what symbol shows up on screen for those that have them).

Table 4-7

Invisible formatting characters

Name	Keystroke	Invisibles Symbol
Return	Return	¶
Soft Return	Shift-Return	↵
Tab	Tab	→
Indent here	Command-\	‖
Discretionary new line	Command-Return	
Discretionary hyphen	Command-hyphen	
Nonbreaking hyphen	Command-=	
Nonbreaking space	Command-space	
New column	Enter	↓
New box	Shift-Enter	⤓
En space	Option-space	
Nonbreaking en space	Command-Option-space	
Flex space	Option-Shift-space	
Nonbreaking flex space	Command-Option-Shift-space	
Current page number	Command-3	
Previous text box page number	Command-2	
Next text box page number	Command-4	

Return. Sometimes known as a "carriage return" or a "hard return," this is the key to press when you're at the end of a paragraph. In fact, the Return character delineates paragraphs from each other. Most people don't think of the Return key as a character, but you can see it and select it with Show/Hide Invisibles turned on.

QuarkXPress is great at wrapping characters onto the next line, so don't press Return after each line like you would on a typewriter. Also, don't press Return twice in a row to add extra space between paragraphs. Instead, use Space Before and Space After (see "Space Before and After," page 259).

Soft Return. Holding down the Shift key while pressing Return results in a soft return, often called the "new line" character. A soft return forces a new line without starting a new paragraph with all its attendant attributes: Space Before and After, First Line Indent, paragraph rules, and so on. For example, we use soft returns for tabular text or for forcing a line break in justified text. This is a character that takes some getting used to, but we recommend you play with it until you do, because it really comes in handy.

Tab. People also rarely think about tabs as separate characters, but that's just what they are. We talked about tabs in "Tabs," page 263, so we don't need to go into it now, other than to say you should really know your tabbing and never (never) use the spacebar to align columns.

Indent Here. There's a great invisible formatting character called Indent Here which you get by pressing Command-\ (backslash). This character causes the rest of the lines in a paragraph to indent to that character. We find this feature particularly useful for hanging punctuation or inline graphics, drop caps, or headings (see Figure 4-58).

In versions of QuarkXPress before 3.3, there was a bug in the Indent Here character that could mess you up: if you indented a paragraph's lines using the Indent Here feature, and the paragraph spanned two text boxes, the indents were dropped for any lines in the second text box. Fortunately, they've fixed that problem now, and all the lines of the paragraph (after the Indent Here character) get indented, no matter what text box they're in. The Indent Here character appears as a single vertical gray line when Show Invisibles is turned on.

Discretionary new line. You can place the discretionary new line character (Command-Return) within a word to suggest places to break that word if QuarkXPress needs to. It's much like a discretionary hyphen, but without the hyphen.

Figure 4-58
The Indent
Here character

How do I love thee? Let me count the ways: ¶

1) ⌃This is the first one. I can't remember quite
 ⌃what it is, but I'm sure I mean well. ¶

2) ⌃Here's the second one. Hmmm. Can't
 ⌃quite remember it, either, but now at the
 ⌃very least I know exactly how to ↵
 use the Indent Here character.

Arrows indicate positions of Indent Here characters.

How do I love thee? Well, don't you think that's a bit of an impertinent question? I mean, if I'd asked *you* that, you'd have every right to throw me out. I mean, such nerve . . .

"We, the curmudgeonly, having solemnly sworn to

For example, if you type an en dash and feel comfortable about the surrounding words breaking at a line end, you can press Command-Return after the en dash (en dashes won't break without this, though em dashes will). If QuarkXPress determines that it needs to break the line at this point, it does. If it doesn't need to break the line there, it doesn't break it (and the character, being invisible, has no other effect on your text). Figure 4-59 shows an example of this character in action. Note that this character doesn't appear, even with Show Invisibles turned on.

Discretionary hyphen. The discretionary hyphen character (Command-Hyphen) acts in the same manner as the Discretionary New Line character, but if the line needs to break at that point,

Figure 4-59

The discretionary new line character

Whilst shaving at Schenectady–on–Thames, the cat ran into the room.

En dashes in the text cause the line to break.

Whilst shaving at Schenectady–on– Thames, the cat ran into the room.

Discretionary new line character here allows the line to break differently.

QuarkXPress adds a hyphen at the break. This is the only way to suggest hyphenation for a particular instance of a word (Hyphenation Exceptions changes the hyphenation of that word throughout the document).

Discretionary hyphens also play another role in QuarkXPress. If you place a discretionary hyphen before a word, that word will never hyphenate at the end of a line. In other words, the discretionary hyphen also acts to turn hyphenation off for a single word.

▼ ▼

Tip: Watch Out for the Hyphen Key. When you need to add your own hyphenation to some text, don't go in and add regular hyphens. Why? What happens if the text reflows for some reason (like you add a word)? All of a sudden, you have hyphens scattered throughout your text (see Figure 4-60. Instead, use discretionary hyphens (Command-Hyphen). These become real hyphens if they need to, but "disappear" when they're not needed (even Find/Change ignores the character).

▼ ▼

Nonbreaking hyphen. You will probably come upon a word which should be hyphenated, but shouldn't be broken at the end of a line. A nonbreaking hyphen is placed within text by pressing Command-= (equals sign). For instance, you typically don't want figure references, such as "Figure 99-3" to break at the end of the line, so you can use the Command-= instead of a normal hyphen.

Figure 4-60
Reflowed hyphens

Greetings, and congratulations on your purchase of **KvetchWrite**, the absolutely
sensational new product for word processing, desktop publishing, object
oriented-drawing, outline processing, flowchart creation, indexing, database
man-agement, telecommunications, and prac-
tically anything else you can imagine

*Hard hyphens
used here.*

*This text should have discretionary
hyphens in it instead of hard hyphens.*

Greetings, and congratulations on your
purchase of **KvetchWrite**, the absolutely sensational new product for word pro-cessing,
desktop publishing, object oriented-drawing,
outline processing, flowchart creation, indexing,
database man-agement, telecommunications,
and prac-tically anything else you can imagine

Nonbreaking space. A nonbreaking space (Command-Space, Con-
trol-Space, or Command-5) looks just like a normal space character (and it expands and contracts as necessary in justified copy).
However, it never breaks at the end of a line. A great use of this is
in company names which include spaces, but shouldn't be broken over several lines (unless you absolutely have to).

New column and new box. If your text box contains multiple columns or is linked to other text boxes, you can use the New
Column and New Box characters to force text to jump from one to
the next. Pressing Enter forces a text jump to the next column. If
the character is placed in the last (or only) column of a text box, it
will force a jump to the next linked text box. Otherwise, pressing
Shift-Enter forces a jump to the next linked text box.

En space. As we mentioned earlier in the chapter, an en is half an
em, which—to QuarkXPress—either equals the width of two
zeros or the height of the font you're working with (depending on

how you've set up Typographic Preferences). Pressing Option-spacebar results in an en space, which acts just like a space character in justified copy. Command-Option-spacebar gives you an en space that doesn't break at the end of a line. Note that an en space is rarely the same width as an en dash, even when Standard Em Space is turned on in the Typographic Preferences dialog box.

▼ ▼

Tip: Nonbreaking Spaces on Foreign Keyboards. Apple pulled a fast one on us: in System 7.1, the keystroke Command-Option-spacebar was appropriated for switching keyboard layouts (located in the Keyboard control panel). There's no way that we can figure out for turning this off. Fortunately, Quark has added a back door: you can use the Control key instead of the Command key when typing various nonbreaking spaces (flex space, punctuation space, and en space).

▼ ▼

Flex space. When you press Option-Shift-Space you get what's called a flex space. You can specify how wide you want it to be (it flexes to your will). Also, once you specify its width, this space is fixed; it won't change width, even in justified text, unless you allow letterspacing in your H&Js. (It's treated like just another character, so if QuarkXPress adds letterspacing in justified text, it adds it to the flex space, too. The space then appears to expand.)

The control for this character's width is in the Typographic Preferences dialog box (Command-Option-Y). The percentage is based on the width of an en space. Therefore, the default value, 50 percent, is half an en space. 200 percent makes the flex space an em space. Note that when you change the width of a flex space in the Typographic Preferences dialog box, QuarkXPress changes the widths of flex spaces throughout that document.

Punctuation space. The punctuation space (Shift-Space)—sometimes called a thin space—is often confused with the flex space while typing, and looks similar. They're both fixed-width characters so they don't expand in justified type (unless you allow letterspacing in the H&J specs), but you can't specify the size of a punctuation space. Typically, it's the same width as a comma or a period, but it's really up to the font designer. Punctuation spaces are often used in European typesetting, especially when setting numbers. For example, you might type "1 024.35" (where a punctuation space is used as a delimiter rather than a comma).

Page numbers. QuarkXPress lets you use three characters to display page numbering (see Table 4-8). As we noted in Chapter 2, *Document Construction,* these are not only page-dependent, but also text box-dependent. For example, you can place a text box with the next text box character (Command-4) on top of a linked text box and the page number will register the link of the text box under it. Current text box (Command-3) is good for automatic page numbers on master pages; and previous text box (Command-2) is good for "Continued from . . ." messages.

Table 4-8 Page-numbering characters	Press . . .	To get the page number of the . . .
	Command-2	Previous text box
	Command-3	Current text box
	Command-4	Next text box

Punctuation and Symbols

A typographer shouldn't feel limited using a Macintosh. The typefaces from the major vendors (Adobe, Bitstream, Monotype, and so on) are loaded with the characters you need to create excellent type, including proper quotation marks, ligatures, and em dashes. If you aren't already a typographer, you'll want to pay careful attention to the tips and examples we show. Using some simple techniques—such as Smart Quotes and automatic ligatures—may make the difference between a piece that looks like it was desktop published (in the worst sense of the phrase) and a piece that is professional.

We can't discuss every special character that appears in a font, but we'll hit on a few of the important ones. Table 4-9 shows how to type each of these, plus a good number of additional characters.

	Name	Looks like	Press . . .
Table 4-9 Special punctuation and symbols in most fonts	Opening double quote	"	Option-[
	Closing double quote	"	Option-Shift-[
	Opening single quote	'	Option-]
	Closing single quote	'	Option-Shift-]
	Em dash	—	Option-Shift-hyphen
	En dash	–	Option-hyphen
	Ellipsis	…	Option-;
	Fraction bar	/	Option-Shift-1
	Vertical bar (pipe)	|	Shift-\
	Capital ligature AE	Æ	Option-Shift-'
	Small ligature ae	æ	Option-'
	Ligature fi	fi	Option-Shift-5
	Ligature fl	fl	Option-Shift-6
	Bullet	•	Option-8
	Copyright symbol	©	Option-G
	Registered symbol	®	Option-R
	Trademark symbol	™	Option-2
	Degree mark	°	Option-Shift-8
	Section mark	§	Option-6
	Paragraph mark	¶	Option-7
	Dagger	†	Option-T
	Cents sign	¢	Option-4

Em and en dashes. An em dash, made by pressing Option-Shift-hyphen, should be used in place of double hyphens to indicate a pause or semi-parenthetical. For example, don't do this: "Villain-ous-looking scoundrels - - eight of them"; instead, use an em dash. An em dash is named for how long it is (one em).

An en dash (Option-hyphen) should generally be used for duration and distance—replacing the word "to"—as in "August–September," "45–90 weeks long," and "the New York–Philadelphia leg of the trip." It's half as long as an em dash, so it doesn't stand out quite as much.

QuarkXPress breaks a line after an em dash when wrapping text, but not after an en dash (unless you put in a discretionary soft return after it; see "Discretionary New Line," above).

Ligatures. Ligatures are to type what diphthongs are to language. That is, they slur characters together by connecting them. While many classic typefaces would contain up to 10 ligatures, most typefaces on the Macintosh include only two basic ligatures (fi and fl) and Expert Sets from Adobe and others usually have three more (ff, ffi, and ffl). However, most people don't bother to use them, for some obscure reason. It's a pity, because they really can help a piece of text look great.

The two ligatures found in every standard typeface are the "fi" and the "fl" combinations. They can be made by pressing Command-Shift-5 and Command-Shift-6. Figure 4-61 shows these ligatures in action. However, there are problems with using these "hard coded" ligatures. First, QuarkXPress can't correctly check the spelling of, or hyphenate words that have the ligature in them. Second, words with hard-coded ligatures in them might look strange in justified text if the program adds a lot of letter spacing. Third, you can't easily edit the word (if you want to delete just the "f" or "i," you must retype both characters) or search for it in the Find/Change dialog box.

Fortunately, Quark has added a great feature that gives you the best of all worlds: automatic ligatures. QuarkXPress can automatically use the "fi" and the "fl" ligatures in place of these character pairs where needed. It doesn't actually replace "f" and "i" in the text with the "fi" symbol, but it substitutes the symbol on screen and in output as if it did.

The key here is the Ligatures popup menu in the Typographic Preferences dialog box (Command-Option-Y). This popup menu contains three items: Off, On, and "On (Not ffi Or ffl)". Off is pretty self-explanatory: QuarkXPress won't replace any characters for you. If you select On, QuarkXPress replaces every "fi" or "fl" with a ligature (as long as your typeface has those ligature characters).

Figure 4-61
Ligatures

Officially, the finalists were affluent flounder

Without ligatures

Officially, the finalists were affluent flounder

With ligatures

The third choice, "On (Not ffi Or ffl)", is for some finicky folks who think that those particular combinations should not get the ligature treatment. We disagree (see "Tip: Pull Those Ligatures Tighter," below).

The first wonderful thing about automatic ligatures is that they work at all. The second wonderful thing is that you can search for and edit character pairs that are turned into ligatures. You can click between the characters, edit one of the characters, and so on. The third wonderful thing about automatic ligatures is that words containing them pass a spelling check and hyphenate properly.

The Ligatures feature in the Typographic Preferences dialog box includes a small text field off to the right that becomes active when you turn automatic ligatures on. The number in this field tells QuarkXPress the letterspacing level above which to break the ligature apart. For example, suppose the field contains "1". If the ligature is kerned or tracked more than one unit, the ligature breaks apart, becoming two separate characters. If you change the number to "5", then QuarkXPress maintains the ligature until tracking or kerning has reached six units.

This is an important feature because you don't want two characters stuck together in "loose" text (it stands out too much). This spacing limit also applies to justified text. That is, if a text block is justified by adding space between characters, the ligatures break apart when necessary.

Note that some fonts have ligatures, but they look just like their character pair equivalents; this is especially true in sans serif typefaces, such as Helvetica. Also some typefaces don't have built-in ligatures, and others have them but QuarkXPress doesn't "see" them (this is especially true with some older Type 3 fonts). So the system's not foolproof, but it's still pretty good.

▼ ▼

Tip: Pull Those Ligatures Tighter. Ligatures generally make pages nicer looking, and automatic ligatures generally make life nicer to live. There are still two instances (actually there are many more, but we'll just focus on two here) where you need to look carefully at your ligatures: the "ffi" and the "ffl."

As we mentioned above, you can turn automatic ligatures off for these character combinations, but we really can't see why you'd want to do this. Instead, we sometimes like to go in and pull the two "f's" slightly tighter together, often so that the crossbars touch (see Figure 4-62). This gives the impression of a three-character ligature. However, many typefaces aren't malleable enough to do this. Either you have to kern in so tightly that the letterspacing looks odd, or you end up with the serif of the first "f" bumping into the second "f," and the whole thing looks even uglier than before. Therefore, in this tip, as in so many others, we urge you to take care with your typography; look closely, and keep your fingers on the Command-Z (Undo) keystroke.

Figure 4-62
The ffi and ffl ligatures

The Affluent Officer
The Affluent Officer

Another option for true typophiles is to purchase the Expert Set that accompanies some of the more extensive font families, such as Adobe Minion, Adobe Garamond, and Adobe Caslon. The Expert Sets have small caps, oldstyle figures, and the additional ligatures ff, ffi, and ffl. Unfortunately, these can't be automatically replaced—yet. When Apple introduces the Line-Layout Manager, which will be part of QuickDraw GX, typefaces may be modified to include all five basic ligatures as part of a larger character set.

▼ ▼

Quotation Marks. The first tip-off that someone is green behind the ears in desktop publishing is his or her use of straight quotes instead of proper "printer's quotes." Straight quotes, which is what you get when you press the ' and " keys, should be used for notation of measurements (inches and feet) or for special typographic effect (some fonts' straight quotes look great in headline type). Printer's quotes, or curly quotes, should be used for English/American quotations. Quark has made it much easier to use curly quotes with two features—Convert Quotes and Smart Quotes.

The Convert Quotes checkbox in the Get Text dialog box lets you convert all straight quotes into proper curly quotes when you import text. Second, you can turn on Smart Quotes in the Application Preferences dialog box. This automatically converts quotes as you type them. We always leave both of these on, unless we specifically need to use straight quotes (see "Tip: Getting Your Quotes Straight," below).

▼ ▼

Tip: Getting Your Quotes Straight. When Smart Quotes is turned on, every time you type a single or double quote it comes out curly. QuarkXPress is replacing the straight quote with the Option-[or -] and the Shift-Option-[or -] keys behind the scenes. However, if you really need a straight quote someplace, you can get it by pressing Control-' or Control-" (that's Control, *not* Command). This keystroke does just the opposite when Smart Quotes is turned off; then you get curly quotes. Unfortunately, this feature doesn't work with some foreign-language keyboard layouts (we've even had complaints about the UK keyboard not working).

▼ ▼

Registration, Copyright, and Trademark. The registration, copyright and trademark characters are found by pressing Option-R, Option-G, and Option-2 keys. We have only one thing to say about using these characters: be careful with your sizing and positioning. We recommend immediately assigning the superior type style to the character, then determining whether it should be kerned or not (see Figure 4-63).

Figure 4-63

Special symbols

KvetchWrite™ is a product of No Accounting For Taste, Eh?®
Documentation © Copyright 1990 No Class Productions.

Trademark and registration characters re-done as superior characters:

KvetchWrite!™ is a product of No Accounting For Taste, Eh?®
Documentation © Copyright 1990 No Class Productions.

Registration mark kerned +12 to give it a little room to breathe.

Result without kerning: Eh?®

▼ ▼

Tip: Key Caps and PopChar. Anyone who can remember every character in a font, including all special symbols and characters, is no one to borrow money from. We can never remember most of the characters we need, so we use Key Caps. Key Caps comes free with your system—it's installed under the Apple menu—and shows you a keyboard map for every character in any font you choose (see Figure 4-64).

To use Key Caps, select it from the Apple menu, then select the font you want to see from the Key Caps menu. When you hold down the Shift key, you see the map of all the uppercase characters. If you hold down the Option key, you see the Option characters, and so on.

Another little utility that does the same thing better is called PopChar (see Figure 4-65). Written by Günther Blaschek (one of our favorite names), PopChar takes a couple steps off the process

Figure 4-64

Key Caps

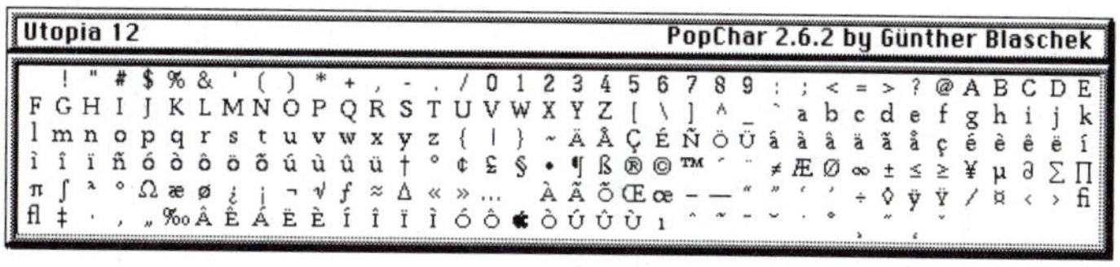

Figure 4-65

PopChar utility

of finding a character. When it's loaded in your system, you only have to click in a corner of your screen and you can immediately see the whole character set (and how to type the characters) for whatever typeface you're working in. We use it all the time. It's on the Quark Goodies Disk from Peachpit Press (see the tear-out coupon in the back of the book).

▼ ▼

Foreign Punctuation and Accents

Working in a foreign language is really a trip. Foreign languages have a different word for everything. Many foreign languages, like French and Spanish, contain accented characters that are built into fonts from the major type vendors. For example, you can type *élève* without switching to some obscure font. Table 4-10 lists the characters that you would most likely use in a foreign language.

Many people don't fully understand how to type these characters. Several of them aren't as easy as just pressing a key, or even a key with Option or Shift held down. For example, "é" is typed by first typing Option-E, then typing the letter "e." It's a two-keystroke deal. If you don't want the hassle of remembering the characters, you might want to use PopChar for this, too (see "Tip: Key Caps and PopChar," above).

▼ ▼

Tip: Get it Right for Overseas. We, in the United States, grew up with the ethnocentric viewpoint that the way we write and typeset is the way everybody does it. Not so. For example, double quotation marks are used in America where single quotation marks are used in Britain. In other European countries, our quotation marks are replaced with guillemets («, », ‹, and ›—Option-\ and Shift-Option-\, and Shift-Option-3 and Shift-Option-4; note that Smart

Name	Looks like	Keys to press
Table 4-10 Foreign accents and punctuation		
Left double guillemet	«	Option-\
Right double guillemet	»	Option-Shift-\
Left single guillemet	‹	Option-Shift-3
Right single guillemet	›	Option-Shift-4
Base double quote	„	Option-Shift-W
Base single quote	‚	Option-Shift-0
Question mark down	¿	Option-Shift-?
Exclamation point down	¡	Option-1
Acute vowel	áéíóúÁÉÍÓÚ	Option-E, then vowel
Umlaut vowel	äëïöüÄËÏÖÜ	Option-U, then vowel
Grave vowel	àèìòùÀÈÌÒÙ	Option-`, then vowel
Circumflex vowel	âêîôûÂÊÎÔÛ	Option-I, then vowel
Cedilla C	Ç	Option-Shift-C
Cedilla c	ç	Option-C
Capital slashed O	Ø	Option-Shift-O
Small slashed o	ø	Option-O
Double s (German)	ß	Option-S
Dotless i	ı	Option-Shift-B
Tilde	˜	Option-Shift-M
Tilde N	Ñ	Option-N, then Shift-N
Tilde n	ñ	Option-N, then N
Circumflex	ˆ	Option-Shift-N
Macron	¯	Option-Shift-comma
Breve	˘	Option-Shift-period
Ring accent	°	Option-K
Ring a	å	Option-A
Ring A	Å	Option-Shift-A
Dot accent	·	Option-H
Pound sterling	£	Option-3
Yen	¥	Option-Y

Quotes lets you set these to appear automatically when you press the quote keys). The Spanish language sets a question or an exclamation point at both the beginning (upside down, keyed with Option-Shift-/ or Option-Shift-1) and at the end of sentences. Figure 4-66 shows examples of each of these styles.

Figure 4-66
Foreign punctuation

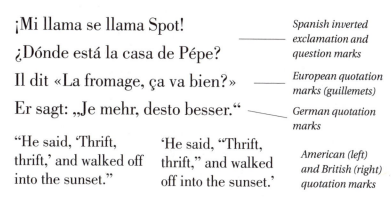

¡Mi llama se llama Spot!

¿Dónde está la casa de Pépe?

Il dit «La fromage, ça va bien?»

Er sagt: „Je mehr, desto besser."

Spanish inverted exclamation and question marks

European quotation marks (guillemets)

German quotation marks

"He said, 'Thrift, thrift,' and walked off into the sunset."

'He said, "Thrift, thrift," and walked off into the sunset.'

American (left) and British (right) quotation marks

If you do a lot of foreign-language work, and especially work that has multiple languages in the same document, you should check out Quark Passport—the multilingual version of Quark-XPress. This program lets you set a language as a paragraph attribute, and will then check spelling and hyphenate that language properly. It comes with about 12 languages built in. (You may run into some difficulties exchanging files in those languages with Passport if you don't have all of the versions synchronized.)

Other languages, such as Hebrew, Farsi, Russian, and Greek, must be typed using a non-Roman font specific to that language, and may require specialized software. QuarkXPress is presently available in 14 languages, including Japanese and German. (In case you're curious, Passport does not include Japanese.)

▼ ▼

Math Symbols and the Symbol Font

QuarkXPress is the wrong program in which to produce a mathematics textbook. You can use utilities such as Expressionist or MacΣqn to help create equations, but they're not set up for doing heavy-duty math typesetting as in FrameMaker. Nonetheless, you can still do a pretty good job in QuarkXPress, as long as you don't have to produce 2,000 different equations in a document.

The keys to doing a good job are the use of the correct symbols and good typography. Most typefaces come with a wide variety of built-in math symbols. Table 4-11 provides a list of the most common of these and how to type them.

Table 4-11

Commonly used math symbols found in most fonts

Name	Looks like	In most fonts	Symbol font
Division	÷	Option-/	Option-Shift-P
Plus or minus	±	Option-Shift-=	Option-Shift-=
Greater or equal	≥	Option-period	Option-period
Lesser or equal	≤	Option-comma	Option-3
Approximate equal	≈	Option-X	Option-9
Not equal	≠	Option-=	Option-P
Infinity	∞	Option-5	Option-8
Partial differential	∂	Option-D	Option-D
Integral	∫	Option-B	Option-Shift-;
Florin	ƒ	Option-F	Option-7
Capital omega	Ω	Option-Z	Shift-W
Capital delta	Δ	Option-J	Shift-D
Product	Π	Option-Shift-P	Shift-P
Summation	Σ	Option-W	Shift-S
Pi	π	Option-P	P
Radical	√	Option-V	Option-/

If you want to typeset an equation of any complexity (such as multiplication), you will quickly want to learn about the Symbol font. Symbol is a Greek and math font that comes with your Macintosh system. It includes such characters as a multiplication sign (×), which you can create by pressing Option-Y. Use Key Caps or PopChar, mentioned earlier, to examine the other characters in this typeface. Even better are pi fonts, such as Universal News with Commercial Pi, which gives you better spacing and more flexible character weights. You can also purchase specialized math pi fonts, like Lucida Math.

▼ ▼

Tip: One-Stroke, One-Character Font Change. QuarkXPress has so many keystrokes and shortcuts that we can never remember them all. Here are two that David always forgets about: pressing Command-Shift-Q sets the next character you type in the Symbol font, while pressing Command-Shift-Z sets it in Zapf Dingbats. After you type the character, QuarkXPress automatically reverts to the typeface you were in. If you have one or more characters already selected when you press these keystrokes, QuarkXPress simply changes them to the desired font.

▼ ▼

Dingbats

Letters, numbers, and symbols do not a funky design make. Oft-times you need dingbats. Dingbats, or pi fonts, are collections of interesting and useful shapes, pictures, graphics, and so on. The most popular dingbat font by far on the Macintosh is Zapf Dingbats—because it comes with most printers. Table 4-12 shows a listing of about a third of the Zapf Dingbats characters and how to type them. The other two-thirds are mostly variations on what is shown here.

Other examples of dingbat or pi fonts are Carta, Bundesbahn Pi, and Adobe Woodtype Ornaments (see Figure 4-67 for a few examples of various pi faces).

Figure 4-67
Some other dingbats

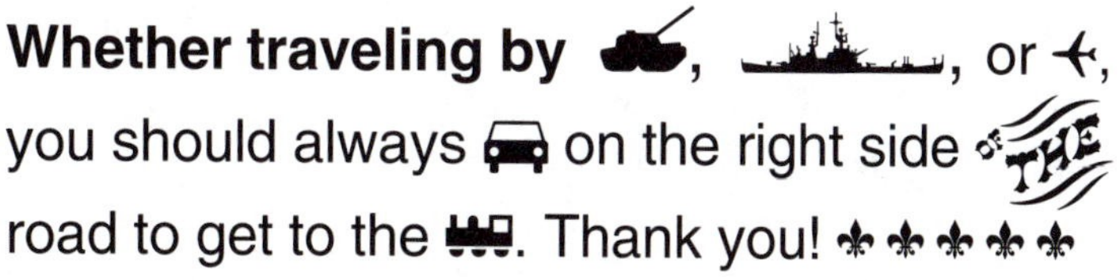

Symbols from Carta, Bundesbahn Pi, and Adobe Woodtype Ornaments.

You can use these fonts for fun, but you'll more likely want to use them in a very functional way. Most people use them for bullets (those round Option-8 bullets get tiring to look at pretty quickly). David's favorite for this function is the lowercase "v" from Zapf Dingbats (❖).

Table 4-12

Useful Zapf Dingbats characters

Press Command-Shift-Z followed by the key or keystroke at right. Or, select a range of characters already typed and then press Command-Shift-Z.

Name	Looks like	Key or keystroke
Shadow ballot box up	❏	O
Shadow ballot box down	❐	P
3D ballot box up	❏	Q
3D ballot box down	❐	R
Filled ballot box	■	N
Hollow ballot box	□	N (apply Outline style)
Opening great quote	"	Shift-]
Closing great quote	"	Option-N
Opening single great quote	'	Shift-[
Closing single great quote	'	Shift-\
Great bullet	●	L
Great hollow bullet	○	L (apply Outline style)
Great shadow bullet	◗	M
Filled arrowhead	➤	Option-Shift-E
Right arrow	→	Option-]
Fat right arrow	➡	Option-Shift-U
3D right arrow	⇨	Option-Shift-I
Speeding right arrow	⇢	Option-Shift-7
Triangle up	▲	S
Triangle down	▼	T
Love leaf	❧	Option-7
X-mark	✗	8
Check-mark	✔	4
J'accuse	☞	Shift-=
Victory	✌	Comma
Scissors	✂	Shift-4
Pencil straight	✏	/
Pen nib	✒	1
Telephone	☎	Shift-5
Cross	✚	Shift-;
Star	★	Shift-H
Big asterisk	✻	Shift-Z
Circled sun	☢	B
Snowflake	❄	D

You can also use these characters as graphics on your page (see Figure 4-68). Don't forget you can shade and color type to act as a background or foreground graphic.

The Sunflower Institute

Dear Alumni/ae,

As you know, times are tough and sunflowers don't grow on trees. Let me rephrase that. They

Tip: Ballot Boxes and Custom Dingbats. Many people create blank "ballot" boxes by typing a Zapf Dingbats lowercase "n" and setting it to outline style, or by buying a separate font package such as Caseys' Page Mill's Bullets and Boxes. The problem with the first method is that imagesetting the outline often results in a hairline that is too thin to reproduce well. The only problem with the second method is that it costs something to buy it (the package itself is great, though). Nonetheless, there's a better option.

1. Create a picture box of any size.

2. Give the picture box a border (Command-B); we like to use .5 points.

3. Select the Item tool and cut the box (Command-C).

4. Using the Content tool, select where in the text you want the box to go, and then paste the box in (Command-V).

5. Resize it to suit your needs.

Not only can you make box characters this way, but any polygon, or anything else you can create within the application. Also, by importing a graphic into the picture box before you cut and paste it, you can create your own custom dingbats (Figure 4-69).

And re*mem*ber! 👤 The *"cornier"* your Presentation, the less likely it is to be *Taken Seriously!*

Custom dingbat created by placing an EPS (Encapsulated PostScript) file within an anchored picture box. Picture box has been resized and its baseline shifted until the block of text looked appropriately corny.

☐ *Ballot box made with an outlined Zapf Dingbat ("n")*

☐ *Ballot box made with an anchored (square) picture box having a half-point (.5) frame.*

▼ ▼

Typographic Special Effects

QuarkXPress is not a typographic special-effects program, such as TypeStyler or LetraStudio. But this doesn't mean that it can't give you the power to create many exciting effects with your type. In this section, we're going to look at a few of the possibilities, like drop caps, rotated text, shadowed type, and type as a picture. But we can't cover everything that you can do. This, especially, is an area in which you have to play around.

Chapter 7, *Where Text Meets Graphics,* covers a few other special effects, such as text runaround, that you can create using QuarkXPress.

Fractions

Desktop publishing isn't so young that it doesn't have some hallowed traditions. One of the most hallowed is groaning in pain at the mention of creating fractions. But, as with most traditions, you shouldn't let that frighten you off. The "fraction problem" in desktop publishing arises because most Macintosh fonts do not come with prebuilt fraction characters.

You can create your own fractions in a number of ways. Let's take a look at each of these, and discuss why you'd want to use some and avoid others.

Pseudo-fractions. You can create pseudo-fractions by typing in numbers separated by a slash. Let's be frank: they look awful, and are considered bad form. But in some cases, such as simple word-processed documents or manuscript text, they're perfectly acceptable. Opinion varies on how best to type these characters, especially when you have a fraction following a number. We generally like to add a hyphen between a number and its fraction. For example, one and one-half would be typed "1-1/2."

Don't try to use the "fraction bar" character (Option-Shift-1) for this kind of fraction. It almost always bumps into the second number and looks like *shmatta* (like junk).

Proper fractions. You can create proper fractions—such as ½, ¾, or ²⁹⁄₃₂—by applying specific character-level formatting to each character in the fraction. The following example shows you how.

1. Type the pseudo-fraction; for example, "3/8". In this case, you should use the fraction bar character (Option-Shift-1) rather than the normal slash character.

2. Select the numerator—in this case, the "3"—and set it to Superior.

3. Select the denominator—in this case, the "8"—and change its size to match the numerator. You can figure out what this size is by examining the Superior settings in the Typographic Preferences dialog box. For example, at the default Superior settings of 50 percent, you would need to change a 12-point denominator to six points.

4. Kern the fractions as desired. The spaces between the numerator and the fraction bar, and the fraction bar and the denominator almost always need to be tightened up.

You can change the size of the numerator by changing the Superior settings in the Typographic Preferences dialog box. But remember to reset your denominator to the proper point size. Differently sized numbers in a fraction look very weird.

When a proper fraction follows a number, you probably don't want any sort of hyphen or even a space (see Figure 4-70).

Figure 4-70

Fractions

They tell me getting there is 3/8 of the fun.

A pseudo-fraction

I went to see *8-1/2* but only stayed for ¾ of it.

A pseudo-fraction, followed by one created via the method noted in the text (see "Proper Fractions")

About ¼ of the time, I won't even give him a dime.

A fraction generated with Make Fraction (from the free FeaturesPlus or Thing-a-ma-bob XTension) plus some manual kerning within the fraction.

Fractions via an XTension. Quark's free FeaturesPlus and Thing-a-ma-bob XTension contain a feature that creates fractions for you (Features Plus was made for version 3.1, but it works fine in version 3.2, in 3.3, you should use Thing-a-ma-Bob). It essentially acts as a macro, performing the procedure outlined above. To let QuarkXPress make the fraction for you, follow these steps.

1. Type the fraction as two numbers separated by a slash.

2. Place the cursor in the fraction or just to the right of it.

3. Select Make Fraction from the Type Style submenu (under the Style menu)

Even though this feature is under the Style menu, Make Fraction is not really a character attribute; it's just a shortcut. Therefore, there's no way to Undo the fraction.

Stacked fractions. QuarkXPress also lets you create stacked fractions, such as $\frac{1}{4}$ and $\frac{3}{4}$. Here's a quick formula for making them.

1. Type the numerator and denominator, separated by an underline (Shift-Hyphen).

2. Change the point size of these three characters to 40 or 45 percent of original size. For example, 12-point type gets changed to five-point type.

3. Select the numerator and the underline, and apply a baseline shift equal to the point size.

4. Leave the numerator and underline highlighted and apply -90 units of tracking.

5. At your discretion, apply extra kerning between the characters to achieve a more precise look. You may want to zoom to 400 percent or print a test sheet.

Chances are, you'll need to adjust the numbers we provide for different typefaces and number combinations. Note that this method of creating stacked fractions only works when both numbers are single digits.

Expert Set fonts. Adobe and other companies have released Expert Sets that complement some of their normal font packages, such as Minion and Minion Expert. The Expert Sets contain some prebuilt fractions and a full set of correctly drawn and scaled super- and subscript numerals, as well as the correct fraction bar for use with them. This really is the best way to make fractions, and it's what we used throughout this book. (The Expert Set also contains oldstyle numerals, small capitals, and other special symbols and ligatures.) However, most fonts don't have Expert Sets; check with the font vendor for specifics.

Fonts and utilities. Some fonts, such as EmDash's Hfraction, consist entirely of fractions. Usually, these fonts are set in Times or Helvetica, so unless you're using those typefaces, they won't perfectly match your text.

You can also create your own fraction fonts with a utility program such as FontMonger, Fontographer, or FontStudio. This method allows you to use any font that you're already using to generate custom fraction characters. See Robin Williams's book, *How To Boss Your Fonts Around*, for details on creating a custom font.

Initial Caps

Initial Caps are enlarged characters at the start of a paragraph that lend a dramatic effect to chapter or section openings. There are four basic types of initial caps: raised, dropped, hanging, and contoured. Each of these styles is made considerably easier to create with the automatic drop caps feature and the Indent Here character (Command-\).

Let's look at several initial caps and how they are made.

Standard raised caps. Raised caps can be created by enlarging the first letter of the paragraph (see Figure 4-71). It's important to use absolute leading when creating standard raised caps. If you don't, the first paragraph's leading gets thrown way off.

Figure 4-71
Standard raised caps

Unaccustomed as I am to public speaking . . . but that never did prevent me from running off endlessly at the mouth . . . you, sir! Stop that hideous snoring! But I digress . . .

14-point copy with a 30-point initial capital.

Hung raised caps. A spin-off of the standard raised cap is the hung raised cap (see Figure 4-72). You can hang the letter "off the side of the column" by placing an Indent Here character after it or creating a hanging indent with indents and tabs. The rest of the text block's lines all indent up to that point.

Figure 4-72
Hung raised caps

Unaccustomed as I am to public speaking . . . but that never did prevent me from running off endlessly at the mouth . . . you, sir! Stop that hideous snoring! But I digress . . .

14-point copy with a 30-point capital. Indent Here character has been placed to the immediate right of the raised cap.

Standard drop caps. The Drop Caps control is located in the Paragraph Formats dialog box (see Figure 4-73). To create a drop cap in a paragraph, place the text cursor in the paragraph, bring up Paragraph Formats, and turn on Drop Caps. You can then modify two parameters for this feature: Character Count and Line Count.

Figure 4-73
Standard drop caps

L et it never be said that the Koala tea of Moishe is not strained. Should this be said, it is entirely possible that the very fabric of civilization would fall utterly into the hands of the

Drops Caps is set in the Paragraph Formats dialog box. Note that the font size is replaced with a percentage.

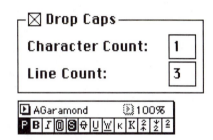

The character count is the number of characters made to drop. The line count is the number of lines that they drop. For example, specifying "3" in Character Count and "4" in Line Count makes the first three characters of the paragraph large enough to drop four lines down. You don't have to worry about sizing the character, aligning it, or specifying the space between the drop cap and the rest of the text. In this example, the baseline of the drop cap aligns with the fourth line down, and the ascent of the drop cap aligns with the first line's ascent. Note that some fonts have ascents that arc taller than their capital letters. This may make the process slightly more difficult, depending on what effect you're trying to achieve.

▼ ▼

Tip: Adjusting Space After Caps. We often find that the space between the initial cap and the text that's flowing around it is too small. People have tried all sorts of weird workarounds for moving the two apart, but we prefer the simple method: add kerning between the drop cap and the character after it. The more kerning you add, the farther away the flow-around text is set.

▼ ▼

Hanging drop caps. You can make these in the same way as the hanging raised caps: place an Indent Here character (Command-\) directly after the dropped character (see Figure 4-74). You can adjust the spacing between the drop cap and the following text by adjusting the kerning value between the drop cap and the next character (in this case, the Indent Here character).

Figure 4-74
Hanging drop caps

Three-line drop cap with Indent Here character placed here, creating hanging drop cap.

L et it never be said that the Koala tea of Moishe is not strained. Should this be said, it is entirely possible that the very fabric of civilization would fall utterly into the hands of

Scaled drop caps. You have one hidden feature on drop cap characters and drop cap characters only: percentage scaling. After creating a standard drop cap (as described above), you can select the drop cap character(s) and change the point size to a percentage of the original drop-cap size. For example, Figure 4-75 shows

Figure 4-75
Scaled drop caps

L et it never be said that the Koala tea of Moishe is not strained. Should this be said, it is entirely possible that the very fabric of civilization would fall utterly into the hands of its

The same, with the capital "L" enlarged to 150 percent of its normal size:

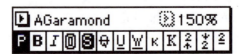

The Measurements palette reflects the change—again, as a percentage of the normal drop-cap size (not in points).

a paragraph first with a standard drop cap, and then with the drop cap scaled to 150 percent. You can change the percentage of the drop cap character(s) to anything you want, and the baseline will always align with the Line Count line.

Anchored raised caps. Another way of making a raised cap is to create it in a separate text box, then anchor that box to the beginning of the paragraph (we discuss anchored text and picture boxes in Chapter 7, *Where Text Meets Graphics*). The raised cap in Figure 4-76 is actually a separate text box containing a large capital letter on a tinted background. The character is centered horizontally and vertically within the frame. We also applied other formatting to the initial cap, such as kerning and baseline shift.

Figure 4-76
Anchored raised caps

e fully recognize that the message "Now formatting your hard disk. Have an *exceedingly* nice day," appearing during the **KvetchPaint** installation, is a bit alarming. Rest assured that it is a harmless prank by one of our programmers—who is, you can also rest assured, no longer with us. As soon as we can break the encryption he used, we

Anchored drop caps. After creating an anchored raised cap, you can make it drop by selecting Ascent in the Anchored Text Box Specifications dialog box (select the anchored box and press Command-M, or double-click on the anchored box). Figure 4-77 shows an example of this, along with an anchored drop cap which has been hung.

Wraparound dropped caps. When using letters such as "W" or "A" you may want to wrap the paragraph text around the letter (see

Figure 4-77

Anchored drop caps

e fully recognize that the message "Now formatting your hard disk. Have a *very* nice day," appearing during the **Kvetch-Paint** installation, is a bit alarming. Rest assured that it is a harmless prank by one of our programmers—who is, you can also rest assured, no longer with us. As soon as we can break the encryption he

Figure 4-78). Using the Drop Cap option in Formats and the non-breaking space, you can easily wrap and rewrap text without having to draw or anchor text boxes.

1. Set Drop Caps under Paragraph Formats (in this example, it's set to one character, three lines deep).

2. Move the cursor to a point immediately following the drop cap. You'll notice the insertion cursor stays the same size as the drop cap.

3. Use kerning to pull or push the copy to the left. All of the lines to the right are kerned in.

4. Use a combination of kerning and nonbreaking spaces to move the lines to be wrapped left or right as needed.

This is only one of many variations on a theme for creating wraparound drop caps. Another is to use an initial cap brought in from an illustration program (as any sort of graphic file). You can then use QuarkXPress's automatic runaround or manual run-around features to control the text runaround (we discuss text runaround in detail in Chapter 7, *Where Text Meets Graphics*).

Figure 4-78

Wrapping drop caps without using anchored boxes

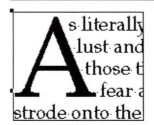

You can make a text wrap around a capital by inserting nonbreaking spaces and kerning closer or farther apart as necessary.

Illuminated caps. We've just seen the use of graphics "disguised" as text. Figure 4-79 shows a graphic as text, but with no disguise at all. This fancy illuminated capital letter is an EPS image from a clip-art library.

Figure 4-79

Illuminated caps

Salivating in public is not only discouraged, but is, in fact, morally wrong. In fact, I think I could go so far as to say that the entire salivation process is, on occasion, a work of the devil. For example, when I see a chocolate sundæ, I know I should not eat it. My rational mind takes a very definite stand on that point. However, my salivary glands pay no mind.

Mixed-font caps. We've already cautioned you about using too many fonts on a page. But if there was ever a time to break the rules, it's with initial caps (see Figure 4-80). If you want your initial caps in a different font, simply change the font for those characters. However, note that when you change the initial cap's typeface, the character may not align properly with the rest of the text.

Figure 4-80

Mixed font initial caps

Zapf Chancery   *Adobe Garamond*

*S*conce, call you it? So you would leave battering, so I would rather have it a head. And you use these blows long, I must get a sconce for my head, and ensconce it too, or else I shall seek my wit in my shoulders. But, I pray, sir, why am I beaten?

Multiple initial caps. Character Count in the Drop Caps feature lets you drop up to eight letters in your paragraph. So a drop cap could be a drop word, if you like (see Figure 4-81).

Figure 4-81

Multiple initial caps

Five-character drop cap. Horizontal scaling of 75%; font size changed from 100% to 87.5%

Comma scaled down to 75% of normal font size, (it's less obtrusive that way).

What, gone in chafing, and clapped to the doors? Now I am every way shut out for a very bench-whistler; neither shall I have entertainment here or at home. I were best to go try some other friends.

Playing with initial caps. Like we said, initial caps are great opportunities to play and come up with creative ideas. Can you recreate the initial cap examples in Figure 4-82?

Figure 4-82

More initial caps

A POOR MAN IS OBSERVED STARING in admiration at the large and ornate tombstone of the richest man in town. he shakes his head slowly and mutters, "Now, that's what I call living!"

Of course, the last time I went to one of those big banquets, I lost my wallet. I went up to the microphone and announced "Ladies and gentlemen, I've lost my wallet, with eight hundred dollars in it. Whoever finds it will get a reward of fifty dollars!"

Then a voice from the back of the room yelled out, "I'll give seventy-five!"

Shadow Type Alternatives

Applying the Shadow type style to any range of selected type creates a generic shadow that cannot be customized. For example, you cannot change its thickness, shade, or offset. Although this is a perfectly nice shadow effect and is useful for many purposes, you may occasionally want more control over your shadows.

You can have total control over your shadows by using duplicate text boxes. Here's one way to do it (see Figure 4-83).

1. Create a text box with some solid black text in it.

2. Duplicate the text box (Command-D).

3. Select the text within the second text box and modify it (change its color or tint, etc.).

4. Send the second text box to the back (choose Send to Back in the Item menu).

Make sure that the topmost boxes have their Runaround and Background Color set to "None". You can then move the second text box around until you have it placed where you want it. Remember that you can click through the top text box by clicking with Command-Option-Shift held down. You might also want to group the two text boxes together in order to move them as if they were one item.

Figure 4-83
Alternative shadows

Introducing

"You've tried the best, now try the rest!"

Pricing

Quark's free FeaturesPlus and Thing-a-ma-Bob XTensions let you automate one other common text formatting function: pricing (use Thing-a-ma-Bob for version 3.3). It's simple to make a number into a "price" (see Figure 4-84). Just type the value, place the cursor within the number or just to the right of it, then select Make Price from the Type Style submenu under the Style menu.

You have several options for how QuarkXPress formats the character, including whether it should take out any decimal point you've included and whether the numbers after the decimal point (the "cents") should have an underline or not. These controls are located in the Fraction/Price Preferences dialog box, under the Edit menu.

Figure 4-84

Make Price example and preferences

"Okay, look, I'll give you $4.74 for it."
"How much did you say? I don't understand."
"I meant 4^{\underline{74}}$."
"Oh! Sure. It's a deal."

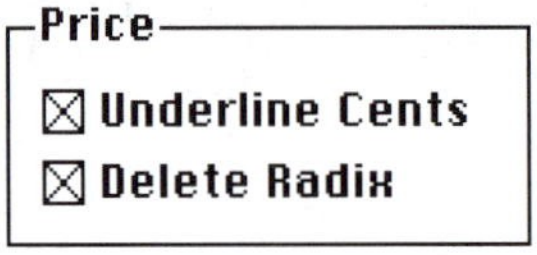

```
┌─Price──────────────┐
│ ⊠ Underline Cents  │
│ ⊠ Delete Radix     │
└────────────────────┘
```

▼ ▼

Text Greeking

After all this talk about making text look better on the screen and on your printed output, you probably need a relief from type. Let's talk about how to make type go away.

Designers have long worked with a concept known as greeking. Greeking is a method of drawing gray bars to represent blocks of text, rather than taking the time to image them all on the screen. QuarkXPress can greek text under a specific size limit, which you define in the General Preferences dialog box (Command-Y). The default value for text greeking is seven points; you can set it from two to 720 points.

Unless you really want to see every character of every word at every size, there's hardly any reason to turn text greeking off. However, depending on what your page design is like, you may want to adjust the Greek Below values at different times. We typically change it to about five points.

▼ ▼

Putting It Together

If you got through this entire chapter and are still not too bleary-eyed to read this, you must really be a QuarkXPress die-hard. After having learned about QuarkXPress's word-processing capabilities in the last chapter and what you can do to those words in this chapter, you're ready to move on to the theory and practice of style sheets and copy flow—automating all this formatting so you don't have to do it all manually every time you need it. There's working with type, and then there's working hard at type. We're trying to get your work to be as easy as possible.

C O P Y   F L O W

As you've learned in preceding chapters, you can do all sorts of wonderful things to type in QuarkXPress. But there's more to the intelligent handling of your copy in QuarkXPress than simply setting it in exquisite type. You have to get the document produced on time.

In the development of a publication, copy is almost never static. For any number of reasons, you may have to make drastic changes in the formatting or content of the copy (usually at or beyond the last minute). Your success in meeting deadlines (and getting paid) can often depend on how carefully you've anticipated such changes. If you don't plan from the very beginning to manage the flow of your document's copy, it will surely end up managing you, and in ways you won't like.

Managing Copy

QuarkXPress has two very powerful tools for automating the formatting and management of your document's copy: Style Sheets and XPress Tags. Use them wisely, and you'll soon make your copy jump through hoops at the snap of your fingers (or the click of your mouse). Use them poorly, or not at all, and you'll be the one jumping through hoops, probably at three in the morning before a major job is due. In this chapter, we'll tell you how to make the best use of these features. The key is learning to work smart.

Working Smart

Simply put, there are two ways to handle your copy in Quark-XPress: the dumb way and the smart way. What's the main difference between the two? Working the smart way, you make the computer do your work as much as possible. Working the dumb way, you take it on yourself to do the kind of mindless, repetitive tasks computers were meant to take off your hands—in this case, the repetitive formatting and reformatting of copy.

It takes a bit more time at first to set up a document to take advantage of QuarkXPress's automation, but it is well worth it if you ever need to make even the simplest document-wide change in the way your text is formatted. Of course, if you're the kind of person who always gets everything right the first time, you'll never, ever need to change any formatting once you've entered it, so you may not find this chapter of much use. The rest of you should pay careful attention.

The dumb way. The dumb way to format your copy is the way you most likely learned earliest: by selecting text and directly applying various attributes. Want a paragraph to be centered? Go to the Style menu and center it. Need to change the typeface? Go to the Font menu and do it.

"What's so dumb about that?" you may ask. It's not that there's anything inherently wrong with applying formatting directly to your copy; it's just that by doing so, you doom yourself to performing the same selecting and modifying actions over and over again whenever you need to format another text element with the same formatting, and whenever you need to make major changes to your document. For instance, if the paragraphs you centered now have to be made flush left, you must select and change each paragraph individually.

Another way of working dumb is to carefully format your text in QuarkXPress, and then, when heavy editing is required, export the copy to a word processor, edit it, then re-import it into Quark-XPress. Suddenly you may notice that you've lost most of your special QuarkXPress formatting (such as horizontal scaling, superior characters, kerning, etc.), and it's time for another long, painstaking formatting pass through your document.

The smart way. The smart way to handle your copy is to take the time to be lazy. Make QuarkXPress's features work for you. Whenever you create a new paragraph format, for any reason at all, assign a style to the format (we cover how in the next section). The next time you need to make another such paragraph, you can simply apply the appropriate style, and QuarkXPress will instantly apply the correct formatting.

And if you've been religious about creating and applying styles for all your document's paragraphs, you can then make sweeping formatting changes throughout your document with only a few keystrokes. Change a style, and all the paragraphs formatted with that style change—maybe not instantly, but almost. Also, be sure to use XPress Tags in exporting your text. This will keep your formatting information intact, even if you send stories out to be edited on a dreaded DOS or UNIX computer.

The following sections reveal the best ways to work smart with QuarkXPress.

Style Sheets

A style sheet is a collection of formatting attributes with a name. For example, a style sheet named "Heading" might be a bunch of formatting like: "14-point Helvetica Bold, centered, with a half-inch of Space Before." Every time you apply that style sheet to a paragraph, the paragraph is assigned that formatting. You can create one style for titles, another for footnotes, and more for different levels of subheads. In fact, you can (and probably should) create a different style sheet for each and every sort of paragraph in your document.

Warning: A Style Is a Style Sheet Is a Style

For some reason, Quark decided not to follow accepted terminology when it named its Style Sheet feature. It is commonly understood in desktop publishing that the group of formatting attributes for a particular type of paragraph is called a "style." Furthermore, the list of all the styles in a document is called a "style sheet."

However, in QuarkXPress's language, each paragraph has its own "Style Sheet" and the collection of these is also referred to as the "Style Sheet." Generally, we'll use the more commonly accepted terminology, as the distinction between style sheets and styles is a useful one. However, when you see the term "Style Sheet" with initial caps, we will be referring to that particular feature of QuarkXPress.

The Benefits of Style Sheets

Working with Style Sheets is the smart way of working for two reasons: applying formatting and changing formatting. We typically say that if your document has more than two pages of text, you should be using Style Sheets.

Applying formatting. Let's say we've hired you to work on creating this book. We've specified three levels of headings, two kinds of paragraphs (normal paragraphs and paragraphs that come right after headings), and a specification for how the figure numbers and titles should look. It's your job to apply those styles to all the text we give you.

If you went through all 780 pages, fastidiously setting the font of each paragraph, the size of each paragraph, the alignment of each paragraph—and so on—we'd be calling you Rip Van Winkle before too long. Instead, you can define all the character and paragraph attributes for each paragraph in a style, then apply all those attributes in one fell swoop by applying that style to a paragraph.

Changing formatting. Of course, the real nightmare would be when you hand us a draft copy of the book and we ask you to bring the size of the headings down half a point (of course, we'd wait to ask you until 5 PM on the Friday before Christmas). But if you're using styles, you'd smile and say, "Sure thing!"

Whenever you make a change to a particular attribute within a style, those changes are automatically applied to every paragraph that uses that style. Because you've had the foresight to create a "Heading" style which is applied to every heading in the book, you need only change the attributes of that style—in this case, the point size—and it gets changed throughout the entire document.

Local Formatting Versus Style Formatting

A key point to remember about QuarkXPress styles is that the character formatting contained in a style is applied to an entire paragraph. If the style calls for Times Roman, the entire paragraph will be in Times Roman. However, you can override the style's font for specific text within the paragraph. This "local" or "hard" formatting remains, even if you change the style's font definition, or apply a different style to the paragraph. (But if a paragraph has the QuarkXPress option "No Style" applied to it, *all* local formatting will be wiped out when you apply a style to it. (See "Normal Style and No Style," below.) In other words, hard formatting stays around for a long time, so you have to mind it carefully.

Local formatting is the *only* way to format just part of a paragraph; QuarkXPress doesn't have styles that can be applied to selected characters. Some programs, such as FrameMaker and the DOS version of Microsoft Word, have both paragraph and character styles. This can be extremely useful for applying specific formatting to elements within a paragraph, such as bold run-in heads at the beginning of a paragraph.

▼ ▼

Tip: Seeing Local Formatting. If there are any local paragraph-formatting or character attributes in the selected text or paragraph containing the insertion point (formatting that overrides the current style's formatting), a plus sign appears to the right of the style's name in the Style Sheets palette. This is a handy way of knowing if you're looking at a paragraph formatted according to its style, or at formatting that's been applied locally (see Figure 5-1).

▼ ▼

Figure 5-1

Local formatting flag

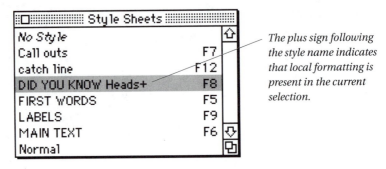

The plus sign following the style name indicates that local formatting is present in the current selection.

Unfortunately, there is one instance in which QuarkXPress loses track of local formatting. If you apply a style to a paragraph which contains the same formatting information as you've used in local formatting, and then you apply a style with different formatting, your original local formatting will be lost.

For instance, assume you have a paragraph whose style calls for plain text (that is, neither bold nor italic), and you've made a few words in the paragraph bold. Now you apply a style that makes *all* the text bold, and then you apply a style that *isn't* bold. All of the text in the paragraph will no longer be bold, including the text to which you originally applied the bold formatting. This doesn't just apply to making text bold or italic, but to any local formatting which can also belong to a style.

It seems that QuarkXPress simply says to itself, "Aha, this text which once contained local formatting should now have the same formatting as all the text around it. So I don't have to remember the local formatting anymore." And it doesn't (see Figure 5-2).

Tagging Paragraphs

It's important to understand that there's a difference between paragraph formatting and the style name. When you apply a style to a paragraph, you're only *tagging* it with that name—essentially identifying *what it is*, not necessarily what it should look like. QuarkXPress has an internal Style Sheet list that tells it what collection of formatting should go with that name. If you tag the paragraph with a different name, the formatting automatically changes. Or, if you change the formatting within the Style Sheet, QuarkXPress updates the formatting throughout the document.

Figure 5-2
How QuarkXPress loses
local formatting

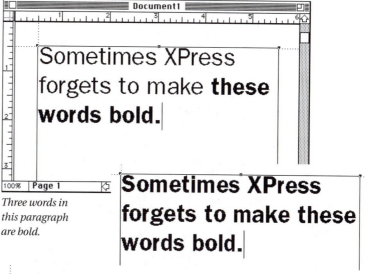

*Three words in
this paragraph
are bold.*

*Apply a style which
calls for all text to
be bold.*

*Now apply a style that calls for plain text. See your
local formatting disappear.*

Therefore, when you begin to work on a document, it's not really that important what formatting is associated with each style, since you can always change the formatting later. Once you've tagged all the paragraphs in your text, you can experiment by modifying the formatting of their styles at your leisure.

There are three ways to apply style sheets from within Quark-XPress: by the menu, the palette, and with keystrokes.

Style Sheets menu. The most basic—and probably the slowest—method for applying a paragraph style is to select the style name from the Style Sheets submenu (under the Style menu; see Figure 5-3). Like any other paragraph formatting, your text selection or cursor must be somewhere within the paragraph.

Figure 5-3

The Style Sheets menu

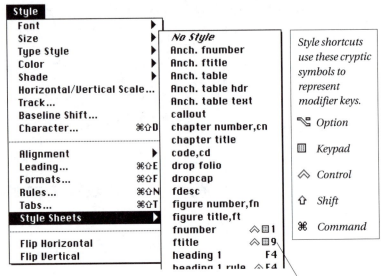

A style can be applied by selecting it in this menu or by using a keyboard shortcut.

Style Sheets palette. The Style Sheets palette lets you apply, edit, and view styles on the fly without having to go to any menus (see Figure 5-4). The palette lists all the styles in your document, along with their keyboard shortcuts if they have any. If you have lots of styles, you can make the palette larger or just scroll through them.

The beauty of this floating palette is that you can put it right next to (or on top of) your text box while you work. To apply any style to a paragraph, put the text cursor somewhere in that paragraph and click on the desired style in the palette. To apply "No Style" to a paragraph, click on "No Style" in the palette. The paragraph is no longer tagged with the style, but the formatting from the style remains as hard, local formatting.

As you move through your text, the style sheet for each paragraph is highlighted in the Style Sheets palette; you can quickly see what styles are applied. This is especially helpful if local formatting overrides styles (see "Local Formatting versus Style Formatting," below), or if you have two styles that are similar and you want to know if a paragraph is tagged with one or the other.

Figure 5-4

The Style Sheets palette

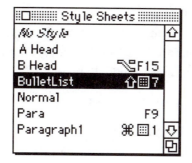

▼ ▼

Tip: Jump to Those Style Sheets. While we're happy that the Mac has menus, we often don't want to use them. Why? Because navigating the mouse (actually, David uses a trackball and a pen system now) over to the menus is a slow and tedious process. Instead, we try to use as many shortcuts as we can. Here's one: To edit a style, Command-click on that style in the palette. This brings up the Style Sheets dialog box with the style highlighted. Then you can click Edit, or press Return or Enter to edit that style sheet (pressing Return or Enter here is often one step easier than clicking the Edit button).

▼ ▼

Keystrokes. The third method of applying styles to paragraphs is by using keystrokes. Each paragraph style can have its own key-strokes command (see "Creating a New Style," below). Then, you can select a paragraph and press that keystroke. In case you forget the keystrokes, they appear as reminders in both the Style Sheets submenu and the Style Sheets palette.

▼ ▼

Tip: Copying Styles from One Paragraph to Another. In addition to using the Style Sheets palette and keyboard shortcuts to apply a style to a paragraph, you can also use a nifty shortcut to copy formats from one paragraph to another, click in the paragraph whose format you want to change, then Shift-Option-click on any other paragraph whose format you want to copy.

Not only is the paragraph's style copied, but any local paragraph formatting (margins, tabs, leading, etc.) is also applied to the destination paragraph. No local character formatting in the destination paragraph is changed.

▼ ▼

Defining Styles

To create or edit styles in a QuarkXPress Style Sheet, select Style Sheets from the Edit menu, Command-click on any style in the Style Sheets palette, or press Shift-F11. This calls up the Style Sheets dialog box (see Figure 5-5). If you call up this dialog box when a document is open, you'll see all the styles for that document. You can use this dialog box to create, edit, and delete styles, and, by using the Append button, import all of the styles from another QuarkXPress (or even Microsoft Word) document.

If you use this dialog box with no open documents, you can edit and add to QuarkXPress's default style-sheet list, which will be automatically included in all new documents.

Figure 5-5

The Style Sheets dialog box

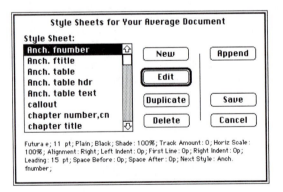

Creating a New Style

To create a new style sheet, click the New button in the Style Sheets dialog box. Or, if you want to copy another style, you can click the Duplicate button. Either way, the Edit Style Sheet dialog box appears (see Figure 5-6). Enter the name of the new style in the Name field. If you want to define a keystroke combination that will automatically apply the style, click in the Keyboard Equivalent field, and press the combination you want.

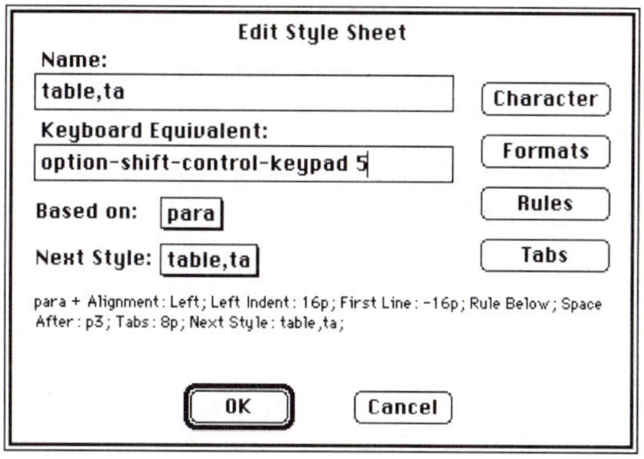

Figure 5-6

The Edit Style
Sheet dialog box

It's often a good idea to use a key in combination with the Control key, because keystrokes defined this way won't conflict with QuarkXPress's other key commands, almost none of which use the Control key (see the keyboard shortcuts tear-out card in the back of the book).

▼ ▼

Tip: Keys You Can Use for Style Shortcuts. You can only use certain keys for applying styles—the function keys (F1 through F15) and the numbers on the numeric keypad. In combination with the Control, Command, Shift, and Option keys, that provides for a lot of shortcuts. However, because QuarkXPress uses the function keys for its own shortcuts (both with and without Option and Shift), we suggest that you use function keys as style sheet hotkeys only in conjunction with the Control key.

There's no way to print a listing of what keystrokes go with what styles (see "Tip: Printing Your Style Sheet," page 362) so we just print a screen shot of the Style Sheets palette and tape it to our wall. If you have a really long style sheet, you may have to take a couple of screen shots.

▼ ▼

Once you've named a style, you can define it by clicking the Character, Formats, Rules, or Tabs buttons. Each of these buttons calls up dialog boxes with the same names as those under the Style menu for text. You can use these boxes to define your new style, just as you would to format any paragraph of text.

When you're finished defining the style, click OK or press Return, and you'll be brought back to the Style Sheets dialog box, where the style sheet has been added to the scroll list. Click the Save button. If you look in the Style Sheets palette, you'll see your new paragraph style ready to use.

▼ ▼

Tip: Creating Styles by Example. Instead of using the Edit Style Sheet dialog box to define the format of a style, you can create a style based on an existing paragraph in your document (see Figure 5-7). This way you can format a paragraph just the way you want it, and then create a style that has all those attributes.

Figure 5-7
Creating a style
by example

Place the insertion point in a paragraph.

When you click the New button from the Style Sheets dialog box, you'll see an Edit Style Sheet dialog box listing all the attributes of the selected paragraph.

Edit Style Sheet

Name:

| Title |

Keyboard Equivalent:

| |

Based on: *No Style*

Next Style: *Self*

Character

Formats

Rules

Tabs

Syntax Black; 24 pt; Plain; Black; Shade: 100%; Track Amount: 0; Horiz Scale: 100%; Alignment: Centered; Left Indent: 0"; First Line: 0"; Right Indent: 0"; Leading: auto; Space Before: 0"; Space After: 0"; Next Style: Self;

[OK]   [Cancel]

To create a style based on an existing paragraph's formatting, position the insertion point anywhere in the paragraph, then create a new style. When you get to the Edit Style Sheet dialog box, you'll see all of the formatting that's applied to the current paragraph listed at the bottom of the box. All you have to do is name the new style, click OK, and save your changes. Note that this doesn't automatically apply the style sheet to that paragraph; you have to then apply that style through any of the methods described earlier.

▼ ▼

Normal Style and No Style

Every QuarkXPress document has a default style, the "Normal" style. This is the style that is automatically applied to all the text in a document if you don't specifically apply a style. You can edit the "Normal" style just like any other.

"No Style" is different; applying it removes *all* style information from a paragraph. All the formatting is then treated as hard local formatting. Normally, local formatting doesn't change when you apply a style to a paragraph. However, if the paragraph has "No Style" applied to it, applying a style wipes out local formatting.

▼ ▼

Tip: Totally Overriding Local Formatting. The fact that a paragraph that has "No Style" applied to it loses all local formatting (including bold and italic) when it's tagged with another style is, more often than not, a pain in the butt and causes much confusion. However, there are some powerful uses for this feature, such as stripping out all local formatting that some dumbbell put in for no good reason.

Always on the lookout for a faster way to do something, we were pleased to find that we could apply "No Style" to a paragraph and then apply a style sheet in one stroke by Option-clicking on the style in the Style Sheets palette.

▼ ▼

Appending Styles

The Append button in the Style Sheets dialog box (brought up by choosing Style Sheets from the Edit menu) lets you import styles from other documents into your QuarkXPress document. You can import styles from other QuarkXPress documents, as well as from Microsoft Word files. Clicking the Append button brings up a standard directory dialog box, which you can use to choose the file whose styles you want to import.

When you bring styles into a document using the Append command, QuarkXPress checks to see if there are styles in your target document with the same name as any you're importing (see Figure 5-8). If it finds such a conflict, it displays a dialog box showing the name and characteristics of the conflicting styles, and gives you two options.

Figure 5-8

Conflicting style sheets
dialog box

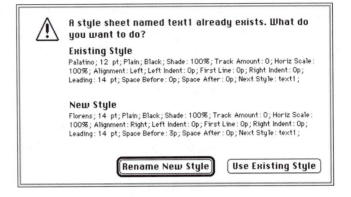

⚠ **A style sheet named text1 already exists. What do you want to do?**

Existing Style
Palatino; 12 pt; Plain; Black; Shade: 100%; Track Amount: 0; Horiz Scale: 100%; Alignment: Left; Left Indent: 0p; First Line: 0p; Right Indent: 0p; Leading: 14 pt; Space Before: 0p; Space After: 0p; Next Style: text1;

New Style
Florens; 14 pt; Plain; Black; Shade: 100%; Track Amount: 0; Horiz Scale: 100%; Alignment: Right; Left Indent: 0p; First Line: 0p; Right Indent: 0p; Leading: 14 pt; Space Before: 3p; Space After: 0p; Next Style: text1;

[Rename New Style] [Use Existing Style]

▶ **Rename New Style.** Rename the style that's being imported. If you rename the style, QuarkXPress imports it with an asterisk appended to its name.

▶ **Use Existing Style.** Ignore the incoming style's formatting, and use the formatting from the existing style in the document.

Another way to move styles from one QuarkXPress document to another is to copy text containing those styles. You can either use Copy and Paste or drag a box containing the text from document to document. However, if you import a style sheet way, QuarkXPress won't alert you that there is a style-name conflict (it just throws away the incoming style's information and replaces it with the existing style's attributes plus local formatting on top).

For example, let's assume that the "Normal" style in the original document calls for 12-point Helvetica, and the "Normal" style in the target document is set for 10-point Palatino. If you move text from the originating document to the target, any "Normal" text you bring over won't change to 10-point Palatino. It will remain 12-point Helvetica (set with local, hard formatting). Even though these paragraphs are tagged with the "Normal" style, you'll have to re-apply the tag to these paragraphs (by Option-clicking on "Normal" in the Styles Sheets palette) in order for the correct formatting to appear.

We'd love it if QuarkXPress allowed you to actually replace style definitions when there are style-name conflicts (see "Tip:

Overwriting Existing Styles," below). Most word processors let you do it, and it's a handy way to quickly change all the formatting in a document. You import a new set of styles, and the whole document reformats automatically.

Note that the renaming of appended paragraph styles only works in version 3.2 and later. In earlier versions, the incoming appended styles are handled as though you dragged them across (in other words, the program handles it really poorly).

Deleting (and Replacing) Styles

When you delete a Style Sheet, the program asks you if you want to replace it with another one. That is, all the text that is tagged with the deleted style is assigned a new style sheet, rather than going to "No Style". If you're using a version earlier than 3.2, the program won't ask you what style to replace it with; it just replaces it with "No Style".

▼ ▼

Tip: Overwriting Existing Styles. As we said earlier, we wish that there were a little more control over how QuarkXPress handles importing style sheets. But take heart: there are always workarounds. For example, here's a little number that lets you import style sheets which override the ones within your document.

1. Import the new style sheets from another document by clicking the Append button in the Style Sheets dialog box. When it asks you whether you want to rename the incoming styles or use the existing styles, click Rename. As we said earlier, QuarkXPress adds an asterisk after the name of each renamed style. For instance, if the style were named "Callout", the program would add a new style called "Callout*".

2. Delete the original style (in this case, "Callout"), and tell QuarkXPress to replace all instances of that style with the new asterisked style ("Callout*").

3. Select "Callout*", click Edit, and remove the asterisk from the Name field.

4. Click Save.

Now the old style is the same as the newly imported style. In effect, the old style sheet name has been overwritten by the new one. This technique works great as long as you don't have to go through it for 125 different styles. We still wish there were an Override Existing option when importing styles.

▼ ▼

Tip: Replacing Style Sheets. We find it rather odd that you can search and replace style sheets in Microsoft Word but not in QuarkXPress. Or can you? Here's a quick search-and-replace procedure to change all instances of one style to another. Let's say you want to replace every instance of "Heading3" with "RunInHead".

1. Open the Style Sheets dialog box and duplicate "Heading3" (select the style and click the Duplicate button).

2. When the Edit Style Sheets dialog box appears, leave the name set to "Copy of Heading3" and click OK.

3. Select the style you want to replace (in this case "Heading3") and click the Delete button. Don't worry; because you created a duplicate of this style, you'll be able to get it back after deleting it.

4. QuarkXPress asks you what style you want to give to the paragraphs tagged "Heading3"; specify the replacement style in the popup menu (in this case "RunInHead"). This is the key to this tip.

5. Click Save.

6. Go back to the Style Sheets dialog box and edit the duplicate style sheet: remove the "Copy of" from the front of the name, and click OK.

You have now replaced all instances of "Heading3" with "RunInHead". You can also find and change styles using the technique described in "Tip: Find/Change H&J settings" in Chapter 4, *Type and Typography*. Note that this tip also works for replacing colors and H&J settings.

▼ ▼

Tip: Style Sheet Page Breaks. PageMaker has a kind of cool feature that we like: you can specify a paragraph attribute that forces the paragraph to start on a new column or page. That is, any paragraph tagged with this attribute will always start at the top of a page or column. As it turns out, you can do a similar thing in QuarkXPress. Many readers pointed out that you can simply make the Space Before value in the Paragraph Formats dialog box as large as the text column is tall. For example, if your text box is 45 picas tall, make the Space Before value 45 picas. You can set this as a paragraph style or as local formatting for particular paragraphs.

▼ ▼

Basing One Style on Another

A powerful feature of QuarkXPress's style sheets is the ability to base one style on another. By basing many styles on, say, the Normal style, you can quickly change many elements in your document by simply changing the "Normal" style.

For example, let's say you want all your subheads to be the same as the "Normal" style, only bold and in larger type. By basing the subhead style on the "Normal" style you can ensure that every change you make to the "Normal" style is instantly reflected in the subhead style. If you change the "Normal" style's font from Helvetica to Franklin Gothic, the font of the subheads based on the "Normal" style automatically changes from Helvetica to Franklin Gothic as well. The subheads retain their larger size and boldness, however.

To base one style on another, use the Based On popup menu in the Edit Style Sheet dialog box to select the style on which you want to base your new style (in this case, "Normal"). Next, use the buttons in the dialog box to change only those attributes you want to be different in the new style (in this case, increasing the type size, and making it bold). Notice that the text at the bottom of the Edit Style Sheet dialog box shows the style that your new style is based on, along with all the additional formatting you've applied to the new Style Sheet (see Figure 5-9).

Figure 5-9

Based On styles

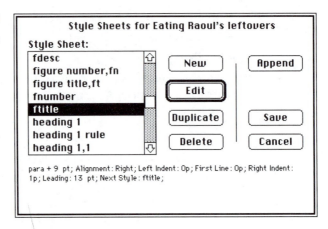

Style Sheets for Eating Raoul's leftovers

Style Sheet:

| fdesc |
| figure number,fn |
| figure title,ft |
| fnumber |
| **ftitle** |
| heading 1 |
| heading 1 rule |
| heading 1,1 |

New   Append

Edit

Duplicate   Save

Delete   Cancel

para + 9 pt; Alignment: Right; Left Indent: 0p; First Line: 0p; Right Indent: 1p; Leading: 13 pt; Next Style: ftitle;

If you plan your styles carefully, you can use the Based On feature to create nested hierarchies of styles based upon one another, so that a simple change to one style will be applied to all the styles based on it, and the styles based on those, *ad infinitum*. This "ripple effect" is a great time-saver, so it's well worth your while to carefully plan your styles to take greatest advantage of this effect.

▼ ▼

Tip: Based on Differences. Note that styles that are based on other styles are primarily defining differences between the base style and the new style. Let's say you have a style called "Head1" and it's 18-point Futura with the bold style applied, and a style called "Head2" that's based on "Head1", except that it's 12-point Futura and is not bold. The difference between the two is the point size and the style.

If you change the font of "Head1 to Franklin Gothic, then the font of "Head2" changes, too, because they're linked by their differences. There's one exception: if you change the parent style to have attributes that are the same as the child style, the difference link is broken. If you change "Head1" to "not bold," for example, then there's no difference in style between the two and the link is broken. Then, if you go back and change "Head1" to bold again, "Head2" follows suit and becomes bold. This is much the same as what happens when local formatting within a paragraph matches the formatting of the style.

▼ ▼

Tip: Use Search and Replace to Fake Character Styles. Although Quark-
XPress doesn't have character styles, it is possible to use the Find/
Change command to achieve some of the functions of character
styles. If you regularly use text with specific local formatting within your paragraphs, with a specific font, size, and weight, the
Find/Change command can save you a lot of keystrokes. Use it to
replace a unique, easily applied style (such as outline or shadow)
with formatting that can require multiple keystrokes or trips to
the Style menu (such as 12-point New Baskerville Bold).

1. In your word processor or in QuarkXPress, assign an otherwise unused character style, such as underline, outline, or
   shadow, to the text to which you want to apply your special
   local formatting.

2. Bring the text into QuarkXPress, if necessary.

3. Select Find/Change from the Edit menu. Uncheck Ignore
   Attributes. Check the appropriate boxes to replace the style
   you originally applied with the new formatting you want.

4. Click the Change All button.

Unfortunately, you can't use this method to apply the more
sophisticated of QuarkXPress's typographic controls, such as
tracking or horizontal scaling.

▼ ▼

Next Style

There's a popup menu in the Edit Style Sheet dialog box that you
can use to select the style that QuarkXPress automatically applies
to the next paragraph you create after one with the style you're
defining. For example, if you've created a style called "Heading"
to be followed by one called "Normal", you can apply the "Heading" style to a paragraph, and when you press Return after you've
typed your heading copy, QuarkXPress applies the "Normal" style
to the new paragraph as it creates it.

Note that this only works if the insertion point is at the very end of a paragraph when you press Return (turn Show Invisibles on to see where the current Return character is). If the insertion point is anywhere else when you press Return, you'll simply break that paragraph in two, and both new paragraphs will have the same style as the original one.

Also, note that when you're defining a new style, one of the choices in the Next Style popup menu is "Self". It's only available when you're creating a new style and haven't yet named it. The "Self" choice does just what it sounds like: it makes the Next Style the style being edited, so that when you're typing and press Return, the style is set to same style as in the previous paragraph.

Combining Paragraphs for Run-In Heads

Another way to fake character styles—this time to create run-in heads—is by combining paragraphs. If you have two consecutive paragraphs with different text formats and you combine them by deleting the carriage return that separates them, the text within the new paragraph will retain the formatting of the paragraph it originally belonged to. For example, you could create a head using a paragraph style calling for 14-point Futura Bold, and follow it with a body paragraph whose style calls for 12-point Garamond. By deleting the return after the Futura Bold paragraph, you end up with the Futura Bold text as a run-in head for the body text set in Garamond (see Figure 5-10).

Note that if you put some special character or series of characters at the end of heads that you want to be run in, you can use the Find dialog box (Command-F) to get rid of the carriage returns. (Remember: "\p" is the code for carriage returns in the Find/Change dialog box.)

There are a few drawbacks to this paragraph combination trick, however. You must be aware that you're basically fooling QuarkXPress. When you combine two paragraphs, QuarkXPress applies all the settings for the first paragraph to the new, combined paragraph. QuarkXPress also applies the style for the first paragraph to the new paragraph. So in our example, QuarkXPress

Figure 5-10
Automating
run-in heads

When a body meets a body.
If you plan on coming through the rye—or just visiting—you
might think about the package deal in which we provide you—
no extra charge—with a genuine imitation camel's hair jacket

Heading as it's typed in the text—styled on a separate line.

When a body meets a body. If you plan on coming through
the rye—or just visiting—you might think about the package
deal in which we provide you—no extra charge—with a gen-

Heading after being run-in.

thinks that the 14-point Futura Bold is the default font for the
entire new paragraph, even though part of it appears as 12-point
Garamond. QuarkXPress doesn't consider the Garamond formatting to be local, hard formatting, and if you apply a new style to
this paragraph, *both* the Futura and Garamond will be changed to
the font called for in the new style.

Since the fake character styles created by this technique are
rather fragile (this really is tricking QuarkXPress), you should
probably not use this technique unless you're certain that you
won't have to ever change the style that's applied to the combined
paragraph.

Xstyle

The Style Sheets palette is great, but this discussion wouldn't be
complete if we didn't mention Em Software's Xstyle XTension. This
add-on takes the Style Sheets palette concept and runs with it,
adding all sorts of functionality (see Figure 5-11).

For example, Xstyle has popup menus that work the way all
popup menus should: just type the first couple of letters of the
style sheet's name and it figures out which one you want. Plus,
you can quickly add or change local paragraph and character formatting. There's even a built-in method for creating pseudo-char-
acter styles. This XTension still has its limitations, but it's made
life a lot nicer for us.

Figure 5-11
Xstyle's floating
palettes

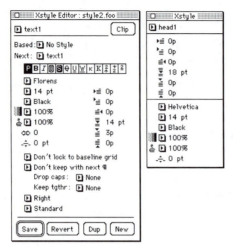

▼ ▼

What Word Processor to Use

Although QuarkXPress can import formatted text from several word processors, it can only interpret the styles of Microsoft Word files. (If you have another word processor that uses styles and can save them as Microsoft Word formatted files, you're in luck, too.) Since styles are so important to the proper management of your copy, Word automatically becomes the best word processor for working with QuarkXPress. (Unless you decide to work exclusively with XPress Tags, which we cover in the next section. These can be used, albeit awkwardly, by any word processor that can import and export ASCII files—that is to say, nearly all word processors).

Another plus for Word is that QuarkXPress correctly imports pictures contained in Word files as inline graphics, and can even export inline graphics to the correct location in a Word file.

How QuarkXPress's Style Sheets Work with Word

When you bring a Word document into QuarkXPress and you've checked Include Style Sheets, QuarkXPress takes every style from the Word file into its own style sheet, incorporating as much of Word's formatting as QuarkXPress can handle.

Character formatting. QuarkXPress can import a great deal of Word's own formatting. All of the character attributes available in Word can be carried over into QuarkXPress, with a few exceptions (see Table 5-1).

Table 5-1
What QuarkXPress does with Word's formatting

Word's formatting	What QuarkXPress does with it
Double and dotted-line underlines	Turns them into normal underlines.
Super- and subscript settings	Applies whatever values you've specified for them within your QuarkXPress document (in Typographic Preferences).
Expanded and condensed type settings	Converts them to tracking values in QuarkXPress. Since you specify these values using points in Word, and Quark-XPress uses $\frac{1}{200}$ of an em, there is usually only a very rough correlation between how tightly type is set in Word, and what you get when you bring it into QuarkXPress.
Footnotes	Numbers are changed to superscript style; footnote text is added at end of story.

Paragraph formatting. For paragraph formats, QuarkXPress brings in most available Word settings, except that it ignores the Page Break Before setting (see "Tip: Style Sheet Page Breaks," earlier in this chapter), and only the top and bottom rules set for boxed paragraphs will be imported (though QuarkXPress does a good job of interpreting the correct size and weight of rules). Quark-XPress ignores any values you've set for space between rules and their paragraphs.

Style formatting. Any of Word's attributes which can be applied to styles can be successfully imported as styles by QuarkXPress, with the exceptions noted above.

If you import a Word file which has styles with the same name as styles already in the QuarkXPress document, you are given the choice to import or override those Word styles. If you click Use

Existing Style, the style already within QuarkXPress will be applied. The QuarkXPress styles predominate. However, any local formatting you've applied in the Word document is imported. Option-clicking overrides all incoming Word styles' formatting.

If you click Rename New Style, the text is imported and the style name has an asterisk appended to it. Option-clicking renames all incoming Word styles in this manner.

This ability to replace Word styles with QuarkXPress styles is important, as you can use Word's style sheets to tag paragraphs with style names, and have QuarkXPress apply the appropriate formatting as soon as you import the text (see the following tip).

▼ ▼

Tip: Don't Worry About Word Styles. Remember that QuarkXPress can override Microsoft Word's formatting for style sheets. Let's say that your Microsoft Word document's "Normal" style is 18-point Helvetica (for easy reading and editing on screen), and your QuarkXPress document's "Normal" style is 12-point Palatino. When you import the file into QuarkXPress and click Use Existing Style in the alert dialog box, the text that is tagged as "Normal" appears in Palatino (like you'd want).

The implication of this is that you never really have to worry about what the styles look like in Word. For example, in this book, our Microsoft Word text was all in Geneva and New York, but when we imported the text files into QuarkXPress, they came out in the fonts you're reading (Utopia and Futura).

▼ ▼

Exporting Text

After you go through all the trouble of bringing copy into Quark-XPress and formatting it, why would you want to then export it? Aside from administrative reasons (backups, use in a database, archiving the text, etc.), there are two major situations in which exporting text can be important.

First, if you encounter sluggishness when working with text in

QuarkXPress (although we still think it's better to keep the text within QuarkXPress; see "Using Dummy Text Boxes" in Chapter 3, *Word Processing*).

The second reason you might want to export text is if you work in a busy workgroup-publishing environment. You may find it absolutely necessary to pull text out of QuarkXPress so that editors can work on it while you continue to refine a newsletter's or magazine's layout.

How to Export Text

Exporting text from QuarkXPress is pretty much the opposite of importing it.

1. With the Content tool, select a text box containing the story you want to export.

2. Choose Save Text from the File menu. The Save Text dialog box will appear.

3. Enter the name you'd like the exported text to be saved under. Click either the Entire Story or Selected Text button.

4. Use the popup Format menu to choose the format for the exported file. The formats listed in the menu will depend on which filter files you have in the QuarkXPress folder.

5. Press Return or click OK.

Pitfalls

The most important consideration when bringing text out of QuarkXPress and then back in is how to accomplish this without losing all the formatting you've applied within QuarkXPress. No current word processor can handle horizontal scaling or kerning properly, for instance, and such formatting could easily be lost during the export/re-import process. There are ways to keep this formatting intact no matter where your QuarkXPress text ends up, however, by using style sheets or XPress Tags.

Exporting to Word

One solution is to export to Microsoft Word. Word files made from QuarkXPress contain style-sheet information, and, as mentioned above, the appropriate formatting is automatically applied when you bring the text back into QuarkXPress. But using Word is only a partial solution to the formatting problem, since only formatting that's applied to an entire paragraph can be stored in styles. If you've applied special local formatting to individual characters or words (such as, for instance, superior type, tracking, kerning, or scaling), it will be lost during the export/re-import process, even if you use Word and take full advantage of styles.

To be honest, we've had lots of trouble exporting files into Word's format. We're not entirely sure why, but styles are often applied incorrectly in the process. It appears as though this is due to Quark's buggy filter. Hopefully, by the time you read this they'll have fixed it up.

▼ ▼

Tip: Exporting Styles. We often use QuarkXPress's Export feature to export all our styles to Microsoft Word. This saves us having to re-create every style name on Microsoft Word's style sheet. For instance, we can design a whole book or magazine, then export the styles for writers and editors to use when creating copy, and be assured that the style names will match when we import the files. To export styles, create a little one-line paragraph for each style. Apply the style, then export that text in a Word format. When you open the file in Word, all the styles are there.

▼ ▼

Tip: Printing Your Style Sheet. We can't find any way to print a listing of every style on our style sheet along with descriptions from QuarkXPress. However, if you export the styles as described in the last tip, you can print the styles from Word. When you've opened your Word document with each of the styles, go to the Define Styles item under the Format menu (Command-T), and select Print from the File menu (Command-P). A lot of the formatting in QuarkXPress styles doesn't get passed through to Word, of course, so the printout isn't complete. But it's better than nothing.

▼ ▼

A Solution: XPress Tags

There is a solution to the problem of losing formatting when exporting and re-importing text, however: export the file in the special ASCII format called XPress Tags. XPress Tags uses special—and complicated—coding that records every single one of QuarkXPress's text-formatting attributes, from style sheets to local formatting (see Figure 5-12).

You may find an ASCII file with XPress Tags confusing to look at, with its multitude of arcane numbers and codes. However, there are many reasons why XPress Tags is the best format to use when you need to edit and then re-import copy.

▼ ▼

Tip: Style Tags Versus XPress Tags. Do not under any circumstances have both the Style Tags and XPress Tags filters in the same folder with QuarkXPress. You can have one or the other, but if both are there, you have a good chance of crashing.

▼ ▼

Why Use XPress Tags?

Not only do files using XPress Tags contain all of a story's QuarkXPress formatting, but because ASCII is a universal file format, these files can be edited by virtually any word processor—Macintosh, MS-DOS, or UNIX. Although the coding may appear daunting if you're used to the WYSIWYG world of the Macintosh, professional typesetters have been working with code-based systems for years, and tagged files can be easily integrated into such an environment.

So if you find yourself regularly needing to export QuarkXPress stories with sophisticated text formatting, XPress Tags is clearly the way to go. While it may take a while to get used to editing an XPress Tags file, it's a lot less work than having to painstakingly reformat your copy every time you bring it back into your QuarkXPress document. Table 5-2, found at the end of this chapter, is a comprehensive list of the codes used in XPress Tags.

Figure 5-12

XPress Tags

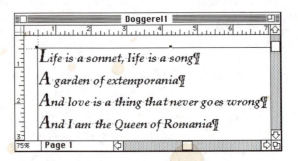

When you save this file in XPress Tags format . . .

. . . the text file looks like this.

```
@Normal=<*L*h"Standard"*kn0*kt0*ra0*rb0*d0*p(0,0,0,
0,0,0,g)*t(0,0," "):¶
Ps100t0h100z24k0b0c"Black"f"BI Palatino BoldItalic">¶
@Normal:<*L*h"Standard"*kn0*kt0*ra0*rb0*d0*p(0,0,0,
0,0,0,g)*t(0,0," "):¶
Ps100t0h100z36k0b0c"Black"f"BI Palatino
BoldItalic">L<z24>ife is a sonnet, life is a song¶
<z36>A<z24> garden of extemporania¶
<z36>A<z24>nd love is a thing that never goes wrong¶
<z36>A<z24>nd I am the Queen of Romania¶
```

▼ ▼

Tip: Automate Your Copy Processing with XPress Tags. Once you're familiar with the coding format used by XPress Tags, you can easily set up a QuicKey to apply formatting codes to an ASCII file in your word processor. If you're more ambitious and handy with database programs, you can design a report format that creates a file that incorporates XPress Tags, so you can export data from your database and have it land on your QuarkXPress pages fully formatted and untouched by human hands.

▼ ▼

Tip: Importing Text from Ventura Publisher. XPress Tags uses almost the same coding format as that powerhouse of DOS-based desktop publishing, Ventura Publisher (recently revitalized by Corel's purchase of it). That's right: if you take a tagged, coded ASCII file from Ventura Publisher, you can import that file into QuarkXPress using the XPress Tags filter. You won't get the proper formatting, and you certainly won't get page layout, but you can save yourself a bundle of time in applying style sheets!

The trick is to alter the tags slightly before importing the file. Here's what you do.

1. Open the Ventura text document in a word processor, or import it as straight ASCII text into a QuarkXPress text box.

2. Search for all instances of " = " (there's a space on either side of that equals sign) and replace it with ": " (that's a colon followed by a space).

3. Save that document as ASCII text (Text Only) again.

4. Import it into a QuarkXPress text box with Include Style Sheets checked.

When you import the file, all of the style sheet names are automatically brought into the QuarkXPress document. However, if you've already created style sheets with the same names as the Ventura document, then QuarkXPress uses the style definitions that you've created in QuarkXPress.

You can also perform a reverse procedure to bring tagged text from QuarkXPress into Ventura.

▼ ▼

Tip: Workgroup Publishing with QPS. Workgroup publishing is another one of those phrases that has been bandied about for some time now. It's really pretty simple: if you're working with a bunch of other people to publish stuff, you're doing workgroup publishing. The biggest problem with workgroup publishing is moving files, pictures, and text from one person to another in an organized way. It seems like something's always getting lost, and hardly anyone knows where things are (or even should be).

Quark is coming to the rescue with a product called Quark Publishing System (or QPS for short). This is a whole networked system that's designed to solve many of these workgroup issues. If you're in such a situation, we urge you to call Quark and ask

them about QPS and how it can help you. It's not inexpensive—
it's estimated at about $1,100 per user for the basic setup—but it's
cheaper than the high-end, proprietary systems like Atex. Plus,
it's centered around QuarkXPress, a program you already know.

▼ ▼

Getting Your Stories Straight

Once you've taken advantage of some, if not all, of these features
of QuarkXPress, you may still find it necessary to burn the mid-
night oil making last-minute changes. But at least you'll have the
full power of QuarkXPress on your side, not buried within a user's
guide. Get to know styles, import and export filters, and especially
XPress Tags, and you can go a long way toward being lazy: making
your computer do the work, rather than having to do it yourself.

Table 5-2

XPress Tags codes

*Note: All codes that are in angle brackets can be combined within one set of angle brackets. For example, <BI*d(1,3)> changes the formatting to bold, italic, and with an initial cap.*

Character Formats	
Style	**Code**[1]
Plain	<P>
Bold	<B>
Italic	<I>
Outline	<O>
Shadow	<S>
Underline	<U>
Word underline	<W>
Strikethrough	</>
All caps	<K>
Small caps	<H>
Superscript	<+>

[1] *These codes act as toggle switches; the first time they're encountered, the format is activated. The second time, the format is deactivated. Note the similarity to formatting keystrokes.*

Table 5-2

XPress Tags codes
(continued)

Style/Attribute	Code[2]	Value set in . . .
Subscript	<->	
Superior	<V>	
Type style of current style sheet	<$>	
Typeface	<f"name">	Name of font
Size	<z#>	Points
Color	<c"name">	Name of color (the four process colors and white can be specified by C, M, Y, K, and W, without quotes, as in <cY>)
Shade	<s#>	Percentage
Horizontal scale	<h#>	Percentage
Kern next 2 characters	<k#>	$\frac{1}{200}$ em
Track	<t#>	$\frac{1}{200}$ em
Baseline shift	<b#>	Points

Paragraph Formats

Attribute	Code[3]	Value
Left-align	<*L>	None
Center-align	<*C>	None
Right-align	<*R>	None
Justify	<*J>	None
Paragraph formats	<*p(#,#,#,#,#,#,G or g)>	Left Indent, First Line, Right Indent, Leading, Space Before, Space After, Lock to Baseline Grid (G=lock, g=don't lock)
Drop cap	<*d(chars,lines)>	Character Count and Line Count

[2] *In these codes, "#" should be replaced with a number. This number can be set to the same precision as QuarkXPress's measurements (tenths, hundreths, or thousandths of a unit). The measurement units used are shown. If you replace "#" or any other code value with a dollar sign ($), QuarkXPress uses the formatting of the current style sheet.*

[3] *In these codes, "#" should be replaced with a measurement in points. If you replace "#" or any other code value with a dollar sign ($), QuarkXPress uses the formatting of the current style sheet. If the code requires multiple values, every value must be present and delineated by a comma.*

Table 5-1

XPress Tags codes
(continued)

Attribute	Code	Value
Keep With Next ¶	<*kn1> or <*kn0>	1=keep with next, 0=don't keep with next
Keep Lines Together	<*kt(A)> or <*kt(start,end)>	"A"=all; start and end are number of lines
Set Tab Stops	<*t(#,#,"character")>	Position, Alignment (0=left, 1=center, 2=right, 4=decimal, 5=comma), Fill character[4]
H&J	<*h"name">	Name of H&J specification
Rule Above	<*ra(#,#,"name",#,#,#,#)>	See "Rule Below"
Rule Below	<*rb(#,#,"name",#,#,#,#)>	Width, Style (from 1–11), Name of color, Shade (percent), From Left, From Right, Offset (if you specify Offset as a percentage place a percent sign after the number)

Special Characters	
Character	**Code**
Soft return	<\n>
Discretionary return	<\d>
Discretionary hyphen	<\h>
Indent Here	<\i>
Previous text box page #	<\2>
Current text box page #	<\3>
Next text box page #	<\4>
New column	<\c>
New box	<\b>
@	<\@>
<	<\<>
\	<\\>

[4]*Align on is specified by replacing the alignment number by the character contained within quotation marks. QuarkXPress 3.3 allows two-character tab leaders.*

Table 5-1
XPress Tags codes
(continued)

Character	Code
ASCII character	<\#decimal value>[5]
Standard space	<\s>[6]
en space	<\f>[6]
Flex space	<\q>[6]
Punctuation space	<\p>[6]
En dash	<\#208>[7]
Em dash	<\#209>[7]
Return (new paragraph)	<\#13>[7]
Tab	<\#9>[7]
Right-aligned tab	<\t>

Style Sheets

Description	Code	Values
Define style sheet	@name=	Name of style sheet; follow the equal sign with definition
Use "Normal"	@$:	
Use "No Style"	@:	
Apply style sheet	@name:	Name of style sheet

General codes

Code	Means . . .
<v#>	XPress Tags filter version number. QuarkXPress 3.2 came with version 1.60; QuarkXPress 3.3 comes with 1.70.
<e#>	Platform version number. 0=Mac, 1=Windows.

[5] Note that the number sign must precede the ASCII character value.

[6] Precede these codes with an exclamation point to make them nonbreaking. For example, <\!s>.

[7] You can also type type the character itself on the Macintosh.

PICTURES

We've been talking a lot about text and rudimentary graphic elements such as arrows and ovals, but let's not forget that, ultimately, QuarkXPress is designed to integrate not only text and lines, but also graphics from other programs, and it contains many powerful features to aid in this task. QuarkXPress handles line art and images such as four-color photographs with a power and feature set previously only attainable by using several programs in conjunction.

In this chapter, we'll cover almost everything you can do with pictures other than running text around them (which we cover in the next chapter).

▶ Importing images into QuarkXPress

▶ Rotating picture boxes and their contents

▶ Precision placement of images and picture boxes

▶ Horizontal skewing of graphic images

▶ Automatic re-importing of modified pictures

▶ Working with System 7's Publish and Subscribe

▶ Picture greeking

CHAPTER 6

Here are the three basic steps of importing pictures into your documents.

1. Create a picture box.

2. Select the box with the Content tool, and bring in a picture by either pasting from the Clipboard or using the Get Picture command.

3. Size, skew, rotate, and crop the image until you like the way it looks on the page.

But what types of pictures are available for use? And how to accomplish the desired look? In this chapter we explore the full range of possibilities for bringing graphics in from other applications and manipulating them on the page. In Chapter 8, *Modifying Images,* we'll talk about some of the effects you can achieve by modifying graphics once they're ready to be printed.

Let's first take a close look at the different types of pictures on the Macintosh applicable to QuarkXPress users.

▼ ▼

Macintosh Graphic File Formats

If there is a question we're asked more often than "why won't my file print?" it's "what's the difference between all those different graphic formats?" The question refers to a host of formats with names such as EPS, TIFF, PICT, PNTG, LZW TIFF, JPEG, and Mac-Paint. No one can be blamed for being confused when faced with such a list! Some of these are different names for the same thing, others are subtly different, and a few represent totally, to-the-core, different concepts.

The fundamental question when considering a graphic file on the Macintosh is whether it is bitmapped or object-oriented.

Bitmaps

Bitmapped images are the most common type of file format. When you use a scanner and scanning software, you are generating a bitmapped image. When you use an image-editing and painting program such as Adobe Photoshop, MacPaint, or ImageStudio, you are working with and generating bitmapped images. However, no matter how ubiquitous bitmapped images are, you are still strictly limited as to how you can use them.

Bitmapped images are just that: images made of mapped bits. A *bit* is a small piece of information. To begin with, let's think of it as a single pixel, or dot, which can be turned on or off. When you look very closely at the screen of a black-and-white Macintosh, you can see that the screen image is made up of thousands of these tiny bits. Some are turned on (black), and some are off (white). The *map* is the computer's internal blueprint of what the image looks like: "bit number one is on, bit number two is off," and so on (see Figure 6-1).

Figure 6-1
Each pixel sits on the grid

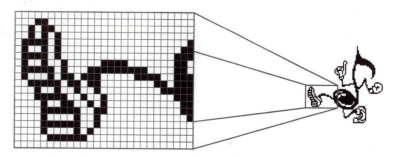

Bitmapped images are complicated creatures. David covers them in much more depth in the book he wrote with Steve Roth called *Real World Scanning and Halftones.* You might want to check that out. However, in the meantime, here's a quick rundown. There are three primary pieces of information which are relevant to any bitmapped image: its dimensions, resolution, and pixel depth.

Dimensions. The bitmap is a rectangular area which describes every dot (pixel) in and around the image. This area is broken down into a grid of many square pixels. Every pixel is whole and not fractured. You can describe the dimensions of the gridded area in several ways, but it is most often specified in the number of pixels or sample points per side, or in inches per side.

Resolution. The resolution of the bitmapped image is usually defined as the number of pixels, or sample points, per inch on the grid (of course, this is different in countries using the metric system). A low-resolution bitmapped image may have 72 pixels per inch; however, this measurement is usually defined as either dots per inch (dpi) or samples per inch (spi). A picture described using only 72 dpi looks very rough. A higher-resolution bitmapped image may be 300 dpi or higher (many film scanners scan images at over 4,000 dpi). These images, when printed, are much crisper and cleaner, with fewer jaggies (see Figure 6-2).

Figure 6-2
Low resolution versus high resolution bitmapped line art.

72 dpi   *300 dpi*

Pixel depth. Each pixel is specified as a specific color. The range of colors available is determined by the type of bitmapped image it is (see "File Types," below). In the simplest bitmapped images, each pixel is defined as either black or white. These are called bilevel, or one-bit, images, because each pixel is described with one bit of information, and as we mentioned above, that one bit can be either on (one) or off (zero).

Bilevel images are *flat*; they have little depth. More complex bitmapped images are *deep* because they contain pixels that are defined with multiple bits, enabling them to describe many levels of gray or color. For example, an eight-bit image can describe up to 256 colors or shades of gray for each pixel (those of us in the

Northwest, having to look at gray a great deal, can identify and name most of those shades). A 24-bit image can describe more than 16 million colors (see Figure 6-3).

Figure 6-3
The number of bits determines the number of gray levels

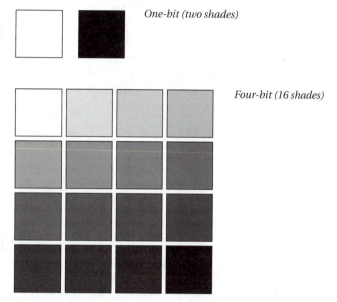

One-bit (two shades)

Four-bit (16 shades)

Manipulating bitmapped images. The limitations inherent in bit-mapped images become most clear when you manipulate the picture in some way, such as enlarging it significantly. The key is that the picture's resolution is related directly to its size. If you double the size of a bitmap, you cut its resolution in half; if you reduce the size of the picture to one-quarter its original size, you multiply its resolution by four. For example, a 72-dpi, one-bit graphic when enlarged 200 percent becomes a twice-as-rough 36-dpi image. However, when reduced to 50 percent, it becomes a finer 144-dpi image (see Figure 6-4).

A grayscale or color image becomes *pixelated* when enlarged, rather than looking more jaggy. That is, you begin to see each pixel and its tonal value (see Figure 6-5).

Object-Oriented Graphics

Instead of describing a picture dot by dot, object-oriented files specify each object in a picture on a coordinate system. A bit-

Figure 6-4
Scaling a bitmap
affects its resolution

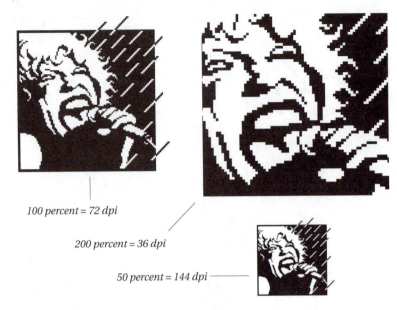

100 percent = 72 dpi

200 percent = 36 dpi

50 percent = 144 dpi

Figure 6-5
Pixelization from
enlarging a
grayscale image

*72 dpi, four-bit
grayscale TIFF
at 100 percent*

*72 dpi, four-bit
grayscale TIFF
at 400 percent*

mapped picture could take an enormous amount of space describing one circle (this dot on, this dot off, and so on), but an object-oriented file could describe it in one line: "draw a circle of this size with a center at x,y." The computer knows what a circle is and how to create it. Different object-oriented formats can describe different things, but most can easily specify objects such as lines, curves, and type, as well as attributes such as shading and object rotation angle.

Most object-oriented graphics can also contain bitmapped graphics as objects in their own right, though you may or may not be able to edit those bitmaps with a paint program. These files are almost always created by an application such as FreeHand or Illustrator.

The magic of object-oriented graphics is that you can stretch them, rotate them, twist them into a pastry, and print them on various resolution printers without worrying about how smoothly the lines will print. That is, when you print on a 300-dpi, plain-paper laser printer, you get a full 300 dpi; when you print to film with a 2,540-dpi imagesetter, you get beautifully smooth lines at 2,540 dots per inch. There is no inherent limit of information for the picture, as there with bitmaps (see Figure 6-6). Theoretically, there are no inherent limits to the number of gray levels in an object-oriented picture. Realistically, however, each format has upper limits.

File Types

On the Macintosh, each files is identified by its *type*. When we talk about file types in this book we're talking about two things: how the information is formatted within the file, and how the file is saved to disk. The common usage of file type—such as Illustrator or QuarkXPress—refers to the way in which the information is formatted. Then there is the way the Macintosh system names files when it saves them to disk; it gives every file an actual, technical, four-letter file *type*. For instance, files generally referred to as Paint or MacPaint files are type PNTG; Illustrator files are either EPSF or TEXT. For the sake of simplicity, we use the terms *type* and *format* interchangeably.

Figure 6-6
Object-oriented
graphics versus
bitmapped images

Object-oriented   *Outline*   *Bitmapped*

You can examine the file type of a file using several different utilities, such as Apple's ResEdit or PrairieSoft's DiskTop (our favorite utility for this sort of task; see Figure 6-7). It's important to understand and identify file types for the discussion below, where we cover the main graphic file formats used with QuarkXPress.

We suggest that you use either EPS or TIFF images for the bulk of your work; anything else is too unstable.

Paint. The Paint format is ultimately the most basic of all graphic file formats on the Macintosh. When the Mac first shipped in 1984, it came with two programs: MacWrite and MacPaint. The latter was a very basic painting program that let you paint bitmapped images, cutting and pasting these pictures into Mac-Write files or saving them as Paint-format (PNTG) files.

Paint files are black and white (one-bit), 72 dots per inch, eight by 10 inches (576 by 720 dots). That's it. No more and no less. Even text is handled like bitmapped graphics; the only way to edit it is to edit the pixels that make it up. Clearly, this format has some stringent limitations which restrict the usefulness of the images. It's sometimes useful for black-and-white screen shots, however.

TIFF. The Tagged Image File Format (TIFF) is another form of bitmap with significantly more support for high-quality images. First off, instead of the standard eight-by-10-inch, 72-dpi, black-and-white PNTG image, a TIFF file can be created at any size and resolution, and include grayscale or color information.

Figure 6-7

PrairieSoft's
DiskTop 4.5

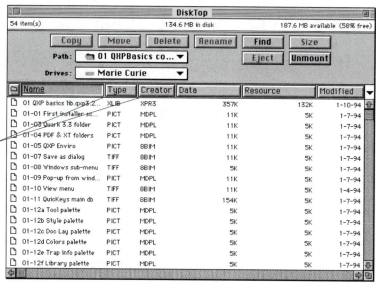

You can view and change
file types easily.

Because of the flexibility of TIFF files, all scanning and image-editing programs such as DeskScan, Photoshop, PixelPaint Pro, and Ofoto can save and open the TIFF format.

TIFF files can seem simple until you really need to work with them in a variety of environments. As it turns out, there are several different TIFF formats, including compressed and uncompressed, and TIFF-6. QuarkXPress imports both standard TIFF and LZW-compressed TIFF files.

PICT. The PICT format, also a part of the original Mac system, but first made easy-to-use with MacDraw, tackles graphic images on an object level as opposed to a bitmap level. However, a PICT image can contain bitmaps alongside object-oriented drawings, or they can be comprised completely of a single bitmap ("bitmap-only PICT"). So PICT files can be either bitmap or object-oriented. Unlike most programs, QuarkXPress can "see" when a PICT file is bitmap-only, and lets you manipulate it as such (we'll see later in this chapter that you can manipulate bitmapped images differently than object-oriented ones). PICT images can be any size, resolution, and color (like TIFFs or EPS files).

Ultimately, the biggest problem with the object-oriented PICT format is its unreliability. For example, line widths can change when moving a picture from one program to another, and text spacing can change, sometimes drastically. Also, printing to imagesetters (1,200+ dpi) can be troublesome. Remember that when you print a PICT to a PostScript imagesetter, the computer has to convert from one object-oriented language to another. We trust these conversions about as far as we can throw them. Nonetheless, PICT is the primary format for printing to non-PostScript devices. Because of this, we suggest you avoid using PICT formats as much as possible, unless they're bitmap-only PICTs from Photoshop or DeskPaint or some other paint program.

For the completeness' sake, we should note that it is also possible to attach a PostScript description of the image to a PICT image (see "Encapsulated PostScript" and " The Clipboard," below).

Encapsulated PostScript. Encapsulated PostScript (EPS) format is the most robust format for putting images on paper or film. Post-Script is an object-oriented page-description language, though its files may contain bitmaps as well. Although it has built-in font-handling features, it ultimately treats type as a graphic made of lines and curves. This makes working with fonts in a PostScript environment a joy, with many possibilities. It is easy to create a PostScript file on the Macintosh, but to print it out you must have a PostScript-compatible printer.

EPS images come in two basic varieties: EPS without a preview, and EPS with a preview. The preview-enclosed feature in many EPS files allows you to bring that file into QuarkXPress and see a low-resolution representation of the image on the screen. When the file is printed to a PostScript printer, however, the bitmap is ignored and the underlying PostScript is used.

If a preview image—which is generally a PICT or TIFF file—is not available, then you see a big gray box on the screen, which may contain some basic information, such as the file's name.

DCS. We'll talk about Desktop Color Separation (DCS) in Chapter 9, *Color*, but let's go over it here quickly. The DCS method is based on preseparating color images into five separate EPS files (which is why DCS is sometimes called "EPS-5" or five-file EPS). Four of the files contain high-resolution information for each of the process colors (cyan, magenta, yellow, and black). The fifth file contains a low-resolution composite image (for proofing), a screen representation of the picture, and pointers to the four higher-resolution files. This fifth file is the file that gets imported into QuarkXPress.

When you print your file, QuarkXPress replaces this representation file (sometimes called the "main file") with the four high-resolution files. This means you can print the separations directly from QuarkXPress to an imagesetter.

Now there is the DCS 2.0 file format, which is basically a revised version of the DCS specification. In DCS 2.0 images, the four process plates and the preview "master" image are all rolled into one big file. Plus, DCS 2.0 lets you include spot-color plates, varnish plates—as many plates as you want. That means that you can create an image in Photoshop that includes spot colors, export it with PlateMaker from In Software as a DCS 2.0 file, and separate the whole thing from QuarkXPress.

QuarkXPress 3.2 and later not only understands DCS documents, it can also create them when you save a page as EPS (see "Page as Picture," page 412).

Windows Bitmap. Windows Bitmap (.BMP) is the bitmap format native to Windows Paint, but isn't usually encountered outside of Windows and OS/2 Presentation Manager. You can, however, bring .BMP files to the Macintosh and use them in QuarkXPress. We just don't think you should; we still prefer TIFF to this format.

Windows Metafile. Closely tied to graphics technology underlying Windows, Windows Metafile (.WMF) is a relatively reliable object-oriented format to use in Windows. However, when you take it out of that environment and onto the Macintosh, things get a little weird. Fonts that are embedded in the graphic really get messed up, and colors can get screwy, too. We suggest leaving this at home on the PC.

Scitex CT and LW files. QuarkXPress can import both Scitex CT (con-tinuous-tone) and LW (line-work) files. However, it can only separate CT files. Note that when we say CT files, we are actually referring to CT HandShake files. We know one guy who got burned because he asked a color house for CT files and got Scitex's propri-etary format instead of the open-format CT Handshake files.

Photo CD. If you have the Photo CD XTension loaded in your QuarkXPress folder, you'll be able to open images made using Kodak's Photo CD format through the Get Picture dialog box. We think Photo CD is really cool, but we can't recommend acquiring images this way. Instead, it's much better to open them in Photo-shop using the Acquire module first. Then you can adjust levels, do color correction—Photo CD images are typically oversatu-rated because they're designed to be shown on a television—sharpen, and save the images as TIFF or EPS at an appropriate resolution (see our book *Real World Scanning and Halftones* for entire chapters on these subjects). You can also use Apple's PhotoFlash software or Kodak's under-$40 Photo CD Access ap-plication to acquire images from Photo CD.

JPEG. JPEG is a file format with built-in compression so that these images can be a tenth of the size or smaller of a non-compressed image. However, the compression in JPEG is "lossy," which means the more it's compressed, the worse the image looks. When you have the JPEG filter (it comes with 3.3) in your QuarkXPress XTension folder, you can import images that were saved in the JPEG format. Photoshop has a JPEG option, and JPEG is built into QuickTime, as well, so PICT files can be saved with various de-grees of JPEG compression.

Once you've imported the picture into QuarkXPress, the pro-gram decompresses it every time you print it (which can take a while). Note that JPEG files are different than JPEG EPS files; the latter only print correctly on PostScript Level 2 printers because the printer itself decompresses the file—QuarkXPress doesn't have to do anything with it.

PCX. PCX is the granddaddy of bitmapped formats, and the current version supports 24-bit and 256-color palettes. Since a variety of color-model techniques have been applied to PCX over the ages, files from earlier programs can have some serious color-mismatch problems. If you're satisfied with the results of importing PCX images, then go for it. If not, see if your source can provide files in TIFF, which is an all-around better format. To make QuarkXPress open PCX files, you have to have the PCX filter in the XTension folder within the QuarkXPress folder.

▼ ▼
Importing Pictures into QuarkXPress

Now that we know the types of pictures we'll be dealing with, let's look at how we'll deal with them. As we mentioned, the first step in importing a graphic from another application is to create a picture box within your QuarkXPress document. This is covered in Chapter 1, *QuarkXPress Basics,* in the discussion of rectangles, ovals, and polygons. When you have an empty picture box on your page, you can see an "X" in the middle of it. At this point you're ready to bring a picture into the box.

Note that we're bringing a picture *into* the box, rather than replacing the box or even "melding" the two together. The picture box is one entity and the picture is another. You might think of the box as being a window frame through which you see the picture. You can manipulate either the picture box or the picture, or both.

The two primary ways to bring a picture in are to paste from the Clipboard or use Get Picture. In order for either of these methods to work, you must have the picture box selected with the Content tool. This, of course, makes some inherent sense: if you're trying to manipulate (in this case, import) the contents of a picture box, you want to use the Content tool.

Pasting Pictures
There are four problems with pasting in pictures rather than using Get Picture. First, because the image is pasted in, there is no

disk file for it; if you want to edit the image, you have to copy it, paste it into a program that can edit it, make changes, copy it again, and paste it back into the picture box. Second, pictures that are pasted in are slightly less reliable at print time than those that are imported. We're not entirely sure why this is, but it's probably related to the instability of PICT images. (Most images, when you cut and paste them, are converted to PICT.) The third problem is that if you paste in a big picture, your QuarkXPress document balloons in size because the document has to hold the whole image. With Get Picture, just a low-resolution image is imported with a pointer to the full file on disk (see "Picture Management," page 404). And, fourth, color images that are pasted in cannot be separated at all.

So, while we'll cover copying and pasting here, we recommend that you avoid it (at least don't use it often and certainly not for big, important jobs).

The Clipboard. The Macintosh system has a storage area called the Clipboard that lets you take information from one place and put it in another. Whenever you cut, copy, or paste, you're using the Clipboard. Thus, you can cut or copy a picture from one application into the Clipboard, and then paste it from the Clipboard into another application.

One of the problems with cutting and pasting is that the Clipboard only handles certain types of picture formats between multiple applications. If you are trying to bring an outline illustration over from Aldus FreeHand, for instance, you cannot simply cut and paste because outside applications (for example, QuarkXPress) don't understand FreeHand's outline format (see "Tip: Clipboard PostScript," below).

▼ ▼

Tip: Clipboard PostScript. As we mentioned above, QuarkXPress can't understand the native Illustrator or FreeHand formats, so when you copy an object out of those programs and paste it into QuarkXPress, you either get an error or a simple PICT image. Neither one will do. QuarkXPress does, however, understand the PICT/

EPS format. You can create a PICT/EPS version of an object with-in Illustrator or FreeHand and add it to the Clipboard by holding down the Option key while selecting Cut or Copy from the menu (you have to do it from the menu, not using the Command-C or Command-X keyboard shortcut). This is usually reliable, but we have heard of some problems with it—especially images getting distorted when you Option-copy them out of Illustrator 5.0. You can also run into problems with font downloading using this method. Once again, saving as EPS and importing using Get Picture is more reliable (also, as we said earlier, images pasted in—even like this—cannot be color separated).

▼ ▼

To get your picture from the Clipboard into the picture box, select the box with the Content tool, then select Paste from the Edit menu (Command-V). QuarkXPress places the upper-left corner of the picture in the upper-left corner of the picture box. (If you can't see the picture, then see "What Happened to My Picture?" below.)

Get Picture

When creating high-quality documents, you will almost always be working with EPS files and high-resolution TIFF images. These, of course, output as grayscale halftones for photographs, with smooth edges at any resolution, and—for EPS pictures—clean and dependable type at any size.

With your picture box created, and the Content tool selected, you can select Get Picture from the File menu (or be like the pros and press Command-E). A directory dialog box appears, allowing you to find the file you wish to import. When a file of a type that QuarkXPress recognizes is selected (see "File Types," above), the file's type and size are displayed.

You also have the option to turn on the Picture Preview checkbox, which lets you see a thumbnail view of PICT, EPS, TIFF, and RIFF image files. This feature is, of course, a great help in finding a particular picture when you're not sure of the file's name. However, it does slow down the process, especially for files with complicated images, such as large color PICT files. Similarly, if you're accessing images over a network it gets really, really slow. Clearly, judicious use of Picture Preview can save you time.

Once the file is selected in the dialog box, click the Open button or just double-click on the file, and the image appears in your picture frame. QuarkXPress shows you its progress in the lower-left corner of the window, so if you're importing a three-megabyte file on your Mac IIsi, you can see how quickly (slowly) it is processing (perhaps this is the best time of the day to make an espresso). For large files, there's a lengthy delay before "0%" shows up while QuarkXPress does some internal monkeying about (especially if EfiColor is turned on); don't conclude the application's crashed until several minutes go by.

▼ ▼

Tip: Grab That Pencil. You will undoubtedly find yourself in a situation at some point where you want to manually re-import a picture or import a new picture into an already used picture box. Problem: you lose the specifications for the original picture box (scaling, offset, rotation, and so on)! This is a case where you can use the most technologically advanced tools available to humankind, but all you really need is a simple notepad and a pencil. Just jot down all the specs for the previous picture (nice of Quark-XPress to show them to you in the Measurements palette), then, after you bring in the new picture, retype the original specs (remember, if you have multiple changes to the picture box, it's usually quicker to make them in the Picture Box Specifications dialog box all at once). It's also worth noting that the XState XTension can retain all of your specs when importing a different image (see Appendix D, *Resources*).

▼ ▼

What Happened to My Picture?

When you import a picture, you may not see exactly what you were expecting or wanting in the picture box. It may be that you see only a gray box with some type, or that the image is misplaced, or even that you can't see it at all. Remember the First Rule of Computer Anomaly: Don't Panic.

Can't see the picture at all. The first thing to check for is whether or not the big "X" is still in the picture box; if it is, then Get Picture didn't work. Maybe you accidentally clicked Cancel instead of OK. (Don't laugh; this often happens around the same time you get what our friend Greg calls *pixel vision*: eyes that are glazed from looking at the screen too long.) If this happens, just try again.

If what you see is just a blank frame, then the picture is probably somewhere in the box but you can't see it yet. The Get Picture feature automatically places the image in the upper-left corner of the bounding box of the frame. Note that we say the "bounding box" and not the box itself. The bounding box is the smallest rectangle which completely surrounds the frame. It's what you see when you are looking at your frame with Reshape Polygon (under the Item menu) turned off (see Figure 6-8). If you have an oval or a polygonal box, and the image is rather small, then you may have to move the object into the frame (see "Moving Your Pictures Around," later in this chapter).

Often, if you center the image in the box you'll be able to see it better (see "Centering," in the next section).

There's no picture—just a gray box. If the image you imported was an EPS file with no preview image attached for screen representation, then QuarkXPress represents the image as a gray box with the note "PostScript Picture" and the name of the file directly in the center of the gray box. This gray box shows the bounding box of the image, as defined in the header of the EPS document (see "Tip: Invisible EPS Files").

Another cause of the gray-box effect is looking at a complex picture from too far back. That is, when you look at the page in Fit in Window view, it looks like a muddled gray box, but when you go to Actual Size, it looks like what you were hoping for.

The third cause of the gray-box effect is that the picture you imported was, in fact, a gray box. In this case, we can only suggest you think carefully about whether or not you really consider a gray box an exciting enough graphic for your publication.

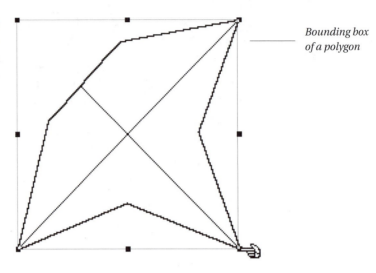

Figure 6-8
Polygons have
rectangular
bounding boxes

*Bounding box
of a polygon*

Working with Pictures

Now that you have brought something (which may or may not look like the graphic you wanted) into the picture box, you can manipulate it in more ways than you ever thought you could, and certainly in more ways than in any other page-layout program.

Moving Your Picture Around

In Chapter 1, *QuarkXPress Basics*, you learned about moving your picture and text boxes around on the page. You can also move the picture itself around within the picture box. You may want to do this for two reasons: for picture placement and for cropping out a portion of the image. Several methods for moving your image within (or even outside of) the box follow. Remember that the picture and the picture box are two different entities, and you can move and manipulate them using different tools: the contents (picture) with the Content tool, the box itself with the Item tool.

Centering. Often the first thing you'll want to do with a picture, whether or not you can see it on screen, is to center it within the picture box. Designers and computer hackers alike have muddled through various tricks to center graphics perfectly within boxes, with varying degrees of success. We suggest you just press Command-Shift-M and let QuarkXPress do it for you. QuarkXPress centers the picture based on its bounding box (its lower-left and upper-right corners). Therefore, pictures which are oddly shaped (for example, an L-shaped picture; see Figure 6-9) may not be centered where you'd expect them to be.

Figure 6-9

Centering an oddly-shaped graphic

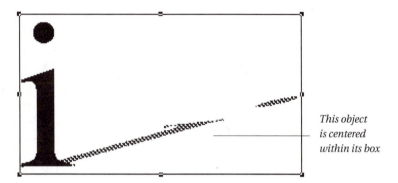

This object is centered within its box

Moving the picture. If you want the image somewhere other than the upper-left corner or in the center, you can use the Content tool (which switches to a Grabber hand when placed over the picture box) to move the picture around. Anyone who has ever done this can tell you that if the image is a large one, it can take quite some time for the picture to respond to the hand movements. If you're thinking about zooming in for precision alignment, remember that what you're really looking at is only a low-resolution (36- or 72-dpi) rendition of the real picture. That means that you can't truly be precise, no matter what you do. The only good solution is to print out proof sheets (see Figure 6-10).

If you know exactly how far you want to move the picture, you can type the offset amounts in either the Measurements palette or in the Picture Box Specifications dialog box (press Command-M or hold down the Command key while double-clicking on the picture). This method is a real godsend when precision is the key, but there are some pitfalls to look out for. One such pitfall is expecting to know where the graphic image is either by the screen

Figure 6-10
Minor picture
offsetting within
the box

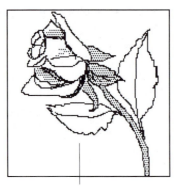
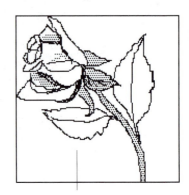

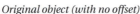

Original object (with no offset)   *Moved horizontally*

representation or the original placement (thinking it's up against the left edge of your box). In the first case, again remember that you're only looking at a 72-dpi image. In the second case, remember that an EPS image almost always has some white space surrounding it. Therefore, when you import it, the image itself is slightly farther to the right than the left edge of the picture box.

▼ ▼

Tip: Minimoves. When you have the Content tool selected and have selected a picture box, you can "nudge" the picture within the box in tiny increments by clicking the arrows in the Measurements palette. Each click moves the image one point in that direction. Holding down the Option key while clicking moves the picture in .1-point increments.

However, we typically find it even more useful to use the arrow keys on the keyboard. Again, each time you press a key it moves it one point; each time you press the key with Option held down, the selection moves .1 point. There are XTensions, such as Nudge-It, that let you customize how far each click or press moves the selection; see Appendix D, *Resources*, for specifics.

Note that if you have the Item tool selected when you do this, you actually move the picture box itself.

▼ ▼

Cropping

If you only want a portion of the picture, then you can "cut out" the unwanted areas by reducing the size of the box and moving the picture so that you only see the area you want (see Figure 6-11). However, there are those who crop out 90 percent of the image in order to use one flower in a bouquet! Then they duplicate that image 12 times and wonder why their file doesn't print. (Don't laugh too loudly; we've seen highly paid professionals do this!)

Remember that unless you're working exclusively with TIFF images, QuarkXPress doesn't get rid of or forget the parts of the picture that aren't shown. That's why you can always go back and change your cropping or picture specifications. But the upshot of this is that it still has to process the entire image, which can take quite some time. So remember to use cropping judiciously. If you only want a small portion of the file, then use an editing program such as DeskPaint or Photoshop to cut out the other parts before you import the image.

If you're using TIFF images, this isn't so much of a problem, because QuarkXPress literally crops down the data at print time, so that the printer only has to chew on what it needs. Note that in versions earlier than 3.3, the program couldn't do this for rotated images (only images at zero degrees would get cropped down; but they fixed this).

Figure 6-11
The edge of the picture box crops the picture

Picture box

Cropped area

Resizing Your Picture

After placing the graphic image where you want it, you may want to scale it to some desired size. QuarkXPress allows you to resize the image within the picture box, stretching or compressing it in the horizontal and/or vertical directions. Most often we find ourselves wanting to enlarge or reduce the picture the same amount in both directions in order to best fit the available space.

If the picture box you created is just the size you want your picture to be, you can quickly and automatically resize the picture to fit the box by pressing Command-Shift-F. However, because this usually stretches the picture disproportionately (adjusting the horizontal and vertical sizing measures differently in order to fill the box), you probably want to press Command-Shift-Option-F (that's a handful!), which makes the picture as large as it can be within the box without distorting it. Note that if you've rotated or skewed the picture first (see "Rotating, Skewing, and Distorting" below), autoresizing may not work exactly as you'd expect it to.

Eric almost never uses the simple and quick keystroke method, however, preferring to type the particular percentages he wants into the Measurements palette or into the Picture Box Specifications dialog box (Command-M). Of course, you can use a combination of these two methods, or even use a third: resizing the picture box.

Usually when you resize the picture box it has no effect on the image which is in it, other than possibly cropping out areas of the picture. However, if you hold down the Command key while resizing (clicking and dragging on one of the control handles), the image resizes along with the box (see Figure 6-12). As usual, holding down the Shift key constrains the picture box (and image) to a square or circle; holding down the Option key along with the Command and Shift keys constrains the picture box (and image) to its proper proportions.

▼ ▼

Tip: Watch 'Em Change. Back in Chapter 1, *QuarkXPress Basics*, we told you about how to watch the changes as you perform them (see "Tip: Viewing Changes as You Make Them"). In case

Figure 6-12
Resizing a picture by
dragging the picture
box handles

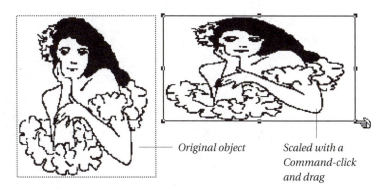

Original object

Scaled with a
Command-click
and drag

you don't remember, the key is to hold down the mouse button for about a half-second (until you see the cursor flash once). Then, when you scale or crop the image by dragging, you can actually see the image get scaled or cropped (otherwise, Quark-XPress just shows you a gray-outline box).

▼ ▼

Resizing for better print quality. As we mentioned earlier, changing the size of a bitmapped image can significantly alter its appearance, either for the better or for the much worse. In general, reducing the size of a bitmapped image, especially if it's a low-resolution graphic improves its output quality by effectively increasing its resolution (a 72-dpi image printed at 50 percent becomes a 144-dpi image).

However, sometimes even a slight reduction can make a big difference. Low-resolution (like 72-dpi) bilevel images containing repeating patterns can come out in plaid patterns when imageset (see Figure 6-13). This is due to the incongruity between the resolution of the image and the resolution of the printer, and can be fixed by scaling the image by a specific percentage. The reduction can be calculated using this formula.

$$(\text{Picture resolution} \div \text{Output resolution}) \times \text{Any whole number} \times 100 = \text{Scaling percentage}$$

You can use Table 6-1 to determine the best reduction for you, or you can create your own chart using the equation above. Note that this is true *only* for one-bit black-and-white images.

Figure 6-13
Nonintegral scaling
ratios can cause
patterning

Rotating, Skewing, and Distorting

QuarkXPress has some amazing graphic manipulation tools; but don't put away your other programs quite yet. For example, let's look at two other modification techniques: rotating and skewing.

Rotation. QuarkXPress lets you easily rotate your imported pictures to a degree unheard of (and certainly rarely needed): $\frac{1}{1,000}$ of a degree. Once again, you are able to set the rotation of the image in several ways.

The first question you'll want to ask yourself is whether you want to rotate the frame, and along with it the image, or just rotate the image itself. You can accomplish either of these by typing in the rotation angle in the appropriate place in the Measurements palette or the Picture Box Specifications dialog box (see Figure 6-14).

While it's really great that you can rotate images in Quark-XPress, you should be careful with this power. When you use QuarkXPress to rotate large bitmapped images, your files can slow to a crawl when printing. Instead, try to rotate these images

When printer resolution is	Scale 72-dpi bilevel images to
635 or	34.02%
1270 or	56.69
2540	79.37
	96.38
	102.05
	119.06

When printer resolution is	Scale 72-dpi bilevel images to
300 or	12.00%
600	24.00
	48.00
	72.00
	96.00
	120.00

When printer resolution is	Scale 300-dpi bilevel images to
635 or	23.62%
1270 or	47.24
2540	70.87
	94.49
	118.11
	141.73

Table 6-1

Integral scaling for bilevel bitmapped images

in Photoshop (or another image-manipulation program) first, and then import them (prerotated) into your picture boxes. This typically isn't a problem with illustrations from FreeHand or Illustrator, because they aren't usually bitmapped.

▼ ▼

Tip: Rotating Your Picture Boxes. Rotating the frame rotates the image, too! The quickest way to "straighten out" your image is to rotate it back by the same amount. That is, if you rotate your box 28 degrees but you want the picture to be straight, then rotate the image -28 degrees.

▼ ▼

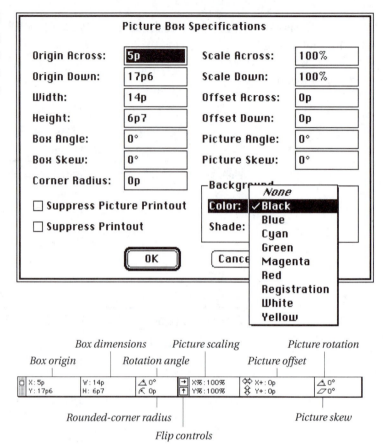

Skewing. Technically, skewing is the process of rotating the two axes differently, or rotating one and not the other. That is, if you rotate just the y-axis (vertical axis) of the coordinate system to the right, everything you print out is "obliqued" (see Figure 6-15). QuarkXPress only allows you to skew in the horizontal direction (rotating the y-axis), which is not a hindrance, as vertical skewing (or "shearing" as it is often referred to) is rarely required. Clearly, skewing an item is not called for every day, but it can be useful in certain situations, enabling you to create interesting effects.

You usually use only one of these effects at a time, perhaps in conjunction with scaling (resizing), but using all three together can make a graphic look quite unusual (see Figure 6-16).

Figure 6-15
Skewing rotates
the vertical axis

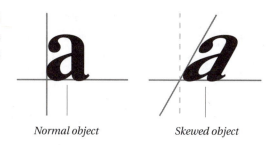

Normal object   *Skewed object*

One of the great advantages of these features is that they're
not incremental. In FreeHand and Illustrator, rotation is cumulative. If you rotate something to 60 degrees and later want to rotate
it to 55 degrees, you have to enter -5 degrees. QuarkXPress, on the
other hand, keeps track of the current rotation, so you just enter
the actual rotation you want. This makes it incredibly easy to get
back to where you started with an image when you've distorted it
beyond recognition: just reset the scaling to 100 percent, and the
rotation and skewing to zero degrees (if you really want to reset
everything about a picture, try reimporting it).

Figure 6-16
Using all of the tools

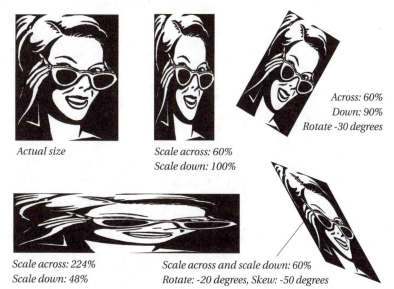

Actual size

Scale across: 60%
Scale down: 100%

Across: 60%
Down: 90%
Rotate -30 degrees

Scale across: 224%
Scale down: 48%

Scale across and scale down: 60%
Rotate: -20 degrees, Skew: -50 degrees

▼ ▼

Tip: Faking Perspective. To make a picture look like it's lying hori-zontally, change picture rotation to -15 degrees, picture skew to 45 degrees, and vertical scaling to 70 percent (see Figure 6-17).

Figure 6-17
Pseudo-perspective

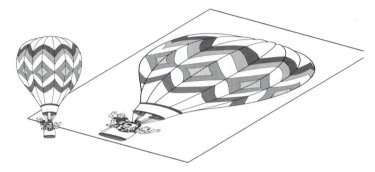

▼ ▼

Tip: Making Multiple Changes to Your Picture. If you know you are going to make multiple changes to your graphic image—changing the skewing, rotation, scaling, and offset, for example—you can speed up your formatting by making those changes in the Picture Box Specifications dialog box (Command-M or double-click on the object while holding down the Command key) so that Quark-XPress processes all changes at once rather than one at a time.

▼ ▼

Publish and Subscribe

Publish and Subscribe is a System 7-only feature that can be really helpful in some ways and really awful in others. How to know the difference? We'll lay it all out for you in this section.

Publish and Subscribe Basics

Let's start out with a quick vocabulary lesson. Subscribe is the second half of Publish and Subscribe. The idea is that you can publish a picture in one program, subscribe to it in QuarkXPress, and then whenever that picture is updated, QuarkXPress can automatically update itself. The file itself is called an *edition*.

The original problem with Publish and Subscribe was (and is) that most edition files are PICT files, which we like using about as much as being bludgeoned by large computer manuals. PICT files and PICT editions are just plain inconsistent when it comes to fonts, line weights, tints, and so on, making them less than useful for graphic arts production work.

However, editions can now be in the form of an EPS. An EPS edition is much, much more consistent and useful. We'll look at just how useful in a moment. Several programs can publish EPS editions, including Adobe Photoshop, Aldus FreeHand, Adobe Illustrator, and Brøderbund's TypeStyler. (Photoshop can also publish TIFF editions, but we don't know of any program that can subscribe to that type.)

How to Be a Publisher

Here's a (very) quick lesson in how to publish an edition. Create a picture in your graphics application. You can select all of it, or a portion of it, and publish it (usually done by selecting Create Publisher from the Edit menu). When you publish it, you create an "intermediate" file: an edition file. You can't edit this file, but whenever you save a change to the source document, the edition gets updated (the update can be automatic if you want). When you create the edition, you usually have to specifically create it as an EPS edition rather than as a PICT edition.

Many programs also let you set some options for editions by selecting Publisher Options from the Edit menu.

Subscribing

In QuarkXPress, subscribing to an edition is much the same as importing a picture, except that you use the Subscribe To command under the Edit menu, rather than Get Picture. They put it in the Edit menu because that's where Apple wanted all Publish and Subscribe controls, unfortunately. The edition looks like a picture, it acts like a picture, it even shows up in the Picture Usage dialog box like a picture. In fact, there's only one little clue that tells you it's an edition: if you go to the Subscriber Options dialog box (see below), there's a little gray square next to the graphic's name, indicating that it's an edition.

Subscriber Options

Subscriber Options is a dialog box that lets you do a number of nifty things (see Figure 6-18). You get to it by choosing Subscriber Options from the Edit menu, or by double-clicking on the picture box with the Content tool (you have to have the picture box selected first to do either of these). The cool thing here is that this dialog box works whether you've got an edition or a normal picture selected.

Figure 6-18
The Subscriber Options
dialog box

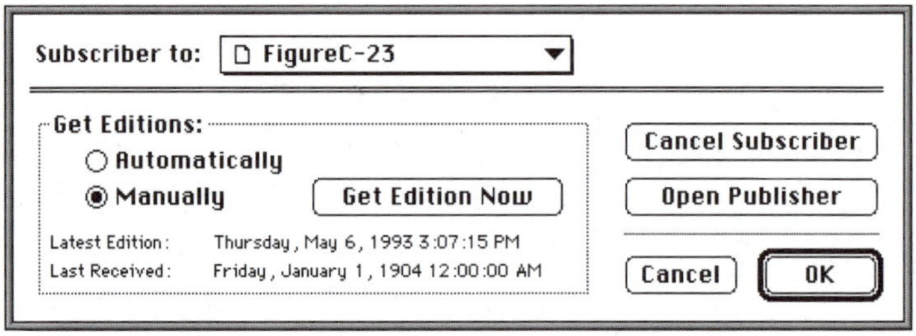

At the top of the dialog box is a popup menu showing the path to the selected picture. Sometimes this can be handier than puzzling out a picture's path from the often-truncated listing in the Picture Usage window. You can tell whether the image is an edition or a regular file by what icon is sitting next to its name. A little icon of a document page means it's a regular picture. A little gray square means it's an edition.

There are several important features in the Subscriber Options dialog box, including Get Editions, Cancel Subscriber, and Open Publisher.

Get Editions. Below the path display are two radio buttons in the Get Editions area. These buttons determine whether Quark-XPress automatically updates that picture every time the edition file is changed, or whether you must update the picture manually.

The Subscriber Options dialog box shows you the last time that QuarkXPress imported or updated the picture (Latest Edition). If you select the Manually button, then QuarkXPress also gives you the Last Received information. To tell you the truth, we can't figure out when this value would be different from the Latest Edition value, so we just ignore it.

If you tell a picture to update manually, then the only time the picture gets updated is when you click the Get Edition Now button in this dialog box.

Cancel Subscriber. The Cancel Subscriber button in the Subscriber Options dialog box supposedly breaks the links between the picture in your QuarkXPress document and the edition upon which it's based, but it actually doesn't appear to do anything more than change Get Editions from Automatically to Manually. Well, it's always nice to have an extra button lying around.

Open Publisher. Eric's favorite button in this dialog box is the Open Publisher button. When you click it, QuarkXPress automatically launches the application that created the picture, and loads the original picture file upon which the edition is based. You can change the picture, and when you save your changes, the edition is updated for you. When you return to QuarkXPress, you'll see that the program has automatically updated your picture (unless you've selected manual updating; then you'll have to click the Get Edition button in the Subscriber Options dialog box).

The only real problem with Open Publisher is that you have to have a lot of RAM for it to work.

▼ ▼

Tip: Use Subscriber Options for Any Picture. What David likes most about the Subscriber Options dialog box is that it works with *all* kinds of imported pictures, not just with edition files. That's right, you can access Subscriber Options for any picture you've imported into your document using the Get Picture command as well as the Subscribe To command. Therefore, Auto Update can work for any picture, rather than just for editions (David never uses editions). Subscriber Options makes working with all of your pictures easier and faster.

▼ ▼

Tip: Subscribing to Non-Native Formats. Since the Open Publisher command works equally well on artwork you've imported or subscribed to, what's the advantage of subscribing? Not much, if your graphics program can directly edit the file you've brought into your QuarkXPress document. Let's say that you have an EPS file from Adobe Illustrator that you import onto your QuarkXPress page. If you select Open Publisher from the Subscriber Options dialog box, the system launches Adobe Illustrator and opens the file so that you can change it. When you're done, you simply save it again, and QuarkXPress can update the picture. This works because Adobe Illustrator can properly open its own EPS files.

But some programs (such as Aldus FreeHand before version 4.0) can't properly read their own EPS format. They can export the EPS file with no problem, but can't open that EPS from within the program. Instead, you have to keep the original file separately, find it, open it, make changes, and then export a new EPS that can be updated in QuarkXPress.

However, like many things, there's a simple solution. If you *publish* your picture from FreeHand or TypeStyler as an EPS rather than *exporting* it as EPS, the Open Publisher command usually works just like it does with an Illustrator or Photoshop EPS.

So while subscribing to editions from Adobe Illustrator or Adobe Photoshop is an often-needless complication, publishing and subscribing from programs such as Aldus FreeHand (pre-4.0) or Brøderbund's TypeStyler can be quite effective.

▼ ▼

Tip: Out of One, Many. We can think of one good reason to use Publish and Subscribe with applications such as Illustrator. The reason lies in the ability to create many editions from a single file. Suppose you have a large, complicated Illustrator picture, and you want to get different parts of it into different places within your QuarkXPress document. You could just import the entire picture to each location, and crop it as desired. But that's wasteful: printer still has to image the whole picture, no matter what's cropped out. You could cut and paste each element from the main picture into smaller picture files, but that's quite inefficient.

An easier solution is to simply select each discrete area of the picture you want to bring into your document, and publish it as an edition. Whenever you change the master, all the published editions get updated, and then are automatically updated in your QuarkXPress document as well.

▼ ▼

Don't Publish or Subscribe to PICTs

We've told you a few reasons why you should consider using Publish and Subscribe, but there's one very major reason why you shouldn't. Most programs that publish graphics only publish in PICT format. By now you know how we feel about PICT, much as the child in the famous New Yorker cartoon did about broccoli. Check the Publisher Options dialog box or user manual of the application from which you want to publish, and see if it supports publishing as EPS. If it doesn't, don't bother publishing. Odds are you'll have only grief when it comes time to print. As nifty as Publish and Subscribe can be, don't publish an Excel spreadsheet or Word table as a PICT and expect it to look acceptable after you subscribe to it and print it from QuarkXPress.

Printing Editions

Note that editions act just like EPS or TIFF images when you print them. That is, QuarkXPress doesn't embed the whole picture into your document; it only creates a link from the document to the picture on your disk. If you send your document to a service bureau to print it, you need to send that edition file, too. No, you don't have to send the original picture file.

▼ ▼

Picture Management

Possibly the worst nightmare of a desktop publisher is arriving at the local service bureau to pick up 300 pages of film negative output, only to see that every illustration has come out as a low-resolution bitmap. Throwing away a thousand dollars is one way to learn some basics of picture management. Reading this section is another.

To Represent

The verb "to represent" means to stand in place for or to act as a placeholder. It is important to note that QuarkXPress represents high-resolution images (including TIFF and EPS files) as low-resolution pictures on screen when you import them using Get Picture. When it's time to print, QuarkXPress searches to find the original high-resolution image and uses it instead of the low-resolution image. It looks first in the folder where the document was originally imported from, then in the same folder as the document you're printing, and finally in the System Folder. If QuarkXPress is successful in this search, your output will look beautiful. If it cannot find the original, it uses the bitmapped 36- or 72-dpi representation for printing. In this case your output will look ugly.

Here are a few items to keep in mind when you use these sorts of pictures.

▶ Don't trash your picture file after importing it, assuming that it's placed for all time.

▶ Don't import your picture and then move the picture file into another folder titled "Picture Folder" (though doing the reverse of this is probably all right).

▶ Do be sure you know where your picture files are.

▶ Do keep your picture files together if possible, to avoid confusion if you need to move your document someplace (like a service bureau).

▶ If you send your document to a service bureau (or any-where else, for that matter), put the document and all of the image files you imported using Get Picture together either in the same folder or on the desktop. You may want to visu-ally segregate the document from its pictures, but keep them in the same folder (see Figure 6-19, and also "Collect for Output," in the "Working with a Service Bureau" section of Chapter 10, *Printing*).

Figure 6-19
Sending your disk to a
service bureau

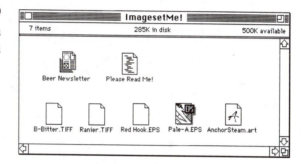

Picture Usage

Submitted for your approval: you've just completed a 600-page document with FreeHand illustrations on every page. The day before sending it to the imagesetter you realize that you have to make changes to every other picture. Tearing your hair out in clumps, you stay up all night changing all the pictures and re-creating new EPS documents to replace all the old ones. But now it's dawn and you have to send it off or risk ruining the whole office's schedule. How will you re-import all those graphics in time? What about replacing and rotating and skewing them all to the correct positions? What will you do? What *will* you do?

Fortunately, you used QuarkXPress, which can automatically re-import every image which has changed since the last time you saved the document. QuarkXPress keeps a running tally of all imported pictures in a document, including when they were last modified. This information is found in Picture Usage in the Utili-ties menu. The Picture Usage dialog box lists several important items about each image in the document (see Figure 6-20).

Figure 6-20

The Picture Usage
dialog box

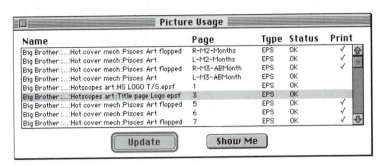

▶ Where the image was originally imported from (its hierarchical disk path, starting from the disk name and moving folder-to-folder, down to the file).

▶ The page number of the document where the picture is located.

▶ The status of the picture: OK, Modified, or Missing.

▶ A column where you can turn Suppress Picture on or off.

We'll cover picture suppression later in this chapter. Here's a quick rundown on the meanings of the various status messages.

OK. This is what you always hope for, especially before printing. QuarkXPress looks for the picture file first in the same place as the file was imported from, then in the same folder as the document, and finally in the System Folder. If it finds it in any of these places, the Status column displays OK.

Modified. If QuarkXPress finds the file but it's been changed in any way since you imported it (the modification date has changed), you see the Modified notice in the Status column. You have two options at this point.

▶ **Ignore the "problem."** Remember that because QuarkXPress uses the external file for printing, the document prints with the updated version rather than the original. However, if you've changed the image's resolution or proportions you shouldn't ignore it; the results are unpredictable.

▶ **Update the image.** All this really means is that you get a new representation image in your document. This approach may help you avoid the annoying dialog box at print time, "Some pictures have been modified or missing." To update the file, select the name and click the Update button. Note that if you've changed much about the image, you should make sure all the rotation, scaling, and cropping attributes you've applied to it are still relevant.

Missing. If QuarkXPress cannot find a file with the same name, it tells you that the file is missing. Again, you have two options.

▶ **Ignore it.** This method is appropriate if you are trying to get some wild artsy effect using low-resolution printing, but is inappropriate for anyone trying to achieve a normal, good-looking, high-resolution print. Remember that if the image is missing, QuarkXPress can only print what you see on the screen: a low-resolution representation.

▶ **Update the image.** If the picture has just been moved to another folder, you can update the link by selecting the file and clicking Update. Here, you're not just bringing in a new representation, but actually relinking the missing picture to the document. The Picture Preview used in Get Picture is also included in the Missing Picture dialog box.

Picture Usage is also valuable when you want to jump to a particular image, if you aren't sure where it is. For example, if you have many figures on many pages, and you want to go to the page which contains "Figure 28b," you can select that item in the Picture Usage dialog box and click the Show Me button. This results in the document displaying the appropriate page and highlighting the picture box which contains that figure. This also works for graphics which have been anchored to text and have flowed to unknown places.

A dagger (†) appearing next to the page number in the Picture Usage dialog box signifies that the picture is on the pasteboard as opposed to on the page itself.

▼ ▼

Tip: Finding Picture Paths. The Picture Usage dialog box is helpful in an indirect way, too. If you're trying to find where a picture came from—that is, where it is on disk—you can select the picture on the page and open the Picture Usage dialog box. That picture is highlighted in the list, so if you have a whole mess o' pictures in your document, you don't have to go scrolling through the list to find the one you want (this also works if you have multiple picture boxes selected). The disk path name is displayed on the left side of the dialog box.

▼ ▼

Tip: Relinking with a New Picture. When you update an image in the Picture Usage dialog box, you don't have to relink with the same picture. You can relink with any other picture, and that image comes in using the same picture specifications as the original (scaling, skewing, and so on). Of course, like many other power tips in this book, this technique can really screw up your image if you don't pay attention.

▼ ▼

Tip: Finding a Bunch of Missing Files. If you move image files or rename the folders they reside in (or even rename the disk they're on), you can wind up with all of your pictures missing. There are two easy ways to relink images.

The first method is the coarser solution, and works if all of your image files are in one folder. Move your QuarkXPress document inside that folder and open it. QuarkXPress looks for missing pictures first inside the folder where the document is located; it automatically relinks them. Save the document, and then move it wherever you like; the images stay linked.

The second method is more subtle, and works if you have clumps of missing files in one or more folders. When you find one missing file inside a folder, QuarkXPress "sees" the other missing files and prompts you whether or not you want to relink them all in one fell swoop (see Figure 6-21). You can then repeat this for other folders with missing images in them.

▼ ▼

Figure 6-21
Updating missing files

Additional missing pictures are located in this folder. OK to update these as well?

OK

Cancel

Auto Picture Import

If you don't want to be bothered by checking Picture Usage all the time, you can use QuarkXPress's internal checking tool: Auto Picture Import. When you have Auto Picture Import turned on in the General Preferences dialog box (Command-Y), each time you open that document QuarkXPress checks to see if any of the linked pictures have been modified. If they have, QuarkXPress brings the new copy in transparently and seamlessly. You won't even know that anything has changed.

Clearly, sometimes not knowing what QuarkXPress is doing behind the scenes is disconcerting or frustrating. There's another option here, which is to set your document preference to "On (Verify)." With this selected, QuarkXPress checks for modified or missing files and, if it finds any, asks you whether you want to re-import them. As with all QuarkXPress features, there is no one "right" way to set up your documents; in some situations you want verifiable auto-importing, and in some you want none at all.

Auto Picture Import Versus Get Edition Automatically

At first glance, the Auto Picture Import and Get Edition Automatically features seem so similar that you might think they're basically equivalent (see "Publish and Subscribe," earlier in this chapter). Not so! Here's the difference. Auto Picture Import only updates pictures when you open your document. You can have your document open for seven hours during a day while you or someone else changes the images, and QuarkXPress never gets the chance to update its pictures.

However, if you turn on Get Edition Automatically for a given picture box, QuarkXPress updates the image anytime it "sees" that the picture has changed.

While Get Editions Automatically might seem like the clear winner here (who wants to wait to have pictures updated?), we think there are good reasons for being judicious with its use. First of all, if you have a document with dozens or hundreds of pictures all set to be automatically updated, QuarkXPress could become so busy checking and rechecking for modified artwork, it might begrudge you the time for trivial tasks such as editing your page.

Another good reason not to use Get Editions Automatically is that there are many times when you don't want images to be changing in your document (especially if the changed images have different aspect ratios—height to width—than the originally imported images). For example, if you've imported images for position only (FPO), then you don't want them suddenly changing and messing up your text runaround and so on.

Greeking and Suppression

There are times when we'd really rather not see all those pictures. Perhaps the screen redraw or printing time is taking too long. Or perhaps we want to use the picture for placement only in the electronic document and don't want it to print out. Or perhaps we just hate the pictures. Whatever the case, QuarkXPress has solutions for you: picture greeking and picture suppression.

Picture greeking. Back in Chapter 4, *Type and Typography*, we discussed replacing text with gray bars. We called that *greeking the text*. Now, with Greek Pictures you can basically replace anything with a gray box. The primary benefit of doing this is speeding up screen redraw: it takes much longer to redraw a detailed picture than it does to just drop in a gray box where the picture should be. Another benefit is found in designing your pages. Sometimes having greeked pictures allows you to see the page layout, including its balance and overall tone, better than if you are looking at "the real thing."

To greek the pictures in your documents, check the Greek Pictures item in the General Preferences dialog box (Command-Y). Note that with this checked, all picture boxes—except for empty and selected ones—are greeked. Selecting a picture box with either the Item tool or the Content tool ungreeks the picture while it's selected.

▼ ▼

Tip: Invisible EPS Images. There are times when you not only don't want to see the images on the screen, but don't even want to see the grayed-out box described above. For example, you might want to place a particular image on your master pages that needs to print out, but doesn't need to be shown on the screen. You can create a screen-invisible EPS document (one which doesn't show on the screen but prints out properly) using ResEdit.

1. Copy the EPS file (when working with ResEdit, always use a copy of the file).

2. Use a paint program such as DeskPaint or Photoshop to select a white rectangular area of the paint document and copy it into the Clipboard.

3. Open the copy of the EPS file with ResEdit.

4. Open the file's PICT resource by double-clicking on it.

5. Select Clear from the Edit menu.

6. Create a new PICT resource by pressing Command-N, then paste the white square into it.

7. Go to the Get Info dialog box by pressing Command-I; change the PICT's number to 256.

8. Save the changes to the file.

Now when you import this EPS file into your QuarkXPress document you won't see anything, but it will successfully print.

▼ ▼

Suppress Printout. In the instances when you want the picture on the screen but not on your printouts, you can turn on Suppress Picture Printout in the Picture Box Specifications dialog box (press Command-M, double-click on the image using the Item tool, or select Modify from the Item menu). You can also select Suppress Printout in this dialog box, which suppresses both the picture contents and the frame itself. Or, even easier yet, you can turn off the checkmark in the Picture Usage dialog box's last column. This is equivalent to checking Suppress Picture Printout in the Specifications dialog box.

Page as Picture

David worked on a book recently which required taking illustrations which were created in QuarkXPress and bringing them into PageMaker (horrors!). This is not an uncommon thing, of course; there are many times when you'd like to move text or graphics from QuarkXPress into other applications, or even bring a page of a QuarkXPress document into another QuarkXPress document as a picture. QuarkXPress allows you to take care of these situations with the Save Page as EPS feature.

Selecting Save Page as EPS in the File menu brings up a dialog box in which you can select a page of your document and save it as a separate EPS file. There are loads of ways to tweak this EPS image.

Page and Scaling

The first two items in the Save Page as EPS dialog box (besides where to save the file) are Page and Scaling. EPS files are only one page long; the Page field in this dialog box lets you specify which page in your document you want to encapsulate.

When you adjust the scaling of the page (for example, make the page 25 percent of full size), the page size is displayed in the dialog box so that you know how large the bounding box of the EPS image is. You can adjust this by changing the scaling. Remember: because this is PostScript, you can scale your EPS page down to 10 percent, bring it into another program, scale it back up to original size, and you won't lose any quality in your output (though your screen preview image may look pretty awful). Figure 6-22 shows a QuarkXPress page that was saved and brought back into another QuarkXPress document.

▼ ▼

Tip: Bleeds in EPS Images. If your page has items that bleeds off the sides, don't expect the bleed to appear in the EPS files. When you save a page as EPS, QuarkXPress cuts the edges of the EPS off right at the edge of the page (the objects still jut out, but Post-Script's clip command doesn't let the printer image them). Unfortunately, there are times when you want to export an EPS and take the bleed with you. For instance, you need those bleeds if you're printing an EPS with OPI comments from Aldus PrePrint or Aldus TrapWise.

You've got two choices in this case. First, there's a great little shareware utility called EPS Bleeder that lets you move the clipping boundary farther out. Second, Quark has promised us that they'll release an XTension very soon (perhaps even before you read this) that will let you specify a bleed distance. This might take the form of an additional field in the Save as EPS dialog box.

You can get these utilities from various on-line services or on the Quark Goodies Disk (see the offer at the back of this book).

▼ ▼

Formats

When you save a page as EPS, the dialog box gives you the option of saving the file in eight—count 'em, eight—different formats: Macintosh Color, Macintosh B&W (black and white), Macintosh DCS, Macintosh DCS 2.0, PC Color, PC B&W, PC DCS and PC DCS 2.0. Let's look at some of these.

Macintosh Color/B&W. If you choose Macintosh Color or Macintosh B&W, you get a normal ol' EPS file. As it turns out, choosing between Color and B&W doesn't just affect the screen preview image. The choice also affects the way that QuarkXPress writes the PostScript code. If you choose B&W, color items are actually changed into black-and-white (or gray) items.

Figure 6-22

QuarkXPress page as
EPS document

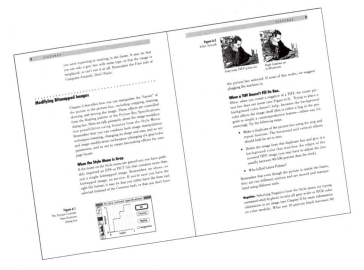

DCS. Choosing DCS causes QuarkXPress to save five files to your disk: one master file that contains a preview image, and four files (one per process color) that contain the actual image data (see "DCS," earlier in this chapter). If you set the Target Profile in the Save as EPS dialog box to SWOP-Coated (or to some other process-color profile), the EfiColor processor converts RGB TIFF and PICT images into CMYK (see Appendix D, *EfiColor*). That means you can save an EPS-5 (or DCS) file that will separate properly in other programs.

Note that because the DCS file format only handles the four process colors, any spot colors you assign get separated into process colors via EfiColor, and placed on the CMYK plates.

DCS 2.0. As we said earlier, DCS 2.0 handles cyan, magenta, yellow, black, and as many spot colors as you want. The cool part about this is that all your spot colors get put on their own plates. The not-so-cool part about this is that RGB images may not get separated correctly. We say "may not" because this might actually just be a bug in the program. Perhaps by the time you read this, QuarkXPress and EfiColor will separate RGB images properly in DCS 2.0. On the other hand, another solution is simply to use pre-separated CMYK images (TIFF or DCS) instead of RGB.

And, as we also noted earlier, selecting DCS 2.0 results in only one file on your hard drive, rather than five or more.

PCs. Earlier in this chapter, we skipped over the whole notion of EPS images for the PC because we didn't think it was really relevant. Of course, in these days of cross-platform compatibility issues, it most certainly is. Preview images on the Mac are low-resolution images placed in the resource fork of the picture's file. PC files don't have resource forks, so this method doesn't work. Instead, the preview image is placed as a header in the beginning of the EPS file. In other words, it's kind of like putting a low-resolution TIFF at the beginning of the EPS file.

QuarkXPress can create EPS and DCS images in a format that retains its preview image when transferred to the PC. Don't forget to give your image a name that's not longer than eight letters, followed by ".EPS" (see Appendix B, *Mac/PC File Transfers*).

Data and OPI

There are two last popup menus in the Save Page as EPS dialog box: Data and OPI. Both of these functions affect only bitmapped image data in TIFF and EPS file formats, so you can ignore them if you're not using one of the two.

ASCII versus Binary. The first choice is whether to include TIFF images in ASCII or Binary format. What's the difference? Bitmapped images saved in binary format are half the size of ASCII. So why use ASCII? You need to if the image will ever be printed over a serial connection (from a DOS or UNIX box, for instance). Binary images won't print over a serial connection.

OPI. The OPI method is based on postseparating full-color pages that include color bitmapped images—especially scanned images. For example, you can import a low-resolution RGB TIFF file into a QuarkXPress document, save that page as EPS, and separate it on either a high-end color system—such as Hell or Crosfield—or on your imagesetter using a program like Aldus PrePrint. Instead of

Quark including the whole TIFF image in the PostScript file, it just throws in OPI comments that say what the name of the scanned image file is, and where the separation program can find it.

This is nice for a couple of reasons. First and foremost is file size. An EPS file with the image date included can be enormous. Sometimes it's nicer to leave the image data on disk somewhere else and just manipulate a minimal EPS file (one that just includes OPI comments about where to find the image data). Another good reason is to work with the file on a system such as Kodak's Prophecy.

The trick to building a PostScript file with OPI comments is the OPI popup menu in the Save Page as EPS and Print dialog boxes (see Figure 6-23). You have three choices in this menu: Include Images, Omit TIFF, and Omit TIFF & EPS.

Include Images. When Include Images is selected in the OPI popup menu, QuarkXPress acts naturally. That is, it works the way it always has, and prints all the TIFF and EPS pictures (or includes them in an EPS).

Omit TIFF. This is the basic setting for OPI comments. When Omit TIFF is selected, QuarkXPress replaces all TIFF images with OPI comments that can be read by an OPI reader like Aldus PrePrint.

Omit TIFF & EPS. Apparently the OPI specs talk about OPI comments for EPS images as well as for TIFF images. However, at this time, no software pays any attention to those specs. So this selection (as far as we can tell) is useless for the time being. Well, it's always nice to have the option . . .

A Warning

A word of warning here about EPS files from QuarkXPress. Some people get overly optimistic about what's possible with PostScript. If you save a full-color QuarkXPress page as EPS, place it in Adobe Illustrator, save, place that on a PageMaker page, and then send it through Aldus PrePrint for final color separations—well, don't be shocked if it doesn't work.

Figure 6-23

OPI popup menu

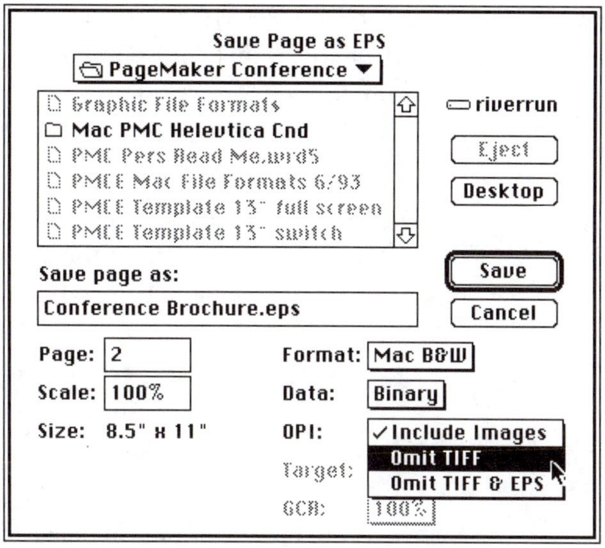

Each of these programs was written by a different group of people and, consequently, handles color, type, and graphic elements differently. Even though, theoretically, the above process should work (PostScript is PostScript, right?), there is almost no way that it ever would (if you can do it, send us a copy!). So, be careful and prudent when you combine programs and nest EPS files within EPS files; the Macintosh platform is not as integrated as it sometimes seems.

▼ ▼

Tip: Suppressing Pictures in EPS Pages. Creating an EPS file of a page with a graphic which has been suppressed does not suppress the screen image of that graphic (although it still suppresses the printing of the picture). If you don't want to see the screen-placement picture, you can cover it with another picture box (a rectangle or a polygon perhaps) with a background color set to zero-percent black (nontransparent) before creating the EPS file.

▼ ▼

Tip: Turning Text to Pictures. You can bring text into QuarkXPress as a PICT image by using a feature of Microsoft Word. Select the text you want in Word and press Command-Option-D. This converts the text to a PICT and places it in the Clipboard. Then move into

QuarkXPress, select a picture box, and press Command-V (Paste). The picture (text) may look odd and jagged on the screen, but it will print out much smoother. You can also manipulate the picture, rotating or scaling it, as described throughout this chapter.

The caveat here, of course, is that we hate PICT images. They are unreliable, so sometimes these words that you'll get from Word look wrong or are set in the wrong typeface. There's not much you can do about it; it's just the state of that art.

▼ ▼

Image on the Half Shell

Now that your understanding of images has risen from the murky oceanic depths to the clear, naked light of day, it's time to take a step forward onto dry land, and—in the next chapter—put them together with text on your page.

WHERE TEXT MEETS GRAPHICS

I t's a curious place, the wild frontier. Whether it's the border between Mexico and the United States, or the border between our tiny planet and the great unknown of Space, we humans strive to conquer and control. This book takes a slightly more microcosmic stance: we're only trying to conquer and control the text and graphics on a page. Nonetheless, it's a task that has been known to make designers shudder. This chapter will show you how this seemingly hostile frontier can be easily subdued.

In QuarkXPress, putting text and graphics together on a page can yield four results.

► They can be positioned so that they don't interact at all.

► They can intrude on one another, with either the picture or the text prevailing (the text flows on top of the graphic or the graphic sits on top of the text).

► They can bump into one another with the text keeping its distance (called *text runaround*).

► One can become embedded in the other and move wherever the other goes.

QuarkXPress allows for each of these possibilities with features such as transparent boxes, text runaround, and anchored boxes. In this chapter we look at each of these features and how they affect your pages.

So, let's take a step forward to those vast frontiers where text meets graphics.

▼ ▼

Transparency

It's easy to make a text or picture box transparent. Just give it a background color of "None" in the Text or Picture Box Specifications dialog box (double-click on the box with the Item tool, or select it with the Item or Content tool and press Command-M).

If one transparent picture box sits on top of another picture box, you can see the second picture box behind it (unless there's a picture in the way). On the other hand, if a transparent picture box sits on top of a text box, the text behind the picture can do two things: it may run around the picture or the picture box, or it may sit there quietly and be trounced on (in which case you'd be able to see the text behind the picture box). Fortunately, you get to control what happens using the Runaround feature.

▼ ▼

Text Runaround

Text can flow around any object on a page: text boxes, picture boxes, and lines. Each item can have its own runaround specification, controlled by the Runaround Specifications dialog box (select the text or picture box and choose Runaround from the Item menu, or press Command-T). For example, if you want to wrap text around a picture box, you should apply a runaround setting to the picture box. Note that the text box has to sit *behind* whatever it's running around.

Figure 7-1 shows the Runaround Specifications dialog box for a picture box. Note that each picture or text box has its own text runaround specification. The Runaround Specifications dialog box gives you four text runaround options for picture boxes and two options for text boxes. Text boxes have the option of None and Item. Picture box options are None, Item, Auto Image, and Manual Image. Let's look at each one of these options in detail.

Figure 7-1
The Runaround
Specifications
dialog box

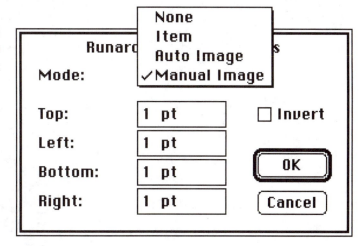

None

When you specify None as the Runaround mode, text that is "behind" a runaround box flows normally. No text is offset, nothing is different. You may not be able to see much of the text behind the item, but . . . hey, that may be your design choice (see Figure 7-2). This option is available for picture and text boxes, and lines.

Item

The Item runaround specification is also available for text and picture boxes, and lines. The key here is to remember that Item refers to the box itself. That is, it doesn't matter what's in the box. Any text that bumps into it flows around the edges of the box (see Figure 7-3). When you have Item specified in the Mode popup

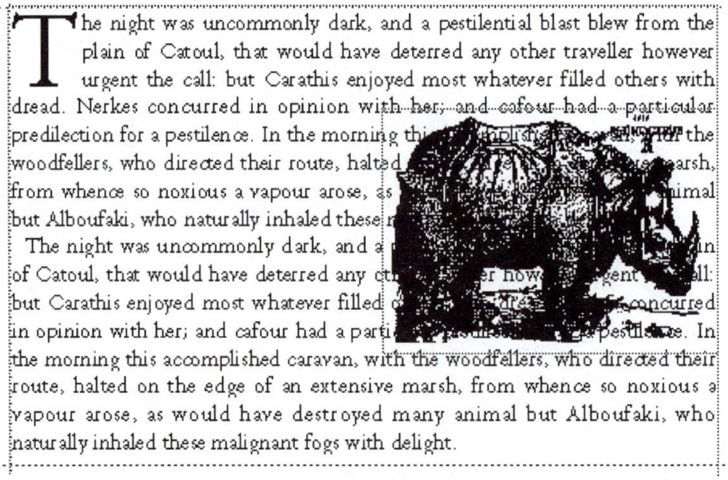

Figure 7-2

Text Runaround
Mode: None

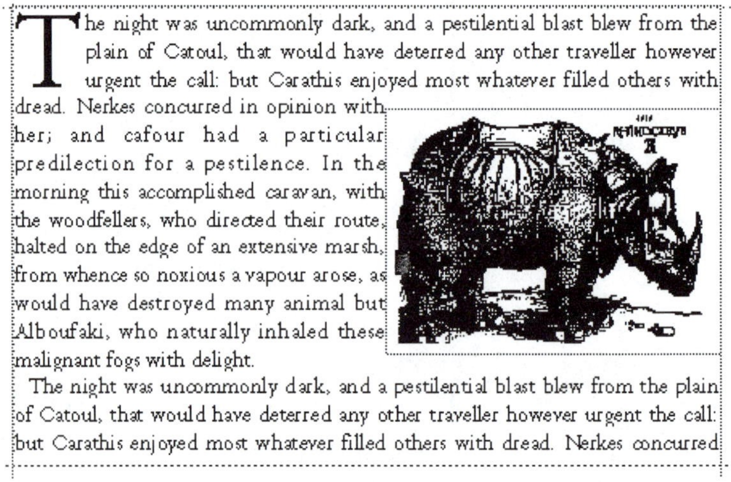

T he night was uncommonly dark, and a pestilential blast blew from the plain of Catoul, that would have deterred any other traveller however urgent the call: but Carathis enjoyed most whatever filled others with dread. Nerkes concurred in opinion with her; and cafour had a particular predilection for a pestilence. In the morning th... ...the woodfellers, who directed their route, halted... ...arsh, from whence so noxious a vapour arose, as... ...imal but Alboufaki, who naturally inhaled these... The night was uncommonly dark, and a... ...in of Catoul, that would have deterred any ot... ...r how... ...ent... ...ll: but Carathis enjoyed most whatever filled... ...concurred in opinion with her; and cafour had a parti... ...pesti... ...e. In the morning this accomplished caravan, with the woodfellers, who directed their route, halted on the edge of an extensive marsh, from whence so noxious a vapour arose, as would have destroyed many animal but Alboufaki, who naturally inhaled these malignant fogs with delight.

Figure 7-3

Text Runaround
Mode: Item

T he night was uncommonly dark, and a pestilential blast blew from the plain of Catoul, that would have deterred any other traveller however urgent the call: but Carathis enjoyed most whatever filled others with dread. Nerkes concurred in opinion with her; and cafour had a particular predilection for a pestilence. In the morning this accomplished caravan, with the woodfellers, who directed their route, halted on the edge of an extensive marsh, from whence so noxious a vapour arose, as would have destroyed many animal but Alboufaki, who naturally inhaled these malignant fogs with delight.
  The night was uncommonly dark, and a pestilential blast blew from the plain of Catoul, that would have deterred any other traveller however urgent the call: but Carathis enjoyed most whatever filled others with dread. Nerkes concurred

menu, you can change how far away the text should flow from the box on each of its four sides. This distance is called the *text outset.*

Auto Image

The Auto Image text runaround mode is available only for picture boxes (that's why the word "image" is in the title). You can specify the text offset for the runaround, and QuarkXPress automatically determines where the image is and how the text should flow around it (see Figure 7-4).

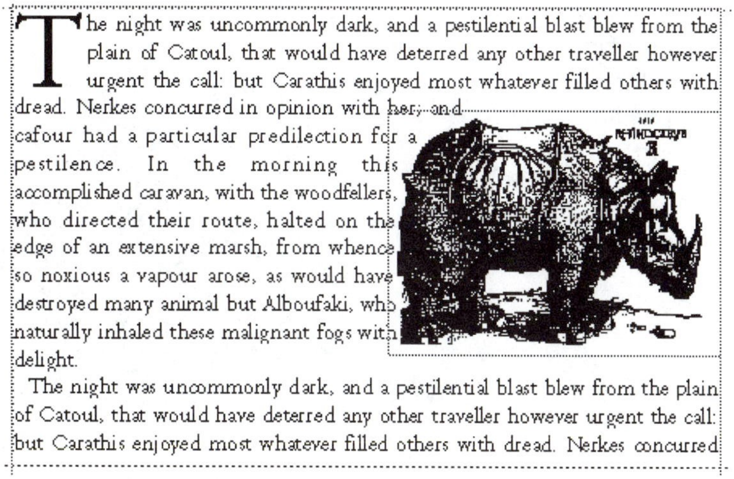

Figure 7-4
Text Runaround
Mode: Auto Image

The image is defined by its screen representation. That is, if you have an EPS picture with a preview, QuarkXPress uses the low-resolution bitmapped image to figure out where the text should run around. If the EPS picture has no screen representation and you only see a gray box, QuarkXPress cannot figure out what the image looks like "inside" the gray box. In this case, it just uses the gray rectangle as the runaround boundary.

Although TIFF images are defined by a rectangle, QuarkXPress treats white space as "blank" space. That is, if you have a black-and-white, grayscale, or color TIFF image which has a lot of white space around the edges, QuarkXPress "sees" the boundary of the nonwhite image. However, even a single gray pixel apart from the main image can cause havoc with text runaround because QuarkXPress sets the text to run around that pixel, too (see Figure 7-5). Sometimes increasing the contrast of an image can help remove unwanted stray pixels (see Chapter 8, *Modifying Images*).

Manual Image

The Manual Image text-runaround feature is one of the coolest features in the program. It lets you specify exactly where you want a runaround to be, using a *text runaround polygon*. These polygons are similar to the polygonal picture boxes we discussed in

Figure 7-5

A couple of misplaced pixels in a TIFF file can throw off the runaround.

These pixels are causing trouble.

Chapter 1, *QuarkXPress Basics*, except that they are used only for text runaround purposes. Figure 7-6 shows an image with a Manual text runaround. Note the handles and dotted line specifying the corners and segments of the text-runaround polygon.

It's important to remember here that QuarkXPress is creating a second box that specifies the text-runaround path. This box is tied inherently to the picture box. If you move the picture box, the text-runaround polygon moves, too. However, you can resize or reshape either the polygon or the picture box without affecting the other.

For those of you who were in such a hurry to get into the book that you skipped Chapter 1, *QuarkXPress Basics*, here is a quick rundown of the necessary concepts and tools for working with polygons.

Figure 7-6

Text Runaround set to Manual Image

- ▶ Polygons are made up of segments joined by corner points.

- ▶ You can move a corner point by clicking and dragging on it.

- ▶ You can also move a line segment of a polygon by clicking and dragging on it. This moves the corner points at both ends of the segment.

- ▶ Moving corners or line segments while holding down Shift constrains the movement horizontally or vertically.

- ▶ You can add a corner point by holding down the Command key and clicking on a line where you want the corner point. When you hold down the Command key, the cursor turns into a hollow circle.

- ▶ You can delete a corner point by holding down the Command key and clicking on it.

- ▶ On text-runaround polygons, you can delete the entire polygon by holding down the Shift and Command keys and clicking on the polygon. This deletes just the text runaround polygon, but not the picture box or the picture itself. The picture box then has no runaround assigned to it (this is the same as changing the Runaround specification to None).

When you specify Manual Image for a picture box's runaround specification, QuarkXPress gives you the text runaround polygon that it uses internally for the Auto Image specification. You can then alter the polygon, using the techniques outlined above, so that the text runaround meets your design needs. Don't worry about getting it perfect the first time; you can always go back and change it.

Note that even though the text-runaround polygon and the picture box are linked together when you move them, the picture box in no way restrains the movement of the polygon. For example, corner points and segments can be placed inside or outside the picture box (see Figure 7-7). In fact, you can use the Content tool to drag a picture and its text runaround polygon anywhere you want on the page (the picture disappears outside the picture box, but the text-runaround polygon is still visible and active).

Figure 7-7

Polygon not restrained by its picture box

You are too simple. Why, you might have said—Oh, a great many things! Mon dieu, why waste your opportunity? For example, thus: Aggressive: I, sir, if that nose were mine, I'd have it amputated on the spot! Friendly: How do you drink with such a nose? You ought to have a cup made specially. Descriptive: 'Tis a rock—a crag—a cape! Kindly: Ah, do you love the little

▼ ▼

Tip: Speed up Polygon Editing. Every time you change a corner or a line segment of a text runaround polygon, QuarkXPress redraws the polygon and recomposes the text to go around it. This quickly becomes tedious. You can make the program hold off on reflowing the text until you've finished editing by holding down the spacebar. When you're finished, let go of the spacebar and Quark-XPress reflows the text.

▼ ▼

Tip: Picture Wrap with No Picture. After you have built a text runaround polygon around a graphic image, you can delete the picture and the polygon remains. Remember to delete the picture while the Content tool is selected, or else you'll delete the picture box (and the picture and polygon with it) instead of just the contents of the box.

If you're using this method to form text into a shape, however, you might as well create a polygonal text box instead (see "Tip: Use Polygonal Text Boxes," below).

▼ ▼

Tip: Polygons from Empty Boxes. If a picture box is empty when you apply Manual Image text runaround, the text-runaround polygon is created in the shape of the picture box itself. We find this handy for creating quick, custom text-runaround paths that don't necessarily have anything to do with a graphic. It's useful, for example, to force a block of text to justify at an angle or wrap around a large drop cap (see Figure 7-8).

Figure 7-8

Text runaround polygons with no images attached

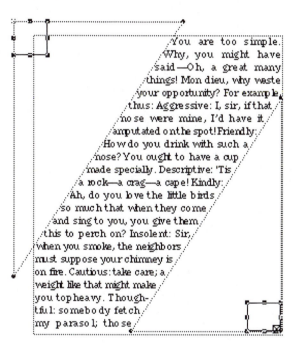

▼ ▼

Inverting the Text Wrap

Each of the types of text runaround we've discussed is based on wrapping text around the outside of an object or polygon. The text flows on one side of the object only, whichever side is the wider and fits more text. However, you can also flow text inside a text runaround polygon (see Figure 7-9). This is called inverting the text wrap. Inverting text wrap is less important than it used to be when you couldn't make polygonal text boxes (see "Tip: Use Polygonal Text Boxes," below); however, it still comes in handy sometimes.

The trick to understanding how to quickly and easily invert a runaround is remembering that text flows where it has the most space. First, select the picture box and give it a Manual Image text runaround (Command-T). Before you click OK in the Runaround Specifications dialog box, check Invert to make it possible to invert the runaround. When you click OK, your text may or may not run inside the text-runaround polygon. If there is more space for the text to run outside the picture box, it'll do that.

To ensure that the text runs on the inside of the text-runaround polygon, first confirm that Invert is checked. Then resize the picture box (not necessarily the runaround polygon) so that the text has little or no room to flow around it.

▼ ▼

Tip: Use Polygonal Text Boxes. Instead of using complicated inverted text wraps, we like to use the polygonal text-box feature introduced in QuarkXPress 3.3. Make a regular text box, then select the last item in the Box Shape submenu (under the Item menu). This turns the text box into a polygon. To alter its shape, you have to turn on Reshape Polygon (select it from the Item menu).

Some XTensions, such as PixTrix, let you convert polygonal picture boxes into text boxes, retaining their shape automatically. This could be very helpful if you wanted to make a complicated polygonal text box (see Figure 7-10).

▼ ▼

Tip: Disappearing Runaround Text. Remember that text runaround is based entirely on box layering. A runaround box must be on top of a text box in order for Auto or Manual Image text runaround to have any effect. One problem many seasoned veterans of QuarkXPress have is that they forget they can assign a runaround to a box or line while the box still has an opaque background (in ear-

Figure 7-9

Text flowing inside
a text runaround
polygon

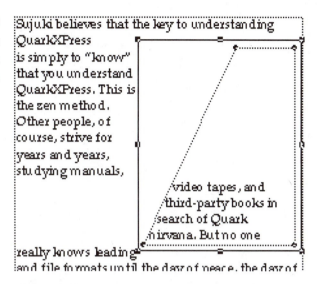

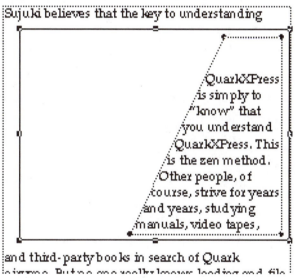

lier versions, opacity and runaround were inextricably linked). If
you assign a text runaround and find that you can't see the text
behind the picture box, make sure your box has a background
color of "None".

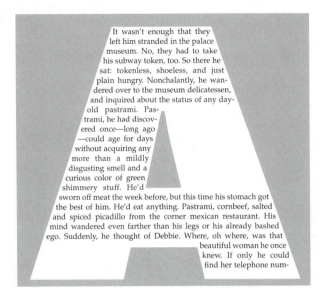

Figure 7-10
Polygonal text boxes

Anchored Boxes

You probably don't think we can come up with a decent encore after those cool Manual Image text-runaround polygons. Well, here's another cool effect: anchored boxes. Many programs let you paste graphic images directly into text. These are usually called *inline graphics.* QuarkXPress takes this concept one step further, however, by letting you paste either a picture or a text box directly into the flow of text. These boxes become anchored to the point where they have been pasted. In other words, as you type, they flow along with the text in the same position.

Anchored boxes can be used in many situations: placing small pictures in text as icons, creating picture drop caps, or allowing tables and figures to keep their place in text. Let's look at how these anchored boxes are created and how to work with them.

Turning a Box into a Character

We like to think of anchored boxes as turning a picture or a text box into a character that can be manipulated in a text block. This proves to be a useful model for working with anchored boxes. There are two steps involved with turning a picture or text box into an anchored box character.

1. Cut or Copy. The first step in creating an anchored box is to cut or copy the picture or text box using the Item tool. Click on the picture or text box and select Cut or Copy from the Edit menu (or press Command-X or Command-C). Because you're using the Item tool rather than the Content tool, the box itself is being cut or copied along with its contents.

2. Paste. The second step is to paste the box into the text using the Content tool. Select the text box and place the cursor where you want your anchored text box to sit, then select Paste from the Edit menu (or press Command-V). Because you're using the Content tool, the box is pasted in as a character in the text block, rather than as a separate box.

What you can't do. QuarkXPress prohibits you from making certain objects into anchored boxes. First of all, you cannot anchor a group of objects. Secondly, anchored boxes are just that: boxes. Therefore, you cannot anchor something that can't be defined as a box, like a line. And, even though QuarkXPress calls polygons and ovals "boxes," it doesn't really let you anchor them (it turns them into rectangular picture boxes). A third function the program won't allow is anchoring text boxes that have anchored boxes within them.

Modifying Anchored Boxes

While anchored boxes can do many things that normal picture and text boxes can't do, they sacrifice some abilities as well. For example, you cannot select and drag an anchored box to a new location. Nor can you rotate anchored boxes (unless you rotate the text box that they are pasted into); though you can still rotate and skew the image within the box. And you can only resize anchored boxes using the sizing handles on the right and bottom sides.

But don't let all these "no-can-do's" dishearten you. There's still lots you can do.

The root of every change you can make with anchored boxes is the Anchored Box Specifications dialog box (there is one for picture boxes and another for text boxes; see Figure 7-11). Selecting the anchored box with either the Item or the Content tool and choosing Modify from the Item menu (or double-clicking on the box with the Item tool, or pressing Command-M) brings up the appropriate dialog box for the type of box that is anchored.

Resizing. You can resize anchored boxes by either dragging one of the three handles, or by specifying a width or height in the Anchored Box Specifications dialog box or the Measurements palette. Remember that anchored boxes are just like normal picture or text boxes in most ways. For example, you can scale both the box and its contents by holding down the Command key while dragging one of the three control handles.

Contents modification. Both anchored text and picture boxes are fully functional. That is, you can edit, import, or reformat the contents of any anchored box. To alter the contents of an anchored box, you must use the Content tool, just as if you were altering a normal box.

There are several features you cannot take advantage of, however. One thing you can't do is change an anchored box's text runaround specification (see "Tip: Adjusting Runarounds for Anchored Boxes," below). The text runaround for an anchored box is determined primarily by its alignment within the text box (see "Alignment," below). Another prohibited function is text linking: you cannot link to or from an anchored text box.

▼ ▼

Tip: Adjusting Runarounds for Anchored Boxes. It took us almost forever to figure out that QuarkXPress ignores any runaround specification you give an anchored box except for one: the Top field when Runaround is set to Item. If you want to set a runaround for an anchored box, you have to set it before you paste it

Figure 7-11

The Anchored
Box Specifications
dialog boxes

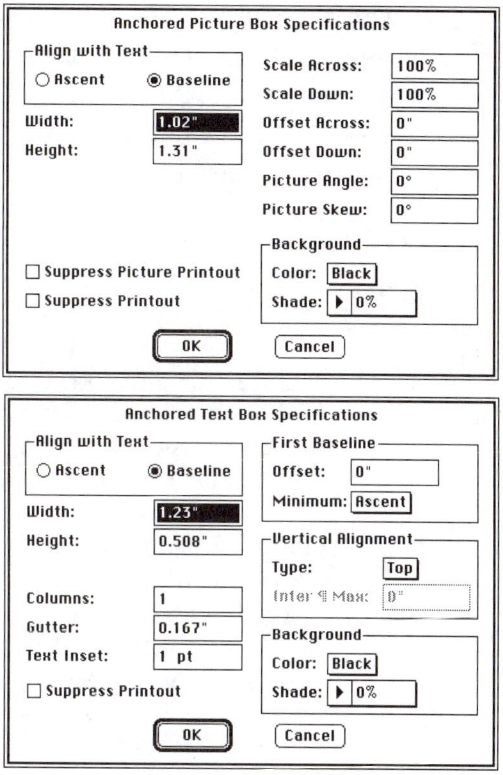

```
┌─────────────────────────────────────────────────┐
│          Anchored Picture Box Specifications      │
│ ┌─Align with Text──────┐                          │
│ │ ○ Ascent  ● Baseline │  Scale Across:  [100%]   │
│ │                      │  Scale Down:    [100%]   │
│ │ Width:   [1.02"]     │  Offset Across: [0"]     │
│ │ Height:  [1.31"]     │  Offset Down:   [0"]     │
│ │                      │  Picture Angle: [0°]     │
│ │                      │  Picture Skew:  [0°]     │
│ │                      │ ┌─Background──────────┐  │
│ │ ☐ Suppress Picture Printout  │ Color: [Black] │ │
│ │ ☐ Suppress Printout          │ Shade: [▶ 0%]  │ │
│ │                              └────────────────┘ │
│           ( OK )    ( Cancel )                     │
└─────────────────────────────────────────────────┘
```

```
┌─────────────────────────────────────────────────┐
│           Anchored Text Box Specifications        │
│ ┌─Align with Text──────┐ ┌─First Baseline──────┐  │
│ │ ○ Ascent  ● Baseline │ │ Offset:  [0"]       │  │
│ │                      │ │ Minimum: [Ascent]   │  │
│ │ Width:   [1.23"]     │ └─Vertical Alignment──┐  │
│ │ Height:  [0.508"]    │ │ Type:    [Top]      │  │
│ │                      │ │ Inter ¶ Max: [0"]   │  │
│ │ Columns:   [1]       │ └─Background──────────┐  │
│ │ Gutter:    [0.167"]  │ │ Color: [Black]      │  │
│ │ Text Inset: [1 pt]   │ │ Shade: [▶ 0%]       │  │
│ │ ☐ Suppress Printout  │ └─────────────────────┘  │
│           ( OK )    ( Cancel )                     │
└─────────────────────────────────────────────────┘
```

into the text block (you can't change it once it's pasted in). Whatever you have set for the Top runaround value is set for all four sides of the runaround box.

▼ ▼

Tip: Backgrounds in Anchored Boxes. Note that the background color for an anchored box is not necessarily the same of that of the text box in which it is located. For example, if your text box is set to 10-percent gray and you anchor a zero-percent black picture box into it, the anchored picture box won't match its surroundings (you'll get a white box on a gray background). If you can think of a better word than "tacky" to describe this, let us know. Instead, be sure to specify "None" for the background in all anchored boxes.

▼ ▼

Alignment. You can align an anchored box in two ways: Ascent or Baseline.

▶ **Ascent.** When you specify an anchored box to align by Ascent, the top of the box aligns with the ascender of the tallest font in that text line. The rest of the figure drops down and text wraps around it. This is most commonly used for creating initial caps and heads (see Figure 7-12).

Figure 7-12

Initial head using an anchored picture box

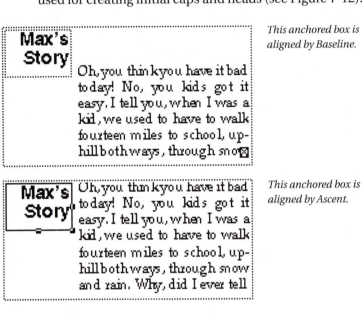

This anchored box is aligned by Baseline.

This anchored box is aligned by Ascent.

▶ **Baseline.** When you specify an anchored box to align by Baseline, the bottom of the box aligns with the baseline of the line it's on. This is very helpful if the anchored box is attached within a line of text and is acting as if it were a special text character.

How the text in previous lines accommodates this baseline alignment depends on the leading in the paragraph. If you specify absolute leading, the anchored box may overlap the text above it (see Figure 7-13). If you are using automatic or relative leading, the space between lines is increased to accommodate a larger anchored box. Again, the model of the anchored box as text character is particularly fitting, as these are exactly the effects you would achieve by using an oversized character in a text block (see "Initial Caps" in Chapter 4, *Type and Typography*).

Figure 7-13
Anchored box
alignment

F ⌐ ⌐ ⌐ /e thy father lies;
(are coral made:
T rls that were his eyes:
    Nothing in him that doth fade,
But doth suffer a sea-change
Into something rich and strange.

Box is aligned by baseline;
text has absolute leading.

Full fathom five thy father lies;
Of his bones are coral made:
Those are pearls that were his eyes:

    Nothing in him that doth fade,
But doth suffer a sea-change

Also aligned by baseline, but
text has automatic leading.

When using a baseline-aligned anchored box that acts as a character within a line, we recommend that you use absolute leading for your paragraph. Otherwise, all hell can break loose and text is shoved all over the place (however, see "Tip: Anchored Figures on Their Own Line," below).

You can choose the anchored box's alignment in two places: the Anchored Box Specifications dialog box or the Measurements palette. To change the alignment using the Measurements palette, click on one of two icons on the far left of the palette. The top icon represents Ascent, and the bottom icon represents Baseline.

▼ ▼

Tip: Anchored Figures on Their Own Line. You might use anchored boxes within a line of text for symbols, complex dingbats, or company logos, but more frequently you'll use them as single "characters" within their own paragraph.

We know we said we hated automatic leading and that you should never use it, but here's an exception. Setting the paragraph that contains the anchored box to Auto leading ensures that there is enough space above the image so that it doesn't overlap any text. The anchored box's alignment should be set to Baseline, too (see Figure 7-14).

Figure 7-14

Setting leading for
anchored boxes

The night was uncommonly dark, and a pestilential blast blew from the plain of Catoul, that would have deterred any other traveller however urgent the call: but Carathis ... s with dread. Nerkes conc ... cafour had a particular pr ... morning this accomplished ... directed their route, halted ... from whence so noxious ... troyed many animal but A ... se malignant fogs with del ...

The night was uncommonly dark, and a pestilential blast blew from the plain of Catoul, that would have deterred any

Absolute leading

The night was uncommonly dark, and a pestilential blast blew from the plain of Catoul, that would have deterred any other traveller however urgent the call: but Carathis enjoyed most whatever filled others with dread. Nerkes concurred in opinion with her; and cafour had a particular predilection for a pestilence. In the morning this accomplished caravan, with the woodfellers, who directed their route, halted on the edge of an extensive marsh, from whence so noxious a vapour arose, as would have destroyed many animal but Alboufaki, who naturally inhaled these malignant fogs with delight.

The night was uncommonly dark, and a pestilential blast blew from the plain of Catoul, that would have deterred any

Automatic leading

▼ ▼

Tip: Aligning Anchored Text Boxes. If you're trying to align the baselines of text in an anchored text box with text that surrounds it, you need to make sure of three things.

▶ The leading in the anchored text box and the surrounding text box must be equal.

▶ The Top text outset value in the Runaround Specifications dialog box must be set to zero for the anchored text box. Note that this is *not* the same as selecting None. Because you cannot specify runaround for a box once it's anchored, you should set this before you cut and paste it.

▶ The anchored text box must have a text inset of zero. You enter this value in the Text Inset field in the Anchored Text Box Specifications dialog box.

▼ ▼

Tip: Anchored Boxes as Initial Caps. In Chapter 4, *Type and Typography*, we implied that you could use anchored boxes as initial caps simply by pasting them in as the first character of a paragraph and setting their alignment to Ascent. However, you may run into a problem if you're using a pre-3.3 version of QuarkXPress. In those versions, if your paragraph has any sort of left indent, some text lines that wrap around the anchored box are indented from the anchored box itself (see Figure 7-15).

There are a few workarounds for this problem, but none other is so easy and elegant as this one: upgrade to the newest version of the software.

▼ ▼

Working with Anchored Boxes

David had a professor once who maintained that when someone reaches perfection, the skies open and he or she is lifted into the heavens in perfect bliss. Given that you're reading this book, you probably haven't reached that pinnacle yet. So what happens if you don't place the anchored box exactly where it should be? Or if you decide to change your mind and delete the anchored box?

Figure 7-15
Anchored boxes can
cause problems
before version 3.3

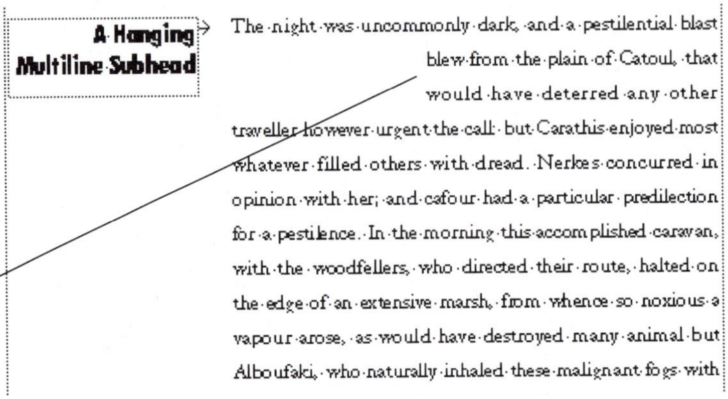

A Hanging Multiline Subhead

The night was uncommonly dark, and a pestilential blast blew from the plain of Catoul, that would have deterred any other traveller however urgent the call but Carathis enjoyed most whatever filled others with dread. Nerkes concurred in opinion with her; and cafour had a particular predilection for a pestilence. In the morning this accomplished caravan, with the woodfellers, who directed their route, halted on the edge of an extensive marsh, from whence so noxious a vapour arose, as would have destroyed many animal but Alboufaki, who naturally inhaled these malignant fogs with

*The text is indented
from the anchored box
(this is a bug in pre-
version 3.3 releases)*

Don't worry, we've got answers for all of that (even though the skies aren't opening here, either).

Moving Anchored Boxes. As we said earlier, you cannot move an anchored box by just dragging it around like you would any other box. There are two ways to move an anchored box: the way that the documentation says you can, and the way that makes most sense.

Quark's documentation says you must select the anchored box with the Item tool, select Cut from the Edit menu, and then switch to the Content tool to position the cursor and paste it. This is consistent with the way that anchored boxes get placed in text in the first place. However, using the model that once an anchored box is placed in a text block it behaves like a text character, we prefer to move this anchored box "character" by cutting and pasting it with the Content tool alone. This just seems more intuitive to us, and it works just fine.

▼ ▼

Tip: Dragging Anchored Boxes. Actually, it turns out you *can* drag anchored boxes to where you want them. The key is the program's Drag-and-Drop text-editing feature, plus a little ingenuity. When Drag and Drop is turned on in the Application Preferences dialog box (Command-Option-Shift-Y), you can select a range of text and drag it to where you want it. If an anchored box is part of that text, it goes, too. However, because there's no way to drag only the anchored box—with no other text going along for the ride—you have to select at least one other character (even a spacebar) and then drag *that* character.

▼ ▼

Deleting Anchored Boxes. We'll say it just one more time: anchored boxes are just like text characters. Do you delete text characters with the Delete function from the Item menu (or press Command-K)? No. A character is not an item; it's a character, and should be treated as one. If you want to stamp out the measly existence of an anchored box, place the cursor after it and press the Delete key—or before it and press Shift-Delete.

Also, after turning a box into a character to anchor it, you can't cut it and paste it somewhere else as a standalone graphic.

▼ ▼

Tip: Getting an Anchored Box Out Again. We like to say, "There's always a workaround." As it happens, there are actually two ways to get an anchored box out as a standalone graphic. The first way is to select it with either the Content or the Item tool (click on the box rather than dragging over it like a character) and select Duplicate from the Item menu (Command-D). This makes a copy of the box, but in a standard (nonanchored) form.

The second method is to select the anchored box with the Item tool (just click on it), copy it, and then select Paste while still using the Item tool.

▼ ▼

Paragraph Rules

While it's true that you can't paste rules (lines) into text to anchor them, you can actually produce anchored rules using a different method. You can set anchored rules through paragraph-level formatting in text, and build them into style sheets. Unlike so many other features in QuarkXPress, you can only set anchored paragraph rules in one way. Unfortunately, these rules can only be horizontal (see "Tip: Vertical Rules," later in this chapter).

Rule Above/Rule Below

The one way to set anchored paragraph rules is via the Paragraph Rules dialog box. While your text cursor is in a paragraph or highlighting it, you can select Rules from the Formats menu (or press Command-N). You then have the choice whether to place a rule above the paragraph, below it, or both. When you select one of these rule positions, QuarkXPress expands the dialog box to give you more choices (see Figure 7-16).

Figure 7-16

The Paragraph
Rules dialog box

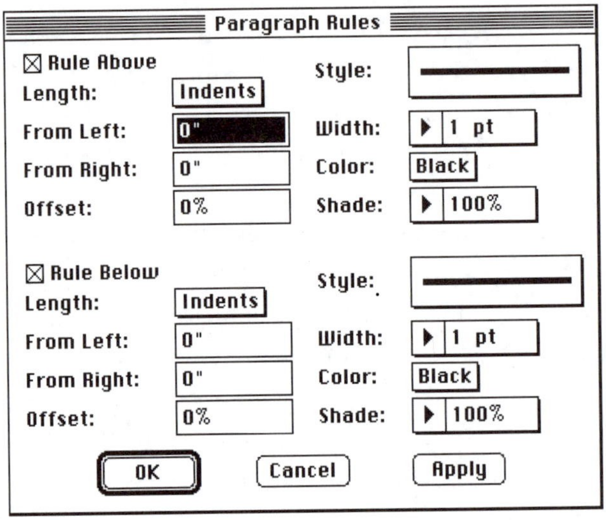

The expanded Paragraph Rules dialog box gives you many options for the placement, size, and style of your horizontal rules. Let's look at each element of the dialog box.

Style. The right side of the Paragraph Rules dialog box contains the style specifications for the rule. You can choose the line style, width (thickness), color, and shade for the rule using the popup menus. You can also type in your own value for the Width and Shade fields, to the thousandth of a point or tenth of a percent.

The line styles available are the same styles available for all lines (see "Lines" in Chapter 1, *QuarkXPress Basics*).

Length. You can specify the length of the rule and its horizontal position using the Length popup menu and the From Left and From Right fields. The initial decision you need to make is whether you want the rule to stretch from the left indent of the paragraph to the right indent (select Indents in the Length popup menu) or only to stretch as far as the text (select Text in the Length popup menu). Figure 7-17 shows examples of these settings.

Figure 7-17

The Length setting in Rules Above/Below

Rule Above: Length set to Text

The night was uncommonly dark, and a pestilential blast blew from the plain of Catoul, that would have deterred any other traveller however urgent the call: but Carathis enjoyed most whatever filled others with dread. Nerkes concurred in opinion with her; and cafour had a particular predilection for a pestilence. In the morning this accomplished caravan, with the woodfellers, who directed their route, halted on the edge of an extensive marsh, from whence so noxious a vapour arose, as would have destroyed many animal but Alboufaki, who naturally inhaled these malignant fogs with delight.

Rule Below: Length set to Indents

Horizontal offsets. The next considerations in determining the length of the rule are its offsets from the left and right. You can specify how far from the left or right the rule should start (or end) by typing a measurement into the From Left and/or the From Right fields. Your only limitation in offsetting the rule is that the rule cannot go outside the text box. For instance, if your paragraph is set to a left indent of "1p6", the minimum left offset you can type is "-1p6" (anything more than that would extend the rule out of the box).

Vertical position. The third specification you can make for an anchored paragraph rule is its vertical position relative to the paragraph to which it is attached. This concept is a little tricky, and Quark's documentation doesn't do a lot to help clarify the idea. Let's break it down into pieces.

The vertical positioning of the rule is set in the Offset field. We don't like the word "offset," as it confuses the issue. We prefer the term *positioning,* so that's what we'll use. Just remember that these values go in the Offset field. You can specify positioning with either an absolute measurement or a percentage. QuarkXPress handles each of these very differently.

▶ **Absolute.** Let's take absolute positioning first. An absolute measurement for a rule above is measured from the baseline of the first line in the paragraph to the bottom of the rule. An absolute measurement for a rule below is measured from the baseline of the last line in the paragraph to the top of the rule (see Figure 7-18).

▶ **Percentage.** Specifying the vertical position of a rule by percentage is slightly more complex. The first thing to remember is that the percentage you are specifying is a percentage of the space between the paragraphs. This space is measured from the descenders of the last line of a paragraph to the ascenders of the first line of the next paragraph.

Let's look at an example. If you set Rule Below for a paragraph with an offset of 60 percent, QuarkXPress measures the distance between the two paragraphs (descender to ascender) and places the top of the rule 60 percent of that distance down. The rule grows *down* from that position as you increase its weight. Rule Above is placed with its bottom in the appropriate position, rather than the top, and the rule grows *up* from that position. A rule above and a rule below, when both set to 50 percent, fall at exactly the same place (halfway between the paragraphs).

To us, percentage-based positioning is equivalent to automatic leading: we don't like it or its kind. We don't think it should be run out of town, because there's always a place for that kind of feature, but—in general—we don't like to use it.

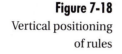

Figure 7-18

Vertical positioning of rules

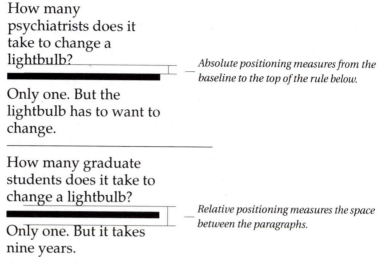

How many psychiatrists does it take to change a lightbulb?

Absolute positioning measures from the baseline to the top of the rule below.

Only one. But the lightbulb has to want to change.

How many graduate students does it take to change a lightbulb?

Only one. But it takes nine years.

Relative positioning measures the space between the paragraphs.

Why? There are some problems with percentage-based rules. For example, if a paragraph is specced to have a rule 30 percent above it, the rule doesn't show up if that paragraph sits at the top of a text box. A paragraph rule set some percentage below a paragraph doesn't appear if that paragraph is the last paragraph in the text box.

It is nice that positioning a rule based on a percentage ensures that the rule doesn't overlap any text (it pushes the paragraphs away from each other if it needs to). But all in all, we would rather have complete control over the rule's position and feel sure that the rule is there, no matter what happens to the paragraph.

On the other hand, if you want a rule halfway between two paragraphs, setting the Offset to 50 percent is much faster than trying to figure out what absolute value you should enter.

▼ ▼

Tip: Reversed Type in Rules. This is one of the oldest tricks in the book. You can make reversed type that is anchored to text by assigning a thick rule above or below a paragraph and setting the type in the paragraph to white. You need to specify a vertical position for the rule so that it "overlaps" its own line. Out of habit, we always use a rule above about four or five points larger than the text size, and specify a -2 or -3-point offset (vertical position). You can use this same technique to create multiple-tinted tables (see Figure 7-19).

Figure 7-19

Type in a rule

SPRING—1624		
Spread	750	1000
Full page	600	800
Half page	400	500
Quarter page	275	375
Spot	175	250

Rule Above with an Offset of -2 points

These are rules, too!

▼ ▼

Tip: Vertical Rules. Nope, there's no way to cajole, coerce, or configure QuarkXPress to paste or place an anchored vertical line in a text block. Or is there? We work around this problem with the following technique.

1. Create a picture box as thin (or thick) as you want your rule.

2. Give the picture box the background color you want the rule to be (for example, 80-percent magenta). Make sure it has a frame width of zero.

3. Copy and paste this empty picture box into the text block as described in "Anchored Graphics," above. You'll probably want to paste it either at the beginning of a paragraph or in a paragraph of its own.

4. Set the anchored box to Ascent alignment, and the text in the text box to absolute leading, so it wraps around the picture box/rule.

Figure 7-20 shows a sample vertical rule made using this method. Note that in this example, the rule appears as if it is set off from the left text margin. Actually, the text is set off from the rule using a nine-point left indent together with a first line indent of -9 points. The picture box/rule is the first character in the paragraph.

Figure 7-20
Anchored vertical rule

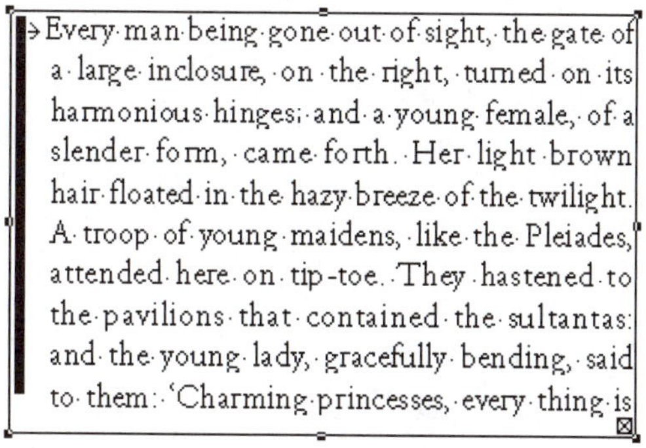

> Every·man·being·gone·out·of·sight,·the·gate·of
> a·large·inclosure,·on·the·right,·turned·on·its
> harmonious·hinges;·and·a·young·female,·of·a
> slender·form,·came·forth.·Her·light·brown
> hair·floated·in·the·hazy·breeze·of·the·twilight.
> A·troop·of·young·maidens,·like·the·Pleiades,
> attended·here·on·tip-toe.·They·hastened·to
> the·pavilions·that·contained·the·sultantas:
> and·the·young·lady,·gracefully·bending,·said
> to·them:·'Charming·princesses,·every·thing·is

▼ ▼

Tip: Return of Vertical Rules. If you need a vertical rule thinner than one point, you're out of luck with the last tip. One point is the minimum thickness of a picture box. It's obviously time to resort to drastic measures: build the rule in another program, and then import it into a picture box before anchoring it in a text box. Make the picture box transparent. If you need to lengthen or shorten the rule, just change the vertical scaling of the picture.

▼ ▼

Poking and Prodding

Where text meets graphics. Like we said, it's a wild, woolly frontier just waiting to be mastered. We've explored how different boxes and page elements can interact, but these are mysterious regions where there is no substitute for poking and prodding about on your own.

The next two chapters deal with a few of the more detail-oriented features in QuarkXPress: modifying bitmapped images and working in color. After reading those, you'll be able to create any page known to humanity (and a few that aren't).

CHAPTER 8

MODIFYING IMAGES

To be honest, many of you will never need to read this chapter, but we think you should anyway. Although image modification is an aspect of QuarkXPress which can only be described as fine tuning, we cover some important areas here, including an in-depth discussion of halftoned images.

In Chapter 6, *Pictures,* we discussed several graphic file formats, how to bring them into your QuarkXPress documents, and how to do basic manipulations with them, such as rotating, skewing, and scaling. In this chapter we look at how you can use QuarkXPress in place of other image-editing software to modify the imported image itself. Bear in mind that we're not talking here about image *editing.* You can't actually change the contents of imported graphics in QuarkXPress. You can, however, change some of their overall parameters, such as contrast, color, and halftone screen.

We start this chapter by examining the types of images we can modify, and then we move into how to modify them. Much of this is potentially confusing, but bear with us, read carefully, and you'll be an inexorable image-modifier faster than you can say, "Phylogeny recapitulates ontogeny."

▼ ▼

The Picture File

In this chapter, we are *only* concerned with bitmapped images. Bitmapped images, as far as QuarkXPress is concerned, are black and white, grayscale, or color, and are found in TIFF, RIFF, PNTG, and PICT files. In the case of PICT files, however, note that when it comes to image control, QuarkXPress only recognizes bitmap-only PICTs. That means that no object-oriented graphics are recognized for the purpose of image modification. But let's be frank: you'd be foolish to be using PICT images anyway. They're very unreliable, and nearly impossible to do color separations with. Due to the nature of bitmapped PICT files, QuarkXPress can import them (see Chapter 6, *Pictures*), but does not allow any modifications such as contrast control to be performed on them. Use TIFFs whenever possible.

Bitmapped Images

You may want to take this opportunity to refresh your memory from Chapter 6, *Pictures*, about bitmapped images and the particular file types of PNTG and TIFF. Here are the highlights.

▶ Bitmapped images are simply rectangular grids of sample points (dots).

▶ The resolution of the image is the number of these sample points per inch (spi).

▶ Each sample point can be black, white, a level of gray, or a color. This color is represented by a number; for example, in a file with 256 gray levels, black would be 255.

▶ Scaling the image has a direct effect on its resolution. Enlarging the picture to 200 percent cuts the resolution in half (same number of samples in twice the space), which may result in jaggies or pixelation. Reducing the image to 50 percent doubles the resolution, which may improve image quality (see Figure 8-1).

Figure 8-1
Resolution and scaling
for bitmaps

▶ A PNTG (Paint-type) file has a fixed size of eight by 10 inches at 72 dpi (576 by 720 pixels), and each pixel can be only white or black. These are said to be "flat" or bilevel bitmapped images.

▶ A TIFF file can be any size rectangle with any number of dots per inch, and each pixel can have any level of gray or color which is definable by the color models described in Chapter 9, *Color.* TIFF files are said to be "deep" if they have four or more gray levels (over two bits per sample point).

Modifying Images

It is rare that a scanned image prints the way you want it to without some modification. You may also want to apply image-modification techniques to synthetic pictures created with a paint program. QuarkXPress lets you alter an image in several ways. Here's what you can do.

▶ Replace its contrast curve with preset high-contrast or posterized effects.

▶ Apply a custom contrast curve.

▶ Invert the image.

▶ Change the picture's on-screen or printed resolution.

▶ Apply a color or tint to the picture.

▶ Change the picture's halftoning parameters.

Each of these features is not only related, but fully interdependent on the others. Let's take a look at these controls and how you can use them to your benefit.

Welcome to the world of image modification!

Importing High-Resolution TIFF Graphics

The first alteration you can make to your file is to up- or downgrade high-resolution TIFF files. This control is available only when you first import the picture (see "Get Picture" in Chapter 6, *Pictures*), so we had better cover it quickly before we move on.

Downgrading screen quality. QuarkXPress normally brings in a screen representation of a high-resolution TIFF or RIFF file at 72 dpi. This low-resolution screen image provides for a relatively quick screen-refresh rate (when, for example, you move around the page). However, if the image is really big or your computer is really slow, importing and displaying an image at even 72 dpi can be time-consuming. You can halve the screen resolution by holding down the Shift key while clicking the Open button in the Get Picture dialog box. This doesn't have any effect on your printed output, but it may speed up your screen redraws (those of you who have a superfast PowerPC machine can stop chuckling).

Changing TIFF types. If you are heavily into image editing and control, you will undoubtedly want to change the bit depth of a TIFF image at some point. Following are two tricks for changing the bit depth as you import the image.

▶ Holding down the Option key when clicking Open in the Get Picture dialog box changes a TIFF line-art image (one bit) into an eight-bit grayscale image. (We can't think of a single use for this feature, but we bet someone can.)

▶ Holding down the Command key when clicking Open in the Get Picture dialog box changes TIFF grayscale images to line art (one bit), and TIFF color images to grayscale. (Changing from color to grayscale is sometimes helpful.)

The Style Menu

Chapter 6, *Pictures,* describes how you can manipulate the "layout" of the picture in the picture box, including cropping, rotating, skewing, and moving the image. These effects are controlled from the floating palette or the Picture Box Specifications dialog box. Here we talk primarily about the image modification possibilities using features from the Style menu. Remember that you can combine both image-manipulation techniques (rotating, changing its shape and size, and so on) and image-modification techniques (changing its grayscale/color parameters, and so on) to create fascinating effects for your page layout.

Tip: When the Style Menu Is Gray. If the items on the Style menu are grayed out, you have probably imported an EPS or object-oriented PICT file. Remember: No shoes, no bitmapped image, no service. If you're sure you have the right file format, it may be that you either have the Item tool selected instead of the Content tool, or that you don't have the picture box selected. If none of this works, we suggest plugging in the machine.

Color. We cover color fully in Chapter 9, *Color.* So at this point, suffice it to say that changing the color of a grayscale or black-and-white image using QuarkXPress's color feature replaces all black (or gray) samples with ones of a particular color.

For example, if you have a black-and-white image and you change the color to red, you then have a red-and-white image. Contrary to some forms of logic, selecting "White" from the menu does not have the same effect as reversing the image; it just makes all the pixels in the image white, and—believe us—there are easier ways of making white boxes!

▼ ▼

Tip: Making Your Grayscale Picture "Transparent." The simple answer to "How do I make my grayscale TIFFs transparent?" is, "You can't." Grayscale TIFFs are not and cannot be transparent. The reason for this is that every pixel has been assigned a gray level (whereas, in black-and-white, one-bit TIFFs, the "white" pixels *are* transparent; white pixels in one-bit, black-and-white EPS bitmaps *can* be transparent—it's an option in Photoshop's EPS Save As dialog box).

However, you can fake a transparent look in some situations by importing the picture into a polygon which just wraps around the edges of the graphic. One way we've found to do this is to import a graphic into a rectangular picture box, trace the edges using the Polygon Picture Box tool, then cut the graphic out of the first box and into the new picture box (see Figure 8-2).

Figure 8-2

Making a fake transparent grayscale TIFF

happiness runs in a circular motion; life is like a little boat upon the sea; everything is a part of everything anyway; you can have everything if you let yourself be; happiness runs in a circular motion; life is like a little boat upon the sea; everything is a part of everything anyway; everything if you let yourself be; happiness runs in a circular motion; life is like a little boat upon the sea; everything is a part of everything; have everything if you let yourself be; happiness runs in a circular motion; life is like a little boat upon the sea; everything is a part of everything anyway; you can have everything is you let yourself be

Of course, the problem with polygonal boxes is that they can only have straight-line segments. If you need to clip the image out with curved lines, we suggest using clipping paths in Photoshop. Make a path, save it, and set it as a clipping path (this is all done in the Paths palette). When you save as EPS, the clipping path is saved with the image.

You can also use a mask in Illustrator or a Paste Inside in Free-Hand to do a similar sort of clipping (but we think Photoshop's approach is the most elegant).

▼ ▼

Tip: More Transparent TIFFs. You create a grayscale image in Photoshop, save it as a TIFF, import it into QuarkXPress, set the background of the picture box to "None", and put it on top of another colored box. When you print it, it looks awful (see Figure 8-3). What went wrong? QuarkXPress is not very good at figuring out what should or shouldn't be transparent in TIFF images, but when you set the picture box background to "None", it tries its darnedest anyway.

Figure 8-3
Grayscale TIFFs with
background of None

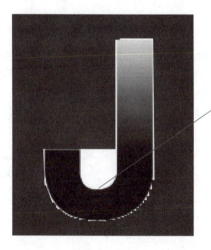

Edges get jaggy when Quark-XPress tries to make the edge around a TIFF transparent. Also note the white space at the bottom of the J, where the program got confused.

QuarkXPress makes something "transparent" in a similar way to the polygon tip above, though it uses lines and curves behind the scenes to "cut out," or clip, the image. However, because it has only the 72-dpi screen image to work with, the program cuts a very rough outline around the picture. This has tripped up more than one unsuspecting soul. The solution? Same as we talked about in the last tip: either save the image as an EPS (with or without a clipping path), or set the background of the picture box to something other than "None".

▼ ▼

Shade. In the same spirit as changing each pixel's color, you can change the gray value for each pixel in the image. The method varies depending on whether you're working with flat or deep bitmapped images.

▶ **Flat bitmaps.** With flat, bilevel, bitmapped images, you can select one of the percentages from 10 percent to 100 percent from the hierarchical menu, or choose "Other" and type in a tint value in one-percent increments. This alters the printed output; every place there was a black pixel in your graphic, a gray pixel prints. Shading line art can present a classier look than you get with just black and white.

▶ **Deep bitmaps.** The Shade menu item is grayed out in versions before 3.3 when you have a grayscale image selected. The only way to handle it there is through the Other Contrast dialog box (see "Other Contrast," below). However, starting in version 3.3, you can apply a shade to a grayscale image (color images are still difficult; see "Tip: Applying a Shade to a Grayscale or Color Picture," later in this chapter). This is called ghosting or screening back an image.

When you set a shade for a grayscale image, it multiplies that shade for each sample point. A 50-percent shade of a 100-percent black sample point is 50 percent; 50 percent of a 60-percent sample is 30 percent, and so on. You hardly ever have to think about this, because it looks just like you'd expect it to.

Negative. Selecting Negative from the Style menu (or typing Command-Shift-Hyphen) inverts all grayscale or color information in an image (see Chapter 9, *Color,* for more information on color models). What was 10-percent black becomes 90-percent black, what was 20-percent red becomes 80-percent red, and so on.

▾ ▾

Tip: When a TIFF Doesn't Fill Its Box. Often when you create a negative of a TIFF, the entire picture box does not invert (see Figure 8-4). Trying to place a background color doesn't help, because the background color affects the image itself (this is either a bug in the program or simply a counterproductive feature—either way it's annoying). Try the following steps.

Figure 8-4

When a TIFF image doesn't fill its box

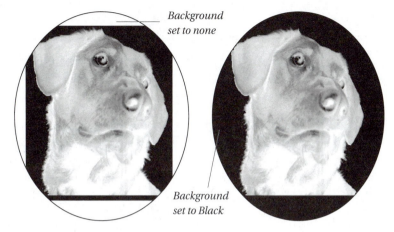

Background set to none

Background set to Black

1. Make a duplicate of the picture box using the Step and Repeat function. The horizontal and vertical offsets should both be set to zero.

2. Delete the image from this duplicate box and give it a background color that matches the edges of the inverted TIFF image (you may have to adjust the tint; usually between 90 and 100 percent does the trick).

3. Send the duplicate box behind the original picture and change the original picture box's background color to "None" (transparent).

This also works to blend normal images into the background.

▼ ▼

Tip: Other Negative Images. Here's another way to invert an image: color it white. This is often not only easier, but also more desirable. For example, if you want a white image on a blue background, you can select the picture box with the Content tool, change the shade of the picture to zero percent (or change the color to "White"), then change the background color to some shade of "Blue" (such as 100 percent).

▼ ▼

Tip: Color Blends in Black-and-White Bitmaps. Carlos Sosa, that hip designer who did those interesting polygon illustrations in the back of this book, turned us on to a very odd and potentially useful technique of putting blends inside of images. (This tip only works with one-bit images. In Photoshop, these are images in Bitmap mode.)

1. Import a one-bit (black-and-white) image into a picture box and set its color to "White".

2. Set the image to Invert (Command-Shift-hyphen).

3. Give the picture box a blended background (see Chapter 9, *Color*, on how to do this).

The background blend actually pokes through the image itself, making it appear as though the image were blended (see Figure H on the color pages). Note that you can fake this effect for a grayscale image by first converting the image into a bitmap in Photoshop (change Mode to Bitmap, and select the Halftone Screen technique).

▼ ▼
Contrast

The Style menu also lets you change the contrast of grayscale and color images. If you are working with a one-bit (black-and-white) picture, these elements are inaccessible.

Contrast refers to the relationships among the tonal values of a picture. A high-contrast picture divides up the gray shades or color saturation of an image into a few sharply distinct tones; a low-contrast picture has little differentiation between tones, and looks grayed-out. You should try to strike some balance between these two, though you may want to create an unnatural-looking image by drastically altering the contrast controls.

The basic concept to remember regarding contrast controls is "input/output." For example, David likes to think of these controls as a machine into which he is inserting his TIFF or PICT images, and out of which comes what is going to print on the page. Other people sometimes think of this process as that of a filter through which the image is poured each time the page gets printed. Remember, though, that neither you nor QuarkXPress actually alters the picture file itself whatsoever; you only alter the "filter" or the "machine" through which the image passes for display and printout. Let's look at the controls QuarkXPress offers.

Normal Contrast. This filter leaves well enough alone and doesn't affect the image at all. This is the default setting for every grayscale and color picture you import.

High Contrast. Selecting High Contrast from the Style menu has the immediate effect of making your grayscale pictures look like they were badly scanned at a one-bit (black-and-white) setting, and your color pictures look like poorly designed psychedelic flyers.

The literal effect of this filter is to change all values under 30-percent gray to white, and all values greater than 30-percent gray to black. Color images are affected in the same way: the saturation levels are broken down so that all colors with over 30-percent saturation are transformed to 100 percent, and so on (see Chapter 9, *Color* for a more in-depth discussion of color and its saturation levels). Why Quark chose the 30-percent mark is beyond us; it makes for some really ugly looking images. We'll look at how to change this "break" point later in this chapter.

Posterized. Whereas the High Contrast setting breaks down the image into only two gray or saturation levels—zero percent and 100 percent—Posterized divides the tonal values into six levels of gray or color saturation: zero, 20, 40, 60, 80, and 100 percent. Gray levels or color saturation in the original picture are mapped to these levels based on what they're closest to (for example, a 36-percent saturation of a color maps to the 40-percent level). Posterization is a common technique for special effects, though it should be used carefully (see Figure 8-5).

Figure 8-5

Posterization of a
grayscale TIFF image

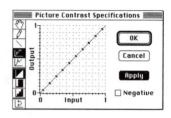

Normal contrast
Normal screen

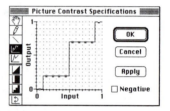

Standard posterization setting
Normal screen

Other Contrast. The ultimate contrast control within QuarkXPress comes from the Picture Contrast Specifications dialog box, which you can get by selecting Other Contrast from the Style menu. This dialog box shows you the mechanism or the filter through which you are putting the picture. If you select Other Contrast after selecting High Contrast or Posterize from the Style menu, you see the contrast curve for those items. Otherwise, with Normal Contrast selected, you see a 45-degree line on the graph (see Figure 8-6).

Looking carefully at the graph, we see that the axes are labeled Input and Output, and each is defined from zero to one (meaning zero to 100 percent). Tick marks are shown in increments of five and 10 percent.

The basic 45-degree Normal Contrast line defines a filter which makes no change to gray levels. For example, a gray level of 20 percent in the input picture is mapped (output) to 20 percent,

Figure 8-6

The Picture Contrast
Specifications
dialog box

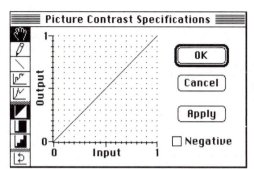

40 percent to 40 percent, and so on. By changing this line, we can change the mapping of the gray levels, affecting the contrast and shading of the printed picture.

Following are some basic tips and tricks to help you when you're modifying images using the Picture Contrast Specifications dialog box.

▼ ▼

Tip: Applying Your Changes. We've said this before, but it's worth repeating here: The Apply button is one of the all-time most helpful features that we've ever had the pleasure to use, especially on a screen larger than nine inches. It's especially useful with the Picture Contrast Specifications dialog box.

You can move the Picture Contrast Specifications dialog box out of the way of the picture you're working on, then make changes to the curve and click the Apply button (or press Command-A) to see the change take place. If you don't like that effect, change the curve again or press Command-Z to undo that change. And don't forget Continuous Apply (Option-click Apply or press Command-Option-A).

▼ ▼

Picture Contrast Specifications Dialog Box

As we mentioned above, the Picture Contrast Specifications dialog box (Command-Shift-C) is the representation of the overall contrast filter through which the picture is processed. With the nine tools in this dialog box, you can create all sorts of filters for both grayscale and color images.

▼ ▼

Tip: Don't Use Other Contrast. There are a half dozen problems that make the contrast controls in QuarkXPress less than useful, the most essential of which is sharpening. Scanned images always need to be sharpened with a sharpening filter (preferably Photoshop's Unsharp Mask filter) before they're printed. Unfortunately, you need to apply sharpening *after* tonal correction. Since QuarkXPress doesn't have a sharpening filter, that's impossible.

So if you need to perform tonal correction on a scanned image (you almost always do), don't use the controls in QuarkXPress. Do it in an image-manipulation program, which probably has better tonal correction tools, and where you can also sharpen the image. Then save the file and place it in QuarkXPress, fully corrected, sharpened, and ready to print.

▼ ▼

You can use the tools to change the contrast curve into either a straight line or a curve. By definition, any contrast curve which is not a straight line is a *gamma curve*. There's nothing mysterious about a gamma curve: it's simply a nonlinear curve with a fancy name. However, when it comes right down to it, QuarkXPress's tools for making curves don't let you do much more than either very basic modifications or very weird ones (see Figure 8-7).

Let's look at how the tools work.

Hand tool. You can use the Hand tool to move the curve (or straight line) around on the contrast graph by selecting the tool, positioning it over the graph, and dragging. You can constrain to either

Figure 8-7
Way-out contrast
correction

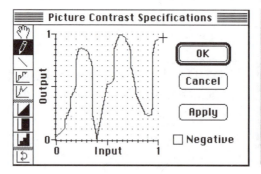

horizontal or vertical movements by holding down the Shift key while dragging. The Hand tool is the easiest way to make adjustments to the contrast curve as a whole. For an example, see "Tip: Adjusting the Break Point on a High-Contrast Image," below.

Pencil tool. If you've ever used a paint program, you're already familiar with the Pencil tool. By selecting this tool and dragging over the curve, you can make both large and small adjustments. With the Pencil tool you can draw curves which adjust for problems in the original scan (see Figure 8-8). Or you can draw wild and bizarre roller-coaster curves which map the gray levels in weird ways. You can also make small corrections in the curve by carefully drawing over areas. Remember, though, that you don't need to have a perfectly smooth curve all the time; slight bumps and dips have little effect on the final output.

Figure 8-8
Gamma curve created with the pencil tool

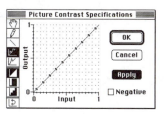

Default settings

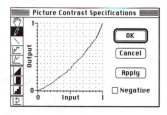

With a gamma contrast curve

Straight Line tool. If you can't figure out that the Straight Line tool draws straight lines, we wish you the best of luck with the program. However, it is not so obvious what these straight lines are good for. Think of the slope of a line in the same way as you think of the slope of a hill. A steep slope steepens very quickly; a shallow slope steepens slowly. You can draw steep and gentle slopes easily with the Straight Line tool.

The steeper the slope, the higher contrast the image has. The gentler the slope, the less contrast; that is, the "grayer" the picture looks. However, remember that by using the straight line rather than a curved line, you are losing tonal values pretty indiscriminately. A steep, contrasty line loses the highlights and the shadows; a flat, low-contrast line loses midtones (see Figure 8-9).

Figure 8-9
Linear adjustment

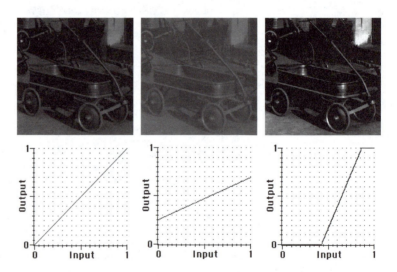

Posterizer tool. As we described earlier, posterization is the act of cutting out or dividing an image's gray or color levels into a few basic tonal values. By selecting Posterize in the Style menu, QuarkXPress divides the gray or color levels into six tonal values. When you select the Posterizer tool, QuarkXPress adds handle points to your line or curve at 10-percent increments. By moving these handles, you flatten and move that entire 10-percent area. By lining up multiple handles, you can easily create posterized effects with any number of levels up to 10 (see Figure 8-10).

Figure 8-10
Using the
Posterizer tool

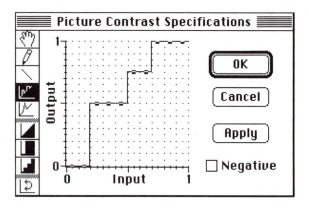

Spike tool. Whereas the Posterizer tool places handles between the
10-percent marks and levels out (flattens) that 10-percent area,
the Spike tool places handles directly on the 10-percent marks
and has no affect on the area between the handles other than to
adjust the lines to keep them contiguous. David thinks this is the
best tool for creating smooth curves—much easier than the pencil tool. Spiking a line is also pretty good for boosting particular
tonal values. For example, if you wanted a 60-percent gray area to
appear black, you could spike it up to 100 percent. Similarly,
if you wanted to drop out all the dark areas of the cyan, you might
use this tool.

Normal Contrast tool. Clicking on this icon reverts the contrast curve
back to its initial 45-degree straight line.

High Contrast tool. Clicking on this icon switches the curve to the
standard bilevel high-contrast "curve" as described above. The
break point is set to 30 percent (see "Tip: Adjusting the Break
Point on a High-Contrast Image").

Posterized tool. When you click on this tool, the curve you're working on switches to the standard posterized curve. Tints under 10
percent go to white, above 90 percent go to black, and other tints
round off to the nearest 20 percent.

Inversion tool and Negative checkbox. Contrary to popular belief, these two items in the Picture Contrast Specifications dialog box do not perform the same task, though in many instances you may achieve the same result. By using either of these, for example, you can invert grayscale files. That is, where there was white, there is black, where there was 20-percent black, there is 80-percent black, and so on. Switching to Negative and inverting the curve also creates the same effect while altering all three RGB values at once (see "Color," below, for more on the RGB contrast curve).

However, inverting color images while using other color models can give you varying effects. Simply put, clicking on the Inversion tool on the Tool palette flips the curve you are working on. Checking Negative has the same effect as selecting the Negative item in the Style menu (see "Negative," above).

▼ ▼

Tip: Adjusting the Break Point on a High-Contrast Image. As we described above, the cutoff point on a high-contrast image is 30 percent, which does hardly anyone any good. Using the Hand tool in the Other Contrast dialog box, you can adjust this point horizontally to anywhere on the scale. Try moving the vertical line over to around 60 percent. This cuts out most of the lower gray values and gives you a clean and recognizable image for many grayscale or color pictures (see Figure 8-11).

This technique is also of great help when working with line art which was scanned as a grayscale image. By adjusting the cutoff point, you can alter the line thicknesses in the artwork (see Figure 8-12). Remember that holding down the Shift key while using the Hand tool constrains the movements to horizontal or vertical.

Of course, to get a really good-looking image, you'd have to start with an 800-dpi gray-scale image (because you want to end up with a minimum of 800 dpi for line art). This would be a really enormous file! So, once again, the caveat to the tip is: this gray-scale-to-bilevel bitmap conversion is better done in Photoshop or other image-editing program.

Figure 8-11
Adjusting the high-
contrast break point
for a grayscale image

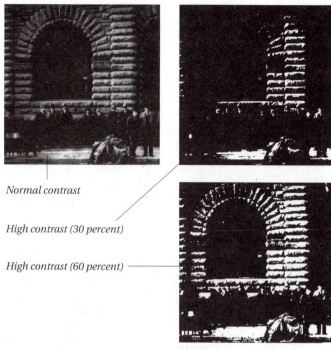

Normal contrast

High contrast (30 percent)

High contrast (60 percent)

Figure 8-12
Line art scanned as
a grayscale image

High contrast (30 percent)   *High contrast (60 percent)*

▼ ▼

Tip: Applying a Shade to a Grayscale or Color Picture. In versions of QuarkXPress earlier than 3.3, the Shade item is grayed out (unusable) for grayscale and color TIFFs and PICTs. If you need to tint—or ghost, or screen back, or whatever you want to call it—a grayscale image but are using an earlier version, you can adjust shading through the Picture Contrast Specifications dialog box.

Use the Hand tool to move the contrast curve vertically (see Figure 8-13). Moving the whole curve up makes the image darker, and down makes it lighter (lower gray levels).

Note, however, that when you move the curve up or down, you're likely to cut out possible gray levels. If you make the image darker, for instance, dark areas go black; make it lighter, and light areas go white. In either case, you lose detail. Because of this, you may want to adjust the curve using the Pencil or Spike tool instead (or use an image-manipulation program), as described above.

If you are using version 3.3 or later, you can set the shade (tint) of a grayscale image using Shade in the Style menu, but you still have to use the technique described above for color images.

Figure 8-13
Shading a
grayscale TIFF

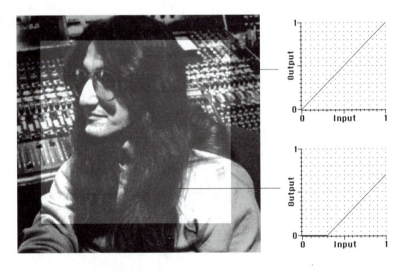

Color

If you aren't familiar with working with color and the various color models that QuarkXPress supports, you may want to skip over this section until you've read Chapter 9, *Color.* In this section we discuss contrast modification of color images using the various color models and their components.

QuarkXPress allows you to modify color TIFF and bitmapped PICT images using the same tools you use for grayscale images, except that you can alter one color at a time. This clearly allows significantly greater control over the way your images print.

We can't think of any reason to use these controls in QuarkXPress other than to create really weird-looking images—especially given the lack of a sharpening filter in QuarkXPress (see Figure J in the color pages). Rather, Photoshop is the tool of choice for making color correction and adjustments. Nonetheless, let's look at the steps you can take to modify these pictures.

Model. This item in the Picture Contrast Specifications dialog box appears when you are modifying a color bitmapped image. You can work with four different color models: HSB, RGB, CMY, and CMYK. When you change between the models, the image resets back to Normal. Thus, you cannot make changes to an image in more than one color model.

Color. When you click one of the color models, QuarkXPress brings up the appropriate color selection checkboxes. That is, when you click HSB, Hue, Saturation, and Brightness checkboxes appear. Clicking CMY gives you Cyan, Magenta, and Yellow checkboxes, and so on. Each checkbox can be on or off, and you can have any number of checkboxes turned on at one time.

The theory is simple: the checkboxes you turn on control which items change when you alter the contrast control curve. In the RGB, CMY, and CMYK models, QuarkXPress gives you color checkboxes. If you check Magenta and Yellow, for example, and change the contrast curve using the tools described above, you change the curve for only those two colors. Everything else remains the same.

The HSB model's checkboxes have slightly different functions. Changing the contrast curve with only Hue turned on maps various colors to other colors. This can be seen on a color screen by examining the color spectrum on the horizontal and vertical axes as well as the curve itself. The Saturation checkbox lets you map various saturations from zero to 100 percent, and the Brightness checkbox lets you map the brightness levels (levels of black) to other brightness levels. Once again, you can adjust these with any, some, or all turned on.

▼ ▼

Halftones

Let's face it. Every high-resolution imagesetter on the market prints only in black and white. And almost every laser printer prints only in black and white. There's clearly a lot to be said for black and white. What we need to realize, however, is that black and white is not gray. Real laser printers don't print gray (at least not the ones we're going to talk about).

So how do we get a picture with grays in it into the computer and out onto paper? The answer is halftones. The magic of halftoning is that different levels of gray are represented by different-sized spots, which, when printed closely together, fool the eye into seeing the tint we want.

Take a look at any photograph in a newspaper, and it's easy to see the halftoning. Notice that the spacing of the spots doesn't change; only their size changes. There are large spots in dark areas and small spots in light areas.

David and Steve talk about halftones in great detail in their book, *Real World Scanning and Halftones*. However, let's take a quick overview of the elements that make up digital halftones here, just in case you don't have that book . . . yet.

Dots. A laser printer prints pages by placing square black dots on a white page (remember, this is the simple approach, and we're not getting into film negs and whatnot yet). Each and every dot on a 300-dpi printer is $\frac{1}{300}$ of an inch in diameter (or thereabouts). That's pretty small, but it's still more than 120 times larger than what you can achieve on a Linotronic 330 ($\frac{1}{3,384}$ of an inch, which is almost too small for the human eye to see). The primary factor concerning how large the dot is is the *resolution* of the printer (how many dots per inch it can print).

Spots. As was said before, a halftone is made up of spots of varying sizes. On a black-and-white laser printer or imagesetter, these spots are created by bunching together anywhere between one and 65,000 printer dots. They can be of different shapes and, to be redundant over and over again, different sizes. We'll look at several different types of spots later in the chapter.

Screen frequency. In the traditional halftoning process, a mesh screen is placed in front of the photograph to create the desired effect of spots (albeit rather square ones) all in rows. Keeping this process in mind can help you understand this concept. The *screen frequency* of a halftone is set by the mesh of the screen, and is defined as the number of these rows per inch. The lower the screen frequency, the coarser the image looks. The higher the screen frequency, the finer the image looks (see Figure 8-14).

Figure 8-14
Various screen
frequencies

 20 lpi   *75 lpi*   *120 lpi*

To complicate issues a bit, the screen frequency of a halftone is often called its *line screen*. Whatever you call it, it's still calculated in the number of lines per inch (lpi). See Table 8-1 for information about when to use a particular screen frequency.

Table 8-1

Screen frequencies to use for different printing conditions

Output	Lines per inch (lpi)
Photocopier	50–90 lpi
Newspaper quality	60–85 lpi
Quick-print printer	85–110 lpi
Direct-mail pieces	110–150 lpi
Magazine quality	133–175 lpi
Art book	175–300 lpi

▼ ▼

Tip: Gray Levels in Your Halftones. Picture this: each spot is made up of tiny dots, and different gray levels are achieved by turning dots on and off (at a 10-percent tint, 10 percent of the dots within a spot's cell are turned on). Okay, now remember that the lower the screen frequency, the bigger the spot, and the more dots are used per spot. The higher the frequency, the fewer dots are used. Thus, the higher the screen frequency, the fewer possibilities for levels of gray there are.

To find out how many levels of gray you can achieve, divide the resolution by the screen frequency, square it, and add one. For example, you can get 92 levels of gray when you print a 133-line screen at 1,270 dpi ($(^{1,270}/_{133})^2+1$), but only 6 levels of gray when you print a 133-line screen at 300 dpi ($(^{300}/_{133})^2+1$). The output is clearly posterized. To get 92 levels of gray on a 300-dpi laser printer, you would need to print at 30 lines per inch! It's an unfortunate fact, but this is one of the inherent tradeoffs in digital halftoning.

▼ ▼

Angle. The halftone screen does not have to be horizontal or vertical—in fact, it rarely is. It's normally rotated to other angles (see Figure 8-15), which are used in both special-effects halftoning and color separation (see Chapter 10, *Printing*). Zero and 180 degrees are horizontal, 90 and 270 degrees are vertical (some types of spots look the same in all four of these, and others look different at each angle). A 45-degree angle is most common because it is the least

Figure 8-15
Rotating the halftone
screen to zero-, 30-,
and -45-degree angles

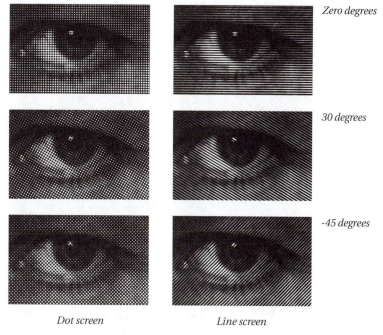

Zero degrees

30 degrees

-45 degrees

Dot screen　　　　*Line screen*

distracting to the eye. Remember that changing the angle of the
halftone screen doesn't change the angle of the picture itself!

Making Halftones Work for You

Once again, just to be clear: anything that contains gray requires
halftoning. Even a simple box or piece of type with a 10-percent
tint comes out as a halftone. There's no other way to render grays
on a black-and-white output device. With bitmapped images,
QuarkXPress lets you change the parameters of the halftones:
spot type, line screen, and angle.

The first four items in the screen section of the Style menu (see
Figure 8-16) are preset combinations for you to choose. By choosing the fifth item, Other Screen, you access the Picture Screening
Specifications dialog box, which allows you to input your own
choices, giving you the greatest amount of flexibility.

Figure 8-16

Halftoning control
under the Style menu

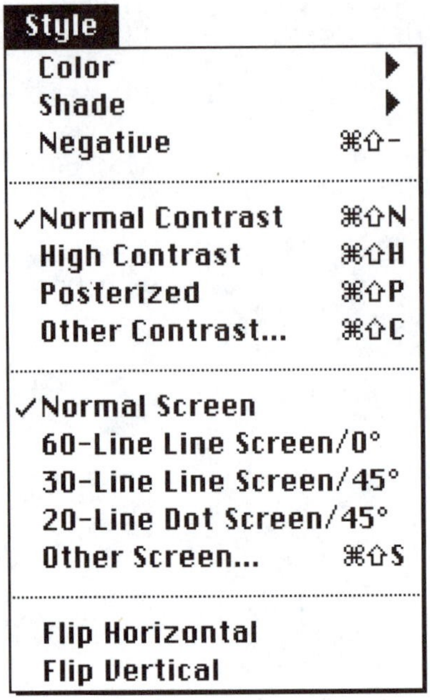

Style

Color	▶
Shade	▶
Negative	⌘⇧–
✓Normal Contrast	⌘⇧N
High Contrast	⌘⇧H
Posterized	⌘⇧P
Other Contrast...	⌘⇧C
✓Normal Screen	
60-Line Line Screen/0°	
30-Line Line Screen/45°	
20-Line Dot Screen/45°	
Other Screen...	⌘⇧S
Flip Horizontal	
Flip Vertical	

Preset Screen Combinations

Let's look at QuarkXPress's preset screen frequency and angle combinations first. Figure 8-17 shows a sample picture for each setting.

Normal Screen setting. Normal, in this case, means default. This is the setting all pictures automatically print in unless you specifically change them. The spot is a round dot (see further description of the round-dot shape below), the angle is 45 degrees, and the screen frequency is whatever you chose in the Page Setup dialog box (move like the pros: press Command-Option-P). In most cases you will find yourself using the Normal Screen setting.

60-Line Line Screen, 0° setting. Why conform to Normal Screen when you have a choice like this? This screen setting uses a line screen using lines rather than round dots. We often call this a "straight-line screen" just to differentiate it from screen frequency, which, as mentioned above, is also sometimes referred to as the "line

Figure 8-17
The halftoning presets

Normal Screen

60-Line Line Screen/0º

30-Line Line Screen/45º

20-Line Dot Screen/45º

screen." This particular straight-line screen is set at a screen frequency of 60 lines per inch (lpi), each line being set to a zero-degree angle (horizontal). Printing at 60 lpi is coarse enough for the eye to easily see each line, but fine enough so that a casual observer won't notice it immediately. Nonetheless, the picture definitely looks different than if you used a round spot.

30-Line Line Screen, 45° setting. We're now in the realm of a very coarse straight-line screen. If you look too closely at this picture you won't even be able to tell what it is. This is a popular screen for special effects, though an angle of -45 (or 315) degrees is often used instead (see below on how to change the angle). Because it's easy to see where the lines in the straight-line screen get fatter and thinner, the eye lingers longer on how the image was created than what the image represents.

20-Line Dot Screen, 45° setting. Here's another potentially confusing term. Here we have a "dot screen," which just means a round spot (the dots which make up the spot haven't changed any). A screen frequency this low can really only be used for special effects, unless you're printing on a billboard or other signage which won't be looked at up close.

Other Screen Options

We now come to the powerhouse behind QuarkXPress's screen features. Using the Other Screen feature under the Style menu (Command-Shift-S), we can choose between five screen patterns, and select any screen frequency or angle we like. Well almost any. Because of limitations in PostScript and the laser printer hardware, there are certain screen frequencies and angles which cannot be achieved (see *Real World Scanning and Halftones*—listed in Appendix D, *Resources*—for a detailed discussion of this problem). When this occurs, the printed output is as close as possible to what you requested.

Following is an in-depth description of these settings.

Screen. David's dream is to print out a halftone image with a screen frequency of one, with each spot having a diameter of one inch. He doesn't have a particular reason for this; he just thinks it would be neat. Unfortunately, PostScript won't presently handle anything below eight lpi, and QuarkXPress won't accept any value under 15. The upper range of 400 lpi is less of an inconvenience, though you may never have the urge to approach either of these limits. Select the screen frequency you want by typing it in, or type "0" (zero) or "default" to defer to the setting that is assigned in the Page Setup dialog box.

Angle. We discussed angles several sections ago, and we'll discuss them again in Chapter 10, *Printing,* when we talk about color separations, so we won't discuss them here. Just type in a number from zero to 360 (or zero to -360 if you think backwards). Once upon a time when you specified a particular angle, the angle would not rotate along with a page printed transversely (see Chapter 10, *Printing*). This caused much consternation for people using coarse screens. We're happy to say that this is no longer the case, and when you specify an angle you get that angle no matter how you print it.

Pattern. Pattern here refers to the spot shape. You have five shapes to choose from (see Figure 8-18).

▶ **Dot pattern.** This is the round spot which you see in almost all PostScript output. At low tint values, it's a round black spot. As the tint level increases, it gets larger. At 50 percent, it changes to a square. At higher levels, it inverts to a progressively smaller white spot.

▶ **Line pattern.** Straight-line screens seem to go in and out of fashion, but they're always good for waking up your audience and, if you use too low a line screen, making eyeballs fall out. The line is thick at high tint values and thin for low values.

Figure 8-18
Various halftone spot
shapes (patterns)

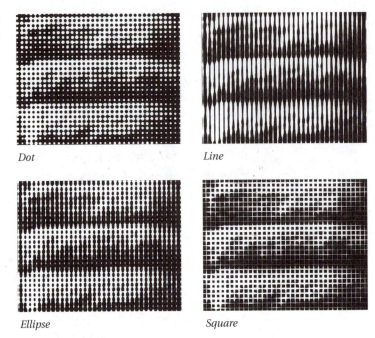

Dot

Line

Ellipse

Square

▶ **Ellipse pattern.** No, this is not a traditional elliptical spot. Printers have used elliptical spots for years and customers have grown accustomed to asking for them by this name, even though the shape of the spot is more of a rounded-corner diamond. The spot which QuarkXPress creates is an oval. We haven't found any good use for this.

▶ **Square pattern.** Here's another funky special-effect spot which may come in handy some day. Each spot is square: lower tint values are little squares, higher values are big squares. Try really coarse screen frequencies for this one.

▶ **Ordered Dither pattern.** This spot shape is actually an attempt to go beyond traditional halftoning. It's a dither pattern optimized for printing on 300-dpi laser printers. Because the pattern adjusts to the resolution of the laser printer, you shouldn't use this if you're planning on printing to an imagesetter (you'd get a dither at over 1,000 dots per inch, which could not be reproduced). The Ordered Dither pattern is also not optimal for offset printing.

When should you use this? QuarkXPress maintains that you should use it when you are printing to a QuickDraw (non-PostScript) laser printer for making multiple copies on a photocopier. Don't even bother if you have a Post-Script printer; it looks terrible. Well, we guess it's nice to have the option.

Display Halftoning option. In most programs on the Macintosh, you cannot see the halftoning settings you choose until you print out a page. However, QuarkXPress can display a representation of the halftone if you turn Display Halftoning. How well it displays the halftone type depends primarily on the resolution of your screen. You almost never need this to be turned on, unless you're working with low screen frequencies for special effects. Once again, it's sometimes nice just to have the option.

▼ ▼

Many Colorful Shades of Gray

We've taken a pretty good look at the options you have for working with images in your QuarkXPress documents, from rotating them to changing their halftone spot shape. Next we go to the world of color and discuss how to bring color onto your pages. Finally, we'll move on to what is perhaps the culmination of all we have learned in this book: printing our documents out.

CHAPTER 9

480

C O L O R

Look around you. Unless you're fully color-blind, everything around you has color. It's not surprising that people have wanted to work with color in their documents since . . . well, since people were creating documents! What *is* surprising is how complicated working with color can be, especially with all this computer equipment that's supposed to make life easy for us.

The complicated issues in desktop color range from specifying the color you want; to getting that color to print on a color or—more likely—a black-and-white laser printer; to producing separated films ready for offset printing. Getting color off the desktop was once a joke among the few people who had actually tried. However, as the '90s rolled in, people's success stories outnumbered their failures and we knew that desktop color was here to stay. Of course, achieving quality color from your Macintosh is still not as easy as turning on the computer; we still have our work cut out for us. But at least we know it's possible now.

We begin this chapter with an overview of some basic theories of color, including the various color models (ways in which you specify color on the computer). This leads us into the color components of QuarkXPress's feature set, including building a color palette and building traps for better print quality. Although we

479

discuss the fundamentals of color separation here, we'll cover the area of actually generating color separations of your documents in Chapter 10, *Printing*. Also, we won't cover the EfiColor color matching system much here; rather, we discuss that in Appendix A, *EfiColor*.

▼ ▼

What You See and What You Get

Before we even begin talking desktop color, it's important for you to know that the color you see on the screen is almost never what you'll get out of your color printer or slide recorder, much less what you can expect to see off a printing press.

The medium is the message. The primary reason is the difference in medium. Colors are displayed on the screen by lighting up phosphors, which emit colored light, which then enters your eyes. This is significantly different from printed material, which depends on other light sources to reflect off it into your eyes. If you use a different method of showing color, you'll see different colors.

Pantone colors are a great example of this: take a Pantone swatch book and pick a color. Hold that color up to the screen next to QuarkXPress's Pantone color simulation. Chances are it'll be a totally different color. Even color proofs created from your final film aren't completely reliable (though they're the best predictor you can hope for). What comes off press may look different.

RGB versus CMYK. Another reason for the difference in color correspondence is that representing four process color plates with three colors (red, green, and blue) just doesn't work. The eye sees and processes the two differently.

Want more reasons? Okay, how about the monitors and imaging devices themselves: take a color document on your color Macintosh and bring it to someone else's computer; it almost undoubtedly looks different, especially if the monitor is a different brand. Take that a step further and image the document using a high-end slide recorder: the device uses light, just like your monitor, but the colors you get off it are very different from what you see on your computer.

Calibration and color management. Some monitors are better than others at displaying certain colors. And a monitor with a 24-bit color card is probably one step more accurate than an eight-bit video card. Some companies, such as Kodak, EFI, and SuperMac, sell monitor-calibration systems to adjust the screen colors so that they'll more closely match your printed output. However, many of the best calibration systems are cost-prohibitive for most people.

Another solution is color management, using a system like Efi-Color (see Appendix A, *EfiColor*). These systems adjust the colors that show up on the screen to more closely match the final output colors. However, even these are limited; they're really more useful for getting consistent color between color printers than from a screen.

Whatever you use, remember that what you see is *rarely* what you get.

Use swatch books. The solution to all this uncertainty is to specify your colors from a swatch book. Look at the book, see what color you want, and spec it. If possible, create your own swatch book, and print it on your final output device—offset press, color printer, slide recorder, whatever. If you're printing with process inks, spec your colors from a process swatch book such as TruMatch. If you're printing with PMS inks, use a PMS spot-color swatch book.

▼ ▼

Tip: Taking a Color Reality Check. Russell Brown, senior art director at Adobe Systems, has some interesting things to say about working in color. To begin with, here are some questions to ask yourself before you consider working in color.

▶ Do I really want to do my own production?

▶ Will I save time?

- ▶ Will I save money?

- ▶ Am I using color as a design solution?

- ▶ Am I crazy?

Clearly, the last question is the most relevant one. Jumping into desktop color is like roller skating on the seven hills of San Francisco: if you don't really know what you're doing, it'll get ugly.

▼ ▼

Describing Color

In a perfect world you would be able to say, "I want this object to be burnt sienna," and your computer, service bureau, and lithographer would know exactly the color you mean. Outside of picking Crayola-crayon colors, however, this just can't be done. Everyone from scientists to artists to computer programmers has been trying for centuries to come up with a general model for specifying and re-creating colors. In the past 50 years alone these color models have been created: HSB, NTSC, CMYK, YIQ, CIE, PAL, HSL, RGB, CCIR, RS-170, and HSI, among others. (And we thought that Macintosh graphic file format names were far-out!)

QuarkXPress presently handles three color models (RGB, CMYK, and HSB), plus several color-matching systems, or libraries: FocolTone, TruMatch, Toyo, DIC, Pantone, Pantone Process, Pantone ProSim, and Pantone Uncoated. Because these color models are intimately connected with printing and other reproduction methods, we'll first discuss the particulars of printing color, then move into each color model in turn.

Spot Versus Process Colors

When dealing with color, either on the desktop or off, you'll need to understand the differences between process and spot color. Both are commonly used in the printing process. Both can give you a wide variety of colors. But they are hardly interchangeable. Depending on your final output device, you may also be dealing with composite colors. Let's look at each of these, one at a time.

Process color. Look at any color magazine or junk mail you've received lately. If you look closely at a color photograph or a tinted color box, you'll probably see lots of little dots making up the color. These are color halftones made up of one to four colors: cyan, magenta, yellow, and black (see Chapter 8, *Modifying Images,* for further information on halftones). We'll talk about this color model (CMYK) a little later on; what's important here is that many, many colors are being represented by overlaying tints of the four basic colors. The eye blends these colors together so that ultimately you see the color you're supposed to.

Cyan, magenta, yellow, and black are the process colors. The method—or process—of separating the millions of colors into four is referred to as creating *process-color separations.* Each *separation,* or plate, is a piece of film or paper that contains artwork for only one of the colors. Your lithographer can take the four pieces of film, expose plates from each of the four pieces, and use those four plates on a press.

Don't get us wrong: process color is not just for full-color photographs or images. If you're printing a four-color job, you can use each of the process colors individually or in combination to create colored type, rules, or tint blocks on the page. These items appear as solid colors to the untrained eye, but are actually made from "tint builds" of the process colors.

Spot color. If you are printing only a small number of colors (three or fewer), you probably want to use spot colors. The idea behind spot colors is that the printing ink is just the right color you want, which makes the need to build a color using the four process colors unnecessary. With spot color, for example, if you want some type colored teal blue, you print it on a plate (often called an overlay) which is separate from the black plate. Your lithographer prints that type using a teal-blue ink—probably a PMS ink (see "Pantone," below) like PMS 3135 or 211, and then uses black to print the rest of the job.

Once again, the difference between process and spot colors is that process colors are built using overlaid tints of four separate inks, while spot colors are printed using just one colored ink (the color you specify). In either case, your lithographer runs the page through the press once for each color's plate, or uses a multicolor press that prints the colors successively in a single pass.

Mixing process and spot colors. There is no reason why you can't use both spot and process colors together in a document, if you've got the budget for a five- or six-color print job. Some lithographers have five- or six-color presses, which can print the four process colors along with one or two spot colors. In fact, one book we know of—Edward Tufte's *Envisioning Information*—was printed with 12 solid spot colors.

Composite color. If your final output is created on a film recorder (slides or transparencies) or a color printer, you may well encounter what we call composite color. Composite color is color which falls between spot color and process color. For example, most film recorders print using the RGB format (more on this format a little later on), whether your color is specified as CMYK or RGB or anything else QuarkXPress allows you to do. Similarly, the QMS ColorScript 100 represents both spot and process colors alike using colored waxes; depending on what type of wax-transfer colors you have loaded, it simulates RGB or CMYK colors.

The key here is that the colors you specify are being represented using some color model which you may not have intended. If you know that you are printing on such a device, you should refer to the service bureau and/or the owner's manual for tips on how to work best with that device.

Color Models

Before we jump into how to specify the colors you want, let's talk a bit about each of the color models that QuarkXPress handles and what each is good for.

RGB. Color models are broken down into two classes: additive and subtractive systems. An *additive* color system is counter-intuitive to most people: the more color you add to an object, the closer to white you get. In the case of the RGB model, adding 100 percent of red, green, and blue to an area results in pure white. If you have a color television or a color monitor on your computer, you have already had a great deal of experience with the RGB model. These pieces of equipment describe colors by "turning on" red, green, and blue phosphors on the screen. Various colors are created by mixing these three colors together.

▶ Black = zero percent of all three colors

▶ Yellow = red + green

▶ Magenta = red + blue

▶ Cyan = green + blue

Color TIFF files, such as color scans of natural images, are often saved using RGB specs. All slide recorders image film using this method.

CMYK. *Subtractive* colors, on the other hand, become more white as you subtract color from them, and get darker as you add more color. This is analogous to painting on a white piece of paper. CMY (let's leave the K aside for a moment) is a subtractive color model: the more cyan, magenta, and yellow you add together, the closer to black you get.

The connection between RGB and CMY is interesting: they are exact opposites of each other. In other words, you can take an RGB color and mathematically invert each of the RGB values and get the same color in the CMY model (see Figure 9-1). If this doesn't come intuitively to you (it doesn't to us), don't worry. The theory behind this is much less important than what it implies.

The implication of RGB and CMY having an inverse relation is that colors in either model should be easy to convert. This is true. They are easy to convert. The problem is that the CMY model has few practical applications because cyan, magenta, and yellow inks don't really add up to make black in the real world because

Figure 9-1
Complementary colors

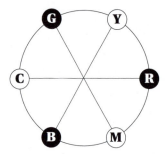

Emitted and reflected (additive and subtractive) colors complement one another. Red is complemented by cyan, green by magenta, and blue by yellow.

ink pigments are never pure cyan, magenta, or yellow. Adding CMY together makes a muddy brown. Thus, lithographers over the years have learned that they must add a black element to the printing process, and that's where the K comes in. (K stands for black because B might be confused for blue.)

CMYK is the standard in the printing world, and the basis of process-color separations. However, the conversion between RGB and CMYK is nowhere near as precise as one could hope. In fact, different programs use different conversion algorithms, so an RGB color from QuarkXPress prints differently from how it would from another application.

You can describe many colors using this method. The following is how Quark describes a few, to the nearest percent.

▶ Red = 100 percent magenta + 30 percent yellow

▶ Green = 77 percent cyan + 100 percent yellow

▶ Blue = 100 percent cyan + 96 percent magenta

Almost every full-color job that gets printed on paper uses the CMYK process.

HSB. Rather than breaking a color down into subparts, the HSB model describes a color by its hue, saturation, and brightness. The *hue* is basically its position in a color spectrum, which starts at red, moves through magenta to blue, through green to yellow, and then through orange back to red. The *saturation* of the color can be described as the amount of color in it. Or, conversely, the amount of white in it. A light pink, for example, has a lower saturation than a bright red. The color's *brightness* reflects the amount of black in it. Thus, that same bright red would, with a lower brightness, change from a vibrant red to a dark, dull, reddish-black.

You could also say that mixing a color (hue) with white produces a *tint* (a degree of saturation). Mixing it with black produces a *tone* (a degree of brightness).

HSB is not easy to understand intuitively, especially when it comes to specifying colors. For example, here are the hue values for the same colors specified above.

▶ Red = zero

▶ Green = 21,845 (QuarkXPress calls this 33.3 percent)

▶ Blue = 43,690 (QuarkXPress calls this 66.7 percent)

You may find HSB useful if you're creating slides on a film recorder or the like, but it's not of much use for print publishing.

Color-Matching Systems

In addition to the three color models in QuarkXPress that you use to define colors, there are also eight color-matching systems—essentially libraries of predefined colors that are based on actual, printed color swatch books. Four of these systems—Pantone, Pantone Uncoated, Toyo, and DIC—are for use with spot color printing. The others—TruMatch, Focoltone, Pantone Process, and ProSim—are for process-color work.

While software companies love to top the feature lists on how many color libraries they offer, they're really little more than conveniences. You can specify process colors by simply typing in the values, for instance, without ever going near the color libraries. And with spot colors, you can use any name and any color specifications you want; the spot-color plates still print out as black. There are some advantages to using these libraries, however, aside from their paint-by-the-numbers simplicity.

▶ **Spot-color libraries.** With spot-color systems like Pantone Coated and Uncoated, using the library ensures that the right color name prints on each overlay, and makes it more likely that the name will match the color name in imported EPS graphics (see "Color from Outside Sources," later in this chapter). Also, the spot colors are set up with color specifications designed to give you the best output that's reasonably possible on screen and on color printers; you don't have to figure it out yourself.

▶ **Process-color libraries.** With process-color work, the only two advantages to using the color libraries are that you don't have to type in the color name and color specification by hand, and that you can easily communicate a color to someone else who also has your kind of swatch book.

Again, these color libraries are merely conveniences. No matter what method you use for specifying colors, you should be looking at printed swatch books to decide what color you want.

Given those caveats, here's a rundown of the color libraries available in QuarkXPress.

FocolTone. Developed in Wales, FocolTone is a process-color matching system used widely in Europe, and very little in North America. After buying FocolTone's rather expensive cross-referenced swatch books, you have to wade through them to find the color you want (you have a choice of 763 colors). These are similar to the Pantone books (see below), which are also in disarray—at least from a user's standpoint. We can't explain FocolTone's numbering system or color sequence to you, because we just can't figure them out.

TruMatch. TruMatch is a system for specifying process colors that was built by people who know and use color from the desktop (especially color from QuarkXPress, as it turns out). This is more important than it might seem. Creating tint builds from the desktop has a particular advantage over having a printer build tints traditionally: we can specify (and a properly calibrated imagesetter can provide us with) a tint value of any percentage, not just in five- or 10-percent increments. The folks at TruMatch took advantage of this and created a very slick, very easy-to-use system with over 2,000 evenly gradated colors (see the sample swatch in Figure D in the color plates).

The TruMatch swatch books tuck this information away, so we want to explain the TruMatch system here. The colors in the swatch book (and in the TruMatch color selector in the Edit Color dialog box) are arranged in the colors of the spectrum: from red through yellow to green through blue to violet and back to red. The first number in a TruMatch code indicates a color's hue (its place on the spectrum). These numbers range from one to 50.

The second item in a color's TruMatch code indicates its tint or value strength, which ranges from "a" (saturated, 100-percent value strength) to "h" (faded, unsaturated, five-percent value strength). The third item, a number, indicates the color's brightness (the amount of black). Black is always added in six-percent increments. The brightness code ranges from one (six percent black) to seven (42 percent black). If there's no black in a color, this third code is left off.

So why is this so great? Well, first of all, you can quickly make decisions on the relativity of two colors. For example, you can say, "No, I want this color to be a little darker, and a little more green." When you go back to the Edit Color dialog box, you can quickly find a color that suits your desires. Compare this to the Pantone or FocolTone matching systems and you'll understand. TruMatch gives us hope that there really is a positive evolution in electronic publishing.

Pantone and Pantone Uncoated. One of the many subsidiaries of Esselte, the largest graphic arts supplier in the world, is Pantone, Inc., whose sole purpose in life (and business) is to continue to develop, maintain, and protect the sanctity of the spot-color Pantone Color Matching System (PMS for short).

Printers and designers alike love the PMS system for its great simplicity in communicating color. As a designer, you can look in a Pantone-approved color swatch book, pick a color, then communicate that color's number to your printer. He or she, in turn, can pull out the Pantone color-mixing guidelines, find that color's "recipe," and dutifully create that exact ink for you. Almost all spot-color printing in the United States is done with PMS inks.

Bear in mind that you can simulate many PMS inks using combinations of process inks. Some simulations are better than others. A pale blue is fairly easy to simulate with process inks, for instance; a rich, creamy, slate blue is almost impossible; and you'll never get anything approaching copper or gold with CMYK (see "ProSim," below).

Pantone, knowing a good thing when it sees it, has licensed its color libraries for coated and uncoated stocks to Quark so that you can specify PMS colors from within QuarkXPress. However, the color you see on the screen may have little correlation to what the actual PMS color is on paper. A computer screen is no substitute for a swatch book, especially when you're dealing with custom-made spot-color inks (we'll talk more about this later).

There are three problems with PMS color.

▶ Only certain colors are defined and numbered. If you want a color which is slightly lighter than one described, but not as light as the next lightest color in the Pantone book, you have to tell your lithographer to tweak it.

▶ Color fidelity of the specification books decreases over time. The books are printed under tight press, paper, and ink conditions, but the colors change as the ink and paper ages, and entropy increases in the universe. Pantone recommends buying a new book every year for this reason—of course, they have a bias: they make a lot of money off selling the books. Just make sure at the beginning of a job that your book and the printer's book are fairly close—or plan to leave your book for the printer to match the color.

▶ We've never met anyone who actually understood the PMS color-numbering scheme. For example, PMS 485 and PMS 1795 are very similar, though every number in between is totally different.

The only good reason to use Pantone books is if you're printing with Pantone inks. In that case, go ahead and use the Pantone color pickers in QuarkXPress; that way the right color name will print on each piece of overlay film, and your printer won't get confused. If you're printing process, don't use PMS specs.

Pantone inks are great for two-and three-color jobs, of course, but they're also worth considering if you have the budget for four or more colors—especially when you consider that you can create tint builds between the various PMS inks. For example, The Understanding Company's road maps are often designed and printed using one to five different Pantone colors in various carefully chosen tints and combinations. This minimizes both the potential moiré patterning (see Chapter 10, *Printing*) and the possible loss of detail in small colored type.

Pantone Process and ProSim. When Pantone realized that they were being left behind (by TruMatch) in the process-color game, they shifted into first gear and released two process-color libraries. The first, ProSim, is designed to simulate the PMS spot colors with the four process colors. It's based on the Pantone Process Color Simulator swatch book, which shows Pantone spot colors printed side-by-side with their process simulations. The second, Pantone Process, is a process-color matching system much like TruMatch's, and has no relationship to the Pantone spot colors; it's just a CMYK swatch book.

There are three problems with spot-color simulation systems like ProSim. The first problem is that it's really hard to simulate spot colors with the four process colors. The second problem is that the team of people Pantone hired to create these simulations seemed to include one person who was (in Steve Job's infamous words) brain-damaged. It's very strange . . . many of the simulations are as good as they could be. Others are so far off the mark that we really had to marvel at the scheme. The third problem is that these systems still use the incredibly strange numbering system that Pantone spot colors use.

Note that ProSim's two primary benefits are that it tries to be more consistent between screen and final output, and that it tries to simulate the PMS colors more closely. The first, as we know, is a lost cause (see "What You See and What You Get," earlier in this chapter). The second benefit is marginal. We feel that trying to match spot colors is typically difficult and unwieldy at best. You're best off using a swatch system that was designed from the start to be used for process color.

Pantone Process, on the other hand, is process color from the ground up (it doesn't try to match anything but itself). It has a new numbering scheme, but this is hardly worth describing because it doesn't appear to make any sense. Fortunately, this system does have a few things going for it. First, it's generally easier to find colors in it than in the Pantone spot-color swatch books (which are arranged with some semblance of order). Second, there are more colors to choose from than in any previous process-color matching system. Third, because Pantone is so well established, it's sometimes easier to find Pantone's swatch books.

We personally feel that the TruMatch system is the best process-color system for designers; it's more intuitive and easier to use than Pantone's. However, both work in more or less equivalent ways. They're just process-color swatch books, though both are produced with rigorous quality-control standards.

Toyo and DIC. Toyo and DIC are both spot-color matching systems from Japan, created by the Toyo Ink Manufacturing Co. and DIC (Dainippon Ink and Chemicals, Inc.), respectively. These spot-color inks have a built-in feature which is kind of helpful: their names reflect how closely you can simulate them in process colors. If the name (number, really) is followed by one asterisk, it means that the color cannot be closely matched in process colors.

If the number is followed by two asterisks, it means that the color that you see on screen isn't even close to the spot color. For instance, metallic colors can never be represented on screen, so they're followed by two asterisks.

If you're creating documents that will be printed in Japan, then you may want to specify spot colors in either of these systems rather than with an American system like Pantone (so the proper spot-color name prints on each overlay). Otherwise, you can probably relax and keep reading.

▼ ▼

Specifying Color

In previous chapters we've discussed applying colors to objects using the Style menu and the Specifications dialog boxes (we'll talk about the Colors palette later in this chapter). Here we'll discuss how to create colors in QuarkXPress over and above the nine which come as default settings.

The Color List

Before you can use a color in QuarkXPress, you have to create it, so it appears in your document's color list. QuarkXPress allows up to 127 different colors on this list, including the six colors which must be present: "Cyan", "Magenta", "Yellow", "Black", "White", and "Registration" (we'll talk about this last "color" later in this chapter). You can access this list—and thereby add, delete, and modify colors—by selecting Color from the Edit menu.

The Colors dialog box (see Figure 9-2) contains the color list (you can scroll through them if there are more than eight entries), plus several buttons to manipulate them. Let's discuss each feature, step by step.

▼ ▼

Tip: Making Your Colors Stick Around. You can alter the default color list—the list with which all new documents open—by adding, deleting, and modifying colors while no document is open. These

Figure 9-2
The Colors dialog box

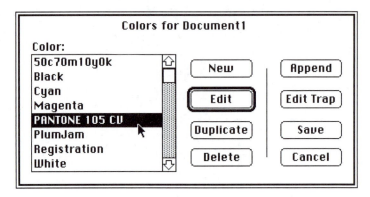

changes stick around forever, or at least until you either change
them again or reinstall QuarkXPress. Changing the color list while
a document is open only changes that document's list; it does not
affect the defaults.

▼ ▼

New

Clicking the New button in the Colors dialog box brings you to the
Edit Color dialog box (see Figure 9-3, and Figure I on the color
pages). Here's a rundown of the choices offered in this dialog box.

Color name. The name that you type in the Name field appears on
the Color scroll list and the color lists in other menus throughout
the program. You can call your color anything you want. For
example, when David is working with process colors, he usually
defines the color he wants using CMYK, then names it something
like "10c80m0y20k". (See "The Right Way" below on how to define
colors.)It's a bit cryptic at first, but he seems to like it. Eric, on the
other hand, likes to just call the color by some name; for example,
he might have a palette full of "fuchsia", "royal blue", and so forth.

If you use the latter method for spot color, you'll want to be
sure you know what the corresponding color in your color swatch
book is. For example, if you use the name "Copper", you'll want to
remember that it represents PMS 876 so that you can communi-

Figure 9-3

The Edit Color
dialog box

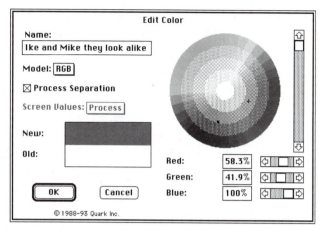

cate this to color identifier your printer. If you use the name "PMS 876", on the other hand, that's what prints out on the edge of the sheet when you pull seps. "Copper" would print out otherwise.

Process or spot. Probably the most important choice in this dialog box is whether the color is a spot color or will be separated into process colors at print time. You use the Process Separation checkbox to determine whether a color is process or spot. When it's turned off, the color is a spot color (that is, it won't separate into CMYK). When it's turned on, the color is never a spot color (it always separates).

Note that you can create a Pantone color—which usually would be specified as a spot color—as a process color, thereby forcing it to separate into four plates at print time. What results is a process simulation of the Pantone color. Similarly, you could create a CMYK color which would print as a spot color on its own plate. The first example has some usefulness; the second has almost none.

Spot-color screen values. When you're creating a spot color (the Process Separation checkbox is turned off), the Screen Values popup menu becomes active. This has been a mystery to a lot of people, so let's explain it carefully. Spot colors aren't always solids, of course; often you'll have tints of them. For instance, you could have a blend from "White" to "Red" (see "Cool Blends," page 507), and the "Red" spot color would be tinted from zero to 100 percent. The only way you can adjust the halftone screen angle and frequency of these tints is to set this popup menu. If you leave it set to "Black", tints of that spot color are always the same as "Black" (usually 45 degrees and the screen frequency set in the Page Setup dialog box). If you set it to "Magenta", then the spot color has the same angle/frequency combination as "Magenta".

The Screen Value is especially important when the spot color is involved in either a blend or an overprint situation (we cover overprinting later in this chapter).

Color specs. Once you've named a color and decided whether it's process or spot, you have to spec the color itself. There are several methods for doing this, and you can choose which system you're going to use by selecting one from the Color Model popup menu. We're going to start out by telling the wrong way to choose a color.

The wrong way to define colors is to use the mouse to click on an area on the color wheel (see Figure 9-3, above). Note that the farther towards the center of the circle you go, the less saturated the colors are. In the center, all colors have zero saturation; they're white. You can choose a pink color by clicking in the red area (near the label "R") and then moving the pointer left until you find a saturation level you like. When you have the general hue and level of saturation you want, you can specify the level of brightness by using the scroll bar to the right of the wheel. The lower the box in the scroll bar goes, the darker the color you get (remember, the lower the brightness, the higher the concentration of black).

This is the wrong way because what you see on the screen probably has no relation to what you'll actually get on paper or film. We should add a caveat here, though. We call this method the wrong way only because amateurs and professionals alike are easily fooled into believing that what they see on the screen is what they're going to get off the press. They (we know you wouldn't) use this method to define process colors, but they shouldn't. Even if you're paying attention to EfiColor's gamut map and gamut alarm, which show what colors can be reproduced with your printing method (see "Gamut Alarm" in Appendix A, *Efi-Color*), choosing a color by how it looks on screen is a mistake.

You can, however, use this color-picking method for coming up with spot colors, because the color specs for spot colors only matter on screen and on color printers; the plates all print as black. For example, in a job we finished recently, we knew we wanted a greenish background printed with a Pantone color, but we didn't know which one. So we picked a color which looked about right on the screen, and set it to a nonseparating spot color called "Kelly Green". We then discussed the color choice with our lithographer, and decided on a Pantone ink. This is a fine way of working with color. But, as we've said, it's too often used wrongly.

Okay, now here's how to define colors the right way.

▶ If you're printing process, specify CMYK values for your colors in the lower-right corner of the dialog box (choosing a color from one of the process-color matching systems is a shortcut). Of course, you need to switch to CMYK mode in the Model popup menu in order to do this. As an alternative to typing your own percentages in these boxes, you can use the scroll bars to raise or lower the values.

▶ If you're printing with spot inks, you can specify colors any way you like, though the built-in spot-color matching systems make it easy to choose one with values predefined for screen and color-printer output.

▶ When you have a color-matching system selected as the color model, you can select the color by either clicking on the color in the Selector box (see Figure 9-4) or by typing the desired number into the field in the lower-right corner of the dialog box. When you type in the number, Quark-XPress automatically jumps to that color. If you're working in Pantone and type "312", it jumps to that number; then, when you type another "5", it jumps to PMS 3125.

In any case, you need to be looking at a printed swatch book.

Figure 9-4
Pantone selection
in the Edit Color
dialog box

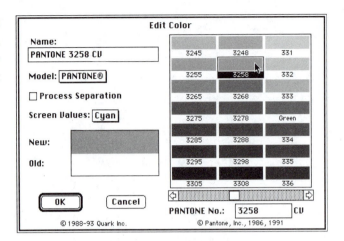

▼ ▼

Tip: Importing Colors from Other Programs. It turns out that you don't have to create the colors from within QuarkXPress. With version 3.3, you can just as easily import an entire color library from an illustration program such as Illustrator or FreeHand. QuarkXPress imports the colors and places them on the color list when you import an EPS file that uses them. The key is that the colors must be named colors in those programs. In Illustrator, you need to create the colors through the Custom Color item, or they don't come in as named colors (though the color specs come in just fine). Likewise, in FreeHand, only named spot colors (Custom or PMS) come across into QuarkXPress.

Only colors that are actually used in an EPS file are imported (see "Color from Outside Sources," later in this chapter). If you just want to import the colors, but don't need the picture itself, you can make a few rectangles and apply the colors you want to those objects. Then save the page as an EPS file (with or without a preview). When you import the EPS into QuarkXPress, those colors are added to the color list. You can then delete the picture from the document, and the colors remain.

▼ ▼

New/Old preview. The final element in the Edit Color dialog box is the New/Old preview. When you are creating a new color, the lower half of this rectangle remains white (blank), as there was no "old" color to show. When you specify a color using one of the methods described above, the upper rectangle shows what that color looks like. You can specify a color, look at this preview window, then change the specifications and actually see the change in the way the color looks.

When you have the color the way you like it, clicking OK closes this dialog box and adds your color to the palette.

▼ ▼

Tip: Multiple Models. We include this tip with a caveat: it's fun and somewhat educational to play with color on the screen, but as we've said repeatedly, it often has little relationship to what you get on final output.

Sometimes you get a color just the way you want it in RGB, except you want a slightly darker tone. At this point you can switch to HSB by selecting it from the Model popup menu, then lower the brightness level slightly. The same applies for any combination of models. For example, start with a Pantone color, then get the CMYK values for it by selecting CMYK from the Model popup menu, alter it, then translate to RGB for further changes. Every color model can be translated into the others.

▼ ▼

Edit

Once you have a color on the color palette, you can edit it by clicking on that color's name in the Color scroll list, then clicking Edit (or just double-click on the color's name). In the default color palette (the one that's there when you first open QuarkXPress) you can edit four of the colors: "Red", "Green", "Blue", and "Registration". The other five colors, which include the four process colors plus White, cannot be edited or deleted. When you edit a color, you see the same Edit Color dialog box as described above, but with several basic differences.

▶ The name of the color already appears in the Name box. Changing the name here changes the color name in the Colors scroll list.

▶ Both the upper and lower halves of the New/Old preview
rectangle fill with the color. When you change the color
specifications using the methods described above, only
the upper half—the New preview—changes. In this way,
you can quickly see a representation of the old versus the
new color.

▶ The model is set to the model of the original color. For
example, if the color was last modified using CMYK, it
appears based on the CMYK model.

▶ The color's RGB and process-color breakdown specifications are displayed.

You can change any of the color's specifications using the same
methods described above. When you like the new color, click OK
to save these changes to the color palette.

▼ ▼

Tip: Color Tricks the Eye. Placing a colored object next to a different
colored object makes both colors look different from how each
would if you just had one color alone. Similarly, a color can look
totally different if you place it on a black background rather than
on a white one. These facts should influence how you work in two
ways. First, when you're selecting colors from a swatch book, iso-
late the colors from their neighbors. We like to do this by placing a
piece of paper with a hole cut out of it in front of a color we're
considering. Secondly, after you've created the colors you're going
to work with in your document, try them out with each other. You
may find that you'll want to go back and edit them in order to
create the effect you really want.

▼ ▼

Duplicate

Let's say you love the color blue. We do. You want a new blue color
that's really close to the one which is in the color palette, but you
don't want to change the one already there. Click on the color

"Blue", then click Duplicate. This opens the Edit Color dialog box, just as if you were editing the color, but the name of the color is changed to "Copy of X" In this case: "Copy of Blue". As long as you don't change the name of your new color back to its original (or any other color already specified), you can change the specifications, and save it onto the Color scroll list without replacing the original color.

QuarkXPress won't allow you to replace a color on the Color scroll list with another of the same name, but it does allow you to merge colors with a workaround, as we discuss in "Delete," next.

Delete

Is this button self-explanatory enough? Click on the color you hate most, then click Delete. If you've assigned this color to any object in your document, QuarkXPress prompts you with a dialog box asking you if you want to replace all instances of the color you're deleting with another color.

Note that you cannot delete the four process colors, "White", or "Registration". And if you delete a color that's not used anywhere in the document it's removed without a prompt, so make sure you really don't need it before clicking Delete. Also note that in versions 3.0 and 3.1, when you delete a color that has been already used within your document, QuarkXPress changes objects of that color to Black (we like the way it handles it now much better).

▼ ▼

Tip: Search and Replace Colors. Because QuarkXPress can merge colors—that is, you can replace one with another when you delete—you can search and replace all the colors in your document pretty quickly with a little workaround. However, instead of repeating the whole workaround here virtually word for word, just look back at the tip called "Replacing Style Sheets" in Chapter 5, *Copy Flow*. Everywhere it says "Style Sheet," mentally replace it with the word "Color." The tip works in just the same way.

▼ ▼

Append

When you click the Append button, QuarkXPress lets you find another QuarkXPress file. Then, when you click Open, that document's colors are added to your color palette. Starting in version 3.2, if the incoming color has the same name as but a different specification from one in your document, the program prompts you to either merge them (Use Existing Color) or to rename the ones you're importing (see Figure 9-5). If you choose Rename New Color, it adds an asterisk to the incoming color name.

▼ ▼

Tip: One More Way to Append a Color. If you want just one or two colors from another file and don't want to append the entire list, you can copy and paste, or drag across an object filled with that color from another document. The color and its specifications come across too, and are added to the color list. Delete the object, and the color remains on the list.

▼ ▼

Tip: Libraries of Colors. Here's one more way to save your colors so that you can bring them into a new document. Place an object (even just a picture box with a colored background) in a Library. David has a Library named "David's Colors" into which he places colors he knows he'll use in various documents, but which he doesn't want to place in the default color palette. When he wants a particular color, he'll open the Library, pull that color's object out onto the document page, and then delete it. The object is gone, but the color stays in the color palette. Within the Library , you can group your colors into types such as "Warm Colors", "Cool Colors", or "Newsletter Colors" using the Library's labeling feature.

Figure 9-5
Appending colors with
the same name

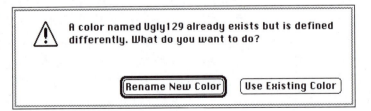

You can even make one library entry contain a number of different colors. For instance, if you apply three different Pantone colors to three different boxes, you can put all three in one library item (select all of them and drag them in all at once). When you pull that library item out into a new document, all three PMS colors are added.

▼ ▼

Edit Trap

Selecting the Edit Trap option in the Colors dialog box brings up the Trap Specifications dialog box. Trapping is a whole other *mishegoss* (Yiddish for "craziness"), so we'll put it off for now and discuss it at some length later in this chapter.

Save

When you are finished with adding, deleting, or editing your colors, you can click Save to save those changes to your document's color palette. Remember that even when you save the changes, you can still come back and edit them later. If you made these color changes while a document was open, the changes only apply to the document's color palette. If no documents were open, then they're added to the default color palette.

Cancel

Almost every dialog box in QuarkXPress has a Cancel button. This one works the same as all the rest: it cancels your entries without saving any changes.

▼ ▼

Special Colors

QuarkXPress has two special colors that aren't really colors. They are "Registration", which we have mentioned above; and "Indeterminate", which we'll talk about soon in "Trapping," below.

Registration

This "noncolor" appears in the Colors scroll list and on all color selection lists throughout the menus. When you apply this color to an object or text, that object or text prints on every color separation plate you print. It's especially nice for job-identification marks, and for registration or crop marks (if you are creating your own rather than letting the program do it for you; see Chapter 10, *Printing,* for more information on these special marks).

For example, Eric sometimes likes to bypass QuarkXPress's regular crop-mark feature and draw his own crop marks in the border around the finished piece. Then he colors these "Registration," and they print out on every piece of film that comes out for that job.

▼ ▼

Tip: Editing the Registration Color. If you use the "Registration" color regularly, you might want to change its color so that you can tell it apart from normal Black. You can use the Edit feature described earlier to change the on-screen color of "Registration" to anything you like. However, note that you can only use the color wheel to choose colors for "Registration". Also, because "Registration" is originally black, the Edit Color dialog box appears with the brightness scroll bar down to zero. Just raise the brightness to the level you want, and then change the color.

No matter what color you specify, objects with the color "Registration" always print on every plate. Changing the color changes nothing but the screen representation for that color. Use a color that is distinctly different from anything else in the document you're creating. That way you always know at a glance what's normal black stuff and what is colored "Registration".

▼ ▼

Indeterminate

When QuarkXPress looks at a selection and finds that either several colors are specified within that selection, or that it's a color picture, it calls this an "Indeterminate" color. This is not something you can change in any way. It's just a definition that the program uses to tell you there are several colors in the selection. In "Trapping," below, we'll see the great benefits of the Indeterminate "color."

Colors Palette

Just like style sheets, you can apply and edit colors with a click using the Colors palette (see Figure 9-6). This floating palette contains a list of every available color, along with a tint-percentage control popup menu, and three icons. These icons gray out depending on what object you have selected. When you select a text box, the icons represent frame color, text color, and background color for that box. When you select a line, two icons gray out, and only the line-color icon remains.

To apply a color to an object, first click the correct icon for what you want to change, then click on the desired color in the color list. If you want a tint of that color, first change the percentage in the upper-right corner, then press Return or Enter to apply the change. You can also just click somewhere other than on the palette. For example, let's say you want to change one word in a text box to 30-percent cyan.

1. Select the word in the text box.

2. Click the center icon in the Colors palette, which represents text (it looks like an "A" in a box).

3. Click on "Cyan" in the colors list.

4. Select "30%" from the popup menu, or type "30" in the field and press Enter.

It's funny, but those four steps are often much faster than selecting a color and tint from the Style menu. Note that you can

Figure 9-6

The Colors palette

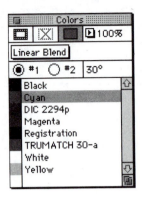

change the color of a text or picture box frame, even if the box doesn't have a frame. If you later add a frame, it will be the color you designated.

▼ ▼

Tip: Jump to Edit Colors. The Colors palette is more like the Style Sheet palette than meets the eye. In both palettes, Command-clicking on an item in the palette quickly brings you to a dialog box. In this case, Command-clicking on any color brings up the Colors dialog box, in which you can edit, duplicate, append, delete, or create new colors. This is also the fastest way to the Edit Trap dialog box.

▼ ▼

Tip: Drag-and-Drop Color Application. Sometimes we think the folks at Quark like to toss in features just because they're cool—for example, drag-and-drop color application. Try it: hold your mouse down on one of the tiny color squares on the Colors palette, and drag it over your page. Notice that as you drag, the image of that color square stays attached to your pointer. As you move the pointer over objects, their color changes to the color you're dragging. Move the pointer past an object, and its color reverts to whatever it was before. It really doesn't add a tremendous amount of what we in the software-pontificating business like to call "functionality," but it's a heck of a lot of fun to play with.

To apply a color to an object, just let go of the mouse button. Note that you can apply a color in this way to backgrounds and borders, but not to text, even if you have the text icon selected in

Figure A
Process-color
separations

Process-color image (four colors)

Cyan, 15 degrees

Magenta, 75 degrees

Yellow, zero degrees

Black, 45 degrees

Figure B
The elegant solution
for shadow type with
process colors

*Normal shadow style applied
(background color is
80-percent magenta)*

*Shadow is in separate text box
(text color set to 30-percent black
and 80-percent magenta)*

Figure C
Separations made
with Photoshop
and EfiColor

*Scan was made on a
Hewlett-Packard ScanJet
IIc desktop flatbed scanner.*

*Adobe Photoshop
(default separation settings)*

*EfiColor XTension
(Calibrated RGB profile)*

*EfiColor XTension
(ScanJet IIc profile)*

*EfiColor XTension
(Wrong profile; Solid Rendering)*

Figure D
A color swatch page
from the TruMatch
color selection book

*You can type this number directly in the Edit
Colors dialog box with TruMatch selected.
(Or you can type in the CMYK values.)*

Figure E
Linear color blend between two process
colors with an EPS image over it

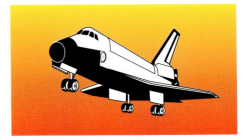

Figure F
Rich black versus 100
percent black

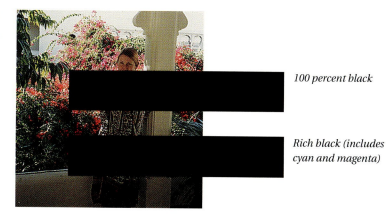

100 percent black

*Rich black (includes
cyan and magenta)*

Figure G
Trapping with process
color on and off

*These traps are
much larger than
you'd generally use.*

No trap (just knocks out)

Process Color turned on

*Box spreads with Process
Color turned off*

Process Color turned off

Figure H
Blend inside
one-bit image

Figure I

EfiColor's gamut alarm

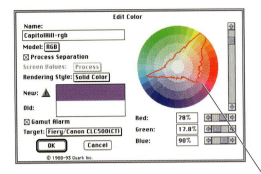

EfiColor's gamut alarm prompts you when a color cannot be printed on the target device.

Figure J

Modifying color images using Picture Contrast controls

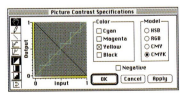

the Color palette. And since the palette is grayed out until you select an object, you can't drag anything until you've selected at least one object.

▼ ▼

Cool Blends

You can call them fountains, dégradés, gradations, or graduated fills, but the concept is always the same: the background of a text or picture box can make a gradual transition from one color to another (see Figure 9-7). Unlike some other programs that create graduated fills, in QuarkXPress you can blend any combination of spot colors, process colors, "White", or "Registration". In fact, QuarkXPress is the only program we know of that lets you blend between a process and a spot color.

Figure 9-7
Color blends

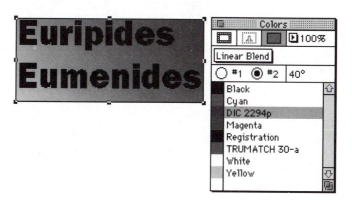

QuarkXPress has a dizzying array of blends: Linear (straight blend), Mid-Linear (goes from one color to another, then back again), Rectangular, Diamond, Circular, and Full Circular. See Figure 9-8 for examples of these various blends.

Creating a blend is easy. Just follow these steps.

1. Select the text or picture box to which you want to apply the blend.

2. Click the background icon in the Colors palette if it's not already selected.

3. Select the blend you want from the popup menu in the Colors palette.

4. Click button "#1", then click on the beginning color of the blend (you can adjust the tint level, too).

5. Click button "#2", and select the ending color of the blend (and adjust the tint, if necessary).

6. Specify the angle of the blend. For Linear and Mid-Linear blends, zero degrees (the default value) puts color "#1" on the left and color "#2" on the right. Increasing the value rotates the blend counter-clockwise (so that at 75 degrees, color "#1" is almost at the bottom of your box). Surprisingly, the angle value you enter has an effect on any kind of blend. It rotates Diamond and Rectangular blends, and affects how the Circular blends spread out within a box.

That's it. If you don't see the blend on your screen, it means one of two things. First, you might have done this procedure wrong. Second, you might have the Content tool selected. When the Content tool is selected, the active item (the text or picture box you have selected) only shows you the beginning color of the blend. This is so screen redraw can take place quickly and efficiently. To see the blend, either deselect the active picture or text box, or switch to the Item tool.

If you want to change one of the colors in the blend, click button "#1" or "#2"; then you can select the color, change its tint, or adjust the angle.

A warning for those placing blends behind grayscale TIFFs: our experience has shown that this usually results in something that looks as pleasant as a baboon's behind. The problem is that color "#1" gets mixed in with the TIFF itself. Quark thinks it should work this way; we think it's crazy. Proceed at your own risk.

▼ ▼

Tip: Accurate Blends. If you've got an eight-bit color monitor (256 colors), QuarkXPress lets you speed up your screen redraw by sacrificing on-screen color blend quality. You do this by turning

Figure 9-8
The cool blends

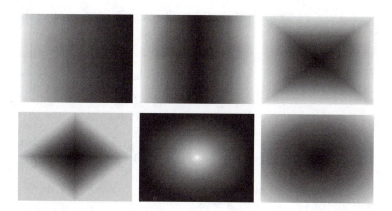

Accurate Blends on or off in the General Preferences dialog box (Command-Y). When Accurate Blends is on (the default is on), all blends appear on the screen as smoothly as QuarkXPress can make them (some are better than others; it depends on what colors you use). When you turn it off, the program just spits out a quick-'n'-dirty representation of the blend. This feature doesn't affect printing at all—just the speed at which your screen re-draws. Note that if you're using a 16-bit (thousands of colors) or 24-bit (millions of colors) monitor setting, this feature doesn't do anything.

▼ ▼

Tip: A New Dimension. Okay, maybe we're just easily amused, but we think this trick for creating three-dimensional buttons in Quark-XPress is pretty keen.

1. Draw a rectangle or oval (we think it looks best with a square or circle).

2. Give it a straight Linear blend. We like to set it at 45 degrees, but it's up to you.

3. Duplicate the object, and make it smaller. The amount you make it smaller is up to you. Remember that if you want to reduce it to 80 percent, you can simply type "*.8" after the measurement in the Width and Height fields.

4. To figure out the second object's blend angle, subtract the first object's blend angle from 270. So if the first object had a 45-degree blend, the second object should have a 225-degree blend $(270-45=225)$. You don't have to do the math if you don't want to; just type "270-45" in the angle box of the Color palette.

5. Space/Align the two objects so that their centers are equal (set Vertical and Horizontal alignment to zero offset from the objects' centers in the Space/Align dialog box).

You can really see the effect best when the page guides are turned off (see Figure 9-9). It's even nicer when you add a .25-point white frame around the inside object (sort of a highlight to the button's ridge).

Figure 9-9
Three-dimensional
buttons

The process   *The result*

Trapping

Nothing is perfect, not even obscenely expensive printing presses. When your print job is flying through those presses, each color being added one at a time, the paper may shift slightly. Depending on the press, this could be an offset of anywhere between .003 and .0625 inches (.2 to 4.5 points). If two colors abut each other on your artwork and this shift occurs, then the two colors may be moved apart slightly, resulting in a white "un-printed" space. It may seem like a $3/1,000$-of-an-inch space would look like a small crack in a large sidewalk, but we assure you, it could easily appear to be a chasm. What can you do? Fill in these potential chasms with traps and overprints.

The concept and practice of traps and overprints contain several potential pitfalls for the inexperienced. Up until now, most designers just let their lithographers and strippers handle it. There is a school of thought that says we should still let them handle it. But you know these desktop publishers; they always want to be in control of everything. The problem is that designers weren't trained to do trapping! Let's look carefully at what it's all about.

▼ ▼

Tip: Just (Don't) Do It. Trapping is as much art as science—in fact, if you look up "difficult" in the dictionary, it offers the synonym: "trapping." We often don't have time to mess around to make sure our traps are proper throughout a document, and sometimes even if we have time, it'd just be too much of a hassle.

QuarkXPress's trapping is pretty good, all in all, but it's lacking in some important areas, such as blends, choking type, and partially overlapped objects. Ultimately, QuarkXPress isn't designed to be a great trapper. If you want to spare yourself a lot of hassle, you can turn auto trapping off (see "Tip: Turning Auto Trapping Off," below), and use a program like Aldus TrapWise.

You probably won't want to own TrapWise yourself (it costs several thousand dollars), but your service bureau will. Find out how much it costs for them to trap the page for you, and then compare that with how much it's worth to you not to worry about it anymore.

▼ ▼

Overprinting. Picture the letter "Q" colored magenta on a cyan background. Normally, when creating color separations, the cyan plate has a white "Q" *knocked out* of it, exactly where the magenta "Q" prints (we'll talk more about color separations and plates in Chapter 10, *Printing*). This way the cyan and the magenta don't mix (see Figure 9-10). You can, however, set the magenta to over-

Figure 9-10
Knocking out and
overprinting

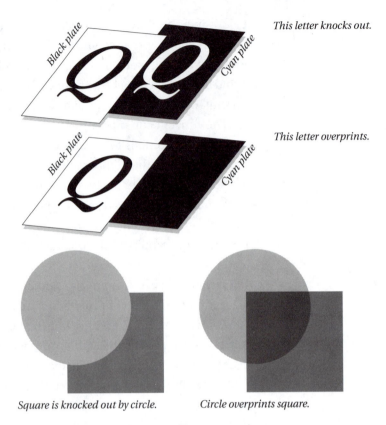

This letter knocks out.

This letter overprints.

Square is knocked out by circle.

Circle overprints square.

print the cyan. This results in the "Q" not being knocked out of the cyan; the two colors *overprint* in that area—resulting in a purple "Q" on a cyan background.

Trapping. A trap is created by very slightly overprinting two colors right along their borders. Then, when the paper shifts on the printing press, the space between the colors is filled with the additional trap color (see Figure 9-11). The trap can be created using two methods: choking and spreading. *Choking* refers to the background area getting smaller. *Spreading* refers to the foreground object (in the above example, the "Q") getting slightly larger.

Simple idea, right? But not necessarily a simple process when you're just beginning. In the sections that follow, we'll look at the various ways to trap objects in QuarkXPress.

Figure 9-11
Trapping two
colored objects

Untrapped

Trapped

Edit Trap

QuarkXPress has a built-in automatic trapping feature that you can control in the Trap Specifications dialog box, which is found by clicking the Edit Trap button in the Colors dialog box. The key to automatic trapping is that you are creating trapping and over-printing parameters for *pairs* of colors: the foreground and the background color. For example, picture some red type on top of a blue area. The blue is the background color; the red is the fore-ground color.

You edit the trapping and overprinting parameters for back-ground/foreground pairs by selecting the *foreground* color from the Colors scroll list and clicking Edit Trap. You are then shown the Trap Specifications dialog box for that color (see Figure 9-12). The list on the left side of the dialog box is the pairing list: each of the colors is a potential background color.

Note that the color "Indeterminate" is listed. This "color" refers to three cases: a color picture in the background, a background where several different colors are present, or an item only partially covering a background color when Ignore White is turned off (see "Trapping Preferences," later in this chapter). If you leave this set to Automatic, then QuarkXPress doesn't include trapping at all when it sees an indeterminate color pair.

Figure 9-12

The Trap Specifications
dialog box

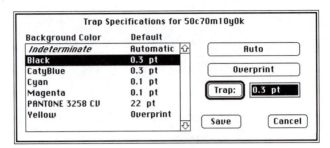

You can edit one, some, or all foreground/background pairs with three buttons: Auto, Overprint, and Trap.

Auto. When you first open the Trap Specifications dialog box for a color, each of the colors on the background list is set to Automatic trapping. If you change the trapping parameters with the tools described below, you can change a color pair back to Automatic by clicking the Auto button. "Automatic" refers to the following built-in trapping algorithm.

▶ Translate each color to its CMYK values.

▶ Note the darkness (luminosity) of each color.

▶ If the foreground color is lighter, then spread it so that it slightly overlaps the background color.

▶ If the background color is lighter, then choke it so that it slightly "underlaps" the foreground color.

This algorithm is based on the rule that in trapping, lighter colors should encroach on darker ones. That way the dark element defines the edge, and the lighter color overlapping doesn't affect that definition (see Figure 9-13).

If the foreground object's color is black and its shading is set to 95 percent or greater, then the automatic trapping algorithm sets it to fully overprint the color beneath it. In all other situations, though, the amount of trapping that the automatic algorithm uses varies depending on how you have your Trapping Preferences set (see "Trap Preferences," below).

Figure 9-13
Traps should go
from light colors
into dark colors

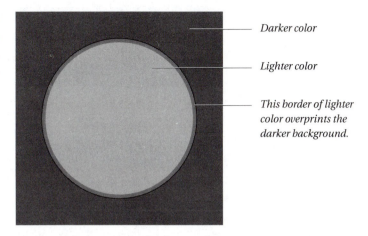

Darker color

Lighter color

*This border of lighter
color overprints the
darker background.*

▼ ▼

Tip: Trapping Small Type. You can run into trouble when you're
using small type, especially serif type, in a color document. Since
the type is so fine—especially the serifs—even a small amount of
trapping can clog it up. The counters can fill in, and the serifs can
get clunky (see Figure 9-14). If you try to choke the background
rather than spread the type, you're in for a nasty surprise: you
can't choke type in QuarkXPress. You can only spread it. Bear this
in mind when you're setting up your trapping preferences, and
when you're specifying colors for type.

Figure 9-14
Trapping serif type

Monsieur de Bergerac
Untrapped

*Serif type can clog
up, and the serifs
can get clunky
when trapped.*

Monsieur de Bergerac
Trapped

▼ ▼

Overprint. As we described above, telling QuarkXPress to overprint
a color pair has the effect of printing the background color with
no knocked-out white space. The foreground color fully overlaps
the background color.

There are a few very important times when you'll want to
overprint colors. If you overprint red on blue, for instance, you get

purple, which is probably not what you intended. The most important of these times, perhaps, is printing fine black lines or type on a colored background. In fact, almost any time you have a black foreground object, it should overprint the background.

To set a color pair to automatically Overprint, select the background color from the list, and click the Overprint button.

▼ ▼

Tip: An Overprinting Black. There are times when we want black to overprint and times when we don't. To give ourselves the option, we added a color to our color palette called "Knockout Black", which is a duplicate of the color "Black". We then edited the trapping specifications for each of the blacks: "Black" would always overprint (as usual), and "Knockout Black" always knocks out (or chokes slightly).

A large black box overprinting a multicolored background may look mottled, so we'd use "Knockout Black". However, fine black type over the same background will probably look just fine, and we'd use normal ol' "Black".

▼ ▼

Tip: Four-Color Black. Even better, you can create a much richer black color by defining a separate black in your color palette which contains a bit of other process color in it. The standard rich black that color strippers use is 100-percent black along with 40-percent cyan. We sometimes like to get complicated, though, and add 20 to 30 percent each of magenta and yellow, too. When a plain black (100-percent K) object overlaps colored objects, it can look mottled and can look different over different colors (see Figure G in the color pages). Adding color to your blacks solves the problem.

This trick not only achieves a richer black on a printing press, but also better blacks from a thermal color printer. However, if the thermal color printer is your final destination, you might boost the additional colors between 50 and 100 percent each.

Note, though, that you should think carefully about how you apply this rich black. A potential problem lurks behind this technique: the cyan can show up from behind the black if (or when) the printing press is misregistered (see "Tip: Knockout Lettering from Rich Black," next).

▼ ▼

Tip: Knockout Lettering from Rich Black. The biggest problem with rich black is that when you have text or an object knocking out the black, any misregistration on press results in the cyan peeking out horribly from behind the black. The engineers at Quark have built a very cool internal solution to this problem.

QuarkXPress checks to see if an object is knocking out of a rich black. If it is, it only spreads the cyan, magenta and yellow plates of that rich-black color by the amount specified in the Auto Amount field, leaving the black plate alone. You need this kind of help most when you're placing a white object (such as white, reversed text) over a rich black. (See Figure F on the color pages.)

If you don't understand what we're talking about, try it yourself with proofs from a laser printer (but change the trap to something enormous that you can easily see—like three points).

▼ ▼

Trap. If you want to set your own specification for an automatic trapping pair, select the background color you want to apply the trap to, then type the amount of trap you want into the space provided. You can select any value between -36 and 36 points, in .001-point increments (why anyone would want a trap over one or two points is beyond us). A positive value spreads the foreground object (making it slightly larger by drawing a line around it). A negative value leaves the foreground object alone and chokes the background object. Don't click OK yet, though: you must first click the Trap button to activate the change (this last step has been the downfall of many a trapper).

The amount of trap you need depends a great deal on your lithographer. No printer worth their salt would say that their printing presses are dead on, and that you don't need to build in any trapping. Chances are that a value between .2 point and one point is adequate. Just as a reference, for almost every color job we do, we set all the trap values to .3 point.

One fine point on trapping: if you are familiar with trapping using illustration programs such as FreeHand or Illustrator, you know that when you apply a trapping stroke to an object, your trap is really only one half of that thickness (the stroke falls equally inside and outside the path). If you're in the habit of using one point when you want a half-point trap, break it when you use QuarkXPress. This program handles the conversion for you.

Trapping Preferences

So who says Quark's default trapping values will work for you? They certainly don't work for us; so we change them. You can change the way that QuarkXPress traps in the Trapping Preferences dialog box (select Trapping from the Preferences submenu under the Edit menu). These changes—like most other preferences—are specific to only the document that you have open at the time; if you want them to apply to all future documents, change them while no other documents are open.

The Trapping Preferences dialog box contains six controls: Auto Method, Auto Amount, Indeterminate, Overprint Limit, Ignore White, and Process Trap (see Figure 9-15). These let you get pretty specific about how you want QuarkXPress's trapping to act.

Auto Method. The Auto Method control is a two-item popup menu that determines how automatic trapping should be handled. Your two choices are Proportional and Absolute. The first choice, Proportional, tells QuarkXPress to look at how different the two colors are and adjust the amount of trap accordingly. Because the program looks at the "darkness" of a color (which is difficult to quantify), it's a little hard for us to describe the exact mathematics here on paper without getting really technical. Basically, though, QuarkXPress takes the difference between the two darkness values and multiplies that by the amount in the Auto Amount field (see below). For example, if the background color were 80-percent dark, the foreground object were 20-percent dark, and the Auto Amount setting were one-half point, then the background would choke by .3 point ($.8 - .2 = .6 \times .5$ point $= .3$ point).

Figure 9-15
Auto Trap Preferences

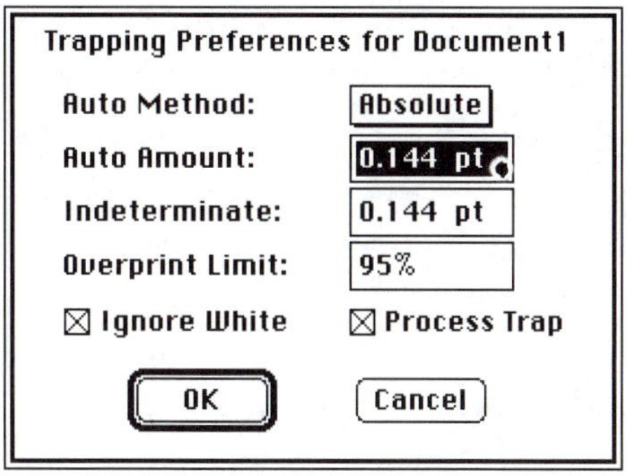

Trapping Preferences for Document1

Auto Method:	Absolute
Auto Amount:	0.144 pt
Indeterminate:	0.144 pt
Overprint Limit:	95%

☒ Ignore White   ☒ Process Trap

OK   Cancel

The second choice, Absolute, tells QuarkXPress to always use the same trapping value. This trapping amount is the value in the Auto Amount field. As far as we're concerned, there's rarely a reason to use Proportional trapping, so we always leave the Auto Method set to Absolute.

Auto Amount. The value that you set in the Auto Amount field tells QuarkXPress the maximum value that Proportional automatic trapping can use, and the specific value that Absolute automatic trapping should use. The default value of .144 point (about $\frac{2}{1,000}$ of an inch) seems a little small to us, so we usually change this to .3 point. However, remember to check with your printer first.

Indeterminate. The value that you set in the Indeterminate field sets the amount of trap that QuarkXPress uses for objects which are placed over indeterminate colors. Note that this is an absolute (not relative) value. That is, any object that sits over an indeterminate color is trapped by this amount (unless you specifically change that object's settings in the Edit Trap dialog box); it doesn't change depending on luminance or blackness. The definition of Indeterminate, however, is slightly more complex than we mentioned previously; it depends on whether Ignore White is turned on (see below).

▼ ▼

Tip: Turning Off Auto Trapping. Depending on your page design, trapping can occasionally cause problems or slowdowns at print time. You can turn it off entirely, however, by setting the Auto and Indeterminate trapping values to zero in the Trap Preferences dialog box. If you're having strange slowdowns at print time and are working with colored type on colored backgrounds, you might try this. Note that you won't get any trapping, which causes its own problems.

▼ ▼

Overprint Limit. Just because a color is set to overprint in the Edit Trap dialog box doesn't mean that it'll really overprint. The key is this Overprint Limit value in the Trapping Preferences dialog box. QuarkXPress overprints the color black and any other color that is set to overprint only when their tint levels are above the Overprint Limit. For example, let's say you have the color Green set to overprint. If you screen it back to 50 percent, QuarkXPress knocks the color out rather than overprinting it, because the tint falls below the Overprint Limit (the default amount is 95 percent). Likewise, when the color black is set to Automatic, it always overprints any color, as long as the black is above this Overprint Limit.

Ignore White. Let's say a red picture box only lies partially on top of another page item, and partially on the white page background (see Figure 9-16). In the Trapping Preferences dialog box, Quark-XPress gives you the choice as to whether it should consider the background color "Indeterminate" or not. When the Ignore White is turned on, QuarkXPress won't call a partial overlap "Indeterminate" because it just ignores the white page background; it traps based on the color of the overlapped object. If you turn this off, however, it "sees" the white background page, and considers the mix of background colors to be Indeterminate.

Process Trap. Take a look at the two process colors (foreground and background) listed in Table 9-1. If you spread this foreground color (a yellow) into the background color (a muddy brown) using with Process Trap turned off (this was the default in earlier versions of QuarkXPress), the trap area doesn't mesh the two colors the way you'd want. That is, the slight sliver of trap (where the col-

Figure 9-16
Ignore White

When Ignore White is turned on, the trap value for this circle is determined by its relationship to the box, rather than "Indeterminate".

Table 9-1
Color breakdown for trapping example

Color	Foreground box	Background box
Cyan	0	30
Magenta	20	50
Yellow	100	90
Black	5	0

ors overlap) is made up of magenta, yellow and black (the foreground color spreads). However, since there's no cyan in the foreground color, the cyan from the background shows through, making a really ugly puke-green trap area. Now you might say: For a quarter-point trap, who cares? No one will see it anyway. Think again. That greenish line stands out clearly around the edge of the yellow object. (See Figure G on the color pages.)

However, when Process Trap is turned on, some process colors get spread while others are choked. Here's how it works. Any process color in the foreground object that is darker than the same color in the background object is spread by half the trapping value (if you're using automatic trapping, it's half the value in the Auto Amount field; otherwise it's half of whatever trapping value you specify). Any process color that's lighter is choked by half that value.

In the example above, the cyan plate is choked by half the trapping value (let's say half of .25 point, or .125 point) because there is less cyan in the foreground box than in the background box. Magenta also chokes. However, the yellow and black plates spread by .125 point.

The result is a trap area as wide as the specified trapping value (in the example above, .25 point), centered on the edge of the foreground object, and with the darkest process colors of each of the objects.

If you don't understand this, read the last few paragraphs over several times. If you still don't understand it, then give up and believe us when we tell you that it's a really good thing. Leave Process Trap turned on (see Figure G on the color pages).

A couple of notes on this feature. When all the process colors in the foreground object are darker or they're all lighter than in the background object, then QuarkXPress doesn't trap at all. This is because it doesn't need to. Also, Process Trap doesn't do anything for spot colors, again because it doesn't need to.

Object-Level Trapping

Instead of just specifying trapping color pairs (all reds over all blues, all blacks over all yellows, and so on), you can specify trapping on an object-by-object basis. For example, if you want one green line to overprint a yellow area, and another similar line to knock out, you can specify that. You do this in the Trap Information palette.

Unlike most palettes in QuarkXPress, where you can either use them or use menu items, the Trap Information palette is the only way that you can use object-by-object trapping. Let's take a gander at this palette's anatomy (see Figure 9-17).

The Trap Information palette shows you the current trap information for a selected page object, gives you "reasons" for why it's trapping the object that way, and lets you change that object's trap value. You can change the trap values, depending on the object you have selected. For example, for a text box with no frame, you can adjust the trap for the background color of the box and the text in the box. For a box with a frame, you can set the

Figure 9-17

The Trap Information palette and its popup information balloons

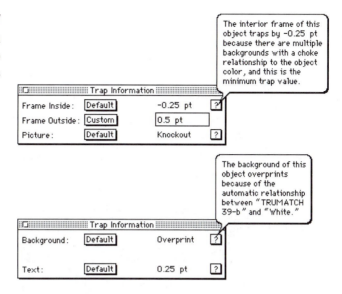

The interior frame of this object traps by -0.25 pt because there are multiple backgrounds with a choke relationship to the object color, and this is the minimum trap value.

The background of this object overprints because of the automatic relationship between "TRUMATCH 39-b" and "White."

trap for the inside of the frame (trapping to the background color of the box), the outside of the frame (trapping to anything behind that box), and the text (trapping to the background of the box).

Unless you've changed the trap value, the Trap Information palette displays all objects at their Default trap. This means that the objects trap at whatever value is set in the Edit Trap dialog box. QuarkXPress displays the trap value to the right of the word Default, and then displays a gray button labeled with a question mark. If you click this button and hold it down, QuarkXPress gives you a balloon message explaining why it's trapping the object this way. For example, if you have a black line selected, the balloon might tell you that it's overprinting the black line because of the relationship between black and the background color. It doesn't usually go into much more detail than that, but it's better than just leaving you up in the air.

To change the trap value for part of an object (e.g., the inside frame of a picture box), you use the mini-popup menu in the Trap Information palette. The menu is usually set to Default, but you can change this to Overprint, Knockout, Auto Amount (+), Auto Amount (−), or Custom. Overprint and Knockout are pretty self-explanatory. The two Auto Amount values use the value in the Auto Amount field of the Trapping Preferences dialog box (the value is either positive or negative, denoting a spread or a choke). When you select Custom, QuarkXPress gives you a field in which to type any trap value you want (from -36 to +36 points).

Note that text can be trapped character by character (see Figure 9-18), and that one black object can be overprinted where another black object knocks out (this kills the need for our tricky tip for a non-overprinting black).

Figure 9-18
Trapping type
character
by character

Trapping to Multiple Colors

We said earlier that when QuarkXPress sees one colored object only partially covering another colored object, the program thinks of this as "Indeterminate" trapping. We then went further and said that when Ignore White is turned on in Trapping Preferences, the program ignores the white background entirely, making it *not* "Indeterminate". Now we have the final word on the subject.

If the foreground object partially overlaps two colored objects, QuarkXPress still doesn't always think of this as "Indeterminate". First it looks at the trapping relationships between all the colors. If the foreground color chokes to both background colors, then the foreground object gets choked. If the Edit Trap specifications are set to spread to both background colors, then QuarkXPress spreads it. If it's supposed to spread to one and choke to the other, *then* the program defaults to the "Indeterminate" color.

Also, just for the sake of completeness, if you set the Edit Trap specifications so that the foreground color spreads one value (let's say one point) to one background color, and a different value (let's say two points) to the other background color, QuarkXPress uses the lesser of the values (in this case, one point).

None of this may apply to you, but it's still good information to tuck into the back of your brain . . . just in case.

▼ ▼

Color from Outside Sources

Up until now in this chapter we have concentrated our discussion on color items—text, boxes, rules, and so on—which are built entirely in QuarkXPress. But what about bringing color graphics in from other programs? And although we discussed modifying color bitmapped images in Chapter 8, *Modifying Images,* what about being prepared for creating color separations? We'll address these points now.

One area you won't read about here is working with object-oriented color PICT images. Why? First, because we think they're kludgey (that's pronounced "cloodgy"), and so unreliable that we wouldn't use them for our own QuarkXPress documents (see Chapter 6, *Pictures,* for a slightly longer discussion of this format). Second, because the only thing you can really do well with a color PICT image is print it on a color laser printer or film recorder which handles QuickDraw well (or as well as could be expected).

Object-Oriented EPS Files

We've avoided the subject of object-oriented graphic files for several chapters, but now it's time to dive back in. Designers frequently generate color artwork using programs such as Adobe Illustrator or Aldus FreeHand, saving them as Encapsulated PostScript (EPS) files. QuarkXPress can not only import files from these programs, but can also generate color separations of them.

Once again, the details of generating color separations (or "seps," as they're often called) is covered in Chapter 10, *Printing,* and Appendix A, *EfiColor.* But while we're talking about color on the desktop, we need to cover some general information about using these programs with QuarkXPress. We'll tackle this discussion one color method at a time: process first, and then spot (we're including Pantone colors in the spot-color discussion, though you can also create process simulations of Pantone inks).

Process color. QuarkXPress can create color separations of illustrations built in FreeHand or Illustrator which contain process colors. Period. All you have to do is specify your process colors in either application, save them as EPS, and import them into your QuarkXPress document using Get Picture. Nice and easy. As we noted earlier in this chapter, if the colors are named (process colors in Illustrator or spot colors in FreeHand), the colors are added to the QuarkXPress document color list.

Note that we say you must use Get Picture. If you use Option-Copy and Paste to paste an EPS graphic into a picture box, QuarkXPress won't separate it (holding down the Option key while copying from Illustrator or FreeHand copies the graphic in PostScript format). In fact, while we're on the subject, we should note that QuarkXPress may not be able to separate color EPS files from applications other than Illustrator and FreeHand. It depends entirely on whether those applications create EPS files according to Adobe's document structuring specifications.

Spot color. The key to working with spot colors brought in from either FreeHand or Illustrator is being careful with your naming. In order for QuarkXPress to separate the spot colors properly, you have to have a color in your QuarkXPress document named *exactly* the same as the color in the illustration. Fortunately, starting in version 3.3, named colors from illustrations are added to your color list automatically upon importing the picture.

If you don't have a same-named color in QuarkXPress (if you're using a pre-3.3 version of the program), the spot color separates into a process color in QuarkXPress. Remember that with spot colors, the colors' actual specifications make no difference except for screen display and color-printer output.

The same goes for the Pantone colors. If you use a Pantone color in your Illustrator file, just make sure it's named the same thing in your QuarkXPress file and it'll print fine. Fortunately, Illustrator, FreeHand, and QuarkXPress name their Pantone colors the same, so if you're using the color libraries included in each program, the names will probably match.

What You Can and Cannot Change

QuarkXPress prints exactly what is specified in every EPS file. In fact, QuarkXPress has no way to change them: encapsulated PostScript files are totally self-contained and cannot easily be modified from outside sources. All the halftoning information for objects and bitmapped images (if it's included in the EPS), all the trapping and tinting information, and all the color specifications are set in hard-packed mud (we like to think that you at least have a chance with hard-packed mud; "stone" is a bit too final).

All this means that you must take a little more control into your own hands. You must specify your own trapping from within FreeHand or Illustrator, and make sure that these EPS images contain traps for their surroundings in QuarkXPress documents.

Luckily, all overprinting specified in Illustrator or FreeHand (or any other program which handles its color PostScript properly) is handled correctly when generating color separations from QuarkXPress. An object that's set to overprint in a FreeHand EPS file not only overprints objects within that EPS, but also QuarkXPress objects. Conversely, if an object is not set to "Overprint," it knocks out any background colors or objects within QuarkXPress.

You cannot adjust any trapping for EPS files from within QuarkXPress. For example, if your EPS picture contains a spot color (PMS 345), and you have set up the equivalent spot color in QuarkXPress as described above, any trapping or overprinting assignments you make to PMS 345 in the Trap Specifications dialog box do not (and actually cannot) make any difference to the EPS file. They do, however, make all the difference to any objects created within QuarkXPress that are colored PMS 345.

The same is true with EfiColor's color correction: it has no effect on the colors in EPS graphics (see Appendix A, *EfiColor*).

Bitmapped Images

Let's cut to the chase: process colors are CMYK (cyan, magenta, yellow, and black). A picture saved in any other color model (most TIFF images are, especially scans) has to be translated into CMYK mode before it can be imageset. QuarkXPress has no built-in method for creating separations of these RGB images because it can't translate them into CMYK by itself. It gladly prints a grayscale representation of the entire picture, but when it comes to pulling it apart, it gives the big "no dice, dog lice."

If you're working with RGB scanned images, you have three options for performing RGB-to-CMYK conversion.

▶ Preseparate the image using Photoshop, PrePrint, or the like, and import it into QuarkXPress as a CMYK TIFF, EPS or DCS file.

▶ Place the image as an RGB TIFF in QuarkXPress and let the EfiColor XTension do the process-separation work (see Appendix A, *EfiColor).*

▶ Place the image as an RGB TIFF in QuarkXPress, print PostScript to disk with EfiColor turned off, and pass the resulting PostScript dump through a postprocessor such as Aldus PrePrint.

Although we'll really be talking about color separation in detail in Chapter 10, *Printing*, and Appendix A, *EfiColor*, let's explore these three methods briefly here.

Preseparating. Adobe Photoshop allows you to translate RGB images into CMYK using the Mode menu (you can tweak the settings it uses in Photoshop's Preferences dialog boxes). Once the image is converted to CMYK, you can save it in several formats, including DCS, EPS, and TIFF. Because the RGB-to-CMYK translation is so difficult, people have developed their own religious preference about what program does it best. We do most of our work in Photoshop, though some people will tell you that Photoshop's separation (translation) technique isn't as good as those in Color Access, Aldus PrePrint, or EFI's Cachet (which is the same as EfiColor's; see below).

Once you've separated a file in one of these programs, you can save it in one of three formats—EPS, DCS, or TIFF—and import it into QuarkXPress, fully separated and ready for output. We discussed these formats in detail in Chapter 6, *Pictures,*.

When you save color bitmaps as Desktop Color Separation (DCS) files, you end up with five EPS files—one for each of the process colors, plus one which includes a pointer to each of those other files and supplies a low-resolution representation of the image. This last file is the one that you import into your QuarkXPress document. When you go to print, QuarkXPress sees the pointers and goes in search of the preseparated files, one at a time.

The key to saving DCS images in Photoshop is to save them as EPS files and select the proper settings in the Desktop Color Separation section of the Save as EPS dialog box.

Note that you don't have to save as five-file DCS to make EPS images separate. The difference? Straight CMYK EPS files can separate fine; their biggest drawback is that they consist of one gigantic file. DCS 1.0 files have the added benefit of letting you work with a small master file while the large CMYK files can be sitting someplace else.

DCS images will print proofs faster because QuarkXPress just uses the low-resolution image when printing to a color printer. And, finally, separations from QuarkXPress print faster with DCS because instead of sending one enormous file down for each plate (as with straight EPS files), the program can just send down the information it needs when it needs it.

Of course, we've already said that color separation is not as easy as clicking a button. If you're looking for quality color, you had better know Photoshop well enough to work with its under-color removal and color-correction settings. Remember: QuarkXPress cannot apply any image modification on the EPS files that you import. All of that must be done before importing the picture.

Preseparating as CMYK TIFF. Once you've switched to the CMYK mode in Photoshop, you can also save files as CMYK TIFF images. We find CMYK TIFFs to be a bit easier than DCS files for several reasons. First, you only have one file to work with. Second, Quark-XPress can do more with TIFF files than it can with EPS or DCS images. For example, QuarkXPress downsamples at print time works when you use TIFF images. Also, you can make tonal and screening adjustments to TIFF images from within the program. Finally, if you're working with an OPI system (see "OPI" in Chapter 10, *Printing*), you can use TIFF images as for position only (FPO) images and let another program strip them in at print time.

Separating with an XTension. If you want to postseparate your RGB images, you can import them directly into QuarkXPress without worrying about the translations beforehand. There are two XTensions presently available for separating your files: EfiColor and SpectraSeps QX.

▶ **EfiColor.** This solution requires that you have the EfiColor XTension loaded in your QuarkXPress folder and the Efi-Color Processor and database in your System Folder. QuarkXPress 3.2 and later include it as part of the package (see Appendix A, *EfiColor*). If you're relying on EfiColor to also handle tonal correction, you might have a problem: EfiColor doesn't sharpen images (image sharpening should always be the last step in the process, after any tonal correction). If the image is already adjusted and sharpened, however, there shouldn't be a problem.

▶ **SpectraSeps QX.** If you need additional controls and are willing to spend a few hundred bucks, you should examine PrePress Technology's SpectraSeps QX XTension. It gives you some controls that you can't get in EfiColor, including sharpening and tonal correction; however, we personally prefer to do these sorts of adjustments in a program like Photoshop.

Postseparating. Finally, you can use a postprocessing utility such as Aldus PrePrint or Kodak's Prophecy system to separate the RGB images. Again, typically this means you make a PostScript dump or save an EPS file with OPI comments. You then open it in your postprocessor or transfer it to a high-end computer for the high-resolution substitution and RGB-to-CMYK conversion.

The Aldus PrePrint utility is a good postprocessing solution for a number of reasons. First, it can read OPI files. That means you can print PostScript to disk from QuarkXPress with OPI comments but without the huge image files (see Chapter 10, *Printing*), and PrePrint can read that and strip in the high-resolution images where necessary. Second, PrePrint has a great tonal adjustment feature called Balance to Sample (our officemate, Ole Kvern, just calls this the "Make Better" command). However, many people find it cumbersome to have to print PostScript to disk and run it through a separate utility just to make separations.

Which to Use? Do we suggest using preseparation (with Adobe Photoshop or Color Access) or postseparation (with EfiColor or PrePrint)? The first issue is which method is more convenient and appropriate for your workplace. The biggest argument for preseparation is the translation time: preseparating your bitmapped images requires translating them from RGB to CMYK only once. Postseparating them with either an XTension or a utility requires that translation time every time you print. This translation is incredibly time-consuming. Given a choice, we'd rather just have to deal with it once and get it over with.

However, which of these methods results in the superior separation? Here we get to the aesthetics of color separation, and we wouldn't want to sway your opinion (which is the nice way of saying that, just this once, we're not going to preach our opinions).

▼ ▼

Tip: Duotones from Photoshop. Many people create duotones or tritones in Photoshop, and then save them as EPS files (you have to save them as EPS files) before importing them into QuarkXPress. If the duotone uses spot colors, such as Pantone colors, you have to make sure you've got the same-named color in your Quark-XPress document. People have had difficulty with this in the past because the two programs sometimes named their Pantone colors differently.

Fortunately, QuarkXPress 3.3 now automatically imports the color names into your document so you're sure to get a match. Even though Photoshop's Pantone color names can be slightly different from QuarkXPress's (Photoshop's have an extra letter at the end of some the colors), QuarkXPress is smart enough to import them in the way it names them.

Also note that if your duotones are set to a spot color and a process color (like black), you have to adjust the halftone screen for the spot color so that you don't end up with moiré patterns (see "Spot color screen values" in the "Specifying Colors" section earlier in this chapter).

Deciding to Work in Color

We started this chapter with a comment from Russell Brown, so we think it's only fair to end with what he considers to be the most logical steps to successful color publishing.

1. Complete a black-and-white project with text only.

2. Complete a black-and-white project with text and graphics.

3. Complete a project with several spot colors.

4. Complete a project with process color tints.

5. Finally, attempt the use of color photography.

The Macintosh, no matter how powerful a tool, is still no substitute for experience. Work slowly and carefully, and you will become a raging color pro in time.

CHAPTER 10

PRINTING

Once upon a time, probably somewhere at some university, someone had an idea and named it "the paperless office." People wouldn't be bothered anymore with having to store the thousands (or millions) of pieces of paper which come through their offices each year. Instead, the information would all be placed on some sort of storage medium, easily referenced by computer. It was a magic concept; everyone agreed that it would make life easier, more efficient, and certainly more fun.

Go ahead and ask people who have been involved with electronic publishing for a while if they have seen any sign of the paperless office. As an example, in our offices, the ratio of expended paper to normal refuse is such that we empty our small garbage cans every couple of weeks and the voluminous paper-recycling boxes weekly. When it comes right down to it, in our business every piece of work that we do is based, ultimately, on a printed page or an imaged piece of film (which will probably be used to print on paper later).

How do we extract the digitized information on disk to print onto paper? Many people mistake the process as being as easy as clicking Print. In this chapter we'll discuss what's behind those two actions, and go into some depth on how to get the most efficient and best-quality printing you can for your document. We'll also touch on tips for working with service bureaus and printers—both the mechanical and the human types.

Before we get into anything too complex, though, let's deal with two simple yet crucial issues in most people's print jobs: PostScript and fonts.

▼ ▼

PostScript

To put it simply, PostScript is what makes desktop publishing with QuarkXPress possible. PostScript is a page-description language—a bunch of commands that PostScript laser printers understand. When you tell QuarkXPress to print a page, it writes a computer program in PostScript describing the page, and sends that program to the printer. The printer (or imagesetter), which has a PostScript interpreter inside it, interprets the PostScript describing the page, and puts marks on the paper (or film) according to that description.

For instance, the PostScript command *lineto* tells the printer to draw a line from one place to another; *curveto* draws curves, and *setlinewidth* changes the thickness of the line the printer is about to image. You don't really need to know much about PostScript in order to get your job done, but it's important to know that it's there working behind the scenes.

This chapter is dedicated, in part, to Chuck Geschke, John Warnock, and the other people who created PostScript. And we need to say one thing up front: we're not talking PCL here. We're not talking CORA or even SGML. Those languages were also designed for putting marks on paper or film. In this chapter, however, we're talking PostScript.

Actually, we do talk about the QuickDraw page description language some, too, since it's integral to the Macintosh system. But mostly we're going to assume you're working with an Adobe PostScript printer. There are other interpreters out there, such as those from RIPS, CAI, or Hyphen, and they've gotten much better over the past couple of years. However, we still prefer printers that include Adobe PostScript over other types because they're typically more reliable. However, sometimes you have no choice; if you're printing to a large-format color plotter, there's a good chance you'll be using Freedom of Press.

▼ ▼

Fonts

Almost everyone uses QuarkXPress at some point to work with text. It's a given. When you work with text, you work with typefaces. Choosing a particular font was covered in Chapter 4, *Type and Typography.* Printing that font is covered here.

If you don't fully understand how bitmap and outline fonts work together, we recommend that you go back and look over the beginning of Chapter 4. Working with each of these requires slightly different approaches to the printing process and results in drastically different printed pages. For those of you who kind of remember, but need a reminder, here's a recap.

Bitmap Versus Outline

When you're working with the Macintosh and PostScript printers, you need two kinds of fonts—bitmapped screen fonts and outline printer fonts. The bitmapped fonts display on screen; the outline fonts are used for printing. If you're using ATM (you should be) or TrueType fonts (you probably shouldn't be), the outline font is also used to image on the screen. That's how you can get smooth type at any size.

Bitmap-only fonts are to outline fonts as bitmapped images are to object-oriented images (see Chapter 6, *Pictures*), and what goes for bitmapped images goes for bitmapped fonts. For example, scaling has a direct effect on the resolution of the image, and rotation can cause severe changes in the placement of the bits. You don't see many bitmap-only fonts these days.

▼ ▼

Printer Fonts

Bitmapped fonts work in tandem with outline fonts. QuarkXPress uses the bitmapped screen font to reference the outline font at print time. But to be able to make this switch, it must be able to find the outline printer font—either in the printer's permanent memory, or in a file on disk.

David thinks of downloading as sending the font file *down* the network lines to the printer (especially because his printer sits *down* under his desk). Any way you think of it, the action is the same. QuarkXPress tries to find the outline information, which is encapsulated in the printer font file. See Chapter 4, *Type and Typography*, for where these fonts should be located depending on the system version and font utilities you're using (if any).

If QuarkXPress can find the printer font, it downloads the font information to the laser printer along with your document. Post-Script laser printers have memory allocated for font storage. However, printers vary in their available memory—and thus, the number of fonts they can hold. For example, the original Laser-Writer could keep only three or four fonts in memory at a time, while an Apple LaserWriter IIf can keep over 13 fonts in memory. Exceeding the amount of memory available causes a PostScript error (which shows up as "VMerror" in the print status dialog box), flushing your job and restarting the printer. (See the "Troubleshooting" section, page 603.)

You don't need the outline printer fonts in your System Folder for any font that is resident in your printer. For example, all Post-Script printers come with Times, Helvetica, Courier, and Symbol encoded directly into the printer's memory, so you don't need a printer font to use these typefaces. Most also come with several other fonts, including Palatino, Bookman, and Zapf Chancery. The page that prints out when you start up your printer usually can tell you which fonts are resident. If the startup page is turned off, you can use Adobe's Font Downloader, PrairieSoft's LaserStatus, or Apple's LaserWriter Utility to retrieve a font list.

Printing Ugly

When you have neither a printer font nor a printer-resident font available, QuarkXPress has two options.

▶ Print using the Courier typeface. This happens when your document contains an EPS file with fonts that you don't have available.

▶ Print the text using a scaled version of the bitmapped screen font that is closest in point size to that you have in your document. QuarkXPress prints the text almost exactly as it appears on screen.

We're not sure which of these is uglier. We tend to break into hives at the sight of either. However, perhaps Oscar Wilde said it best when he noted, "For those who like that kind of thing, that is the kind of thing they like."

More Font Downloading

Ordinarily, when your printing job is done, the fonts that you used are flushed out of the printer's memory. Then, next time you print the document, QuarkXPress has to download the fonts all over again. Downloading one time may not seem like a long process, but having to download the fonts repeatedly starts to make chess look like a fast sport.

But you don't have to wait. You can do something about your predicament. You can download the fonts yourself.

Manual downloading. You can download a typeface to your printer's RAM (which works just like a computer's RAM) and keep it there until you turn off the printer. Several utilities let you do this. We like LaserStatus because it's really simple, but you can also use Font Downloader or LaserWriter Utility. Typically, these sorts of utilities call this "permanently" downloading, even though you can only "permanently" download to a hard drive, as described below. When you download to a printer's memory, the fonts disappear when the printer is turned off or gets reset.

Downloading a font manually is particularly helpful for type-faces which you use many times throughout the day. If Goudy is your corporate typeface, you can manually download it from one computer at the start of each day. And, as long as no one resets the printer, you can use it to your heart's content from any of the computers hooked up to the network (whether or not they have Goudy's printer font on their hard disks).

Hard-disk storage. If you have a hard disk connected to your printer, you can download a printer font to the printer's hard disk where it resides until you delete it (or drop the hard drive on the ground). Some downloading utilities, such as Font Downloader and LaserWriter Utility, have the extra features necessary for this task. If you have some odd sort of printer, you may have to get special software from the manufacturer. Note that any normal SCSI hard drive works fine for this. It doesn't even have to be for-matted or a Mac drive; you format the drive with the printer software. So if you have an extra 20- or 40-megabyte hard drive sitting around, you could hook it up to the SCSI port on your printer (assuming that the printer has a SCSI port, of course).

Choosing a Printer

We're going to leave the choice of lithographers up to you. If it's MinutePress, good luck. If it's a really good printer, just listen to what they tell you and follow obediently. Instead, we want to talk here about what electronic-imaging device you use to output your document.

Clearly, the most important feature of a printer is its imaging resolution. Whereas many high-resolution imagesetters offer a variety of resolutions, most desktop laser printers are only happy when they're printing 300 or 600 dots per inch. Table 10-1 lists several printers with their resolutions.

Table 10-1

Resolution choices for
some imaging devices

Device	Printing resolutions (dpi)
Apple StyleWriter II	360
Desktop laser printers	300, 400, 600
Varityper VT-600	600
Linotronic 300/500	635, 1270, 2540
Compugraphic CG9400	1200, 2400
Varityper VT6000	1200/2400, 1270/2540, and six others
Linotronic 330/530	1270, 2540, 3386
Film recorders	1024, 2048, 4096, 8192, and higher

We, like most people, use a desktop laser printer to print proof copies of our QuarkXPress documents before we send them to a service bureau to be imageset onto RC paper or film. Every once in a while we meet someone who prints first to a StyleWriter, DeskJet, or a QuickDraw laser printer, and then uses a service bureau to get PostScript laser proofs made. If you haven't got a PostScript printer yourself and are forced to do this, then so be it; but be sure to take some precautions.

Before doing anything else, make sure you know what device your Chooser is set to. The Chooser is part of the Macintosh system software that lets you choose what kind of printer you want to use. You can also specify which printer, if there is more than one on a network. You can access it by selecting Chooser from the Apple menu (see Figure 10-1). The icons on the left are the types of printer drivers you have installed in the Extensions folder of your System Folder (printer drivers tell your computer how to drive your printer). When you click on one, the computer asks you for more pertinent information in the rectangle on the right.

For example, if you click on the LaserWriter icon, you'll get a list of all of the available LaserWriters (even if only one printer is attached, you still need to select it by clicking on it before closing the Chooser). If you have a large network which is split up into zones, you may need to select a zone—which shows up in the lower left of the window—before selecting a printer in it. The changes take effect as soon as you click on the printer's name.

Figure 10-1

The Chooser

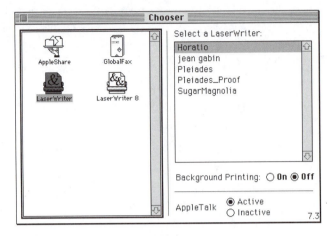

If you are working with just a single PostScript laser printer, you hardly need to worry about the Chooser. Just set it once and forget it, except when you want to switch between PostScript printers on the network. However, if you are printing to a Quick-Draw printer (for example, a DeskJet) with the aim to later print to a PostScript printer for final output, see "Tip: Switching Printer Types," below.

▼ ▼

Tip: Switching Printer Types. If you are creating a document on a machine with one type of printer attached to it and printing to a different printer for final output, make sure that you create your document with a printer driver compatible with the final output device. For example, if you are proofing on an Hewlett-Packard DeskJet and will later print to a Linotronic imagesetter, create your entire document with a LaserWriter driver selected in the Chooser (you don't actually have to own the laser printer or have it on hand to use its driver). Then, when you want to print your document, switch to the DeskJet driver, and don't change your Page Setup dialog box settings. Call it superstition, or what you like, but it has taken care of some major printing problems in the past for us. Note that when you're switching among printer drivers in the Chooser, you can press Tab to move between the various windows, and you can type a few letters of a driver or printer's name to select it.

▼ ▼

Every time you make a different printer-driver selection in the Chooser, you receive a dialog box noting that you should be sure to check your Page Setup dialog box (see "Page Setup," below). There are several reasons for this, the most important of which is that when you switch printer types, QuarkXPress needs to register that you've done this. It can then calculate the image area and other important controls. Otherwise, QuarkXPress sends a set of instructions to the printer which may be totally incorrect.

▼ ▼

Page Setup

Okay: you've got your document finished and you're ready to print. But wait! Don't forget to check the Page Setup dialog box. Some people choose the Page Setup feature by selecting it from the file menu. However, when we're doing demos, we like to look like pros and confuse the audience by just pressing Command-Option-P (see Figure 10-2).

The Page Setup dialog box changes depending on what printer driver you have selected in the Chooser. We're going to focus on the LaserWriter 8 driver that ships currently with System 7.1. If you use an older or different driver, much of the following discussion is relevant, but it may not mirror exactly what you see on your screen.

The Page Setup dialog box is divided into five areas, although the it doesn't delineate them very well. The areas are: paper/page specs, output specs, roll-fed printer specs, screen/color settings, and printer options; the last is a separate dialog box. Let's take a look at each of these in turn.

Paper/Page Specifications

There are two sections in the Page Setup dialog box that let you choose paper size: one is at the top of the dialog box and is put there by the printer driver, the other is lower and is put there by QuarkXPress. The form the first one takes depends on the printer

Figure 10-2

The Page Setup
dialog box

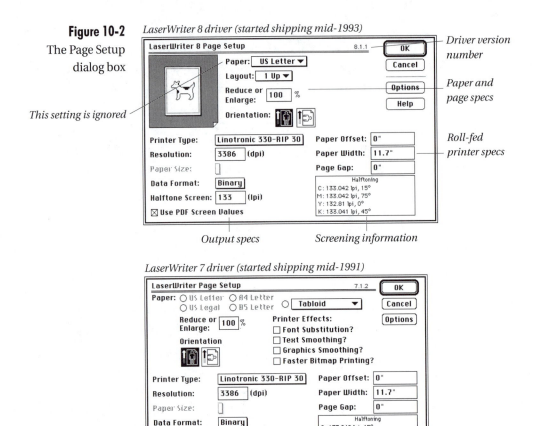

This setting is ignored

LaserWriter 8 driver (started shipping mid-1993)

*Driver version
number*

*Paper and
page specs*

*Roll-fed
printer specs*

Output specs   *Screening information*

LaserWriter 7 driver (started shipping mid-1991)

driver. If you're using LaserWriter 8, it's a popup menu; all the drivers before that made it a set of radio buttons. Which one do you pay attention to? QuarkXPress ignores the top one, and uses its own instead, so that's what we do, too.

Contrary to popular belief, the paper size that you choose in the Paper Size area is not necessarily the page size of your document. It is, instead, the *paper* size onto which you want to print your document (see Table 2-1 on page 137 for the detailed measurements). For example, if your newsletter is set up on a regular 8.5-by-11-inch page, you can have it printed onto as large as a tabloid-size area, or as small as a No. 10 envelope.

The page size you choose determines the printing area. So, if you choose Letter from the pull-down menu, but your document is actually tabloid-sized, your page is cropped down to 8.5 by 11 inches. Selecting a page size does not, however, determine where the automatic crop marks are placed (see "Registration and Trim Marks," page 582).

Where your page actually gets imaged on the paper depends on the relative sizes of the document and the paper.

► If your document is smaller than the paper selected, the document is centered on the paper.

► If your document is bigger than the paper selected, your page is cropped. The upper-left corner of the document is matched to the upper-left corner of a normal, letter-sized page. Confusing? Take a look at Figure 10-3 for a visual explanation of this.

If the Paper Size popup menu is grayed out, then QuarkXPress knows that the printer either only prints on one size paper or is a roll-fed device that can print any size you want. If it's not grayed out, the available choices are determined by information in the Printer Description Files or internally in QuarkXPress. Once again, you don't need to select a paper size that is consistent with your document's size (though the paper size must be larger than your page size). This only determines the image (or printable) area.

Output Effects

Directly under the Paper Specifications popup menu in the Page Setup dialog box are ten popup menus, icons, checkboxes, and fields that give you control over the overall printing of the document. The controls are: Layout, Reduce or Enlarge, Orientation, Halftone Screen, Printer Type, Paper Size, Data Format, EfiColor Profile, GCR, and Use PDF/EfiColor Screen Values.

Layout. The LaserWriter 8 driver can print multiple-up pages. 1 Up means that only one page appears on the printed sheet; 2 Up

Figure 10-3

Printed page size determined by paper selection

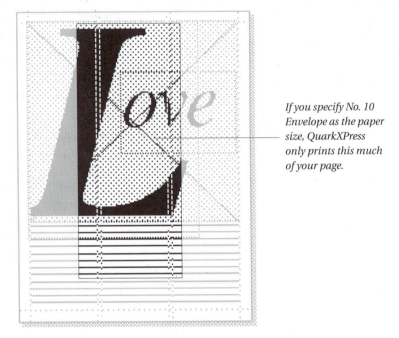

If you specify No. 10 Envelope as the paper size, QuarkXPress only prints this much of your page.

means two pages appear on the sheet together (page one and two). If you have an eight-page document and you select 4 Up from the Layout popup menu, only two sheets print out: the first has pages one through four on it, the second contains pages five through eight. Of course, to fit more than one page on the sheet, the program has to shrink the pages down. It figures out how to do this automatically.

This isn't something you'd use very often. However, we find it more useful than printing thumbnails (which we'll talk about more later) because the pages appear much larger than thumbnails do. Watch out, though, for leaving this value at 4 Up when you send the document to a service bureau; if they don't remember to change it back to 1 Up, your document might come out somewhat differently than you expected.

Reduce or Enlarge. Changing the Reduce or Enlarge field value affects the scaling of the document when you print. You can enter any whole number (no decimal points) between 10 and 400 percent. This is especially nice when printing proofs of a larger-format document, or when trying to create enormous posters by tiling them (you could create a four-by-four-foot poster in Quark-XPress and then enlarge it to 400 percent, so that when that last sheet printed out of your printer and you'd tiled all 439 sheets together, you'd have a poster 16-feet square). Table 10-2 shows several page-size conversion settings.

Table 10-2

Converting page sizes

To print this sized page	Onto this sized page	Reduce/Enlarge to
Legal	Letter	78%
Tabloid	Letter	64%
A4	Letter	94%
Letter	Tabloid	128%

Orientation. Remember back to the first day of high school when they had Orientation Day? The idea was to make sure you knew which way you were going while walking around the school grounds. Well, this Orientation is sort of the same, but different. The idea is to make sure QuarkXPress knows which way you want your document to go while it's walking through the printer. You have two choices: portrait and landscape. Luckily, this feature has its own icons so that you don't have to think too hard about which to choose. We've included some samples in Figure 10-4 so you can see what each does.

▼ ▼

Tip: Save the RC Trees. When you're printing onto a roll-fed image-setter (more on these later), you can save film or paper by printing your letter-size pages landscape rather than portrait. That way you only use around 8.5 inches on the roll rather than 11. It may not seem like a great difference, but those 3.5 inches really add up when you're printing a long document. For example, a 100-page file will save more than 300 inches of film or paper. Printing the pages landscape also makes it easy to cut them apart and stack them. Check with your service bureau to see if they'll give you a discount for the time and energy you've saved them.

▼ ▼

Figure 10-4
Page orientation

*The left column is
"portrait" or "tall";
the right column is
"landscape" or "wide."*

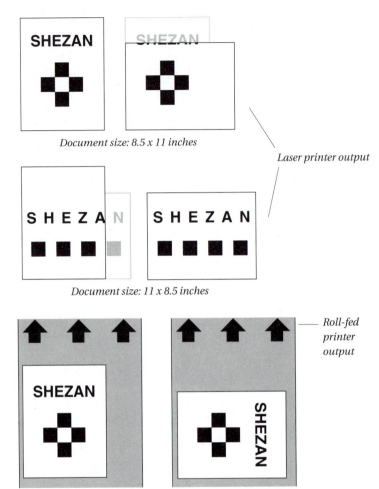

Document size: 8.5 x 11 inches

Laser printer output

Document size: 11 x 8.5 inches

*Roll-fed
printer
output*

Document size: 8.5 x 11 inches

Halftone Screen. We talked at some length about halftones and halftone screens back in Chapter 8, *Modifying Images*. In the Page Setup dialog box, this specification determines the halftone screen frequency of every tint in your document (except for those graphic images which you have set using the Other Screen features, and EPS graphics that have their screen specified internally). This includes gray boxes, tinted type, screened colors, and so on.

The default value for the halftone screen (the one that Quark-XPress uses unless you specify something else) is 60 lpi. On a

300-dpi laser printer, this almost always gives you an actual screen frequency of 53 lpi. That's just the way it works. You can type your own setting from 15 to 400 lines per inch. Raising the screen frequency nets you "smoother" grays, but you'll find you have fewer gray levels to work with (we talk about this tradeoff in the book *Real World Scanning and Halftones*).

You should note that the screen frequency value is "sticky." If you set it in one document, save the document, then open a new document, the value is still there. Thus, it is advisable to always check the Page Setup dialog box, just to make sure you're getting a proper halftone screen (what if the last person to use the computer set it to a 15-lpi screen?).

▼ ▼

Tip: Maintaining Resolution. When you print a document that in-cludes TIFF images, QuarkXPress may downsample the image data behind the scenes. The program figures that you'll never need more resolution in your images than two times the halftone screen frequency, so it cuts off the data at that point. If you have a 200-dpi image reduced to 50 percent on your page (which makes it a 400-dpi image; see Chapter 6, *Pictures*), and you're printing at an 80-lpi screen frequency, QuarkXPress chops off the image res-olution at 160 *dpi* (two times the frequency).Typically, that's okay. In fact, it's great if you're proofing high-resolution images on a laser printer. However, every now and again, this feature can jump up and bite you.

For example, if you reduce an image considerably in a picture box, you can sometimes get mottling or jaggy artifacts from the downsampling. Or, if you're purposely printing at a very low screen frequency because your color printer requires it (some do), your images may look really weird because QuarkXPress has downsampled them so much.

Fortunately, Quark has provided a workaround, even if it is a klunky one. Part of the Bobzilla XTension is a feature called Full Resolution TIFF. If you select a picture box and turn this on (by selecting it from the Item menu), QuarkXPress won't downsample that image at print time. Unfortunately, at this time you have to do this for each picture individually rather than set it for the whole document at once.

Note that this effect (and solution) only affects TIFF images. EPS pictures don't get downsampled because QuarkXPress can't touch the data that's encapsulated in them.

▼ ▼

Tip: A Colorful Shade of Gray. A couple of caveats to this tip, before we get to it: this is helpful primarily if you're printing proofs which won't be reproduced, and if you don't need a wide spectrum of gray values in your output. That said, we think a great screen frequency to use for printing to a 300- or 600-dpi printer is 106 lpi. Go ahead and try it. We think you'll like the tone of the gray.

▼ ▼

Tip: Changing Spot Functions. QuarkXPress uses a standard round halftone spot when it tints type, rules, boxes, and other elements on the page (everything except halftoned bitmapped images, which you can control; see Chapter 8, *Modifying Images*). You can change the type of halftone spot that QuarkXPress uses by modifying the PostScript print-to-disk file. Search for "sp0 setscreen" (don't include the quotation marks; note that in earlier versions of the program, it was "xpspot0"). The first two numbers on that line are the screen frequency and the angle. The screen frequency should be the same as what you specified in the Page Setup dialog box. The angle should be 45 degrees. You can change both of these to whatever you want them to be.

If you change "sp0" to "sp1," your halftones are printed with a straight-line spot; "sp2" is an oval; "sp3" is a square spot; and "sp4" is a weird random spot. If you are working with a screen frequency over 30 or 40, you probably won't be able to tell the difference between any of the spots, so this is mainly for special effects at low frequencies.

You can add your own spot functions by replacing the word "sp0" with a procedure. For example, you can create a triangular spot by replacing "sp0" with "{1 exch sub exch 1 exch sub sub 2 div}".

Note that if your PostScript file has multiple color separations in it, each plate has its own setscreen command. For more on spot functions (lots more), see David and Steve's book *Real World Scanning and Halftones.*

▼ ▼

Printer Type. Specifying the type of printer you'll be printing to with this popup menu lets QuarkXPress optimize the way it prints your document. It also determines several other factors in the print job, including activating or deactivating the roll-fed printer specifications features (see below). To explain here what changes are made to each printer would probably not be productive; just pick one and take a leap of faith that it's really doing something. Do note, though, that changing the printer type here does not change the Chooser selection. The type of driver selected in the Chooser should properly reflect the printer selected here.

If the type of printer you're using is not listed on the menu, you can call Quark to see if they have a Printer Description File (PDF) for you (see just below for the difference from PPDs). These are often included these days on a disk shipped with the printer. Or your service bureau can give you one for their device, as well. If your printer is basically the same type of printer as the one listed, go ahead and use the one that's there. For example, David prints to his Ricoh PC 6000/PS using the LaserWriter II selection since both printers are 300-dpi desktop laser printers of comparable speed, and so on. An Agfa Matrix SlideWriter is not comparable to a StyleWriter, so call your service bureau first.

QuarkXPress 3.3 lets you use Adobe's PPD (PostScript Printer Description) files, so if you don't have a PDF file for your printer and Quark or the vendor can't supply one, try finding a PPD. The difference? PDFs contain slightly more information relevant to QuarkXPress, so they're typically better to use. However, PPDs are simpler and they're editable (they're just text files that you can edit with any word processor). If you have a PPD and a PDF for the same printer, the program uses the PDF.

Also note that PDFs must be stored in either the PDF folder in the QuarkXPress folder, or loose in the QuarkXPress folder itself.

PPDs can be in either of those places, or in the Printer Description folder that sits inside the Extensions folder in the System Folder. (Do these lists sometimes sound to you like "Abe begat Herbie; Sarah begat Izzy; and so on"? They do to us.)

Paper Size. We talked about Paper Size in "Page/Paper Specifications," earlier in the chapter.

Data Format. We talked about binary versus ASCII data formats back in Chapter 6, *Pictures*, when we discussed QuarkXPress's Save as EPS feature; here the choice appears again. To recap, this only pertains to how bitmapped TIFF and PICT images are sent to the printer. While sending the information in ASCII format is more reliable over some networks, binary is almost always fine and has the benefit of creating a much smaller PostScript file (the images are half the size of ASCII). We just leave this set to Binary. You may also want to send as ASCII if you're making PostScript files for your service bureau and they're going to transfer the files to a PC- or UNIX-based system for output.

EfiColor. If you have the EfiColor color-management system installed (see Appendix A, *EfiColor*), the Page Setup dialog box includes two extra controls: EfiColor Profile and GCR. We cover both of those in Appendix A, *EfiColor*.

Use PDF/EfiColor Screen Values. In the lower right corner of the Page Setup dialog box sits a field that displays screen angles for each process color. The default angles are: cyan at 105 , magenta at 75, yellow at 90, and black at 45. If the PDF or PPD for the printer you've chosen contains alternate screening information, and you've checked the Use PDF Screen Values box, the new screen angles and halftone screen appear in this field. Sometimes this means that QuarkXPress will override the line-screen value you've entered in the Halftone Screen field. For example, the LaserWriter IIf-g PDF uses a halftone screen of 106 lpi (to take advantage of Apple's PhotoGrade technology in those printers).

If you have EfiColor turned on and the output device has a color profile, this checkbox changes to Use EfiColor Screen Values (see "EfiColor or PDF Screen Values" in Appendix A, *EfiColor*).

Roll-Fed Printer Specifications

These features apply only to—you guessed it—roll-fed printers. These are imagesetters, such as those in the Linotronic, Agfa, and Varityper lines, that feed paper and film off rolls rather than one sheet at a time. The four choices available to you when you have a roll-fed printer selected in the Printer Type menu are Resolution, Paper Offset, Paper Width, and Page Gap.

Resolution. Don't change this number with the expectation that it has any major significance to how your job prints. It doesn't determine the resolution at which your job prints. However, it does determine some important issues when printing bitmapped images. Paint and 72-dpi PICT images can be smoothed with Quark's proprietary bitmap-smoothing algorithms, which depend on knowing the resolution of the image. Also, bitmapped images that have a very high resolution may print significantly faster when you include the right printer resolution. For example, QuarkXPress internally reduces the resolution of a 600-dpi line-art image when it prints to a 300-dpi printer. The printer doesn't need any more than 300 dots per inch anyway, and you save time because QuarkXPress only has to download half as much information (and the PostScript interpreter has to wade through only half as much).

Paper Offset. This feature controls the placement of your document on the paper or film. The printer's default paper offset, even when set to zero, is actually enough so that you don't have to worry about changing the value of Paper Offset here. For example, on a Linotronic imagesetter, when Paper Offset is set to zero inches, the file is printed ¼-inch from the edge. If you want it farther from the edge, change this value.

However, the Paper Offset setting shouldn't exceed the document height subtracted from the paper width (that is, if you have a 10-inch tall document printing on 14-inch paper, your offset certainly should not be more than four inches, or else you'll chop off the other end of the page).

Paper Width. The Paper Width specification is not an actual control so much as a description of the device you'll be printing to. A Linotronic 300, for example, can image to 11.7 inches ("70p2" in QuarkXPress's pica notation). An Agfa CG9400 images to 14 inches, and a Linotronic 530 images to 17.5 inches. Whatever the case, and whatever the measurement style, just replace the default number with the proper paper width.

David fondly recalls the time when he printed several pages with Paper Width set to "11p7" (11 picas, 7 points; or 139 points), instead of 11.7 inches. Everything on each page was cut off at exactly "11p7" from the left edge. The rest of the page was blank. He wasn't happy, and has been studiously monitoring this feature ever since.

Page Gap. The last roll-fed printer specification determines the amount of blank space between each page of the document as it prints out on the roll. Initially, this value is zero. We recommend changing this to at least ¼-inch ("1p6") so you can cut the pages apart easily. If your document contains spreads, this gap between pages is placed between the spreads (more on printing spreads later), not between each page within the spread. Some imagesetters suppress this value, however, and rely on lower-level settings that an operator has to change via proprietary software or front-panel settings. Check with your service bureau before output— they may have advice on the correct setting.

Printer Options

This last set of Page Setup features is again direct from Apple's LaserWriter driver. You access this "second page" by clicking the Options button in the Page Setup dialog box (see Figure 10-5).

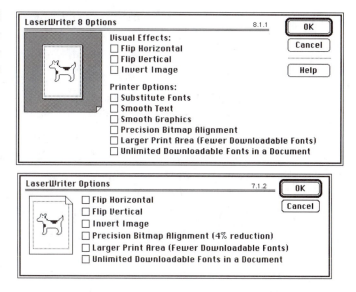

Figure 10-5

The LaserWriter
Options dialog box for
versions 7 and 8

The checkboxes in this dialog box are separated into two areas: Visual Effects and Printer Options. Note that the Printer Options have consequence only when you're printing to a PostScript printer (for most of you, that means all the time).

On the left of the dialog box, a graphic shows you a tiny representation of what each of these effects will do to your page. For instance, checking Invert Image inverts the picture in the box. If you're using Apple's LaserWriter driver, the graphic you'll see is sort of a weird-looking animal. The hallowed halls of Macintosh folklore may someday be cluttered with speculation on what particular animal this is. While the consensus seems to be dog, we prefer the rare dogcow (it says, "Moof!"). Whatever the case, this is the animal to watch when you check boxes in Options.

Here's a discussion of all of the options in order, starting with the visual effects.

Flip Horizontal/Flip Vertical. We'll meld these two into one description, as they are really doing the same thing. Flipping an image is used primarily for creating from imagesetters either wrong- or right-reading film, or film with emulsion side up or down. The differences? Let's look at what happens when you print onto film.

As the film moves through the imagesetter, the side of the film that is coated with a photographically-sensitive emulsion is exposed to a laser beam. If you have neither Flip Horizontal nor Flip Vertical selected, the film is imaged right-reading, emulsion up (or wrong-reading, emulsion down if you prefer). This means that when you are holding the film so that the type reads from left to right and graphics are oriented correctly ("right-reading"), the emulsion of the film is facing you. If you select either Flip Horizontal or Flip Vertical, the film emerges right-reading, emulsion down (which is how most printers want it). To look at it in a different way, this means that when you hold the film with the emulsion away from you, the text and graphics look correct ("right-reading"). See Figure 10-6 for a quick graphical reference.

Figure 10-6
The effects of Flip Horizontal and Flip Vertical

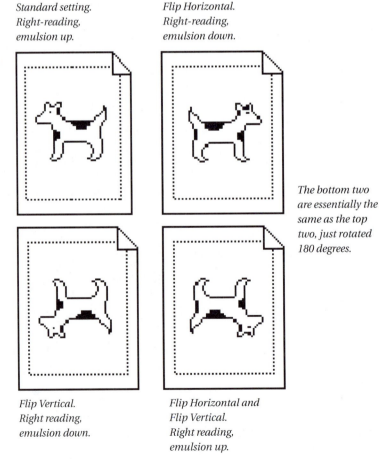

Standard setting. Right-reading, emulsion up.

Flip Horizontal. Right-reading, emulsion down.

The bottom two are essentially the same as the top two, just rotated 180 degrees.

Flip Vertical. Right reading, emulsion down.

Flip Horizontal and Flip Vertical. Right reading, emulsion up.

If you want to know why you'd ever care whether the emulsion is up or down, check with your lithographer (and then talk to a screen printer; you'll see they need different film output for similar but different reasons). Providing film in the right format could reduce the reproduction generations at the printer—saving time and money, and improving quality.

Invert Image. Clicking this checkbox inverts the entire page so that everything that is set to 100 percent black becomes zero percent black (effectively, white). It is the same as selecting the Inversion tool from within the Contrast Specifications dialog box, except that it affects the entire page. In some countries—most notably Italy, Switzerland, Hong Kong, and Singapore—lithographic plates are typically made from positive film (rather than film negatives, like we use in North America). The end result is the same, but they use different techniques to get there. Always check on this specification if you're printing outside of North America.

▼ ▼

Tip: Negatives of Low Screen Frequency Halftones. If you are printing halftones or tints at very low screen frequency (anything coarse enough to actually see the spots), you should be aware of an important fact about Invert Image. This feature does not actually invert pixels from black to white or white to black. It inverts gray levels. For example, a 70-percent black elliptical spot does not actually become a white elliptical spot 70-percent "large," but instead a white elliptical spot 30-percent large. It seems like a minor point, but it has caused enough difficulties around our offices. In cases like these, we now print to film positive and then take it to a stat house to get a negative shot of it. Note that some imagesetters actually have a button that lets you invert the image. This sort of inversion often gives you a true inversion and you probably wouldn't have the same sort of problem.

▼ ▼

Substitute Fonts. Before System 7, New York, Geneva, and Monaco were bitmap-only fonts (read: "ugly"). Now they're TrueType outlines, but we still think they're pretty ugly. Checking Font

Substitution allows QuarkXPress to substitute Times Roman for New York, Helvetica for Geneva, and Courier for Monaco. The problem is that the letterspacing is all thrown off when you do this, so it's hardly worth it (see Figure 10-7). The solution is to "just say no" to using those TrueType fonts in the first place.

Figure 10-7
Font substitution

Text prints with the wrong character widths when fonts are substituted.

I, sir, if that nose were mine, ¶
I'd have it amputated on the spot!

Typeface is New York. Screen display is New York.

I, sir, if that nose were mine,
I'd have it amputated on the spot!

Typeface is New York, but printed with font substitution. Output font becomes Times Roman, badly letterspaced.

I, sir, if that nose were mine,
I'd have it amputated on the spot!

Typed in Times Roman and output as Times Roman with excellent spacing.

Smooth Text. If you *must* use a bitmapped font on a PostScript laser printer, you may want to enable Smooth Text. This feature tells the printer to attempt to smooth out the bitmaps, so they don't look too jagged. We've seen both excellent and awful results with this. It works best with small-size fonts with few "stairstepped" areas, and it's terrible with fonts that are out of their size ranges (that is, if you have a bitmapped font which was designed for 14 point and you're using it at 39 point). In general, if it looks okay on the screen, it'll look at least decent in the output. On the other hand, if you're trying to reproduce a bitmap-only font, like one of Emigre's cool fonts, make sure that Smooth Text is *not* checked.

We just leave this turned off all the time, even though we haven't used bitmap-only typefaces in years.

Smooth Graphics. As the name would suggest, the Smooth Graphics feature does to bitmapped graphics what Smooth Text does to bitmapped fonts. The QuarkXPress documentation mentions that this is effective for "some bitmap pictures." What that means is it only works for 72-dpi black-and-white bitmapped PICTs and MacPaint graphics. Many people who are creating newsletters or flyers use this feature to smooth out inexpensive Paint-type clip art (however, people who use MacPaint and PICT images aren't the typical users of QuarkXPress). There's no doubt that this sometimes helps a bit (okay, sometimes more than just a bit), but don't expect to get really smooth curves or diagonals from this method. Also, if there are gray areas or patterns in the art, smoothing can really mess them up. Plus, you should note that this function can significantly increase printing time (it takes a lot of calculations to smooth those puppies out). Again, we typically just leave this turned off.

Precision Bitmap Alignment (4% reduction). We talked about printing bitmapped images back in Chapter 6, *Pictures*. The problem, in a nutshell, is that bitmapped images that don't have an integral relationship with the printer's resolution often print out with ugly tiled patterns. This is especially a problem with dithered black-and-white scans. For example, a 300-dpi printer attempting to print a 72-dpi picture has to resolve a discrepancy of .17 points per inch ($300 \div 72 = 4.17$). When you select Precision Bitmap Alignment, the entire document is scaled down four percent, which raises the effective resolution of the bitmapped image to almost 75 dpi, and that image now prints with few or no ugly patterns.

The problem is that now the rest of your document has been scaled down four percent. If you're printing a small company newsletter and you don't care how bad it looks, this might make no difference to you. Otherwise, it would be unwise to use this feature. Besides, QuarkXPress's ability to perform scaling on images makes the Precision Bitmap Alignment feature obsolete (few of your images are 72 dpi after you've scaled them, so the feature doesn't help anyway). Just reduce the graphic images to an appropriate size and leave well enough alone. For more information on integral scaling of bitmapped images, see Chapter 8, *Modifying Images*.

Larger Print Area (Fewer Downloadable Fonts). When you print a page to a desktop laser printer, you are only able to print up to approximately .5 inch from the page edge because of the limited memory within the PostScript printer. The largest chunk of memory is reserved for storing the actual bitmapped image of the page. If you're working with a 300-dpi printer, it has to store around 7.5 million bits of information for each page it prints. The rest of the printer's memory is split up between the amount of space required to process the job (interpret the PostScript data) and to store the needed fonts.

By checking Larger Print Area, you tell the laser printer to alter the memory allocation slightly, giving a bit more memory to the image area and a bit less to the font area. You can then print out to the very minimum ¼-inch border, but you have less room to store your downloadable fonts, so the number of downloadable fonts you can use on a page is reduced. In other words, a page which may print fine without the Larger Print Area box checked may now cause an overload in printer memory and a PostScript error. We suggest you leave this turned off unless you really need it. And after using it, don't forget to turn it off again.

Unlimited Downloadable Fonts in a Document. Checking this feature is a last resort when you really have too many fonts on a page to print it successfully. The issue here is time. Normally, Quark-XPress downloads all the fonts it needs for a job as it needs them. If the printer's memory runs out, then it runs out, and you get a PostScript error telling you that you can't print the job.

If you have the Unlimited Downloadable Fonts in a Document feature enabled, QuarkXPress downloads the font when it needs it, then flushes it out of printer memory. Next time the document needs the font, QuarkXPress downloads it again. The problem is, that might be 10 times on a single page, making your job print very slowly. So, while you gain the ability to print as many fonts as you want, you pay a hefty price in printing time.

Also, just to be precise, it's not QuarkXPress that is using such a slow method here; it's the Apple LaserWriter driver. Well, someday someone will build some intelligence into these things.

This feature can be a godsend in getting a page printed out on your laser printer (even if it does take a long time to print). However, make sure you turn it off before sending the document to an imagesetter; there it can cause troubles.

Faster Bitmap Printing. The Faster Bitmap Printing feature only appears in pre-8.0 LaserWriter drivers. We can't be sure, but we think Faster Bitmap Printing is a feature that someone at Apple thought would be funny, so Apple included it in their early LaserWriter drivers. Hey, who wouldn't want their bitmapped images to print faster? Why would anyone ever want to turn this off? In fact, turning it on does seem to speed up printing time from anywhere between .003 and one second on every test we conducted. There is slightly more speedup if your bitmapped images have an integral relationship with the printer's resolution (for example, 75-dpi bitmapped images sometimes print better and faster than 72-dpi images, because 75 goes evenly into 300; though sometimes they won't). Whatever the case, the whole thing makes us nervous—always has. We automatically turn it off when we print.

In the latest printer drivers, this feature has been removed (again, probably because it wasn't really doing anything).

▼ ▼

Print Dialog Box, Part 1: Apple's Stuff

The Print dialog box has changed significantly over the past few years, partly because Quark has added so many new features and changed the interface, and partly because the new LaserWriter drivers have changed. The top half of the Print dialog box (see Figure 10-8) in QuarkXPress is standard to almost all Macintosh

Figure 10-8

The LaserWriter 8
Print dialog box

*The LaserWriter 7 dialog
box offers most of the
same options.*

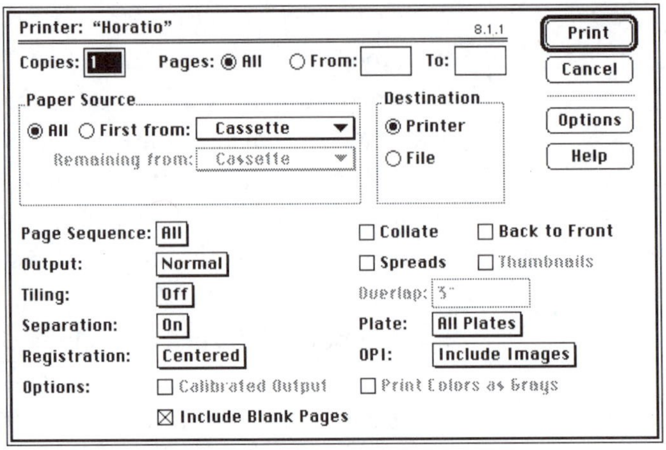

applications because it's connected directly to Apple's LaserWriter driver (if you use a different driver, these items may change). Let's look at these items one at a time.

Copies. We might as well start with the simplest choice of all. How many copies of your document do you want printed? Let's say you choose to print a multiple-page document, specifying four copies. The first page prints four times, then the second page prints four times, and so on. In other words, you may have a good deal of collating to do later (see "Collate," below).

Pages. You can specify to print all pages in a document, or a range of pages. The values you type in for the From and To range must either be exactly the same as those in your document or be specified as absolutes. If your document starts on page 23, you can't type "1" in the From field; it must be either "23" (or whatever page you want to start from) or "+1" (the plus character specifies an absolute page number). Similarly, if you are using page numbering in an alphabet system (such as a, b, c, etc.), or using a prefix (see "Section and Page-Numbering Systems" in Chapter 2, *Document Construction*), you have to type these sorts of numbers into the slots. It's annoying, but if you don't type the page number exactly the way it's used in the program (or use absolute numbers), the program tells you that "no such page exists."

▼ ▼

Tip: From Beginning or End. If you want to print from the first page to a specified page, you can leave the From field empty in the Print dialog box. Similarly, if you leave the To field empty, QuarkXPress assumes you want to print to the end of the document.

▼ ▼

Paper Source. This feature specifies where you would like the printer to get its paper. Normally, you'd have this set to Paper Cassette. However, if you are using a printer that can take manual feed pages, you may want to select this at various times—for example, when you print onto a single sheet of special stationery or onto an envelope.

When Manual Feed is selected, the printer waits for a designated time—usually 30 seconds or a minute—for you to properly place the sheet of paper at the manual feed slot. If you don't place the page in time, the PostScript interpreter returns a timeout error and flushes the rest of the print job.

Destination. Remember that earlier in this chapter we discussed the idea that when you print, QuarkXPress and the Macintosh printer driver create a PostScript file that contains the description of each page of the document. It turns out that this PostScript file can be either sent to a printer, or saved on disk so that you (or your service bureau) can download it later. The Destination section of the Print dialog box lets you choose between these two.

If you know about creating PostScript dumps (those of you who don't will learn about them later in this chapter), this is the place to do them. If you're used to creating PostScript dumps with earlier drivers than version 7, don't bother to try holding down the F or the K key. They don't work anymore.

Note that when you select File as your destination, the Print button changes to Save. When you click that, the Macintosh gives you the option of where you want the file to go and what you want to name it. The file that the Macintosh saves to disk contains the entire PostScript LaserPrep header (as holding down the K key would do using pre-7.0 versions of the LaserWriter driver).

Print Dialog Box, Part 2: Quark's Stuff

The second half of the Print dialog box is specific only to Quark-XPress (where the first half was common to all Macintosh programs).In this section there are 13 popup menus and checkboxes that let you tweak your print job to perfection. All of these break down into three basic areas: output, tiling, and color.

Output

Output covers the details of how QuarkXPress prints your job: which pages, more detailed page selection, in what order the pages should print, and whether or not you want registration marks. Let's go over each control in order.

Page sequence. The first popup menu in this section is Page Sequence, which gives you slightly more control over which pages in your document get printed. You have three choices: All, Odd, or Even.

▶ **All.** This is the default position for printing pages from QuarkXPress. It means "all pages that you have selected above." In other words, if you have selected a page range from 23 to 28, having All Pages selected won't counteract your desires; it'll just print all those pages.

▶ **Odd/Even.** These two choices are mutually exclusive. We sometimes joke about this feature when we're working on jobs with several strangely designed pages: "Just print the odd ones, and leave the rest." The only real value we've ever gotten out of this feature lies in the following tip, "Printing Double-Sided Documents."

Tip: Printing Double-Sided Documents. You can print double-sided pages with the following technique.

1. Print all of the odd-numbered pages (select Odd).

2. Place these pages back into the printer, face down.

3. Select Back to Front (we discuss this feature later in this chapter).

4. Print all the even pages (select Even).

If everything is set up right, and your document has an even number of pages, the second page should print on the back of the first, and so on.

You can use this same technique to print documents when photocopying onto two sides of a page (if your photocopier handles automatic two-sided copying, then ignore this). Print the odd-numbered pages first, then the even-numbered pages, then ask your local Kinko's person what to do next.

▼ ▼

Output. The Output popup menu gives you the opportunity to speed up your printing significantly . . . but at the cost of the pictures in your document. Pictures are often the single most time-consuming part of printing a page; but if you're only printing rough proofs, you may be able to cut corners.

▶ **Normal.** What can we say about Normal? It's normally how you'd want your normal documents to print out. This is the default setting in the Print dialog box, and the only times you change it are when you want special printing effects like those listed below. You get just what you created—no better, no worse.

▶ **Low Resolution Output.** If you select Low Resolution from the Output popup menu, QuarkXPress prints your document using the picture-preview image built into the document, rather than the source picture file. If you've imported a huge high-resolution TIFF or EPS, Low Resolution mode prints the document using the low-resolution (36- or 72-dpi) screen image that QuarkXPress creates when you import the picture.

This is a godsend if you have to make many proofs to a low-resolution desktop printer. We can't tell you how much time we've wasted either sending documents with high-resolution pictures to low-resolution devices (it takes forever for them to print), or manually hiding the pictures somewhere on our hard disks so QuarkXPress can't find them, then telling it to print anyway (that was the old trick for making QuarkXPress use the internal low-res image).

▶ **Rough.** If your document has many illustrations or special frames in it, you may want to print your proof copies with Rough selected. This feature automatically replaces each picture in your document with a big "X," and every complex frame with a double line of the same width (see Figure 10-9). Clearly, the pages print significantly faster than with Normal or Low Resolution.

Collate. We said earlier that when you printed multiple copies of your document you would receive x number of the first page, then x number of the second page, and so on, leaving you to manually collate all the copies. You can have QuarkXPress collate the pages for you, instead, so that the full document prints out once, then again, and again, and so on.

The problem with Collate is that it takes much longer to print your complete job. This is because the printer cannot "remember" what each page looked like after it goes on to the next page, and so it has to reprocess the entire document for each new copy. How long this takes depends on the number of fonts and pictures you use, among other things. On a long document, the time difference becomes a toss-up: do you take the time to collate the pages yourself or have the printer take the time to process them?

If you have Background Printing turned on in the Chooser, your Mac will handle printing in the background, though it may annoy you by making your mouse cursor jump around erratically.

Back to Front. The problem with talking about printing from QuarkXPress is that each PostScript printer model is slightly (or

Figure 10-9

Page printed with
Rough selected

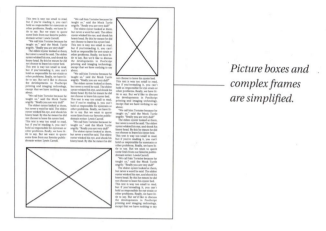

*Picture boxes and
complex frames
are simplified.*

not-so-slightly) different from the next. For example, when you print a multiple-page document on your laser printer, does the first page come out face up or face down? Some printers do one, some the other, and some give you a choice. If the pages come out face up, you'll love the Back to Front feature. Selecting Back to Front prints the last page of your page selection first, then prints "backwards" to the first page. The stack of pages that ends up in the output tray will be in proper order.

Note that you can't select this feature when you are printing spreads or thumbnails (if you want a good brain twister, try to think of how pages would print if you could select these together).

Spreads. This is a powerful but potentially dangerous feature, so it should be used with some care. Checking Spreads in the Print dialog box tells QuarkXPress to print spreads as one full page rather than as two or three pages. For example, printing a two-page, facing-pages spread with registration marks normally results in one page printing with its set of crop marks, then the next page, and so on. When Spreads is turned on, both pages abut each other and sit between the same crop marks. This is useful in a number of instances, perhaps the best of which is printing a spread that has text or a graphic across the page boundaries (see Figure 10-10).

Figure 10-10
Printing spreads
versus printing
individual pages

*Two pages printed as a spread; this only works for center spreads, or when
you've set up panels of a brochure or poster as individual pages.*

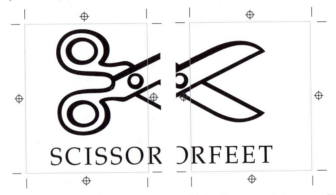

*A reader spread printed as two pages. This is what your printer generally wants
when you supply output. Note the bleed for images that cross the page break.*

However, there's a potential problem lurking behind the
Spreads feature. Let's say you're laying out a magazine with a
standard facing-page format, except in the middle of the document you have a fold-out, resulting in two three-page spreads.
You send the file off to be imageset, specifying that Spreads
should be checked. When you get the film or paper back you find
everything worked just like you thought it would: two-page
spreads spread across two pages, and the two three-page spreads
spread all the way across three pages (never mind that this is definitely not how you'd want to print a magazine; it would be a
stripping nightmare).

But when you get your bill, it's hundreds of dollars more than
you expected. What happened? What went wrong? This is the

dangerous part of printing contiguous spreads. When you specify Spreads, QuarkXPress tells the roll-fed imagesetter to advance the film the width of the widest spread in the page range specified. So in the example above, each two-page spread actually took three pages of film; hence it was much more expensive.

There's also the chance that printing spreads can confuse the imagesetter entirely. Some people have reported that they've had problems printing spreads to imagesetters, and almost all report slow printing.

▼ ▼

Tip: Printing Spreads in a Document. Don't waste paper or film when you print contiguous spreads from a single document; if for no other reason, it's expensive. If you have a multiple-page spread crossing pages 45 through 47, have your service bureau print the pages from one through 44, and 48 through the end as single pages, and then print the three-page spread on a separate pass.

▼ ▼

Tip: Imposition. While there are some great page imposition tools out there—including Aldus PressWise and the InPosition XTension—sometimes you just want to do a quick little booklet at just as little a cost. You can use the Spreads feature in conjunction with the Document Layout palette to "strip" together pages which will be double-sided and saddle-stitch bound. We think this is one of the coolest things you can do with the Document Layout feature anyway. Just follow these steps.

1. Create your document as usual, but with no facing pages (see Chapter 1, *QuarkXPress Basics*).

2. When you're finished, use the Document Layout palette to move the last page to the left of the first page. Then move the second-to-last page (which has now become the last page) up to the right of the second page (which is now the third page). Then, move the next last page to the left of the next single page, and so on.

3. When you're done, every page should be paired with another page, and the last pages in the document should be the middle-most pages. For example, in an eight-page booklet, the final pages would end up being the spread between pages four and five.

4. Make sure the Spreads feature is selected in the Print dialog box when you print the document page.

Note that this method won't work if you are using automatic page numbering (because you're moving pages around; for example, the final page ends up being page one).

Ultimately, however, if you're going to be doing imposition like this very often, we do suggest using an XTension or utility (see Appendix D, *Resources*, for more information).

▼ ▼

Thumbnails. Selecting Thumbnails shrinks each page of your document down to 12.5 percent of its size and lines up each page next to each other. It then fits as many as it can onto each printed page. This is great for an overview of your file, though the output you get is usually too small to really give you much of an idea of anything except general page geometry (see "Faster, Larger Thumbnails," below). Note that on PostScript printers, it takes just as long to print this one sheet of many pages as it does to print every page individually, so plan your time accordingly. If you just want to look over the pages, it would probably be faster to see them on screen in Thumbnails view. Remember that you don't have to print all your pages when you select Thumbnails. We often find it helpful to just print one or two pages at a time to see how they're looking.

▼ ▼

Tip: Faster, Larger Thumbnails. We find the size that Thumbnails usually gives us pretty useless; they're just too small! And if we have pictures on the pages, the job takes too long to print. So we use this feature in conjunction with two others: Rough and Reduce or Enlarge. Rough is nearby in the Print dialog box in the Output popup menu (see above). Just make sure this is selected, and your thumbnails print with "Xs" through the pictures, and with simplified frames. The Reduce or Enlarge feature is found in the Page Setup dialog box and is covered earlier, in that section. Change Reduce or Enlarge to 200 percent, and your thumbnails are printed at 24 percent instead of a little over 12 percent. This is just about the right size for most letter-size pages.

▼ ▼

Tip: Two Thumbnails per Page. If you want your thumbnails much larger, you can up the scaling factor to 375 percent and turn the page landscape in the Page Setup dialog box. With this value, you can get two letter- or legal-size pages on one page. You can get two tabloid-size pages on one letter-size landscape page with an enlargement of 300 percent. If your document is made of two-page spreads, then you can print letter- and legal-size pages up to 400 percent (the maximum allowed for enlargement), and tabloid-size pages up to 350 percent.

However, if you're using the LaserWriter 8 driver, there's an easier way to do this: just select 2 Up or 4 Up in the Page Setup dialog box and ignore QuarkXPress's Thumbnails feature all together. That's our favorite method. (Remember to turn it back to 1 Up before sending it to be output later!)

▼ ▼

Include Blank Pages. As we write, our white-paper recycling bins overfloweth. We go through so much paper that we feel guilty every time we drive through a forest (which is difficult to avoid in the Pacific Northwest). Therefore, whenever we have the chance to save a tree here and there, we jump at it. QuarkXPress is giving us just this chance with the Include Blank Pages control in the Print dialog box. When you turn on Include Blank Pages (it's on by default), QuarkXPress prints as it always has: every page, no matter what is (or isn't) on it. When you turn off Include Blank Pages, QuarkXPress won't print a page if there isn't anything printable on it. This includes pages whose only objects are colored white, or are set to Suppress Printout. We've gotten in the habit of always turning this off when we print.

Calibrated Output. If you've ever printed a 50-percent gray box on your desktop laser printer, you've probably noticed that the box doesn't come out 50-percent gray. This is because of Quark-XPress's built-in printer-calibration settings. When you select the LaserWriter printer in the Page Setup dialog box, QuarkXPress alters all its gray levels when printing. Fortunately, enough people threw fits, and Quark has now made this an option. Most service bureaus use imagesetter-linearization software that lets them calibrate the imagesetter, so that its output of a 50-percent gray is really a 50-percent gray; Quark's scheme just interferes with this.

When Calibrated Output is checked in the Print dialog box, QuarkXPress performs as it always has (it calibrates for the printer it's set to). When you turn off this checkbox, QuarkXPress doesn't change a thing. There are benefits to both sides, we suppose, but we'd just as soon leave this on as we'd use Microsoft Word to produce books (yeah, we've done it, but we didn't want to).

By the way, turning off Calibrated Output is just the same as temporarily resetting the printer calibration curves to straight lines using the Printer Calibration XTension. We'll discuss calibration and dot gain a little more in "Color Separation," below.

Tiling

What's a person to do with a 36-by-36-inch document? Printing to paper or film is . . . well, almost impossible (to be thorough we should mention it can be done through systems such as the Scitex ELP printer or Colossal System's giant 300-dpi electrostatic printer). You can break each page down into smaller chunks that will fit onto letter-size pages. Then you can assemble all the pages (keep your Scotch tape nearby). This process is called *tiling*, and is controlled in the Print dialog box. The three options for tiling are Off, Auto, and Manual.

Off. Off is off. No shirt, no shoes, no tiling. QuarkXPress just prints as much of the page as it can on the output page, starting from the upper-left corner.

Auto. Selecting the Auto tiling feature instructs QuarkXPress to decide how much of your document to fit onto each printed page. You do have some semblance of control here: you can decide how much overlap between pages you would like. Remember that you have a minimum of ¼-inch border around each page (at least on most laser printers), so you'll probably want to set your overlap to at least ½-inch to get a good fit. We generally use a value of four picas, just to be safe.

Note that QuarkXPress does not make an intelligent decision as to whether it would be more efficient to print the pages landscape or portrait, so you'll want to be careful to set this appropriately in the Page Setup dialog box (see Figure 10-2).

Manual. Most people seem to overlook the value of Manual tiling, skipping over it to Auto tiling. But there are times to trust a computer and times not to, and when it comes to breaking up our pages into manageable sizes, we generally prefer to make the choices ourselves.

When Manual tiling is selected, QuarkXPress prints only as much of the page as fits on the page selected, starting at the ruler coordinate "0,0." You can then move the "0,0" coordinate to some other place on the page (see "Rulers" in Chapter 1, *QuarkXPress Basics,* for more on this) and print the page again. In this way you can manually perform the same task as Auto tiling does, or you can be specific about what areas of the page you want to print. Note that if you have a six-page document and print using Manual tiling, you receive (for example) the upper-left corner of each of the six pages before the printer stops. If you only want one page or a smaller range of pages, use the From and To specifications at the top of the Print dialog box.

We should point out that where you place the "0,0" point is usually not where QuarkXPress starts printing. It actually tries to give you a little extra room so that the area you selected prints on the imaged area of the printer. For example, if you're printing to a desktop laser printer with Larger Print Area turned off, Quark-

XPress actually moves your starting point a couple of picas up and to the left. This is another area where QuarkXPress tries to be helpful, but ends up just being confusing and difficult to predict.

▼ ▼

Tip: Printer as Magnifying Glass. You can use Manual Tiling and Enlarge to blow up a particular area of the page for inspection (when 400-percent magnification on the screen still doesn't suit you). Change the enlargement factor in the Page Setup dialog box to 400 percent (or whatever enlargement you desire), then move the "0,0" point of the rulers to the area which you want to inspect. Now print that page with Manual Tiling on, and—*mirabile dictu*! A super-size sectional.

▼ ▼

Tip: Assembling Your Tiled Pages. This really has nothing to do with the use of QuarkXPress, but when it comes to assembling tiled pages, we find it invaluable. The idea is simple: when fitting two tiled pages together, use a straight-edge to cut one, then use the other blank border area as a tab.

▼ ▼

Print Options

The LaserWriter driver has even more goodies in store for us when we click the Options button of LaserWriter 8's Print dialog box (earlier versions of the driver don't have this): Cover Page, printing color, and PostScript error handling. You may never use a single one of these, but they're certainly worth knowing about.

Cover Page. This feature is usually set to No, and we almost never change it. But then again, we don't work in large workgroups. Each cover sheet includes the name of the person who sent the job—determined by the name set in the Chooser in System 6 or the Sharing Setup control panel device in System 7—and a date/time stamp, along with other information (see Figure 10-11). If you have several (or many) people printing to one printer, using cover sheets can be a real lifesaver. Not only does the cover page

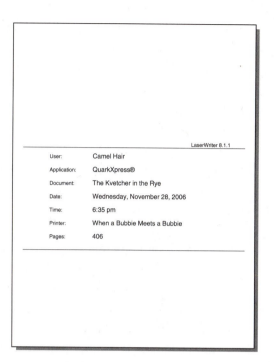

Figure 10-11

Cover page for
LaserWriter 8
print job

LaserWriter 8.1.1

User:	Camel Hair
Application:	QuarkXpress®
Document:	The Kvetcher in the Rye
Date:	Wednesday, November 28, 2006
Time:	6:35 pm
Printer:	When a Bubbie Meets a Bubbie
Pages:	406

act as a label for each print job, but it separates each job so that one page from one document doesn't get mixed up with pages from the next document.

Note that you can set the cover page to print either before the first page or after the last page. Take your pick, depending on whether your printer dumps paper face up or face down. But, if you're in a workgroup situation, you probably want everybody to use the same setting to avoid confusion.

On the other hand, why use extra paper if you don't need to? If you're the only person using the printer and you don't need to document each print cycle, just leave this feature off.

Print. Apple is amazing: they seem to be able to get away with just about anything, including throwing a feature into their Print Options dialog box that doesn't really do much of anything. The Print popup menu is one of those things. The truth is that no matter what we do, we can't get this to affect our output, so the three values in the popup menu—Color/Grayscale, Black & White, and Calibrated Color/Grayscale—are more or less useless. (If you know something we don't know about these, call us!)

PostScript Errors. We can't all be perfect, even—especially?—if we're computers. Sometimes errors arise when printing, and it's difficult to know what has happened because the computer doesn't tell you very much. Often, the only message you'll receive is, "This file generated a PostScript error. The file is okay but cannot be printed." Helpful, right?

The more recent LaserWriter drivers have included basic PostScript error handling that can give you more information. We're going to talk more about how to fix errors in "Troubleshooting," later in this chapter. However, getting information like what kind of PostScript error you've encountered is often the first step. Here's how you can do that.

The PostScript Errors popup menu in the Print Options dialog box lets you choose one of three items.

▶ **No Special Reporting.** The default setting for PostScript Errors is No Special Reporting, which gives you what you've always had: almost no information at all. At best, you'll find out that a PostScript error occurred; at worst, you'll get an error number -8133 or the page just won't print at all.

▶ **Summarize on Screen.** If you get a mysterious PostScript error, the first course of action is to switch the error handling to Summarize on Screen. Instead of just getting a message that the file could not be printed, a dialog box appears prompting you with what the particular PostScript error was. If you don't know anything about PostScript, this might not help you anyway (or it might just make you feel better). If you *do* know something about PostScript, it's the first step in fixing the problem. Note that after you click OK in this alert dialog box, Print Monitor still tells you that the page couldn't be printed (we haven't found a way to get around that inconvenience yet).

▶ **Print Detailed Report.** If you know something about Post-Script, or you're really into trying to troubleshoot the print job, after finding a summary of the PostScript error on screen, you'll want to jump into a detailed report. When this feature is selected and the printer comes up with an error, the printer is forced to spit out the page with however much was imaged, along with a note saying exactly what the PostScript error was and what command in the file triggered it. Then it tells you what was currently on the stack at the time of the error (if you don't know what the stack is, this won't help you; it's central to the way that PostScript works).

Print Status

We don't know, but we have an inkling that Print Status is another feature that former PageMaker users talked Quark into throwing in so they'd feel more at home. The concept is as simple as its execution. Concept: We want QuarkXPress to show us its progress as it downloads a print job to a PostScript printer. Execution: Just print. In version 3.1, you needed to hold down the Shift key as you clicked the Print button. But in every version since then, it's just the opposite: you get Print Status automatically every time you print, unless you hold down the Shift key. The Print Status dialog box not only tells you what page it's printing, but also what color plate, tile, and EPS/TIFF images it's working on (see Figure 10-12).

Remember that no program can know how long a page will take to print on a PostScript printer, so there's no way to show how much longer the print job will take. Instead, the status bar in the Print Status dialog box only displays the percentage of pages that have been printed (for example, if you have two pages in your document, the status bar is 50-percent full after the first page, even if the second page takes ten times longer than the first one to print). Nonetheless, this is a nice intermediate step, and often makes us feel better when we're waiting for those long jobs to print.

Figure 10-12
Print Status dialog box

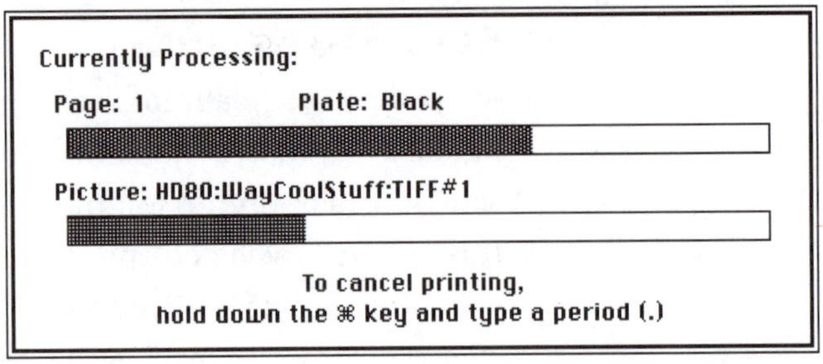

```
┌─────────────────────────────────────────────┐
│  Currently Processing:                        │
│                                               │
│  Page: 1                 Plate: Black         │
│  ▐█████████████████████████▌          │       │
│                                               │
│  Picture: HD80:WayCoolStuff:TIFF#1            │
│  ▐███████████████▌                     │      │
│                                               │
│            To cancel printing,                │
│    hold down the ⌘ key and type a period (.)  │
└─────────────────────────────────────────────┘
```

▼ ▼

Color Separations

We come now to the last area of the Print dialog box, which, as a subject, deserves a whole section of the book to itself: color separation. The concept behind color separation is simple, and Quark-XPress does a pretty good job of making the practice just as easy, but the truth is that this is a very complicated matter which, in the space of this book, we can only touch on briefly. Let's take a look at what color separation is all about, then move on to how Quark-XPress and various third-party products handle the process.

The Basics of Color Separation

A printing press can only print one color at a time. Even five- and six-color presses really only print one color at a time, attempting to give the ink a chance to dry between coats. As we discussed in Chapter 9, *Color*, those colors are almost always process colors (cyan, magenta, yellow, and black), or they may be spot colors, such as Pantone inks. Colors that you specify in your QuarkXPress documents may look solid on the screen, but they need to be separated and printed onto individual plates for printing. If you print color separations for a job with only process colors, you output four pieces of film for every page of the document. Each spot color requires adding another plate to the lineup.

Print Colors as Grays

Before we go any farther, we should jump to the last, but certainly not least, item in the Print dialog box: the Print Colors as Grays feature. Be sure to check this if you are proofing your color document on a black-and-white printer. This prints each color as a shade of gray rather than a solid black or white. You don't have too much control over which shades of gray go with which color, so subtle differences in colors (such as between a pink and a light green) may blend together as one shade of gray, but it's better than printing the file out as a page of solid black (see Figure 10-13).

Figure 10-13

Printing colors as grays

Print Colors as Grays turned off

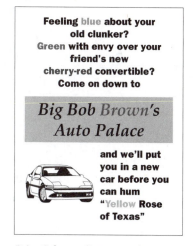

Print Colors as Grays turned on

Another Look at Colors

If you haven't read Chapter 8, *Modifying Images*, and Chapter 9, *Color*, we recommend you go back and look them over before getting too in-depth with color separation. But given that you probably have as busy a schedule as we do, here's a quick rundown of the most important concepts.

▶ Process colors are colors that may look solid on the screen, but will break down into varying tints of cyan, magenta, yellow, and black (CMYK) when printed as separations.

   Each of the four process colors is printed as a tint or a halftone (if you don't understand the fundamentals of halftoning, we *really* recommend you look at Chapter 8, *Modifying Images*). By overlapping the screened tints, a multitude of colors is created.

▶ Spot colors are colors which don't separate into tints of process inks at print time. Instead, each spot color prints on its own plate. These are typically Pantone (PMS) colors which will be printed with PMS inks. In Japan, they might be Toyo or DIC colors.

Printing Color Separations

Let's start with the most basic method of printing color separations, and then move on to more complicated concepts.

To print color separations, you set the Make Separations popup menu in the Print dialog box to On. This activates the Plates popup menu, giving you a choice of which color plates you want to print. By default, it's set to All Plates, which includes the four process colors plus any spot colors you have defined.

Even if you have All Plates selected, QuarkXPress only prints plates for the colors that are actually used in your document. If you create custom spot colors, but don't actually use them in your document, they appear on the Plates menu. But don't worry: they won't print when you specify All Plates.

We can't really call it a bug when the documentation goes right ahead and says that it is supposed to work this way, but the fact that QuarkXPress prints a black plate when you select All Plates even when you don't have anything black on the page is really annoying, if not downright crazy. But that's the way it goes, and the only way around it is to print each separate plate one at a time, selecting only the plates that actually are necessary.

The Rosette

When the process color plates are laid down on top of each other, the halftones of each color mesh with each other in a subtle way. Each plate's halftone image is printed at a slightly different angle, and possibly at a different screen frequency as well. The result is thousands of tiny rosette patterns (see Figure 10-14). If this process is done correctly, the separate colors blend together to form one smooth, clean color. If the angles or screen frequency are slightly off, or the registration (alignment) of the plates is wrong, then all sorts of chaos can ensue. Both of these problems can come about from errors on the lithographer's part, but more likely they are problems with your imagesetting process.

Figure 10-14

A simulated process-color rosette

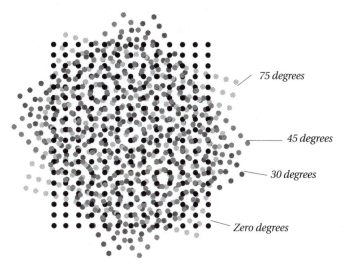

75 degrees

45 degrees

30 degrees

Zero degrees

The most common effect of the above problems is a patterning in the color called a *moiré pattern*. There's almost no good way to describe a moiré pattern: it's best to just see a few of them. They might be pretty subtle, but it would behoove you to learn to identify them and learn how to make them go away. Figure 10-15 shows an outlandish example of this patterning caused by the screen frequency and angles being set completely wrong.

Making sure you don't get moirés has been a major undertaking over the past few years in the color prepress industry, and has resulted in screening technologies that are often built right into the imagesetters themselves. Balanced Screens, ESCOR screening, and High Quality Screening (HQS) are three examples of this from the three major imagesetter vendors: Agfa, Varityper, and Linotype-Hell. For these technologies to work, you need to make sure that QuarkXPress is using its default screening angles (black, at 45 degrees; cyan at 75; magenta at 105; and yellow and 90). If you know that your service bureau is *not* using one of these sys-

Figure 10-15
Moiré patterning

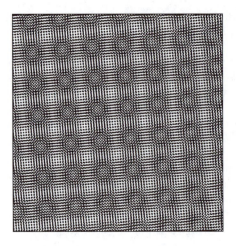

tems, you'll probably want to turn on Use PDF/EfiColor Screen Values in the Page Setup dialog box (see "Page Setup," page 541). Screening and moiré problems are discussed in much more depth in Steve and David's book *Real World Scanning and Halftones.*

▼ ▼

Tip: Changing the Color Sep Angles. If you don't want to use the angles that QuarkXPress sets up for you (or that you get when Use PDF Screen Values is turned on), you have two choices: either go into the PostScript code and change them yourself (sounds painful, doesn't it?) or use an XTension to do it. Quark's own QuarkPrint XTension lets you do this, as does the fcsAngles XTension. Typically, unless you have a really good reason to do this, you shouldn't mess with it at all. Also, some imagesetters override these settings regardless of what you change them to.

▼ ▼

Dot Gain and Printer Calibration

It's easy to confuse the concepts of dot gain and printer calibration. They have similar effects. To put it simply, both of these have to do with why the tint levels you specify in your files are not always what come out of the imagesetter or off the printing press. For example, you might specify a 40-percent magenta, and your final printed output will be 60 percent. Don't kick yourself for typing "60" when you meant "40"; remember that the problem could be in three places: dot gain, printer calibration, or your glasses might just be dirty. Let's look at each of these and then explore what we can do about them.

Dot gain. Dot gain (sometimes called *spot gain* or *spot variation* because it deals with how halftone spots grow or shrink) occurs while your artwork is actually on the press, and ink is flying about. The primary factors are the amount of ink on the press and the type of paper you're printing on (or, to be more specific, your lithographer is printing on). If there's too little ink on the press, your tints may print too light. If there's too much ink or if you're printing onto very absorbent paper, such as newsprint, your tints may print much too dark. A good lithographer can control the ink problem, but the issue of what kind of paper you're printing on must be kept in mind while you're outputting your finished artwork. This is another issue that's covered in much greater depth in the book *Real World Scanning and Halftones.*

Printer calibration. Just to be clear, we're talking here about imagesetter calibration. The idea is this: when the imagesetter's density knob is cranked up too high, the service bureau's densitometer is broken, or the film processor's chemicals are depleted, your delicate halftoned color separations are going to print less than optimally. All this equipment is so nifty that we sometimes forget that we're actually dealing with precision instruments designed to be able to produce very high-quality artwork. If neither you nor your service bureau understands how to take care of the equipment, the artwork suffers.

Glasses. The third possibility listed above is dirty glasses. In this busy world of contact lenses and corrective eye surgery, you have to stop yourself and ask: Why am I wearing these things, anyway? Then remember that if your computer explodes, the shattering glass will harmlessly bounce off those plastic lenses. But remember to keep them clean, or no matter what you do about dot gain and printer calibration, the colors will still look muddy.

Adjusting for Dot Gain and Printer Calibration

We live in a less-than-perfect world, and so we require adjustments to compensate for reality. What exactly can we, as QuarkXPress users, do to ensure high-quality printed output?

First of all, we highly recommend that whoever is doing your imagesetting use a calibration utility such as Kodak's Precision Imagesetter Linearization Software. Proper use of this keeps the output from the imagesetter relatively consistent on a day-to-day basis. You can then concentrate on your efforts to compensate for the natural dot gain your art experiences while on the press.

The primary method of adjusting for dot gain is Quark's Printer Calibration XTension. We find using this for imagesetter calibration (which it seems to be intended for) useless unless you have an imagesetter in-house and cannot use a utility like the one described above. However, as a tool to combat dot gain, it's just great. The problem, though, is cost.

To successfully adjust your printed output for the dot gain on various papers, you need to output the sample calibration guide which comes with the free Calibration XTension on a *calibrated* imagesetter. Then—and this is the expensive part—have your lithographer print this guide onto a sample of the stock you plan to use. Take density readings of this printed sample and then adjust QuarkXPress's internal printer settings by following the directions for printer calibration in the XTension's Read Me file. Does this sound like too much work to you? It does to us, except for the most demanding jobs. Talk the issue of dot gain over with your printer, and see what he or she says.

Registration and Trim Marks

Before we move on, we need to cover one last section of the Print dialog box: registration marks. In addition to the text and graphics of the pages themselves, your printer (we're talking about the human lithographer here) needs several pieces of information about your camera-ready work. One fact is where the sides of the printed page are. If you're printing multiple colors, another piece of information your printer needs is how each color plate aligns with the other. Additional job and page information may be helpful also. Selecting the Registration Marks feature answers all of these needs—QuarkXPress places *crop* (or *trim*) *marks, registration marks,* and page information around your document (see Figure 10-16).

Figure 10-16

The Registration Marks feature places items around your page

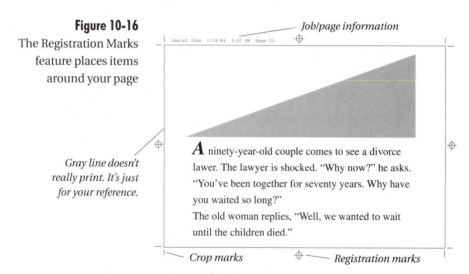

Job/page information

Jewish Joke 1/24/84 3:20 PM Page 23

A ninety-year-old couple comes to see a divorce lawer. The lawyer is shocked. "Why now?" he asks. "You've been together for seventy years. Why have you waited so long?"
The old woman replies, "Well, we wanted to wait until the children died."

Gray line doesn't really print. It's just for your reference.

Crop marks   *Registration marks*

Crop marks. Crop marks specify the page boundaries of your document. They are placed slightly outside each of the four corners so that when the page is printed and cut to size, they will be cut away. These are also called trim or cut marks.

Registration marks. Registration marks are used primarily for color-separation work, but you get them even if you just need crop marks on a one-color job. These are used by your printer's stripper to perfectly align each color plate to the next (see "Tip: Better Registration Marks," below).

Page and job information. The page and job information that is printed in the upper-left corner of the page includes the file name, a page number, and a date and time stamp. If you want more job information than is listed here, see "Tip: Additional Job Information," below.

Centered/Off Center. To make QuarkXPress add all these marks to your printed page, you need to select either Centered or Off Center from the Registration Marks popup menu in the Print dialog box. These features refer to the placement of registration marks. If you select Centered, each registration mark is centered exactly in the center of each side of the printed page. This is where most strippers need it. Others, because of their pin-register systems, need the registration marks slightly off center. Ask your printer.

▼ ▼

Tip: Better Registration Marks. The registration marks that Quark-XPress creates for you are okay, but not great, and certainly not optimal from a stripper's point of view. This is how you can make a better registration mark directly in QuarkXPress (you can also make one in FreeHand or Illustrator, and bring it in as an EPS; see Figure 10-17).

1. Draw a line about ½-inch long. Set width to .25 points with Midpoints selected in the Measurements palette.

2. Use the Step and Repeat feature from the Item menu to create one copy with no horizontal or vertical offset.

3. Make this second line perpendicular to the first by adding or subtracting 90 degrees from the line angle in the Measurements palette. Color the lines "Registration" (see Chapter 9, *Color*).

4. Draw a square picture box about ¼-inch large (hold down the Shift key to maintain a square) and center it over the lines. You could center it by either using the Space/Align feature (see Chapter 1, *QuarkXPress Basics*) or by just aligning the box's handles directly over the lines.

5. Set the box's background to 100-percent "Registration."

Figure 10-17

A more versatile registration mark

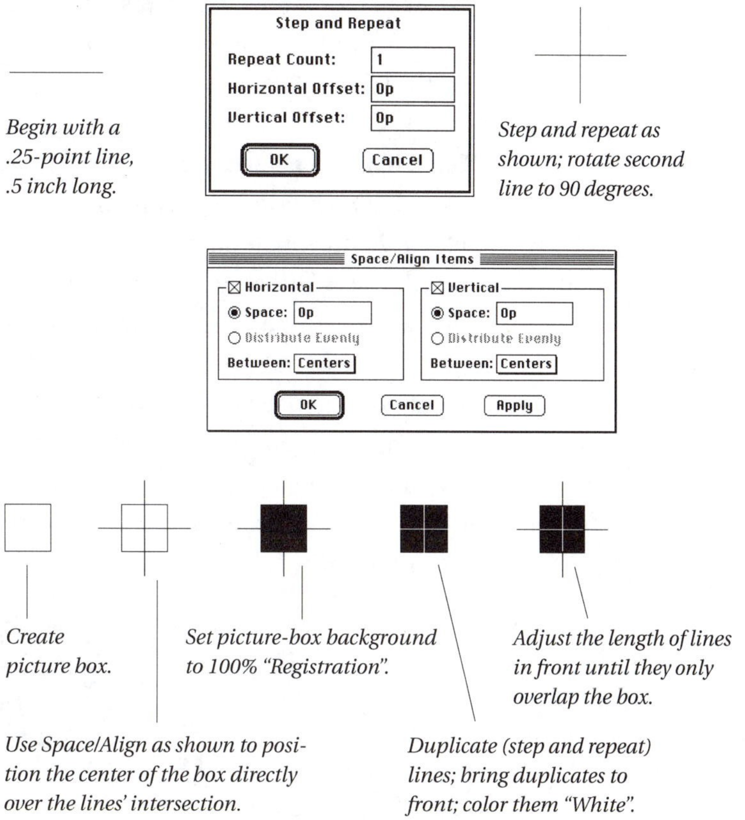

Begin with a .25-point line, .5 inch long.

Step and Repeat

Repeat Count: 1

Horizontal Offset: 0p

Vertical Offset: 0p

[OK] [Cancel]

Step and repeat as shown; rotate second line to 90 degrees.

Space/Align Items

☒ Horizontal
● Space: 0p
○ Distribute Evenly
Between: Centers

☒ Vertical
● Space: 0p
○ Distribute Evenly
Between: Centers

[OK] [Cancel] [Apply]

Create picture box.

Set picture-box background to 100% "Registration".

Adjust the length of lines in front until they only overlap the box.

Use Space/Align as shown to position the center of the box directly over the lines' intersection.

Duplicate (step and repeat) lines; bring duplicates to front; color them "White".

6. Select the two lines, and step-and-repeat both of them once with no offsets. Bring these lines to the front, if they're not already there.

7. Color the second set of lines "White", and shorten them so that they only overlap the box.

The great benefit of this registration mark is that when you print negatives, your printer can still align black crosshairs on a white background. After you create one of these, you can duplicate it as needed. Also, you can save it in a library or make an EPS out of it so that you can import it quickly onto other pages.

Going this route is clearly more work, as you sometimes need to build your page larger than necessary, then add your own crop marks and registration marks (and job info, if you want it), but it could be rewarding, depending on your situation.

Even better than going this route is using an XTension such as MarksXT (see Appendix D, *Resources*), which gives you even more control (but, of course, costs more, too).

▼ ▼

Tip: Additional Job Information. We discussed bleeds in Chapter 1, *QuarkXPress Basics*, as items which are mostly on the page, but bleed slightly off it. But you can also create items that are mostly off the page, and only slightly on it. This is ideal for adding additional job information on your documents. As long as at least a bit of a picture or text box is on the page, it will be printed along with what's on the page (see Figure 10-18). For this trick to work, the part that's touching the page has to be a nonprinting color. For instance, if you hang a text box off the top of the page, the bottom of the box might touch the page, but the text at the top of the box sits off the page.

Figure 10-18
Hanging items
off the page to
print with jobs

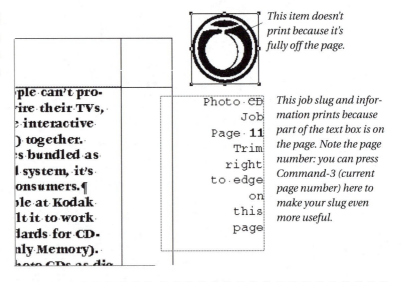

This item doesn't print because it's fully off the page.

ple·can't·pro-
·ire·their·TVs,·
·interactive·
)·together.·
·s·bundled·as·
·l·system,·it's·
onsumers.¶
·le·at·Kodak·
lt·it·to·work·
lards·for·CD-
ly·Memory).·

Photo·CD
Job
Page·**11**
Trim
right
to·edge
on
this
page

This job slug and infor-mation prints because part of the text box is on the page. Note the page number: you can press Command-3 (current page number) here to make your slug even more useful.

▼ ▼

OPI

The OPI popup menu that appears in the Print dialog box is exactly the same as the one in the Save Page as EPS dialog box, so we'll save our breath here by referring you to "Page as Picture," in Chapter 6, *Pictures*.

▼ ▼

Working with a Service Bureau

The existence of service bureaus with imagesetters (sometimes called imaging centers, imaging service bureaus, or "lino parlors") has mushroomed over the past five years. The phenomenon has grown from a storefront where you could rent a Mac and print on a laser printer to a specialty service where you can send your files to be imageset or color-proofed on a number of medium- and high-end imagesetters and other output devices. Alongside this growth has developed standard etiquette and rules spoken only in hushed voices (and usually after the customer has left the shop). In this section we bring these rules out into the open and take you through, step by step, how to best send files to your service bureau, and how to ensure that you'll receive the best quality output from them.

The first thing to remember when dealing with service bureaus is that they don't necessarily know their equipment or what's best for your file any better than you do. That's not to say that they are ignorant louts, but we are of the opinion that good service bureaus are few and far between, and you (the customer) have to be careful and know what you're doing. The principal relationship we talk about in this section is that of you, the customer, sending your QuarkXPress files to a service bureau to be imageset. We'll talk first about sending the actual QuarkXPress file, and then about sending a PostScript dump of the file. Many of our suggestions may be totally wrong for the way your particular service bureau works, so take what works and leave the rest. Some prefer PostScript dumps, for instance, while others opt for the QuarkXPress files themselves.

One other thing: you might also want to check out another book that David co-authored (with Peter Fink and Glenn Fleishman) called *WYSIWYG*, also from Peachpit Press. It covers not only how to make sure what you see on your screen is what you get, but how to make sure your files print at the service bureau successfully. (Okay, that's the end of this commercial break.)

▼ ▼

Tip: Does Your Service Bureau Have a Densitometer? A densitometer is a piece of equipment that you won't want to spring for unless you've got an imagesetter and you're outputting your own film. Generally, it's the responsibility of the service bureau to check their output regularly (at least daily) to make sure their density is correct, and that when you specify a 20-percent tint in your document, you get a 20-percent tint on your film (unless you're adjusting for dot gain, as described above).

If you are working with halftones or tints—especially with color separations—going to film, make sure your service bureau owns a *transmission* densitometer (as opposed to a *reflection* densitometer), knows how to use it, and does so frequently, especially when moving between film and paper. If they don't, go elsewhere.

▼ ▼

Tip: Some More Questions for Your Service Bureau. Here is a list of a few more questions which you may want to ask when shopping for a service bureau.

▶ What imagesetters do they have available, and what resolutions do they support?

▶ Do they have dedicated equipment just for film, and do they calibrate it using imagesetter linearization or other software? If they're using other software, do you need a component on your system when making files to output with them?

▶ Do they have an in-house, color-proofing system? Is it a laminate system (like Match Print or Press Match) or digital composite (like the 3M Rainbow or Iris printers)?

▶ Do they have a replenishing processor, or do they use the same chemicals continually? If it's the latter, how often do they clean their wash?

▶ Do they inspect their film before it is sent out?

▶ Do they have a customer agreement that lists what they're responsible for and what the customer is responsible for?

▶ Do they have a job ticket for output that lets you fill in all the details of your particular project?

There are no right or wrong answers to any of these. However, asking the questions not only tells you a lot about the service bureau, but also teaches you a lot about the process they're going through to output your film or RC paper.

You should make decisions about where to run each print job. For example, if a service bureau doesn't calibrate their equipment, you probably don't want to use them for halftoning or color separation work. If their top resolution is 1,270 dpi, you may need to go elsewhere for high-quality grayscale images. You can weigh these items against the cost of the film or paper output, the distance from your office, the friendliness of the staff, and so on.

▼ ▼

How to Send Your File

You have two basic choices in transporting your QuarkXPress document to a service bureau to be imageset: sending the file itself or sending a PostScript dump of the file. Let's be clear right off the bat that we strongly recommend sending a PostScript dump. Why? Mostly because we want to be in control of our document's printing.

When we send the file off to be printed using someone else's system, we don't know whether their fonts are different, whether the text will reflow, whether they'll forget to set up registration marks, or whether they'll print the file at the wrong screen frequency. By sending them a PostScript dump (see "Sending a PostScript Dump," below), you put yourself in the driver's seat: you can control almost every aspect of the print job.

Sending QuarkXPress Files

Though we prefer to send PostScript dumps, we know that many service bureaus prefer to receive the actual QuarkXPress file. And the truth is that many QuarkXPress users don't want to be responsible for checking all the buttons and specifications necessary to create a PostScript dump. If you find yourself in either of these situations, you'll need to know what to do in order to optimize your chances of success. Let's look at the steps you need to take.

Check your fonts. We can't tell you how important it is to keep track of which fonts you've used and where they are on your disk. Make sure that your service bureau has the same screen fonts as you, and has the printer fonts (downloadable fonts) that correspond to each and every font you've used in your document. We sometimes send our own fonts along with our job to the service bureau because we believe that sometimes screen fonts that are supposed to be the same simply aren't. Either they've gotten corrupted, or it was a different release, or something. But we'd rather be overly careful than have film come back totally wrong.

Chooser and Page Setup. We've always found it helpful to make sure we've got a LaserWriter driver selected in the Chooser, and that we've at least checked the Page Setup dialog box once before proceeding to the next step. You don't need to specify which printer you're using in the Page Setup dialog box if you're not sending PostScript dumps (the service bureau has to select theirs on their machine; the Chooser settings aren't carried with document files).

Look over your document. Take the extra time to perform a careful perusal of your entire document. If you need to, zoom in to 200 percent and scroll over the page methodically. Many problems with printing occur not with the printing at all, but with that one extra word that slipped onto its own line, or the one image that was "temporarily" set to Suppress Printout, and then never switched back.

Print a proof. If you can print the document on a desktop laser printer, chances are the file will print at your service bureau. That's not a guarantee, but it's usually a pretty good bet. When you print this proof, go over it, too, with a fine-tooth comb. You might have missed something in the on-screen search (see "Tip: Laserchecking with LaserCheck," below).

XPress Data. If you're still using QuarkXPress version 3.0, you'll need to find a service bureau that actually supports that version (few, if any, do). When you do, you'll have to include a copy of your XPress Data file with your document. In 3.1 and later, you *don't* have to send any XPress Data, Preference, or program files.

Include your illustrations. If you have imported pictures into your document using Get Picture, you need to include the original files on the disk with your document. Remember that QuarkXPress only brings in a representation image for the screen, and then goes to look for the original at print time. You can use the Picture Usage dialog box to see which graphic images you imported, and whether they are missing or present.

The idea is to send your service bureau a folder rather than just a file. Give them everything they could ever think of needing, just in case. The Collect for Output feature can really help this process along (see "Collect for Output," below).

▼ ▼

Tip: Catching all the Fonts and Pictures. You can find out what fonts and pictures you used in the Font Usage and Picture Usage dialog boxes. However, there's no way to print them without making screen captures. Or is there? When you select Collect for Output from the File menu, QuarkXPress prompts you for a place to save a report file. If you click OK and then press Command-period as soon as you see the progress bar graph appear, the program saves the report file and then cancels the operation. You can open that report in a word processor and find the names of the fonts and the graphics (as well as a lot of other information).

▼ ▼

Tip: Check Your Compatibility. Fonts change, colors change, everything changes except change itself (if you've seen one cliché, you've seen them all). If you're working with a service bureau regularly, you'll want to make sure that their equipment and system setup is compatible with yours. One way of doing this is for you to use the same files. That is, copy every file off their disk onto yours. This is clearly tedious, possibly illegal, and certainly never ending. You could perform periodic tests with a test sheet which includes the fonts you regularly use, a gray percentage bar, some grayscale images, and perhaps some line art (just for kicks). The idea is to see whether anything has changed much between your system and the service bureau's. If fonts come out different, the tints are off, or the density is too light or dark, you can either help them correct the problem or compensate for it yourself.

▼ ▼

Tip: Laserchecking with LaserCheck. LaserCheck lets you print a document on your desktop laser printer that was meant for an imagesetter. That is, you can actually set up the Page Setup and Print dialog boxes just as though you were printing on an imagesetter, and your laser printer not only handles it correctly, it tells you—with the help of LaserCheck—more than you'd ever want to know about the PostScript file it printed. We've found this handy for checking whether our tabloid-sized pages were going to come out lengthwise or widthwise on the L330, and for seeing whether a file would just plain print. Generally, if it prints with Laser-Check, there's a good chance it'll print on the imagesetter.

If you get an error with LaserCheck, you not only know that it probably wouldn't have output on the high-res device, but you get detailed information on what PostScript problem caused the error. Your service bureau may be able to help you solve your problem if they know a little about PostScript.

For more advanced and detailed information, you might look into two PostScript error handlers: PinPoint XT from the Cheshire Group, and the Advanced PostScript Error Handler from Systems of Merritt (see Appendix D, *Resources*). David loves these, but he's a PostScript hacker and likes to muck about with *movetos* and *curvetos*.

▼ ▼

Checklists for Sending QuarkXPress Files

We find checklists invaluable. Not only do they improve your method by encouraging you to do the appropriate task in the right order, they're satisfaction guaranteed every time you can check an item off the list, which in itself is a boon to flagging spirits as a deadline looms. Below are examples of checklists we use before sending files to a service bureau.

Fonts

▶ What fonts did you use in your document?

▶ Does your service bureau have your screen fonts? (If not, send them.)

▶ Do they have your printer fonts? (If not, send them; some service bureaus may not take them because of the ongoing confusion over copyright and copying of fonts. If that's the case, you'll have to make a PostScript dump which includes your fonts.)

Printer Type

▶ Chooser setting to LaserWriter or other appropriate driver?

▶ Page Setup to appropriate printer?

▶ Printer options checked in Page Setup dialog box? LaserWriter Options "second page" dialog box?

Document Check

▶ Check for text and picture boxes set to Suppress Printout.

▶ Check for text-box overflows.

▶ Check for missing or modified pictures in the Picture Usage dialog box.

▶ Check for widows, orphans, loose lines, bad hyphens, and other typographic problems. (Use Line Check if you have the FeaturesPlus or Thing-a-ma-bob XTension installed.)

Proof

▶ Print a proof on a laser printer, preferably using Laser-Check or another imagesetter-on-a-laser-printer utility.

▶ Check it carefully to make sure it's what you want. If you're working with a client, have them look over the proofs and sign off on them.

Relevant Files

▶ Did you include EPS and TIFF files?

▶ Did you include the document itself? (Don't laugh; sometimes this is the one thing people *do* forget after a long day.)

Collect for Output

To make the above process significantly easier for y'all, Quark has added a cool feature called Collect for Output. This feature first saw life as a free XTension from Quark for version 3.1; it's been a full-fledged part of the program since version 3.2. Selecting this command from the File menu copies your document and all the picture files necessary for its output to a folder of your choice—it doesn't move or remove the original files. It also creates a report containing detailed information about your document, from fonts and pictures used to trapping information. Then all you have to do is get the folder to your service bureau or color prepress house by modem, messenger, or carrier pigeon.

Using this command is simplicity itself. When you select it, it prompts you to find a folder, and asks you to specify a name for the report. We typically just use QuarkXPress's default name; it's simply the name of your document with "report" stuck on the end. Once you've selected a folder, QuarkXPress copies your document and all picture files, wherever they might reside, to that target folder. If you haven't saved your file before selecting Collect for Output, QuarkXPress asks you if you want to save first.

Note that to avoid potential copyright problems, QuarkXPress doesn't copy any fonts to the folder. That's up to you to do yourself, if necessary. The legal ramifications are between you, your service bureau, and your font vendor. We don't blame Quark for wanting to stay out of this one!

Collecting files for output often takes longer than manually copying each file, as QuarkXPress does a very thorough search for each file it needs. This may take a bit longer, but the process does give you the satisfaction of knowing you haven't forgotten to copy that little bitty logo illustration hidden at the bottom of page 32.

Also note that you may need lots of space on your hard drive to do this. David recently worked on a job in which the combined size of the document and all the pictures in it was over 200Mb. When he went to Collect for Output, not only did it take almost forever to do, but he ran out of hard-drive space halfway through the procedure. If you're working with big files like this, it's probably easier and less painful for you to simply copy files yourself.

Sending a PostScript Dump

It's probably clear that we not only don't trust many service bureaus to do the right thing, but we also don't trust ourselves to always remember everything we need to while standing at the service bureau counter. Because of this, we strongly urge you to use PostScript dumps. A PostScript dump, also known as a print-to-disk, when performed correctly, almost always ensures a better print, and is sometimes even preferred by your service bureau.

In fact, many service bureaus now give big discounts to people who bring in PostScript dumps as opposed to the actual files. (Our neighborhood service bureau cuts five dollars a page off their single-page price.) Instead of having to open your file, make sure all the correct fonts are loaded, check all your settings, and then print it, they can simply download the PostScript dump to their imagesetters.

The biggest difference is that with PostScript dumps you have the responsibility for making sure your file is perfect for printing. However, this isn't as difficult as it may seem. Let's go through the steps you need to take to create the perfect PostScript dump. At the end we'll include a checklist that you can copy or re-create for your own use.

System setup. Make sure you have enough memory on your disk to save the PostScript dump. With the LaserWriter 7 and 8 drivers, you can tell it where you want the file to be saved (earlier drivers saved the dump in the same folder as your copy of QuarkXPress). PostScript dumps are often large. To figure out how large a print to disk file will be, you can usually add up the size of all the figures, add the size of the file itself, then tack on another 10 percent. If you've got a 30Mb image in your file, your PostScript dump has to include that too, and will be accordingly enormous.

Note that with the LaserWriter 8 driver, you have to have twice as much space on your hard drive because the driver spools the information to disk first, then writes the PostScript file afterward. The file is spooled to your startup disk (whatever disk shows up on top and has your System Folder on it), while the PostScript dump can be to any volume, cartridge, floppy, etc. If you're using very large files, it's probably not worth making PostScript dumps.

Chooser setup. Because you're printing to a PostScript device, you need to have the LaserWriter driver selected in your Chooser. Background Printing can be set to On or Off. It doesn't matter whether you actually have a PostScript printer hooked up or not. (David makes PostScript dumps on his PowerBook while traveling on the road, then compresses those files and sends them to service bureaus to be imageset.)

Page setup. Check your Page Setup dialog box. The proper printer should be selected in the Printer Type menu. This determines how large the printed page should be. Be sure to set the halftone screen frequency you want; this is an area where many people screw up. Read over "Page Setup," page 541, for more details. Also, don't forget to set the correct orientation, Options, Enlarge or Reduce settings, EfiColor controls, and so on. Remember, if you don't set these correctly now, no one else can later.

Fonts. You must have the screen font loaded for every font you use in your document. One way to check which fonts are in your document is with the Font Usage feature in the Utilities menu. However, this method won't always give you fully accurate results, so it's best to keep a running list of fonts you use. If you don't have the screen font for a document, try to get it; without it, you run the risk of having your document print in Courier. In addition, all your line spacing will be messed up due to a difference in character widths. Note that this means you have to have the fonts loaded for typefaces used in EPS files, too.

▼ ▼

Tip: Telling Fonts Not to Download. When QuarkXPress prints a Post-Script file to disk using LaserWriter drivers before LaserWriter 8, it attempts to include any outline printer font information it can find. For example, if you used Courier in your file and have the Courier printer font in your System Folder, QuarkXPress includes that font's information in the file. However, if your service bureau already has the font, you don't need to include it in your Post-Script file. It just makes the file bigger. Disk space might not be an issue to you, but if it is, you might want to *dis*-include those fonts.

In the LaserWriter 8 driver, the default setting is not to include any fonts (see below). However, if you're using an earlier version of the driver, you can still leave the fonts out. There are two ways to make sure QuarkXPress doesn't include any printer fonts you have floating about. The first option is to move the printer fonts someplace where QuarkXPress can't find them. This means putting them anywhere but in the System Folder, the QuarkXPress folder, and the folder where you keep your screen fonts. This is another instance where PrairieSoft's DiskTop seems impossible to live without. With it, you can quickly move these files anywhere you want, then return them after you create the print-to-disk.

LaserWriter 8 avoids this whole problem by offering you three options in a popup menu (see Figure 10-19).

> ▶ **None.** The default setting in this dialog box is None, and—just as the name implies—no fonts get included in the PostScript file when you chose this. If you and your service bureau are sure that they have all of the fonts downloaded

Figure 10-19
Saving a PostScript
dump using
LaserWriter 8

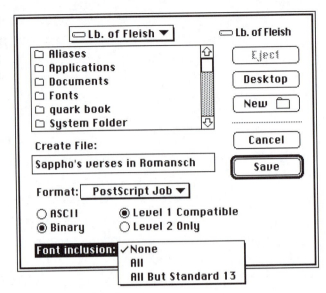

to their imagesetter's hard drive (or if you provide the printer fonts so they can download them in advance of your job), then you may be safe selecting None. Your file will be substantially smaller with this option selected.

▶ **All.** The polar opposite of None is, of course, All. If you select this, then all the fonts get included in the PostScript dump. It makes for a big file, but we sometimes use this method because neither we nor the service bureau needs to worry about downloading fonts. They're all in the file.

▶ **All But Standard 13.** Almost every PostScript printer has a core of 13 basic fonts: Courier, Helvetica, and Times (each in four styles), plus Symbol. If you select All But Standard 13 from the popup menu, all the fonts in the document are included unless they're one of these 13 typefaces. When we send PostScript dumps to a service bureau, this is the method we prefer. If you have All selected, you may end up including Helvetica, Courier, and Times repeatedly, even though you're not using them.

▾ ▾

Pictures. The next step in making a PostScript dump is to check your Picture Usage dialog box to see if all the pictures you used in your document are available. This is a suggested step but is not crucial, because if you don't do this, QuarkXPress checks for you at print time and then gives you the opportunity to find any that are missing (see Chapter 6, *Pictures*, for more information on this dialog box).

Print. The most common mistakes in creating PostScript dumps are made in the Print dialog box. Be careful with the buttons and menus here. If you want registration marks (along with trim marks and job information), you must turn them on here. If you want multiple copies (not likely, for high-resolution output), choose your value here. But if you only want one copy of each page, make sure that you specify "1" here! We've had friends who've gotten 10 copies back from their service bureau simply because they didn't check this carefully. Expensive mistake.

Be careful, too, with the tiling features. You may be printing to a roll-fed imagesetter that can handle a full tabloid-size page, and if you were printing tiled proof copies earlier, Manual or Auto tiling might have been left on.

If you're making color separations, read over the section "Color Separation," page 576.

Finally, as we noted earlier in this chapter, to make the PostScript dump select File in the Print dialog box's Destination area. When this is selected, the OK button changes to Save.

Making dumps with early drivers. If you're using a printer driver before 7.1 you won't see have the option to save a file in the Print dialog box. We highly recommend upgrading your system and print drivers. However, if you can't do that for some reason, here's how to make a PostScript dump.

▶ **The F key.** When you are finally ready to print the file, click OK, and immediately press the F key. Keep holding down this key until you see the message "Creating PostScript file." If you start to see messages such as "Preparing Data," you waited too long to press the F key. Cancel and try again. Some people like to press the mouse button down, then hold down the F key, then let go of the mouse button. This way they ensure that they'll catch the computer in time.

▶ **The K key.** If you are transferring the PostScript dump to a non-Mac machine before printing, or are printing to a printer that doesn't have Apple's LaserPrep downloaded to it, you should press the K key rather the F key. Hold down the K key after clicking OK, and QuarkXPress includes Apple's LaserPrep information at the beginning of the file. This information is vital to the way that your PostScript file runs. When you make a PostScript dump using the later version printer driver, the LaserPrep header is always included automatically.

▶ **The "PostScript0" File.** We mentioned above where the file would be saved to, but not what it would be called. The first time you do a PostScript dump, the file is called "Post-Script0". The second time, it's called "PostScript1", and so on. After "PostScript9" the computer starts over, erasing "PostScript0" and replacing it, and so on.

▼ ▼

Tip: When Your File Is Too Big. It's easy to make PostScript dumps that are too big to fit onto a floppy. Add a TIFF or an EPS here and there, forget to turn off access to printer fonts (see "Tip: Telling Fonts Not to Download," above), or even just try to print a large file. Don't fret: there's always a workaround.

First of all, if you're going to work with the Macintosh, you must own a copy of Compact Pro. It's shareware, which means that you can get it almost anywhere (user's group, dealer, online service), but if you use it for more than 15 days, you are honor-bound to send Bill Goodman (his company is Cyclos) his $25. Compact Pro has become the shareware standard on the Macintosh for compressing files. Some TIFF files can compress as much as 90 percent, but most files compress by around 30 to 60 percent. You can also use Compact Pro to break up files onto several disks, then join them up again to fit back onto a hard disk. (For those of you who always want alternatives, there's also the shareware version of StuffIt called StuffIt Lite, which doesn't always achieve the same speed and compression factor.)

Several commercial compression packages have gotten rave reviews recently, including AutoDoubler, TimesTwo, DiskDoubler, and StuffIt Deluxe. The central issue is often not which is better to use, but which program the person on the receiving side owns. If you're not sure what your service bureau has, save the compressed file as a "self-extracting archive." Those can be decompressed by double-clicking on the icon. Most of the commercial packages have a freeware decompression module, too.

If you're going to be sending lots of large files to your service bureau, we recommend a removable hard disk, such as a SyQuest cartridge or magneto-optical drive. Make sure the type you get is compatible with what your service bureau uses. SyQuest cartridges come in 44, 88, and 105Mb flavors, but most people can at least read the 44Mb variety. Magneto-optical (MO) cartridges can hold from 128Mb on a 3.5-inch cartridge to over one gigabyte on a 5.25-inch cartridge. Removables are also great for backing up your data.

DAT (digital audio tape) drives have made a big impact lately as the price tumbled. A DAT drive uses a data-grade tape (it's a better grade than that used to record audio digitally) to hold from 1.2 gigabytes (without compression) to as much as 8Gb (with compression). The tapes cost $12 to $20, so the cost is minuscule per megabyte; they're also tiny—smaller than a pack of cards. Many service bureaus have started supporting these tapes because of the ease of transporting vast amounts of data on them. However, because these tapes aren't Finder-mountable without special software, most people use backup software to write to them. You have to make sure that you and your service bureau are using either the special Finder-mountable software or the same backup program before you send them data on a tape.

Finally, you can always just send a big hard drive to the service bureau. One friend recently completed a job too big to easily handle even on removables, so he just brought his one-gigabyte drive to the service bureau to print.

▼ ▼

Checklist for Sending PostScript Dumps

Your service bureau will appreciate you for checking these items.

System and Font Setup

▶ Do you have enough memory on your disk to save the PostScript dump?

▶ Do you have the proper screen fonts loaded for the fonts that are in your document? EPS files?

▶ Have you disabled the printer fonts, so that they don't get included in the PostScript dump? (Or, if you're using Laser-Writer 8, have you selected the proper font-inclusion setting in the Save as PostScript dialog box?)

Chooser and Page Setup

▶ Do you have the LaserWriter or other appropriate driver selected in the Chooser?

▶ Do you have the proper settings in the Page Setup dialog box? LaserWriter Options "second page" dialog box?

Pictures

▶ Do you have all the EPS, TIFF, and other image files available? Check the Picture Usage dialog box.

Print Dialog Box

▶ Are all the proper settings made? Registration marks? Page range? Color separations?

▶ Have you selected File in the Destination area?

Sending the File

▶ Do you want to compress or segment the file?

▶ Rename the file to something appropriate.

▶ Make sure that your service bureau has the same kind of removable media or tapes that you're going to send.

Troubleshooting

After all of this, printing should be a breeze, right? Well, we wish it were. Too often, we get phone calls from our service bureau saying, "Your job wouldn't print." Back in the good old days, a service bureau would offer to fix it for you. Now life has gotten busy for them, and they often expect you to do the fixing. Here are some tips that we've found to work over the years.

Graphics Look Awful

One of the most common problems with print jobs from Quark-XPress has never had anything to do with QuarkXPress itself. The problem is with the person sending their files. Remember that QuarkXPress does not actually suck in any EPS or TIFF files that you have imported. It only brings in a low-resolution representation for the screen image, and maintains a link with the original file. If that file changes or is missing when QuarkXPress tries to print it, the graphic will look different from what you expected.

Two notes to write on your forehead follow.

▶ If you're going to send your QuarkXPress document, then send a folder, not a file. The folder should include the document, all EPS and TIFF images you used, and possibly the fonts, too. You might want to use the Collect for Output feature that we discussed earlier in this chapter.

▶ If you can, send PostScript print-to-disk files (PS dumps) instead of the document itself. The PostScript dump *does* contain the TIFF and EPS files, as well as all the information QuarkXPress needs from the preferences file, and fonts, and so on.

Because QuarkXPress downsamples TIFF images to two times the halftone screen frequency, sometimes you can get strange mottling or jaggy images, especially if you've scaled down an image considerably (see "Tip: Maintaining Resolution," page 547).

Memory Problems

QuarkXPress has gotten a bad rep in the past for causing Post-Script errors at print time. Almost all of these errors are the result of printer-memory problems (called VMerror), and almost all of them can be avoided with a few tricks.

Reset the printer. Our favorite technique for avoiding memory problems is simply to turn the printer off, wait a few seconds, and turn it back on again. This flushes out any extraneous fonts or PostScript functions that are hogging memory. It's sort of like waking up after a good night's sleep, but different.

Use minimum settings. Using the minimum settings means turning off all the printer options in the Page Setup dialog box, including the LaserWriter Options "second page" dialog box.

Rotate your own graphics. If you've scanned in big bitmapped graphics, and need to rotate them, you should use Photoshop or another image-manipulation program rather than doing it in QuarkXPress. Rotating large bitmapped images in QuarkXPress may or may not choke the printer, but it certainly slows it down a lot—an important point if you're paying a per-minute surcharge at a service bureau. (Note that we're not talking about object-oriented pictures here, such as those from Illustrator or FreeHand.)

Take care in selecting your fonts. If you play around with a lot of different fonts trying to find one you like, you may inadvertently leave remnants of old fonts lying around. For example, a space character may be set to some font that you don't use anyplace else. Nonetheless, QuarkXPress must download that font along with every other font you use. This takes up memory that could be used for something else. Try using the Font Usage dialog box to see which fonts are sitting around in your document. Then purge the ones you don't need.

Use Unlimited Downloadable Fonts. If you must have many fonts on a page, you might want to enable the Unlimited Downloadable Fonts feature in the LaserWriter Options dialog box under Page Setup. See the section on this earlier in the chapter before you use it, though, as there are some serious drawbacks to it.

Print fewer pages at a time. We have successfully coached long documents out of an imagesetter by printing two to 10 pages at a time, rather than all 500 pages at once. This is obviously a hassle, but it's better than not getting the job printed at all. Much of the work can be done early by creating multiple PostScript dumps, then queuing them up on a spooler at the service bureau.

Remove enormous graphics. One of the great promises of desktop publishing was that we could print an entire page with every graphic and text block perfectly placed. Remember that promises are often broken. Case in point: large graphics (and even small graphics) sometimes choke the printer. These graphics often print all by themselves, but when placed on a page they become the chicken bone that killed the giant. Yes, using every trick possible you might get the page out, but is it worth the time? Perhaps it's more efficient to let your printer or stripper handle that graphic. Or, god forbid, hot wax that puppy and paste it down yourself.

Make sure you're current. Someone recently called Eric and asked him why her file wouldn't print (this is, by the way, almost impossible for anyone to answer over the telephone). He suggested a few things, and then asked what version of QuarkXPress she was using. It turned out she was using an older version of the program, and as soon as she updated, the printing problem went away. This is not uncommon. They don't talk about it much, but the engineers at Quark are constantly trying to make their program print better. In fact, the "patch level 2" release of version 3.2 solved several major printing problems. We've included this on the Quark Goodies Disk for those of you still using QuarkXPress 3.2 (although it's better just to upgrade to version 3.3).

PostScript Problems

There are some PostScript problems that aren't memory-related, even though just about everyone at Quark will tell you they don't exist. One is the infamous *stackunderflow* error. Another is the *undefined* command error. These are significantly harder to track down and fix. However, here are a few things you can try.

Save As. Logically, resaving your document under a different name doesn't make any sense, but it does work sometimes.

Selective printing. You can try to pinpoint what page element is causing the error by printing only certain parts of the page. For example, select Rough in the Print dialog box to avoid printing any pictures or complex frames. If the page prints, chances are one of the graphic images is at fault. You can also use Suppress Printout to keep a single image from printing.

If the page still doesn't print after printing a rough copy, try taking out a text box at a time, or changing the fonts you used. If you are printing color separations, try printing a single plate at a time.

Re-import. If the problem turns out to be a graphic you've imported, you might try re-importing it. If the image is a PICT, you might have better luck using Get Picture than Paste. Even better, convert the PICT into a TIFF (for bitmaps) or EPS (for object-oriented graphics) file. Then re-import it.

Check printer type. Make sure you have the correct printer type selected in the Page Setup dialog box. Often, this won't have any effect on your output, but it's worth checking.

Big Ugly White Gaps Appear Between Colors

You've output your four-color separations and sent the file off to your lithographer. A few days later you show up for the press check and you see, much to your surprise, big ugly white gaps appearing between each of the colors. What happened? You forgot about traps. It's easy to do, believe us. The remedy? Go read the section on trapping in Chapter 9, *Color*, and redo your negatives.

Irregular Lines

If you have a number of thin lines next to each other, some may appear thicker than others when printed on a low-resolution printer (such as a 300-dpi laser printer). If you need them to look the same, and don't mind a little PostScript hacking, insert the following code directly after the header (right before the line that includes *mddict begin*).

```
/roundme {.25 sub round .25 add} bind def
/transthese {transform roundme exch roundme exch itransform} bind def
/moveto {transthese moveto}bind def
/lineto {transthese lineto}bind def
```

Wrong Screen Frequency

QuarkXPress can neither read your mind nor the mind of your lithographer. If you print your file out with the default halftone screen frequency setting of 60 lpi, that's just what you'll get. This is coarse, but fine if you're just going to photocopy your page. However, it looks pretty awful compared to the 120 or 133 lpi (or higher) used in most print jobs. Check with your lithographer for what screen frequency to use, then check your Page Setup dialog box before you print your job. Note that this is usually not a function that your service bureau can change if you provide a PostScript dump.

Not Enough Space Between Pages

If your pages are printing too close together from a roll-fed printer, you may have to adjust the Page Gap value in the Page Setup dialog box. Note that QuarkXPress prints your document only as wide as it needs to. For example, if your page is four by four inches, QuarkXPress only tells the imagesetter to print four inches of film. This is a great saving for film or RC paper, but sometimes it's a hassle to handle the output. It's worth talking to your service bureau before you set the gap; with some setups you actually need to ask them to adjust settings using utilities such as LinoUtil or Varityper Imagesetter Utilities instead of you worrying about it yourself.

Document Settings

Back in the age of version 3.0, people were constantly complaining about their spacing being off, kerning pairs disappearing, and custom frames getting screwed up when they sent their documents to the service bureau. The problem was that they weren't sending their XPress Data files along with their documents.

Fortunately, these are the salad days, the happy-go-lucky days, the days of wine and roses. These days there is no XPress Data file, and all the information that was in that file is now stored within the document file itself. However, there's one caveat to this story: when your service bureau (or whoever else is looking at your file) opens your document, they're presented with an alert dialog box asking which to use: the document's settings, or the settings of the computer they're opening it on. If they choose the latter, then your painstaking work may be screwed up.

A service bureau that doesn't know to always select Use Document Settings is not a service bureau we'd want to work with.

Three separate XTensions can help eliminate this confusion for your service bureau (or for you, if you're constantly customizing). Quark sells QuarkPrint, which offers a number of print job options, but also has a setting so that Use Document Settings is selected whenever you open a file. Two third-party XTensions, SpeedOpen (which is freeware) and XState (which is not), also let you set a similar preference (see Appendix D, *Resources*).

Fonts Come Out Wrong

Don't forget that you have to have the screen and printer fonts loaded for every font in the document available to QuarkXPress and the printer when you print. That means the fonts you selected, those that were imported, and those that are stuck somewhere in an EPS document. "Available" means that they should be where your system wants them; see Chapter 4, *Type and Typography*, for a rundown on where the printer font needs to be depending on your system version and font utilities.

Also, watch out for EPS files nested inside of EPS files nested inside of EPS files. Depending on which application created each EPS file, QuarkXPress may or may not be able to dig deep enough to find every font used.

Registration Problems

Imagine the Rockettes, kicking their legs to chorus-line stardom in perfect synchronization. Then imagine the woman at one end having no sense of rhythm, kicking totally out of sync with the others. This is what happens when one color plate is misregistered from the others. When a sheet of paper is rushed through a printing press and four colors speedily applied to it, there is bound to be some misregistration—sometimes up to a point or two. However, you can help matters considerably by making sure that your film is as consistent as possible.

Whenever we are told that a job printed great "except for one plate that was off-register," we immediately ask if that plate was run at a different time than the others. The answer is almost always yes. We realize it's expensive and time-consuming to print four new plates every time you want to make a change to a page, but it is a fact of desktop life that you can almost never get proper registration when you reprint a single plate. One service bureau we know of also had this problem when they ran two or three plates at the end of a roll of film, and the rest of the job at the start of the next roll. Why? The weather, roll stretch, alignment of the stars . . . all sorts of reasons contribute to this massive hassle.

Output devices that use cut sheets of film (drum imagesetters) often have better luck matching film done at different times than roll-fed or capstan-mechanism imagesetters, because the factor of roll stretch is eliminated, and the film is often registered with pins rather than rubber rollers.

▼ ▼

"Job Finished"

As we said way back at the beginning of the book, don't give up until you get it to work. If you run into difficulty, there is almost always a workaround solution. Working through to that solution almost always teaches a valuable lesson (as grandma used to say, "It builds character"). However, remember that the solution is sometimes to just print the job in pieces and strip them together traditionally. It feels awful when you have to clean off your drafting table and dust off your hot waxer, but efficiency is often the name of the game.

One last note: when the last page comes out of the imagesetter, don't forget to thank your computer, QuarkXPress, the service bureau, and yourself for a job well done.

APPENDIX A

EFICOLOR

For years, "What You See Is What You Get," or WYSIWYG (pronounced "wizzy-wig"), was one of the key buzzwords of desktop publishing. It meant that the page layout you saw on your computer screen was, more or less, what you'd get out of your printer. WYSIWYG works fine for a page with any color of ink—so long as it's black (to paraphrase Henry Ford). But it's significant that nobody felt the need to come up with a similarly cute acronym to describe color fidelity between computer and printer. We considered "Color You See Is Color You Get," but we wouldn't want to be responsible for unleashing "kissykig" on the world. Our editor, Steve Roth, says he prefers WYGIWYG: "What You Get Is What You Get."

Silliness aside, the main reason nobody's come up with such an acronym is that until recently, it would have described a condition that didn't exist. If you've ever created color pages, you've learned—probably with no little pain—that the colors you see on your screen have little more than a passing resemblance to what comes out of your printer or off a printing press. In fact, a major part of working with color on Macs has been learning through trial and error that when you see color A on your Mac screen, you'll actually get color B out of your color-proofing printer, and color C off of a four-color press run. Your only guides were process-color swatch books, test prints, and bitter experience.

611

▼ ▼

Managing Color

Well, the times they are a-changing, and the hottest things on the Mac market today are color-management systems (CMS) that promise to provide fidelity between the colors on your computer screen and those of your printed output. Apple, Eastman Kodak, Pantone, and Electronics for Imaging (EFI), among others, have management systems that sometimes actually cooperate with each other. Frankly, we're more than a little skeptical of some of the claims made by marketers of these products ("No more Match Prints; proof colors right on your computer screen!"), but color-management systems are clearly a step in the right direction.

And if you own QuarkXPress 3.2 or 3.3, you already have one such system, or at least major components of it: EfiColor from EFI, supported in QuarkXPress by the EfiColor XTension.

What EfiColor Attempts

As a color-management system, EfiColor is designed to make the colors on your document's page consistent—from your Macintosh screen to a color proof to your final output device. If you're creating a document to be output on a four-color press, EfiColor makes the colors on your screen look more like those that will emerge from your press run. If you use a color printer such as a QMS ColorScript for comps, EfiColor ensures that your color printout also bears more than a passing resemblance to your final four-color output.

Note that we're saying "look like" and "passing resemblance." EfiColor can remove a lot of the guesswork from working with color. So instead of few of the colors on your screen looking like your final output, many of the colors you see may be significantly closer to what you'll be getting than they would otherwise. In photographic images—images that use a lot of subtle tonal changes, not flat tints—you'll have a better idea of what the over-all look and color cast of the final image is.

Why Color Management "Can't" Work

If there's one thing we want you to get out of reading this appendix, it's that it's just plain not possible for computer monitors, thermal wax color printers, color copier/printers and four-color printers to exactly match each other, color for color. Each device uses different technology to create color, and each uses differing methods of specifying its colors. Monitors display colors as values of red, green, and blue (RGB). Printers usually use cyan, magenta, yellow, and black (CMYK). The colors emitted from a monitor use light and are additive: the more color you add, the closer to white the screen gets. On the other hand, printers that apply ink, wax, powders, or toner to paper generally create colors by combining values of cyan, magenta, yellow, and black. This color model is subtractive: the more of each component you add, the darker your final color becomes. When you try to create the same color using two different methods, there's really no way that the two can look exactly the same.

Plus, the same RGB values on two different monitors might not look like each other at all, because the screen phosphors and technology might be slightly different. Similarly, the same CMYK values printed on a thermal wax transfer printer such as a QMS ColorScript look very different from "identical" values printed on a four-color press on coated stock, and those colors also look different than colors printed on newsprint.

We call each of these color systems *device dependent* because the color is specific to only one device—a brand of monitor, color printer, or whatever. EfiColor tries its best to create consistency among various devices, but you need to understand that it's not entirely possible.

"I Only Paint What I See"

Matching colors might be a hopeless comparison of apples, oranges, and grapefruits, except that there's one constant shared by every method of creating colors: the human eye. The fact is that your eyes don't care what technology a monitor or printer uses to create a color; they just see colors. Just as monitors and printers are device *dependent,* your eyes are device *independent.* They're the one constant in this whole *mishegoss,* and not surprisingly, they're the key to many color-management systems such as EfiColor.

No, EfiColor doesn't try to calibrate your eyes with some sort of cybernetic gizmo. Rather, it uses a color-space model based on a statistical analysis of how most people perceive differences between colors. This model was designed by the Commission Internationale de l'Eclairage (that's the International Commission on Color, or CIE, to you and me) in the 1930s. The CIE color space describes every different color the human eye can see, using a mathematical model that isn't dependent on fickle things like the density of phosphor coatings or the amount of ink spread on certain paper stocks.

Unlike RGB or CMYK values, which don't really describe a color (the same values might look quite different on different devices), CIE values actually describe a color's appearance, not just the values that make it up.

Color-Management Concepts

Before we go further into this discussion, we have to take a break and define a couple of important words: *gamut* and *profile.* We'll use these words a lot throughout this chapter.

Gamuts. A device's color *gamut* describes the range of colors which that device can create or sense. Since the CIE color space describes every perceivable color, by default it has the largest gamut. No device—monitor, scanner, or printer—can come close to reproducing this range of colors, and so the gamut of any specific device is smaller than the CIE gamut. Plus, different devices are able to image different sets of colors (the available colors are spread out differently). So one device may be able to reproduce many hues of red, while another may be weak in reds, but especially competent in producing a wide range of blues.

Profiles. EfiColor uses files called *device profiles* to keep track of not only the color gamuts of particular devices, but also other information about their capabilities and limitations. Most of the profiles you use with EfiColor are actually device characterizations, rather than calibrations. In other words, they're generic descriptions of Apple 13-inch monitors, or printing presses that use SWOP (Standard Web Offset Press) coated inks, not specific descriptions of your personal device or your lithographer's press. With the pending release (at this writing) of EfiColor Works, however, tools will be available to build custom scanner and monitor EfiColor profiles for your devices.

Another development promises to provide even more flexibility in choosing, using, and customizing profiles. As of January 1994, the four primary color-management software companies (EFI, Eastman Kodak, Apple, and Pantone) have agreed in principle to standardize on Apple's ColorSync profile system. The profiles to be provided in EfiColor Works are actually ColorSync profiles. Many scanner- and monitor-calibration systems can already create ColorSync profiles. And because other color-management vendors are starting to sell their hand-built output profiles in ColorSync format, in the not-so-distant future (perhaps by the time you read this) you'll be able to mix and match profiles from every company, or even make your own. Like your Uncle Jack used to say, you can buy your razors from one company, and your blades from someone else.

From Device to Device

EfiColor actually adjusts colors depending on what it knows about certain printers and monitors. It does this by converting color information to and from its native CIE color-space format (see Figure A-1). If you've installed the appropriate device profiles on your Macintosh, EfiColor can transform the color you see on your screen into CIE color, then turn around and convert it to a similar color on your color printer.

Note that a color monitor can display a different set of colors than a desktop color printer, which, in turn, has a much greater

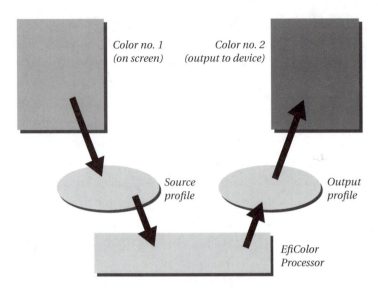

Figure A-1
EfiColor's
transformations

Color no. 1
(on screen)

Color no. 2
(output to device)

Source
profile

Output
profile

EfiColor
Processor

gamut than a four-color press. EfiColor's color transformations work best when they reduce one device's gamut to match another; it's just not possible to *increase* a device's gamut to match another's, although there are ways of faking it. That is, a color monitor is good at displaying the limited gamut of a four-color press, but a four-color press is hard-pressed (no pun intended) to simulate a display.

Perhaps the most important aspect of this technology is the conversion between RGB and CMYK color models. Once EfiColor transforms a color into its internal CIE color space, it can transform it to any other color model it knows about. And while the RGB-to-CMY conversion is relatively simple (see "Color Models" in Chapter 9, *Color*), converting to CMYK has traditionally been quite difficult. EfiColor does this for you behind the scenes.

Whether or not you want EFI to do this conversion is a legitimate question; people have argued for years over which program does the best conversion. Some say Adobe Photoshop, some say EfiColor, and some say forget all desktop solutions and hire a traditional color separator to do it for you. You'll forgive us if we just stay out of this argument. But do note that EfiColor gives you the choice by letting you turn its transformations on or off.

Metric Color Tags

If all the colors you ever use are created on your own Mac using QuarkXPress, then the color transformations we just described would be all you'd ever need. But life (and desktop publishing) is more complicated than that. Most of the time you'll be importing artwork created or scanned elsewhere. How will your EfiColor XTension know what sort of display this artwork was created on, and what kind of printer it was designed for?

The answer is supplied through a tagging format called Metric Color Tags (MCT): applications that support EfiColor can tag a graphics file with profile information. Then, when you import a picture into QuarkXPress, the EfiColor XTension automatically reads the MCT information from the picture and uses the appropriate device profile to transform the picture's colors when it's displayed and printed, to simulate the colors of the output device you've specified. At least that's the way it's supposed to work.

The important thing to understand here is that specifying a color with RGB or CMYK values alone doesn't really mean anything. For example, it's meaningless to say, "This color has such-and-such RGB values," because there's no basis for comparison. The RGB values as displayed on one device are totally different from those values displayed or printed on other devices. However, if you say, "This color is defined by these RGB values *as displayed on this particular device*," then you've got something to work with. Knowing both the values and the device profile sets the groundwork for knowing what the colors really look like.

Using EfiColor

OK, so now that you have an idea of what EfiColor is supposed to do, let's talk about how it works with QuarkXPress 3.2 and later, and how you tell it what you want.

Installing EfiColor

Note that EfiColor is not built into the QuarkXPress application itself. Rather, it's a combination of an XTension and some files placed in the System Folder. Therefore, in order to use EfiColor, you must first make sure it's installed properly. This isn't difficult: when you run QuarkXPress's Installer, the first dialog box asks you which file sets you want to install. Make sure the EfiColor XTension has a checkmark next to it, and the Installer does the rest.

What You Get

There are three parts to the EfiColor color-management system for QuarkXPress: the EfiColor Processor, the EfiColor DB (database) folder (which includes all the device profiles), and the EfiColor XTension itself.

EfiColor Processor. The main components of the EfiColor system are the EfiColor Processor file and the EfiColor DB folder, both of which live in your System Folder. The EfiColor Processor file is accessed by any application on your Macintosh which uses EfiColor, such as QuarkXPress's EfiColor XTension or EFI's Cachet. The EfiColor DB folder contains folders for all the profiles currently installed on your Mac, as well as ancillary files used by EfiColor. In your QuarkXPress folder are the EfiColor XTension and its help file. (EfiColor help is found under the Balloon Help menu; this is another one of those weird and unfortunate standards that Apple is trying to promote.) Note that the EfiColor processor is backward-compatible, so that you don't have to worry if some other program (like EFI's Cachet) has already loaded a processor into your System Folder.

Profiles. QuarkXPress ships with a number of profiles, including profiles for two scanners, five printing devices, and a bunch of different monitors. If your monitor's or printer's profile is not included with QuarkXPress, then you should either contact the manufacturer or EFI (see Appendix D, *Resources*, for their telephone number). The profiles cost anywhere from $129 to $329 each.

For example, QuarkXPress comes with the SWOP-Coated profile, but there's no profile for uncoated stock. You can purchase that profile separately, or you can get it by buying either EFI's Cachet or EfiColor Works program. Monitor profiles may be available free from online services and user groups. Some monitor calibrators, such as the SuperMatch Display Calibrator, let you create custom profiles for your monitor.

Remember that in order to transform colors correctly, the EfiColor XTension must have profiles available for whatever monitors, color printers, and whatnot that you're using.

▼ ▼

The EfiColor XTension

The EfiColor XTension adds many dialog boxes and commands to QuarkXPress. Rather than tackle them on an item-by-item basis, we'll take you on a tour of how we think you'll most likely use the XTension's features.

Although the range of choices you can specify with EfiColor seems daunting, you can break EfiColor's choices into three broad categories: telling it about your monitor, telling it about your printer(s), and telling it how it should modify colors within your document. When the EfiColor XTension knows all these variables, then it can correctly transform color between color spaces and gamuts, resulting in closer color matching between all the devices.

Telling EfiColor About Your Monitor

The first step in getting consistent color is to tell EfiColor about your monitor. When EfiColor is turned on, the Display Correction checkbox is active in the Application Preferences dialog box under the Edit menu (or press Command-Option-Shift-Y). You can then turn Display Correction on or off, and select the profile for your monitor from the popup menu (see Figure A-2).

Because EFI's monitor profiles are designed to work with properly calibrated monitors, your screen color looks the best when

you have calibrated your monitor to match the values specified in the reference card for your monitor's profile (these reference cards come with the profiles and with the EfiColor XTension's documentation). On most monitors, in fact, if you haven't calibrated properly, or if you're using an Apple 13-inch monitor, chances are that turning on Display Correction won't make any difference. Note that Apple's 13- and 14-inch monitors are basically identical.

Telling EfiColor About Your Printers

The next step in the consistent color game is to tell EfiColor what printer you're printing to. Of course you don't need to do this until you're actually ready to print a proof or your final piece. You give EfiColor this information in the Page Setup dialog box. (See Figure A-3 for the LaserWriter 8 version of the dialog box; see Chapter 10, *Printing*, for LaserWriter 7 dialog boxes). The EfiColor XTension adds two items to the Page Setup dialog box: one popup menu for selecting the desired EfiColor profile, and another for specifying the percentage of gray component replacement (GCR) you want to use. If you've selected a color printer from the Printer Type popup menu, the XTension also changes the checkbox labeled Use PDF Values to Use EfiColor Screen Values.

EfiColor Profile. After you use the Printer Type popup menu to select your printer, you can use the EfiColor Profile popup menu immediately below to select that device's profile. However, note that you should always choose the profile associated with the printer you've selected. If you select the QMS ColorScript from the Printer Type popup menu, then you should always pick a ColorScript profile, too. (EfiColor helps you out by making an educated guess as to which profile you want.) If you select a profile that isn't set up for the printer—for example, if you select SWOP-Coated—you'll probably end up with garbage.

Figure A-3
EfiColor in the Page
Setup dialog box
for LaserWriter 8

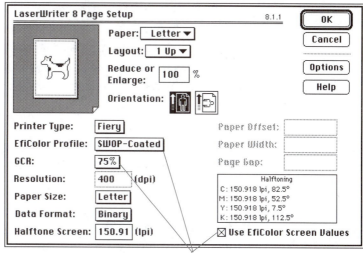

EfiColor output controls

In the future, you may be able to choose a different profile so that one printer can simulate another—like a CLC 500 outputting colors that look like they're from an offset press. Note that the Efi-Color Profile popup menu changes, depending on what printer type you have selected. If you're printing to an imagesetter (which, by definition, prints only black and white), you can't select a profile for a color printer.

Gray Component Replacement (GCR). If you select a SWOP-Coated or other four-color-process profile, QuarkXPress lets you specify a value for Gray Component Replacement (GCR). You can choose zero, 25, 50, 75, or 100 percent. This process replaces areas of neutral gray that are made up of cyan, magenta, and yellow inks with equivalent tints of black. The two greatest benefits of GCR are saving ink on long press runs and creating richer, crisper dark areas.

Some people argue that EfiColor's GCR isn't precise enough for high-quality work. If you feel that way, you probably want to use a different program for your color separations, such as Color Access or Photoshop. For most color work, one of these five GCR values is reasonable. Typically, leave this set to about 75 percent.

When you set GCR to 100 percent, you often lose some of the soft, natural-looking shadow areas because black is replacing almost all the cyan, magenta, and yellow tones.

The key to GCR is that it only works for RGB to CMYK conversions—and curiously enough, they don't talk about this in the documentation. Colors and images that are already specced in the CMYK color model don't get adjusted at all. If you specify a GCR value, QuarkXPress either applies those GCR values to your process-color separations or simulates the effect when printing to a color printer.

EfiColor or PDF Screen Values. Whenever you select a color printer in the Printer Type popup menu, QuarkXPress changes the checkbox labeled Use PDF Screen Values checkbox in the Page Setup dialog box to Use EfiColor Screen Values. When this checkbox is turned on and you're making color separations, QuarkXPress prints your document using the halftone screen frequency and angle values built into the EfiColor profile, rather than using either QuarkXPress's built-in values or those in the PDF or PPD. We prefer to use the EfiColor values, but it's really up to you.

Regardless of whether you check the box, angles and screen frequencies are displayed in the Halftoning field at the lower-right corner of the dialog box.

▼ ▼

Tip: QuickDraw Printers. If you're using a QuickDraw (rather than PostScript) printer, you can still specify an EfiColor profile. Once you've selected a QuickDraw printer in the Chooser, you can access an abbreviated Page Setup dialog box. Turn color printing on with the radio buttons, and select the EfiColor Profile you want from the EfiColor Profile popup menu. If the profile reference card for your printer profile has instructions for Special (or Printer) effects, make sure to apply them in this dialog box before proceeding with printing. Also, you'll get more accurate color if you use the inks and papers specified on the printer's profile reference card.

▼ ▼

Tip: Turn Off Calibrated Output. If you're using the EfiColor XTension, we recommend that you turn off Calibrated Output in the Print dialog box. Some people use the calibrated output feature to adjust for dot gain, but the way that QuarkXPress handles it just isn't as powerful as other calibration software such as the Precision Imagesetter Linearization Software from Kodak. Whatever the case, if you leave Calibrated Output on, then it may further adjust your color correction, messing up what the EfiColor XTension is trying to do.

▼ ▼

Telling EfiColor About Pictures

Once you've told EfiColor about your monitor and printer, you need to tell it a little about the pictures you're importing. You can do this in several ways, but when you import a picture, typically you'll assign it a profile and rendering method in the Get Picture dialog box.

Selecting a Profile

The EfiColor XTension adds two popup menus to the Get Picture dialog box (see Figure A-4). These popup menus let you assign both an EfiColor profile and a rendering style to pictures as you import them (we'll explain what rendering style is in just a moment). If a picture didn't have a profile or rendering style assigned to it, then EfiColor couldn't transform its colors because it wouldn't know what to transform *from* (it doesn't know what the colors are *supposed* to look like). Therefore, no color matching would be possible. Again, the point is that when you tell EfiColor where the image came from, here in the Get Picture dialog box or elsewhere, you're telling it how the colors should really look.

For instance, when we scan an image on our Hewlett-Packard ScanJet IIc, we can assign the ScanJet IIc profile when we import

Figure A-4
The Get Picture dialog
box's EfiColor controls

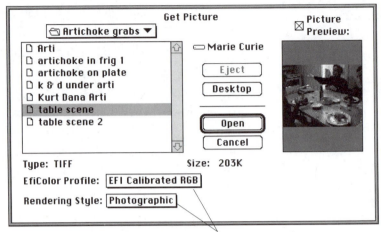

EfiColor picture-import controls

it into a picture box. EfiColor then knows not only the RGB values in the image but also what device created those values—hence, what the colors really look like.

In general, you should select a profile that corresponds to how the picture was saved. EfiColor is smart enough to examine the format of a file and only display acceptable profiles. That is, it lets you choose process-color profiles such as SWOP-Coated only when you're importing a CMYK image, and RGB color profiles when the image is stored in an RGB mode.

You can change the default settings (the ones that come up automatically) by going to the EfiColor Preferences dialog box (see "EfiColor Preferences," page 634).

Note that if the picture you're importing has a Metric Color Tag (MCT) attached to it, the profiles popup menu automatically changes to that profile. Also, the profile's name is displayed with an underline, just to show you that it's a special case. You can change to a different profile if you want to, but we wouldn't advise it.

Rendering Style

What are rendering styles, anyway, and how do you know what kind to assign to a picture? The *rendering style* of a picture tells EfiColor how to convert colors in a picture when the gamut of your printer isn't big enough to print those colors. For example, it's easy to pick an RGB color that cannot be printed in CMYK on a press. So the EfiColor XTension can transform that color into a color that a press can print. EfiColor has two methods for converting colors like this: Photographic and Solid Color.

Photographic. If the image you're importing is a scanned photograph, you probably want to use the Photographic rendering style. That seems obvious enough. But why?

When EfiColor needs to transform a color into a smaller gamut, it has to deal with colors that fall outside that gamut—and their relationships to other colors. Photographic rendering compresses the entire color range of your picture to fit into your printer's gamut (see Figure A-5), maintaining the balance of color throughout the picture. All the colors in the picture change, but they maintain their relationships to each other, resulting in a more true-to-life rendition of color photographs.

Balance, it turns out, is often more important to maintain in photographic images than the colors themselves. For example, the colors in a picture of a face can be pretty far off, but as long as the colors maintain a relative balance—among the skin, the eyes, the hair, for instance—our eyes adjust to it fine.

Solid Color. If your picture contains only a few colors that must be matched as closely as possible between your proofs and your final output, select Solid Color for the rendering style. When Solid Color is selected, colors in your image that are within the output device's gamut stay just the same; no color adjustment is made. Any color that is outside the printer's gamut gets mapped to the nearest possible color.

You end up with fewer colors using the Solid Color rendering method, because some colors are mapped to the same values as existing colors. Most colors don't change at all, and every color is mapped to its closest equivalent. The relationship between colors changes, but that's less important with a non-photographic image.

Figure A-5

Solid versus Photographic rendering

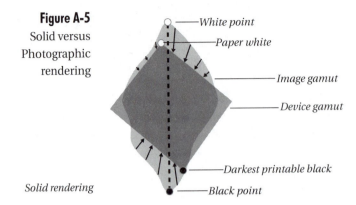

Solid rendering

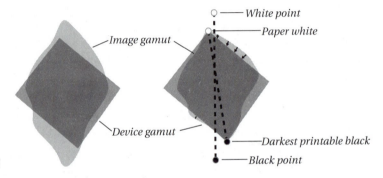

Photographic rendering

Images from FreeHand or Illustrator that have been turned into TIFFs are often perfect for Solid Color rendering (especially if they don't include graduated fills), because you want the colors to be as close as possible to your original specifications. On the other hand, if you specify that a photograph should be transformed with Solid Color rendering, the colors in the picture that are inside the printer's gamut will be maintained perfectly, whereas any color outside the printer's gamut will be mapped, throwing the balance way off.

Changing the Profiles for a Picture

What happens if you've imported a picture, and then realize you've chosen the wrong profile or rendering style for it? You could reimport the picture and spend a lot of time (importing pictures takes somewhat longer with EfiColor; see "Before You

Use EfiColor," page 639), or you could simply select the picture and choose the Profile command from the Style menu. The Picture Profile dialog box (see Figure A-6), has the same two popup menus—Profiles and Rendering Styles—as the Get Picture dialog box. Simply change the values to whatever you want.

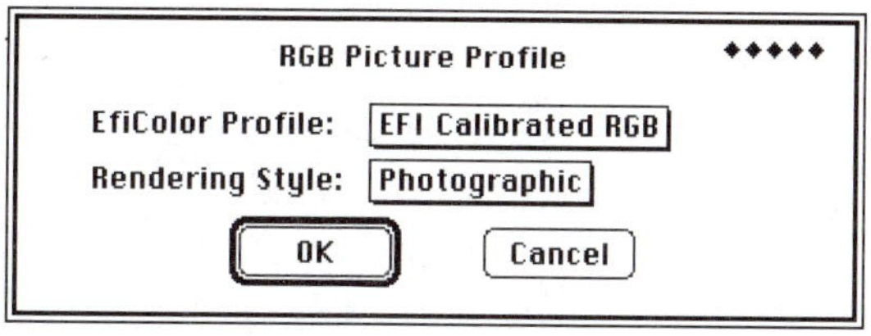

Figure A-6
The Picture Profile
dialog box

If you want to change a lot of pictures at the same time, you can use the Profile Usage dialog box (see Figure A-7), found under the Utilities menu. You look for and replace profiles in much the same way that you identify and update missing pictures or fonts. The Profile Usage dialog box contains information about your document's pictures and profiles, and lets you replace profiles quickly.

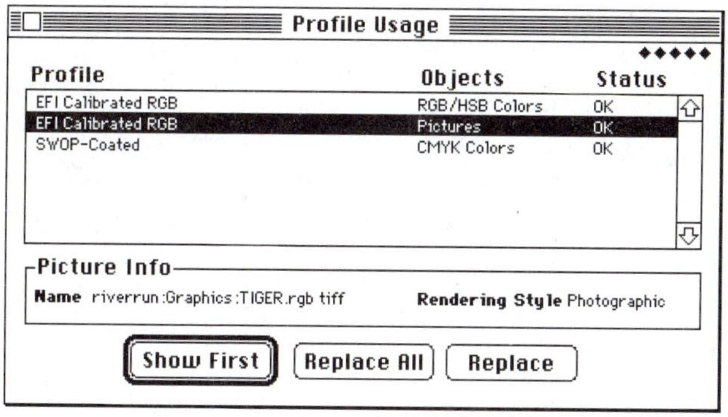

Figure A-7
Profile Usage
dialog box

Profile. The first column in the Profile Usage dialog box lists all the profiles used in the current document. Even if you don't have any items in a document, the default profiles for RGB and CMYK images are always listed in the dialog box. Note that a profile can be listed more than once, depending on the kinds of objects to which it's applied. For example, all the QuarkXPress items that have a profile assigned to them are listed, as are all the pictures that have a certain profile, and so on. That makes it easy to change all of one kind of object from one profile into another.

Objects. These are the kinds of color models to which a profile's been applied in a document. The possibilities are pictures (imported graphics), RGB/HSB colors, and CMYK colors. Note that you can't apply the same profile to both RGB/HSB and CMYK colors.

Status. Status in the Profile Usage dialog box means almost the same thing as in the Picture Usage dialog box. However, instead of pictures, QuarkXPress is looking for the availability of profiles. OK means that the necessary device profile has been installed in your EfiColor DB folder (usually in the System Folder); Missing means it's not there (see "Missing Profiles," page 637).

Show First. The Show First button is active only when you've selected a profile that's applied to pictures. Clicking it takes you to the first picture in a document that uses the profile you've selected. After you've displayed the first picture, the button changes to Show Next, so you can use it to cycle through all the pictures that use a specific profile. Of course, if there's only one picture in a document that uses that profile, the button remains Show First. And, just as in the Find/Replace dialog box, you can change the button back to Show First at any time by holding down the Option key.

Replace All. This button lets you automatically replace the selected profile for the entire object class on that line. For instance, if you want to change all the CMYK pictures in your document from a SWOP profile to a Canon CLC 500 profile (we don't know why you'd want to do this), you can select SWOP pictures and click Replace All.

This dialog box has the familiar popup menus for selecting profiles and rendering styles. If you've selected a profile that's missing, it appears grayed-out in the menu. If you've chosen Replace All for several pictures which use different rendering styles, then the word Mixed appears in the Rendering Style popup menu.

Note that it's possible to change the profiles for RGB/HSB Colors and CMYK Colors. If you change these, QuarkXPress goes through your document and changes both the colored elements (the ones you colored in QuarkXPress) and the default profiles in the EfiColor Preferences dialog box.

Replace. This button is only active when you've selected a profile that is applied to pictures. First, use the Show First or Show Next button to select the picture you want to change. Next, click the Replace button. This brings up the Replace Profile dialog box (see Figure A-8).

Figures A-8
Replace Profile
dialog box

```
┌─────────────────────────────────────────────────┐
│   Replace Profile "EFI Calibrated RGB"   ♦♦♦♦♦    │
│            for TIGER.rgb tiff                     │
│                                                   │
│   EfiColor Profile:  │Apple 13" RGB│              │
│   Rendering Style:   │Solid Color│                │
│                                                   │
│        ( ⦿ OK  )        ( Cancel )                │
└─────────────────────────────────────────────────┘
```

Picture Info. Underneath the profiles section of the Profile Usage dialog box are two pieces of information titled Picture Info. These fields display the path leading to a selected picture file, and the rendering style applied to it. Note that you can only see Picture Info after you've selected a picture with Show First or Show Next.

Pictures EfiColor Understands

The EfiColor XTension really only works with images that QuarkXPress itself can change. If you remember Chapter 8, *Modifying Images*, QuarkXPress can only modify TIFF, Paint, and bitmap-only PICTs. That means that EfiColor won't even attempt to transform any EPS, DCS, or object-oriented PICTs. (As we finish this edition, EfiColor Works is in beta. It includes an XTension for color management of EPS images.)

Although the EfiColor XTension can recognize EPS and DCS images that have had MCTs assigned to them, you can't change the profile for these pictures, nor can you assign a profile to EPS or DCS files that don't already have one. Also note that the profile name for an MCT file will appear grayed out if it's a profile not available on your system.

By the way, the EfiColor documentation says that when you print your document using the preview image of an EPS or DCS picture—that is, if either the high-res picture is missing or if you turn on Low Resolution in the Print dialog box—then EfiColor transforms the colors of the preview image. They're wrong. Apparently, that's the way that it was originally supposed to work, but it doesn't yet. Oh well. Perhaps someday.

Editing Colors in QuarkXPress

Objects that are built or colored directly in QuarkXPress can always be transformed by the EfiColor XTension. The key to making this work is correctly setting up the Edit Color dialog box for each color (see Figure I on the color pages). The EfiColor XTension adds a few new features to this dialog box: Target, Gamut Alarm, and Rendering Style.

Note that every color you create in the Edit Color dialog box is automatically assigned a profile based on the defaults you have selected in the EfiColor Preferences dialog box. If the color is set using CMYK, TruMatch, FocolTone, or Pantone ProSim, Quark-XPress assigns the default CMYK profile. If the color is set using RGB, HSB, or one of the color-matching systems (Pantone, DIC, or Toyo), the RGB/HSB default profile is assigned.

Target

Before you even begin to pick a color, you should select a profile from the Target popup menu; the profile that you select should be for your final output device. If your final artwork is on a Canon

CLC 500 with a Fiery RIP, then select Fiery. If your final destination is a four-color press run, then select SWOP-Coated or another four-color process.

You want to set the target profile because that's how EfiColor figures out whether colors are within the device's gamut (see "Gamut Alarm," below). If Gamut Alarm is turned off, then you don't need to set the Target—in fact, you can't; it's grayed out.

Gamut Alarm

The Gamut Alarm checkbox lets you turn on and off one of the neatest features of the EfiColor XTension. The Gamut Alarm shows you whether the color you specify can be printed on the target printer. There are two ways to see if your color is within gamut: the alarm and the gamut map.

Alarm. The alarm shows up as a little triangular icon with an exclamation point in it, sitting to the left of the New or Old color field. When either the old color (if you're editing a color) or the new color is out of gamut (outside of the possible color spectrum of the target device), the Gamut Alarm icon appears, warning you that the color cannot be printed on the target printer.

The Gamut Alarm takes two profiles into consideration: the default color profile and the target profile. The EfiColor XTension essentially compares the two profiles to see if a color created with the default profile falls inside the gamut of the target profile. If it doesn't, then the Gamut Alarm shows up. (The default profile set up in the EfiColor Preferences dialog box is the "source" profile automatically assigned to all colors created within the program.)

Gamut outline. The second part of the gamut-alarm system is the gamut outline, which is basically a graphic representation of the available color gamut. If you're specifying an HSB, RGB, or CMYK color, the EfiColor XTension displays a red border on the color wheel that shows you where the edges of the gamut are (see Figure A-9). Note that if you select a color near the border of the gamut outline, the outline and the triangular gamut alarm might

Figure A-9

Gamut outlines

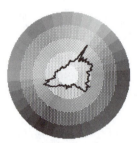

RGB gamut map
Target: SWOP-Coated

RGB gamut map
Target: Fiery/CLC

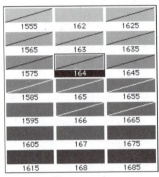

1555	162	1625
1565	163	1635
1575	164	1645
1585	165	1655
1595	166	1665
1605	167	1675
1615	168	1685

6-a	6-a1	6-a2
6-b	6-b1	6-b2
6-c	6-c1	6-c2
6-d	6-d1	6-d2
6-e	6-e1	6-e2
6-f	6-f1	6-a5
6-g	6-d5	6-b5
6-h	6-e5	6-c5

Pantone gamut map
Target: CLC/Fiery

TruMatch gamut map
Target: QMS ColorScript

disagree. The gamut alarm is always the final judge in these dis-
putes. If you're using color swatches—such as TruMatch, Pantone, or FocolTone—diagonal lines cross out swatches that don't
fit in the gamut of the target device.

Once again, this gamut outline takes into account both the
default color profile (the one assigned to the color) and the target
printer. If you change one or the other, the gamut outline
changes, too.

Rendering Style

There are times that you want to specify a color, even if the gamut
alarm says it won't print correctly. Perhaps you don't have the correct profile to select in the Target popup menu, or perhaps you trust
yourself more than you trust the Gamut Alarm. (Who are we to stop
you if you know what you're doing?) If the color you pick *is* inside

the gamut, you can just leave Rendering Style set to Solid (see "Rendering Style," page 624). However, if it isn't, you need to think for a moment about which rendering style you want.

You can determine which rendering style to choose based on the source of the color, and how you'd like it to finally appear.

Solid Color. If you're specifying a color using a matching system such as TruMatch or Pantone, you probably want your final output to appear as close to those colors as possible. In that case, you should probably select Solid Color in the Rendering Style popup menu. Likewise, if you're trying to match a color to one in an imported graphic that's assigned the Solid Color rendering style, you should also apply the Solid Color rendering style to your color. Otherwise, the picture's color and the color you're creating may not match properly.

Photographic. On the other hand, if you're creating a color that matches one in a continuous-tone image (a photograph or piece of artwork), you should use the Photographic rendering style (see "Matching Colors in Pictures," below). EFI advises that if your color doesn't fit in your device's gamut, you should use the Photographic rendering style. However, while this does maintain the overall color balance of your document's colors, it may not provide the best match to that one particular color.

Note that Rendering Style is only available when your color is set to Process Separation. That's because EFI figures that if you're creating a solid Pantone spot color, you're always going to want Solid rendering. So that's what it gives you. We can't think of a reason why you wouldn't want this, but if you like, you can call them and complain.

▼ ▼

Tip: Matching Colors in Pictures. Suppose you've imported a picture into your QuarkXPress document, and you want to create a color in QuarkXPress that exactly matches a color in the picture. If you've used named colors such as TruMatch or Pantone to define a color in a graphics program, all you need to do in QuarkXPress is specify the same color with exactly the same name, and assign to it the same rendering style and device profile as you've used for the picture.

However, if you're matching colors in a scanned photograph, you have a little more work cut out for you. The problem is that your graphics program probably defines color differently than QuarkXPress does. Therefore, you have to convert the color from the way it's described in your graphics program to the way it's described in QuarkXPress.

1. Open the image in a program like Photoshop.

2. Use the eyedropper tool to find the exact RGB or CMYK values of the color you want to match. Write those values down (yes, you may have to actually use a pen—so much for the paperless office).

3. In QuarkXPress, create a color based on those RGB or CMYK values and set it to the Photographic rendering style. Some photo-manipulation programs define RGB colors as numbers on a scale from zero to 255, while QuarkXPress defines them as percentages from zero to 100. To convert the former to the latter, divide the color's value by 255 and multiply by 100; for example, the color value 129 divided by 255 and multiplied by 100 gives you 50.6 percent.

4. Make sure the Process Separation box is checked.

EfiColor Preferences

The EfiColor Preferences dialog box found under the Edit menu is the Command Central of the EfiColor XTension (see Figure A-10). Here's where you get to set the default EfiColor settings, and also tell EfiColor how and when to do its thing. Note that this preferences dialog box works just like QuarkXPress's: if a document is open, then any changes you make in the EfiColor Preferences dialog box change only that document. If no documents are open when you change something, then that change is good for all subsequent documents you open (older documents retain their settings). Let's examine what the various options in this dialog box do.

Figure A-10
EfiColor Preferences
dialog box

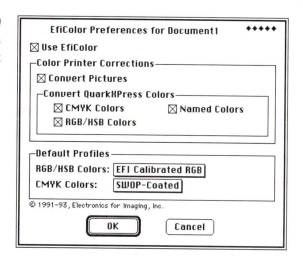

Use EfiColor. The first item in the EfiColor Preferences dialog box is Use EfiColor. This is almost entirely self-explanatory: check this box to turn EfiColor on; uncheck it to turn EfiColor off. When EfiColor is off, the XTension doesn't transform any colors at import, on screen, or during printing. Note that any pictures you've already imported into your document look the same on screen even after you turn EfiColor off. You can't reset them to a pre-EfiColor screen rendition without re-importing them. However, if EfiColor is turned off, the picture won't get transformed when you print the document.

Convert Pictures. The upper half of the EfiColor Preferences dialog box is labeled Color Printer Corrections, which is really a misnomer because it's not just color printers that this affects. The changes you make in this area of the EfiColor Preferences dialog box alter the way that EfiColor transforms colors anytime you use a profile.

The first checkbox in the Color Printer Corrections section is Convert Pictures. Check this box to have EfiColor convert colors in imported graphics. (EfiColor can't transform EPS graphics without the EfiColor EPS XTension that ships with EfiColor Works.)

Convert QuarkXPress Colors. The three checkboxes in the Convert QuarkXPress Colors section let you tell EfiColor which kinds of colors created within QuarkXPress to convert. Turning these on or off won't change anything except tint builds or colors that you actually specify in QuarkXPress. The three checkboxes are labeled CMYK Colors, RGB/HSB Colors, and Named Colors.

The trick here is that while Pantone is a named color, Tru-Match and FocolTone are not. Why? Because the Pantone system actually defines a set of distinct, named ink colors, whereas Tru-Match and FocolTone colors are built from CMYK inks.

Default Profiles. The Default Profiles section of the EfiColor Preferences dialog box lets you set which profiles the EfiColor XTension will use whenever you create new colors or import artwork. You can always override these profiles for individual pictures later on, but you can't override them for colors created within QuarkXPress (those are always assigned with whatever you have Default Profiles set to). Also, pictures that already have profiles assigned to them via an MCT ignore the default profiles on import.

If you don't want CMYK colors that you specify within Quark-XPress to be modified at all on your final output device, be sure to select that device's profile as your CMYK default. For instance, we send our final film to an imagesetter and then take that film to a printer, so we set the default CMYK profile to SWOP so that Efi-Color doesn't alter the CMYK values when we print; it assumes that they're already set up for that output. However, when we print to a color printer, the colors *do* get altered (because we're not printing seps).

▼ ▼

Missing Profiles

Progress is never without a price. When you use a new typeface, you have the burden of making sure your service bureau and other people who receive your documents have that typeface as well. It turns out that EfiColor profiles are the same way. When you send a file to another QuarkXPress user, you must make certain that your recipient has legal copies of all the EfiColor profiles you've used in your document (see "Tip: Moving Profiles," below). Just as with fonts, the Collect for Output feature (see "Collect for Output" in Chapter 10, *Printing*) doesn't automatically assemble all the profiles used in a document. You're on your own.

What To Do

So let's say you've received a document without all the needed profiles. How will you know? What can you do about it? If you're familiar with the ways QuarkXPress handles missing fonts and pictures, you should have no trouble coping with missing profiles.

When you open a document that uses one or more profiles that are not in your EfiColor DB folder, an error message appears indicating the missing profile or profiles (see Figure A-11). If you can obtain the proper profile from someone—perhaps from the person who sent you the QuarkXPress document, or from EFI, or maybe even from the manufacturers of the device—then do it (see "Tip: Moving Profiles," below). You just have to put that profile in your EfiColor DB folder (in the System Folder), and re-launch QuarkXPress.

However, if you can't obtain the profile, you can either go ahead and do nothing about it, or replace it with a profile that is active in your system. If you're only interested in a fast and dirty proof—let's say you're proofing page geometry or type—then there's no need to replace profiles. But if you need EfiColor's color matching, you must replace the missing profiles (see "Changing the Profiles for a Picture," earlier in this chapter).

Figure A-11
Mising profile alert
when opening a
document

mycolormag.qx3.2 uses profiles not
installed in your EfiColor DB folder:
• Fiery/Canon CLC500(CT)

[OK]

▼ ▼

Tip: Moving Profiles. EfiColor profiles are little pieces of software. And, like most pieces of software, they're copyrighted. Like fonts, you're not really supposed to copy them from one machine to another; you're supposed to buy a profile for each machine you use. However, EFI is being somewhat generous: they're encouraging people to freely pass around monitor and scanner profiles. But restraint is the name of the game when it comes to output device profiles.

While this isn't supposed to be a commercial plug, EFI really makes its money through sales such as these, and we shouldn't begrudge them that. If you need a profile, call them (their number is in Appendix D, *Resources*) and order one. Plus, EfiColor Works includes a large set of output profiles, for a variety of color-proofing and printing methods.

▼ ▼

Printing with Missing Profiles

If you attempt to print a file which uses profiles that are missing from your system, you'll get an alert very similar to the one displayed when you try to print a document with missing or modified pictures (see Figure A-12).

You've got three options in this dialog box: click Cancel to cancel the print job, click OK to proceed with printing despite the missing profiles, or click List Profiles to display the missing profiles. If you choose the third option, you get the Missing Profiles dialog box, which is almost identical in appearance and function to the Profile Usage dialog box, with a few changes.

First of all, it only displays missing profiles and the items associated with them. There's also an OK button, which lets you

Figure A-12
Missing profile alert
when printing a
document

proceed with printing the file regardless of the number of profiles you've replaced. And there's a Cancel button, to stop replacing profiles; however, this also stops your print job.

▼ ▼

Tip: Pre-EfiColor Documents. It's easy to take advantage of EfiColor's capabilities in a document created by previous versions of Quark-XPress. When you open an old document, the EfiColor XTension may be turned off. Go to the EfiColor Preferences dialog box and turn it on. Once EfiColor's on, and you've chosen appropriate profiles for the colors in your document, EfiColor converts the document's colors when you print. If you're not happy with the results, and would rather have the colors print as they did in previous versions of QuarkXPress, simply turn EfiColor off in the Preferences dialog box.

▼ ▼

Before You Use EfiColor

If EfiColor is so great and wonderful, why would you ever *not* want to use it? There are lots of reasons, from speed to consistency. In this last section of this appendix, we want to look at a few things that you should think about before you jump in and start using EfiColor.

Performance

Every time EfiColor transforms a color to look right on your screen or your proofing printer or your final output device, the color gets *processed*. That takes time. And time is something we often don't have enough of.

Imagine converting a 30Mb image from RGB mode to CMYK mode in Photoshop or Cachet. It takes a long time, doesn't it? Efi-Color can't do it any faster than those programs can, and that's just what it's doing when you print an RGB TIFF from Quark-XPress with EfiColor turned on. And it has to make that conversion every time you print.

Similarly, when you import any sort of TIFF or PICT image, EfiColor has to convert the screen preview to look correct on the screen. That can easily make importing pictures take four or five times as long as without EfiColor. You can speed the process a little by pressing the Shift key while clicking Open in the Get Picture dialog box; that imports the picture at half the screen resolution. However, you then get a low-resolution image to look at on the screen, which sort of defeats the purpose.

Dollars and Sense

Time, we all know, is money. And if EfiColor is a hit to our performance at output time, then money may be at stake. Many service bureaus were bewildered soon after EfiColor first appeared on the scene and they started receiving documents that suddenly took five or 10 times longer to output than they expected. The culprit? The EfiColor XTension. Although EfiColor Cachet had been released months before, and Quark had announced the incorporation of EfiColor support with the XTension, service bureau operators weren't prepared for the amount of time it could take to convert even moderately sized RGB images to CMYK separations. Their clients weren't prepared for the kinds of charges they could incur.

Service bureaus usually charge a per-page amount which is based on how much an average page takes to imageset. If your job goes over their time limit—say 10 minutes—the service bureau might charge you an additional per-minute charge that can range as high as two or three dollars a minute. If you're relying on the EfiColor XTension to separate your RGB images, and that adds an additional ten minutes to the print time . . . well, you can see the dollars adding up.

So for those of you who operate a service bureau: warn your clients in advance about using the EfiColor XTension (or against it, if you aren't willing to support it). You might suggest they make PostScript dumps, so it's *their* machine time that's being eaten. For those of you using a service bureau, investigate the excess-time charges to see if it's worth the extra money. Plus, you should consider doing PostScript dumps rather than paying per-minute charges on the service bureau's Mac.

▼ ▼

Tip: Don't Remove the XTension. With most XTensions, if you don't want to use what they have to offer, you can just delete them or, better yet, move them into another folder so that QuarkXPress can't "see" them. However, you shouldn't do this with the EfiColor XTension. That's because Quark actually uses part of the XTension to make preview images for pictures on your screen. So if you don't want EfiColor to function, don't move the XTension; just turn it off in the EfiColor Preferences dialog box. By the way, QuarkXPress still functions fine if you *do* move the XTension. It's just that it functions even better when the XTension is around.

▼ ▼

Incompatible File Formats

What happens when you import a color EPS image from Aldus FreeHand or Adobe Illustrator onto your page, and surround it with colors that you've matched exactly within QuarkXPress? You can throw the words "matched exactly" out of your vocabulary. The colors you assign in QuarkXPress are transformed according to the profiles you choose. The colors in the EPS image are not transformed at all. Why? Because the EfiColor XTension never transforms EPS or DCS images. Never ever. Well, maybe their screen-preview renditions, but probably not even those.

You have to understand the philosophy of EPS images. The whole idea of Encapsulated PostScript originally, was that a program should never need to look "inside" them, and should certainly never change anything inside them. Therefore, according to this school of thought, EfiColor should never adjust the color inside an EPS or DCS image.

The problem is that people use these images all the time, and go nuts when the colors don't match what comes out of Quark-XPress. Unfortunately, we don't really have a good answer for how to handle this situation right now. If you're using images built with Photoshop or Cachet, you can assign either an MCT or an EfiColor profile to the image (EFI is selling color-separation sets for Photoshop that help you do this; they're also included with EfiColor Works). This allows EfiColor to adjust the screen preview image to more closely match what will come out of the printer. It has no effect on the printed output, however.

Until Aldus and Adobe decide that color management is really worth their time (read: their customers want it), we'll all just have to hold our breath and wait for a whole, integrated color-management system.

▼ ▼

Tip: Don't Convert Pantone Colors. A funny thing happens if you convert a Pantone color to RGB and then try to print it using EfiColor: you get a different color. Now theoretically, this shouldn't happen. However, because of the way that EfiColor "sees" Pantone colors, you get a more accurate Pantone color by leaving it in Pantone mode (you *can* change the name if you want) rather than converting it to RGB or CMYK.

▼ ▼

The Problem with OPI

Trying to manage color with OPI images (see "OPI" in Chapter 10, *Printing*) is even more difficult than with EPS, because Quark-XPress never even touches the final image. Remember that with OPI, you export PostScript from QuarkXPress without image data; only little tags are inserted in the PostScript saying what the name of the image is and how it should be adjusted (rotation, cropping, and so on). That's why QuarkXPress is called an *OPI writer*.

The PostScript that comes from QuarkXPress gets passed on to another program—an *OPI reader*—that interprets the PostScript and substitutes high-resolution images where appropriate. Until OPI readers include the EfiColor color-management system, those images will never get adjusted properly. The solution, again, is to adjust for the target printer when the image is scanned or saved from a image-manipulation program.

Quality of Character

Blends, vignettes, split fountains . . . whatever you want to call them, they're a hassle when it comes to color management. The problem, put simply, is that you can get a nice clean blend, but the colors may be slightly different than you want. Or you can get a weird looking blend, but the colors all along the blend will be as close as they can be to the original colors. EfiColor takes the first path, making the blend look smooth. We agree that this is probably what people want, but you need to at least be aware of it so that you don't get snagged down the road.

▼ ▼
Pros and Cons

When it comes right down to it, we think that the EfiColor XTension is not only really cool, but it can be incredibly useful. However, it obviously has limits and isn't for everyone all the time. One of the most important things to note is that color management works best when you're comparing apples to oranges rather than to salmons or coffee beans. You'll get a better idea of a final color by looking at a printed color proof than at the screen. You can calibrate all you want, and you'll still always get a more reliable image from a printer than from the screen. It still won't be a perfect match to your final output, of course, but it's that much closer. Clearly, as with just about every other aspect of desktop publishing, WYSIWYG color is a relative thing.

MAC/PC FILE TRANSFERS

Although many hard-core Macintosh users may prefer to wear cloves of garlic (or rubber gloves) when working with Windows machines, the fact can't be denied that there are lots more Windows boxes out there than Macs, and an increasing number of them are running the Windows version of QuarkXPress.

From the outset, QuarkXPress for Windows could open files saved by QuarkXPress for Macintosh version 3.1. But it was a one-way trip until QuarkXPress for Macintosh version 3.2 came out. Now, at last, there's decent two-way transferability of files between Macs and Windows machines.

Or is there? While bringing files from your Macintosh to a PC and back again is possible, it certainly isn't a no-brainer. In this section, we want to take a quick tour of the obstacles in your way when transferring files.

You May Get There From Here

There are many ways of transferring files between PCs and Macs, and QuarkXPress is happy with the result no matter how you move your files. If your Macintoshes and PCs share a hard drive on a network through any kind of network software, you can just copy the file, or open it directly. If you have a modem link between the machines, you can use your communication program's file-transfer capabilities.

However, the most popular way to transfer files is via floppy disk. This is easy enough to do if your Macintosh can read 1.44Mb floppies. This kind of floppy drive is called either a SuperDrive or a High-Density Floppy Drive; almost every Mac and PC sold in the past five years has one. The high-density drives can read from and write on PC-formatted floppies as well as the standard Macintosh-formatted ones.

However, even though the Macintosh can theoretically read and write PC floppies doesn't mean that the operating system itself can. Every Macintosh comes with a simple program called Apple File Exchange that lets you access PC disks. Unfortunately, you can only read and write on them from within the program (the disks don't show up on your desktop). When you're running Apple File Exchange, you can insert a PC disk, select files to copy or remove, and so on. The built-in "default translation" usually works pretty well. When you quit Apple File Exchange, any PC disks in your drives are automatically ejected.

This is admittedly kludgey, albeit free. If you're doing a lot of PC transfers on your Macintosh, you should purchase one of three relatively inexpensive programs. PC Exchange, DOS Mounter, and AccessPC let you insert disks and they appear right on the desktop, like Macintosh disks. All three of the programs let you map PC extensions (see "PC Naming Conventions," below) to Macintosh application file types so that you can double-click on PC files to open them (again, just like from Macintosh disks). DOS Mounter and AccessPC let you mount PC SyQuest cartridges, too.

If you're moving a file from your Macintosh and you don't have a PC-formatted floppy handy, you'll have to format one. Any 3.5-inch floppy will do, even one labeled "Mac formatted." In fact, the Macintosh reads PC disks that were formatted on a Macintosh even better than if the disks were formatted on a PC. All the programs we just talked about can format PC disks, too.

There are also programs that let PCs mount Macintosh disks. Our colleague Bob Weibel—the co-author of the Windows version of *The QuarkXPress Book*—uses Mac-in-DOS with pretty good results. However, for various technical reasons we don't really need to get into, we typically recommend that people store and transfer their files using PC disks only.

▼ ▼

Tip: Translations vs. Universal File Formats. While you can now move QuarkXPress files between Macs and PCs, there's still no such thing as a "universal" QuarkXPress document format that's identical on both platforms. Each time QuarkXPress opens a document saved on the opposite platform, it must translate the file. The file name doesn't change, but—as one Quark tech-support person puts it—"the dirty bit is on," so you should immediately save the file. And since some information gets lost (as we'll describe) or needs to be fixed when you translate files, we'd recommend you keep your cross-platform transfers to the minimum necessary to finish a job. Remember: fewer translations equals less clean-up.

▼ ▼

File Names, Types, and Creators

The first hassle (though minor) in moving files from one platform to another is that PCs and Macintoshes "see" files differently. On the Macintosh, every file has several attributes attached to it, including file type and creator. These are four-letter keys that tell the Macintosh what sort of file it is and what program generated it. For example, when you double-click on a file, the Mac looks at the file's creator to see what application to start up.

In the PC world, it's simpler: no file types, no file creators—only file names. PC files all have names that are eight-dot-three. That means that the name can be no longer than eight letters, followed by a period, and ending with a three-letter extension; for example, "8LTRBLUS.TXT". This extension provides all the information (and it ain't much) about the file's type and creator.

Moving from PC to Mac

When you're trying to open a QuarkXPress for Windows document on a Macintosh, you must make certain that the document has either the correct three-letter extension or the correct file type and creator. If you move a file from the Macintosh to Windows without the right extension, and can't see the file in an Open dialog box, you should switch the File Types popup menu option in the dialog box to "All Files *.*".

If you move the file from Windows to the Macintosh, the document icon may look like a blank page. But as long as the file has the proper DOS extension (".QXD") QuarkXPress can still "see" and open the file on the Macintosh.

If you want the file to open when you double-click on it in the Finder, or your PC disk mounter doesn't map the extensions to the proper file type, you have to change the file type and creator. The easy way is to open it with QuarkXPress, if possible, and do a Save As, renaming it if you want (otherwise it overwrites the original). This works as long as the file is a proper QuarkXPress file and has the ".QXD" file name extension.

You can also use utilities such as PrairieSoft's DiskTop (in the Technical mode), Apple File Exchange, ResEdit, or the shareware program FileTyper to manually change the type and creator. Also, the three utilities for mounting PC disks all have a cool feature that lets you automatically assign a proper file type and creator based on the PC file's three-letter extension (see Figure B-1).

So what are the appropriate file types and creators? Documents created in QuarkXPress 3.1 or later on the Macintosh have a creator code of "XPR3"; documents created in version 3.0 have a creator code of "XPRS". The file type depends on what kind of file it is: documents are "XDOC", templates are "XTMP", and libraries are "XLIB". These are the only kinds of documents on your Mac that will ever show up in QuarkXPress's file-opening dialog box; you'll never see a Microsoft Word or FileMaker Pro file in there, because QuarkXPress filters out all files except those which have these three specific file types.

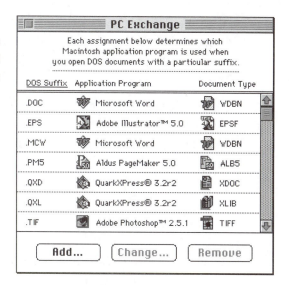

Note that when you open a QuarkXPress for Windows file on the Macintosh, the Open dialog box tells you that it's a PC file; when you click Open, it gives you a message saying it's converting the file.

Mac to PC: Filenames and Extensions

Macintosh users who are used to 31-character names will find the eight-dot-three filename limit for PC files absolutely infuriating. It's one of the reasons why David's PC has a big dent in its side, right about at kicking level. Of course, for some PC users, that limitation is just another creative opportunity. You can use almost any combination of characters you want in a PC filename except punctuation (see "Tip: Careful with Your Naming," below).

It's really easy to change the file type and creator for a PC file while on either a Macintosh or a PC: just change the three-letter extension. The eight-character filename can be whatever you want, but the relevant extensions are ".QXD" for documents, ".QXL" for libraries, and ".QXT" for templates. If you assign a legal name to a document using these extensions, it should be easily opened by QuarkXPress for Windows, either by double-clicking in the Windows File Manager, or from QuarkXPress for Windows. You can also select "All Files *.*" in the popup menu in the Open dialog box, and it shows even files with the wrong extensions.

If you're using a PC-disk mounter or a file server, you can save a little trouble by always adding the dot-three extension name to the Macintosh file. Even though the first part of the name is truncated, the dot-three part is retained. (This won't work when you use communications programs or other means to transfer files.)

If you don't give a proper DOS name and extension to a document while it's still on the Macintosh, its name appears strangely altered and truncated when it's transferred to the PC.

▼ ▼

Tip: Careful with Your Naming. The filenaming conventions used by the Macintosh and the PC are so different that, for some people, they become the central issue in cross-platform compatibility. Macintoshes use 31-character names, while PCs use eight characters plus three extension characters after a period (eight-dot-three). The two most dangerous traps in file naming are name size and characters within the name.

▶ **Name size.** When you move a document from the Macintosh to the PC and the name of that document is longer than eight letters or numbers (alphanumerics), the operating system generates a new name in eight-dot-three form. For instance, if you use Apple's PC Exchange software on the Macintosh, and move a document called "David's Document" to a PC floppy disk, the name comes across as "!DAVID'S.DOC".

If you open this file in QuarkXPress for Windows and then save it again with the same name, chances are the file will return to the Macintosh with its full name. That's because PC Exchange (and other similar utilities) stores the full name inside a directory called "RESOURCE.FRK". However, if you either move the file to a disk without moving "RESOURCE.FRK" or save the file with a different name, the full name is lost.

▶ **Characters.** The only character you can't use in a Macintosh file name is a colon. That's because the Macintosh operating system uses colons internally to keep track of file paths (what files are within what folders). DOS-based systems, however, use lots of these "internal" characters for all sorts of stuff. That means you can't use spaces, question marks, asterisks, slashes, backslashes, equal signs, plus signs, or angle brackets in DOS filenames.

Because of these limitations, we reluctantly recommend that—if you have to move your files around a lot—you use the lowest common denominator for all your graphics and document names. That means only PC filenames (if you can stand it).

▼ ▼

Tip: Previewing DOS Names on a Macintosh. If you're using PC Exchange or another PC disk mounter, you can see how a document name is going to look when it gets to the PC. First, copy it to a PC disk, then select it in the Finder and choose Get Info from the File menu (Command-I). At the top of the dialog box, you can see the name of the file. Click on it and it switches to the eight-dot-three PC name. Click on it again and it switches back.

▼ ▼

What Does (and Doesn't) Transfer

Physically moving your QuarkXPress files between platforms and successfully opening them is only half the job of transferring files. In general, all page-layout, text, and picture information comes across just fine in either direction, as do any changes you've made to the General, Typographic, and Tool preferences. Also, any colors, style sheets, and H&J settings you've defined in the document generally transfer without a hitch. However, you'd better be aware of what doesn't get transferred. QuarkXPress documents on each platform are almost identical, but that "almost" can trip you up if you're not careful.

Frames. We have very mixed feelings about the Frame Editor program on the Macintosh. It can do some nice things, but mostly we think it fits best in the Trash. But who listens to us? Lots of people are using custom frames and getting reasonable results. However, do note that Frame Editor doesn't exist in QuarkXPress for Windows. In version 3.1 of the Windows version, custom frames didn't even show up correctly on the screen, let alone print properly. Now, in version 3.3, any special frames you've created or assigned on the Mac will travel over to the PC, and usually show up and print fine. Of course, you still can't edit those bitmapped frames, as there's no Frame Editor utility on the PC (thank goodness).

Color-contrast adjustment. In QuarkXPress for Windows, you can't adjust the contrast of color bitmap images, as you can in the Macintosh version. However, any brightness/contrast adjustments you've made to a bitmap in the Mac version won't be lost when you transfer your file to Windows; you just can't change them unless you bring them back to your Mac. But let's get serious for a moment: why would you want to use QuarkXPress's color-contrast functions? (See Figure J on the color pages for an example of this feature.)

XPress Preferences. On the Macintosh it's called XPress Preferences; on the PC it's called "XPRESS.PRF". Either way, they do the same thing, but are not interchangeable. There is no good way to move a preferences file from one platform to the other, but fortunately, that's not something that many people need to do. All the document-level preferences are saved within the document itself, and almost all of them translate perfectly (Auto Ligatures is one notable exception). When you open a Macintosh file in QuarkXPress for Windows, you're almost always prompted with the "XPress Preferences does not match" dialog box. We typically just click the Use Document Preferences button.

Character-set remapping. Probably the biggest hassle in transferring files between platforms is character-set remapping. The problem here is that Macintosh and Windows font character sets don't match completely. All the basic "low-ASCII" characters (letters, numbers, punctuation) map just fine, but special characters can sometimes get messed up.

If a special character shows up in both Macintosh and Windows typefaces, QuarkXPress does its best to map it correctly. But there's only so far it can go. Table B-1 shows a list of characters that are commonly found in Windows and Macintosh fonts that have no equivalent on the opposite platform (unless you switch to a special typeface). You can also use this table to select special characters if you know you'll be printing on the other platform.

Table B-1

Special characters that map differently in Windows and on the Macintosh

Windows	ANSI code ◄ maps to ► Macintosh		ASCII Code
Š	138	ˇ	255
š	154	π	185
¦	166	ı	245
²	178	≈	197
³	179	Δ	198
¹	185	◊	215
¼	188	⁄	218
½	189	fi	222
¾	190	fl	223
Đ	208		240
×	215	˘	249
Ý	221	˙	250
ý	253	˝	253

Note that the mathematical symbols that seem to appear in every PostScript font on the Macintosh are often just mapped from the Symbol font. So unless the font you're using has the math symbols built in—unfortunately, there's no good way to find this out without Fontographer or another font-editing program—several characters won't transfer correctly. In Table 4-11 on page

318, we've listed where each math character is found in the Symbol font, so you can search and replace before transferring a file to Windows (or use those characters to begin with).

Ligatures. One of the biggest losses in going from Mac to PC is ligatures. The "fi" and "fl" ligature characters on the Macintosh are not to be found on the PC. That's right: any ligatures used in your Mac document will go bye-bye when they're opened by Quark-XPress for Windows. Because QuarkXPress for Macintosh (version 3.2 and later) has automatic ligature support, there's little reason to actually insert the ligature characters any more (See "Automatic Ligatures" in Chapter 4, *Type and Typography*). However, if you've used them for some reason or aren't sure whether you did, you should use Find/Change to change them back to normal character pairs before transferring the file.

QuarkXPress for Windows doesn't have the automatic ligatures feature, so when you move a Mac file with automatic ligatures turned on over to Windows, your ligatures go away (and because of that, you may get some text reflow; see Figure B-2). But at least you have fi and fl, rather than the "½" and "¾" characters Windows substitutes, and that you have to search for and replace.

Figure B-2
Windows warning
about automatic
ligatures

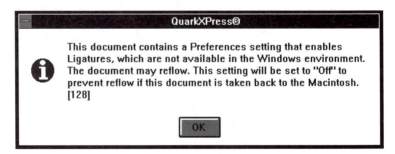

The second solution is to use a program like Fontographer or FontMonger to either mess around with the ASCII numbers assigned to ligatures in Windows fonts, or to create new fonts on the PC that include the ligatures. We only recommend the latter if you're particularly brave, and aren't working on a deadline. (This doesn't work with auto ligatures, however, because QuarkXPress wouldn't know where to find them in the character set.) Or you can resort to Expert Set fonts from Adobe and other font vendors, and use the Find/Change dialog box to replace fi's and fl's with Expert Set characters. The Expert Set characters are typically the same in both Macintosh and Windows versions of the fonts.

Font metrics. Font metrics describe the width of each character in a font, and the kerning pairs for those characters. On the Macintosh, PostScript fonts store their character widths and kerning pair values in the screen font files. Macintosh TrueType fonts store metrics entirely in the printer font (the screen fonts contain just bitmaps). On the PC, the font metrics for PostScript fonts are located in ".PFM" files; metrics for TrueType fonts are found in ".TTF" files.

However, no matter where the metrics of a font may reside, you need to be aware that the metrics of a PC font may differ from those of a Macintosh font, even if they're from the same company. We don't know why this is, but it's certainly a major problem when moving files back and forth. If the metrics change, then the text in a document reflows. Sometimes this is hardly a problem, and other times it can spell hours of work.

It's a good idea to have a printed proof of a Macintosh document handy after you've imported it into your Windows version of QuarkXPress (or vice versa). That way you can check to see if the layout got altered in the transfer. When proofing the document, look for any widows or orphans that may result from minute differences in font metrics. If you notice a problem, you can sometimes adjust the spacing parameters through kerning or tracking to compensate for the differences in font metrics.

Forbidden fonts. There are certain typefaces that exist only on Macs or only on Windows machines. You should never use them on documents that you intend to shuffle between platforms, unless you enjoy spending a lot of time staring at the Font Usage dialog box. On the Macintosh, avoid using system fonts such as Chicago,

Geneva, Monaco, and New York (a good rule, with some exceptions, is never to use a font named after a city). In Windows, avoid
fonts such as "Helv", "System", or "Tms Rmn".

If you open a file and its document fonts are missing, Quark-
XPress gives you a chance to immediately change them. If you
click Continue, it ignores the missing fonts and replaces them with
a default font. If you click List Fonts, you get the Missing Fonts dialog box (see Figure B-3). You can then select fonts that you want
changed, and replace them with a font that you do have available.

Figure B-3
Missing Fonts
dialog box

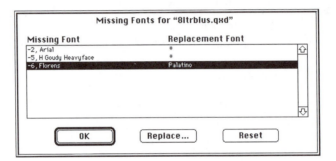

QuarkXPress catches missing fonts if you've used them anywhere in your document, including in style sheets and on master
pages. In other words, even if you don't use a particular style sheet
or master page anywhere in your document, you get notified.

Kerning information. If you've spent a lot of time making kerning
tables within QuarkXPress's Kern/Track Editor, you might want to
save the hassle of doing them over on another platform. We're
happy to note that you can move the kerning information from
the PC to the Macintosh (or vice versa) by exporting the information as a text file (click the Export button in the Edit Kerning dialog
box) and importing into the other program (use the Append button in the same dialog box in the Windows version).

The only problem with this technique is that the fonts on each
platform are sometimes different, even if they're the same font
from the same company—just like with the metrics. Therefore,
the kerning used on the Macintosh might not always apply precisely to the PC font.

Transferring Graphics

The last (but certainly not the least) of your problems when transferring files between platforms is graphics. In fact, this is one of the least-understood issues in cross-platform compatibility. The basic problem is that graphics, like fonts, are described in different formats on the two platforms.

The good news is that QuarkXPress is smart enough to do most of the translation work for you. No matter which platform you're working on, QuarkXPress can import files in either IBM or Macintosh format. It simply doesn't care whether you're on a Macintosh importing a PC format file, or on a Windows machine importing a Macintosh TIFF file. This is great, but if you're using pictures in your documents, you still might have some work ahead of you.

Graphic links. The first and most basic problem is that links to EPS and TIFF images can get messed up in the transfer—the Picture Usage dialog box shows the image as either missing or modified. You can remove the chance of this happening by keeping the images in the same folder as the QuarkXPress document you're opening, and by always naming files with the PC eight-dot-three convention.

If you send a document to the PC to work on it temporarily, the picture links to the files on the Macintosh are retained (as long as they aren't changed on the PC). Similarly, links within Windows documents are retained when you move a file to the Mac and back, as long as you don't change them on the Mac. The trick is to update a picture only if you're certain you won't be sending the QuarkXPress file back to its original location, or if you absolutely must print with current versions of artwork, regardless of the platform.

EPS screen previews. The next thing you need to be careful of is how images are transferred between the Macintosh and PC. Screen previews are handled differently on each platform. When you create an EPS with Macintosh preview, the screen preview is stored in what's called the file's resource fork. The problem is that re-source forks don't exist on the PC, so if you move the graphic over and try to import it into QuarkXPress for Windows, you can't see the preview. In fact, without a screen preview, all you see on the screen is a gray box where the picture should be. Note that the picture still prints properly, even if you can't see it on screen.

There are two solutions to this problem: importing into Mac XPress and then transferring the document to the PC, or saving the picture as PC EPS.

▶ **QuarkXPress for Macintosh.** Because QuarkXPress saves a pre-view image of each picture within your documents, you can bring those documents to the PC and still see the pre-view image on screen. The images are linked to the EPS files, so even if you move the image *and* the QuarkXPress document to the PC, you can print properly, as well. Even auto-runarounds are transferred okay.

▶ **PC EPS files.** The second solution for the EPS screen preview problem is to give your EPS files PC previews. Adobe Illus-trator, Aldus FreeHand, Adobe Photoshop, the LaserWriter 8 driver, and a slew of other programs let you save or export a file as a PC EPS—with a preview that's saved in the data fork rather than the resource fork. Therefore, when you move it over to the PC, you can import it, screen pre-view and all. This is our favorite method because most of the Macintosh and PC applications that we use can read or import this PC format just as easily as the Macintosh for-mat. Again, this is working with the lowest common de-nominator, but there's hardly a penalty paid except for the anemic file name.

File names and extensions. Just as QuarkXPress documents need to have their names changed, graphics that get transferred to the PC also need appropriate file extensions, or else the program won't be able to recognize them as graphics. That means they'll often need to be renamed to have a three-letter ".TIF", ".EPS", or ".PCT" extension (see *The QuarkXPress Book, Second Edition for Windows,* for more information on this).

File types to avoid. Some formats to avoid: PICTs contained in Mac documents and transferred to PCs sometimes print poorly or not at all (just like on Macs!), and, WMF pictures in PC documents may (similarly) not print correctly on the Mac. Sometimes EPS images from the Mac look wrong on screen after they're transferred. Often if you simply re-import the picture, it'll clear up any problems. And when it comes to edition files (with Publish and Subscribe), forget it. If you've subscribed to an edition file on your Mac, that link gets lost for all time as soon as the file is opened and saved by QuarkXPress for Windows. Similarly, if a Windows user has made OLE links (the Windows version of Publish and Subscribe) within a Windows document, that information will be lost when the document's opened on a Macintosh.

▼ ▼

Tip: Transferring Libraries. We love it when the folks at Quark say things like, "You can't do that." We take it as a personal challenge. For example, Quark said, clear as a Texas sky in June, that you can't move libraries from the Macintosh to the PC. After some intense thought, sweat, and caffeine, we found that Quark really should have said, "You cannot move libraries from the Macintosh to the PC *easily.*"

If you have a library that you absolutely must take from one platform to another, you can. However, it's what we call a kludge—pronounced "kloodge." (Our friend Steve Broback recently came up with the best definition of "kludge" we've heard: "It's Yiddish for 'duct tape.'" It's something you use at the last moment to fix a problem, but for which you hope there'll be a better solution soon.) The trick is in understanding what libraries really are.

A QuarkXPress library is simply a QuarkXPress document with some additional preview and labeling information. That means that you can actually open a QuarkXPress library within Quark-

XPress for Windows as a document. If you move a Macintosh library to the PC, open it by either selecting "All Types *.*" in the Open dialog box or by changing the file name extension to ".QXD".

What you see is each library entry on a separate page of a big QuarkXPress document. Each page is the maximum size allowable—48 by 48 inches. If you don't see the library entry, look in the upper-left corner of the page. Now you can open a new library in QuarkXPress for Windows and use the Item tool to drag the old page items into the library, one page at a time. Of course, this is not only a pain in the lower back , but you also lose all your labels.

Modern Myths

We have very mixed feelings about cross-platform compatibility. On the one hand, moving documents and graphics between Macintoshes and PCs sometimes works like a charm. On the other hand, sometimes the strangest things happen and it can cause horrible nightmare scenarios (of course, right on the eve of a deadline). Although QuarkXPress is very similar on the two platforms, and tries its hardest to make cross-platform issues irrelevant, there are clearly issues that are beyond its control.

Nonetheless, because more and more people are finding themselves in that "third-culture" arena—where they are literate on two or more platforms—transferring files is becoming almost commonplace. With the introduction of PowerPC machines that can emulate Windows, we may see an explosion of compatibility problems—or (thinking optimistically) solutions. Whatever the case, with a dose of experience and a patient hand, you may soon find yourself making the process more or less painless.

APPLE EVENT SCRIPTING

We on't know why, but some people just like doing things the hard way. Like those people who insist on doing long division on the back of an envelope rather than using a calculator. Or like folks who scroll around their documents using the scroll bars instead of using the grabber hand. Yes, it's weird, but they seem happy enough; so why bother them by telling them there's an easier way to do it?

We don't know about you, but it drives us crazy doing repetitive tasks in QuarkXPress. Remember that time when you had to select each paragraph in your document and apply the proper style sheet to it? First paragraph, "Heading"; second paragraph, "Subhead"; third paragraph, "Description" . . . "Heading", "Subhead", "Description" . . . and so on, and so on, throughout your 200-page file. It was just one of those monotonous, robotic tasks that we do every day when working on our computer. It seemed like the only way to do it at the time.

We're here to tell you that the days of repetitive monotony; the weeks of dull mechanical routines; the months of dreary, unchanging keystrokes—are over! There are two things that can alleviate these woes: macros and scripting.

Macros Versus Scripting

Before we get into the details of scripting, let's take a quick look at how macros and scripting are similar and different.

Macros. Let's just get one thing perfectly clear: if you don't own and use a copy of QuicKeys, you're just not being efficient in your work. QuicKeys lets you create macros to tell QuarkXPress—and any other program or utility you use, including the Finder—what to do. A macro can be an action or sequence of actions. It can be triggered by a keystroke, by the time of day, or by selecting it from a menu. We have lots of QuicKey macros on our computers. To start QuarkXPress, David presses Control-Q. To create a new text box, put it six picas from the top of the page, and automatically jump into the measurement palette, Eric presses Control-Option-N. To clone an object, we both like Command-= (same as it is in Aldus FreeHand). All of these work on our machines because we've made QuicKeys macros.

Any menu item you can select, any key you can press, any printer or server you can choose on the network, any event you can cause to happen, can be assigned a macro keystroke or be built in to a sequence macro. They're incredibly helpful and can speed up work enormously because they're easy to create and use.

Scripting. There are two basic differences between macros and scripts. First, whereas macros automate particular tasks that you perform on a computer (like select that menu item, push that button, type such-and-such, and so on), scripts let you sneak in the back door of the program and control it from behind the scenes. Second, scripts have flow control. Flow control is a programming term that means you can set up decision trees and loops (you can do some conditional branching and looping with QuicKeys, but it's a pain); plus, scripts often contain variables. You can do much more complex and interesting things with scripting than you can with simple macros.

When people talk about scripting, they're usually talking about either program-specific scripting, or AppleEvents. AppleEvents is a feature in Macintosh System 7 that lets programs communicate with and control one another.

The rest of this chapter is going to focus on AppleEvents-based scripts and scripting, including a description of a bunch of scripts that come with QuarkXPress and on the goodies disk you can get from Peachpit (see the offer in the back of the book). Note that scripting is usually done with either AppleScript or UserLand Frontier, but QuicKeys 3.0, HyperCard, and several other programs also support scripting. So in theory you can control Quark-XPress using scripts sent from FileMaker.

What Comes with QuarkXPress 3.2 and Later

The files that you have in the QuarkXPress folder on your hard disk depends on what checkboxes you selected when installing the program. If you left the two items labeled AppleEvents checked, then you have a full complement of scripting information available to you. If you didn't leave the items checked, you should either run the installation process again with *just* those two items checked, or you can copy the relevant files and folders off the AppleEvents disk manually.

You can find important reference information in the For Advanced Scripting folder. If you're planning on doing your own scripting, you'll want to print out the Chapter 4 document and keep it around for reference (this document is a supplement to Quark's scripting documentation). It was over 75 pages at last count, but you'll need it if you want to script. If you enjoy reading text on screen, you can read the other documents "online"; they're much shorter.

The AppleEvents Preview folder in the gamma of version 3.3 contains the Frontier Runtime application, "Runtime.root," and sample documents. The "Runtime.root" file provides you with a bunch of sample scripts, which are described in Quark's own documentation in greater detail that we can get into here. Note that in order to get the Frontier Scripts menu in QuarkXPress (if you want to use Quark's scripts), you'll need the Frontier Menu Sharing XTension in the same folder as QuarkXPress (with version 3.3, it can go in the XTension folder inside the QuarkXPress folder).

▼ ▼

How to Get Scripting Stuff

Unfortunately, you can't write your own scripts with the files and XTension that come with QuarkXPress 3.2 and later. In order to write or edit scripts, you need to use UserLand Frontier (for UserTalk or Frontier scripts), the AppleScript Editor (for AppleScript scripts), CE Software's QuicKeys (version 3.0 or later), or some other scripting application such as HyperCard.

AppleScript. As it turns out, each of these methods means an additional cost. In this chapter, we're focusing on AppleScript, and all of the scripts listed here are in AppleScript. At this time, the only way you can run or edit them (or write your own) is by purchasing the AppleScript Disk. The Apple Programmer's and Developer's Association (APDA) sells this for about $20. You can call them at (800) 282-2732 from within the United States, (800) 637-0029 in Canada, and (716) 871-6555 from elsewhere in the world.

Other utilities. You can buy UserLand Frontier via mail order for about $185. QuicKeys 3.0 is available mail order for about $90 .

Books. We've only seen two books so far that cover AppleScripting. *The Tao of AppleScript* and *Danny Goodman's Guide to Apple-Script* are reasonably good introductions to scripting, and both of them come with a disk that includes AppleScript. This is probably the cheapest way to get the AppleScript system extension, along with some good information about how to use it. Unfortunately, neither of the books covers working with QuarkXPress.

Writing a Script

The best way to learn how to script QuarkXPress is by first looking at and deconstructing other people's scripts, and then trying, trying, and trying again. Scripting is programming. If you've ever programmed in another computer language, you'll probably pick up AppleScript or UserLand Frontier pretty quickly. If not, it may take you a while to start to understand the concepts. We know it's a cop-out, but there's neither time nor space to teach you how to program.

What we *can* do here is give you a pretty solid foundation on which to build your scripting knowledge. Then you can go off, look through the scripts we've included in this chapter and on the goodies disk, and try your own.

The main concepts you've got to understand are the object model, hierarchies, properties, and events.

The Object Model

Let's get one thing clear: the object model is not a feminist theory regarding the objectification of fashion models in magazines. Rather, the object model describes the way in which AppleEvent scripting works. That is, in order to "get" scripting, you have to think in terms of the object model.

The object model says that everything is an object that you can "talk to." For example, an object might be a text box, or a word, or a picture, or a whole document. Objects can contain other objects; for instance, a page can contain text boxes, which can contain paragraphs, which can contain words.

There are currently 27 kinds of objects in QuarkXPress. Each of these objects can be controlled or queried through basic scripting commands. Although some objects are intuitively similar to items you know in the program, others are a little more obscure. For example, while text boxes and words are clear and you can easily get a handle on what they are, Master Document and Delimit Table may be confusing at first (see "Difficult Objects," below).

▼ ▼

Tip: Naming Objects. One of the coolest things about scripting QuarkXPress is that you can name most objects. You can always identify *text box 1* or *line box 3*, but a text box could be named "Lead story" and a line box could be called "VerticalLine." That makes it much easier to choose and manipulate those objects later, especially in a complicated script.

▼ ▼

Hierarchies, Elements, and Containers

You can't understand the object model and scripting without understanding hierarchies, elements, and containers. Most objects in QuarkXPress contain other objects; for example, a paragraph contains words, which contain characters.

Hierarchies only get complicated when you can't remember what contains what (see Figure C-1).

In working with hierarchies, two terms are helpful to keep in mind: elements and containers. An element is an object that is contained within another object. A text box is an element of a page, for instance. A container is simply an object that has elements. The application QuarkXPress is a container for windows, documents, and so on.

Properties

Every object in QuarkXPress has properties that you can look at and—usually—change. A property is a characteristic of an object. For example, picture boxes have the properties of background color, rotation, placement on the page (called *bounds*), and many more.

Figure C-1
AppleScript hierarchy

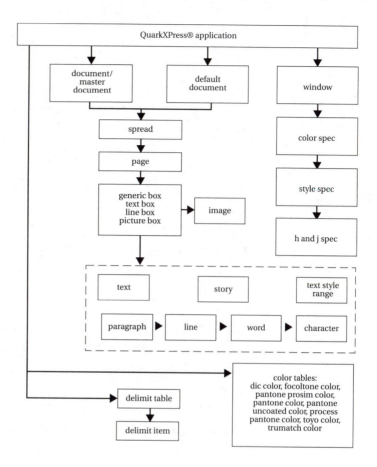

Difficult Objects

As we noted earlier, some objects in QuarkXPress are pretty confusing if you haven't seen them before. Objects such as document and picture box are pretty simple, so we're just going to focus on the objects in QuarkXPress that may raise your eyebrow.

Application. The highest object in the hierarchy is Application. You can think of the QuarkXPress application as being the program with or without a document open; changes made here are application-wide and affect any document that is open or is created from then on. Note that if you've renamed your copy of Quark-XPress, then the application's name might be different for you.

Window. When we first saw the Window object, we thought it was the same as Document. However, that's not the case. Documents are only open documents, but you can control all the windows in QuarkXPress. That includes the palettes and dialog boxes. You can't do a lot to them, but you might want to write a script that brings all the palettes up and then sets their sizes and positions on the screen.

Default document. The default document contains all the preferences and settings for the New dialog box, the H&Js, colors, and style sheets—whether a document is open or closed. For example, with no document open, you can set the default document's settings when you create a new document, it will be configured in that way.

Spread. Spreads are pretty obvious, but here's an important point you should know: items on the pasteboard fall in the domain of the spread, but not the page. So if you change all the text boxes in a spread to red, then the text boxes on the pasteboard get changed, too. If you do it to all the objects on a page, only the ones that are touching the page get changed.

Also note that a spread includes all the pages that are next to each other. So you can have a one-, two-, three-, or more page spread.

Master document. The master document is the object that contains the master pages. What does that mean? Dave Shaver, one of the engineers at Quark who worked on scripting, describes the master document as being a "shadow" of the document. You can talk to its light side (the actual document pages), or you can talk to its dark side (the master pages).

For example, if you want to change something on a master page, you need to address a page or spread in the master document. You can't change a master page from within the document itself. Of course, master document 1 and document 1 are just different parts of the same document. Note that if you're going to change something throughout a document, it's best to change it on the master document pages first, then, if necessary, on the document pages.

Color spec. There are no color objects in QuarkXPress, only color specs (or color spec objects, to be precise). Color specs don't contain anything, but have various properties. You can assign a color spec to something, but Quark was nice enough to let you get by with a shortcut: assigning the color name directly. That's easier and more intuitive. For instance, instead of *set color spec of generic box 1 to "Red"* you can say *set color of generic box 1 to Red*. This applies the properties of the color spec "Red" to the box.

Style spec. A style spec—similar in operation to a color spec or H&J set—is the object that describes a style sheet. While you can set the style sheet of a paragraph to style spec Normal, it's easier to take the shortcut and just say *set style sheet of paragraph 1 to "Normal"* (QuarkXPress is smart enough to know what you mean). However, if you want to change the style sheet itself, you have to specify that it's a style spec.

H&J set. Like color spec and style spec, the H&J set contains particulars of a hyphenation and justification style.

Horizontal and vertical guide. You can create and manipulate ruler guides through scripts by working with horizontal and vertical guides. In fact, you can even do things to guides that you can't do in the program itself, such as make them undeletable or immobile (see "Unmoveable guides," in "Sample Scripts," below).

Line. Don't get fooled: a line is not a rule. That is, the line object is a line of text, not a graphic on the page. The line extends from one margin to another in a column of text.

Line box. For some obscure reason which we haven't figured out yet, lines (graphic rules) are considered "line boxes." We suppose that makes it all consistent under the hood, but it can kind of screw you up if you're not careful.

Image. Each picture box can contain one image. You import a picture into a picture box by setting the image to a file on disk. For example: *set image 1 to alias "myharddisk:picture1"*.

Generic box. A generic box is any page item in QuarkXPress, whether a picture box, a text box, or a rule (see "Line box," above). This can be helpful, especially when you're telling a whole bunch of items to do the same thing. Note that generic boxes take the lowest common denominator properties of all objects. For instance, line boxes don't have a *bounds* property, so neither do generic boxes.

Story. A story is, as you may have guessed, all the text in a chain of boxes. Each text box has only one story (but, of course, a story can go through many text boxes). The nice thing about stories is that you can find and change things in them really quickly (much faster than if you specify changes by word, for instance).

Text style range. Most people who use QuarkXPress don't think in terms of ranges of text. However, there are times when you want to select a block of text that contains all the characters with the same text formatting. This block is called a text style range. Note that the "same formatting" includes color, font, style, kerning, tracking, and so on. As soon as the style changes in any way, QuarkXPress breaks the text down into another style range.

For example, if you set the color of every word whose color is "Red" to "Blue," it won't catch the words whose first three characters happen to be green (because QuarkXPress only looks at the first character of a word when assessing color). However, if you set all the text style ranges whose color is "Red" to "Blue" then, all the red characters change.

Delimit table. The delimit table object seems like one of the more obscure items in scripting, but in fact it's relatively straightforward. The delimit table contains 256 delimit items that tell QuarkXPress what delimiters to use to distinguish where words begin and end. That is, a space, a period, a comma, an exclamation point, a semicolon, and so on, each mark the beginning or end of a word. Each item in the delimit table is an ASCII character specified using its decimal code. Item 32 is a space (ASCII 32), for instance, and so on.

You may never or rarely use this, but it can occasionally come in handy. For example, if you wanted to work with tab-delimited text from a spreadsheet or a database, you can set up your QuarkXPress document so that only a tab character counts as a word delimiter. Then, when you want to do something to the second word in the story, QuarkXPress does it to the second "field," from one tab to the next, whether there is one word or 20.

Note that once you change the delimit table, it will stay that way until you change it back or until you quit QuarkXPress. Also note that changing the delimit table doesn't actually change the way you can select words from within the program—by double-clicking with the Content tool, for instance (we think this would be a really cool feature).

Each delimit table item can be set to one of four possibilities: *not word member, can start or end or be contained in word, can start or end word,* or *can be contained in word.* For example, a quotation mark would probably be set to *can start or end word* because you don't want it to be in the middle of a word. You can set the delimit item by specifying it between quotation marks (e.g., ":") or by its ASCII character number. If you're specifying invisible characters, it's easiest to call them by their QuarkXPress name; a tab is "\t", a return is "\r", and so on.

Events

The way you alter an object is by sending QuarkXPress an "event." Event is AppleEvents-ese for a command. If you want to set the tint of a line on page four, you need to send an event. In Apple-

Script format, the event would be a "set" command (such as *set shade of line box 1 of page 4 to 30*). Events are relatively simple, and there aren't that many of them, but there are enough so that we can't really discuss them here. My only suggestion is that you pick them up as you go along by looking at other scripts and seeing how they work.

▼ ▼

Looking at a Script

Our next step in learning how to script with QuarkXPress is to look at an actual, real, live script and see how it works. We're going to focus on AppleScripting here because Quark focuses on Frontier in their documentation (we always like to be a little ornery).

The following script creates a document, puts a headline on the page (in a tinted red box), and then adds a story and a picture. The story and the picture are pulled from disk files, and the picture box is set to a background of None and a Runaround of Automatic. Let's see how it's done.

```
tell application "QuarkXPress®"
--CREATE AND SET SOME VARIABLES *******
    set picboxwidth to 170
    set picboxheight to 200
    set pgheight to (9 * 72)
    set pgwidth to (7 * 72)
--MAKE A DOCUMENT *******
    set properties of default document 1 to ¬
        {page height:pgheight as points, ¬
        page width:pgwidth as points, ¬
        automatic text box:true, ¬
        left margin:"8p", ¬
        right margin:"1\"", ¬
        bottom margin:"5p", ¬
        facing pages:true, ¬
        ligatures on:true}
    activate
    make document at beginning
    set view scale of document 1 to ¬
```

```
                 fit page in window

--MAKE PAGE 1 *******
        tell page 1 of document 1

--TEXT BOX 1 *******
            make text box at beginning
            tell text box 1
                set bounds to {"6p", "8p", "2\"", "6\""}
                set color to "Red"
                set shade to 40
                set vertical justification to centered
            set properties of story 1 to ¬
                {contents:"The QuarkXPress Book ¬
                    from Peachpit Press" ¬
                , font:"Helvetica" ¬
                , size:29 ¬
                , leading:29 ¬
                , style:bold ¬
                , justification:centered}
            end tell

--TEXT BOX 2 ******* (automatic text box)
            tell text box 2
                set properties to ¬
                    {columns:2 ¬
                    , bounds:{"2.1\"", "8p", "49p", "36p"}}
                set story 1 to (¬
                    choose file with prompt ¬
                    "Please select a text file")
                set properties of paragraph 1 to ¬
                    {drop cap lines:4 ¬
                    , drop cap characters:1}
                set style of line 1 to small caps
                set style of line 2 to plain
                if leading of story 1 as real ¬
                    is greater than 16 then
                        set leading of story 1 to "16 pt"
                end if
            end tell

--PICTURE BOX *******
            set startpicboxy to (pgheight - picboxheight) ÷ 2
            set startpicboxx to (pgwidth - picboxwidth) ÷ 2
```

```
        tell (make picture box at beginning with properties ¬
            {bounds:{startpicboxy as points ¬
            , startpicboxx as points ¬
            , (startpicboxy + picboxheight) as points ¬
            , (startpicboxx + picboxwidth) as points} ¬
            , runaround:auto runaround ¬
            , text outset:"8pt" ¬
            , color:"None"})
            tell image 1
                set contents to ¬
                        (choose file with prompt ¬
                        "Please select an image")
                set bounds to proportional fit
            end tell
        end tell
    end tell
end tell
```

Description of the Script

If you've never programmed before, looking at that script is probably somewhat unnerving. But we assure you that scripting is not
as difficult as it looks, especially in the AppleScript language. After
reading this section, you'll probably be up and running with basic
scripting. Let's look at that script, how it works, and why.

There are two conventions that you should be aware of. First,
all comments in this AppleScript script have two hyphens before
them. QuarkXPress just ignores those lines (they're there just for
"human readability"). Second, the character that looks like a side-
ways "L" is a line-break character (its printable character is made
by pressing Option-L in most PostScript fonts, or by pressing
Option-Return in the AppleScript Editor). It comes at the end of a
line that continues on the next line. If that's not there, then Apple-
Script gets confused at the line breaks. We've used them
extensively here so that the code can all fit into this text column.

Opening. You always need to specify in the script what application
you're talking to with the *tell application* command. In this case,
"QuarkXPress®" is the way that our copies of QuarkXPress are
named. If you change the name of the program without changing
the name in the code, AppleScript won't be able to find it.

Variables. Variables are like little boxes to put something in. Each box has a name, and you can put whatever you want in it. For example, here we create and set four variables and we give them the names *picboxwidth, picboxheight, pgheight,* and *pgwidth.* Each of these "containers" is filled with a number. We'll see later what they're used for. You can set variables at any time, but in this case we want to set them at the beginning so that they're easy to find and change if we want to later.

New document. Before we create a new document, we want to set up the specs of the default document. In this case, we're setting the page height, width, margins, and so on. Note that in this area we're specifying both information found in the New document and Application Preferences dialog boxes.

To set a number of values at once, we use the command *set properties of default document 1 to.* Inside the curly brackets, we specify all the values we want to set, separated by commas. And because we're inside those curly brackets, instead of saying *set facing pages to true,* we simply say *facing pages:true,* and so on.

Note that we're using the variables *pgheight* and *pgwidth* here to specify the height and width of the default document page. If you change the values of the variables in the first section, the page of your document will be different.

The next event you see is *activate.* This simply displays the application (in this case QuarkXPress) in front of the AppleScript Editor.

And, finally, we create the document itself with the *make document at beginning* command, and set the view scale of that document. Anytime you make or create an object, you need to tell QuarkXPress where to do it. In this case, we add "at beginning" even though there is no beginning or end. Yeah, it's weird, but that's just the way it works.

The first text box. Because we want to make a text box on page one, we first specify what page we're talking to with the *tell page 1 of document 1* command. Then we move right into making a text box and filling it. First we make the text box at the beginning of the page (the upper left corner). Then we set its attributes: bounds (placement on the page), color, shade, and vertical justification.

Finally we set the contents of the text box. Here we set a number of attributes at once, so we can say *set properties of story 1 to*. Note that QuarkXPress knows which story we're talking to because of nesting. At the time it sees this event, it knows that we're talking to text box 1 on page 1 of document 1 of application "QuarkXPress®". When we're done working with text box 1, we say *end tell*.

The second text box. The next text box is the automatic text box that was already on the page when the document was created. Therefore, we move directly to setting its properties. In this case, we're setting the number of columns, the positioning, the story that goes in it, and the formatting of that text.

The event *set story 1 to (choose file with prompt "Please select a text file")* brings up a dialog box for the user to select a story from disk. You could also type something like *set story 1 to alias "myharddisk:text files:tuna story"*, which would get a specific story off the disk. (Aliases are the way to tell AppleEvents what a disk path is.)

After we have a story in the text box, the script sets its formatting. First, it gives the first paragraph a drop cap, then it sets the rest of the first line to small caps style. Note that when it does this, there's a pretty good chance that some text from the first line will spill over to the second line (small caps are often wider). So, we add a line that sets the style of the second line to plain; that way, those characters have small caps removed.

Finally, we don't want the leading of this story to be too big, so we alter it some with an *if* statement: *if leading of story 1 as real is greater than 16 then set leading of story 1 to "16 pt"*. If . . . then statements are one of the most powerful features of scripting. When we say "as real" that makes QuarkXPress convert the leading value into a real number (a number that has a decimal fraction, like 12.4, as opposed to an integer which has no fraction) that we can compare against. If the *if* statement comes up "true" (in this case, if the leading is actually larger than 16 points), then we go to the next event, which is to set the leading to 16 points. If the answer is "false," then the script skips all the way to the *end if* statement.

The picture box. Finally, we want to throw a picture in the middle of the page. We start this section by creating two more variables called *startpicboxy* and *startpicboxx*. By letting QuarkXPress do a little math for us, we can set these variables to where the picture box should originate (upper left corner) in order for the box to be centered on the page.

Next, we create a picture box at the beginning of the page and set its parameters. Note that we've used a rather nonintuitive but clever way in which to do this quickly: *tell (make picture box at beginning . . . .* This starts the *tell* event even before the picture box is made. Because the *make picture box* is inside parentheses, QuarkXPress performs that first, then recognizes that this object that it just created is the object that you were referring to when you started the *tell* operation.

Also, once again note that we have to specify that the numbers and variables in the bounds setting are set up for points, so we use the *as points* modifier.

The end. In order to end the script successfully, you need to tie off all the loose ends and close the nested tells. Here we have four *end tell*s in a row: one to finish the operation on the image, next to finish talking to the picture box, third to stop talking to page one of document one, and finally to end the tell to the application itself.

Stuff You Should Know About

Now, before you go off half-cocked with scripting ideas, let us throw a few "things you should know about" at you. This list is going to get bigger and bigger as we all learn more about scripting.

Not completed yet. As QuarkXPress 3.2 shipped—the first version to support AppleEvents beyond the basic four—there were a bunch of things left out. In version 3.2, you couldn't script libraries, groups, auxiliary dictionaries, hyphenation exceptions, box creation defaults, color pair trapping (though you can still trap object-by-object), page setup and print dialog box specifications, EfiColor XTension, blends, anchored boxes, and sections. That's quite a list! In version 3.3, they managed to include some of the missing features (for instance, you can now set the values in the Print dialog box).

Interrupting and canceling. You can always interrupt a script while it's running by pressing Command-period. Note that moving the mouse or typing on the keyboard usually won't do anything, so don't get paranoid about it. Also, remember that you can't Undo a script after it's run, so be careful and make backups.

Line boxes. In version 3.2, line boxes (what mere mortals call "lines" or "rules") can't be rotated. That is, you can't set their rotation angle; they're only specified in scripting by their end points. In version 3.3, line boxes do have a *rotation* property, but it only applies to rotating from the midpoint of a line; in other words, line modes are still not implemented.

Adding pages. If you try to add pages using the *make page at end* command you'll get a potentially nasty surprise. Pages get added into the same spread, making long spreads rather than multiple pages. To add additional pages in the document as though you were using the Insert Page dialog box, you need to make a new spread rather than a page (such as *make spread at end* or *create spread at beginning*). Of course, if you're trying to make multipage spreads, then you can just add pages.

Page names. Pages are named so you can quickly access them even if you've set sections with different pages numbers. If you want to do something to the fourth page, you can script page 4; however, if your numbering system is in roman numerals, you can also call it page "iv". The name of the page (in quotation marks) is whatever is in the lower left corner of the document window in QuarkXPress. This goes for master pages within the master document, too.

Variables. Watch out for what variables you specify within your scripts. Many of the words are already taken by QuarkXPress itself. In fact, when using AppleScript (Frontier doesn't do this) we like to set the formatting for different identifiers so that when we compile or run the script, we can quickly see what is a variable, what is an object, what's an event, and so on. You do this by selecting AppleScript Formatting from the Edit menu in the AppleScript Editor.

Hidden text. You may notice while browsing through the scripting docs that you can make text "hidden." Even though it's tempting, resist it. First of all, it doesn't really do anything to the text. Secondly, hidden text is complicated enough so that it should be kept out of scripting and left to XTension developers (who do use it occasionally).

One more thing about hidden text. There are times that you might search and replace text throughout a story and you might accidentally change some text that was hidden by QuarkXPress or an XTension. For example, anchored picture boxes have hidden text around them, and if you screw it up accidentally, weird things can happen. We can't say what you should and shouldn't do, but it's something to watch out for.

▼ ▼

More Scripts

We love scripting in AppleScript because it's so easy. Even someone like David, who has a degree in Theatre Arts (whatever that means), can jump in and start scripting away. We don't profess to be great programmers, but we do appreciate an elegant, well thought-out script. If you have one (or more) that you'd like to share with us, please send it or e-mail it to David (his address is at the end of the book).

In the meantime, we want to share a few scripts with you. We hope that they'll interest and inspire you to do your own.

Change numbers to old style. David's officemate, Glenn Fleishman, requested this first script in honor of three book designers from Yale (Howard Grala, Greer Allen, and Roland Hoover) because it's such a hassle having to search through a document and change every number to a different typeface just to get old-style numbers. In this case, all characters that fall between "/" and ";" on the ASCII chart (in other words, all numbers) get changed to a different font. This example assumes Minion is the regular text face.

```
tell document 1 of application "QuarkXPress®"
    set font of every character of every text box ¬
        of every page whose (¬
        it is greater than "/") and (¬
        it is less than ";") to "Minion Expert"
end tell
```

Delete all empty boxes. In case you're one of those people who leaves lots of empty text and picture boxes around in your document, this script will clean them up (delete them). Note that it only deletes empty boxes if the background is White (tinted or colored boxes remain). We're almost sure that there's a better way to do this, but we can't figure out how.

```
tell document 1 of application "QuarkXPress®"
    repeat with pg from 1 to count of pages
        tell page pg
            repeat with x from 1 to count text boxes
                if (count of words of text box x) ¬
                        is 0 and (name of color of ¬
                        text box x is "White") then
                        set name of text box x to "Ralph"
                end if
```

```
            end repeat
            repeat with y from 1 to count picture boxes
                if (data size of image 1 of ¬
                        picture box y) is 0 and (name ¬
                        of color of picture box y ¬
                        is "White") then
                        set name of picture box y to ¬
                        "Ralph"
                end if
            end repeat
        end tell
    end repeat
    delete (every generic box of every page ¬
        whose name is "Ralph")
end tell
```

Add a Dingbat. Many magazines and newsletters end every story with a little dingbat character. However it can take a lot of time going through every story in a document just to add a single character. This script does it for you.

```
tell document 1 of application "QuarkXPress®"
    make character at end of every story with data "n" ¬
        with properties {font:"Zapf Dingbats", size:11}
end tell
```

Change Superscript to Superior. Dave Shaver of Quark shared this little script with everyone in the DTPforum on CompuServe. It changes every piece of text throughout your document that's in superscript style into superior style (this is only important because QuarkXPress doesn't have a way to do this in the Find/Change dialog box).

```
tell document 1 of application "QuarkXPress®"
tell every story
    set the style of (every text style range ¬
        whose style contains superior) to ¬
        {on styles:superscript, off styles: superior}
    end tell
end tell
```

Unmoveable guides. As we mentioned earlier in the chapter, you can set guides to be unmoveable and/or undeletable by scripting (you can't do this within the program). Perhaps even better, you can automate the creation of grids throughout a document. Here's a little script that shows an example of both of these tasks.

```
tell document 1 of application "QuarkXPress®"
    tell every page
        repeat with i from 72 to 432 by 72
            make horizontal guide at beginning with properties ¬
                {position:(i as points), unmoveable:true}
        end repeat
    end tell
end tell
```

Rotate everything. In some situations, pictures redraw faster on your screen if the picture box is rotated a little. You can run this script once to rotate them all by a degree, and then run it again when you're ready to print. (But be sure to run it again to set everything back to zero, or else you could have all sorts of trouble printing.)

```
tell application "QuarkXPress®"
    set rotation of every picture box ¬
        of every page of document 1 ¬
        to 1
end tell
```

FileMaker Pro and QuarkXPress. When scripting, you don't have to limit yourself to one application. This script pulls information out of a FileMaker Pro database and plops it into a QuarkXPress document. Pictures are pulled off the hard disk by name (the file name is pulled from FileMaker Pro, as well).

```
set thepath to "riverrun:temp:"
tell application "QuarkXPress®"
    activate
    if not (document 1 exists) then
        open file (thepath & "myfile.qx")
    end if
end tell
```

```
tell application "FileMaker Pro"
    activate
    if not (Window "Sessions.fpro" Exists) then
        Open file (thepath & "Sessions.fpro")
    end if
    tell Layout 1 of Window "Sessions.fpro"
        Show (every Record whose Cell "Day" = "Tuesday")
        set recordcnt to (Count of Record)
        repeat with i from 1 to recordcnt
            copy Cell "Session Name" of ¬
                Record i to session
            copy Cell "Speaker" of Record i to speaker
            tell Document 1 of Application "QuarkXPress®"
                activate
                show page i
                tell page i
                        set text of text box 1 to session
                        set text of text box 2 to speaker
                        set image 1 of picture box 1 ¬
                                to thepath & "pictures:" ¬
                                & speaker & ".tiff"
                end tell
            end tell
        end repeat
    end tell
end tell
```

▼ ▼

The Future of Scripts

Clearly, AppleEvent scripting gives you extremely powerful control over your environment in QuarkXPress (and other programs). As more people learn about it, we're expecting that we'll hear of some amazing applications online and in the press. In fact, if you're looking for a career-shift, we strongly suggest looking into becoming a scripting consultant. David recently sat next to a publisher of a magazine who wanted to start putting stuff on-line. His problem was that he had no good way of automating the process from a database to QuarkXPress to output (like Acrobat). As soon as David started talking about scripting, his eyes lit up. That's one man out of thousands who wants to hire a scripter. Any takers?

RESOURCES

We've always suspected that appendices chock full o' resources are only included in books under the orders of the greedy Publishing Trust—just to increase bulk and justify a book's hefty price. We can't vouch for other books (especially those from publishers we don't write for), but it's not the case here.

As any QuarkXPress Demon knows—and as we've tried to make clear throughout the book—QuarkXPress is not an island. We don't use QuarkXPress for everything, and we don't expect you to, either. And even if you do, there are many add-on XTensions from Quark and other developers that increase your power and efficiency in making pages.

We list here much of the software we've discussed throughout the book, plus some other items we think you should at least be aware of. The last section of this appendix is devoted to books and magazines that we find useful in our work. Perhaps you will, too. Good luck!

▼ ▼

XTensions

We first covered XTensions and how they can add functionally to QuarkXPress back in Chapter 1, *QuarkXPress Basics.* We mentioned several commercial vendors, but there's no way we could talk about them all. Below is a list of some XTensions that we find interesting, along with some general descriptions of what they are, how they work, and why we like them.

We're not necessarily endorsing the use of these XTensions. They're ones that we've worked with or know the most about. There are many more XTensions out there that are worth looking into. To find out more about other available XTensions, contact the XChange at the address below. You can also find many freeware or shareware XTensions on electronic bulletin boards, such as America Online and CompuServe.

▼ ▼

Bob and his many relatives
See Tables D-1 and D-2

Quark Inc.

1800 Grant St.

Denver, CO 80203

303/894-8888

Product Information Line: 800/788-7835

Quark has produced some of the most widely-used XTensions, partly because many of them are "free" (if you buy them directly from Quark, they charge you around $25 to pay for for disk duplication, shipping and handling) and partly because they're really useful. Several of them are simply XTensions we think you *must* have, though others you could easily do without.

One of the frustrating aspects about working with Quark's XTensions is that they are often good for only one or two versions of the product (see Tables D-1 and D-2). For instance, QuarkXTras was a must-have for version 3.0, but was discontinued when version 3.1 came out. Then, some of its functionality was built into QuarkPrint (an XTension sold, not given away, by Quark) and other choice bits were built into the free FeaturesPlus XTension. With version 3.3, Quark disabled the use of FeaturesPlus and rolled many of its features into Thing-a-ma-Bob (the descendant

| Feature | XTension to use in version . . . | | | |
	3.0	3.1	3.2	3.3
Alternate em space	FeaturesPlus	FeaturesPlus	Built-in	Built-in
ASCII PostScript send	n/a	Son of Bob	Built-in	Built-in
Calibration of output	Printer Calibration for all versions[1]			
Change view scale	n/a	Son of Bob	Built-in	Built-in
Collect items for output	n/a	Prepare for SB	Collect for Output	Built-in
Color swatch drag	Bob	Bob	Built-in	Built-in
Cool Blends	Cool Blends for all version[1]			
Full-Resolution TIFF	n/a	Son of Bob	Bobzilla	Bobzilla
Line Check	Bob	Bob	Bobzilla	Bobzilla
Make Fraction/Price	n/a	FeaturesPlus	FeaturesPlus	Thing-a-ma-bob
Multiple Masters font	MMU	MMU	MMU	MMU
Multiply/divide in fields	n/a	Son of Bob	Built-in	Built-in
Network communication	n/a	Net. Comm..	Net. Comm.	Net. Comm.
Notes	n/a	n/a	Notes	Notes
PageMaker file import	PM Import ß2	PM Import ß2	PM Import ß2	Doesn't work
Photoshop plug-ins access	Photoshop Plug-in for all versions			
Popup pages	Bob	Bob	Bobzilla	Bobzilla
Remove Manual Kerning	FeaturesPlus	FeaturesPlus	FeaturesPlus	Thing-a-ma-bob
Slide show presentation	n/a	QuarkPresents	QuarkPresents	QuarkPresents
Smart Quotes	n/a	Son of Bob	Built-in	Built-in
Super Step and Repeat	n/a	n/a	Bobzilla	Bobzilla
Value Converter palette	FeaturesPlus	FeaturesPlus	FeaturesPlus	Thing-a-ma-bob
Windows submenu	FeaturesPlus	FeaturesPlus	FeaturesPlus	Thing-a-ma-bob

Table D-1

Features and where to find them by version number

[1] See Table D-2 for the version number.

of a long series of "Bobs": Bob, Son of Bob, Bobzilla, etc.) Why they couldn't just come out with same-named XTensions and different version numbers is beyond us.

Table D-2 lists Quark's various XTensions, and which you should use with different versions of XPress. Because most of the XTensions listed are for older versions, we'll just focus on a few of them here.

	Version			
Quark XTensions	**3.0**	**3.1**	**3.2**	**3.3**
Bob	●	●		
Bobzilla			●	●
Cool Blends	●	●	●	●
FeaturesPlus	●	●	●	
Multiple Masters (MMU)	●	●	●	●
Network Connection	●	●	●	●
Notes			●	●
Patcher for 3.2			●[1]	
Photoshop Plug-in	●	●	●	●
PM Import	●	●	●	
Prepare for SB		●		
Printer Calibration	● 3.0	● 3.1	● 3.2	● 3.2
QuarkLog	●	[2]	[2]	[2]
QuarkPresents		● 1.0	● 1.1	● 1.1
QuarkPrint ($195)	● 1.01	● 1.02	● 1.03	● 1.04
QuarkXTras	●			
Son of Bob		●		
Stars and Stripes			●	●
SuperXTension	●			
Thing-a-ma-bob				●
Zapper 2.0A	●[3]			

[1] Patches version 3.2 patch level 1 (the release version) to patch level 2.
[2] QuarkLog features were moved to QuarkPrint.
[3] Patches version 3.0 patch level 0 (release version) and 1 (first zapper patch)
to patch level 2.

Thing-a-ma-Bob and Features Plus. These XTensions (use Thing-a-ma-Bob for version 3.3 and Features Plus for earlier versions) include Make Fraction/Make Price, Value Converter, Windows Menu, Remove Manual Kerning, Word Space Tracking, Alternate Em Space. Some, of course, are no longer relevant—Alternate Em Space and the Windows menu feature are now built into the program. No matter which version of QuarkXPress you use, we strongly recommend you get one of these XTensions.

Bobzilla. Bobzilla was released for version 3.2, and includes Go-To-Page (what we call popup page), Line Check, Super Step & Repeat, and Full Resolution TIFF. Many people get by without this, but you shouldn't: it's free, it's cool, it's on our disk (see the disk offer in the back of the book).

Notes. The Notes XTension is sort of interesting, but rather limited in its use. You can use the Notes palette to add notes in text. Then you can show and hide notes (and the palette) at will. The interface is similar to the Quark Publishing System (QPS). However, the notes can be attached only to text, and it's not easy to see where they are (see Figure D-1). Nonetheless, if you're passing your QuarkXPress documents around, it might be helpful to you.

Figure D-1
Notes XTension

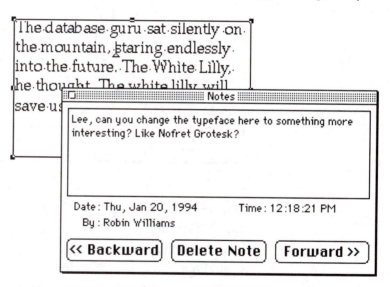

Network XTension. The Network XTension (not to be confused with the Network extension file that sits in the Extensions folder in the System Folder) lets you send messages, pictures, and text stories among a number of QuarkXPress users on a network. It's not used very often, for four reasons. First, almost no one knows about it because Quark doesn't send it out on their Freebies disk. Second, it's not really a finished product. Quark released it a couple of years ago because they thought it was an interesting idea and they were thinking of making a more full-fledged program out of it (it later turned into the massive Quark Publishing System). Third, people don't use it because it has kind of a quirky interface and functionality (see Figure D-2). But, finally, the reason people don't use it is because e-mail systems like CE Software's Quick-Mail are better solutions than using this XTension.

Figure D-2

Network
Communication
XTension

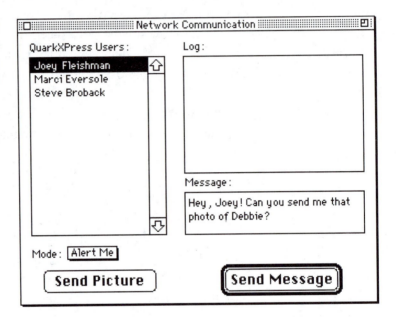

QuarkPrint. The only XTension in Table D-2 that isn't free is the QuarkPrint package. QuarkPrint's predecessor, QuarkXTras, was also a commercial product, but it only works with version 3.0. QuarkPrint's mission in life is to make printing QuarkXPress documents easier for you. It lets you create named sets ("jobs") of Page Setup, Chooser, and Print dialog box settings. It also has some cool extra features like printing discontiguous pages (for instance, printing pages "1, 5, and 9–12").

PageMaker Filter. The PM Import filter is an XTension that lets you convert PageMaker files that were built in PageMaker versions 4.0 or 4.01 only; there's no guarantee it will work with any later version. In fact, it may not even work at all (different people have varying degrees of success). Although it has some limitations, it's great for transferring page geometry. Text is brought in properly, but some typographic values are lost in the translation. Moving text around is probably still performed better by exporting and importing Microsoft Word files. If you do use this XTension, remember to open the PageMaker file first and perform a Save As before attempting to import it into QuarkXPress.

Cool Blends. Cool Blends XTension is now included with Quark-XPress, though it's still a separate file in QuarkXPress's XTension folder. This XTension adds five blend types to QuarkXPress (in addition to Linear, which is built-in): Mid-Linear, Rectangular, Diamond, Circular, and Full Circular. See Chapter 9, *Color*, for more information. If you use a Cool Blend and give the file to someone else, they must have the same or a later version of the XTension for the blends to work correctly.

Photoshop Plug-in. The Photoshop Plug-in XTension is supposed to let you acquire images using Photoshop acquire modules (mainly scanner plug-ins) and place them directly into picture boxes. For example, you should be able to scan something and have it placed immediately into a picture box. Unfortunately, we've never gotten it to work well. Maybe you can. With this XTension and EfiColor, you can scan and separate without leaving QuarkXPress—but we don't recommend it since there's no way to sharpen or adjust images in this scenario).

▼ ▼

XTension of the Month Club
XPress XPerts XChange (X³)
The XChange
P.O. Box 270578
Fort Collins, CO 80527
(800/788-7557 or 303/229-0620; Fax 303/229-9773
CompuServe: 75300,2337 or America OnLine: XChange

If great companies develop out of great needs, then the XChange is destined to fly. One of the biggest problems with getting quality XTensions has been where to go for information, sales, and technical support, since Quark itself doesn't sell third-party XTensions. The XChange is now here on the scene to help. They have agreements with most commercial XTension developers to be XTension Central: they market and sell XTensions (the developers love this because they're usually small shops without the resources to get the word out). And they also handle tech support for many of the XTensions (what they don't know, they know how to find out).

If you need an XTension, but don't know who makes it, or if it even exists, call the XChange. If they don't know of it, they'll pass the idea on to a XTension developer who might create it down the line (or do a custom job for you).

The XChange also has an XTension of the Month Club. As a subscriber, each month you get a free XTension, a demo version of new or existing XTensions, and other software. They'll even send you a newsletter with all sorts of XTension information in it.

The XChange is also the central hub of the XPress XPerts XChange, an international users group for people using QuarkXPress. At the time of this writing, X³ ("ex-cubed") is in its initial formation stages, but it looks like it will be a great place to acquire QuarkXPress information.

(Note: We're leaving all the XTension developers' addresses out for the rest of this chapter. Instead, we suggest you call the XChange for information.)

▼ ▼

Xdata ($299)
Xtags ($299)
Xstyle ($99)
Em Software

Here are three very different XTensions with very different applications. One for anyone publishing data, the second for anyone doing serious work with XPress Tags, and the third is for . . . anyone!

Xdata. Xdata is a powerful yet simple XTension that formats information coming out of a database or a spreadsheet. Its uses vary.

For example, David once built a 270-page, 17,000-name-and-address directory by importing information from a mainframe computer into QuarkXPress. Xdata automatically formatted each record the way he wanted it (name was bold, address was a smaller and different typeface, and so on). It's also an important part of creating catalogs, financial sheets, and even mail-merged documents.

Xtags. Xtags does everything that the XPress Tags filter does (see Chapter 5, *Copy Flow*), and more. The primary additions are creating and filling in-line anchored text and picture boxes, applying master pages, and translating user-defined tags upon import. It also includes error handling, which is sorely missed in Quark's XPress Tags. This last feature can be especially useful.

Xstyle. Xstyle is an XTension that makes style sheets more accessible, and it works beautifully. It adds three new floating palettes to QuarkXPress (though you don't have to have them open all the time): Paragraph Styles, Character Styles, and Style Editor. Note that the character styles palette doesn't offer character-based styles. However, it does let you quickly change character formatting that isn't available in the Measurements palette.

▼ ▼

Kitchen Sink ($39)
faceIT ($99)
a lowly apprentice production

Paul Schmidt has worked for Quark and DK&A, but we'll always remember him as the guy who created the Kitchen Sink and faceIT XTensions. Here are two goodies which we think you should take a careful look at. Like most utility XTensions, these add functionality that probably should be included right in QuarkXPress; but as the features aren't in the program, it's worth a few bucks more to get these.

Kitchen Sink. When David first asked Paul what the Kitchen Sink XTension did, he should have been able to guess the answer: "Everything but the kitchen sink." It's almost true. This little XTension includes a powerful palette for moving around your page and document quickly (see Figure D-3), a dynamically updated palette with lots of buttons that control every function in Quark-XPress, the ability to create and save specs for commonly used document sizes, and lots more. It's great!

Figure D-3

Co-Pilot palette from Kitchen Sink

faceIT. Finally, an XTension for QuarkXPress that makes character styles! faceIT is not a perfect XTension, but it does its job pretty well—better than anything else we've seen. Character styles, like paragraph styles (style sheets), let you name a group of character formatting attributes and then apply them all at once. Then, when you want to change those attributes, you can change them in the faceIT dialog box, and your text gets changed throughout your document (see Figure D-4). This also contains other minor but helpful features. Joe Bob Blatner says Check it Out.

Figure D-4

faceIT XTension's
character styles

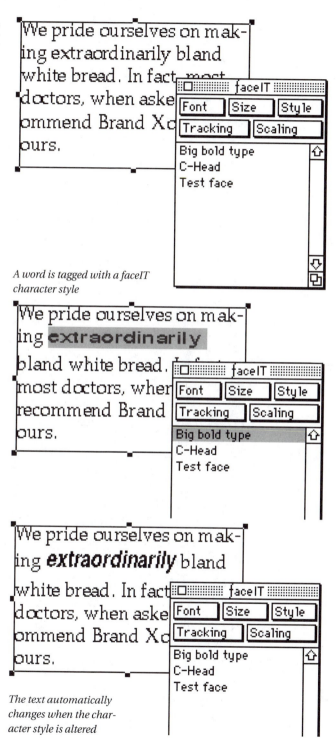

*A word is tagged with a faceIT
character style*

*The text automatically
changes when the char-
acter style is altered*

▼ ▼

Scitex Document Reports ($149)
Scitex Fractions ($69)
Scitex Grides & Guides ($99)
Scitex Image Tools ($199)
Scitex Layers ($99)
Scitex Precision Tools ($199)
Scitex Corporation

You've all heard of Scitex, right? Million-dollar, high-end imaging systems, and so on. Well now you can buy some of their expertise for much less than a milllion bucks. Most of the Scitex XTensions are really, really cool (the others are just plain cool), and can be extremely useful. Let's take a quick look at what they do.

Scitex Layers. This XTension lets you organize the various components on your pages, grouping and ungrouping quickly and easily. What's really great about Layers is that you can make layers disappear and appear at will. Invisible layers also don't print, so you can use Layers to create one document with varying pieces. For example, you could make one document with two different lanuages on the same page. When you want to print the English version, you can turn the French layer off, or vice versa.

Scitex Precision Tools. The Precision Tools XTension lets you do a number of things, including powerful aligning and measuring of items, magnifying areas of your page up to 1600 percent, precision nudging, and fast locking of multiple items in your document. In our judgement, the alignment and measurement tools are the best things about this package.

Scitex Fractions. If you work with text that contains a lot of fractions, you'll love the Fractions XTension. It lets you create fractions quickly and intuitively. Most people will be happy enough with the Make Fraction feature from Quark (see Table D-1), but for others, this hands-on approach will be the cat's meow (see Figure D-5).

Figure D-5
Scitex Fractions

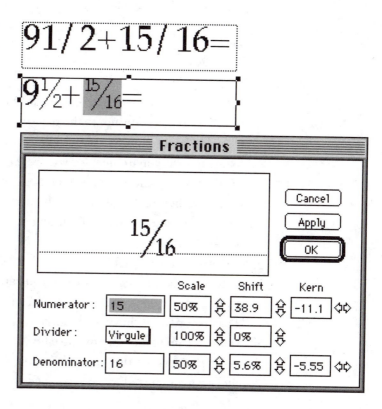

Scitex Grids & Guides. The Grids & Guides XTension from Scitex is the most powerful guide-making XTension that we've seen. It's also the most expensive (certainly a matter of "you get what you pay for"). If you work with a lot of page guides and don't use this XTension, you probably don't know what you're missing.

Scitex Image Tools. The Image Tools XTension from Scitex consists of four parts: blends, silhouettes, picture scaling, and quick proof. If you thought Cool Blends was great, you need to see Scitex Blends, which lets you create complex, multicolored blends (like from red to blue to yellow at the rate you specify). The silhouette tool is extremely powerful for creating complex polygons around pictures, and it has built-in links to high-resolution Scitex silhouetting tools.

▼ ▼

XState ($79)
Markzware

Have you ever been frustrated that an XPress document always re-opens to page one, not to the page you were viewing when you closed it? Xstate to the rescue! When you re-open a document, Xstate returns you to the page you were last viewing and restores the document window size, screen position, and magnification as they were before. It even remembers your last text cursor position. XState can also place a number of QuarkXPress documents in a single Project palette.

Plus, Xstate has a few other side-benefits, such as a "switch to next open document" keystroke. You can set it to automatically select Keep Document Settings when you open documents. And, it can record how long you've worked on a document or a project. Xstate is a great tool for anyone who works on large, multi-document projects. As the manual for the XTension notes, "XState keeps you organized without you even trying!"

▼ ▼

PixTrix
Graham Morgan

If you walk down Normal Street and take a sharp turn to the left, you walk down this little alleyway called PixTrix. Like many other wild and wooley XTensions, this rather cool add-on to Quark-XPress has several different functions, none of which is necessarily dependent on the others. The key is creating and manipulating text and picture boxes. You can transform text into polygonal text or picture boxes; make wild starbursts interactively; propagate an image among a number of different picture boxes (see Figure D-6); and lots more. It's certainly one you should look at.

Figure D-6
PixTrix's Propagate
feature

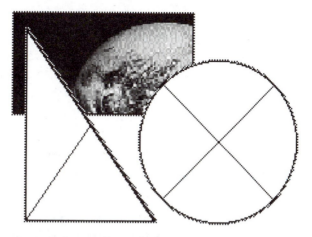

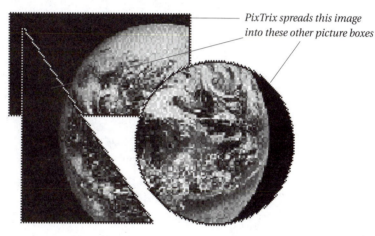

*PixTrix spreads this image
into these other picture boxes*

▼ ▼

CopyFlow ($395)
CopyFlow Reports ($295)
Overset ($69)
North Atlantic Publishing Systems, Inc.

Now here's a company with a mission: to help out the editorial
process with as many XTensions as possible! CopyFlow, Copy-
Flow Reports and CopyBridge are three XTensions designed for
groups of people working together on a project. They're great aids
to any publication that's being edited by one person while
another person is doing page layout.

CopyFlow. If you find yourself frequently needing to export and re-import text from your QuarkXPress document, you should take a look at the CopyFlow XTension from North Atlantic Publishing Systems (NAPS). You can use CopyFlow to record a name and editor for every story in your QuarkXPress document, and specify a folder on your Mac (or on a network server) from which the story should be imported, and to which it should be exported.

Once you've named and specified folders for stories, you can, with a single command, automatically export individual stories, or every named story, to the export folder. You can export to any word processing file supported by QuarkXPress, or to XPress Tags, Style Tags, or NAPS's own tagging format. Then, after the copy's been edited, CopyFlow can automatically re-import the stories into their text boxes, untouched by human hands.

CopyFlow Reports. CopyFlowReports is an add-on XTension that can give you detailed information about all the stories and pictures in your document. This information can be imported into a spreadsheet program for quick reference. CopyBridge is an XTension designed for publishers who are using XyWrite or Microsoft Word extensively, and need a good translator for their Quark-XPress documents.

Overset. Overset is a little XTension in the genre of SetInset (see "SetInset" below): it does only one thing, but it does it well. Overset lets you see the text that won't fit into the text box you're working with. Once you turn this XTension on, when you click on that little "X" that indicates an overflow, Overset pops open another text box and flows the additional text into it. As soon as this auxiliary text box is empty, it disappears.

▼ ▼

Sonar Bookends ($129)
Sonar TOC ($99; must have Sonar Bookends to use)
Virginia Systems, Inc.

The Sonar Bookends XTension purports to create indexes and tables of contents. In our minds, this is more marketing hype than truth. What Bookends does really well is searching. It can search faster than bare feet move on hot asphalt. Not only can you search for things like "storm" throughout multiple documents, but you can search for all the instances of "storm" that are within four words of "warning" but aren't on the same page as "Billy Joel." It also creates a great concordance, and can be a good aid in cross referencing.

To be fair, there are many people who are happy with Sonar-Bookends as an indexer. These people seem to fall into two categories: those who use the XTension as a starting point for their own indexes, and those who just don't care if they have a machine with no intelligence build their indexes.

Sonar TOC can create a pretty good table of contents, but it's a little clunky in how it works. Before you get too excited about these, check out the other index and table of contents XTensions that we talk about later on.

▼ ▼

Tableworks Plus ($310)
Npath, Inc.

For those of you who follow the discussions on nationwide electronic bulletin board systems, you probably know that more people ask about a table-making XTension than anything else. To fill the need, Npath software has released Tableworks Plus, a powerful table creation and editing tool. Tableworks Plus adds a new menu and a new tool to the tool palette which lets you build a table quickly and efficiently. Well, maybe we shouldn't say quickly; QuarkXPress has never been good at handling a large number of text or picture boxes at any great clip. But it's certainly faster than having to do it by hand.

Tableworks Plus also has many table manipulation features. For example, groups of cells can be merged to create straddle-column or -row heads, and column and row heads can be treated differently when defining lines and when importing text. These heads can also be automatically repeated when a table carries over to a new page. Tables created with Tableworks Plus can be a fixed size or can be set up to dynamically grow horizontally or vertically, depending on the text brought into them.

Brad Walrod of High Text Graphics in New York (author of *QuarkXPress Unleashed;* see "Magazines and Publications," page 718) has used Tableworks a lot more than we have. He says, "Tableworks is a must for anyone creating anything but the simplest tables in QuarkXPress."

▼ ▼

PinPointXT ($89)

Cheshire Group

Like Steve Werner, David dreams in PostScript. However, sometimes his dreams turn to nightmares when he encounters PostScript errors in printing jobs. Usually these errors flash on the screen quickly, then disappear, and the print job just dies. But that's where PinPoint XTension comes in handy. When PinPoint is turned on, QuarkXPress downloads some special PostScript code with your print job. This code "catches" any PostScript errors and tells you exactly what's going wrong and where. This XTension is very helpful for service bureaus trying to troubleshoot problems, or for PostScript hackers who are playing with QuarkXPress's code. Also see "Tip: Laserchecking with LaserCheck" in Chapter 10, *Printing*.

▼ ▼

SxetchPad ($229)

Datastream, Inc.

We never though we'd see the day when we could actually draw Bézier curves in QuarkXPress and then curve type around them. Well, believe it or not, that's exactly what SxetchPad lets you do. But wait: there's more! You can also convert type to outline, and then fill and stroke those outlines with colors or fancy blends. Plus, you can edit the curve points at any time (see Figure D-7). This XTension adds to QuarkXPress much of the basic functionality of FreeHand or Illustrator.

Figure D-7
SxetchPad XTenion

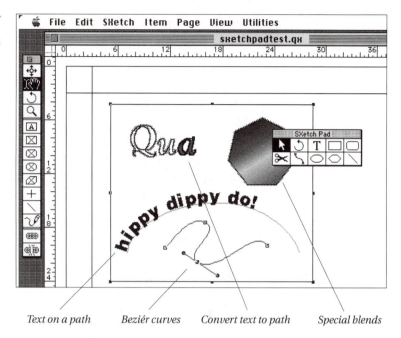

Text on a path   Beziér curves   Convert text to path   Special blends

The next version of SxetchPad, which should be out by the time you read this, will let you open Illustrator 1.1 and 88 documents directly so that you can edit them within QuarkXPress. Very nice.

▼ ▼

SetInset II ($29)
InsertSpace ($49)
XTend, Inc.

SetInset. SetInset is a shareware XTension that lets you define the inset for a text box on the left, right, top and bottom sides of the box. This overrides the single "all-sides" Text Inset value in the Text Box Specifications dialog box. SetInset II does has a better interface, but you have to pay more, too.

InsertSpace. XTend's commercial product, InsertSpace, brings to QuarkXPress a feature that traditional typesetters have been asking about for years. InsertSpace adjusts the tab stops for a line of text so that columns of text have equivalent amounts of space between them.

▼ ▼

Azalea Barcode XTension ($129)

Azalea Software, Inc.

Jerry Whiting, king of barcodes, has brought the realm of the barcode-blessed to QuarkXPress by releasing an XTension to automatically create all sorts of high-quality EPS bar codes directly within QuarkXPress—UPC, ISBN, and many, many more (see Figure D-8). They're really cool.

Figure D-8
A bar code
created using
Azalea's barcode
XTension

▼ ▼

Missing Link ($69)
NavigatorXT ($65)
Vision Contents ($129)
IndeXTension ($99)
ResizeXT ($99)
Textractor ($149)
and lots more!

Visions Edge

This may be the last company to be listed in this appendix, but it's *far* from being the least important or the least cool. Dacques Viker is creating some of the most useful utility XTensions on the market today. Here are descriptions of just a few (call the XChange for information on the others).

Missing Link. The Missing Link XTension lets you do all sorts of things you've wanted to do for years with linked boxes in Quark-XPress. For example, you can copy a text box out of the middle of a text chain and retain just the text that's inside it. To us, the best thing is the ability to link together two chains of text boxes, each of which contain text (see Figure D-9).

Figure D-9
Missing Link XTension

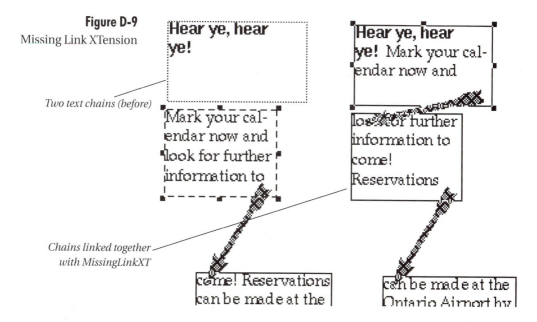

Two text chains (before)

Chains linked together with MissingLinkXT

NavigatorXT. We often find ourselves working on a document zoomed in to 200%. Then, when we want to edit a different part of the page we zoom out to Fit in Window and zoom back in to where we want to go next. This is time consuming, to say the least. That's when we go buy NavigatorXT, which lets us move quickly to various areas of the page without zooming out first. We simply bring up the Navigator palette and click on the area of the mini-page that we want to go to.

Vision Contents. Vision Contents is the table of contents maker that we've been waiting for for a long time. You can quickly create a table of contents based on style sheets, even over multiple documents. So for instance you can ask it to build a TOC that includes paragraphs styled as "Chapter Number", "Chapter Title", "A Head", "B Head", and "C Head". It even pulls out run-in heads if you want it to. Plus, as an added bonus, it can renumber sets of documents. For example, you can build a list of documents, tell it in what order they should flow, and then Vision Contents changes the opening page numbers for each document automatically.

IndeXTension. Ben Taylor originally developed this great indexing XTension for Future Publishing, but now Vision's Edge is expanding it even farther into cool realms. IndeXTension lets you create an index the way most people work: marking words and phrases on your document pages. You can also mark the words from within a word processor such as Microsoft Word. If you have to create an index from a QuarkXPress document, you really should check this out.

ResizeXT. When David gives seminars in various places around the world, he has to answer lots of questions, but the one that almost always comes up is, "How can I resize a group of objects all at the same time?" His answer every time is, "Call the XChange and get ResizeXT." This simple utility XTension is designed to resize pictures, text, lines, and frames quickly and exactly to the size you want them (see Figure D-10). Like many of Vision Edge's XTensions, a similar feature will probably show up in QuarkXPress itself someday, but until then this is the best we can hope for.

Figure D-10

Resize XT

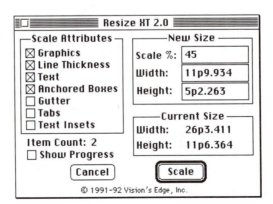

TeXTractor. If you need to pull text out of your QuarkXPress documents—whether for archival, text manipulation, or whatever—you should take a good look at the TeXTractor XTension (gotta' love these names, eh?). It's a powerhouse text extractor, letting you export the text in your document all at once, or by the criteria you specify.

▼ ▼

Quark Lab-Paks

If you're teaching or creating a student publication at a college or university, or are a Quark Authorized Training Center or Consultant, you might qualify to buy a 15-user Lab-Pak from Quark that you can use to teach the program. There are a number of restrictions and difficulties with the Lab-Pak, but there are great benefits as well. Most of all, it's a way to get 15 registered, educational-use-only copies of the program for the retail price of a single copy of QuarkXPress (about $800).

Do You Qualify?

The basic criteria for qualifying to buy the Lab-Pak are pretty simple.

▶ You plan to use the Lab-Pak copies of QuarkXPress in a course for credit; to produce a student publication; or as part of training offered by an authorized training center or consultant.

▶ You agree not to use any of the Lab-Pak copies for anything but learning purposes. That is, the Lab-Pak copies can't be used in offices or outside of classrooms (except to produce student publications).

There are a few other particulars which Quark provides as part of the application form. You can call the Quark's Education Product Manager at 303/894-8888 to get an application form.

Managing the Lab-Pak

When you get the Lab-Pak, you'll find 15 individually serialized, fully functional copies of QuarkXPress. Because they're individually serialized, you should immediately make backup copies of the 15 installation disks with the serial numbers on them. Quark doesn't devote a lot of time and effort to these educational programs, so if one of your serialized disks goes south, it can take four to six weeks to get a replacement.

▼ ▼

Tip: Back up the Programs. If you have a network supporting the classrooms or labs in which you're going to use the Lab-Pak, here's an alternate scheme for making your authorized archival backup.

1. Install one full copy of QuarkXPress (including PDFs, XTensions, and so on) on your server, and customize it the way you want (setting up the XTensions in the various folders, etc.)

2. Install all the other copies of QuarkXPress on the server. This time, uncheck everything, and *only* install the application itself. While you're doing this, put each program into its own folder, and name the folder with the serial number of the program inside it.

3. Finally, you can install QuarkXPress on each of the machines by copying one program and the QuarkXPress folder to each computer on the network. That is, copy "QuarkXPress #1" and the rest of the QuarkXPress folder's files to the first machine; then copy "QuarkXPress #2" and the same folder to the second machine, and so on.

Then, if you have a hard disk crash on one of your machines, you can easily reinstall by dragging the appropriate serialized version of it to the correct machine. (The alternative is to painfully reinstall from floppies.)

▼ ▼

Tip: Answer Your Mail. Quark's support for the Lab-Pak, as we noted, is pretty minimal. However, they take all correspondence very seriously. They send you a questionnaire every fall, which you must fill out in its entirety, enclose the proper documentation, and return within some stated period of time. If they don't receive the form back by the deadline, they may "unregister" your Lab-Pak. It reverts to a single registered copy of Quark; the other 14 serial numbers are removed as authorized numbers from their database. This is an expensive mistake, so make sure and immediately reply to all mail from Quark.

▼ ▼

Quark Multi-Paks

While the Lab-Pak is intended and priced for educational use, Quark does offer a "pack" approach for commercial users, too. If you purchase in increments of five copies, you can get a single serial number that works with multiple copies over a network. The pricing in this system is typically not advantageous until you start purchasing 10 or more copies.

On the other hand, the administrative burden is lower: you can install all 10 users from a single set of installation disks. Note that if you sign up for this, Quark registers the program for you and ships it direct from Denver. Of course, sometime their typists are less than perfect; one of David's colleagues at Kodak purchased a 10-pack and for the next year he saw "Eastman Koday" every time he ran Quark.

▼ ▼

QuarkLibraries

Quark has long been known as a one-product company. However, the truth is, they actually do have other products. One such product is the QuarkLibraries line. These are a series of 15 sets of Encapsulated PostScript (EPS) clip-art, ready-made into Quark-XPress Libraries. Honestly, we don't think many of the images are very good, but some of them could be useful, especially flags, patterns, and maps. See Figure D-11 for a small sampling of the images.

Figure D-11
Library samples

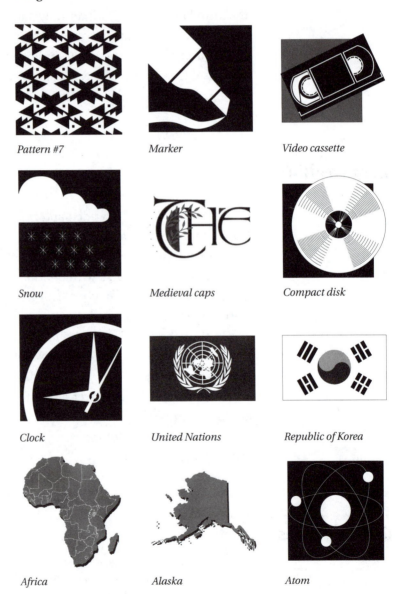

Pattern #7   Marker   Video cassette

Snow   Medieval caps   Compact disk

Clock   United Nations   Republic of Korea

Africa   Alaska   Atom

▼ ▼

Software

QuarkXPress only goes so far, and XTensions—while stretching farther—don't fill all our needs. So we turn to other programs, utilities, and system extensions to make our lives better. In this section, we go over all of the software we've talked about throughout the book, as well as a few other programs or companies you should probably know about. Don't buy software direct from the company unless you want to pay too much for it, or you really want to support the developers directly. Most of this software can be found at your nearby software dealer or from a mail-order house for substantially less than suggested retail price.

FontDownloader
Illustrator
Photoshop
Adobe Dimensions
Adobe Type Manager (ATM)
Adobe Type Reunion (ATR)
Adobe Systems Inc.
1585 Charleston Road
PO Box 7900
Mountain View, CA 94039-7900
415/961-4400

StuffIt
Aladdin Systems, Inc.
Deer Park Center, Suite 23A-171
Aptos, CA 95003
408/685-9175

FreeHand
PageMaker
PrePrint
TrapWise
Aldus Corporation
411 First Avenue S., Suite 200
Seattle, WA 98104
206/622-5500

MasterJuggler
ALSoft Inc.
PO Box 927
Spring, TX 77383-0927
713/353-4090

Fontographer
Altsys Corporation
269 W. Renner Road
Richardson, TX 75080
214/680-2060

LaserWriter Utility
ResEdit
Apple Computer, Inc.
20525 Mariani Avenue
Cupertino, CA 95104
408/996-1010

QuicKeys
CE Software
801 73rd Street
Des Moines, IA 50312
515/224-1995

FontStopper
Compumation, Inc.
820 N. University Drive
State College, PA 16803

Electronic Border Tape
EBT Frame Mover
ShadeTree Marketing
5515 N. 7th St. Suite 5144
Phoenix, AZ 85014
800/678-8848

ParaFont
MathType
Design Science
6475B E. Pacific Coast Highway
Suite 392
Long Beach, CA 90803
213/433-0685

EfiColor profiles
EfiColor Works
EfiColor Cachet
Electronics for Imaging
2855 Campus Drive
San Mateo, CA 94403
415/286-8600

Fraction Fonts
EmDash
PO Box 8256
Northfield, IL 60093
708/441-6699

Suitcase
Symantec
175 West Broadway
Eugene, OR 97401
800/441-7234

PlateMaker
In Software
2403 Conway Drive
Escondido, CA 92026
619/743-7502

Precision Imagesetter Linearization Software
Kodak Electronic Printing Systems, Inc.
164 Lexington Road
Billerica, MA 01821-3984
508/667-5550

Enhance
Micro Frontier
7650 Hickman Road
Des Moines, IA 50322
515/270-8109

Microsoft Word
Microsoft Excel
Microsoft
1 Microsoft Way
Redmond, WA 98052-6399
206/882-8080

Monotype Fonts
Monotype, Inc.
2500 Brickvale Drive
Elk Grove Village, IL 60007
708/350-5600

Super Boomerang (part of Now Utilities)
Now Software
319 SW Washington St., 11th Floor
Portland, OR 97204
503/274-2800

Mac-in-DOS
Pacific Micro
201 San Antonio Circle, C250
Mountain View, CA 94040

DiskTop
LaserStatus
PrairieSoft
1650 Fuller Rd.
PO Box 65820
West Des Moines, IA 50265
515/225-3720

Exposure Pro
McSink
Vantage
Preferred Software, Inc.
5100 Poplar Avenue, Suite 706
Memphis, TN 38137
800/446-6393

LaserCheck
Advanced PostScript Error Handler
Systems of Merritt, Inc.
2551 Old Dobbin Drive East
Mobile, AL 36695
205/660-1240

Color Calibration Software for Postscript Imagesetters
Technical Publishing Services, Inc.
2205 Sacramento
San Francisco, CA 94115
415/921-8509

Images with Impact
3G Graphics
114 2nd Ave. S, Suite 104
Edwards, WA 98020
800/456-0234

DeskPaint
DeskScan
Zedcor
4500 East Speedway, Suite 22
Tucson, AZ 86712
800/482-4567

▼ ▼

User Groups

X³ (X-cubed)
The XChange
PO Box 270578
Fort Collins, CO 80527
800/788-7557 or 303/229-0620; Fax 303/229-9773
CompuServe: 75300,2337 or America OnLine: XChange

QuarkXPress Users International
PO Box 170
1 Stiles Road, Suite 106
Salem, NH 03079
603/898-2822 or Fax 603/898-3393

▼ ▼

Color-Matching Systems

Pantone

55 Knickerbock Rd.

Moonachie, NJ 07074

201/935-5500

TruMatch

25 West 43rd St., Suite 802

New York, NY 10036

212/302-9100

ANPA

Newspaper Association of America

11600 Sunrise Valley Drive

Reston, VA 22091

703/648-1367

Focoltone

Springwater House

Taffs Well, Cardiff

CF4 7QR, United Kingdom

44/222-810-962

Toyo Ink Manufacturing Co. Ltd.

3-13, 2-chome Kyobashi

Chuo-ku, Tokyo 104

81/3-2722-5721

▼ ▼

Magazines and Publications

PostScript Language Reference Manual
PostScript Language Program Design
PostScript Language Tutorial and Cookbook
(also known as the Red, Green, and Blue books)
Addison-Wesley Publishing
6 Jacob Way
Reading, MA 01867
617/944-3700

Digital Prepress Book
Agfa Compugraphic
200 Ballardvale Street
Wilmington, MA 01887
508/658-5600

MacWeek
Coastal Associates Publishing Company
PO Box 5821
Cherry Hill, NJ 08034
609/461-2100

Design Tools Monthly
1332 Pearl Street
Boulder, CO 80302
303/444-6876

Step-By-Step Electronic Design
Dynamic Graphics
6000 N. Forest Park Drive
Peoria, IL 61614-3592
309/688-8800

The Form of the Book
Hartley & Marks, Inc.
79 Tyee Drive
Point Roberts, WA 98281

U&lc
International Typeface Corporation
2 Hammarskjold Plaza
New York, NY 10017
212/371-0699

Macworld
Macworld Communications, Inc.
501 Second Street
San Francisco, CA 94107
800/234-1038

Before and After
PageLab
331 J Street, Suite 150
Sacramento, CA 95814-9671

How To Boss Your Fonts Around
Learning PostScript
The Little Mac Book
The Mac is not a typewriter
The Photoshop Wow! Book
QuarkXPress Tips &Tricks
QuarkXPress Visual Quickstart Guide
Real World FreeHand
Real World Scanning & Halftones
WYSIWYG . . . and many, many more
Peachpit Press
2414 Sixth St.
Berkeley, CA 94710
800/283-9444 or 510/548-4393; Fax: 510/548-5991

Publish!
501 Second Street
San Francisco, CA 94107
800/274-5116

QuarkXPress Unleashed
Random House Electronic Publishing
400 Hahn Road
Westminster, MD 21157

Seybold Report on Desktop Publishing
Seybold Publications
PO Box 644
Media, PA 19063
215/565-2480

MacUser
Ziff-Davis Publishing Company
950 Tower Lane, 18th Floor
Foster City, CA 94404

Index

P

The QuarkXPress Book Doesn't Stop Here Anymore

▼▼▼▼▼▼▼▼▼▼▼▼▼▼▼▼▼▼▼▼▼▼▼▼▼▼▼▼▼▼▼▼▼▼▼▼▼▼▼

We couldn't do it. We just couldn't steer though the twists and turns of all those wild jungle roads just to stroll off at the end of the line. So we ain't stoppin' here! We've hijacked the bus, we're painting it pink and green, and we won't stop drivin' until we reach the top. Stay on board! Give us a shout from time to time and let us know how you've liked the ride so far. Tell us if you've picked up any new XPress Demon machete techniques that make the driving easier. We're always looking out for a new trick or two from a young tyro or a seasoned pro. You can write to David at the following address.

Parallax Productions
1619 Eighth Avenue North
Seattle, WA 98109
CompuServe: 72647, 3302
America Online and AppleLink: Parallax1
Internet: 72647.3302@compuserve.com *or* parallax1@aol.com

Examples of what can (but shouldn't) be done with QuarkXPress's Polygon tool. ©1993 Carlos Sosa

DON'T **B** E **CRUEL**

Colophon

▼▼

If anything shows that we practice what we preach, it's this book. The QuarkXPress Book was created using almost every technique and many of the tips that we divulge throughout the chapters.

Text

Because the pages for the previous edition of the book were in QuarkXPress format, all the text was exported as Microsoft Word 4.0 files (fortunately, the style sheets were exported with the text; unfortunately, XPress's Word filter ain't perfect). Chapters were edited and written in Microsoft Word 5, and then reimported into QuarkXPress to be laid out. The bulk of the work was done on a PowerBook Duo 210 with a Duo MiniDock, a Quadra 650, a Centris 650, and a PowerBook 170.

Artwork

We created all the artwork in QuarkXPress, Adobe Photoshop, Adobe Illustrator, and Aldus FreeHand. Every screen shot in the book was created with Exposure Pro and then converted to TIFF format with DeskPaint or Photoshop. Each figure was imported, cropped, and sized within QuarkXPress, and saved in a library along with its caption and callouts (one library per chapter). For fast access to each figure, we labelled them using the library's labelling feature to speed up page production.

Design

For this revised edition, the body copy was set in Adobe Utopia and Utopia Expert (for fractions, footnotes, etc.); the heads are in Bitstream's Futura Condensed Bold. Chapter numbers and initial caps are set in Adobe's Bodoni Poster Compressed. Universal News with Commercial Pi was used throughout for our bullet symbol (▶), math symbols, and other dingbats.

Output

Color pages were sent as PostScript files to Seattle Imagesetting and set on a Linotype-Hell Linotype 330. They were printed on Luna at 133 lpi on a sheetfed press. The rest of the pages were dumped as PostScript files, proofed with LaserCheck, and sent to Consolidated Printers in Berkeley, California. They imposed the job using ImpoStrip, and output the imposed flats on an Agfa ProSet 9800 imagesetter. Consolidated Printers printed the book on a web press using 50-pound Husky Vellum. The bind-in keystroke card and disk offer card were printed on a sheetfed press. The keystroke card was printed in black and a PMS spot color on a coated stock, then varnished.

More from Peachpit Press...

Camera Ready with QuarkXPress
Cyndie Kopfenstein
A practical guide to creating direct-to-press documents using XPress. Includes QuarkXPress templates disk for many common documents. *(206 pages)*

Four Colors/One Image
Mattias Nyman
Step-by-step procedures for reproducing and manipulating color images using Photoshop, QuarkXPress and Cachet. A terrific, invaluable resource for those who need great color output. *(84 pages)*

Illustrator Illuminated, 2nd Edition
Clay Andres
This full-color book shows how professional artists use Illustrator's tools to create a variety of styles and effects. Each chapter shows the creation of an illustration from concept through completion. Contains new material for Illustrator 5. *(200 pages)*

The Illustrator 5 Book
Deke McClelland
Experienced Illustrator users and novices alike will learn many helpful tips and techniques. Very thorough and comprehensive, *The Illustrator 5 Book* covers Illustrator's latest features. *(660 pages)*

Photoshop 2.5 for Macintosh: Visual QuickStart Guide
Elaine Weinmann and Peter Lourekas
Get started in Adobe Photoshop with an easy, visual approach. Learn how to use masks, filters, tools, and much more. *(264 pages)*

The Photoshop Wow! Book
Linnea Dayton and Jack Davis
Wow! This book is an easy-to-follow, step-by-step tutorial of fundamentals with over 150 pages of tips and techniques. Includes a disk containing Photoshop filters and utilities. *(200 pages & disk)*

QuarkXPress 3.3 for Macintosh: Visual QuickStart Guide
Elaine Weinmann
This award-winning book is often used as a textbook by DTP educators, thanks to its simplicity of style and clarity. *(248 pages)*

QuarkXPress Tips & Tricks
David Blatner and Eric Taub
The smartest, most useful shortcuts from *The QuarkXPress Book*—plus many more—are packed into this book. Provides answers to common questions as well as insights on techniques that will make you a QuarkXPress power user. *(286 pages)*

Real World FreeHand 4
Olav Martin Kvern
The ultimate insider's guide to FreeHand. This authoritative and entertaining book first lays out the basics, then concentrates on advanced techniques. *(600 pages)*

Real World Scanning and Halftones
David Blatner and Steve Roth
From scanning images to tweaking them on your computer to imagesetting them, this book shows you how to master the digital halftone process. *(296 pages)*

Order Form

to order, call:
(800) 283-9444 or (510) 548-4393 or (510) 548-5991 (fax)

#	TITLE	Price	Total
	Camera Ready with QuarkXPress	35.00	
	Four Colors/One Image	18.00	
	Illustrator Illuminated	24.95	
	The Illustrator 5 Book	29.95	
	Photoshop 2.5 for Macintosh: Visual QuickStart Guide	18.00	
	The Photoshop Wow! Book (with disk)	35.00	
	The QuarkXPress Book, 4th Edition (Macintosh)	29.95	
	QuarkXPress 3.3 for Macintosh: Visual QuickStart Guide	15.95	
	QuarkXPress Tips & Tricks	21.95	
	Real World FreeHand 4	29.95	
	Real World Scanning and Halftones	24.95	
	Other:		

SHIPPING:	First Item	Each Additional	
UPS Ground	$ 4	$ 1	Subtotal
UPS Blue	$ 8	$ 2	8.25% Tax (CA only)
Canada	$ 6	$ 4	Shipping
Overseas	$14	$14	**T O T A L**

Name

Company

Address

City   State   Zip

Phone   Fax

❏ Check enclosed   ❏ Visa   ❏ MasterCard

Company purchase order #

Credit card #   Expiration Date

Peachpit Press, Inc. • 2414 Sixth Street • Berkeley, CA • 94710
Your satisfaction is guaranteed or your money will be cheerfully refunded!